BRITISH FURNITURE

1820 to 1920: The Luxury Market

BRITISH FURNITURE

1820 to 1920: The Luxury Market

Christopher Payne

ACC ART BOOKS

Furniture is as much a part of our life as are the trees around us which took many years to grow. It is easy to use furniture on a day-to-day basis without a thought to the quiet peace of the forests of the globe that supplied the timber, cut by long hours of toil, shipped by sail and steam and made by hand or machine by skilled artisans in workshops throughout the land.

Contents

Foreword 7

Acknowledgements 11

Introduction 15

Chapter 1: 1820s 18

Chapter 2: 1830s 64

Chapter 3: 1840s 118

Chapter 4: 1850s 170

Chapter 5: 1860s 224

Chapter 6: 1870s 284

Chapter 7: 1880s 340

Chapter 8: 1890s 390

Chapter 9: 1900–1909 442

Chapter 10: 1910–1920 486

Endnotes 540

Bibliography 556

Index 566

Foreword

It was a great delight to me when Christopher Payne asked me to write a foreword for this remarkable publication. I had known of Christopher and his work for a long time before we met at the first international conference on marquetry in Vadstana, Sweden in 2007. As a researcher and author of many aspects of furniture history, I have used his various publications over the years. I was also fascinated by his depth and breadth of knowledge that was displayed in his appearances and long association with the BBC's *Antiques Roadshow*.

Over the subsequent years we have been "talking furniture" and discussing a whole range of aspects of this mutual interest, including academic and practical matters. We also both have a particular interest in the materials and techniques associated with furniture production. One particularly memorable moment was when Christopher showed me the results of his own Windsor chair making!

While there have been many survey books on numerous aspects of 'Victorian' furniture, as well as books and articles on specific businesses, designers and makers, this volume is important as it offers a new perspective and an overview of British luxury furniture across the period 1820–1920. To some degree it complements Christopher's work on the Paris luxury furniture trades of the nineteenth century. The importance of the great international fairs, the continuation of skilled craftmanship, the role of eminent designers, the growth of specialist businesses, and the range of items purchased and collected by aristocrats and newly wealthy entrepreneurs are all reflected in the operations of the luxury market that is analysed here.

The concept of luxury that is explored in the book underlines how beneath the processes of consumption of luxury and semi-luxury furniture is found an industry of commercial enterprises (furniture makers) who link design, skilled labour, fine materials and the expensive application of time to produce furniture of outstanding quality. The book illustrates how methods of production and marketing were often shared between luxury and semi-luxury goods, using the same patterns and catalogues, the same tools and techniques, and in many cases similar materials, thus demonstrating degrees of adaptability and the exploitation of complex networks of manufacture. In this regard, many of the makers will be familiar to furniture collectors and historians, however, once important but now lesser-known manufacturing and retailing businesses, are also discussed and brought to the fore.

The value in considering the period 1820–1920 through decades, rather than by grouping into stylistic periods such as Gothic revival, Renaissance revival, Art and Crafts, is that a sequence can be traced to show how styles grew, matured, overlapped and changed or were reused over long periods of time. Indeed, the importance of the revival styles and copies, a fundamental part of the furniture trade that has often previously been neglected, is here given the treatment it deserves as a really important part of the business. From the early decades that employed 'old French' styles to the

A detail of the border of the circular centre table designed for Morel & Seddon by the fifteen-year-old A.W.N. Pugin in 1827. Delivered to Windsor Castle the following year, the stylised oak leaf and acorn marquetry in contrasting colours set within pollard oak crossbandings are an indication of Pugin's precocious genius.

(left) **A capstan table**, based on Jupe's 1835 patent, under construction at a Waring & Gillows cabinet workshop in Lancaster. The woodwork is by John Arthur Bates (1897–1978), who worked for Warings from 1911 to 1962. He had started his apprenticeship with the firm at the age of fourteen; his wife's father, two brothers and a nephew all worked for Gillows. Bates served his country fighting in Belgium in the 1914–1918 Great War and in World War II, at Gillows, he was making the de Havilland DH.98 Mosquito aeroplane, dubbed 'The Wooden Wonder'.
[Patricia Mee collection]

(opposite) **London cabinet makers** used the highly figured veneers of coromandel in preference to the more intense shades of ebony preferred by their Parisian counterparts. Here two sheets of veneer have been used in an unusual and inventive form, the marquetry border in a Greco-Roman manner is relieved with interwoven honeysuckle discreetly highlighted with ivory. Made in the mid-1860s and inspired by French Louis XVI Classicism, stylistically and technically the manufacture is attributed to Jackson & Graham; another detail is shown in Fig. 6.94.
[Butchoff Antiques]

less well-known reproductions of eighteenth-century English designs, this book goes further than any previous attempts to explore these fascinating revivals. It is particularly strong in investigating and explaining the rise of copies and reproduction styles between 1880 and 1920.

The work's textual research, evidenced by extensive endnotes, is enhanced by a huge range of over one thousand images that show furniture items, details of individual pieces, drawings, catalogues and interiors. These images are linked to discussions of provenance, maker, style and technique, therefore enhancing the reader's experience. They are themselves an invaluable collection that offer the reader a visual feast that can also stand alone. Of course, there are some images of well-known examples, but the majority comprise a selection of numerous lesser-known pieces that illustrate various styles, manufacturers, or modes of decoration, that are very valuable in order to gain a broader understanding of the variety of British luxury furniture of the period.

Evidence of the author's approach to research is also seen in his engagement with conservators, dealers and auction house specialists, as well as academics and collectors. This has enabled him to write about furniture from an historical perspective, a technical viewpoint, a business angle, and also offers insights into the trades.

It is perhaps no surprise to find that the topic that initially brought me into contact with Christopher is featured throughout the book. Whether it is the mention of the marquetry of Robert Blake in the 1820s, the exhibition works of Jackson and Graham, or the projects of Kallenborn & Sons for the Omega workshops in the 1910s, the design and making of marquetry work for the decoration of furniture is visual evidence of both the nature of the luxury trade and the quality and high skills of the workers who made it.

I know that this celebration of the diversity and quality of British furniture in the period 1820–1920 will add much to our knowledge and be a constant source of inspiration and delight to the reader.

Professor Clive Edwards
Emeritus Professor of Design History
Loughborough
2023

Acknowledgements

Without doubt my greatest thanks are to Ian Butchoff for initiating the concept of this book and his generous sponsorship. He has been affably patient and understanding in the book's long gestation. Ian, a quiet, unassuming bibliophile, has a thirst for antique furniture only matched by his acquisition of books. His well-stocked library was my first port of call when starting the research for this volume. The team at Butchoff Antiques, Adam and James Kaye, have been unfailingly helpful in my requests for information and images. However, this work would have been impossible without the support of Gallery Manager, Rainier Schraepen, with whom I had many useful and detailed discussions about arcane details of nineteenth-century furniture. Rainier has been responsible for the organisation and huge task of co-ordinating over 1,000 illustrations from disparate sources, including the comprehensive Butchoff archive.

The wealth of knowledge amongst those in the antique trade is too often ignored. Dr Mark Westgarth, Associate Professor in Art History and Museum Studies at the University of Leeds, has been a champion of the dealers who are such an integral and oft-underrated part of our world. After all, ACC Art Books (originally known as the Antique Collectors' Club) was started in 1966 by John and Diana Steel, driving around the country loading furniture onto the ubiquitous Volvo estate! There is no substitute for the day-to-day handling of furniture, supervising restoration; putting hard cash down concentrates the mind.

The next vote of thanks is to the Getty Research Institute who invited me to join my wife on a three-month internship in 2018 and allowed me to return on two further occasions to use their world-class facilities in convivial surroundings, cocooned by a wide array of international scholars. I would like to thank Dr Arlen Heginbotham for all his support, and Alexa Sekyra, Head of the GRI Scholars Program, and her team for their welcome, help and kindness. The Special Collections at the Getty Museum is a treasure trove for researchers and many thanks also to them for their patience and understanding.

Many curators of museums and private collections, as well as National Trust houses, welcomed my requests in an area of research that has until now not been given much airtime and I am very grateful to them all. Rufus Bird, former Surveyor of the Queen's Works of Art, and his team went out of their way to help, and supplied numerous photographs. Jon Culverhouse, the curator at Burghley House, always found something new to discuss. Amongst others are Julie Biddlecome-Brown at Raby Castle, and here Lord Barnard provided ready access to the exciting items in the collection. Clare Baxter and the team at Alnwick Castle were equally accommodating. Dr Wolf Burchard responded enthusiastically to my request for help sourcing material in New York and I am grateful to him. Despite her busy schedule, Victoria Partridge, curator at The Higgins Bedford museum deserves

An 1894 photograph of the Music Room at Norfolk House in St James's Square, demolished in 1938, the panelling preserved in the Victoria and Albert Museum. Built between 1748 and 1756, the English Rococo interiors and their French counterparts were an inspiration for the white-and-gold furniture of the 1830s and 1840s. The cabinet maker's plan of the octagonal centre table is seemingly identical to a table stamped by Morant, see Fig. 2.31a. The marquetry, in both cases by the Blake family, is less elaborate in the Norfolk House image. [Historic England (Bedford Lemere)]

a special mention. All were fully cognisant of the strain on funds for the modern author and were generous in their permission to use their photographic material. Dr. Bernard (Bill) Cotton is a fount of knowledge and wide-ranging conversations with him always provided more food for thought and insights. Similarly, John Whitehead has always kindly shared his knowledge and Dr. Diana Davis generously shared her ideas and her thesis, now published as *The Tastemakers: British Dealers and the Anglo-Gallic Interior, 1785–1865*. Professor Clive Edwards agreed to write the foreword for this book. Our discussions about the nitty gritty of furniture have always been a constant source of delight and his 2022 publication *Collinson & Lock: Art Furnishers, Interior Decorators and Designers 1870–1900* is a milestone in the understanding of a major London firm.

Due to Covid restrictions it was impossible to visit as many houses as I would have wished. One significant and vastly important collection stands out and I am deeply grateful to the Duke of Buccleuch for his generosity in sharing his collection with me. The enthusiastic support of the duke and the energies of his curator Scott MacDonald, archivist Crispin Powell, and the Collections Assistant Kathryn Price were key to several important previously unpublished discoveries. The riches of the collection formed by the 5th Duke in the 1830s and '40s are a vital source and worthy of a book in their own right. I would also like to thank Sir Philip Naylor-Leyland and the Duke and Duchess of Rutland for their support.

All the dealers whom I approached were helpful and enthusiastic about the project and their names are cited alongside the photographs that they kindly contributed to the book. Martin Levy of Blairman's was often my first port of call with questions. Auction rooms far and wide also generously contributed, many of their staff fitting in my innumerable requests with their hectic schedules. One nineteenth-century enthusiast deserves a special mention. Giles Forster, latterly of Christie's and now a director of Adrian Alan Ltd, constantly came up with new ideas and suggestions. Henry House of Sotheby's allowed me free access to my old run of bound catalogues and Shiona Fourie went beyond the call of duty in providing images. Malcom Barber was equally generous at Bonhams as was Thomas Moore of their furniture department. Bonhams and Sotheby's allow scholars to have high-resolution images gratis, and without such generosity books such as this would never be published. Special thanks to Daniel Brooke who has been responsible for photography at Butchoff Antiques for many years and has generously provided many of the images in this book. I am very grateful to my old colleague from Sotheby's, Ken Adlard of New Moon Photography, with whom I have worked on several projects and publications, who was always inventive and energetic on location and worked tirelessly to make some of my own images presentable. llustrations in Chapter 10 marked simply 'Frederick Parker Collection' are by kind permission from The Worshipful Company of Furniture Makers, Frederick Parker Collection, London Metropolitan University. Access to the run of *The Cabinet Maker* in the university archives was an immersive experience in a publication that has more to offer for researchers. In and out of Covid restrictions, I was able to have free access to the Victoria and Albert Museum's Department of Furniture and Woodwork makers' files. Leela Meinertas was always able to suggest new directions of research. John Hardy always took time to explain questions about classical references. John and Leela have a depth of knowledge that puts me to shame, as does that of Sarah Medlham. Special thanks must go to the late John Evan Bedford for giving me full access to his wonderful library before it was transferred for posterity and safekeeping to Leeds University.

The bulk of illustrations that were not supplied by Butchoff Antiques or antique dealers were sourced by the highly professional Susannah Stone whose experience, efficiency and contacts made it possible to source many previously unpublished images.

Long before my *Paris Furniture* (2018) I was able to tap into the wealth of practical experience and academic knowledge of the Kent-based conservator Yannick Chastang. In conjunction with Dr Arlen Heginbotham at the Getty Museum, and the Rijksmuseum, their work on X-ray fluorescence (XRF) is breaking new ground. Peter Holmes was always on hand for technical questions, usually about the timbers used in furniture, as was Anthony Beech. The experience of established conservators is an invaluable aid to a writer and happily, over the last decades, their wealth of knowledge has become recognised by a wider audience.

My thanks to Kerry Monaghan-Smith for her valuable comments on my first draft and to Margot Chadwick for painstakingly reading it. Alexander Collins diligently went through the text and endnotes and created the bibliography. Clarissa Ward was always on hand for comments. Ocky Murray brilliantly laid out the pagination of the book and patiently allowed my digital tweaks. My collaboration with ACC spans several decades. Indeed, I handed the text and images for my first book (long before the internet, in two large suitcases) to the Antique Collectors' Club as it was then, at Woodbridge over forty years ago. My thanks to all the people who have supported me there, past and present, most especially the late Diana Steel.

I would also like to thank my long-suffering wife for her forbearance in the gestation of such a large publication. Dr Helen Jacobsen, formerly Senior Curator at the Wallace Collection and now Executive Director at The Attingham

Trust, has been an exacting and knowledgeable editor in her constant revisions of my work and trying to put my scattered thoughts into a logical format.

There is a certain amount of fear and trembling in covering such a wide range of furniture. Many readers will have an in-depth knowledge of certain makers cited in this work. I worry at the shaking of heads on certain points much as on occasion I tut-tutted when I read comments by others on, for example, François Linke. Let this book lead to more areas of specialist research. Since I first published *European Furniture* in 1981, the 1820–1920 period has opened up to new researchers and authorship. Long may it continue.

In 1926 R.W. Symonds wrote that furniture after 1820 had very little interest to the current student and collector.* Although this attitude lasted well into the twentieth century and even later in some circles, interest in the nineteenth century has blossomed. A watershed was an exhibition of Victorian and Edwardian decorative arts at the Victoria and Albert Museum in 1952. By 1962 Symonds was at the forefront of new interest, writing *Victorian Furniture* with B.B. Whineray the same year that Elizabeth Aslin published *19th Century English Furniture*. Both books were my early reading as a teenager when browsing my father's library. Imagine my excitement sixty years later, when I called in to Anthony Beech Restorations at Burghley House and saw Mrs Thornton's *bureau en pente* by Holland & Son, which I remembered was illustrated in Symonds & Whineray (see **Fig. 5.55**), the owner happy to let me take my own colour photographs. A chance visit to Manor House Antiques unearthed the Robert Christie table made for Buscot Park, the *Cabinet Maker* engraving re-published in 1972 by Pauline Agius in *British Furniture 1880–1915* (see **Fig. 8.91**). There are still discoveries to be made and many opportunities for future researchers.

The annual journals of the Furniture History Society, launched in 1964, have consistently carried a wide range of incisive articles. The first two volumes were dedicated to eighteenth-century England, but volume III in 1967 included Lindsay Boynton's work on Marsh and Jones of Leeds. Dr Boynton's opening words were: 'Interest in English furniture used at one time to cease abruptly at 1800'. He added: 'As the Regency became acceptable, the date was advanced to 1820 or so'. Volume I had included *The Overseas Trade in Furniture in the Eighteenth Century* by Edward Joy. By volume VI in 1970, Joy had expanded his work to the nineteenth-century overseas trade and every article in the volume encroached into the nineteenth century. Joy noted that as early as 1840, furniture from England was exported to seventy-one different countries. The Furniture History Society has always been a great presence in my career. The annual journals and regular newsletters are essential reading.

Under the auspices of the Furniture History Society, BIFMO (British and Irish Furniture Makers Online) have compiled a comprehensive website listing makers and suppliers in the furniture trades. The site is updated on a regular basis with thousands of names and cross-references, street names and dates covering 400 years of activity. Before the BIFMO site was announced, it was intended that *British Furniture 1820 to 1920: The Luxury Market* would have a Makers List compiled by Rainier Schraepen. This database will now only be available online and managed by Butchoff Antiques: www.butchoff/makers/1820-1920.

The gestation of this book has taken a long time and I have benefitted from a great many people's help and enthusiasm. If I have left anyone out, please accept my sincere apologies. All errors are my own.

Footnote
* '... the mahogany period is regarded as lasting one hundred years, that is to say it is brought to a close in 1820, furniture after that date having very little interest for the student or collector.' R.W. Symonds, 'The Quality of Mahogany Furniture', *The Connoisseur*, vol. LXXVI, 1926, p. 19.

Introduction

Prior to this publication there have been few books available covering British furniture of the period 1820 to 1920 and it is hoped that this work goes some way to filling the gap for those interested in this fascinating century of innovation and luxury. It is intended to be an illustrated compendium of British furniture spanning the century. The book does not purport to be an encyclopaedic reference of the one hundred years but a rich visual source, highlighting the multitude of different styles that were fashionable over the period; furniture made by a huge variety of skilled craftsmen. These styles often overlapped, running concurrently side by side, sometimes for decades.

No single volume can hope to encapsulate the enormous productivity of the British cabinet maker over the century, a hundred years which witnessed so much technological innovation and economic growth. Over the period, Britain established an empire, and the industry of the Victorian era became a model and influence across the globe. In furniture, the period witnessed both technical and artistic innovation but at the same time relied heavily on past influences, reflecting the glory of the previous centuries and celebrating Britain and its historical past.

This book is set out by decade, each chapter spanning ten years of design and manufacture with the intention of giving each section a visual coherence. Designers and makers, however, do not conveniently separate their work into decades to aid the work of historians. Many designs so often considered 'Victorian' were concepts formulated during the Regency between 1810 and 1820. One particular group of furniture that defies accurate dating within a decade is that produced by the Blake family of marquetry cutters along with furniture supplied and sometimes made by the ubiquitous E.H. Baldock, and I have illustrated their work in various chapters. Few of these pieces are dated and could be interchangeable within several chapters. Such examples are numerous. Thomas Sopwith's 'Monocleid' cabinet (shown opposite) arguably Chippendale in inspiration, was designed in the mid-1830s and exhibited over twenty years later at the Great Exhibition in 1851. At the other end of the century, the carver Gerrard Robinson, who had also exhibited at the Crystal Palace, was making furniture in a similar vein in the 1890s. Towards the end of the nineteenth century and well into the twentieth, the growing influence of the George II and George III periods of Chippendale, Hepplewhite and Sheraton becomes increasingly difficult to separate into convenient ten-year chapters and, without archival evidence, dating of these pieces becomes subjective; it is likely that much of this reproduction furniture is far later in date than generally assumed.

Over the fifty years of my career, I have been constantly reminded of the quality of furniture made in Britain during the period of this book, and it is a celebration of my personal interest in not only the prevailing fashions of the period but also in the technical ability of the crafts people involved in the often-complex production. I have tried to identify as many of the main makers as possible and used lavish images to give some indication as to the quality of their work.

A version of the 'Monocleid' cabinet by Thomas Sopwith. Sopwith originally designed the cabinet to be opened with one single key, hence the name, in the 1830s. Underlining the difficulty of assigning furniture design to a specific decade, this version in mahogany probably dates to the mid-1840s and a variation was exhibited at the Great Exhibition in 1851. Here the cabinet is shown open, the pigeonholes annotated for filing, one marked 'Nether Grange', another 'North Eastern R***', suggesting that this example was in use not far from where it was made in Newcastle (see Fig. 3.90a).
[Casa-Museu Medeiros e Almeida]

CHAPTER 1

1820s

The defeat of Napoleon at Waterloo in 1815 ushered in a prolonged period of peace. The twelve years of the Napoleonic Wars had brought a tremendous social upheaval to Europe, while victory and maritime supremacy enabled Britain to become the dominant economic force. Peace brought prosperity and an opportunity for Britain to greatly expand its luxury market as the growing population became wealthier. Auspicious trading conditions were an opportunity for inventiveness in the decorative arts and in furnishing the homes of the aristocratic and wealthier classes. The essentially French *Expositions des produits de l'industrie française* in Paris had been held erratically from 1798 but it was not until 1828 that Britain attempted a wider based International Exhibition, held near Charing Cross in central London. This first London exhibition was deemed a failure but nine years later one in Manchester met with greater success, followed by another in Leeds in 1839. Perhaps more significant were the increasing number of design books and other printed matter which helped promote and disseminate a wide variety of styles in interior decoration in general and furniture in particular.

Many of the new stylistic traits in Britain in the early nineteenth century were essentially revivalist, whether adaptations of the French Louis styles, the absorption of ancient Greek and Roman culture or the amalgamation of Gothic and Elizabethan motifs. The century was dominated by eclecticism, continually reworking old formats as people's requirements adapted and changed to suit contemporary interiors and an increasing sense of prosperity and comfort. A number of different styles were in varied and common usage as early as the 1820s. In his 1808 publication *A Collection of Designs for Household Furniture and Interior Decoration*, George Smith (1786–1826) described his collection as 'a variety of the newest patterns, combined with Classical taste, for the plainest and for the most superb articles of modern furniture, studied from the best antique examples of the Egyptian, Greek, and Roman styles; and to augment this variety, some designs are given after the Gothic or old English fashion',[1] as well as inspiration from the French designers Charles Percier (1764–1838) and François-Léonard Fontaine (1762–1853). Smith described himself as 'upholder extraordinary to his Royal Highness the Prince of Wales'; his 158 aquatint engravings produced between 1805 and 1807 are in a style that today is unmistakably 'Regency'.

This chapter is intended as a stylistic introduction to the second quarter of the century and serves to illustrate how 'Victorian' in appearance were many of the individual decorative motifs that were used and how furniture increasingly took on a fussy, over-embellished look which

Fig.1.1 **The ultimate prize for British collectors in the 1820s was *ancien régime* furniture by André-Charles Boulle. This cabinet of *c.*1700 has been enhanced and restored for the luxury market. The Egyptomania stand reflects fashionable taste, as evidenced in the Egyptian Hall in Belgravia opened by William Bullock in 1812. After alteration, the cabinet was almost certainly sold to George Byng in 1828 for Wrotham Park.**
[Fitzwilliam Museum, M.2-2010]

1.2a

1.2b

1.2c

Fig.1.2a **A mahogany library bookcase almost 5m (16½ft) wide, with an attribution to Gillows based on a drawing in the Gillow archives of a cabinet with similar carved door panels and capitals. The gilt Roman numerals suggest that it was part of a larger suite of bookcases. It is stamped 'James Winter & Son, 101 Wardour Street Soho London', probably in the role as retailer.**
[Private collection]

Fig.1.2b **The mahogany doors of the bookcase have carefully chosen, beautifully figured veneers, the log cut to show off the rich patterning of the grain, called 'flame figuring' for its similarity to a leaping flame. Only the most affluent workshops would have been able to afford such expensive imported timbers and Gillows, with its proximity to Lancaster docks, was perfectly placed to get first choice.**
[Private collection]

Fig.1.2c **The interior of the Gillows bookcase is fitted with expensively veneered drawers and flush-fitting brass handles typical of Gillows' attention to quality and detail.**
[Private collection]

CHAPTER 1: 1820S

is often misconstrued as dating to ten or even twenty years later. The 1820s was a particularly productive decade with inventive, original and eclectic designs. On the demise of George III in 1820, the Regency of the Prince of Wales ended and he was proclaimed King George IV, reigning for just over ten years. Widely condemned as a profligate spendthrift, George had a wide-ranging and diverse sense of style and was an important influence on the decorative arts. His personal taste encouraged the nobility and newly wealthy industrialists to engage with a myriad of styles, some familiar and reworked, such as those of French and Chinese origin, and some new and innovative, such as those of South Asian origin. From the 1790s he had constantly been looking for new directions in the decorative arts. The furniture and decorations he commissioned were so advanced that he might be regarded as the first 'Victorian'. The extraordinary Brighton Pavilion, with its elaborate riding school and stables, built between 1803 and 1808 in an exotic and romantic Indian style, is a lasting tribute to his extravagance. The Pavilion was redesigned and greatly extended for its patron between 1815 and 1822 by the English architect John Nash (1752–1835), who was also responsible for much of the layout of central London, including the Classical and elegant 'Nash terraces' of Regent's Park. It is Nash's façade at Brighton that can still be seen today with its striking Indo-Islamic outline and an interior by John Crace and his son Frederick, who also supplied much of the furniture. An exhibition at the Queen's Gallery held in 2020, *George IV: Art and Spectacle,* was a modern tribute to the king, marking him as the 'first gentleman of Europe'.[4]

The elegant simplicity of Regency furniture from 1810–20 is much appreciated by collectors today. The lavish and indulgent taste of George IV, not to the liking of Queen Victoria a generation later, was not a style seen in everyday furniture production; even wealthy clients felt the need to water down such extravagance. Furniture of the 1820s is

Fig.1.3 A gentleman's library chair in Cuban mahogany with a similar heavy Rococo Revival design to a chair by Gillows incorporated into a room design for a 'G. Bamford' *c.*1820, the plan for which was prepared by the Oxford Street branch of Gillows between 1815 and 1835, showing a sofa, stool and table with the same bold design.[2] The example here has short stubby legs with eagle's claw talons.[3] [Private collection]

Fig.1.4 A Honduras mahogany cabinet, unusually one of a pair, the quality of the wood suggests the workshops of Gillows. The illustrated example is lined with false book spines, reminiscent of a 'jib' door, whilst its companion is open on all four sides. [Butchoff Antiques]

1.3

1.4

Fig.1.5 **The use of oak veneers and stylised foliate marquetry would support an attribution to George Bullock.** [Butchoff Antiques]

Fig.1.6 **A rosewood writing or sofa table, with Bullock-style marquetry inlay to the top. The table is recorded as being supplied to Burghley House by 'Messrs Town & Emanuel' in 1835.** [Burghley House]

Fig.1.7 **This set of twenty dining chairs made from finely figured *gonçalo alves* imported from South America, is in the style of Gillows. It is not known how many there were originally, or if there were ever any armchairs, but the examples illustrated are numbered in Roman numerals from one to twenty, indicating they have remained together.** [Butchoff Antiques]

Fig.1.8 **One of a pair of dumbwaiters in the manner of George Bullock, made of English oak, inlaid in ebony with ivy leaves.** [The Buccleuch Collections]

surprisingly difficult to date accurately, with many designs of the period appearing 'Victorian'.

Furniture in what is considered to be a more typical 'Regency' form, is illustrated by the expensively made table shown in **Fig. 1.5**, a familiar outline that had become popular at the end of the eighteenth century. More commonly known today as a sofa table, early invoices term them writing tables. The pole stretcher joining the trestle legs is a giveaway as to the date – an eighteenth-century example would have no pole at the bottom of the trestle, the support being concealed under the top. The table, once in the collection of the Londesborough family, has distinct similarities with some of the designs of George Bullock (1783–1818). Tracings by the relatively undocumented Thomas Wilkinson, purchased by the Birmingham City Museum and Art Gallery and a reference source for Bullock's designs, show an identical foliate pattern to that inlaid into the well-figured oak veneers of this table.[5] A table also in a 'Bullock' style at Burghley House has similar inlay, **Fig. 1.6**. However, the stretcher is heavy and placed midway between the top and the base of the trestle. Both this and the table in **Fig. 1.5** would appear to have the same date, sometime in the 1820s. Another

significant firm during the Regency was Town & Emanuel, and the Burghley archives record the sale to the 2nd Marquess of Exeter: 'from Messrs Town & Emanuel 1835 … to a Marquetrie Library table. £21.0.0 Packing case for do. £1.0.0'.[6] Is the table really as 'late' as 1835, or was it old stock or even second-hand at the time of purchase? Another elaboration in this distinctive style is a pair of bookcases made by Bullock for Napoleon during his internment at Longwood House on Saint Helena. They appear similar to a design by Richard Brown on plate XVIII of his *Rudiments of Drawing Cabinet and Upholstery Furniture* (**Fig. 1.10**). Unlike the writing table with applied indigenous veneers, the 'Napolionic' [sic] bookcases were veneered in *gonçalo alves*, a wood with an often dramatically contrasted colour or stripe, often mistaken for the more commonly used rosewood, both imported from South America. The pole stretcher of the Burghley table and the four supports on the lower part of the design in **Fig. 1.10** have a distinctly similar feel.

Bullock, who began his career as a sculptor and wax modeller in Liverpool, was one of the most iconic makers of the late Georgian period and by 1804 had a successful furniture business in the city. In 1810 he described his business as: 'architects, modellers, sculptors, marble masons, cabinet makers and upholsterers'.[7] Like many northern makers, he later established a reputation in London, opening the fashionably named 'Grecian Gallery' in 1812 to his own design in the Egyptian Hall that his brother William had established on Piccadilly. In his short career, Bullock's oeuvre was substantial, including work for Cholmondley Castle, Bolton Hall, Scone Palace, Blair Castle, Armdale Castle, Battle Abbey, Shrubland Park, and Abbotsford, for his friend, the novelist, Sir Walter Scott. The avant-garde Bullock championed the use of oak and other indigenous English timbers in his work. An extensive collection of oak furniture by Bullock, inlaid with native holly, was supplied to Matthew Bolton for Great Tew Park from 1816 to 1818, the year Bullock suddenly died. Bullock used green Mona marble from his own quarries in Anglesey.[8] The table in **Fig. 1.5** uses native-grown oak veneers, holly stringing and ebonised marquetry foliate decoration. In *Rudiments*, Richard Brown praised Bullock: 'He has shewn that we need not roam to foreign climes for beautiful ornaments, but that we have abundance of plants and flowers equal to the Grecian, which if adopted would be as pleasing as the antique'.[10]

Bullock produced comparatively restrained yet bold designs, much of his work influenced by the French Empire style. He also reinterpreted the delicate patterns of brass inlays in a Boulle-revival idiom. English sources that influenced him included those of Thomas Hope,

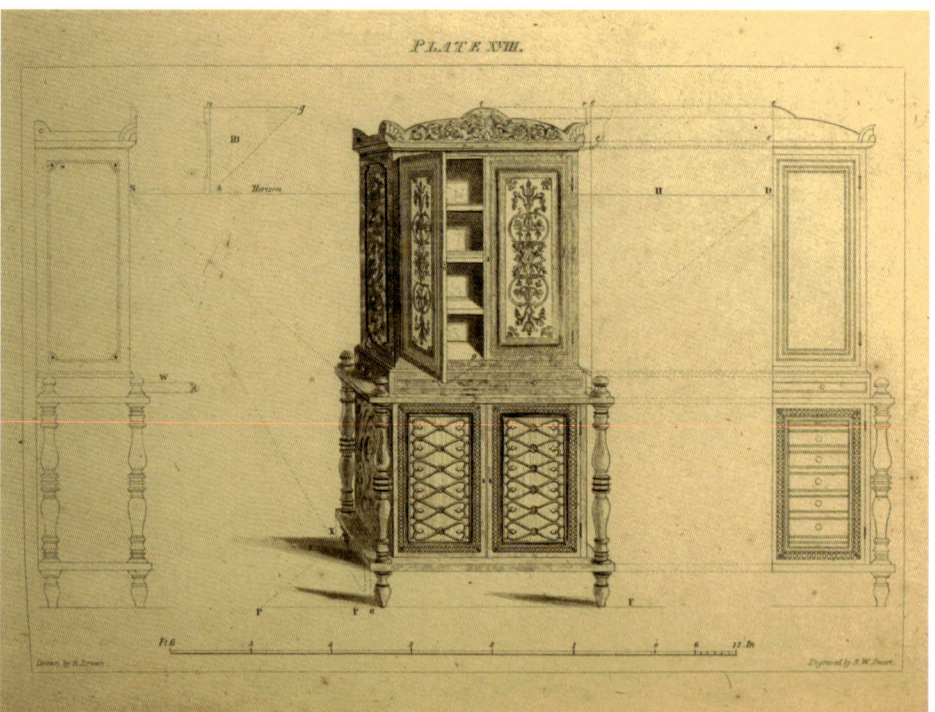

Fig.1.9 **A design by Richard Bridgens, with the Thomas Hope-style triangular concave support which influenced the firm of Morant, in a style often attributed to Edward Holmes Baldock.**
[Getty Research Institute]

Fig.1.10 **Plate XVIII from Richard Brown's** *Rudiments of Drawing Cabinet and Upholstery Furniture* **of 1822. The flanking pole supports seen here are similar to the stretcher on the sofa table in Fig. 1.5.**
[Getty Research Institute]

Fig.1.11 **A set of fourteen mahogany dining chairs from Whitestock Hall,[9] probably made by Gillows of Lancaster. It is probable that the set originally included a pair of armchairs.** [Private collection]

Fig.1.12 **A finely executed bookcase in San Domingo mahogany. Attributed to George Oakley, it may date to the Regency period, between 1810 and 1820.** [Butchoff Antiques]

Sheraton and Henry Holland, who incorporated Greek, Roman, Egyptian, Gothick and Hepplewhite motifs into his work.[11] Hope appears to have been the instigator of the triangular concave table support, identifiable in his *Household Furniture* of 1807, a support which Bullock's former apprentice, Richard Bridgens, developed which is seen on a wide range of tables sometimes ascribed correctly to Morant or, probably in error, to Baldock (see **Fig. 1.9**). It would seem likely that the marquetry-cutter Robert Blake was also influenced by Bullock, either directly or indirectly. Furniture with Blake marquetry often uses the triangular table support and the octagonal tabletop popularised by Bullock and also repeatedly seen on tables by Morant (such as one at Dunrobin Castle) or ascribed to Baldock. The sale of Bullock's effects in 1819, 'All the valuable Unmanufactured Stock in Trade of Mr. George Bullock dec.', would have been the ideal opportunity to purchase mounts, plans and models.[12]

1.13a

Figs 1.13a–c A remarkable mahogany chest of drawers of small proportions that follows the English tradition of identifying and collecting rare specimen woods. During the eighteenth and nineteenth centuries, cabinets and tabletops were constructed in a variety of rare and interesting woods as well as specimen marbles and hard stones. It was a sign of erudition and propensity for scientific inquiry. Both the 2nd and 3rd Dukes of Northumberland shared a deep interest in botany, growing plants and trees often suited to hotter climes. The 3rd Duke of Northumberland grew rare woods for furniture making. An invoice to the 3rd Duke from Morel and Hughes, dated 1823, specifies that a chair intended for the Ante Room to the Crimson Drawing Room for Northumberland House, was to be made from African aburra wood, the timber already in the personal ownership of the Duke.[13]

The small scale, only 31½ in (80 cm) wide, suggests that this chest was made purely as a display item. The drawers are designed without locks, and also without keyhole escutcheons; the complex geometric parquetry design of the drawers is only enhanced by the discreet ebony drawer pulls.

George Bullock was always looking for unusual timbers and prominently displayed wood specimens on his furniture. In an advertisement of 1812, Bullock mentions; 'scarce and valuable wood… Mahogany, Zebra, Topaz and other woods… exhibiting specimens of various fancy woods'.[14] A cabinet by Bullock with specimen wood geometric parquetry is illustrated as Fig. 24 of the exhibition catalogue *George Bullock, Cabinet Maker* (Wainwright, 1988, p. 66). Another Bullock design feature is the use of unusual, disengaged columns, also drawn by Brown, see Fig. 1.10, and is seen on a pair of cabinets supplied by Bullock in 1819 for New Longwood, Napoleon's final home on St Helena. [Carlton Hobbs LLC]

1.13b

1.13c

The San Domingo mahogany bookcase (**Fig. 1.12**), with its original brass trellis grilles on the doors to allow the books to 'breathe', is in the style of George Oakley (c.1760–1840), whose premises were established in 1786 near St Paul's Churchyard. One of many makers patronised by the Prince of Wales, what is known of his output is recorded in detail in the indispensable *Dictionary of English Furniture*.[15] A bookcase of virtually identical form was supplied, as well as wardrobes, to Papworth Hall, owned by Charles Madryll Cheere, who commissioned Oakley to furnish the house during the Regency. This style of brass grille was widely used throughout the early nineteenth century for bookcases and was hand cut from large brass sheets cast in an elaborate process on a flat stone. In contrast, French bookcases of the eighteenth century and revival periods used a light wire twisted together, or used interwoven strips of cut brass, in a myriad of different patterns.

The ports on the north-west English coast were the first landfall after the long voyage from the Caribbean or the Americas and makers such as Gillows of Lancaster were ideally placed geographically to buy the first choice of imported timbers, especially the perennially popular and versatile mahogany. The long set of fourteen dining chairs shown in **Fig. 1.11** are a typical high-quality product and were almost certainly made by Gillows, in their Lancaster workshops. The set was originally at Whitestock Hall, the family home of the portrait painter George Romney. The chairs were still in the house in 1893, when they were listed

CHAPTER 1: 1820S

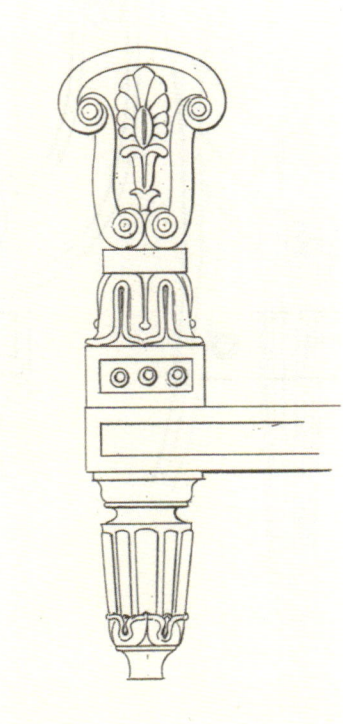

Fig.1.14a **A rare example of a true pair of chaises longues in boldly carved rosewood. The detail borrows from plates in Thomas King's** The Modern Style of Cabinet Work Exemplified **of 1829, plates 9–11.** [Butchoff Antiques]

Fig.1.14b **The rosewood cornucopia on the chaises longues is detachable to allow for re-upholstering. This type of elaborate stylised cornucopia was a form used in Biedermeier furniture and on seat furniture from the Baltic states.** [Butchoff Antiques]

Fig.1.15 **The bold carving and generous form seen in this window seat, or 'causette', are the summit of uninhibited late Georgian design and execution.** [Private collection]

Fig.1.16 **In his 1829 publication,** The Modern Style of Cabinet Work Exemplified, **Thomas King illustrated a 'couch' with Grecian-style carving of similar form to that found on this sofa. This example is in European oak.** [Butchoff Antiques]

Fig.1.17 **A detail of 'sofa ends' from Thomas King's** The Modern Style of Cabinet Work Exemplified, **1829, p. 13.**

Fig.1.18 **An armchair in the French style supplied to Liverpool Town Hall in 1829 for use in the Council Chamber. The top-rail is applied with a gilt-bronze Liver Bird, the symbol of Liverpool, encircled by the city's motto** DEUS NOBIS HAEC OTIA FECIT **('God hath granted us this ease').** [Butchoff Antiques]

in an inventory.[16] Romney was born in Beckside, Cumbria, in 1734 and, aged eleven, was apprenticed for a brief period to his father, who was a cabinet maker. It is interesting to note that Gillows employed seven workmen named Romney between the 1760s and the 1840s.[17]

Whereas the George Oakley-style bookcase in **Fig. 1.12** reflected the taste for ancient Greece, the rosewood window seat (**Fig. 1.15**) looked back to Rome. The design compares to a 'causette' or conversation sofa, illustrated in Ackermann's popular style periodical, the *Repository*

29

Fig.1.19 The design and generous size of this chair, one of a pair, resemble a suite of chairs by Dixwell, see Fig. 1.20, dated to between 1811 and 1820. [Butchoff Antiques]

Fig.1.20 One of a set of twelve armchairs influenced by ancient Greek *klismos* chairs, part of which is now in the Metropolitan Museum. Some chairs include the signature 'C. Dixwell', one dated 1820, referring to Charles Dixwell. Dixwell was a London 'upholder' who was apprenticed to the celebrated furniture maker George Seddon for seven years and is recorded as having subscribed to Sheraton's *Drawing Book* in 1793. [Butchoff Antiques]

Fig.1.21a Nine of this set of ten dining chairs are stamped 'Gillows • Lancaster'. Two of the set have the stamp of James Lawson, a Gillows craftsman. [Butchoff Antiques]

Fig.1.21b The distinctive Gillows stamp, seen on nine of the chairs shown above. The 'dot' separating the two words was used from c.1795. [Butchoff Antiques]

of Arts.[18] The cornucopias on the pair of rosewood chaises longues (**Fig. 1.14a**) are an adaptation of another Ackermann design, the upholstery of which would have been more expensive than the construction of the frame, and incorporates several details from Thomas King's *The Modern Style of Cabinet Work Exemplified* (**Fig. 1.17**).

The large armchair, one of a pair and illustrated in **Fig. 1.19**, carved in the highest quality Cuban mahogany, bears the royal coat of arms. The elaborate decoration might suggest a late date but when compared with a similar suite of armchairs by Charles Dixwell, a London 'upholder', one of the set now in the collection of the Metropolitan Museum of Art,[19] and another in a private collection (**Fig. 1.20**), they can be dated to the 1820s. As two of the Metropolitan Museum of Art chairs are dated, one 1811 and the other 1820, it is clear that such elaboration was incipient in the early 1810s. Both of the pair of armchairs are stamped on the underside 'IMD', and one has the pencil inscription 'Hon Ashton Chase'.

The armchair by Morel & Seddon (**Fig. 1.18**) is a classic example of furniture that at first glance appears to be Victorian but was made in 1829 for Liverpool Town Hall. The top-rail is applied with a gilt-bronze Liver Bird, an ancient mythical creature and the symbol of Liverpool, standing within the city's motto.[20] Made of Cuban mahogany, the chair is a clumsy rendition of the Louis XV mid-eighteenth-century period, with cabriole legs of a form that, with the waisted back, anticipates the ubiquitous Victorian balloon back chair. It was originally one of a set of forty

Fig.1.22 Designed in the 'Old English' style, this pattern of chair is in the Gillows Sketch Book of 1827. With variations to the legs and feet, other versions were made in a variety of woods, including mahogany, walnut, yew or elm. [Christie's]

Fig.1.23 Suggesting a revival of the designs of William Kent from one hundred years earlier, this armchair relates to a pair of rosewood *bergères* supplied by Gillows to the 2nd Baron Newborough for Glynlliffon in 1824. [Peacock's Finest]

chairs (of which ten remain in situ), the cost of which ran to £501 3s 6d.[21] The set of ten dining chairs in **Fig. 1.21a** also anticipates a style that is often mistaken for Victorian, but they date to *c*.1825, midway through the reign of George IV. They have the distinction of bearing not only the Gillows stamp but two also have the stamp of the frame maker, James Lawson.[22]

At the beginning of the nineteenth century there were already rare appearances of variations of early Georgian furniture. A prime example is a type of armchair habitually associated with Gillows and eminently suitable as a desk chair, the overall shape looking back to the 1740s (**Fig. 1.22**). Designed in the 'Old English' style, the chair derives from an example at Boyton Manor.[23] The shaped solid back and shepherd's crook arms are common features from the reign of George II, whereas the use of oak with well-figured wood is more typical of the use of indigenous material favoured in the Regency period and later. In a rare indication of the maker, the chair is signed in pencil on the underside of the seat rail 'Robt Lawson'. The paw feet and knees are by a carver named Rigby. This pattern of chair was revived in the 1820s

Fig.1.24 The Small Drawing Room at Raby Castle was considerably altered in the 1820s when this large giltwood side table was added. The veneered *breccia* marble top is supported by eagles with outstretched wings, in a revival of the William Kent style of one hundred years earlier. The table fits the wall mouldings exactly, probably ordered to fit under the existing mirror. The reflection in the mirror shows the top of two giltwood armchairs, part of a set supplied by Morant twenty years later (see Fig. 3.40).
[Raby Castle, County Durham]

by French and English dealers to suit contemporary aspirations and appealed to largely uninformed buyers for whom 'the look' was more important than authenticity. Many museum collections have several examples of eighteenth-century furniture altered to suit the fashion of the day (**Fig. 1.1**). As in the previous decade of the Regency, in the 1820s French designs were reinterpreted in new furniture alongside forms from ancient Greece and Egypt and the seeds of what is seen as Victorian eclecticism were sown. Luxury was the key for those who could afford it. Huge sums were spent on decorative schemes, not least by the Prince of Wales on projects including Carlton House, Brighton Pavilion, and later, when king, the refurbishment of Windsor Castle. The display of wealth and luxury that was achieved is ably demonstrated by, for example, the magnificent cabinet made in London by, or under the direction of, the carvers and gilders Robert Hume and his son, also Robert, in 1824 (**Fig. 1.28**). The *pietre dure* plaques were originally produced between 1650 and 1700 in the Gobelins workshop, probably by immigrant Florentine mosaicists. The cabinet was delivered to the 10th Duke of Hamilton in 1824.[25] Davis recorded that Hume was buying at principal auctions for his clients, including that of Erlestoke Park in 1832.[26] The side table (**Fig. 1.25a**) is one of a pair originally at Erlestoke that was included in the contents of the house sold by order of George Watson Taylor. The exaggerated cabriole legs can be compared with those on another *pietre dure* side table (**Fig. 1.26**). The winged caryatids on the latter are clearly inspired

and executed in a variety of woods, including mahogany, walnut, yew and elm. Gillows is recorded as making the model in yew and examples are listed in the 'Estimate Sketch Book' of 1827.[24]

Following the lead of the king, English aristocratic collectors embraced the Louis styles from the 1680s to the 1780s. George IV and his circle were active purchasers of French furniture, especially of the *Grand Siècle*, of which André-Charles Boulle's work from the early eighteenth century was the ultimate find. Much furniture was adapted

Fig.1.25a **A side table, richly applied with lapis lazuli, agate, quartz, amethyst and jasper. One of a pair made by Robert Hume c.1825 for Erlestoke Park.** [Fine Arts Museums of San Francisco, 1956.77]

Fig.1.25b **A detail of the Italian hardstones on the console tables made by Robert Hume for Erlestoke Park.** [Fine Arts Museums of San Francisco, 1956.77]

Fig.1.26 **This sumptuous table in the manner of Robert Hume is also lavishly embellished with applied fruit in coloured hardstones. The caryatids at each corner resemble those on the chests of drawers, or commodes, originally conceived and made by Boulle for Louis XIV at Trianon in 1708. The commode was later reproduced for the 4th Marquess of Hertford in the early 1850s (see Chapter 4 – 1850s).** [Carlton Hobbs LLC]

by those on the Trianon commodes, or chests of drawers, made by Boulle for Louis XIV in 1708. The only known version of the Boulle chest of drawers in Britain at the time was at Hamilton Palace, where Hume worked for the 10th Duke of Hamilton. The chest of drawers, now at Petworth, was later sold at the Hamilton Palace sale in 1882,[27] having previously been exhibited at Gore House in 1853. The style of the side table is unquestionably Hume's. It might be suggested that Hume, whose firm did extensive work at Hamilton Palace, was familiar with the Trianon chest of drawers and made the side table, either for the duke or as a speculative enterprise. Hume's work was highly respected in the nineteenth century, as attested by the comments of James Morrison, who visited Hamilton Palace in 1841: 'There is nothing but the Cabinets to envy, and the best of these have been made up by Hume'.[28]

Hume also worked extensively at Belvoir Castle, the seat of the dukes of Rutland. Having been almost completely destroyed by fire in 1816, Belvoir was rebuilt in a romantic Gothic style in the late 1820s and largely completed by 1832. The interior is an early example of the British adaptation of French, especially Louis XIV and Louis XV, taste. Little is

1.27

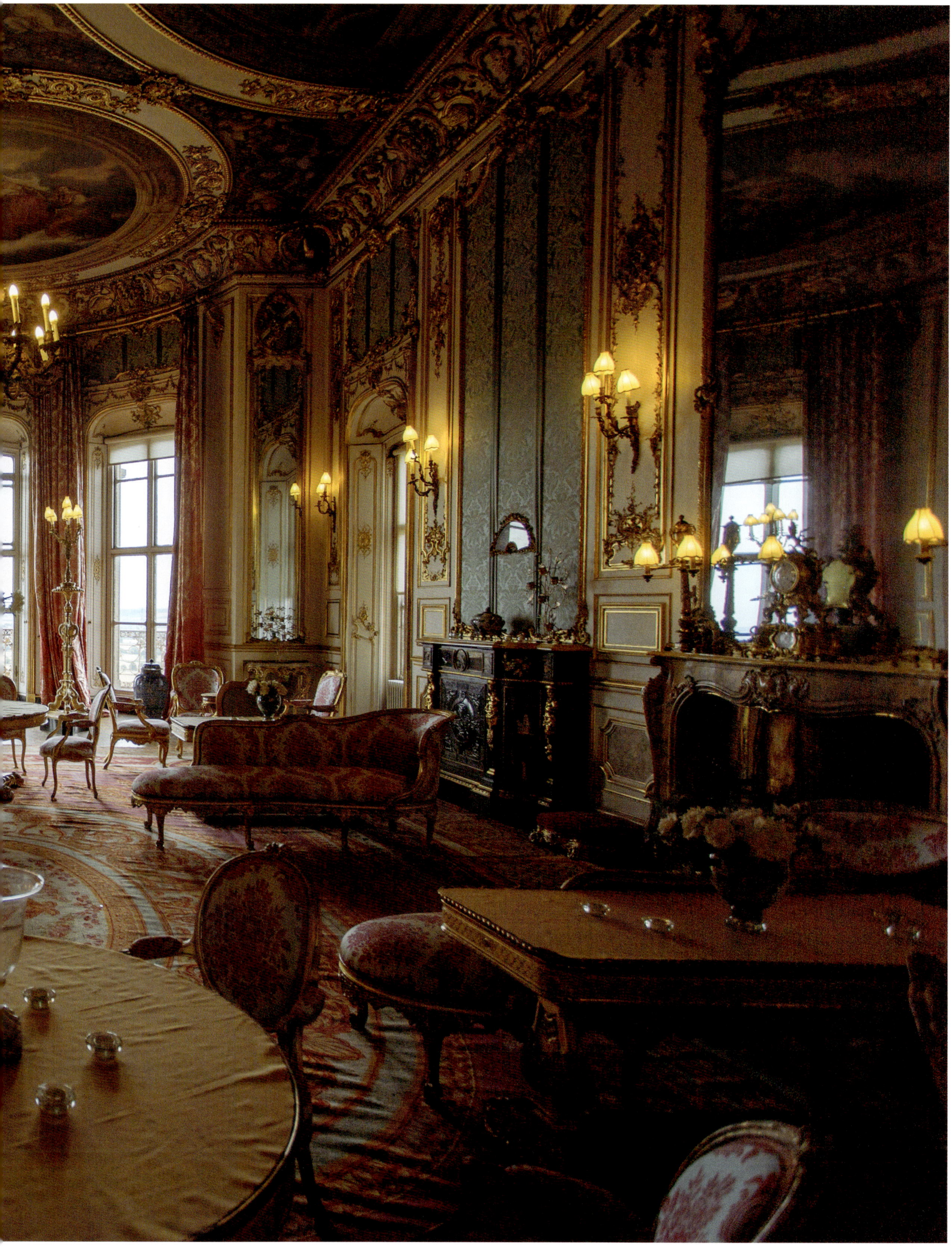

Fig.1.27 (previous spread) The Elizabeth Saloon at Belvoir Castle, showing two of the set of four *pietre dure*-mounted cabinets supplied by Robert Hume *c*.1826. [Belvoir Castle / © Sam Churchill]

Fig.1.28 The London-based Robert Hume incorporated magnificent Gobelins workshop *pietre dure* plaques from the second half of the seventeenth century into this eclectic side cabinet delivered to the 10th Duke of Hamilton in 1824. [© Victoria and Albert Museum, London / courtesy of The Rosalinde & Arthur Gilbert Collection]

Fig.1.29 A 'Buhl' desk in rosewood stamped 'Morant'. The form is based loosely on a French *bureau Mazarin*. Instead of the two clusters of four legs as on late seventeenth-century desks, this example has been 'modernised' with cabriole legs. Every surface is profusely inlaid with brass and turtle shell. [Burghley House]

known about the London-based Robert Hume or his work.[29] Davis has recorded about fifteen pieces by him, made for such celebrated collectors as George Watson Taylor, William Beckford, the 10th Duke of Hamilton and the 2nd Viscount Dungannon (1763–1837).[30] He supplied and produced furniture in a variety of differing styles, such as the cabinet in the Gilbert Collection (**Fig. 1.28**) and the set of four cabinets of the same ilk at Belvoir Castle. The latter cabinets were ordered by the Duchess of Rutland, probably supplied in 1826 and remain in situ today (**Fig. 1.27**).[31] Hume also supplied a simpler suite of Rococo-style giltwood furniture for the Elizabeth Saloon. A Hume sofa table at Belvoir of *c.*1825 is a mixture of Regency taste and the Louis XV Rococo style that, without the provenance, could easily be mistaken for something made a decade later.

The eighteenth-century French style was frequently represented in furniture design of the day and the brass inlays of the Regency period are a constant reminder of the vogue for French-inspired decoration. The British taste for the style inspired by André-Charles Boulle, his name habitually misspelled as 'Buhl' in Britain, was inspired by the grandeur of the *Grand Siècle* and the reign of Louis XIV and became the aspirational choice. The ultimate purchase from the Louis XIV period by an English buyer was the pair of magnificent cabinets designed by Charles Le Brun and made by Domenico Cucci for Louis XIV at the Gobelins workshops, sold by the enterprising London dealer Edward Holmes Baldock to the 3rd Duke of Northumberland in 1822. Baldock, apprenticed as a carpenter between 1792 and 1793,[32] became a dealer-entrepreneur selling and refurbishing eighteenth-century furniture and decorative objects. Despite his distinctive stamp, it is not clear if he actually had cabinet-making workshops on his premises; it is likely that he outsourced most of this work. His name appears as early as 1805 as the freeholder of 7 Hanway Street as a dealer in china and glass. His business expanded and by 1821 the *Post Office Directories* record him as an antique furniture and ornamental china dealer, and in 1826 he described his activities in a bill heading as buying, selling, exchanging and valuing 'China, Cabinets, Screens, Bronzes etc.'[33] Furniture that Baldock handled is frequently seen with his branded stamp 'EHB', but many pieces are attributed to him without firm foundation.

The monumental Alnwick Cabinets are authentic late seventeenth-century pieces but smaller cabinets, also mounted with *pietre dure* plaques made either at the Gobelins or in Florence, were incorporated into new forms such as the Hume cabinet now in the Gilbert Collection or the set of four supplied by Hume to Belvoir Castle. Encrusted with applied and inlaid hardstones and semi-precious stones, their style and glamour reflect the taste of George IV, who had purchased a pair of *pietre dure* cabinets in 1803 through his friend Sir Harry Fetherstonhaugh from the Paris dealer Martin-Eloi Lignereux (1752–1809) for £380.[34] Between 1802 and 1803, during a lull in the Napoleonic Wars, Lignereux's stock was described by an English visitor: 'Nothing can be more beautiful and more costly' he wrote, 'Tables and Secretaires of yew, with gilt and Bronze ornaments for 1000 Louis. For 30 per Ct. advance he will deliver them to England. He says the chief sale is there. The bronze figures supporting candles, the lamps, the clocks, the china tables are all in the richest and best taste'.[35]

The desk or *bureau Mazarin* (**Fig. 1.29**), with *Régence*-style cabriole legs, is from Burghley House, the ancestral home of the marquesses of Exeter. The brass inlay, let into rosewood, is English, but clearly influenced by Boulle. The desk is a finely made revival piece, with mahogany drawer linings, made and stamped by Morant of New Bond Street.

Thomas Chippendale supplied a French-made 'Boulle' desk of similar form to Dumfries House in 1759.[36] Other Boulle-revival furniture made in London at the time was by the French émigré Louis Constantin le Gaigneur (*fl.* 1814–1821), whose work is at first glance similar to the relatively undocumented work of another London maker, Thomas Parker of Air Street (*fl.* 1805–34),[37] and to work attributed to Town & Emanuel, who supplied furniture to Burghley (see **Figs** 1.6 & 2.54). A pair of *première*- and *contre-partie* brass-inlaid games tables, one shown here (**Fig. 1.35a**) is attributed to Parker on stylistic grounds as little of his work is signed. The less well-known John Corfield supplied writing desks in a similar style and a number of small boxes. Baldock also supplied furniture with doors panelled in 'Buhl', including one cabinet with the stamp of Étienne Levasseur, a Parisian cabinet maker.[38] A brass-inlaid table with a Béranesque design by Town & Emanuel, painstakingly inlaid on an ebony ground, is at Hinton Ampner.[39]

Louis Le Gaigneur set up his 'Buhl Manufactory' in London in 1814/15 at 4 Homer Street and 19 Queen Street (now Harrowby Street), shortly after George Bullock had established himself as a maker and designer often using the inlaid brass technique now universally referred to as 'Boulle' work. One of his patrons was the Prince Regent, who bought two writing desks from Le Gaigneur in 1815 for £250 each.[40] Other clients were the Earl of Yarmouth (1777–1842), later the 3rd Marquess of Hertford, who acquired a similar desk now in the Wallace Collection (**Fig. 1.31**).[41] The Prince of

Fig.1.30a Unattributed, but with similarities to the work of Gillows, this rosewood folio cabinet for a gentleman's library has remarkable torsade legs inspired by the twisting of luxurious and expensive heavy silk braid, while the capitals are boldly carved with acanthus. [Butchoff Antiques]

Fig.1.30b The brass inlay and metal marquetry of the 'Buhl' work of this period is characteristically English. [Butchoff Antiques]

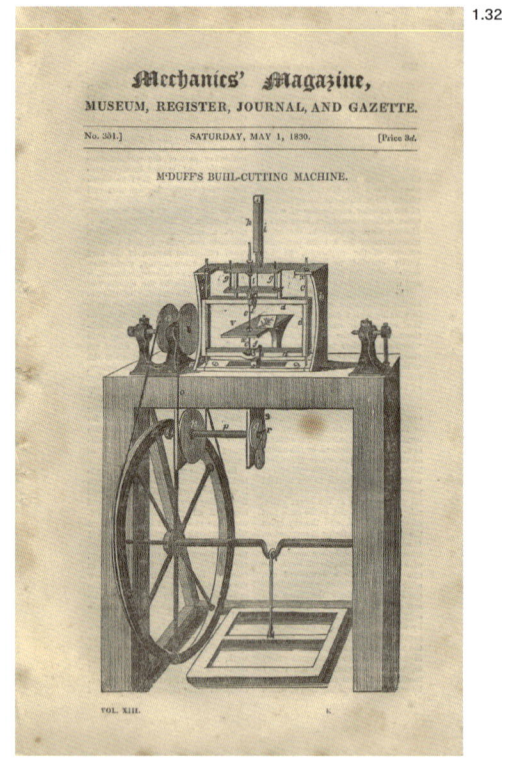

Fig.1.31 **A writing table or *bureau Mazarin*, signed 'Louis Le Gaigneur fecit', almost identical to a pair supplied to the Prince Regent in 1815.** [The Wallace Collection]

Fig.1.32 **A turner by trade, McDuff was awarded a prize of £10 for his invention of a buhl-cutting machine, which he patented in 1829.** [Author's collection]

Fig.1.33 **Attributed to Town & Emanuel, the central brass marquetry panel of this olivewood cabinet is inspired by the designs of Jean Bérain the Elder. Bérain was appointed *dessinateur de la Chambre et du cabinet du Roi* in the Menus-Plaisirs in 1674.** [Butchoff Antiques]

Fig.1.34 **A Louis XV-style writing desk, or *bureau plat*, attributed to Thomas Parker. It demonstrates the taste for the *ancien régime* that became such a strong influence in Britain from the 1820s.** [Carlton Hobbs LLC]

Fig.1.35a & b (overleaf) **Attributed to Thomas Parker, one of a pair of 'Buhl' games tables in** *première-* **and** *contrepartie* **mother-of-pearl and turtle shell, claims inspiration from the early eighteenth century with marquetry panels in the manner of Jean Bérain the Elder. The overall design however is an anglicised interpretation.** [Butchoff Antiques]

Fig. 1.36 **Described in 1827 as 'A MAGNIFICENT TORTOISE-SHELL AND BUHL PARISIAN CABINET With Coved Top And Panels, In Ebony and Rosewood Frame,** *Fitted up inside with Ten Drawers, banded Satinwood and kined Velvet, enclosed by Folding Doors'*,[42] **this cabinet was made in London by Louis Le Gaigneur in** *c.*1820, **almost certainly made for or acquired by Elizabeth Lamb, 1st Viscountess Melbourne, who was part of the Prince Regent's close circle.** [H. Blairman & Sons]

Wales was a close associate of Yarmouth and they appear to have influenced one another's taste. The knee-hole desk once owned by the latter is discreetly signed by the maker 'Louis Le Gaigneur fecit'. The desk is unusual for the extensive use of pewter with idiosyncratic marquetry. With two groups of four legs at either end it is a modern adaptation of a late seventeenth-century form known as a *bureau Mazarin*. However, at 156cm (61½in) wide it is much larger than the earlier examples it seeks to emulate.[43]

Machinery as an aid to the production of furniture had been available as early as the seventeenth century and was constantly being developed for specific tasks. In 1792 a French patent had been taken for stamping brass.[44] In 1803 Thomas Sheraton wrote that 'brass inlay could be cut by gages, made by the cabinet maker for that purpose'.[45] In London Joseph Binns (1776–1829), a 'cabinet inlayer, shell and stringing maker', was making Buhl work in the 1820s and a turner called McDuff patented a buhl-cutting machine (shown in **Fig. 1.32**), essentially a horizontal marquetry 'donkey' for metal, in 1829. The brass marquetry panel on the side cabinet shown in **Fig. 1.33** is inspired by late seventeenth- and early eighteenth-century designs by Jean Bérain and his son and executed in the Boulle metal marquetry technique. Attributed to Town & Emanuel, the cabinet is made of olivewood, almost unheard of at this period. Even after the invention of machinery such as McDuff's, such a large panel would almost certainly have been cut by hand. Machinery was mainly used for the repetitive smaller patterns seen on a variety of different forms of furniture.

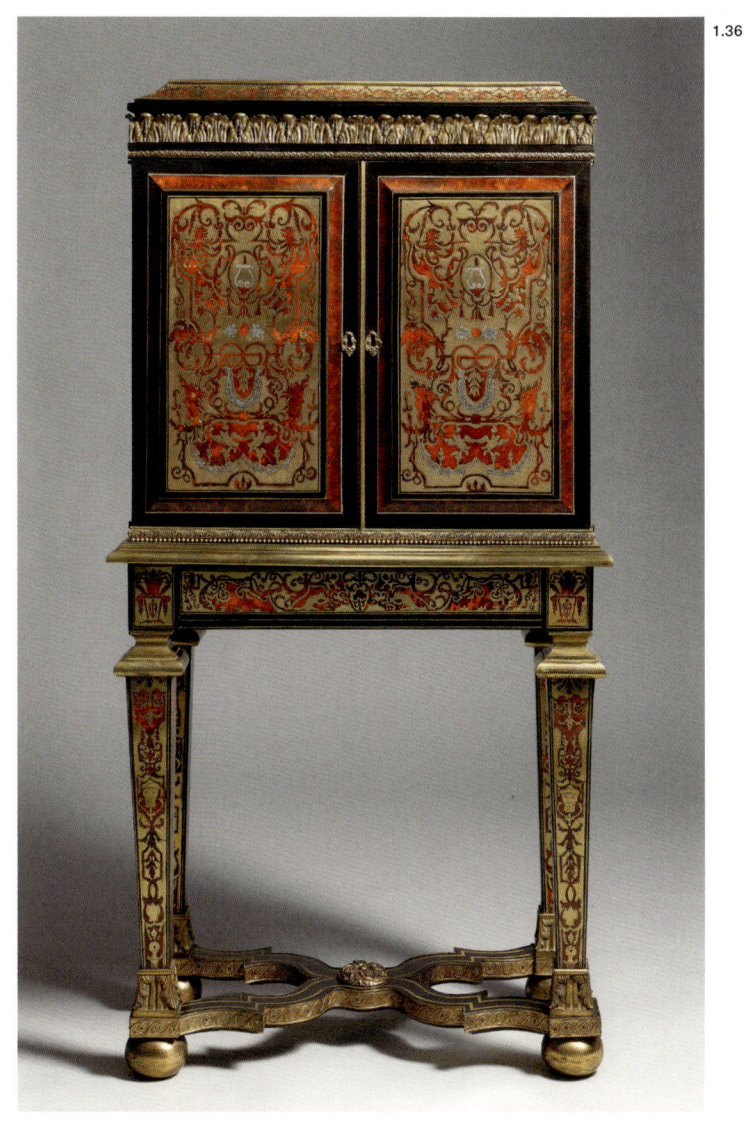

Richard Bridgens is celebrated for his designs in the Gothic, Baronial, Elizabethan and Jacobean styles (**Figs 1.37 & 1.38**). He worked for his contemporaries George Bullock and James Watt at Battle Abbey and for Sir Godfrey Vassal Webster at Aston Hall. His work at Abbotsford, home of Sir Walter Scott, whose novels encouraged a romantic view

1.35b

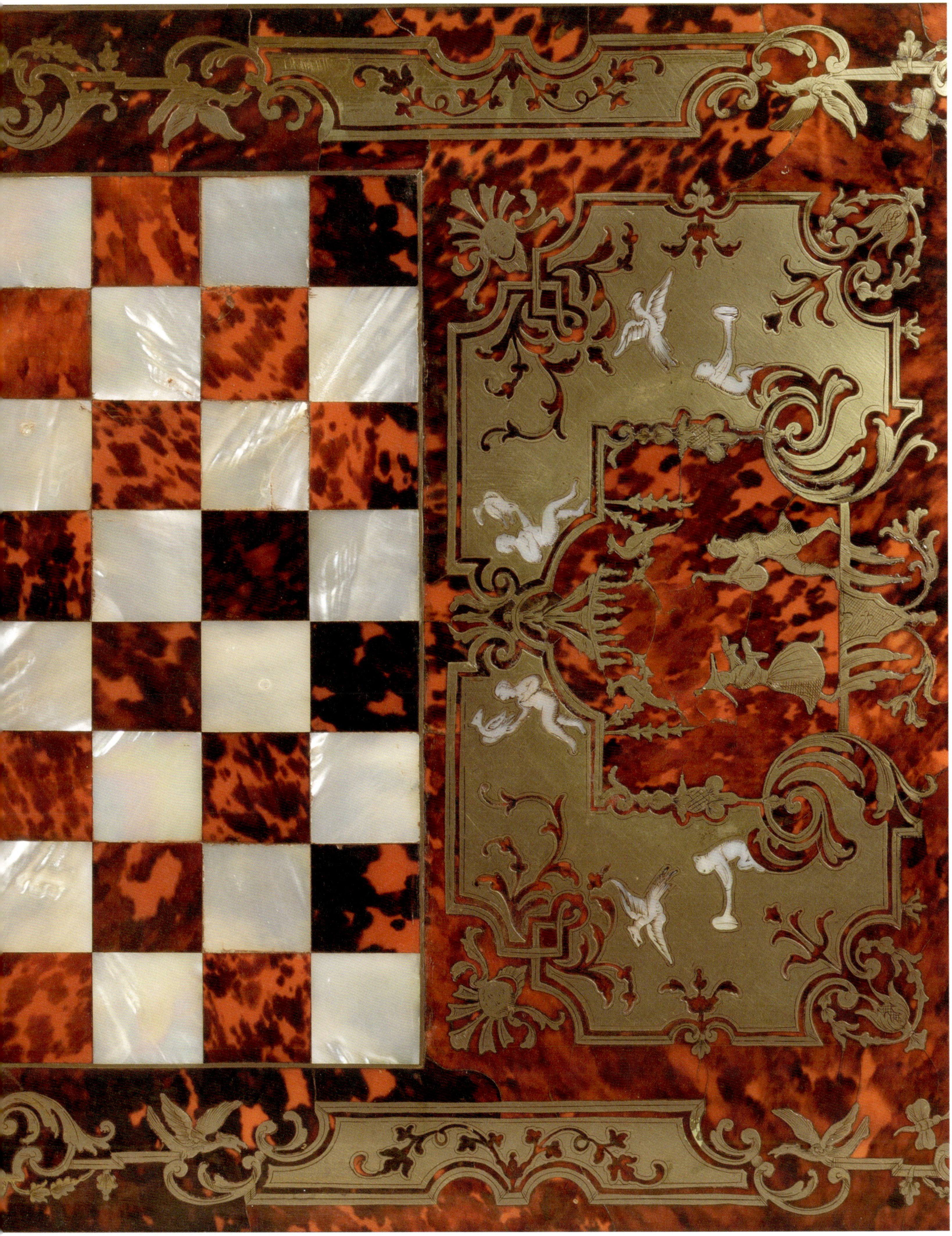

Fig.1.37 **In this design for an elaborate 'window seat', Bridgens has combined decorative elements from the sixteenth and seventeenth centuries, unwittingly inventing the 'Jacobethan' style.** [Getty Research Institute]

Fig.1.38 **Bridgens' interpretation of the Elizabethan Revival, identifiable by the bold strapwork, can be seen clearly on the apron of the sofa in his design.** [Getty Research Institute]

Fig.1.39 **Using the full majesty of home-grown oak, this large library or centre table has a strapwork frieze that is directly comparable to the Bridgens drawings in Figs 1.40a–e.** [Carlton Hobbs LLC]

of Scotland, bolstered support for the Baronial style.[46] In the realm of furniture, other novel and inventive designs had been conceived as early as the late 1810s, but were not disseminated in print until 1825, when Bridgens published *Furniture with Candelabra and Interior Decoration*.[47]

Bridgens' work incorporated and grafted Elizabethan and Jacobean motifs onto familiar forms such as the large oak circular table shown in **Fig. 1.39**, the top lifting when not in use to create space. Similarities can be detected between this table and Bridgens' drawings (**Figs 1.40a–e**). In both instances the carving is directly comparable to two tables at Aston Hall illustrated in the 1838 edition of *Furniture with Candelabra and Interior Decoration*, plates 31–2. The foliate strapwork draws on the style of the late sixteenth and early seventeenth centuries (**Fig. 1.40c**). The decoration on the concave tripod support copies the Elizabethan style of faceted decoration and strapwork imitating jewellery, as drawn in the more fanciful table (**Fig. 1.40d**).

The Elizabethan style favoured by Bridgens was a recurring feature in many of his early designs. The popularity of his work, and the continual reprinting and updating of his book, makes accurate dating of furniture based on his designs difficult unless there is evidence of a specific commission. Although the Elizabethan Revival had its roots in the 1810s, for decades architects continued to admire the Elizabethan era as a truly national style, and many important houses were built accordingly, some furnished to a greater or lesser extent in an eclectic late sixteenth- to late seventeenth-century manner. One later example is Harlaxton Manor, which was built between 1837 and 1845. The design was commenced by Anthony Salvin, who devised the extraordinary façade that drew inspiration from nearby Burghley House. As a sign of one-upmanship, and displaying new wealth as opposed to the aristocratic accumulation of the dukes of Rutland, Harlaxton was engineered to be one room larger than nearby Belvoir Castle. Highclere Castle, better known today as the setting for the BBC television series *Downton Abbey*, was remodelled between 1842 and 1849 by Sir Charles Barry. In the fast-moving fashion of the period, the house had only just been remodelled in the Greek Revival manner by the architect and furniture designer Thomas Hopper. A decade later, Mentmore Towers was completed for Baron Meyer de Rothschild by Sir Joseph Paxton. In the 1820s the huge popularity of novels by Sir Walter Scott encouraged an antiquarian style with an idealised view of life in Britain several hundred years earlier. The antiquarian revival was taken to extremes at the Eglinton Tournament of 1839, a spectacularly extravagant revival of a medieval joust held at Eglinton Castle. However iconic this rain-drenched tournament has become, it should be remembered that it had been prefigured by the antiquarian interests of George IV. Eglinton's festivities pale when compared with the coronation banquet held eighteen years earlier by George IV, specifically the approach of the King's Champion on horseback in full Tudor-style armour (**Fig. 1.43**).[48]

A commonly seen device associated with Victorian furniture is the twist-turned column emulating the Carolean supports typical of the back of caned chairs made from c.1660 to 1700.[49] Wrongly termed by nineteenth-century designers as 'Tudor', these later models epitomise the muddled thinking of the period. They can be seen as early as 1817 in Ackermann's *Repository of Arts* and titled 'Fashionable Chairs', designed by George Bullock. George Smith perpetuated this error in his *Cabinet-Maker and Upholsterer's Guide* of 1826, describing 'the light spiral columns in the backs of chairs…and…in the legs of their tables' as essential elements of the Elizabethan era.[50] The twist turning was confirmed in popularity when Ludwig Grüner furnished the Garden Pavilion in the grounds of Buckingham Palace with a similar chair in 1844 (see **Fig. 3.18**).[51] The same spirals are still evident in Lorenzo Booth's *Exhibition Book of Original Designs for Furniture* of 1864. The pair of side chairs in **Fig. 1.41a**, from a set of ten, is clearly of English construction unlike the numerous Flemish imitations later imported from Malines where such chairs were a speciality. English chairs, even in the late seventeenth century, almost always had square blocks on the stretchers going into the legs, whereas Franco-Flemish chairs have a

1.39

Figs 1.40a–e The frieze illustrated with Elizabethan-style strapwork in plate 31 of *Furniture with Candelabra and Interior Decoration*, is the inspiration for the circular table in (Fig. 1.39). [Getty Research Institute]

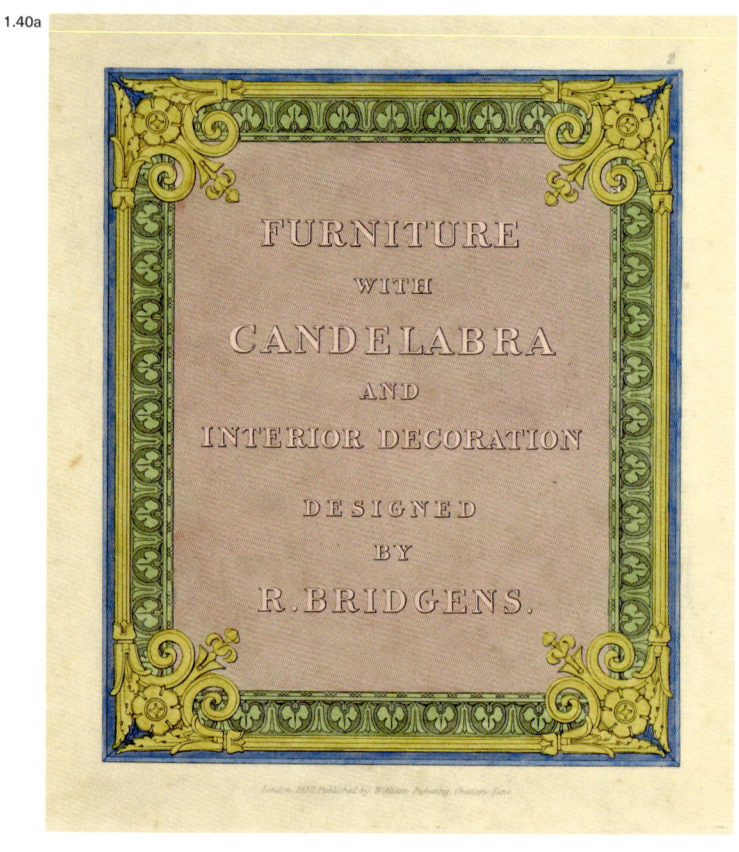

turned tapering end. The twist-turned spirals of the back supports of the nineteenth century run in opposing directions, unlike late Stuart examples where the turning is always in the same direction. Although the illustrated chairs, **Fig. 1.41a**, are a relatively pure late Stuart design, other designs, especially those by Bridgens, are more eclectic. They combine Elizabethan motifs with Stuart (late sixteenth century with late seventeenth century), in a style so aptly named by John Betjeman in 1933 as the 'Jacobethan' style (**Fig. 1.37**).[52]

The Gothic style of architecture and decoration of the eighteenth century can be seen in Chippendale's *Director*, published in the 1750s and 1760s, and Horace Walpole's villa, Strawberry Hill House, rebuilt in stages between 1749 and 1776. In *A Collection of Designs for Household Furniture and Decoration* (1808),[53] Smith illustrated a more robust Gothic style in comparison to the 'Rococo-Gothic' of Walpole's time. The large secretaire bookcase in **Fig. 1.44a**, in richly figured mahogany and over 5.5m (18ft) wide, is in a style of late Regency Gothic that is much heavier than the

CHAPTER 1: 1820S

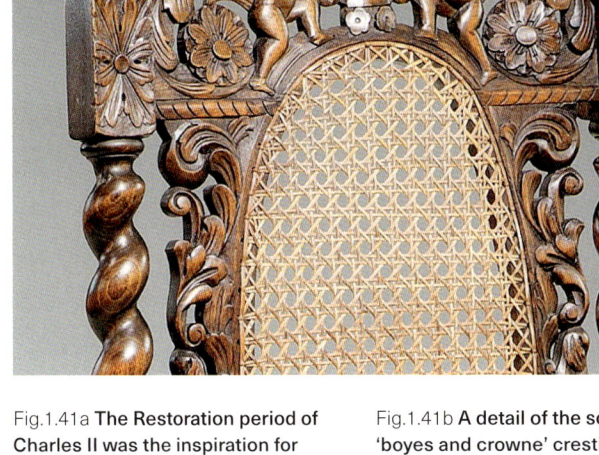

Fig.1.41a The Restoration period of Charles II was the inspiration for numerous sets of caned chairs with tall backs, a style revived from the 1820s onwards. [Private collection]

Fig.1.41b A detail of the so-called 'boyes and crowne' cresting commonly used on copies of Charles II-style caned chairs. In this instance the 'crown' is simply a vase of flowers. [Private collection]

Fig.1.42 As early as 1828, Bridgens designed this ultimate piece of fantasy Elizabethan furniture, complete with coloured detail, a style emulated by Caldecott of Great Russell Street for the Great Exhibition in 1851. [Getty Research Institute]

Fig.1.43 An oil painting by George Jones depicting the antiquarian medieval rite, the entry of the King's Champion, Henry Dymoke, to Westminster Hall during the banquet at the coronation of George IV in 1821. [© His Majesty King Charles III 2023, RCIN 404463]

BRITISH FURNITURE

Fig.1.44a The pinnacle of 'Gothick', this architectural secretaire bookcase, which in part follows the Gillows design shown in Fig. 1.44b, combines idiosyncratic details, notably the astragals, and high-quality mahogany veneers (see also pp.16/17). [Butchoff Antiques]

Fig.1.44b This drawing is the probable inspiration for the bookcase in Fig. 1.44a (above), most notably the oval lobed quatrefoils on the lower doors. The design, dated November 1811, is in the Gillows Sketchbooks. [Westminster City Archives]

Fig. 1.45 Described by George Smith as a 'Sofa Table', this 1807 design, plate 85 of *Collection of Designs for Household Furniture* (1808), has similarities with the pair at Raby Castle (opposite). [Internet Archive Open Library]

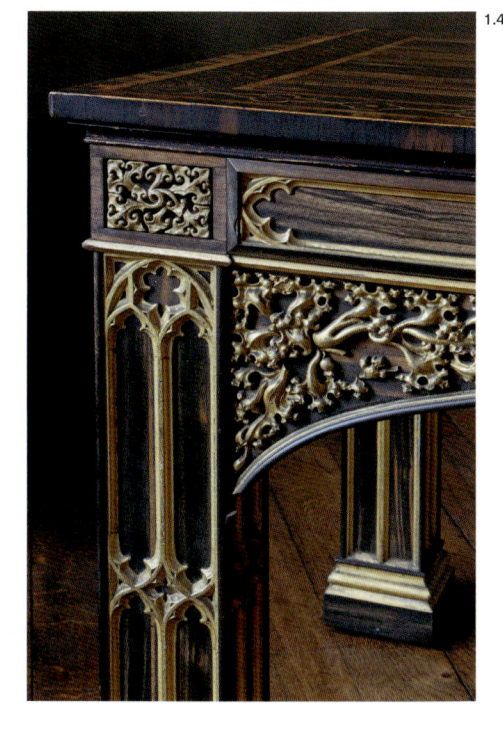

Figs 1.46a–c A stunning calamander-veneered suite comprising a pair of 'Sofa Tables' and an octagonal table with delicately carved applied giltwood tracery. The suite was possibly made for John Carr's octagon room at Raby Castle in c.1820. There are distinct similarities with the George Smith design of 1807 in Fig.1.45 (opposite), and comparisons can be made with a sideboard in the State Dining Room at Windsor Castle, the design attributed to A.W.N. Pugin.[54]

[Raby Castle / Brownlow]

style of eighteenth-century interpretations. The precise date of the piece is unknown. The designer may well have owned a copy of Smith's *Household Furniture*, the only substantially Gothic furniture pattern book of the late eighteenth or early nineteenth centuries. The locks are stamped 'GR', suggesting the date is before 1830. Other possible influences are the Gothic designs by Pugin, published from 1825 to 1828 by Ackermann, but the designer was clearly familiar with mid-Georgian furniture pattern books such as Chippendale's *Director*.

The probable inspiration seems to have been a drawing by Gillows for Edward Hobson in November 1811 (**Fig. 1.44b**).[55] The design has similar elongated quatrefoil panels in the lower cupboard doors, articulated by cluster-column uprights rising to a cornice with three pagoda-style pediments divided by pierced battlements and pinnacles. Another bookcase of similar form was made by Gillows for Daniel Leo of Lannark Park in July 1795.[56] In that example the quatrefoil panels on the cupboard doors were enclosed within ovals. A further model was made by Gillows for Francis Duckinfield Astley in August 1805, again with a crenelated cornice with three crocketed concave-sided triangular pediments.[57]

The suite of Gothic Revival furniture, **Figs 1.46a–c**, now in the Baron's Hall at Raby Castle, is one of the most pleasing reinterpretations of Gothic forms. The use of stunning calamander veneers creates a dramatic effect of contrasting colours and is a rare use of an expensive timber. A species of ebony, alternatively called coromandel, it was mentioned by Sheraton in 1803. More commonly used as a crossbanding due to the expense, the quantity used in the Raby tables is lavish in the extreme. The black and yellow striations of the wood are cleverly contrasted with the applied carved giltwood tracery, complemented by the delicate tracery of marquetry on the tops. The drawer linings of all three tables are in a style suggesting the cabinet maker was trained a generation earlier. The locks on the drawers of the centre tables are stamped 'GR Patent' below a crown, the octagonal table locks are unmarked.

Another early example of the nineteenth-century Gothic Revival is evident in the set of golden oak chairs, one illustrated in **Fig. 1.53a**. Two sets of twelve of the exceptionally long original set of forty-eight chairs are known, this set and the twelve chairs bought in 1979 by the British National Art Collections Fund, which now form part of the permanent collection at Lord Byron's ancestral home, Newstead Abbey. The details are restrained and beautifully worked in a design seemingly ahead of its time. The set was made for Knowsley Hall, the seat of the earls of Derby, considered to be 'one of the great historic houses of England'.[58] The architect John Foster Jr (1786–1846) remodelled the house in the Gothic style, his name appearing in the house account books from 1810 until renovations were completed in 1822.[59] In the time-honoured fashion of an impending royal progress, the house was refurbished for the visit of George IV in 1821. The style suited the king's medieval predilection and the historical symbolism of Gothic design as a 'royally sanctioned aesthetic' heightened its popularity in the 1820s.[60] Foster, like his father, was a

Figs 1.47a & b **The brand on the underside of the Morel & Seddon table in Fig. 1.47c, supplied to Windsor Castle in 1828, branded during the 1866 inventory for Room 235. The paper label indicates that the table was moved in the same year to the next room.** [Butchoff Antiques]

Figs 1.47c & d **A library table by Morel & Seddon of 1828, the firm describing the gilt leaf carving on the top edge as a 'taurus' moulding. It is interesting to contrast this refined and relatively simple table with the rapidly changing taste of the king seen in the table illustrated in Fig. 2.17a.** [Butchoff Antiques]

Fig.1.48 A silver or 'China' table based on an example made by Gillows in 1761 for Thirsk Hall. Popular again in the early nineteenth century, Gillows named this style of table a 'Salisbury Antique Table' in their 1828 Estimate Sketch Book.[61] [Ronald Phillips]

Figs 1.49a & b The outer border of the top of a table almost certainly made by Morel & Seddon is veneered in amboyna. The purpleheart foliage, inlaid into bird's eye maple, is divided by intricate pewter inlay on a red turtle shell ground. The purpleheart would have been a bright and heady hue of vivid purple when new. Over the years it has naturally faded with sunlight and oxidisation. The Grecian-style trestle supports are edged in amboyna. [Butchoff Antiques]

notable Liverpool architect. No doubt his understanding of the Gothic style was guided by his mentor, Sir Jeffry Wyatville (1766–1840).

Furniture such as the Greco-Roman-inspired table (**Fig. 1.47c**), made in the late 1820s, is another example of the eclectic taste of George IV and is very different from the elaborate furniture that might be expected from a seemingly unlimited royal purse and a patron of avant-garde taste. The simple, elegant occasional table resembles the late stylised Empire fashion favoured in Paris under Charles X, making use of distinctive veneers in light-coloured *bois clairs*. Veneered in amboyna, it is an important escapee from the Royal Household, made by Morel & Seddon in 1828 as a part of George IV's revitalisation of Windsor Castle.[62] Paper labels on the underside of the table record much of its history: 'Windsor Castle Room 236, No.4 1866', another '235' and two other labels, 'R235' and '21'; a brand mark, shown here (**Fig. 1.47a**), under the front rail 'V.R. 1866, Windsor Castle, Room 235'; and a pencil notation to the underside 'Room 235, York ***'. The 1866 inventory documented and stamped not only the furniture in each room but also locks and keys. The invoice from Morel & Seddon clearly described this table as 'an occasional table of fine amboyna ... supported on four columns, enriched with carved foliage ... gilt in burnished and matt gold'.[63]

In a similar vein the writing table shown in **Figs 1.49a & b** is an elegant and innovative pseudo-Grecian form from the end of the Georgian era.[64] The self-tapering trestle supports are a familiar theme but the top is of the finest design and quality of execution and clearly of a standard high enough to be a royal commission. Almost certainly by Morel & Seddon, the top is inlaid with an outer band of cut

CHAPTER 1: 1820S

Figs 1.50a & b **This amboyna-veneered centre table has been richly inlaid with a Buhl-style border. It was supplied to George IV between 1827 and 1829 by Morel & Seddon and is now in the Grand Reception Room at Windsor Castle.** [Royal Collection Trust / © His Majesty King Charles III 2023]

Figs 1.51 & 1.52 **Two carved oak tables attributed to A.W.N. Pugin and made by Morel & Seddon between 1827 and 1829 for occasional use in the octagonal Beauffette, the Ante Room to the Dining Room at Windsor Castle. Pugin has used the Tudor rose motif on the table on the right and suspended quatrefoils on the table on the left. As with other tables at the time, he used a wide variation of decoration and supports.** [Royal Collection Trust / © His Majesty King Charles III 2023]

Figs 1.53a & b **This chair is from a long set designed by the Liverpool architect John Foster for the state dining room of Knowsley Hall. The oak has acquired a rich golden glow, a patination built up since the 1820s.** [Carlton Hobbs LLC]

Figs 1.54a & b **In Cuban mahogany with boldly moulded 'Gothick' tracery and a crenelated cornice, this bookcase appears to be influenced by plate 100 in** *A Collection of Designs for Household Furniture and Interior Decoration*, **by George Smith, first published in 1808, revised in 1826.** [Butchoff Antiques / Getty Research Institute]

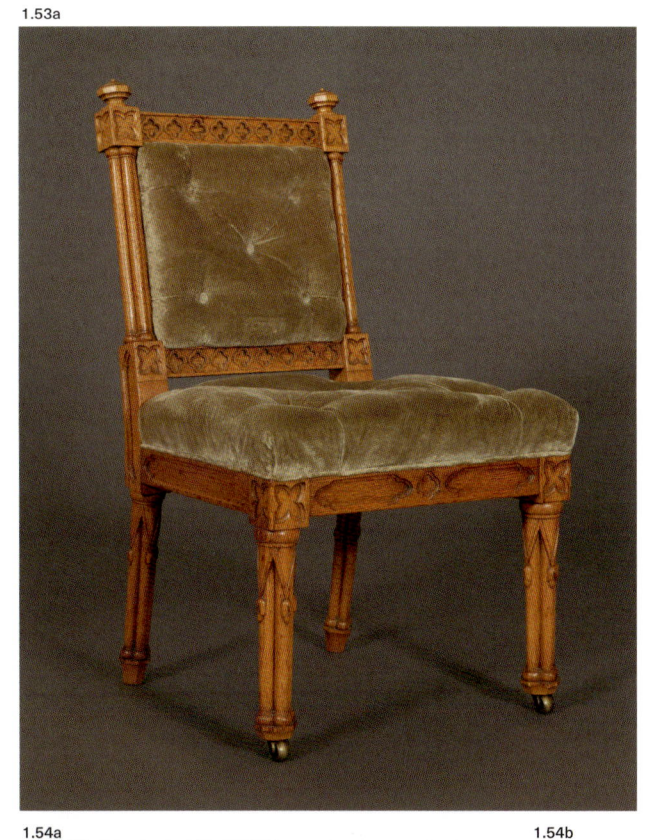

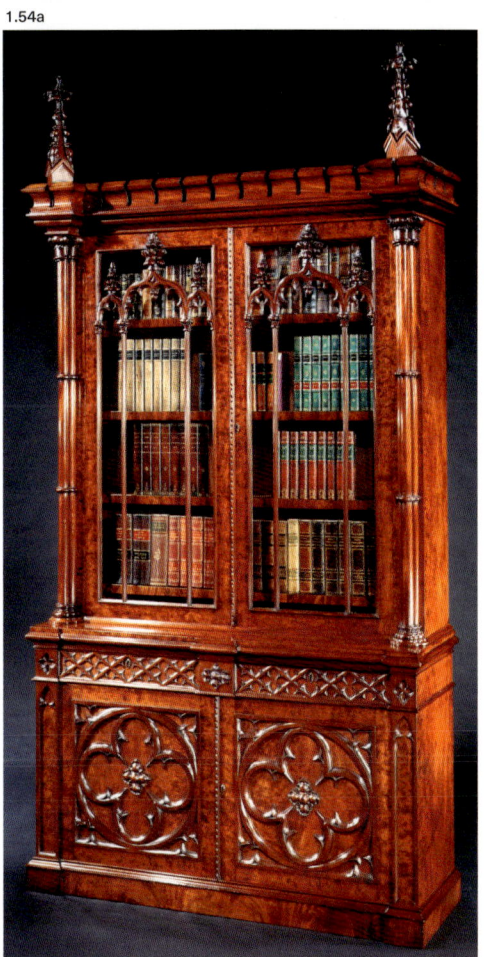

51

BRITISH FURNITURE

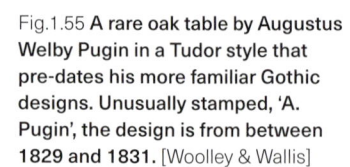

1.55

1.56

1.57

Fig.1.55 **A rare oak table by Augustus Welby Pugin in a Tudor style that pre-dates his more familiar Gothic designs. Unusually stamped, 'A. Pugin', the design is from between 1829 and 1831.** [Woolley & Wallis]

Fig.1.56 **The c.1823 design of this armchair is attributed to Augustus Charles Pugin. Made by Gillows for Eaton Hall, it is directly comparable to an example in the Victoria and Albert Museum.**[65] [The Higgins Bedford]

Fig.1.57 **The Drawing Room, plate 13 in** *Views of Eaton Hall in Cheshire, The Seat of the Right Honourable Earl Grosvenor* **by J. & J.C. Buckler, published in 1826. This view shows the back of a Pugin armchair with an unusual method of fabric hanging. A similar set of chairs, made for dining, were made for Lord Berwick at Attingham Park.** [Alamy Stock Photo]

pewter 'Buhl' work in the French manner, set onto a rich red turtle-shell ground.[66] The table's marquetry decoration again has similarities with numerous French examples of the contemporary Charles X period, and furniture made by Morel & Seddon for Room 231 at Windsor.[67] The mix of amboyna with Boulle marquetry is similar to a table in the Royal Collection, part of the group of furniture and furnishings supplied between 1827 and 1829 to George IV for Windsor Castle by Morel & Seddon (**Fig. 1.50a**). The design was by Nicholas Morel, the furniture made in George Seddon's workshops. Tables like **Fig. 1.49a**, variously called writing or occasional tables in the 1820s, could be easily wheeled in front of chairs or sofas when needed.

Roberts's cataloguing and subsequent publication (2001) of the furniture made by Nicholas Morel and George Seddon for George IV at Windsor is an extraordinary inventory of royal taste. Morel, thought to be of French extraction, had worked for the Prince of Wales at Carlton House and the Brighton Pavilion. Taking advantage of Seddon's large existing workforce at his workshops on Aldersgate Street, the two men formed a partnership to undertake the monumental task of refurbishing the apartments at Windsor Castle, basing the company at Morel's address, 13 Great Marlborough

CHAPTER 1: 1820S

Street. The firm later worked for William IV and, in 1830, on a commission for the acquisitive Francophile, the Marquess of Stafford, later the 2nd Duke of Sutherland, which ran to the value of £15,000.[68] Furniture was supplied by Morel & Seddon to Windsor Castle between 1827 and 1833 for the settled at sum of £180,000, the approximate equivalent of over £19 million today.

A.W.N. Pugin is well documented for his designs and work in the Gothic style, but little is known of furniture made in his Covent Garden workshops during his short-lived furniture-making business. In 1829, at the remarkably young age of seventeen or eighteen, he established workshops at 12 Hart Street (now Floral Street) in London's Covent Garden. The table shown here is a rare and early example of work made in his workshop and is stamped 'A. Pugin' on the underside (**Fig. 1.55**). Possibly, the pedestal is one of two or more made to support dining table leaves. An identical base is in the Victoria and Albert Museum.[69] Although developing his now-celebrated Gothic themes, in these early days Pugin was designing in what he termed the 'James I style'. More gifted as a designer than a businessman, two years later he effectively went bankrupt but was bailed out by his maternal aunt, Miss Welby,[70] who rescued him from the sponging-house, the somewhat unfortunate name for a place of temporary confinement for debtors. The octagonal centre table in **Fig. 1.58a** has the royal stamp for Queen Victoria and an inventory date of 1873. However, it is of a type designed by the precocious Pugin and made for Windsor Castle in the 1820s. The inventory marks also include 'Room 551' which refers to the Brunswick Tower. Pugin wrote in his diary 'went to design and make working drawings for the Gothic furniture of Windsor Castle at £1.1s per day, for the following rooms. The long gallery, the coffee room, the vestibule anti-room, halls, grand staircase, octagon in the Brunswick Tower and Great Dining Room'.[71]

It was generally agreed that the library was the room best suited to the powerful pictorial language of Gothic. As Edward Joy has noted, 'the library became the *locus classicus* of Gothic furniture, which could readily conjure up the quiet

1.58a

1.58b

1.59

Fig.1.58a There are several Pugin-designed pieces at Windsor showing the use of double-ended lancet arches, such as for the drawers and octagonal base of this oak table. The underside has the later stamp 'VR' below a crown, along with the 1873 inventory mark when it was placed in Room 551. [Private collection]

Fig.1.58b Pugin's highly individual brass handles are a unique and specific design, the detail contrasting with the architectural simplicity of the table itself. [Private collection]

Fig.1.59 Possibly designed by William Porden, who designed furniture made by Gillows for Eaton Hall, this half tester bed of oak, applied with Gothick-style foliage highlighted in gold, has similar details, such as the underhanging parcel-gilt arches, to the table in Figs 1.60a–d (overleaf). [Butchoff Antiques]

and studious atmosphere of the monastic scriptorium'.[72] Writing in *The Repository* in March 1827, Ackermann waxed lyrical about a Gothic library bookcase designed by Pugin the Younger.[73] 'No style,' he wrote, 'can be better adapted for its decoration than that of the middle ages, which possesses a sedate and grave character, that invites the mind to study and reflection. The rays passing through its variegated casements cast a religious light upon the valuable tomes on either side.'[74] Such praise was no doubt prompted

Fig.1.60a Designed for Morel & Seddon by the fifteen-year-old A.W.N. Pugin in 1827, this centre table was originally delivered to Room 240, 'The Coffee Room', at Windsor Castle, in July 1828. The pollard oak veneers are complemented by oak leaf and acorn marquetry and highlighted with parcel gilding. [Butchoff Antiques]

Fig.1.60b A similar table to Fig. 1.60a in A.W.N. Pugin's *The True Principles of Pointed or Christian Architecture*, 1841, p. 41. [Getty Research Institute]

Fig.1.60c The cover for the Windsor table, embroidered with the royal coat of arms. [Butchoff Antiques]

Fig.1.60d The elaborate architectural underside of the Pugin table. [Butchoff Antiques]

by Pugin and Wyatville's lavish Gothic remodelling of George IV's state apartments at Windsor, which had started in 1824.

The 'medievalising' of Windsor Castle was the climax of seventy years of Georgian interest in Gothic interiors, but the Gothic style continued to be popular in various forms throughout the nineteenth century. Alongside delicately veneered, inlaid and gilt furniture, Morel & Seddon supplied furniture inspired, and in many cases designed, by Pugin, such as the oak octagonal table (**Fig. 1.58a**). Pugin has borrowed from the uncompromising solidity of exterior stonework and the table has lancet arches similar to those on the balustrade of a staircase salvaged from George IV's Carlton House and reused at Windsor. The photograph in **Fig. 1.61**, taken in *c.*1880, shows **Fig. 1.60a** in the King's State Bed Chamber at Windsor Castle. The Sovereign's Entrance and staircases at Windsor are other examples of rooms furnished by Morel & Seddon in this Puginesque style.

Aged twenty-three, Pugin worked with Sir Charles Barry on the design for the new Palace of Westminster. Here his medieval and Gothic style was heavier than his early phase,

Fig.1.61 **A photograph taken in *c.*1880 of the Council Room at Windsor Castle, now known as the King's State Bed Chamber, with the centre table by Morel & Seddon (Fig. 1.60a) in the foreground. The bed, attributed to George Jacob, was supplied by Dominique Daguerre for the Prince of Wales at Carlton House in the late 1780s and altered and reupholstered by J.G. Crace for the State Visit of Napoleon III in 1855.**
[Royal Collection Trust / © His Majesty King Charles III 2023]

GOTHIC TABLE.

more robust and emphasising constructional details that re-emerged on Arts and Crafts furniture at the end of the century. Despite the inevitable praise in contemporary 'polite' exhibition prose, it is unclear how popular a cabinet designed by him shown by Crace at the 1862 London exhibition, for example, would have been amongst the general public (see Chapter 5 – 1860s). A.W.N. Pugin died at the age of forty and his son Edward Welby Pugin subsequently built up a successful architectural practice. His furniture was more flamboyant than his father's and had a decidedly French twist.

Apart from the obvious need for comfort, elaborately upholstered beds continued to be a status symbol in the nineteenth century. However, the fully upholstered four-poster bed with a canopy, which was an important feature from the late seventeenth century, became less popular over the course of the early nineteenth century, particularly as room heating improved. The bed shown in **Fig. 1.59**, enriched with 'Gothick' tracery, is a half tester in the manner of the architect William Porden, who designed Eaton Hall for the Grosvenor family.

The fashions in France and England for furniture and interiors inspired by the archaeology of the ancient Greek and Roman civilisations, and the Napoleonic campaigns in Europe, continued into the 1820s. The Grecian-influenced work table in **Fig. 1.65a**, veneered in *gonçalo alves* and partly

Fig.1.62 **A plate from Rudolph Ackermann's** *The Repository of arts, literature, commerce, manufactures, fashions and politics*, **published periodically between 1809 and 1829. This illustration of 1826 shows Gothic tracery above gryphons inspired by those at the** *Palais de Justice*, **Rouen.** [from Rudolph Ackermann, The Repository of Arts... Ser. III, vol. VII, March 1826, pl. 17]

Fig.1.63 **One end of a rosewood divan in the Greco-Egyptian taste but inlaid in brass with fashionable 'French Buhl' foliage. The unknown maker has reinterpreted designs created by Thomas Hope.**[75] [Private collection]

1.63

1.64

Fig.1.64 **A pair of unusual Grecian-influenced open bookcases are comparable to a single example formerly at Belton House and bear the label of James Newton, an upholsterer, cabinet maker, appraiser and undertaker at 63 Wardour Street.** [Sotheby's]

Fig.1.66 (opposite) **In this design for a secretaire bookcase, Nicholson has accentuated the decorative possibilities of flame-figured mahogany. The design of the gilded glazing bars could be varied according to the client's wishes.** [Peter and Michael Angelo Nicholson, *The Practical Cabinet-maker, Upholsterer, and Complete Decorator*, 1827, plate XXIII]

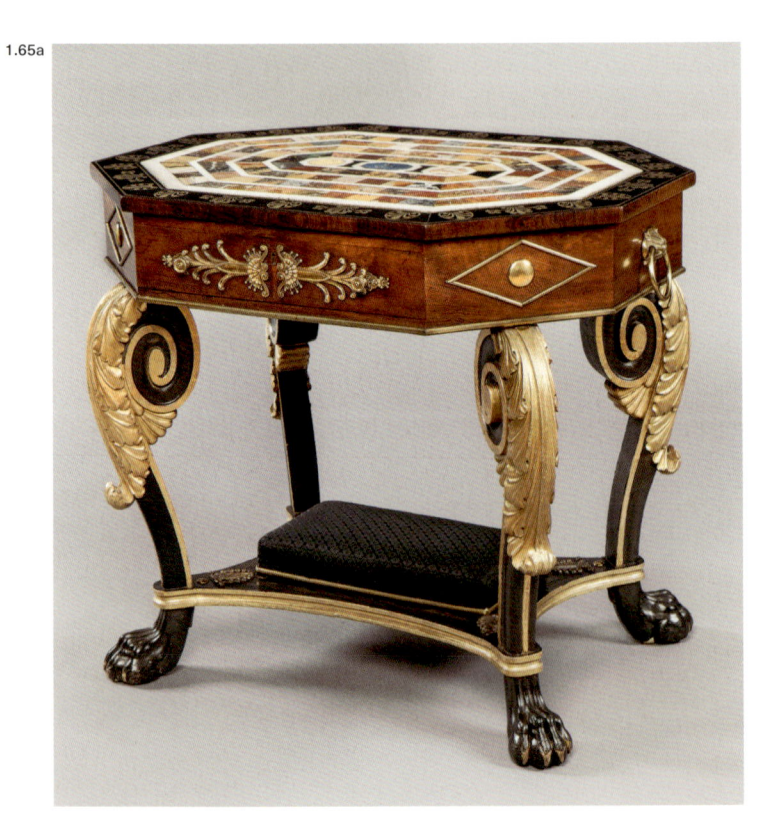

1.65a

1.65b

Figs 1.65a & b **Possibly designed by James Newton, the elongated octagonal top of this table is decorated with specimens of various hardstones including *lapis lazuli*, *antico rosso*, *giallo sienna*, *cipollino*, *mandolato rosso* and *brecciato*. When exhibited at The Regency Festival Exhibition at Brighton Pavilion in 1948, the underhung work bag for knitting and sewing was still present.** [Butchoff Antiques]

CHAPTER 1: 1820S

1.66

1.67

1.68

1.69

Fig.1.67 A plate dated 1827 from Peter and Michael Angelo Nicholson's *The Practical Cabinet-Maker, Upholsterer, and Complete Decorator*. Nicholson has used the ubiquitous 'sabre' leg and Grecian attributes to the back and crossbar highlighted in gold. The decoration of the top-rail is confined in the same manner as the set of chairs by Dixwell (Fig. 1.19). [Peter and Michael Angelo Nicholson, *The Practical Cabinet-maker, Upholsterer, and Complete Decorator*, 1827]

Fig.1.68 A rosewood library table attributed to Morel & Hughes. The original red morocco leather top has a fine gilt-bronze (ormolu) gallery and profuse parcel-gilding. It appears no expense was spared for its original owner, the 3rd Duke of Northumberland. [Private collection]

Fig.1.69 One of a pair of large mahogany wine coolers attributed to Gillows. The designs of the heavy gadrooning and fluted columnar support are drawn from antiquity. [Private collection]

BRITISH FURNITURE

Figs 1.70a–d *The Complete Cabinet Maker and Upholsterer's Guide*, published by J. Stokes in 1829, has sixteen highly coloured plates and 'receipts' [*sic*] for staining various materials, including turtle shell. [Getty Research Institute]

Figs 1.71a & b This day bed, or couch, is made from tigerwood. Termed *gonçalo alves* in Portuguese, it bears a distinct resemblance to rosewood. The apron is decorated with Buhl-style brass marquetry, in a manner similar to work by William Trotter of Edinburgh. [Butchoff Antiques]

60

gilded ebony, is attributable to James Newton (1760–1829).[76] Newton trained under Lawrence Fell and William Turton, rivals of Thomas Chippendale. The Greek style was further perpetuated by Peter Nicholson and his delightfully named son Michael Angelo in their joint publication *The Practical Cabinet-Maker, Upholsterer, and Complete Decorator* of 1826.[77] Full of complex drawings sufficient for a cabinet maker to understand the principles of design, the eighty-one plates, mainly in colour, are highly decorative and appear to be an amalgam of the simpler, instantly recognisable Regency style with a fussiness and over-elaboration anticipating Victorian taste (**Figs 1.66 & 1.67**). Due to the continued popularity of the Nicholson Grecian style, the book was republished as late as 1846. The circular wine cooler, one of a pair, in **Fig. 1.69** is of generous proportions and similar to plate 22 of *The Practical Cabinet-Maker*. The heavy Roman-style gadrooning shows an almost excessive use of expensive mahogany. The fact that they appear to be almost exactly the model of a cooler supplied by Gillows in 1810 to Stephen Tempest of Broughton Hall underlines the difficulty of dating furniture of this period.[78]

In the early nineteenth century, William Trotter was the most successful cabinet maker in Scotland. His premises were described in Thomas Dibdin's *Tour in the Northern Counties of England and in Scotland*. Dibdin wrote that 'The locality of this great … warehouse is rather singular. It is on the ground floor, lighted by a skylight. Of great length, and vistas filled with Mahogany and Rosewood objects of temptation. Of all styles, including the modern form.'[79] Trotter is normally associated with the Grecian Revival style typical of the late Regency and the elegant couch, or chaise longue, in the Greek style (**Fig. 1.71a**) may reasonably be attributed to the Trotter family. The furniture made by Trotter in the 'Chinease' [sic] style in 1825 for Kinfauns Castle overlooking the river Tay appears to have been an idiosyncratic exception.

In 1807, the wealthy Dutch-born financier, Thomas Hope, had published his *Household Furniture and Interior Decoration*. The designs it featured juxtaposed a whole range of styles, including Greek, Roman and Indian, and a

Fig.1.72 **A mahogany table in the manner of George Smith with a** *Saint-Pons-de-Thomières* **marble slab. Smith's contemporary, Bullock, favoured Mona marble from his own quarry in Llanfechell.** [Private collection]

Fig.1.73 **The base of this rare table is vibrantly carved in rosewood with a nod to the French** *Régence* **style. The maker, Saunders & Woolley of 170 Oxford Street, has stamped it twice.** [Butchoff Antiques]

1.74a

1.74b

Figs 1.74a & b **A beautifully figured mahogany wardrobe in the Egyptian style. Its exoticism is enhanced by the pylon-shaped central section that owes much to the influence of Thomas Hope's *Household Furniture* of 1807.** [Butchoff Antiques]

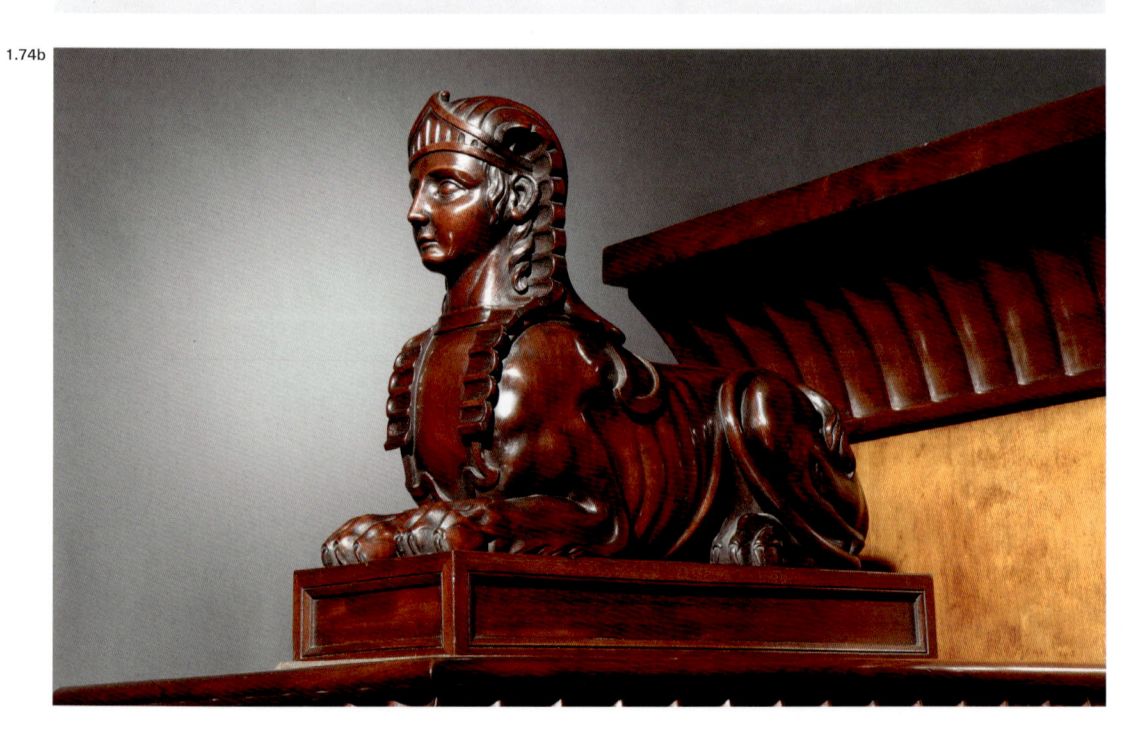

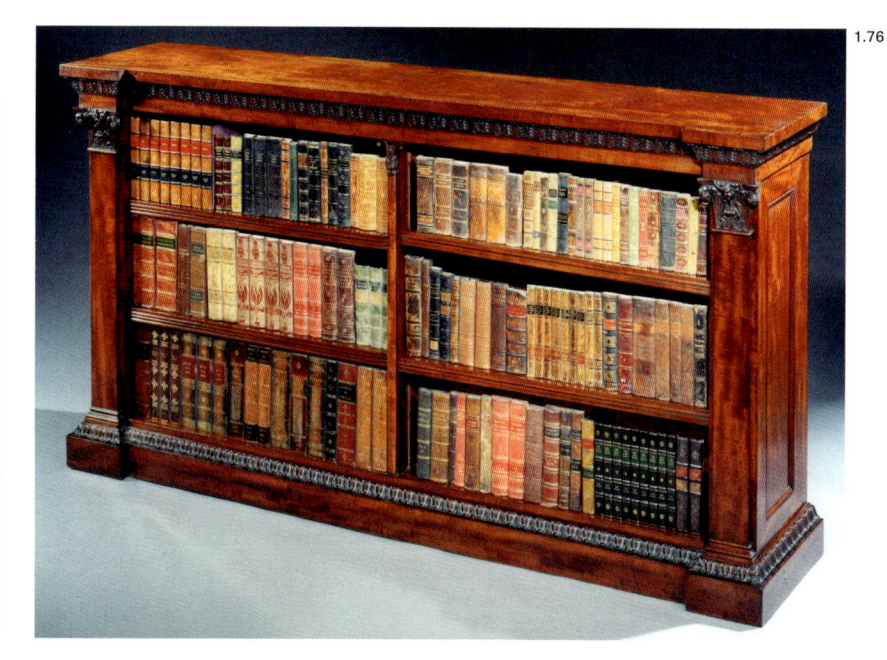

Fig.1.75 **A small mahogany stool with Egyptian overtones, created by an as yet unidentified designer or maker, is a rare anomaly, typical of the inventive period of the early years of the nineteenth century.** [Butchoff Antiques]

Fig.1.76 **One of a pair of library bookcases in richly veneered Cuban mahogany, possibly made by George Seddon. Made to just fit over a dado rail to allow for a picture hang, the form has an affinity with a design** in *The Practical Cabinet-maker, Upholsterer, and Decorator* of 1826. [Private collection]

Fig.1.77 **Two mahogany bench stools of the Rococo Revival of the 1820s and '30's. One is marked 'I and II' and the other 'V and VI', the missing numerals indicating they were part of a larger set. The bearers of each stool are stamped with the workman's initials, 'HH', a mark found on seat furniture by Gillows.**[80] [Private collection]

room devoted entirely to the Egyptian style. In 1812 George Bullock's brother William opened a museum on Piccadilly, the façade partly inspired by Hope's Egyptian Room at Duchess Street. Called the Egyptian Hall, it contained an extensive Roman gallery as well as George Bullock's own showroom. Egyptomania, a fashion resulting from Napoleon's Egyptian Campaign (1798–1801), had been a novel and exotic influence on the decorative arts. In July 1798 Napoleon had landed his *armée d'Orient*, comprising not only 35,000 troops but also a dedicated group of scientists and artists to record the mysteries of the Nile. English and French designers quickly incorporated these new discoveries into the decorative arts.

The eccentric wardrobe illustrated in **Fig. 1.74a** is the zenith of the Egyptomania interest of the Regency period and owes much to the influence of Thomas Hope's 1807 book of designs. The most immediate Egyptian motif is the Sphinx, but a closer look shows pharaonic heads wearing *khat*-headcloths, adorned with the uraeus, a symbol of Wadjet, the goddess of wisdom. The choice of mahogany is exquisite, with carefully matched veneers aptly referred to as 'flame figured'. The pylon form of the central section of the wardrobe is drawn directly from the architecture of ancient Egyptian temples. The pharaonic references are exotic even today and would have had a spectacular impact on audiences in the early nineteenth century.

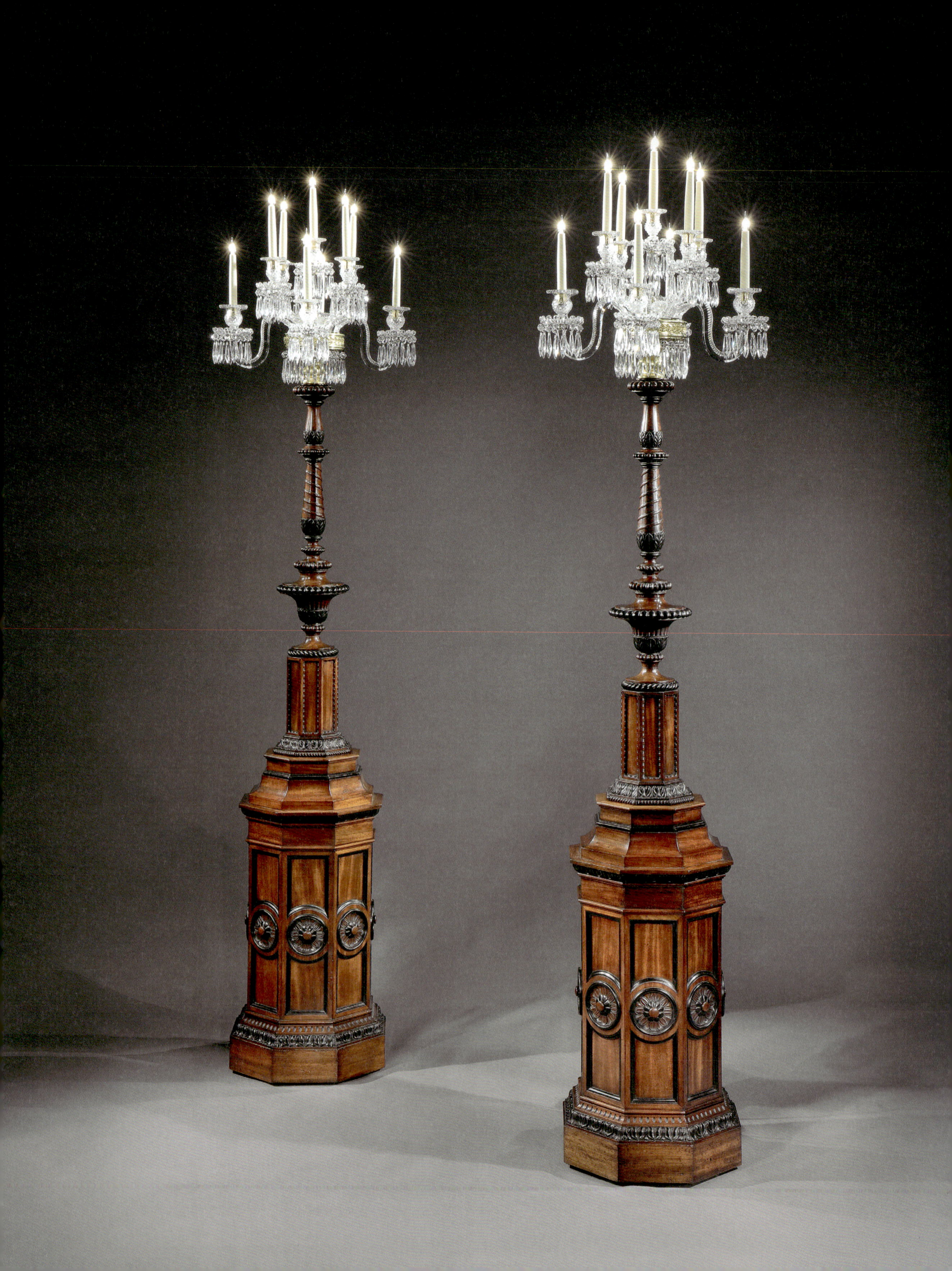

CHAPTER 2

1830s

'I have come from my house to your palace!'[1]

On 26 June 1830, the ailing George IV died and was succeeded by his younger brother William, who by then was sixty-four years old. William died in 1837 and was succeeded by his eighteen-year-old niece, Victoria. A time of innovation, the population was expanding and travel became easier with the first ever intercity line from Liverpool to Manchester opening in 1830. This was followed by the Liverpool to Birmingham line in 1837 and, in 1838, the year of the queen's coronation, the Birmingham to London link opened. Just one year later, participants in the Eglinton Tournament, a re-enactment of a medieval joust, were able to make their way to Ayrshire, with their armour and horses, using special trains laid on by the Glasgow and Ayrshire railway.[2] Shipping also improved; three large wooden-hulled steam liners were launched in 1839 that were able to complete a transatlantic crossing in a quarter of the time taken by sailing ships. Industry was growing at a fast rate, especially in the north of the country, and the furniture industry needed to keep up with demand. The Swing Riots in England, albeit confined to the destruction of new-fangled farm machinery, must have caused nervousness amongst the bosses of the larger furniture firms who were beginning to use steam machinery to speed up production, needing fewer employees. By the end of the decade Britain's influence as a world power had grown enormously, in part due to a booming export industry.

Although the use of machinery brought with it attendant dangers to health and safety, throughout history cabinet-making firms repeatedly suffered from one major danger – fire. The reporting of fires in various newspapers and journals gives a snapshot into their frequency and the financial damage caused. Many firms appear to have had insurance, but this was for loss of stock and buildings, not for loss of trade, although most were able to re-establish their ability to do business quickly. Inevitably furniture workshops, using heat, open furnaces, candlelight and, increasingly, steam, were susceptible to fire. Seddon & Sons suffered several workshop fires with a particularly disastrous instance in 1830. Mahogany to the value of £1,500 was destroyed, and *The Times* reported that as many as one hundred tool chests were lost.[4] The firm, one of the largest and longest standing of all the London firms, had suffered fires in 1768 and 1783.

Despite the rich, ornate decoration and sumptuous excess of much of the furniture shown in this chapter, British makers continued to produce furniture in a more modest style. Most of this output is anonymous but some has similarities with that seen in the plethora of design books published in the

Fig. 2.1 (opposite) **In the Regency period, George Bullock and W. & C. Wilkinson designed tall and imposing candelabra in the Grecian style. This slightly later palatial pair, almost 3m (10ft) tall, each have nine cut-glass candlearms, the glass attributed to Hancock & Rixon. Later exhibiting at the 1851 exhibition, the glass maker had worked at Windsor Castle and St James's Palace and received payment for '2 very thick handsome Maplewood Stands French Polished…'.[3] They made the world's largest chandelier for the Throne Room of the Dolmabahçe Palace in Istanbul, a gift to the Sultan from Queen Victoria in 1853.**
[Butchoff Antiques]

65

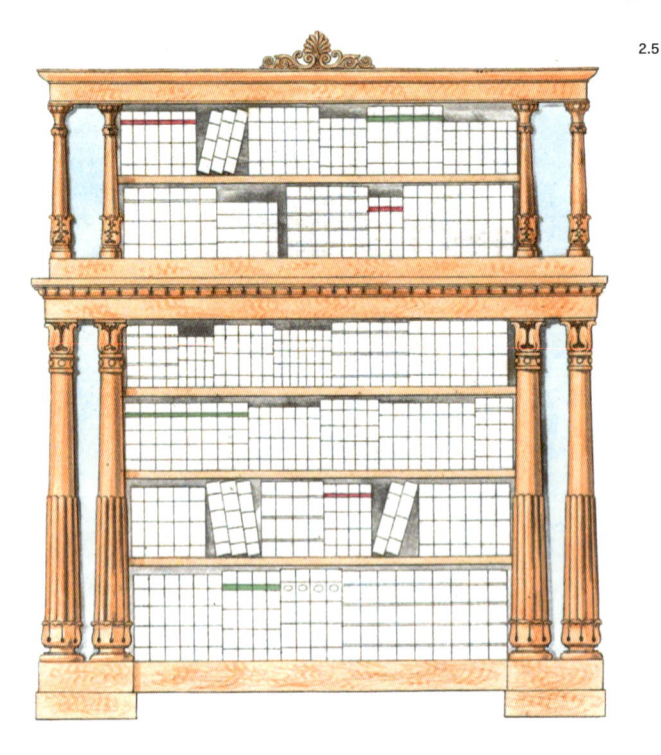

late 1820s and early 1830s. Thomas King's 1829 publication *The Modern Style of Cabinet Work Exemplified* was revised in 1835 and remained in print until 1862, which makes accurate dating on a stylistic ground virtually impossible. As can be seen in the satinwood lady's work table in **Fig. 2.4**, King promulgated what he saw as French design and wrote in his Address: 'As far as possible, the English style is carefully blended with Parisian taste'.[5]

Notwithstanding the necessary ostentation of Queen Victoria's State Throne Chair, made by Dowbiggin in 1837 (**Fig. 2.6**), not all royal taste was extravagant. In 1835 Tatham & Bailey supplied a set of ebonised chairs in the Elizabethan taste for the Royal Pavilion. In 1840, Edward Bailey made a chair of state for Queen Victoria's wedding at the Chapel Royal, St James's Palace. On his sketch is a note showing royal approval of the design.[6] H.L. Goertz of Windsor supplied the castle with furniture for many years, including three simple tripod tables in mahogany, which remain in the Royal Collection today.[7] They are of a type that would have adorned many drawing rooms across the country at the time.

As with the previous two decades of the nineteenth century, the 1830s saw a multitude of styles with varying degrees of eclecticism. Egyptian, Greek, Gothic, Elizabethan and Jacobean, together with other elements, were used as well as what was termed 'Old French'. The rosewood

Fig. 2.2 **It became fashionable for houses to fill an entrance hall with arms and armour. This 1832 watercolour by Sir William Allan shows the panelled hall at Abbotsford filled with suits of armour and Scottish memorabilia. J.M.W. Turner had made pencil sketches of the room the previous year.** [National Galleries of Scotland]

Fig. 2.3 **A set of twelve Cuban mahogany dining chairs, probably an even longer set when originally ordered from John Howard. The firm was established in Leman Street near Aldgate in 1820, moving in 1835 and becoming one of the leading London makers by the 1850s.** [Private collection]

Fig. 2.4 **A satinwood lady's work table with similarities to a plate in George Smith's** *Cabinet-Maker and Upholsterer's Guide*. **This example possibly made by Holland & Sons.** [Private collection]

Fig. 2.5 **'A Dwarf Bookcase' from Thomas King's** *The Modern Style of Cabinet Work Exemplified*. **Several of the plates have been coloured to illustrate the decorative effects of mahogany veneer.** [Thomas King, *The Modern Style of Cabinet Work Exemplified, in New Designs, Practically Arranged*, 1839]

Fig. 2.6 **Queen Victoria's State Throne Chair made by Thomas Dowbiggin of Mount Street in 1837 at a cost of £1,187. The firm supplied furniture to Windsor Castle and upholstery to Buckingham Palace between 1837 and 1853. The Dowbiggin name continued in use on Holland & Sons letterhead until** *c.*1902. [Royal Collection Trust / © His Majesty King Charles III 2023]

2.7

2.8

Fig. 2.7 **One of a pair of Gillow** *jardinières*, the rosewood tops outlined with Chinese *ruyi*-style scrolls, the maker has economised by making the bases in less expensive mahogany. [Butchoff Antiques]

Fig. 2.8 **Made entirely from rosewood, this** *jardinière*, a variation of a model designed by Gillows in 1822, has a removable tray top similar to design number 1970 later repeated by Loudon. The scrolled gallery is divided by four die-stamped inset gadrooned mouldings, a feature repeatedly used by Gillows. [Private collection]

Fig. 2.9 **Veneered in finely grained rosewood, the concave corners of this free-standing bookcase have capitals that retain a hint of Regency Egyptomania.** [Private collection]

2.9

bookstand, **Fig. 2.9**, shows a discreet reference to the Egyptian style with the subtle capitals to the top of the concave corners. Made for a gentleman's library, it could just as easily be thought to date to the 1820s or even the late 1810s.

Due to the sheer quantity of mahogany furniture in Britain, mahogany is often perceived as the main imported timber. However, rosewood, albeit more expensive, was also used in large quantities at this time, usually in veneers, and was equally adaptable to any form. The circular table illustrated in **Fig. 2.10** shows a remarkable display of specimen woods set out in a vortex, most of which have been identified.[8] No expense was spared on the construction of the table so as to ensure the stability of the carcass and to avoid any possibility of the top warping. Solid San Domingo mahogany forms the ground onto which the specimen woods have been veneered, while the outer borders of the table are made from Brazilian rosewood. The swirling pattern in which the veneers have been arranged was promoted in *The Modern Style of Cabinet Work Exemplified*, which in turn influenced Anglo-Indian furniture makers in Sri Lanka's Galle District. The earliest dated example of this type of Sri Lankan furniture is a piece formerly at the Royal Commonwealth Society, with a presentation plaque from 1836.[9] Rosewood was used on the *jardinières* on tripod stands, a form developed in the late seventeenth century, **Fig. 2.7**. The table tops are removable and pop up by pressing a brass-capped button hidden on the underside. The rosewood tops are veneered onto mahogany, not only for stability but also to save costs, as imports of mahogany were more plentiful and cheaper than rosewood. The waved gallery is influenced by the contemporary revival of Rococo scrollwork, as well as Chinese *ruyi*-style scrolls. This form of Chinese-inspired tray top was often used by Gillows.[10] This particular design proved long-lived, remaining available until 1851. The higher cost of rosewood furniture at this time was underlined by Susan Stuart, who noted that a work table in mahogany cost 10s, whereas a work table in rosewood cost twice as much – £1.[11] **Fig. 2.8** also has a pop-up top, the scrolled gallery divided by four die-stamped inset gadrooned mouldings, a feature repeatedly used by Gillows.

One of the most extraordinary publications of the decade was *An Encyclopaedia of Cottage, Farm, and Villa Architecture and Furniture*, first published in 1833 by Scotsborn John Claudius Loudon (1783–1843). He also published from 1834 his *Architectural Magazine and Journal*. The frontispiece of his magazine, **Fig. 2.11**, shows an engraved tablet listing a series of disciplines that interested him. Aside from furnishing and cabinet making, his interests veered from architecture through road making to engineering. He first made his reputation as a garden planner, an agriculturalist and a city planner. The illustrated tablet rests on a Gothic Revival chair; the twist-turned lamp stand behind could as easily be a tripod table support or a post for a tester bed. The magazine has left us an enormously rich legacy from an extraordinary and industrious polymath; many of its engravings, most relating to architecture, have been reprinted numerous times. The title of Loudon's book gives us a sense of the wide variety of styles of furniture described within it, including not only kitchen furniture but 'Grecian and Modern Villa Furniture', 'Gothic Villa Furniture', 'Elizabethan Villa Furniture' and, in 1842, a supplement entitled 'Furniture for Living-Rooms'. He eschewed the ornate carving of the Louis XIV style because 'of the great expense of carrying them into execution'.[12] Loudon appeared to be critical of those 'upholsterers in London who collect, both in foreign countries and in England, whatever they can find of curious and ancient furniture … and adapt them into modern uses'.[13] He cites Wilkinson of Oxford Street, Hanson of John Street and James Nixon of Great Portland Street[14] as likely dealers in such pieces. Despite appearing to be a champion of the working man, Loudon's furniture was hardly 'cottage' furniture, but he felt that the working classes would soon be able to prosper, due to better education, and in turn increase their ability to afford more home comforts.

In 1833 Loudon noted the increased use of springing in furniture and upholstery, with a 'pneumatic' look creeping into chair design that has become a visual hallmark of the Victorian era. Coil springing had been invented in the eighteenth century but patents were taken out in 1826, by Samuel Pratt of New Bond Street, and another by J.P. Gillespie.[15] During this period chairs developed a deeper, heavier apron than their eighteenth-century precedents. This was necessary to accommodate the depth of the steel springs and marked the beginning of a new style of upholstery which replaced the much thinner stuffed or squab seat.

Loudon wrote that the cabinet maker William Dalziel designed and, importantly, made most of the 'Grecian or modern furniture' shown in his *Encyclopaedia*. The Gothic-style pieces were designed by a Mr Lamb, while the Elizabethan-style pieces were designed by both Lamb and Henry Shaw. It is possible that Dalziel designed and made the tray top on the rosewood *jardinière* tripod table shown in **Fig. 2.8**, though it also bears a strong resemblance to work by Gillows. *Jardinières* were explained by Loudon in his *Encyclopaedia* as 'a kind of flower-stand … A tin pan fits into the top, which has a cover of trelliswork … through which cut flowers are put into wet sand'.[16]

The concepts behind the two chairs seen in the engravings from Loudon's *Encyclopaedia*, **Figs 2.13a & b**, are groundbreaking. The engraving on the left shows a chair with the familiar 'Regency' motif of an anthemion, not as a tentative decoration but as the whole of the back support. Could this have been envisaged to be made in cut or pressed metal? The chair on the right was designed to have the back and arms cast in one piece, the supports made from pipes used for gas. Both designs are an indication of what was new and innovative at the very beginning of what we now term the 'Victorian era'. In the 1839 edition of the *Encyclopaedia*, Loudon referred to the plethora of styles available in London's Marylebone area. He noted that Wilkinson of Oxford Street and Hanson of John Street had a mixture of old and new furniture for sale.

The proliferation of design books in the early years of the nineteenth century makes for a rich but confusing source of attributions. A piece of furniture may be *designed* by, for example, Thomas King, but could have been *made* by any competent maker. This is the same practice as in Chippendale's time, but on a wider scale. These publications were printed and available to anyone who could interpret and execute the design. William Smee incorporated much of King's work and it is unreasonable and possibly unnecessary to try to distinguish between the two.[17] His interpretation of the 'Old French' style, combining Louis XIV Baroque and Louis XV Rococo, became a standard form for the new era of luxurious seat furniture that dominated the second half of the century. It is interesting to see how makers as far afield as Sri Lanka appear to have had access to, or were influenced by contemporary design books such as King's, **Fig. 2.14**. The hexagonal top follows King's pattern but the inlay of exotic

2.10

Fig. 2.10 This wonderful centre table of generous proportions demonstrates the use of precious Caribbean veneers available to British craftsmen. The radiating fan motif calls to mind furniture of the same period made in Galle in South West Sri Lanka (formerly Ceylon).
[Butchoff Antiques]

1: Rio Rosewood
2: Unknown
3: Russian Maple
4: Poplar
5: Bird's-Eye Maple
6: Russian Maple
7: West Indian Satinwood
8: Partridgewood
9: Bois Satine
10: Unknown

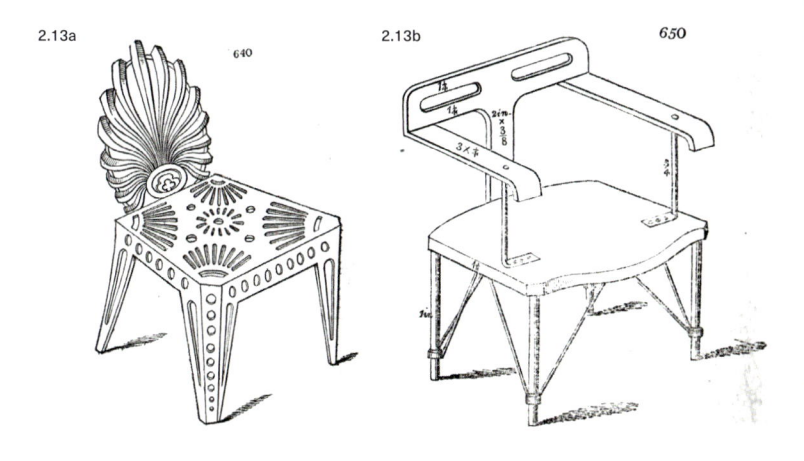

Fig. 2.11 The frontispiece of the 1837 issue of Loudon's *Architectural Magazine*. The tablet in the centre lists the disciplines discussed within the magazine, including furnishing and cabinet making. The tall lamp has spiral turning in a similar vein to the pair of *torchères* by Bullock & Wilkinson, see Fig. 2.1. [The Reading Room / Alamy Stock Photo]

Fig. 2.12 In his *Encyclopaedia* Loudon states that for a library bookcase 'An architectural character should always be given... corresponding with the style of the house'.[18] [J C. Loudon. *An Encyclopaedia of Cottage, Farm, and Villa Architecture and Furniture*, 1833, p. 1053]

Figs 2.13a & b These two designs would have been groundbreaking in 1833. On the left is a chair with an anthemion back, drawn by a 'Mr. Mallet',[19] and on the right is a chair with a cast-iron back and arms that would have been innovative even in the 1930s. [J C. Loudon. *An Encyclopaedia of Cottage, Farm, and Villa Architecture and Furniture*, 1833, pp. 318, 320]

woods, such as using a wide variety of native timbers, the marquetry and the distinctive C-scroll legs, are typical of Sri Lankan furniture.

As Britain grew wealthier, untroubled by war, the sumptuous and rich furniture of the previous decade was surpassed by the luxury market of the 1830s. It is interesting to contrast the refined and relatively simple table shown in the previous chapter in **Fig. 1.49a & b** with the constantly evolving taste of George IV, seen in the sofa or centre table illustrated in **Figs 2.17a–c**. Almost acting as a bridge between the old and the new eras, it is veneered in amboyna, reflecting the *bois clair* used in contemporary France, while holly and various specimen woods are inlaid into the main ground with a rich and extensive use of carving and gilding of exceptional quality. In stark contrast to the formality of the Bullock-like foliage along the outer border of the top, the centre is inlaid with a marquetry posy of spring flowers, anticipating the naturalism of the Great Exhibition of 1851, similar to a style used by the Blake family of marquetry-cutters. Elaborate and beautifully made, the table has many similarities to the type of amboyna-veneered furniture supplied by Morel & Seddon to George IV at Windsor Castle in the previous decade. It has the same Charles X-style marquetry but is more florid, in keeping with the furniture supplied by Morel & Seddon to Stafford House for the 2nd Duke of Sutherland.[20]

BRITISH FURNITURE

Fig. 2.14 One of a pair of work tables inspired by plate 14 of Thomas King's *The Modern Style of Cabinet Work Exemplified*. These examples have distinctive specimen wood tops with a radiating fan motif typical of the Galle district of Sri Lanka and the generous use of ebony.[21] [Christie's]

Fig. 2.15 The extravagant carved rosewood waved top and tripod base of this table was made by Robert Strahan of Dublin specifically for the *pietre dure* marble top by Joseph Darmanin of Malta. The arms are those of General Robert King, 1st Viscount Lorton of Boyle. [Butchoff Antiques]

Figs 2.16a & b Two designs of 1838 by Richard Bridgens in his less familiar 'Old French' style. [The Metropolitan Museum of Art, New York]

Anticipating the revival of the Louis XV Rococo style, it may have been made shortly after Morel appears to have left the firm in 1832.

Stafford House was one of the most magnificent townhouses in nineteenth-century London, prompting Queen Victoria to remark to the Duchess of Sutherland whilst on a visit there that 'I have come from my house to your palace!'[22] The Dining Room was redecorated by Sir Charles Barry in 1838 with large, formal console tables more reminiscent of the Empire style, in complete contrast to the dolphin consoles supported by 'life size' putti supplied by George Jackson & Sons for the Great South Drawing Room in 1842. A smaller example, provenance unknown but similar in style and colouring, is shown here, **Fig. 2.19**. The French style at Stafford House, now known as Lancaster House, is an early and important documentation of French taste as adapted to new and grandiose English interiors. The house's State Apartments and Picture Gallery were supplied with white and gilt Louis XV-inspired furniture by George Morant & Sons to complement the wall decoration by Benjamin Wyatt, while Charles Hindley supplied anglicised 'Louis XV style' furniture, the woodwork of which was overlaid with gold leaf.[23] Belvoir Castle, the rebuilding finished in 1832, is considered the first of the stately new British houses with 'Rococo-style' white and gold panelling, a theme used at Norfolk House in the 1750s and widely in the mid-nineteenth century.

The Whistlejacket Room at Wentworth Woodhouse, **Fig. 2.21**, named after the celebrated racehorse painted by George Stubbs, was furnished in a quasi-Baroque style with a suite of giltwood seat furniture and tables applied with heavy Rococo-style foliage. The account from Gillows was

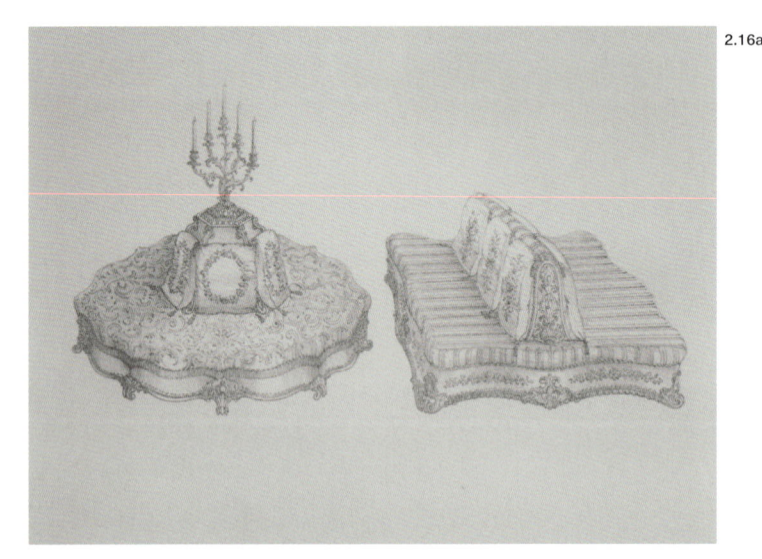

72

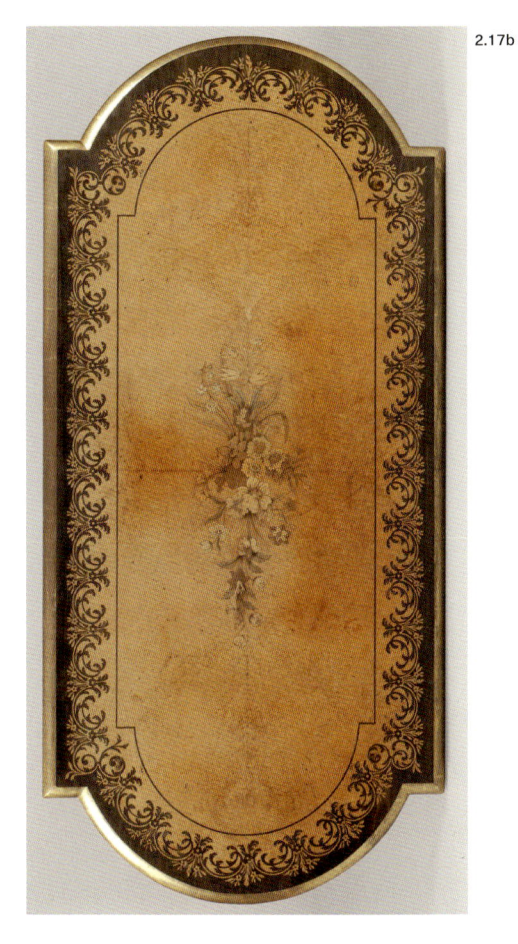

Figs 2.17a–c An elaborate centre table that a slightly later taste than the table of the late 1820s made for Windsor Castle, Fig. 1.47c, or a giltwood table attributed to Hume in the Elizabeth Saloon at Belvoir Castle. The amboyna-veneered top and purpleheart marquetry look back to the previous decade, but the spray of marquetry is more in keeping with the Louis XV Rococo of the mid-eighteenth century, loosely in the style of Louis Tessier. [Butchoff Antiques]

Fig. 2.18 A detail from a writing table lavishly veneered in amboyna with a mother-of-pearl inlaid 'Buhl' border. With its plush footrest, it recalls a table designed by Philip Hardwick and made by Wilkinson for the Goldsmiths' Hall. [Sotheby's]

Fig. 2.19 A small console table with figures finished in white to simulate white statuary marble is similar in style to those supplied by George Morant & Sons to Stafford House in 1838. Not signed, it may be attributable to a 'Mr. Clarke', who exhibited a similar table at the Great Exhibition.[24] Similar white and gold cherubic figures were supplied by Morant to Shrubland Park.
[H. Blairman & Sons]

Fig. 2.20 A pen-and-ink sketch for a sideboard drawn in 1835 by Anthony Salvin for the 10th Lord Falkland at Skutterskelfe Hall. [The Metropolitan Museum of Art, New York. Gift of Royal Institute of British Architects, 1963]

settled by the 5th Earl of Fitzwilliam in October 1833. In the same Neo-Baroque vein, similar furniture was supplied to the Red Drawing Room at Tatton Park and Ickworth, **Figs 2.22 & 2.23**, under the direction of Lewis Wyatt. From a distinguished family of architects, Wyatt appears to have had a close connection with Gillows, who most likely made the furniture.[25] Gillows made a variety of large and heavy sofas, not only in giltwood but also, for example, albuera wood. The wood, also known as zebra wood, is frequently referred to in the Gillow archives from 1832 to the mid-1860s.[26] By 1847, Holland & Sons supplied a less ornate but nevertheless sumptuous carved and gilt sofa for the State Drawing Room at Osborne House, to a design by Henry Whitaker.[27]

The 2nd Duke of Sutherland, like many of his peers, had been on shopping expeditions to Paris and was an ardent advocate of the French style.[28] Benjamin Wyatt provided chairs for Stafford House which he described as being in the 'Louis Quatorze' style but, to the modern eye, are clearly imitations of Louis XV Rococo, a style he also used for the 1st Duke of Wellington at Apsley House. A particularly lavish extant example of the French taste in Britain is the large gilt and patinated bronze clock and chimney piece supplied by the Parisian *fondeur* Crozatier to Stafford House in 1836, where it remains today.[29] One of the best-known dealers in the French style was Edward Holmes Baldock, who supplied at least one French-inspired piece to the house: a 'very rich table made to fit circular plaque of china'.[30] A photograph of the Great South Drawing Room of Stafford House, **Fig. 2.25**, taken in 1895, shows a large circular table with a white marble top, supported by carved and gilt dolphins. Supplied to the duke by Baldock in 1837, it is in an uncharacteristic style, with few, apart from the dolphins, of the attributes with which Baldock's work is so often associated, such as porcelain plaques and foliate gilt-bronze mounts. The pieces that he supplied to the 3rd Marquess of Lansdowne exemplify his typical style of furniture, **Fig. 2.45**. It is clear that Baldock, for his part in creating such furniture, should also have been included on Loudon's blacklist. When 'the remainder of Mr. Baldock's stock' and workshop material were sold at auction in 1843, a Boulle-style chest of drawers and other ornaments from the time of Louis XIV were included, as well as two boxes 'containing a quantity of useful carvings'.[31] Also included were 'Boule [*sic*] panels and Ornaments, Stock of Choice Wood, in Veneers…Tools, Work Benches', which would have provided other dealers with a rich assortment of materials. These descriptions present a tantalising mystery to the modern historian.

CHAPTER 2: 1830S

Fig. 2.21 **The Whistlejacket Room at Wentworth Woodhouse.** The celebrated Arabian chestnut, Whistlejacket, painted by George Stubbs in *c.*1762 overlooks the extravagant suite of giltwood furniture supplied by Gillows in 1833. [*Country Life*, 1924]

Fig. 2.22 **The Red Drawing Room at Tatton Park.** The giltwood seat furniture was probably supplied by Gillows in *c.*1830. [*Country Life*, 1964]

Fig. 2.23 **Almost certainly supplied to the 1st Marquess of Bristol for Ickworth Park,** this pair of large and heavy eclectic Neo-Baroque armchairs are similar to suites supplied by Gillows to Wentworth Woodhouse and Tatton Park, amongst others. [Sotheby's]

Fig. 2.24 **Indistinctly signed and dated 'I Fife, April 3 1830',** this chair, based on *Directoire chaises gondoles*, uses the same white and gold colour scheme advocated by Philip Hardwick at Goldsmiths' Hall. [Carlton Hobbs LLC]

The return of the Rococo in an institutional setting can still be seen at Goldsmiths' Hall in the City of London. Decorated in the so-called 'Louis XIV style' by Philip Hardwick (1792–1870) in the mid-1830s, the main reception rooms are effectively a mixture of Louis XIV Baroque and Louis XV Rococo, and accurately reflect the style of furniture produced in the 1830s to 1850s. The interior of the hall was originally co-ordinated in a red, white and gold colour scheme. Hardwick also commissioned an extensive suite of parcel-gilt furniture from the cabinet-making firm of William and Charles Wilkinson, including window seats, sofas, large armchairs, eighteen 'fly' chairs for ladies and eight chairs of a heavier design for the gentlemen (see pages 101–103).[32] The newly decorated hall opened with a grand banquet in 1835.

Fig. 2.25 **The Great South Drawing Room at Stafford House, taken in 1895. The large circular giltwood table on the right with dolphin supports was supplied by Baldock in 1837.** [Historic England (Bedford Lemere)]

The circular occasional table with a marble top became an integral piece of furniture. They were often on a surprisingly sizeable scale, more suited to large rooms. The most sought-after were, and still are, the examples with *pietre dure* marble tops from Italy. An essential acquisition whilst on the Grand Tour in the late eighteenth century and first half of the nineteenth century, these exquisitely inlaid marble tops were expensive souvenirs often bought directly by the traveller from the maker or retailer in Florence or Rome and shipped back to England where a suitable base was made. The example illustrated (**Fig. 2.26**) has a colourful variation of specimen stones, including lapis lazuli, malachite, porphyry, *breccia* marble, agates and *verde antico*. The marble tops are difficult to date as they continued to be made for many years in a traditional Roman style such as one with a base by Morant, and one by Taprell, **Figs 3.81 & 3.82**.

Edward Holmes Baldock's name has become familiar due to the comparatively large number of extant pieces branded with his 'EHB' stamp. Long thought to have been the mark of a mysterious French cabinet maker or *château*, Geoffrey de Bellaigue correctly identified the stamp as being that of Baldock in a groundbreaking article in 1975.[33] Previously the historian Jean Nicolay had speculated that it was the inventory mark for the Écuries de l'Hôtel Bourbon,[34] and Francis Watson suggested that it was for Queen Hortense of Holland, Eugénie Hortense Bonaparte.[35] Pierre Verlet was

Fig. 2.26 From the 1820s Gillows were making expensive rosewood supports for Italian specimen marble tops brought back from Italy by wealthy travellers. This example with lotus leaf supports is similar to a drawing in the Gillows archives. [Butchoff Antiques]

Fig. 2.27 One of a pair of easily transportable marquetry folding tables. The tops are inlaid with strapwork outlined in metal stringing in the style of the De Lucci brothers, an unusual technique known to have been emulated by Blake. Supplied to John Campbell, 2nd Marquess of Breadalbane, possibly for Taymouth Castle, an account in the Breadalbane records may connect them to Baldock. Dated 1835 it is headed 'Baldock', 'for restoration to two beautiful inlaid tables and regilding of the mounts'. [Anthony Outred]

closer, thinking that it was the stamp of a faker or clever restorer.[36] As a prominent London dealer with a wealthy clientele, Baldock, who was based on Hanway Street in the heart of London, searched actively for antiques and made a practice of incorporating old fragments into modern furniture to suit the taste for 'Old French' that had developed in the Regency period. To augment his stock, and no doubt in a quest for the exotic, Baldock travelled to Italy and other European countries.[37] He described himself in 1805 as a 'dealer in china and glass', and in 1824 his bill heading described his activities as 'buying, selling, exchanging and valuing China, Cabinets, Screens, Bronzes etc.' By 1827 he had expanded his business description to include: 'Seve [sic], Dresden, Oriental China and Antique Furniture Warehouse', with 'China, Cabinets, Screens, Bronzes etc.' which were

'Bought, Sold, Exchanged or Valued'.[38] He was one of the leading dealers of *ancien régime* French furniture in the first half of the nineteenth century and was described in London directories from 1810 to 1844 as an 'Ornamental China-Dealer', 'Furniture Broker and Appraiser', 'Foreign China Furniture Warehouse(man)' and 'Antique Furniture and Ornamental China Dealer'. He had considerable success as a *marchand-mercier*, supplying furniture and ornaments in succession to three monarchs: George IV, William IV and Queen Victoria. He also sold pieces to a wide range of aristocratic houses, not least those of the dukes of Sutherland and Buckingham, the 5th Duke of Buccleuch and most famously the 3rd Duke of Northumberland, to whom in 1824 he sold the magnificent pair of cabinets made by Domenico Cucci in 1683 for Louis XIV. The celebrated collector William Beckford was also a client, as was George Lucy of Charlecote Park, the 2nd Earl of Lonsdale and the 3rd Marquess of Lansdowne. There is no documentary evidence that Baldock actually made furniture on his premises, but it is clear that, although his business was primarily in dealing in furniture and porcelain, his extensive enterprise also included repairing, modelling and altering existing furniture, much of it continental in origin. References in the Lowther, Lucy and Buccleuch papers bear witness to these activities. They itemise the addition of mounts, embellishment of pieces with porcelain plaques and the alteration of desk and cabinet interiors.[39] Bellaigue's discovery of Baldock's invoices to the 5th Duke of Buccleuch, from May 1840 to February 1841,

Fig. 2.28a In Baldock's account of August 1838 to the 5th Duchess of Buccleuch, he writes: 'An inlaid secretaire with a fall down front, making new drawers'. Three years later Baldock supplied a similar desk to the duke, see Fig. 3.75a. [The Buccleuch Collections]

Fig. 2.28b A detail of 'new drawers' made for a desk supplied by Baldock to the 5th Duchess of Buccleuch in 1838. [Author's photograph]

illustrate the scale of Baldock's work. Much of the furniture supplied is still in the ducal collection.

'The modern furniture of E.H. Baldock has a distinct and consistent quality…(with)…two distinctive styles'.[40] Baldock is rightly identified as the supplier and perhaps the maker of much of the French-style porcelain-mounted furniture shown in this and the following chapter. It is not clear, however, that he should be credited with *making* the group of marquetry tables that are often attributed to him, although in many instances he was most probably involved in the supply and sale.[41]

A table now at Temple Newsam was sold to the 5th Duke of Buccleuch and invoiced as follows: 'E. H. Baldock, Chinaman to Her Majesty, Hanway, Oxford Street, London, 30 Sept 1840, A Beautiful Octagon Ebony Table with pictures in each side -- Flowers in centre. Intervals Lined in Green Leather. Gold Borders, 5 ft diam'r £85'.[42] The distinctive form of the table, with an octagonal top and concave sides, self-tapering base, in this instance four-sided but also available with a triangular section, is a design easily identified with the second quarter of the nineteenth century. Several of these are known, including **Fig. 2.31a**. A table of similar design is at Crom Castle in Co. Fermanagh, built in 1837, and another, mounted in gilt bronze but without inlay, was illustrated in a Mayfair house belonging to the dukes of Sutherland in the early twentieth century.[43]

Although the Temple Newsam table was supplied by Baldock, he almost certainly did not make it in his own workshops. The firm of Morant is also linked to a series of octagonal tables with highly individual marquetry such as the one shown here, **Figs 2.31a–2.31r**, stamped 'G.I. Morant, 86 New Bond Street London'. The design of the base appears to have been inspired by an illustration in Bridgens' *Furniture with Candelabra*, where it was described as a 'Marquetrie Centre Table'. In turn, Bridgens had probably been influenced by designs published by Thomas Hope in *Household Furniture and Interior Decoration* (1807).[44] Although similar and characteristic marquetry appears on furniture attributed to Baldock, the complicated and sophisticated inlay work was neither by Morant nor Baldock, but by the Blake family of London. The marquetry on this style of table has a coherence that, like an artist's hand in a sketch or oil painting, appears to have come from one

CHAPTER 2: 1830S

school. The table stamped by Morant, **Fig. 2.31a**, is a typical example. The octagonal tilt, or 'tip'-top, is inlaid in tulip and kingwood, with ivory and mother-of-pearl details on an ebony ground, with copper and pewter stringing. Formerly in the First State Bedroom at Carlton Towers, which was added to the building by the 8th Baron Beaumont in 1842,[45] the table dates to around the time that this enlargement was carried out. It is probable that this type of table, either octagonal or circular, was by Morant with Blake marquetry and retailed by them or other firms such as Baldock. Davis noted twenty-eight Blake marquetry tables in the Miles & Edwards stock list of 1843/44.[46] It is unlikely that such tables sold by Baldock were made in his workshops, since the finish and finesse is completely different to his furniture in the 'Old French' manner.

Fig. 2.29 This table is identical to the Buccleuch example, details of which are below. This example has a paper label reading 'G.J. Morant, Carver, Gilder & Picture Frame Maker to Her Majesty and HRH The Duke of Cambridge 91 New Bond Street London.' [Private collection, photograph Yannick Chastang]

Figs 2.30a & b Two details from a table almost certainly by Morant, which appears to be identical to the example in Fig. 2.29. This example, at Bowhill, is not signed and was supplied by Baldock to the 5th Duke of Buccleuch. The marquetry of addorsed serpents and ivory relieved foliage is typical of the Blake workshops. An undated design for a table with a similar Bridgens'-inspired base is also in The Buccleuch Collections, Fig. 2.35. [The Buccleuch Collections]

79

2.31a

2.31b

Fig. 2.31a **A masterpiece of Blake marquetry, the frame is stamped 'G.I. Morant, 91 New Bond Street London'. With a later Edwards & Roberts stamp, it was formerly in the First State Bedroom at Carlton Towers.** [Butchoff Antiques]

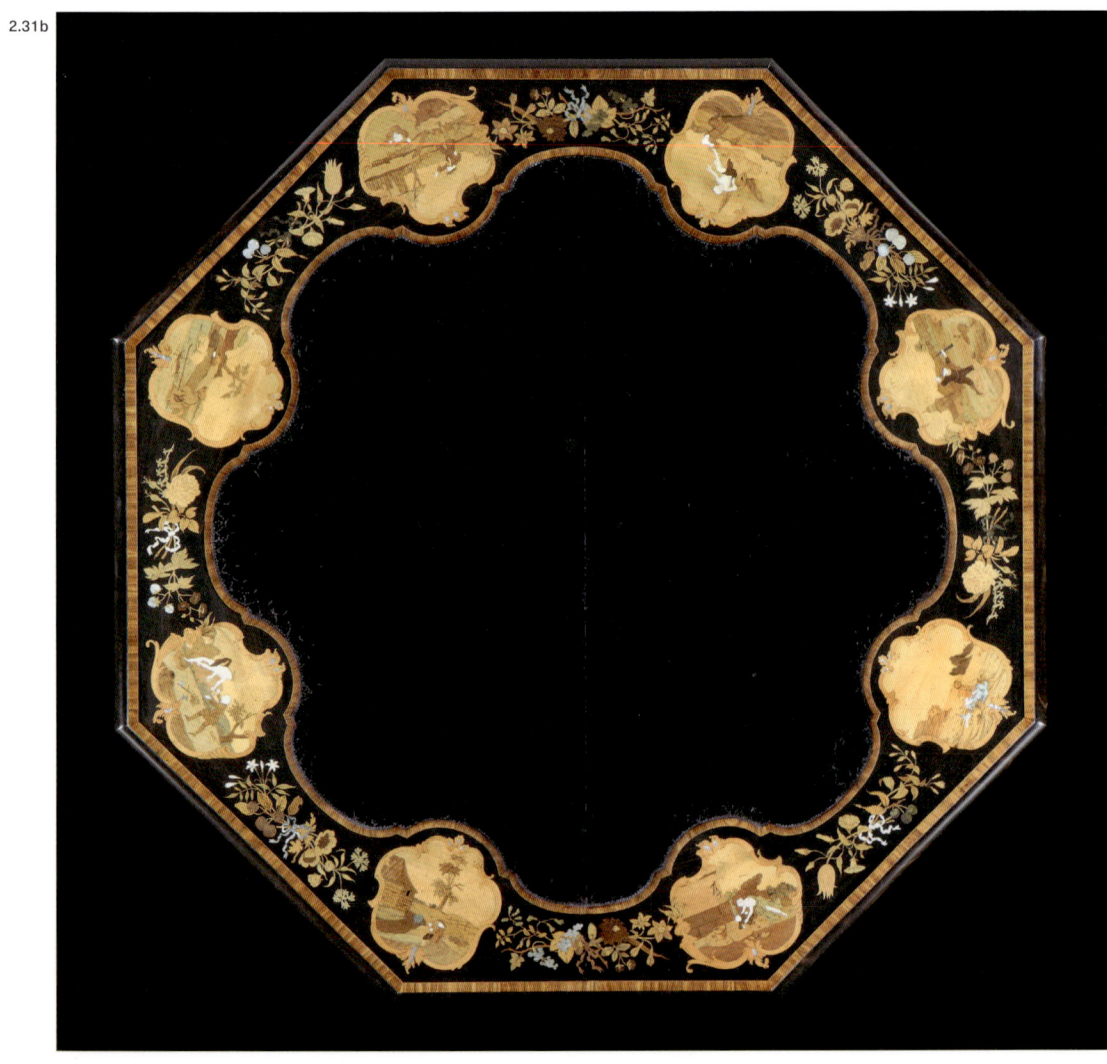

Fig. 2.31b **The top of the Morant table showing eight scenes from Jean de La Fontaine's** *Fables choisies, mises en vers*, **illustrated by Jean-Baptiste Oudry from 1729 to 1734 and published between 1755 and 1760.** [Butchoff Antiques]

Figs 2.31c & d **The Monkey and the Dolphin, Fable LXVII** [Jean de La Fontaine, *Fables choisies, mises en vers*, 1755–1759]

Figs 2.31e & f **The Astrologer who Fell into a Well, Fable XXXV** [Jean de La Fontaine, *Fables choisies, mises en vers*, 1755–1759]

Figs 2.31g & h **The Honest Woodcutter, Fable LXXXIII** [Jean de La Fontaine, *Fables choisies, mises en vers*, 1755–1759]

Figs 2.31i & j
The Wolf Turned Shepherd, Fable XLV
[Jean de La Fontaine, *Fables choisies, mises en vers*, 1755–1759]

Figs 2.31k & l
Jupiter and the Farmer, Fable CVII [Jean de La Fontaine, *Fables choisies, mises en vers*, 1755–1759]

Figs 2.31m & n
The Clay Pot and the Iron Pot, Fable LXXXIV [Jean de La Fontaine, *Fables choisies, mises en vers*, 1755–1759]

Figs 2.31o & p
Fortune and the Young Child, Fable XCIII [Jean de La Fontaine, *Fables choisies, mises en vers*, 1755–1759]

Figs 2.31q & r
The Child and the Schoolmaster, Fable XIX [Jean de La Fontaine, *Fables choisies, mises en vers*, 1755–1759]

The quality of the construction of these tilt-top tables, both the circular and octagonal examples, is far superior to the porcelain-mounted furniture supplied by Baldock, shown in this chapter and in Chapter 3 – 1840s. Despite having cabinet workshops, Baldock was mainly 'improving' earlier furniture; for example, by adding porcelain plaques to suit the taste of the day or restoring or making up pieces from his purchases at home and abroad. Frederick Litchfield cited Baldock as one of the frequent buyers at Christie's auction house in the 1830s, suggesting that he was buying 'old' furniture for 'improvement'. Litchfield's research was based on his access to Christie's catalogue archives and his father's recollections; Samuel Litchfield took over Baldock's business in 1843.[47] Other regular buyers at Christie's during this period were Town & Emanuel, Webb, Morant, Hitchcock,[48] Forrest and Redfearn.[49]

Another example of a table stamped by Morant and modelled on the characteristic Bridgens style of base, but not with marquetry in the Blake manner, is the 'tip'-top circular table in **Fig. 2.33**. The main veneer is amboyna, inlaid with fine marquetry foliage on an ebony ground. Each side of the triangular concave base is inlaid with the interlaced 'LL' of the French Bourbon kings below a royal crown. The royal cipher may be a compliment to King Louis-Philippe of the French, who abdicated in 1848 and, under the patronage of Queen Victoria, was installed in Victoria's childhood home of Claremont. What appears to be the pair to the table, with minor differences, was sold at auction in 2006.[50]

The style of the base of the table by Freeman of Norwich, **Fig. 2.37**, is similarly influenced by the drawings of Richard Bridgens. The publication of Bridgens' designs disseminated this novel and intricate shape, which was to become so

BRITISH FURNITURE

2.32

2.33

influential in the second quarter of the nineteenth century. Of varying form, either tri-form or quadruped, the distinctive downswept legs, with the toes scrolling under the leg, are repeated on a variety of tables including, in a squatter form, the teapoy, **Fig. 2.39a–c**. The Freeman table has fine-quality inlay and crossbanding, but a similar form was often repeated on more widely available commercial furniture. The provincial origins of the Freeman table would make it easy to date this to later than mainstream London examples, but Freeman was established in 1811 and there is no reason to think that he did not have Bridgens' first publication.

The most instantly recognisable features of Baldock's oeuvre appear to have been the addition of porcelain plaques to eighteenth-century French furniture, possibly work initially carried out in the new decades of his career, and the supply of furniture set with old or, more frequently, modern or later-decorated porcelain panels. He sold a Paris-made porcelain-mounted desk by the celebrated cabinet maker Martin Carlin to the 5th Duke of Buccleuch in 1830[51] and appears to have developed this applied porcelain style from

Fig. 2.32 **The library at Charlecote Park.** Although the octagonal table shares the same distinctive style of base as Fig. 2.31a, the marquetry is completely different and the frieze apron is straight, not undulating, to allow for six drawers. [*Country Life*, 1985]

Fig. 2.33 **The bases of this series of Morant tables in walnut heightened by ebony**, are inspired by Bridgens' design of *c*.1828. This example has the historicist royal cipher of the Bourbon kings in marquetry on the top and concave tripod support. [Private collection]

Figs 2.34a & b **A centre table in the same vein as the Baldock drawing shown Fig. 2.35.** Initially imported from Ambon Island, amboyna is here used as the main background for the lively figurative marquetry in ivory, executed to the high standard set for the craft by the Blake family. The marquetry includes motifs that are comparable to the work on the Blake/Érard piano of *c*.1840 in Fig. 3.59a, for example the butterfly and snail in mother-of-pearl and ivory. [Butchoff Antiques]

Fig. 2.35 **An undated pen-and-ink design, most probably in Baldock's own hand, for a marquetry centre table, 1.17m (3ft 10in) diameter.** Inscribed 'amboyna wood ground with coloured flowers', the concave triform base is clearly derived from Bridgens' designs. [The Buccleuch Collections]

this date onwards. Baldock furniture in this manner is almost exclusively in a delicate Louis XV style of small proportions. This was no doubt carefully considered to appeal to the broadening market of the 1830s and 1840s, which was no longer catering just to aristocratic magnificence but also to people with smaller houses and a taste for an aspirational aristocratic lifestyle encapsulated as 'Old French'. Baldock is reported to have used his own cache of eighteenth-century Sèvres blanks,[52] which were then painted by English porcelain artists. The console '*en secrétaire*' shown in **Fig. 2.43** is of English construction and may have been made in Baldock's workshops. Although an unusual model, it is inspired by models by the mid-eighteenth-century cabinet makers Bernard II van Risenburgh and Jacques Dubois.[53] A pair of similar consoles attributable to Baldock also porcelain plaques purportedly by Coalport, the flowers attributed

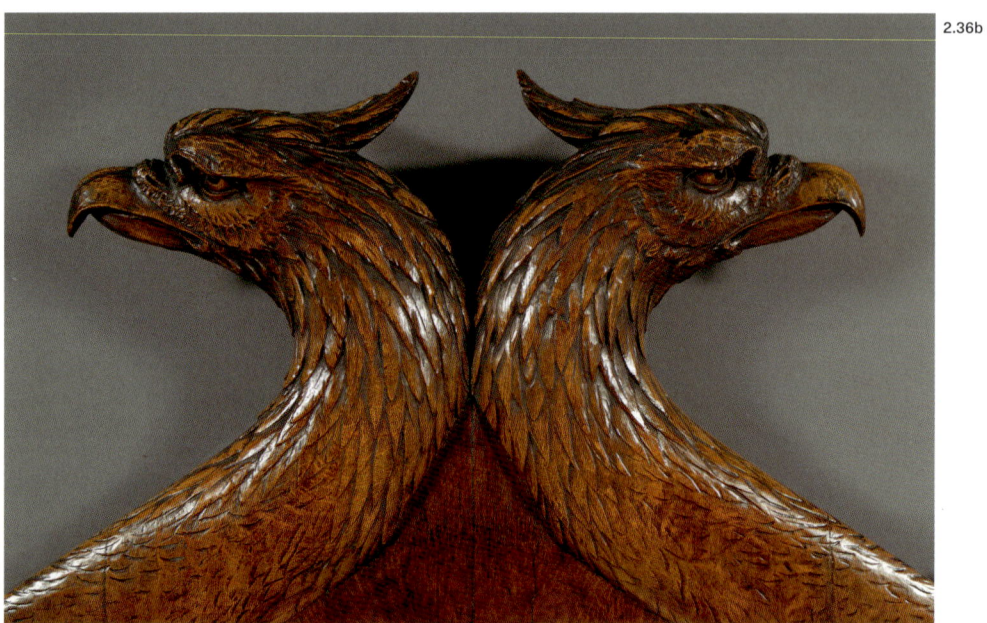

Figs 2.36a & b **Oak is a challenging timber to carve and this mirror frame has been subtly cut to emphasise the decorative medullary rays of the timber.** [Carlton Hobbs LLC]

Fig. 2.37 **A provincial interpretation of Bridgens' designs by Freeman of Norwich. It is veneered in pollard oak, a difficult task to apply to the undulating curved base.** [Butchoff Antiques]

Fig. 2.38 **A lady's work table veneered in *gonçalo alves*, often mistaken for rosewood. The form of the table bears some resemblance to designs by Bridgens, whilst the marquetry is of Dutch inspiration.** [Private collection]

to William Cook and the game birds to Thomas Martin Randall.[54] The pair of display cabinets shown in **Fig. 2.45** are a rare variation of Baldock's work with his typical adaptation of the Louis XV cabriole leg. A paper inventory label attached to the back shows that they were owned by Henry Petty-Fitzmaurice, 3rd Marquess of Lansdowne (1780–1863). A sketch in The Buccleuch Collections, **Fig 2.46**, annotated in what is most probably Baldock's own hand, shows a similar design to the base. More Baldock furniture is also discussed in Chapter 3.

Baldock's account of June 1831 to the Duke of Buccleuch includes '2 Buhl cabinets richly mounted in Egyptian green slabs' and '2 with Siena marble tops'.[55] One of the 'Buhl' cabinets, now at Drumlanrig, is shown as **Fig. 2.49**. The 1843 auction of Baldock's workshop effects also contained a quantity of Florentine *pietre dure* plaques of varying dates. The cabinet with the Baldock branded stamp in **Fig. 2.47a** shows the rare use of *pietre dure* plaques inspired by the engravings of Jacques Callot (*c.*1592–1635), published in 1616. The figures were also executed in marquetry, for example on the table supplied by Baldock to the 5th Duke of Buccleuch in 1841, **Fig. 2.48**. A photograph taken by Charles Thurston Thompson in *c.*1853 shows another cabinet, possibly by Robert Hume, inlaid in *pietre dure* with similar Callot figures practising the art of fencing.[56] The 1831 invoice from Baldock to the duke also includes two pairs of smaller side cabinets. One pair remains in the collection at Bowhill. The shape is in a style perpetuated by Levasseur but they incorporate the finest wood marquetry in the style the Boulle workshops produced in the 1680s.

There has been considerable interest recently in the work of the Blake family, a family of marquetry-cutters who had various addresses in central London.[57] Robert Blake was apprenticed in 1781, he and his descendants were listed at 8 Stephen Street, between 1825–26 and 1880 and as 'manufacturers' and 'buhl-cutters' from 1847 onwards. Stephen Street, off the Tottenham Court Road in the West End of London, was at the heart of the furniture trade, manufacturing for aristocratic patrons in the nineteenth century. Blake was also listed as a 'cabinet inlayer and buhl manufacturer' between 1826 and 1839.[58] There are no early

Figs 2.39a–c Three views of a rare and elaborate table known as a 'teapoy'. The form of the base is an elaboration of Bridgens' design. The marquetry, probably by the Blake family, shows allegories of War, Love, Music and Plenty in satinwood, harewood, ivory, tulipwood and purpleheart. The top is inlaid partly in ivory with a coat of arms, its motto *FIDE ET CONSTANTIA* translates as 'Faith and Determination to Learn'.
[Lennox Cato]

references to the Blakes as cabinet makers but in a recent discovery, Davis found that in his will Robert Blake, who died in 1839, styled himself as a 'Cabinet Maker and Inlayer' and an 1865 bill head reads 'Charles Blake, Late C. & H. Blake Manufacturer of Marquetrie & Buhl Furniture'.[59] To maintain the chronology of this book the Blake family is discussed more fully in subsequent chapters.

As marquetry cutters, the Blakes can be linked to furniture supplied by the dealers John Webb and Baldock but no evidence has been found for their early cabinet-making capabilities despite the description in Robert Blake's will. It must be asked if they actually *made* the carcass furniture at this early stage, but it is entirely possible that they added cabinet-making facilities to their workshops as their business flourished. In the 1820s and 1830s it is likely that marquetry designs were sent to Blake by dealers such as Baldock and John Webb, and furniture makers such as Morant; the finished marquetry sent to the relevant cabinet workshop to be incorporated into furniture. Baldock's workshops were in Hanway Street, a three-minute walk away from the Blake premises. Webb was an established furniture supplier on Old Bond Street, first listed in 1825 as a cabinet maker with a Richard Webb, who might have been a brother.[60] The firm was known as Webb & Cragg between 1831 and 1836, before Webb took over the business alone in 1840. He

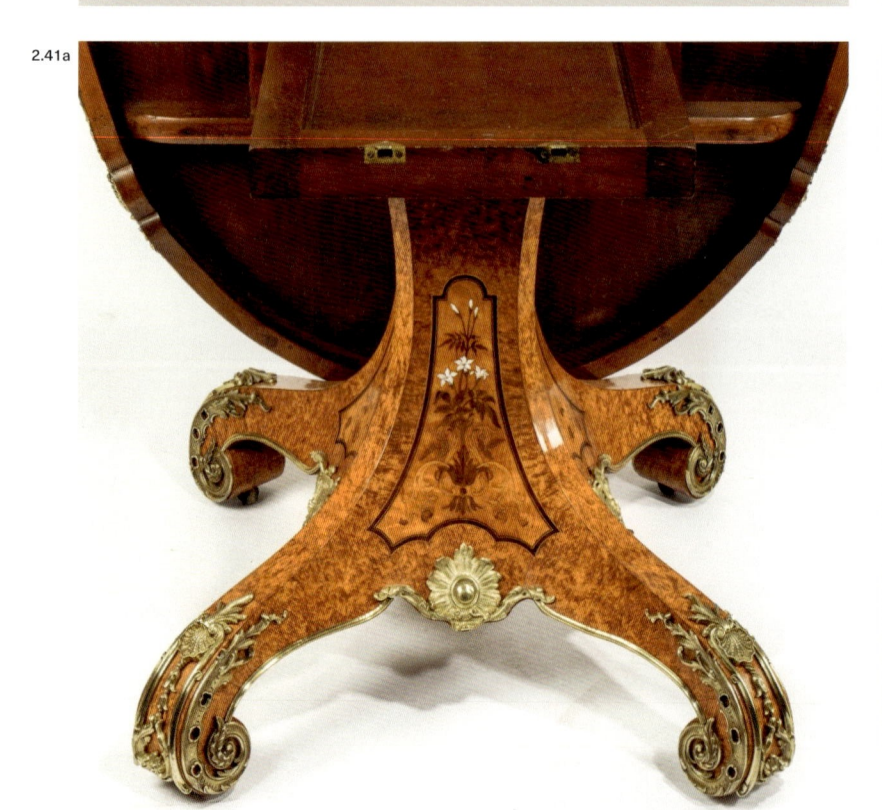

Figs 2.40a & b The dolphin base of this round tip-top table is carved from solid *gonçalo alves*, referred to alternatively as 'tigerwood' or 'zebrawood'. The veneered top is striking and distinct. [Private collection]

Figs 2.41a & b An amboyna-veneered table; the elongated oval top is a form more commonly seen in the 1850s and 1860s. The naturalistic spray of flowers in marquetry, may have been supplied by the Blake family. The base shares similarities with designs Richard Bridgens published in his *Furniture with Candelabra and Interior Decoration* of 1838. [Butchoff Antiques]

2.42a

2.42b

2.43

2.44

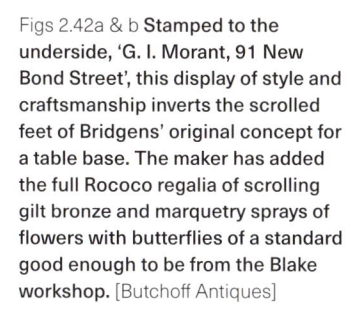

Figs 2.42a & b Stamped to the underside, 'G. I. Morant, 91 New Bond Street', this display of style and craftsmanship inverts the scrolled feet of Bridgens' original concept for a table base. The maker has added the full Rococo regalia of scrolling gilt bronze and marquetry sprays of flowers with butterflies of a standard good enough to be from the Blake workshop. [Butchoff Antiques]

Fig. 2.43 One of a series of unusual *bois de citronnier*, gilt-bronze and porcelain-mounted *bureaux en console*, probably made by Baldock. The porcelain plaques are attributed to Coalport, the game birds possibly painted by John Randall, the flowers by William Cook. [Sotheby's]

Fig. 2.44 One of a pair of side cabinets, formerly the property of the Countess of Munster, both stamped with Baldock's branded 'EHB' mark. Porcelain plaques of this type are often Sèvres, later-decorated blanks. This style of painted decoration on porcelain is often attributed to John Randall of Robbins & Randall. [Sotheby's]

BRITISH FURNITURE

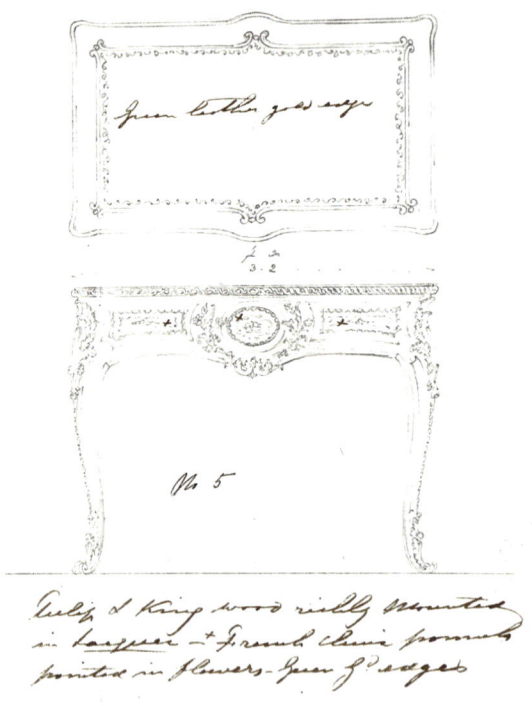

2.45

2.46

Fig. 2.45 The lower portion of this pair of display cabinets is almost the same as the Baldock drawing in Fig. 2.46. Each back has the 'EHB' brand mark and a paper label showing they were owned by Lord Shelburne, the 3rd Marquess of Lansdowne.[61]
[Bamfords]

Fig. 2.46 A rare survival, this pencil sketch has an annotation thought to be in Baldock's own hand. He notes that the top should have a 'green leather gold edge', 'Tulip & King wood richly mounted in Lacquer +/- French china…'. It offers the client a choice between porcelain and lacquer plaques and is similar to desks by Baldock and the base of the pair of display cabinets in Fig. 2.45.
[The Buccleuch Collections]

was cited as the cabinet maker of a Gothic-style extending dining table and matching sideboard in 1841.[62] A somewhat enigmatic figure, Webb became an important dealer, and the most significant and best-recorded pieces associated with him are the copies of French furniture he supplied to the 4th Marquess of Hertford with gilt-bronze mounts some of which are signed 'Blake' (see Chapter 4 – 1850s).

Working in a similar vein to the porcelain-mounted furniture supplied by Baldock, the firm of Town & Emanuel was established in 1830 at 103 New Bond Street in London; it was clearly a thriving business until their closure in 1849.[63] The firm sold a wide range of antique and modern furniture and *objets d'art* and were appointed 'manufacturers of Buhl Ormulu [sic] and Bronze in ordinary' to Queen Victoria in 1838. Davis noted that the will of Edward Emanuel in 1849 described him as a 'manufacturer of antique furniture', something of a contradiction in today's parlance.[64] Christie's held a seven-day auction of the effects of the firm in April 1849, which raised £11,444. The frontispiece of the catalogue has a list of some of the most celebrated auctions held in the early part of the nineteenth century. It noted that 'all these Objects have been selected with the well-known judgment and taste of this house [Town & Emanuel], from different sources on the Continent, as well as from Fonthill, Wanstead, Erlstoke, Grimsthorpe Castle'.[65] The label on one of the pair of side cabinets, or commodes, shown in **Fig. 2.55**, has an extended description of the firm's output which reads: 'Bo of Town & Emanuel, Manufacturers of Buhl Marquetrie, Resner [sic] & Carved Furniture, tripods, screens &c of the finest & most superb designs of the Louis 14th. Splendid cabinets and tables inlaid with fine Sevre [sic] and Dresden china &c. old paintings and bronzes, carvings, oriental and other china, jewellery & curiosities bought and exchanged. Buhl and antique furniture repaired. By appointment to Her Majesty'.[66] It also has traces of a Town & Emanuel label with the pre-printed date of '183_', left blank and the later retailer's stamp of Edwards & Roberts. Such cabinets are in a similar vein to furniture supplied by Baldock but lack his lightness of design. Apart from making new furniture in the 'Old French' style, the firm also dealt in 'curiosities and antiques'. The reference to 'Resner' is interesting, as Riesener's furniture was increasingly in demand on the art market at this time. In 1848 Honoré de Balzac wrote in *Le Cousin Pons* that a single piece of furniture by Jean-Henri Riesener was 'worth as much as three or four thousand francs'.[67]

90

It would seem possible that this is the same Emanuel who supplied George Hammond Lucy when he inherited Charlecote Park in 1823, as he was buying from similar dealers at this time. The firm supplied a mirror to the 3rd Baron Braybrooke in 1830 and 'new furniture' at a cost of 12 guineas to the Francophile 2nd Duke of Sutherland at Stafford House. The firm was also awarded a Royal Appointment to Queen Adelaide, wife of William IV.[68]

Town & Emanuel were dealers, like Baldock, Webb and others, actively buying at auction in the 1830s and 1840s. Despite advertising themselves as having 'superb designs of the times of Louis 14th', their porcelain-mounted furniture, whilst seemingly not as common as that of Baldock, is more identifiable with the transitional Louis XV or Neoclassical Louis XVI styles. Boulle-style furniture, commonly misspelt as 'Buhl' by Town & Emanuel and their contemporaries, was repaired for the Royal Household and supplied to, for example, Hinton Ampner, Hertfordshire. The cost of English-made 'Buhl' work was, not surprisingly, high. *The London Cabinet Makers' Book of Prices*, published in 1831, recommended that 'Buhl' work, even in wood marquetry, should be charged at fifty per cent higher than ordinary bandings.[70]

The work of Town & Emanuel has been recorded by Francis Collard, and the auction of their 'Extensive Stock' in 1849 gives an indication as to the size and style of the firm.

Fig. 2.47a An English cabinet embellished with imported Florentine *pietre dure* plaques, the back of the carcass branded with Baldock's 'EHB' mark. Although made in England, it is similar in shape and proportion to cabinets made by the Befort family in Paris during the same period. [Butchoff Antiques]

Fig. 2.47b The two *pietre dure* figures on the cabinet stamped 'EHB', are in the genre of engravings by Jacques Callot, and often repeated in marquetry by Blake, Fig. 2.48 (above). The figures also appear on a hardstone-mounted table in the Gilbert Collection.[69] [Butchoff Antiques]

Fig. 2.48 A detail of one of four Callot figures, the marquetry attributed to Blake, on a writing table by Baldock to the Duke of Buccleuch. [The Buccleuch Collections]

Fig. 2.49 Probably part of the 1831 invoice from Baldock, one of a pair of English-made Boulle-style side cabinets with Egyptian green marble tops supplied by Baldock to Drumlanrig Castle. The burnished and finely chased gilt-bronze frieze mounts are probably made by the same firm as the pair of *pietre dure* cabinets shown in Figs 2.50a & b (opposite). [The Buccleuch Collections]

They did not confine themselves to 'fancy goods', such as the side cabinets based on a Louis XV *commode à vanteaux*, **Fig. 2.55**. They also supplied period furniture to Burghley, for example a magnificent set of twelve large late-seventeenth-century Venetian armchairs and a pair of stools in the manner of Andrea Brustolon.[71]

Many renditions of furniture in the French Louis XV style were only published as being of English manufacture in the 1980s. The difficulty of identifying the country of origin was compounded by the activities of unscrupulous antique dealers who lightly planed off English makers' stamps from the tops of drawers so as to strengthen their similarity to French furniture, which sold more readily.[72] In 1903, Litchfield noted that Town & Emanuel's 'Old French' tables and cabinets were so carefully finished with regard to style and detail that, with the 'tone' which time has given them, it is not always easy to distinguish them from the models from which they were taken.[73] In the light of present-day expertise this statement seems naïve; although the pieces are well made, none of the extant furniture would appear now to be anything other than nineteenth-century confections and the veneers were not given the faded patination in exact imitation as was the case in Paris copies. The drawer construction of this furniture is also typically and distinctively English, as are the high-quality brass locks, some of which are stamped with the maker's name; other locks, made post-1837, were stamped with Queen Victoria's 'VR' monogram.

The quality of the cabinet making of furniture with Baldock's 'EHB' brand mark is competent, using good-quality veneers, but does not have the highly sophisticated cabinet-making qualities of some of his contemporaries, Morant for example, or Town & Emanuel. His effusive, eye-catching 'ormolu' mounts could be exceptional but not always so, sometimes more show and glow than beautifully chased and burnished. It is not known if the metalwork was made in his own workshops, but it is typically varnished in the English manner, and very different to the mercury-gilded mounts perfected in eighteenth-century France. The presence

Fig. 2.50a One of a pair of large side cabinets supplied by Baldock to Bowhill House incorporating fine-quality *pietre dure* panels, probably part of the 1831 invoice from Baldock. The gilt-bronze mounts on the frieze are subtly burnished and are probably by the same firm as the pair of Boulle-style cabinets at Drumlanrig Castle, Fig. 2.49. [The Buccleuch Collections]

Fig. 2.50b The foliate mounts on both pairs of the Boulle-style and *pietre dure* cabinets appear to be from the same master models, burnished and chased in a similar manner. [The Buccleuch Collections]

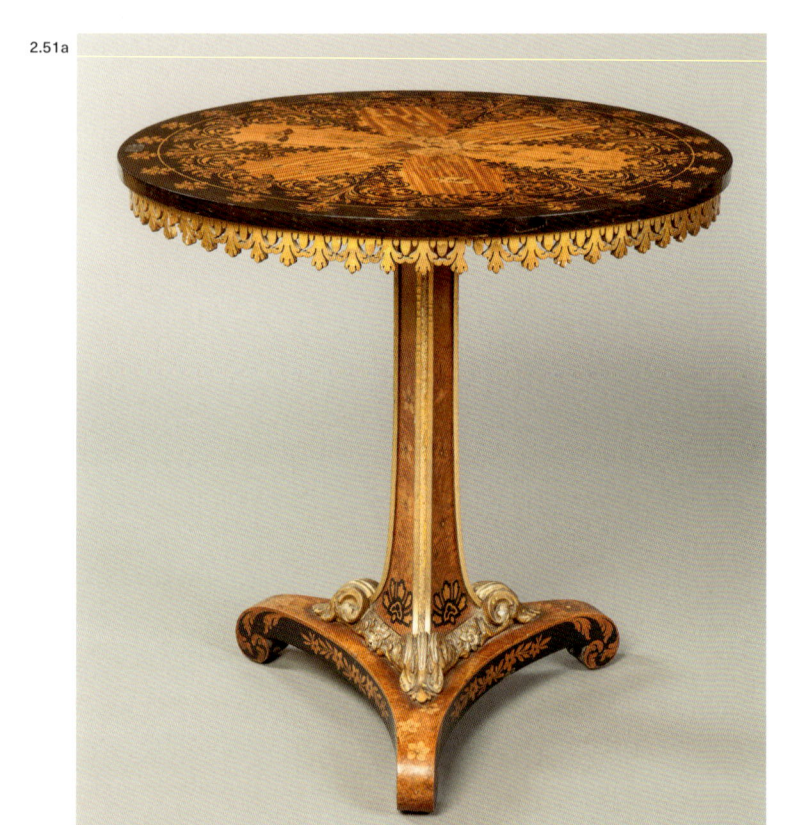

Figs 2.51a & b **The base of this table appears to draw on a design on plate 17 of Bridgens'** *Furniture with Candelabra and Interior Decoration.* **On stylistic grounds it is tempting to attribute the fine-quality marquetry to the Blake family but it is not clear who made or supplied the table; possibly it was Baldock, but more likely Morant. Like Baldock and Blake, Morant worked over a period of several decades and thus his work is difficult to date with a degree of accuracy unless there are extant invoices or records. More of Morant's work can be seen in Chapter 3 – 1840s and subsequently.** [Private collection]

Fig. 2.52 The maker of this tripod table remains a mystery. It combines Blake-style marquetry with a form of base once again adapted from Bridgens' designs, the overall form probably inspired by a centre table by Thomas Hope made for his house, 'The Deepdene'. [Private collection]

of a 'Lackering Stove and a Forge in Braziers Shop' suggests that his workshop was involved in working on at least some of the mounts.[74] The variation in quality of his cabinet making suggests that it was not important to Baldock as long as the overall look was suitable for his clientele. The lack of consistency in the quality of balk's furniture points to his having outsourced much of it, even if it bears his brand mark.

Whereas most of the pieces Baldock is known to have supplied were pastiches of the early Louis styles, a new genre of furniture appeared in the 1830s and 1840s, that of high-quality reproductions faithfully copying eighteenth-century French precedents; for example, the copies of the 'The Master of the Pagodas' desks with Chubb locks dating them to 1848, see **Fig. 3.76**.

Other copies include the pair of large desks, **Figs 2.56a–c**, in The Buccleuch Collection now at Bowhill, originally supplied to Dalkeith Palace. The scale and quality of the desks is remarkable. Could they be the '2 magnificent tables sumptuously mounted in ormolu' noted in Baldock's fourth account book of 1831 to the Duke of Buccleuch?[75] If so, it is the earliest date recorded for this model. Most examples of this large desk, are to a very high standard but the quality of the gilt-bronze mounts on the Buccleuch pair is exceptional. All the bronzes on this series of desks are identical with the exception of the Buccleuch pair, which have distinctive masks at each corner, not the usual foliate capitals. The style and technique of these mounts have similarities with the foliage flanking a clock supplied by Benjamin Vulliamy to the Royal Pavilion in Brighton, ordered by George IV.[76]

The exceptional chasing and burnishing of the gilding, **Fig. 2.56a**, is of the highest standards and of a standard in keeping with recorded work from the Vulliamy workshop or possibly Samuel Parker.[77] Notwithstanding the difference in the leg capitals, the desks are copies of an eighteenth-century precedent formerly in the collection of Lionel de Rothschild.[78] Both the Buccleuch desks and the Rothschild original are veneered in rosewood. The Buccleuch copies are now faded in colour; it is not clear from the black and white photograph in the Rothschild sale catalogue entry whether the original was the Indian rosewood or South American variety. The authenticity of the Rothschild original has been questioned, but there is no reason to doubt the 1937 Sotheby's cataloguing.[79] It may be that all the recorded copies of this desk, including the Buccleuch pair, an example formerly at Clandon Park, a pair still in the collection of the earls of Normanton at Somerley, Hampshire, and one formerly at Powerscourt, Co. Wicklow, are based on the desk sold out of the Rothschild collection.[80] Other variations have been recorded, one in an unidentified veneer, possibly *satiné*, another ebony veneered,[81] all once considered to be of continental manufacture. Another, veneered in coromandel, has German sixteenth-century marquetry inset into the frieze and drawers.[82] It is possible that the eighteenth-century model passed through Baldock's hands and that it was he who supplied the first copies – the Buccleuch pair. It is not improbable that, since he was constantly sourcing old furniture and 'spare parts' from Europe, he could have sourced the German marquetry. Such desks were almost certainly not made in Baldock's workshops; the most likely contender is Town &

Fig. 2.53 Unsigned and without a useful printed label, this side cabinet, one of a pair, is veneered in what originally would have been highly contrasting kingwood and tulipwood. The concave glazed vitrines at either end, in a re-interpretation of a Louis XVI-style *commode à l'anglaise*, suggest the work of Town & Emanuel but Toms & Luscombe are also candidates. [Private collection]

Fig. 2.54 A kingwood-veneered writing desk, made in England in the French Louis XV style, supplied new in 1836 to Burghley House by Town & Emanuel at a cost of £21. [Burghley House]

2.55

Fig. 2.55 One of a pair of commodes, both of which are stamped on the tops of the drawers by Town & Emanuel, and one has their paper label. An extravagant model made in the French Louis XV/Transitional style, they are also stamped Edwards & Roberts, who probably retailed or repaired them at a later date. [Butchoff Antiques]

2.56a

CHAPTER 2: 1830S

2.57

2.56b

Fig. 2.56a A corner mount from the pair of large writing desks supplied to the 5th Duke of Buccleuch at Dalkeith Palace (Figs 2.56b & 2.57), the high-quality gilding contrasting with the Indian rosewood veneer. The stylised capitals are of an exceptional quality such as work produced by Benjamin Vulliamy. There are similarities with florid gilt-bronze foliate mounts flanking the dial on a clock made by Vulliamy to the order of George IV for the Royal Pavilion at Brighton. [The Buccleuch Collections]

Fig. 2.56b A detail of one of the pair of large desks supplied by Baldock to the Duke of Buccleuch in 1831. The distinctive gilt-bronze mounts are exceptional and the chased and burnished gilding of the mounts of outstanding quality. Variations were made later by Toms & Luscombe, one in Boulle marquetry shown in Fig. 4.86. [The Buccleuch Collections]

Fig. 2.57 The Gallery at Dalkeith Palace, photographed in 1911. On the left, surrounded by eighteenth-century furniture, is one of a pair of 'magnificent tables sumptuously mounted in ormolu'. Could they be the pair invoiced by Baldock in 1831? The pair of large *pietre dure* side cabinets, festooned with Baldock-style mounted porcelain, are probably also part of the same 1831 invoice, see Fig. 2.50a. In the background is one of a series of celebrated cabinets on stand of *c.*1680 by André-Charles Boulle. [*Country Life*, 1911]

2.58a

2.58b

Figs 2.58a & b **A large centre table in brilliant red turtle shell with ivory inlay in an unusual style drawn from marine life. A companion and seemingly identical to one in the Royal Collection, the corner mounts are distinctive and reminiscent of the desks supplied by Baldock to the 5th Duke of Buccleuch, Figs 2.56a & b. The bold strap work made by the De Lucci brothers' work of the late seventeenth century as reinterpreted by the Blake family (Fig. 2.27).**[84] [Private collection]

Emanuel. Appointed 'manufacturers of Buhl Ormulu [sic] and Bronze in ordinary' to Queen Victoria in 1838, Town & Emanuel's closing sale in 1849 listed 'A superb ebony library table, with masks and or-molu mouldings, in the taste of Louis Quatorze'.[83] The catalogue reference to 'Louis Quatorze' is misleading as the desks are in the style of a generation later, Régence or even Louis XV. Intriguingly, it is unclear whether the reference to 'masks' in the 1849 catalogue is to the faces on the handles, or to animal masks. The proportions and weight of bronze give the model a Germanic overtone. Another example of this large desk, in Boulle marquetry, was exhibited by Toms & Luscombe in London in 1862, see **Figs 4.85 & 4.86**. Josiah Toms, a former assistant to Town & Emanuel, purchased and continued the Town & Emanuel business with his partner, William Luscombe. Using their former employers' workshops, they would have almost certainly had access to the invaluable master models of the bronzes and the cabinet maker's plans to remake the desk.

Toms & Luscombe are known to have purchased extensively at the auction of Town & Emanuel stock, including a japanned cabinet and a clock in a 'Buhl' case.[85] They took over the old Town & Emanuel premises and continued to make Boulle and marquetry furniture in the vein of their predecessors. They were still advertising exact copies of French eighteenth-century furniture at the 1862 exhibition in London. The intriguing dealer Samson Wertheimer, who later acted for the Rothschild family, was also a purchaser

Fig. 2.59 **The white and gold Picture Gallery of Stafford House, now known as Lancaster House, photographed by Bedford Lemere in 1908.** [The Print Collector / Alamy Stock Photo]

Fig. 2.60 **The Court Drawing Room of Goldsmiths' Hall, finished in 1833, was destroyed in World War II. This photograph of 1892 by Bedford Lemere shows the disposition of the French-inspired Louis XV-style seat furniture with a large set of 'Fly' chairs designed by Philip Hardwick and made by W. & C. Wilkinson. See 2.63a–c.** [Historic England (Bedford Lemere)]

at the Town & Emanuel auction. One lot in particular is indicative of the luxurious and extravagant tastes he catered for: 'lot 68…a cabinet of twenty-four drawers full of precious stones'. Another buyer was Litchfield, presumably the dealer Samuel Litchfield who took over Baldock's business in 1838. He bought 'lot 103…a pair of marqueterie encoingnures' [*sic*]. The name Holland also appeared as a buyer, probably the London furniture-making firm.

One of the most iconic forms of the early nineteenth century is the 'Victorian' chair, with cabriole legs loosely based on those of the Louis XV period. Designed and made in multiple forms, one of the best known is a model designed by Philip Hardwick and made by W. & C. Wilkinson for Goldsmiths' Hall in 1834, **Fig. 2.61**. The model is similar to a line engraving in George Smith's *Cabinet-Maker and Upholsterer's Guide* of 1828, **Fig. 2.62**, and, although a well-documented design of William IV's reign, is often considered to be 'Victorian'. The fly chair also designed by Hardwick for Goldsmiths' Hall has obvious similarities to the ubiquitous 'balloon back' chair, which is the epitome of Victorian design.

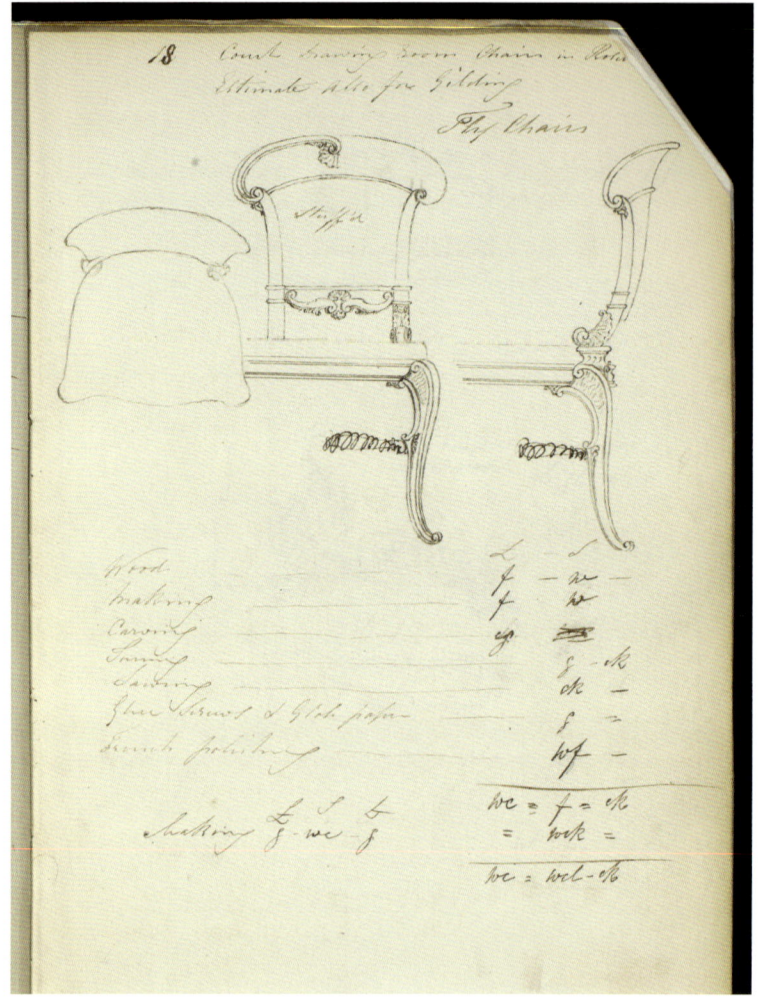

Fig. 2.61 *En suite* with the lighter 'fly' chairs for Goldsmiths' Hall, Philip Hardwick commissioned Wilkinson & Sons to make extensive suites of white-painted and parcel-gilt beechwood chairs to his design. See Fig. 2.60. [© Victoria and Albert Museum, London / Lent by the Worshipful Company of Goldsmiths]

Fig. 2.62 Under the heading 'Antique Chairs', George Smith, in his *Cabinet-Maker and Upholsterer's Guide*, calls this engraving of a fly chair 'French'. [Getty Research Institute]

Fig. 2.63a Hardwick's drawing for the 'fly' chairs at Goldsmiths' Hall, Fig. 2.60. The coded costings even include the cost of 'Glue Screws & Glass paper'. [The Goldsmiths' Company. Photographer: Richard Valencia]

Fig. 2.63b Williamson's full-scale seat plan for the 'fly' chairs at Goldsmiths' Hall. They are signed 'H. Williamson', dated 2 July 1834 and countersigned by Hardwick. The finished set of eighteen was delivered in 1835, at a cost of £23 14*s* each. [The Goldsmiths' Company. Photographer: Richard Valencia]

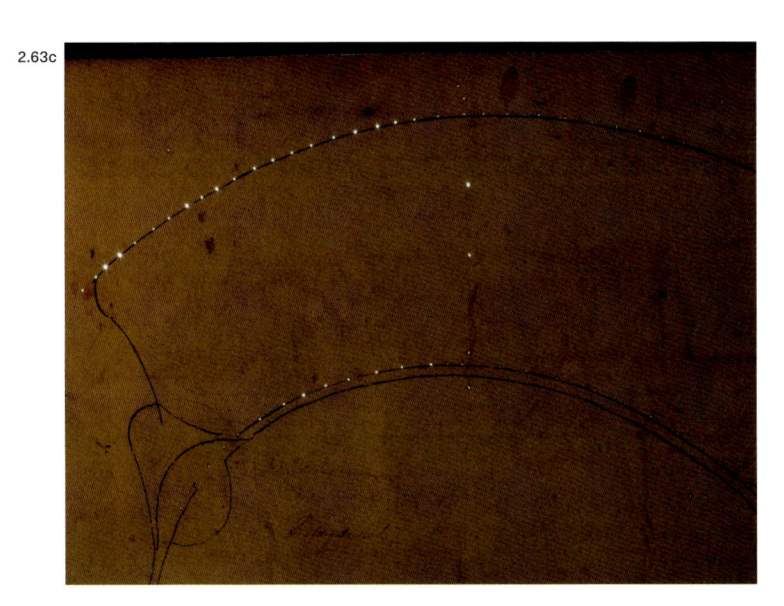

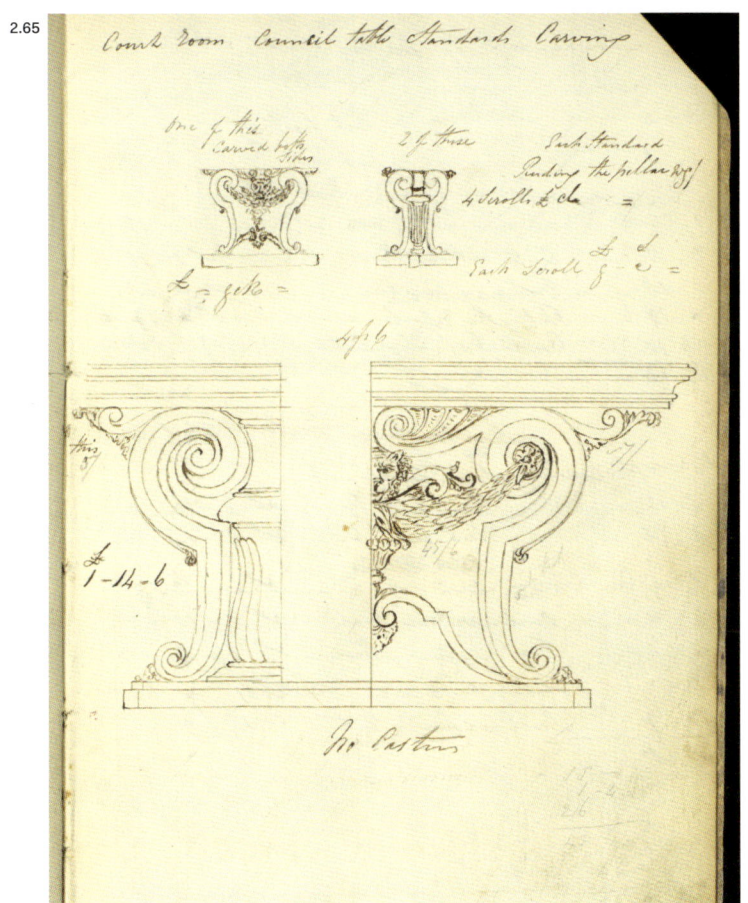

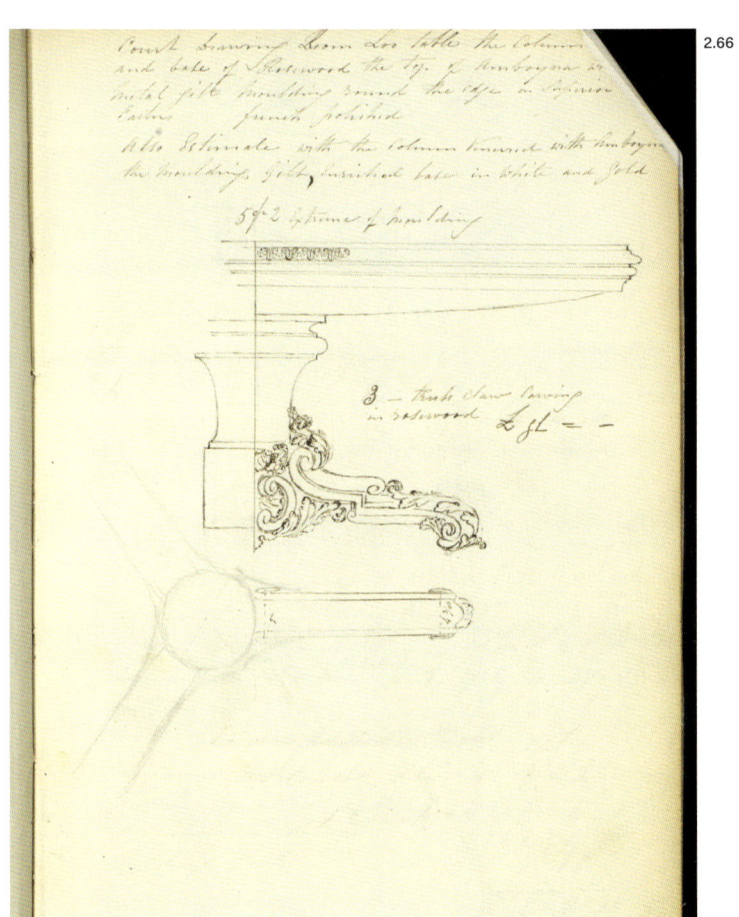

Fig. 2.63c A detail from Williamson's full-scale plan for the fly chairs at Goldsmiths' Hall, Fig. 2.63b, showing the pricked-out holes for the chair maker to transpose the exact curvature and scale directly onto the raw timber for cutting. [The Goldsmiths' Company. Photographer: Richard Valencia]

Fig. 2.64 A design for the standard ends of two rosewood tables for the Court Drawing Room at Goldsmiths' Hall. The tops specified to be amboyna with a gilt border. [The Goldsmiths' Company. Photographer: Richard Valencia]

Fig. 2.65 Designs for the standard ends of the council table made for the Court Drawing Room at Goldsmiths' Hall. They contain detailed instructions and costings for different styles of carved foliage and specify 'no castors'. [The Goldsmiths' Company. Photographer: Richard Valencia]

Fig. 2.66 A design for a Loo Table for the Court Drawing Room at Goldsmiths' Hall in rosewood or alternatively 'the column veneered with Amboyna'. [The Goldsmiths' Company. Photographer: Richard Valencia]

BRITISH FURNITURE

2.67

2.68

2.69a

2.69b

Fig. 2.67 The back of this Irish armchair, in the manner of Mack, Williams & Gibton of Dublin, has rear legs of equine form, possibly borrowed from the French *Directoire* style of the late 1790s. [Private collection]

Fig. 2.68 A substantial library armchair of generous proportions, which would have been equally suitable as a club chair. The frame is in oak boldly carved with acanthus and lotus leaves. [Private collection]

Figs 2.69a & b Although unsigned, judging on elegance and quality of execution this pair of solid oak benches is almost certainly by Gillows. The acanthus-carved arm terminals are very similar to an armchair with carving by Gillows' prolific master carver, Robert Farmer, now in the Judges' Lodgings Museum in Lancaster.[86] [Butchoff Antiques]

Fig. 2.70 An undated oil painting by Richard Lonsdale of the Drawing Room at Whittington Hall. The room was completed in 1836 and furnished to a large extent by the nearby firm of Gillows. In the background are the pair of Elizabethan revival open bookcases designed in 1840 for Conishead Priory, see Fig. 3.9. [Lancashire County Council]

King's and Whitaker's designs promulgated this style, which was seen as being 'Old French' because of the Louis XV-style cabriole legs. Holland was still making such chairs in 1845 when he supplied six to Osborne House for Queen Victoria.[87] As with the royal commission, these chairs were normally supplied in a set of six as salon chairs, not for use in formal dining. In ascending order of cost they were made in either stained beech, mahogany, walnut, rosewood or, in the case of Osborne, satinwood with parcel-gilt highlights. The 'balloon' style was transferred to the numerous parlour suites made during the mid-nineteenth century through furniture types such as chaises longues and 'grandfather' and 'grandmother' chairs. For dining rooms Hardwick designed variations of the Greek *klismos* chair with a distinctive C-shaped top-rail which, at first glance and without documentation, could be misread as dating from the Regency.

The Goldsmiths' Company Library archive holds a unique record of drawings for these and other chairs, as well as tables and curtain pelmets, several of which are shown here in **Figs 2.63a–2.66**.[88] The archive consists of small, beautifully drawn pen-and-ink sketches in a pocketbook, with annotations in code as to the costing of the various components of each item of furniture. Although unsigned, it is probable that these are by Hardwick himself. Such detailed designs are rare but rarer still are the full-scale drawings, presumed to be drawn by the maker Henry Williamson (or his studio). They are signed and dated July 1834 by Williamson and countersigned by Hardwick as commissioning architect. Some of the drawings have been pricked out, suggesting that, as they are exactly the same scale as the finished pieces of furniture, they were used by the maker to cut out the patterns. All instructions by the designer to the maker are specific, for example the chairs are 'all to be made in Fine Rosewood with silk damask or finished in White & Gold' and '2 Pier tables carved in Lime tree and gilt in matt & Burnished Gold with Statuary marble Slabs'.

The 1830s was a productive period for Irish furniture makers, especially those in Dublin. There had been a tradition of Huguenot migration to the city and more French makers came to work and settle after the French revolutions of 1789 and 1830.[89] The oak armchair, **Fig. 2.67**, in the manner of Mack, Williams & Gibton, is an uncompromising rendition of the Louis-XV style. However, its rear legs are of equine appearance, a motif possibly borrowed from the French *Directoire* style. The substantial form of the chair means that it was probably made for a gentleman's club, or for heavy use in a dining room. The partnership of John Mack, Zachariah Williams and William Gibton traded from 1810 in Stafford Street, Dublin, until John Mack's death in 1829, when Williams and Gibton continued to work together until the death of Gibton in 1842. The Williams & Gibton stamp on their solidly made furniture would suggest a date between 1830 and 1844.

The Elizabethan and Jacobean revival designs of the early decades of the nineteenth century were based on a fascination for antiquarian scholarship, some well-informed,

Fig. 2.71 A watercolour by John Scarlett Davis of the library at Tottenham in 1835, seat of the Windus family, with their collection of paintings by J.M.W. Turner. The eclectic interior shows a large antiquarian table in a mixture of 'Old French' and Elizabethan styles, the proportions reminiscent of one made for William Beckford at Fonthill and now at Charlecote Park. [© The Trustees of the British Museum]

Fig. 2.72 The dramatic ribbed buttress supports of this side table in solid pollard oak have similarities to a 1824 design for a table by Richard Bridgens. The bold architectural form is in contrast to the four delicate, Elizabethan-inspired pendants. [James Graham-Stewart]

Fig. 2.73 An etching imagined by A.W.N. Pugin published by Ackermann in 1836. A romanticised image of a fifteenth-century artisan working painstakingly with simple tools. It shows a glimpse of the toil involved in such work. [Getty Research Institute]

Fig. 2.74 A carved oak wardrobe possibly made for Gosford Castle to a design by Hopper. The strongly modelled arch is similar to a late twelfth/early thirteenth-century Norman arch at Norton Priory and has similarities to the distinctive arches in the hall at Penrhyn Castle, Fig. 2.76. [© Victoria and Albert Museum, London.]

Fig. 2.75 Thomas Hopper's robust designs vary between simplified and highly complex as with this carved sideboard in pollard oak. [National Trust]

Fig. 2.76 (overleaf) The hall at Penrhyn Castle, rebuilt between 1821 and 1837 by the architect Thomas Hopper, is one of the most iconic examples of the Norman Revival. Hopper designed a range of idiosyncratic furniture, notably the side table with dolphin supports below the mirror in the background. In the centre is a variation of a Morant octagonal table with Blake marquetry. In contrast to the example formerly at Carlton Towers, this model has flat, panelled sides influenced by Tuscan tables of the seventeenth century. [The National Trust Photolibrary / Alamy Stock Photo]

CHAPTER 2: 1830S

2.73

2.74

2.75

2.76

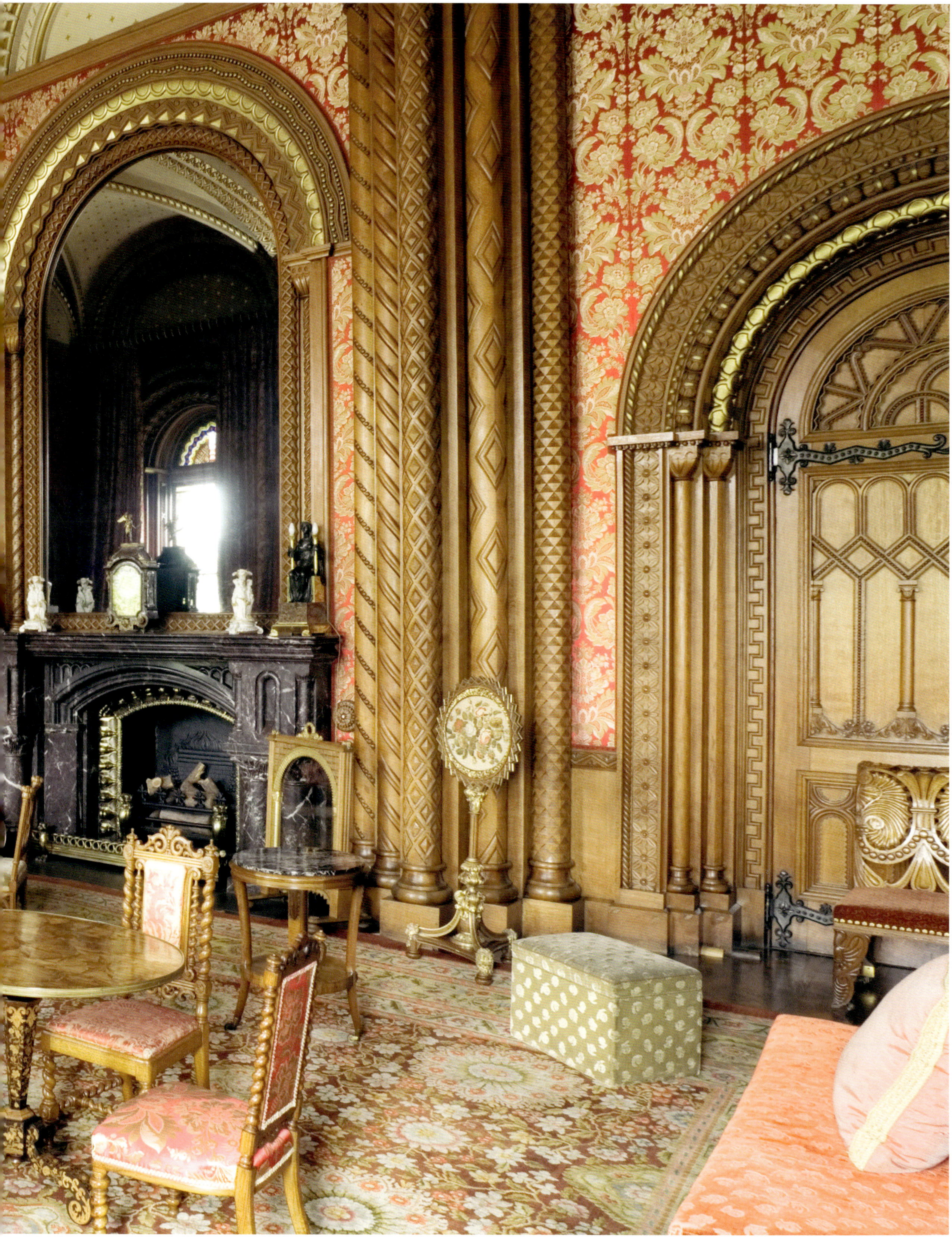

BRITISH FURNITURE

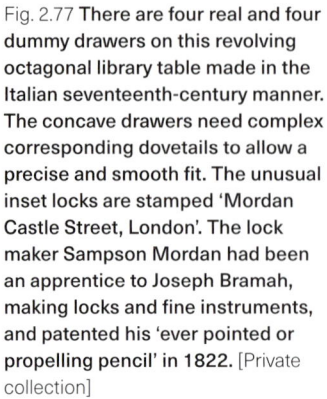

2.77

2.78

Fig. 2.77 There are four real and four dummy drawers on this revolving octagonal library table made in the Italian seventeenth-century manner. The concave drawers need complex corresponding dovetails to allow a precise and smooth fit. The unusual inset locks are stamped 'Mordan Castle Street, London'. The lock maker Sampson Mordan had been an apprentice to Joseph Bramah, making locks and fine instruments, and patented his 'ever pointed or propelling pencil' in 1822. [Private collection]

Fig. 2.78 A parcel-gilt octagonal centre table veneered in maple and thuya that may date to the 1840s and may have formed part of the suite designed by Henry Whitaker for the Conservative and Unionist Club founded in 1844. Another table from this suite, currently on loan to Astley Hall but without any gilding, was acquired by the Victoria and Albert Museum in 1960. Both this table and the one above are directly influenced by Italian seventeenth-century precedents. [Chorley's]

others less so. Anthony Salvin (1799–1881), an architect and, like many of his contemporaries, also a furniture designer 'established a wide reputation as an authority on medieval and Tudor architecture',[90] while the architect T.F. Hunt (c.1791–1831) published the first study of Tudor furniture in 1830 in *Exemplars of Tudor Architecture Adapted to Modern Habitations: With Illustrative Details Selected from Ancient Edifices; and Observations on the Furniture of the Tudor Period*. Seventeenth-century design precedents included furniture with carved decoration, tables often with cup and cover baluster legs, and a mixture of Gothic and Renaissance motifs.

The console table in **Fig. 2.72** illustrates a fashionable trend, favoured by George Bullock, to use indigenous woods in furniture, in this case carefully chosen pollard oak. Although a native timber, it was not necessarily cheaper to produce than the expensive veneers imported from the Caribbean or the Far East, but it had a rugged quality and fitted in better with the fashion for the medieval great hall. In 1831 *The London Cabinet Makers' Book of Prices* stated, 'Work veneered, with English mottled or pollard oak… charged on the shilling extra from mahogany'. Likewise, for oak carved out of the solid.[91] Although not directly attributable to a specific maker, the console table appears

110

CHAPTER 2: 1830S

Fig. 2.79 In beautifully figured San Domingo mahogany, the glazed and lower doors with gothick tracery, this bookcase is stamped by Thomas Willson, a furniture broker and appraiser. The locks are stamped 'Chubb & Son Makers To HRH Prince Albert'. The serial numbers on each lock indicate that they were made between 1839 and 1841. [Butchoff Antiques]

Fig. 2.80 The Bramah locks on this simply panelled mahogany desk, made or retailed by Matthew Willson of London, are clearly visible. The turned wooden knobs have been added at a later date, so often the case when complex Bramah keys were lost. Mathew Willson took over from his father Thomas' business in Great Queen Street in 1830. [Private collection]

BRITISH FURNITURE

2.81a

Fig. 2.81a Veneered in burr elm, this seemingly unique and idiosyncratic table base is flanked by figures of the Duke of Wellington, his arch enemy Napoleon Bonaparte and George Washington. [Butchoff Antiques]

Figs 2.81b–d The base of the table supported by carved figures of the Duke of Wellington, the Emperor Napoleon and President George Washington. [Butchoff Antiques]

2.81b   2.81c   2.81d

Fig. 2.82a 'An improved expanding table so constructed that the sections composing its surface may be caused to diverge from a common centre and that the spaces caused thereby may be filled up by inserting leaves or filling pieces.' The detailed ink and watercolour designs submitted by Robert Jupe who applied for the patent in March 1835. [The National Archives, Kew]

Figs 2.82b & d A fine example of Jupe's patented extending table, made in mahogany by Johnstone & Jeanes, a partnership formed in 1840. It is shown open to receive eight large or, alternatively, eight smaller brass-tipped leaves. Its diameter when closed is 152cm (5ft); when open is either 184.5cm (6ft) or 214cm (7ft), depending on the degree of extension required. [Woolley & Wallis]

Fig. 2.82c The Jupe table closed and with its original cabinet made for the eight small and eight large brass-tipped additional leaves. Both the table and cabinet bear the maker's stamp. [Woolley & Wallis]

2.83

2.84

Figs 2.83 & 2.84 A rare example of two tables made with *première* and *contre-partie* marquetry inlaid in a variety of woods into a Circassian walnut ground. The tripod bases have a fine example of Elizabethan Revival strapwork and foliage. The unknown marquetry cutter may well have been familiar with the designs of 1530 by Francesco Pellegrino. The *première partie* table top Fig. 2.84 has a more complex gadrooned edge; its mahogany-framed platform base with the retailer's stamp 'H Winter, Wardour ST'.[92] [2.83 Nan Xu; 2.84 Butchoff Antiques]

Fig. 2.85 A page from *Livre de Moresques*, reproducing designs by Francesco Pellegrini, first published in book form by the artist in Paris in 1530 under the title *La Fleur de la Science de Pourtraicture* [sic]. The maker of the tables in Figs 2.83 & 2.84 may have been aware of the designs, published in Antwerp in 1543 and in Paris in 1546.
[Metropolitan Museum of New York: Harris Brisbane Dick Fund, 1926. Accession Number: 26.71.8(5)]

influenced by the design philosophy of Bridgens, with its bold incurved buttress support and Elizabethan-style 'jewel-like' carving, in contrast to the overall architectural form.

The unusual mirror with addorsed, fiercely carved griffin heads in **Figs 2.36a & b**, is a subtle reference to the early nineteenth-century antiquarian taste in England. It is made of English oak, emblematic of England and used to underline an association with Elizabethan and seventeenth-century British furniture. To achieve such sculptural precision in oak requires a carver of consummate technical and artistic ability; the wood's coarse grain and very hard inclusions, the medullary rays, make oak one of the most challenging woods to carve.

It was common for designs of Elizabethan-style strapwork, as revived in the second quarter of the nineteenth century, to draw on English architecture and panelling, and an interesting example is the table base made for Warwick Castle.[93] Made on a massive scale and at a lower height than a conventional table, the decoration of the legs pays homage to an important *pietre dure* marble top with the arms and attributes of the patrician Grimani family. The Grimani tabletop represents a pinnacle in the history of the use of hardstones in the decorative arts, and the 3rd Earl of Warwick ordered the new wooden frame in the Elizabethan Revival style, the heavy tapering legs carved with strapwork, to be made to support the top as the Grimani family had retained the original giltwood table base when he purchased it for Warwick Castle in 1829.

In 1836, A.W.N. Pugin published his important volume *Gothic Ornaments of the 15th & 16th Centuries*, marking the arrival of 'Reform Gothic', **Fig. 2.73**. This style of furniture, with clear constructional details, led the way for the Arts and Crafts style of the 1860s, a fashion that continued well into the twentieth century.

The Norman style, based on architecture of the early years of the last millennium, was adopted almost exclusively by Thomas Hopper (1776–1856). Hopper was a surveyor-cum-architect whose first major commission was the Gothic conservatory he added to Carlton House in 1807 for the Prince Regent. However, by 1820, when he started rebuilding Penrhyn Castle for George H. Dawkins-Pennant, Hopper had started to work in the Norman Revival style. Penrhyn is a rare nineteenth-century venture into this style and Hopper's furniture is not often seen. However, much of the original furniture and fittings for Penrhyn remain in situ and are immediately recognisable for their bold, chunky style; the arched doors, mirrors and twist-turned supports of the castle's rooms are echoed in the oak furniture, **Fig. 2.76**. The same arches can be seen in Hopper's interior for Gosford Castle. An oak wardrobe, possibly from Gosford, is in the Victoria and Albert Museum, **Fig. 2.74**.[94] The Norman style is also seen in drawings by Edward Lamb, one of the draughtsmen for Loudon's *Encyclopedia*.

The inventiveness of early nineteenth-century furniture makers and designers saw no bounds. Although Parisian makers in the third quarter of the previous century, such as Jean-François Oeben, had successfully experimented with steel mechanisms for multi-use tables, the essentially English capstan table used mechanics in a novel and convenient form. Although mechanically highly innovative, the table as patented by Robert Jupe in 1835 has a distinctly 'Regency' look to the base, **Fig. 2.82b**. The concept was later taken up by others, presumably after the original patent had expired. The patent was disputed, unsuccessfully, by the inventor Samuel Pratt, who advertised 'their newly-invented circular extending tables' in May 1836.[95] A popular and useful style of table, another example was at Buckingham Palace by 1871, see **Fig. 6.3** and another by Maples in **Fig. 7.50** with variations at Windsor Castle. The circular tops of these tables turn on a complex elliptical iron frame opening so that segments can be inserted, increasing the number of diners from six to eight to ten or more. Less satisfactory are models that allow for further segments to be attached around the rim to accommodate even more diners. Jupe patented his 'Improved Expanding Table' in 1835, and at the same time formed a company with John Johnstone of 67 New Bond Street. Five years later Jupe left the firm, which then became known as Johnstone & Jeanes. A fine mahogany example is shown here open to allow the eight tailor-made segments to be inserted, **Figs 2.82b & d**. It has the rare addition of the original cabinet in which to store the leaves when not in use, **Fig. 2.82c**. All the components of this example are marked: the central brass capstan boss inscribed 'JOHNSTONE & JEANES PATENTEES' and the central block stamped 'JOHNSTONE, JUPE & CO. NEW BOND ST. LONDON 10288'. The bearers have stencilled numbers with corresponding numbers on the leaves. Even the

Fig. 2.86 **This 1904 image of the Drawing Room at Wrest Park shows the Louis XV Revival furniture and mirrors thought to have been supplied by Dowbiggin & Co., in 1839.** [*Country Life*, 1970]

Fig. 2.87 A watercolour, attributed to Thomas Scandrett, c.1840, showing the extravagant rococo decoration of the library at Wrest Park, the Rococo Revival interiors largely designed by its owner, Earl de Grey. The opulence is notable, underlined by the abundance of turquoise-green and silver-coloured damask, the curtains deliberately puddled on the floor to give the room an extra dimension of luxury and extravagance.[96]
[Bedfordshire Archives]

iron extending mechanism is stamped 'JUPE'S PATENT'. The illustrated example is made of solid mahogany. The swirling, intricate expanding mechanism as patented by Jupe is clearly visible. Most of the early models are stamped 'Johnstone Jupe & Co.', with the 67 New Bond Street address that they held from 1835 until 1894. Early Jupe tables appear to have all been made in mahogany and often have an uneven circumference when closed, many with a Regency, Grecian-style base although some with a Gothic-style support.

Idiosyncratic design has long been a feature of English furniture and the nineteenth century was no exception. Indeed, it was an epoch that held the banner of eccentricity high. The table illustrated in **Figs 2.81a–d** is typical of a love for the historic, but the intent of the designer is unclear. Such furniture is difficult to date with any certainty but is clearly Regency in form and the overall shape is common enough. The juxtaposition of the three figures is intriguing.

The seated central figures supporting the base are the Duke of Wellington and Napoleon Bonaparte, opposing leaders, revered both in France and England. The third is George Washington, the first president of the United States who favoured the French, not the English. Each figure sits adjacent to patriotic motifs: the Union Jack, the thirteen stars of the United States and the French Imperial Eagle. A reference to three great leaders, the designer, maker and probable commission remain a mystery.

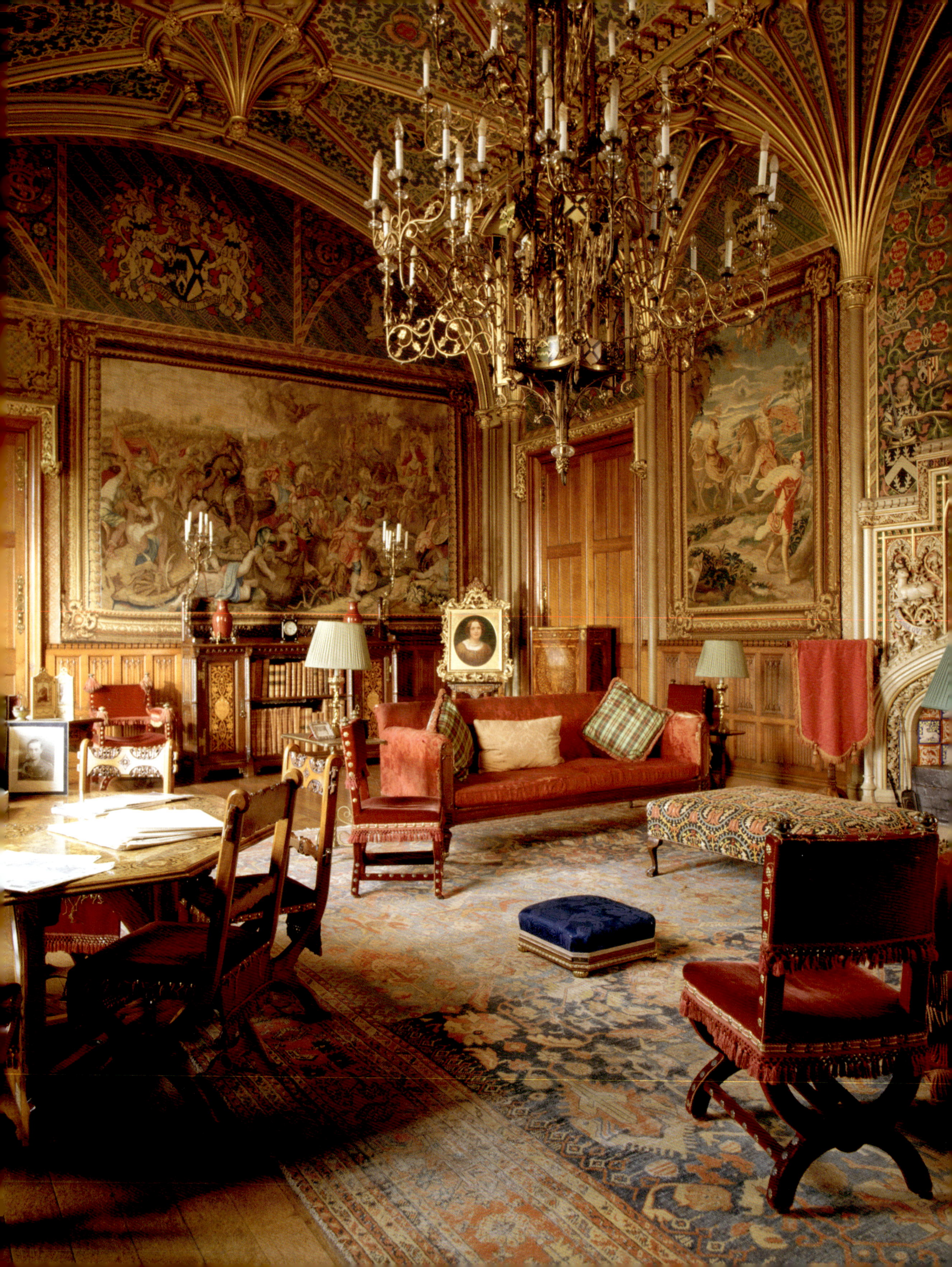

1840s

The life and work of furniture designers, manufacturers and dealers do not fall conveniently within the boundaries of decades. Their work is generational, often spanning only one generation, sometimes a whole dynasty lasting over a century, Gillows being a prime example. Richard Bridgens' iconic designs were first conceived in the 1820s but his *Furniture with Candelabra* was published in a second edition in 1838. His work spanned at least two decades, and his influence continued well into the 1840s. The body of signed furniture made or retailed by Edward Holmes Baldock is frequently catalogued as '1840s', a time when he was nearing the end of his career and many of the extant examples of his work are probably earlier than thought. Unless there is precise documentation, provenance, or an inventory, it is difficult to be certain of the exact date of a piece of furniture. Contemporary criticism of the eclecticism of British furniture design in the 1840s was mixed with praise. One example was the 1841 *Art Union* noting that the refurbishment of York House, later named Stafford House, had 'furniture of no particular style, but, on the whole, there is to be found a mingling of everything, in the best manner of the best epochs of taste'.[1] In 1843, a commentator in *The Builder* wrote that 'We are, however pleased to be able to trace a growing improvement in the taste of the furniture of our living apartments, and a predilection for the rich and elegant designs of the Elizabethan age'.[2] The furniture historian Frederick Litchfield wrote tantalisingly about furniture makers or designers who are little known today, for example the Irish interior decorator Leonard William Collman (1816–1881), whom he described as 'an excellent draughtsman' who 'carried out the decoration and furnishing of many public buildings, London Clubs, and mansions of the nobility and gentry'.[3]

In 1898, Litchfield lamented 'the very low state of Art in England fifty years ago' and quoted a government Select Committee between 1840 and 1841, which hoped that the re-building of the Palace of Westminster would encourage new design.[4] The Gothic, already by then a mainstay of English design, was championed by A.W.N. Pugin. At first his furniture was delightfully simple but as the 1830s and 1840s progressed it became heavier and more elaborate. The Gothic Revival spurred a renewed interest in woodcarving and subsequently increased employment for many craftsmen in London and the provinces, especially in cathedral cities. The Gothic style lent itself to the narrative of a strong and proud country with a long heritage and was used in the architecture and furnishings of many public buildings. The visitor to London familiar with the intricate carved stone exterior of the Palace of Westminster today may be largely unaware of the matching interior and its magnificent woodcarving. In 1847, John Webb of Bond Street supplied, to a Pugin design,

Fig. 3.1 **The Gothic Drawing Room at Eastnor Castle. Between 1849 and 1850, A.W.N. Pugin made alterations to Robert Smirke's original design for the house. The vaulting on the ceiling can be compared with the table Pugin designed for Windsor Castle, Fig. 1.60d.** [*Country Life*, 1993]

3.2a

CHAPTER 3: 1840S

Fig. 3.2a A remarkable marquetry table cabinet made by Berlin-born Friedrich Ludwig Hausburg (1817–1886), who established a workshop in Liverpool in 1840, the year he was naturalised as a British citizen. The primary panel carries his signature 'F. L. Hausburg Fecit Liverpool' and the inscription 'Begun in 1840 Finished in 1857'. [Butchoff Antiques]

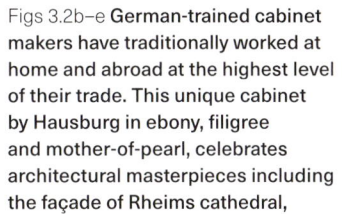

Figs 3.2b–e German-trained cabinet makers have traditionally worked at home and abroad at the highest level of their trade. This unique cabinet by Hausburg in ebony, filigree and mother-of-pearl, celebrates architectural masterpieces including the façade of Rheims cathedral, King's College Chapel, Westminster Abbey, Buckingham, Kensington and Kew palaces, the House of Lords, the Royal Pavilion at Brighton, the castles of Windsor, Dover, Caernarfon and Kenilworth, and St Paul's Cathedral. [Butchoff Antiques]

121

BRITISH FURNITURE

3.3a

3.3b

Figs 3.3a & b **These two cabinets were supplied by Gillows; the first in 1848, the other in 1858 to the 3rd Baron Newborough for Plas Glynllifon. There are slight differences between the pieces, no doubt due to the cabinet maker's personalised interpretation of Gillows' designs and because they were made ten years apart. Each of the glazed panels is divided by the Gillows-pattern die-stamped gadrooned mouldings.** [Christie's]

Fig. 3.4 **The strength and power of the design of the set of chairs in The Prince's Chamber in the House of Lords emphasises why Pugin's interpretation of the Gothic style was deemed so suitable for important public buildings.** [The Metropolitan Museum of Art, New York]

Fig. 3.5 **The Prince's Chamber in the House of Lords, furnished with a set of oak X-frame chairs and an octagonal table designed by A.W.N. Pugin, supplied by John Webb.** [Robertharding / Alamy Stock Photo]

Fig. 3.6 **The giltwood throne, or 'Chair of State', made in 1847 for Prince Albert's use in the House of Lords under the direction of the influential dealer John Webb, to a design by A.W.N. Pugin.** [© Parliamentary Historic Furniture and Decorative Arts Collection, POW 03609]

Fig. 3.7 **A design for a Gothic interior signed by the furniture makers Charles Hindley & Sons. The stag's head with widespread antlers were intended to add a medieval aesthetic to the room.** [The Metropolitan Museum of Art, New York]

the spectacular gilded 'Chair of State' for the use of Prince Albert in the House of Lords,[5] **Fig. 3.6**, as well as a set of chairs and an octagonal table for the Prince's Chamber (**Figs 3.4 & 3.5**).

Antiquarian decoration persisted; a fine architectural example can be seen in the watercolour of the staircase hall at Beaumanor Hall, a stark 'Jacobethan' interior built between 1842 and 1848 by William Railton, **Fig. 3.11**. The Jacobethan style continued in the furnishings, the hall table and chair typical of the seemingly muddled rendition of decorative features. As was often the case, the decoration of the hall contrasted with the soft comfort of the drawing room which was in the full-blown Rococo Revival style. Elsewhere, new furniture in the Elizabethan idiom was designed to fit

122

3.4

3.5

3.6

3.7

3.8

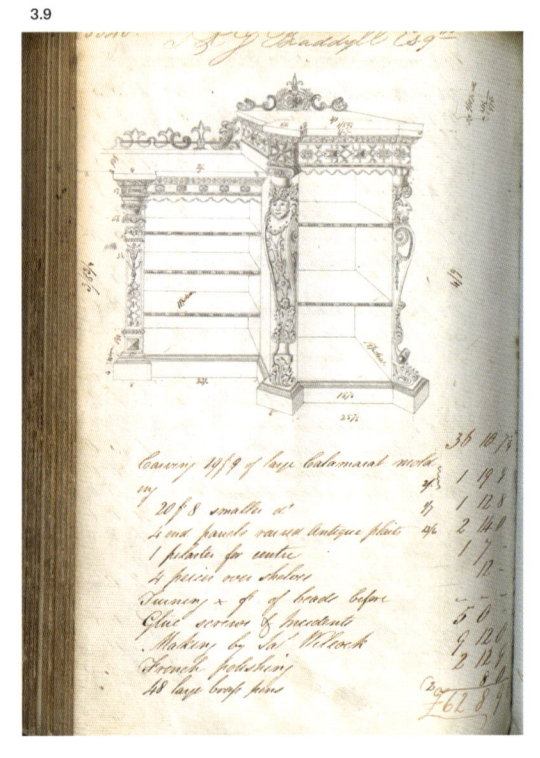

3.9

Fig. 3.8 **This form of pedestal bookcase was used in the Regency but has been adapted here in the Elizabethan style in a similar vein to furniture designed by Gillows between 1840 and 1841 for Thomas Braddyll's Oak Room at Conishead Priory.** [Bonhams]

Fig. 3.9 **Design number 5340, created by Gillows in June 1841 for a pair of bookcases made for Colonel Braddyll at Conishead Priory. The annotations show the exact sizes required for each component. The instruction at the base of the drawing seems to suggest that the carving was to be in calamander, a difficult timber to carve satisfactorily. The total cost for the pair was £62 8s 9d.** [Westminster City Archives]

Fig. 3.10 **The Oak Room at Conishead Priory partly furnished by Gillows between 1840 and 1841.** [Author's collection]

into original late sixteenth- and early seventeenth-century rooms, such as the Oak Room at Conishead Priory, **Fig. 3.10**. However, the elaborately carved panelling at Conishead, although 'period', had been brought from Samlesbury Hall, another of Thomas Braddyll's houses. The panelling dates from 1623, the oldest panels show the three figures of 'Faith', 'Hope' and 'Charity'.[6] A.W.N. Pugin had created a similar room for Scarisbrick Hall between 1837 and 1841. Gillows designed a bookcase for Braddyll's Oak Room between 1840 and 1841, in an ornate Elizabethan style, **Fig. 3.9**. Falling out of fashion in the twentieth century, Elizabethan Revival furniture such as the glazed walnut cabinet once more appeals to collectors, **Fig. 3.13**.

One of the most prominent London interior decorators of the nineteenth century was the Crace family. The table in **Figs 3.15a & 3.15b**, with polychromatic decoration and Elizabethan style 'jewels', can be associated with the work of John Gregory Crace (1809–1889). As a young man John Gregory Crace had assisted his father working at Windsor Castle and Buckingham Palace. He supplied chairs and tables for the palace from 1838, work which continued into the early 1840s. Sir Charles Barry commissioned Crace to work with A.W.N. Pugin on the interiors of the Houses of Parliament in the 1840s. Crace and Pugin formed a partnership in 1844 and made oak furniture in the Crace workshops behind the main showrooms on Wigmore Street. The polychrome table is almost certainly attributable to Crace, but for which patron remains a mystery. The unabashed luxury of the satinwood top, with the original red velvet on the footrest, the mahogany-lined drawers, and the initial 'D' on the cartouches, suggest that the table may have been made by Crace for the 6th Duke of Devonshire at Lismore Castle. The 'Bachelor Duke' had commissioned both Crace and Pugin to work on Lismore, converting the old bishop's palace into a medieval-style banqueting hall. The colour scheme is similar to a pair of side tables at Knebworth House, where Crace worked between 1843 and 1844 for Edward Bulwer-Lytton (see **Fig. 3.16**).

Between 1842 and 1845, a small luxuriously appointed pavilion was erected in the garden of Buckingham Palace for Queen Victoria and Prince Albert. Its German designer, Ludwig Grüner (1801–1882) of Dresden, based in London from c.1842, was much admired by Prince Albert.[7] The interior had an elaborate polychromatic decorative scheme in a High Renaissance Revival style, as seen in the lithograph, **Fig. 3.17**. The frescoes, started in 1843, were designed by eight eminent artists, including Charles Eastlake, William Etty and Edwin Landseer. The pavilion, demolished in 1928, included a dedicated 'Scott room', furnished with an Elizabethan-style 'Abbotsford' Sir Walter Scott chair. Grüner's invoices for work at Buckingham Palace amounted to over £6,000 in the mid-1850s.[8] Varied and eclectic, the Carolean-style chair with twist-turned supports seen on the left of the engraving **Fig. 3.18**, is not a typical English construction and is clearly designed by a European hand. Little of the furniture for the Pavilion has survived; the giltwood centre table, **Fig. 3.19**, is a rare exception. Made for the centre of the pavilion, the Octagon Room under the main

Oak Room, Conishead Priory Hydropathic, Ulverston — Valentine's Series

dome, it would have been the first piece seen by visitors. An attribution to the royal furniture makers George Morant & Sons is based on a similar table by the firm for Great Tew Park (see **Fig. 3.28**).⁹ Grüner published *Decorations of the Garden Pavilion in the Grounds of Buckingham Palace* in 1846. A jewel cabinet designed by Grüner and made by the Birmingham firm of Elkington, Mason & Co. is in the Royal Collection and was exhibited at the Great Exhibition, together with an Axminster carpet designed by him for the Green Drawing Room at Windsor Castle.¹⁰

The strict and disciplined training of apprentice cabinet makers in the German-speaking states made them a valuable asset in other European countries, specifically Paris but also London, one example being Johann Martin Levien. Another was the maker of the remarkable marquetry cabinet illustrated in **Fig. 3.2a–d**, Friedrich Ludwig Hausburg (1817–1886), who was born in Berlin and subsequently worked with his uncle, August Promoli, in Liverpool.¹¹ In 1840, the year he became a naturalised British citizen, Hausburg started the cabinet, which was not finished until seventeen years later. Modelled as a gothic cathedral, and measuring only 45cm by 38cm (approx. 17¾ x 15in), the cabinet is a celebration of architectural history in marquetry. The exterior is ebony, a representation, as Hausburg stated in his will, of the exterior of Reims Cathedral. The turrets have concealed sliding covers, with compartments underneath, and there is a well-hidden spring-operated secret drawer. The exquisite interior is elaborately inlaid with brass, tulipwood and mother-of-pearl, with scenes from the interior of King's College Chapel, Cambridge. The drawer fronts on the left-hand side depict Kew Palace, the entrance to the Old House of Lords, Kenilworth Castle, Brighton Pavilion, Windsor Castle, Dover Castle and Caernarvon Castle. The two hinged doors depict the Palace of Holyroodhouse and Westminster Abbey. On the right are Virginia Water, Hampton Court Palace, Edinburgh Castle, Bushy Park, Kensington Palace, Buckingham Palace and the Tower of London. The doors are representative of St Paul's Cathedral and St James's Palace. Hausburg died in Cannes in 1886, leaving the substantial sum of £180,000.

The interior of grand Scottish Baronial mansions was the perfect setting for the Elizabethan Revival style. The doyen of the style was the energetic Scottish architect William Burn (1789–1870). In 1842, he wrote to Tyndall Bruce with a

Fig. 3.11 **Beaumanor Hall, built in the 1840s by the architect William Railton, continued the quasi-Jacobean/Elizabethan style. In contrast to the staircase hall, the drawing room was in a Rococo Revival style.**[12] [© Leicester Arts and Museums Service / © Leicester Museums & Galleries / Bridgeman Images]

list of suggestions of where to source fittings: 'For old oak carvings go to Messrs. Pratt, No. 47 New Bond Street, Webb and Cragg No. 8 Old Bond Street…For the most Splendid Carvings… to Mr. G. Rogers No 18 Church Street, Soho…'. His lengthy advice continued: 'but for cabinets and china, do not omit going to Baldocks, Hanway Street… which is the *first* place in London'.[13] The area 'was for some time the resort of the highest fashions for mercery, and other articles of dress; and it has continued to this day to be noted for its china-dealers and curiosity shops…'. Edward Walford specifically mentions Baldock 'when it was still called Hanway Yard. It was narrow and dirty, and full of old china-shops, including Baldock's, "a sort of museum for Chinese horses and dragons, queer-looking green vases, and dollsized teacups".'[14]

The Great Hall at Burghley was an impressive venue for a state banquet (**Fig. 3.23**). To furnish it the 2nd Marquess of Exeter bought a large mahogany dining table which extends to over 9 metres (29½ feet) from Edward Holmes Baldock. He also bought a set of carved walnut dining

Fig. 3.12 The often sparse, empty entrance hall was later used as an extra sitting room. This photograph of Shuckburgh Hall shows the entrance hall fitted out with Elizabethan-style furniture, sometime after 1844. [Leicestershire County Council]

Fig. 3.13 Partly of Elizabethan inspiration, this display cabinet with brass-framed doors uses well-figured walnut. The white Carrara marble top is inset in the French style; the outset corners carved with a stylised fleur-de-lys, centred by a heraldic device. The overall form is similar to the cabinet Fig.4.10. [Nan Xu]

Fig. 3.14 A large walnut stool, which mixes Elizabethan with boldly modelled Rococo scroll legs. It is attributed to Arthur Blain & Son, who were established in Liverpool in c.1835. Forty years later, Blain's *The Cabinet-makers' Pattern-book* of 1875 contained over 1,000 lithograph designs. [Nan Xu]

chairs (**Fig. 3.22**), loosely in the style of Daniel Marot, from Samuel Pratt. Exeter recorded the order in his diary: '1840... Twenty-five carved Chairs bought by Lord Exeter of Mr. Pratt for Great Hall dinner Table. 5 guineas each'.[15] Samuel and Henry Pratt were advertised as 'Antique & Foreign Furniture Dealers' in 1839, but it also appears that they were innovators in furniture making. In 1826, Samuel patented the coil spring, an important addition to the comfort of chairs,[16] and in 1843 he and Henry patented a woodcarving machine.[17] Samuel died in 1849, but his sons, Henry and Samuel, continued the business until c.1879.

Similar chairs to Pratt's set for Burghley were made by the Patent Wood Carving Company of Henrietta Street in London's Covent Garden. Such chairs were made in huge numbers, but it is possible, judging by the construction, that the Burghley set were actually produced in France or Belgium. The rounded ends of the stretchers are more typical of continental chairs, whereas in England they would normally have square ends jointed to square leg blocks. However, Pratt worked with William Irving at the time of

Figs 3.15a & b **Possibly designed by Frederick Crace & Son, this richly decorated polychrome table is in a style of furniture made for the 6th Duke of Devonshire at Lismore Castle. The padded footrest suggests that it was intended as a writing table.** [James Graham-Stewart]

Fig. 3.16 **The State Drawing Room at Knebworth House, where Frederick Crace & Son worked between 1843 and 1844. The console table to the right of the fireplace is one of a pair, the polychrome decoration similar in style to the table shown above (Figs 3.15a).** [*Country Life*, 2003]

3.17

Fig. 3.17 **In 1842, Ludwig Grüner designed a splendid pavilion in the grounds of Buckingham Palace, demolished in 1928, the interior decorated in an elaborate Renaissance manner.** [Royal Collection Trust / © His Majesty King Charles III 2023]

Fig. 3.18 **A group of furniture designed by Ludwig Grüner for the Queen's Pavilion in 'Buckingham Gardens' in 1842. The giltwood centre table Fig. 3.19, attributed to Morant, is clearly visible.** [Heidelberg University Library]

Fig. 3.19 **A rare survivor from the Buckingham Palace Garden Pavilion, made to a design by Ludwig Grüner, possibly by George Morant & Sons.** [Carlton Hobbs LLC]

3.18

3.19

the Burghley acquisition, so it is possible that the chairs were machine carved at the Architectural Carving Works in Pimlico or that, as the undersides of the seat rails are made in the English tradition, the frames were imported from Europe in pieces and assembled in England. The price of the comparatively simple new chairs seems high, certainly in comparison to the celebrated set of twelve seventeenth-century armchairs by Andrea Brustolon, bought from Town & Emanuel for Burghley by Lord Exeter in 1836 at 12 guineas a chair.[18] Another long set of chairs with rounded-end stretchers in a similar vein were supplied to the 5th Duke of Buccleuch at approximately the same date.

In 1841, the *Art Union* announced that a 'taste has of late years arisen for carved furniture of the Tudor, Louis Quatorze and Renaissance periods'.[19] This fashion was exemplified by every type of furniture, such as the set of oak, caned-back chairs that were supplied to Charlecote Park in the 1830s seen now placed around a Morant octagonal table, **Fig. 2.32**. This type of chair was made in Britain with endless variations throughout the century with increasing competition from factories in Mechelen, in Belgium. Although much of the furniture of the period was hand carved, steam-driven carving machines were used to reduce the high cost of intricate ornament. Machines would be used for the roughing out, or 'bosting', and the work was hand finished. Another form of decoration was to emboss the wood under machine pressure, giving the initial appearance of hand carving as on the Gillows cabinets, **Fig. 3.3a**. Much of the intricate work at the Palace of Westminster was carried out in this manner, dramatically saving time and expense. Firms specifically advertised woodcarving by machine, such as in *The Builder* in March 1847, placed by Jordan's Patent, the Patent Wood Carving offices and the Architectural Carving Works. It can be remarkably difficult to tell the difference between hand and machine work, except that most machine work appears repetitive. For example, each leaf or flower is identical, whereas hand carving by its very nature is inconsistent, even when executed by an experienced craftsman.

The large mahogany and maple octagonal table made in the Tuscan seventeenth-century style for the Conservative Club by Henry Whitaker in 1844 is typical of the substantial and self-confident furniture thought appropriate for the masculine domain (**Fig. 2.78**). Whitaker also made a set of four library bookcases for the club in St James's.[20] Although some of the furniture Whitaker supplied to the club was decorated with complex sculptural forms, he remarked that such work was of 'comparatively moderate expense' when it could be carried out by a carving machine.[21]

Equally bold are a set of mahogany hall chairs, monogrammed with 'VA', designed by Whitaker and made by Holland & Sons for the Pavilion Entrance Hall of Osborne House, and the heavy and uncompromising mahogany sideboard shown in **Fig 3.25**.[22] For the Osborne chairs, Whitaker used the 'X'-frame form of leg seen in Pugin's chairs for the Palace of Westminster and Scarisbrick Hall, but in a simple Italianate, rather than Gothic, style to appeal to the personal taste of the royal couple. Other furniture made by Whitaker for Osborne includes a large giltwood settee which, at first glance, could be taken for being twenty years earlier.

In 1847, Whitaker published many of his designs in *The Practical Cabinet Maker and Upholsterer's Treasury of*

Figs 3.20a & b The walnut veneer on this parcel-gilt loo table is inlaid with detailed marquetry, while the base combines an eclectic mixture of French eighteenth-century styles. It shares similarities with tables by Holland & Sons but the underside has the stamp of Johnstone & Jeanes who took over from Jupe between 1837 and 1838. [Private collection]

Fig. 3.21 The stamp of Johnstone & Jeanes on this amboyna table gives the address as '67 Bond Street' (actually 67 New Bond Street), the stamp the firm used between *c.*1840 and 1880. The Elizabethan style of the strapwork supports suggests a date in the 1840s. The top has patriotic inlays of English roses and the national emblems of Scotland and Ireland, the thistle and the shamrock. [Butchoff Antiques]

Fig. 3.22 One of the set of walnut dining chairs, in the style of Daniel Marot, supplied in 1840 by the dealer Samuel Pratt to the 2nd Marquess of Exeter for the Burghley House dining table in the Great Hall. [Burghley House]

Fig. 3.23 A watercolour by Henry Bryan Ziegler recording the banquet during Queen Victoria's visit to Burghley House in 1844. The mahogany dining table, which extends to over 9m (30ft), was purchased by the 2nd Marquess from Edward Holmes Baldock. [Burghley House]

Designs, followed by *The Cabinet-Maker's Assistant* in 1853. At the Great Exhibition of 1851, he exhibited a centre table of a very different style, with a tasselled border supported by oversize winged beasts made in the most elaborate and florid manner, and a concave-sided, quadruped base with scrolled feet; an ornate rendition of a design by Bridgens.

Like many of the more established firms, George Morant & Sons were both decorators and cabinet makers who supplied high-quality furniture in a variety of different styles. Amongst their most important patrons were the 2nd Duke of Sutherland, for whom they carried out work at Stafford House between 1836 and 1842, and the 13th Duke of Norfolk (after he succeeded to his title in 1842) at Arundel Castle; they also supplied furniture to Raby Castle in the 1840s. Morant had also worked with George Bullock at Great Tew Park in 1817, and in the early 1840s provided furniture to the house in a modernised but similar style for the Boulton family. The furniture Morant delivered for Great Tew followed Bullock's tradition of inlaying holly marquetry into oak in a 'Buhl' style, while retaining a somewhat Regency appearance. Some of the Morant pieces at Great Tew were branded with the mark that the firm used from 1841 to 1842, or had the name stencilled onto their dust covers, as at Raby where the covers have been carefully put back after the upholstery has been replaced. The set of twelve elegant dining chairs, **Fig. 3.29a**, were designed in *c*.1843 to fit in with the existing pieces that Bullock had made for Tew between 1816 and 1818. Morant has kept to the spirit of the original Bullock commission with the unusual combination of oak and holly and instantly recognisable Regency frames.

The possibility of a royal visit to an aristocratic house was impetus enough to have it redecorated, with guest rooms refurnished to celebrate the occasion. It was also an opportunity to make an impression on the visitor. The splendour of Burghley House needed little or no attention, and when the sixteen-year-old Princess Victoria had visited in 1835 she commented that Burghley was a 'fine, large and handsome house'. Nevertheless, the 2nd Marquess of Exeter had commissioned Morant to supply a new suite of furniture, two years in advance, for the three-day visit of Queen Victoria and Prince Albert in November 1844. The Second George Room was refurnished in a more modern style, one that typified the eclecticism of the period, **Figs 3.37 & 3.38**. Several years previously, Morant had applied successfully for a royal warrant on the recommendation of the Duchess of Gloucester, and this undoubtedly increased his cachet in aristocratic circles and was likely a factor in Exeter's decision to assign Morant the work at Burghley. The suite, still in situ, consists of carved giltwood furniture, **Figs 3.32–3.36**, a type of work which Morant proudly advertised on their bill heads. The State Bed, originally supplied to the room by Fell

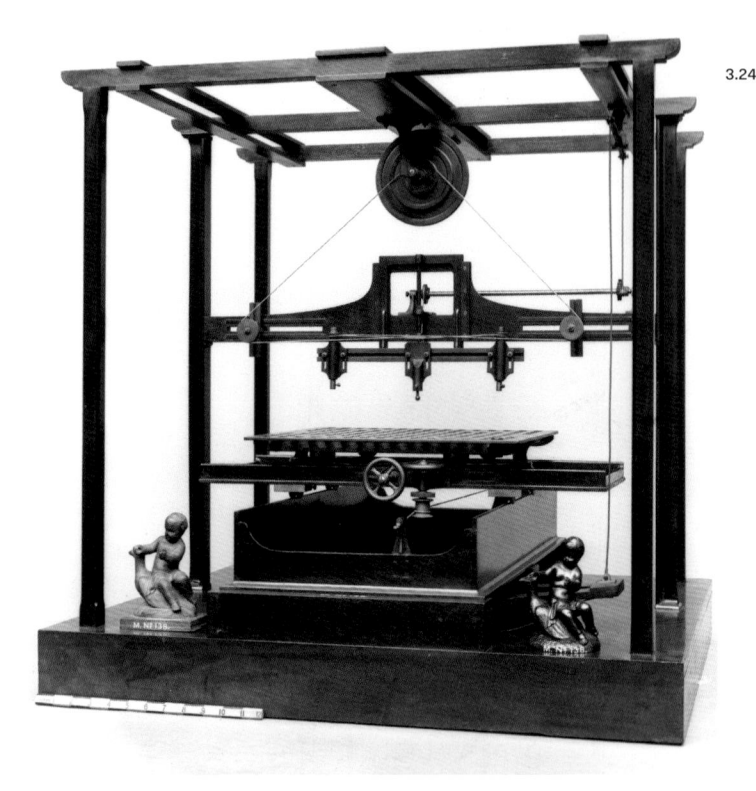

Fig. 3.24 **During the 1840s, machinery became increasingly common in larger and more established cabinet-making workshops. In 1845, T.B. Jordan invented a steam-driven woodcarving machine for which this** 1:4 scale model exists in the Science Museum. Later the machine was improved to carry out the complex operation of undercutting, an effect which helps give carving a lighter appearance when viewed from the front. [Science Museum, London]

& Newton in *c*.1795, was altered by Morant for the royal couple, with a pair of carved lovebirds added to the cornice. The white and gold colour scheme of carved furniture was also used by Morant for furniture supplied to the Duke of Norfolk for Queen Victoria's visit to Arundel Castle in 1846. White and gold had been the colour scheme for carved-wood wall panelling at Norfolk House in the mid-eighteenth century, the French-inspired scheme becoming fashionable again in the 1830s after the examples for the Duke of Rutland at Belvoir started in the late 1820s. This was quickly followed by schemes for the Duke of Sutherland at Stafford House and interiors at the Goldsmiths' Hall. The quality of the Burghley House white and gold bedroom furniture made for Queen Victoria's visit is of the highest London standards as would be expected from Morant. In a similar veing, in 1848 William Burn remodelled the Octagon Drawing Room at Raby Castle, and George Morant supplied cabriole-leg seat furniture (**Figs 3.40 & 3.41**).[23] Burn also worked for the 5th Duke of Buccleuch and the Raby chairs are similar to chairs at Drumlanrig Castle. No doubt under Burn's direction, for Raby Morant also supplied bedroom furniture in white and gold (**Figs 3.39a–d**). Burn had

CHAPTER 3: 1840S

Fig. 3.25 The personal taste of Queen Victoria and Prince Albert was far more traditional than that of George IV but furniture produced for the royal family remained very high quality. This large sideboard and wine cooler were made by Henry Whitaker for Osborne House using the finest mahogany. [Royal Collection Trust / © His Majesty King Charles III 2023]

Fig. 3.26 The rough cutting for the carving of this sideboard was achieved by Jordan's Carving Works, the finishing touches by hand. Makers such as Cox & Son based their steam-driven machinery on the Jordan Patent. [© Victoria and Albert Museum, London]

Fig. 3.27 The ubiquitous fire screen was perceived as essential to prevent ladies' blushes in the winter and provide a draught excluder from an open chimney in the summer. This example by Jennens & Bettridge, painted with the 8th Earl and Countess of Kintore riding in the grounds of Keith Hall, formed part of an extensive suite delivered to Kintore in October 1850. Its elaborate *papier-mâché* frame has Elizabethan-style strapwork, forming a suitable frame for their ancestral home. [© Victoria and Albert Museum, London]

proposed an Elizabethan transformation to the façade of Dalkeith Palace in 1831, a project that was rejected. By the time of Queen Victoria's visit in 1842 the interior had a more feminine interior in white and gold.

An important series of white and gold furniture and fittings was supplied to the 5th Duke of Buccleuch in the early 1840s, mainly for Dalkeith Palace. Much of this furniture appears to have been supplied by Edward Holmes Baldock but some was made locally by the Edinburgh cabinet maker James Morison. Receipted accounts from Baldock in the Buccleuch Archives dating between 1841 and 1842 list, amongst others, 'A very rich white and gold dressing table richly ornamented and a marble top', and a 'Large cheval glass in white and gold', (similar to one at Raby, **Fig. 3.39d**), and include drawings for bedroom furniture. An undated estimate for bedroom furniture in an unidentified hand, headed 'Estimate of Sundry Furniture in White & Gold', lists ten pieces, including a 'Pier Wardrobe' at £25 10s and a larger 'Wing Wardrobe' at £54.0.0, probably those shown in **Figs 3.42 & 3.43b**.[24]

The Buccleuch Papers confirm that Baldock was not the only supplier of this fashionable white and gold furniture to

3.28

CHAPTER 3: 1840S

3.29a

3.29b

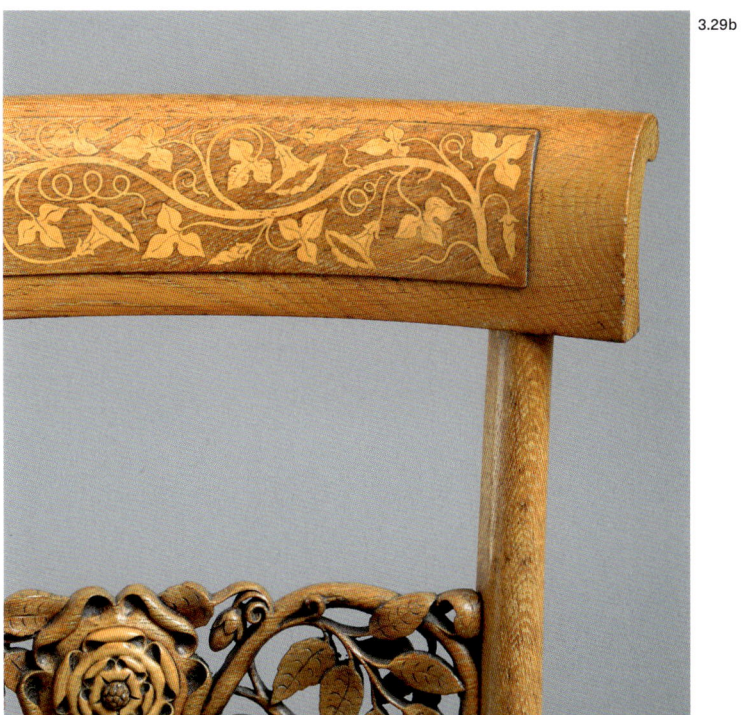

3.30a

3.30b

3.31

Fig. 3.28 **Library at Tew Park refurnished by Morant in** *c.*1843. [Tew Archive, © Christie's 1987]

Fig. 3.29a **One of a set of twelve side chairs supplied in** *c.*1843 **by Morant to complement the original Regency commission by Bullock at Tew Park.** [James Graham-Stewart]

Fig. 3.29b **A detail of the later set of Tew Park dining chairs, the delicate foliage inlaid in holly on an oak frame.** [James Graham-Stewart]

Figs 3.30a & b **Two designs by Morant, on the left a table base for a** *pietre dure* **top with winged griffin supports on lion paw feet. The design for the table on the right has winged rams' heads and cloven hoof feet.** [Tew Archive, © Christie's 1987]

Fig. 3.31 **A library table by Morant made in** *c.*1843 **for Tew Park, the winged chimera supports, a variation of the designs in Figs 3.30a & b.** [Tew Archive, © Christie's 1987]

135

Fig. 3.32 A white and gold wardrobe, in an exuberant Rococo style, signed by Morant and supplied for Queen Victoria's visit to Burghley House in 1844. Morant has refashioned old French wall panelling dating to the second quarter of the eighteenth century to use as the doors. [Burghley House]

Figs 3.33–3.36 Part of the white painted and giltwood bedroom suite Morant supplied to the 2nd Marquess of Exeter for Queen Victoria's use on her visit in 1844. [Burghley House]

Fig. 3.37 (opposite) The Second George Room at Burghley House, the furniture supplied by Morant for the visit of Queen Victoria and Prince Albert in 1844. The state bed supplied by Fell & Newton in *c.*1795, with its extravagant curtaining and fringes, was altered for the occasion, adding a pair of lovebirds to the cornice. [Burghley House / Photo Sam Lloyd]

3.37

BRITISH FURNITURE

3.38

Fig. 3.38 An anonymous watercolour of the newly refurbished Second George Room at the time of Queen Victoria's visit to Burghley House in 1844. The chaise longue in front of the bed and the cabinet and chair to the left are illustrated as Figs 3.34–3.46. [Burghley House]

Fig. 3.39a The Blue Bedroom at Raby Castle. The wardrobe is applied with carved giltwood foliage; of an unusual form, it may have been supplied by Morant in *c*.1848. The suite only matches in colour – white and gold – not in style. Rooms at Burghley, Arundel and other houses have similar colouring, often in anticipation of a visit from Queen Victoria. The grained and pollard oak State Bed bears the coat of arms of the 3rd Earl of Darlington impaled with the arms of his second wife, Elizabeth, dating it to between 1807 and 1827. [Raby Castle, County Durham]

Figs 3.39b & c The dressing table, toilet mirror and gilt overmantle in the Blue Bedroom at Raby Castle were possibly supplied by Morant in the 1840s. The armchair beside the dressing table is French, *c*.1740, re-painted white and gold to match. The giltwood centre table has a Howard & Sons paper label. The carpet is a copy of the original made for the room in 1848, re-woven by the original supplier, Mackay's of Durham. The detail of the dressing table shows mahogany shields painted with the initial 'C' for the Duke of Cleveland. [Raby Castle, County Durham]

Fig. 3.39d A large cheval glass, part of the white and gold suite supplied in *c*.1848 to Raby Castle. It is remarkably similar in style to a *'Large cheval glass in white and gold'*, on a receipted invoice from Baldock to the 5th Duke of Buccleuch, the execution is in the style of James Morison. [Raby Castle, County Durham]

the Buccleuchs. A letter from James Morison, an Edinburgh cabinet maker, to the duchess dated 14 December 1842, includes various sketches, one of which is shown as **Fig. 3.43a**. The letter refers to alternative cornice designs on the drawing of a 'winged wardrobe'; an executed wardrobe, **Fig. 3.43b**, displays the cornice on the left-hand side of **Fig. 3.43a**. A note of July 1833 from Morison to the Duke had explained: 'Sure he (Mr. Burn) will be able to obtain some good substantial furniture equal at least to the best makers in London'.[25]

James Morison was based in Edinburgh. His father Matthew had founded a cabinet-making firm in *c*.1790 in Ayr, some 40 miles from Drumlanrig Castle, and James expanded the firm first to Glasgow and then to Edinburgh.[26]

138

CHAPTER 3: 1840S

3.39a

3.39b

3.39c

3.39d

139

3.40

3.41

Three cabinet makers' day or pocketbooks, brought to the public eye in 1997 but hitherto unpublished, have proved to be an important source of information.[27] The books are unsigned but the hand is that of James Morison in his correspondence with the Buccleuchs. The format of the pocketbooks is typical of the genre and consistent with other known cabinet makers' day books, which were kept by the owner or foreman of the cabinet-making shop as a handy reference to the orders received and which craftsmen were working on which piece, including the cost and the name of the commissioning client. The books date between 1843 to 1845 and contain rough sketches of hundreds of pieces of furniture, most of which are of a form typical of the decade. Each has the name of the client alongside, showing that Morison had a formidable client list. These included the Duke of Hamilton, Sir Robert Abercrombie, the Earl of Glasgow, the Earl of Lauderdale (for whom a considerable amount of furniture was made), Macintosh of Macintosh, and companies such as the Scottish Equitable Life Assurance Society. Amongst these important clients was the 5th Duke of Buccleuch, at the time when he was refurbishing Bowhill

House, Dalkeith Palace and Drumlanrig Castle. It is clear from the ink sketches in the day books that many of the pieces are still now at Bowhill or Drumlanrig.

Perhaps the most intriguing is the entry for 2 February 1843 which describes a 'Wardrobe with wings in the French still finished in White & Gold & varnished for the Queens Room', costing Morison £52.16s to make. It was clearly executed, as the drawing for it is annotated with the name of Veitch, one of Morison's cabinet makers who appears to have been given the most complicated pieces to make, **Fig. 3.45**. It is very similar to a wardrobe now at Bowhill but not the same, with a different cresting and plinth (**Fig. 3.42**). The variations may be due to the fact that the pocket book entry was only a personal *aide memoire* for Morison and not a design drawing. It was destined for Dalkeith Palace, for the bedroom in which Queen Victoria stayed on her visits. In January 1843, the 5th Duchess of Buccleuch wrote to the duke 'I looked over Morison's and Whytock's bills, they are almost all connected with the Queen's visit and are right as far as I know'.

More easily identifiable from a sketch in the Morison day books are a set of *jardinières*, described as '6 Oak Flower Stands' in the carvers' book, **Fig. 3.46a**. No instructions were given as to the decoration. All are now painted white, each with four white and gold porcelain plaques, **Fig. 3.46b**. Morison's business was extensive, and he supplied furniture of all types, including cabinet furniture, chairs, and carved and gilded frames. The Duke of Buccleuch repeatedly appears in the Morison day books as a client for a wide range of furniture, much of which can be identified in situ today.

The revival of interest in the Rococo, a recurring theme from the 1820s, was aided by publications of designs between 1830 and 1860 by John Weale of 59 High Holborn, who adapted earlier designs by Thomas Chippendale, Matthias Lock, Inigo Jones and others. The taste for Rococo lent itself ideally to elaborate and often gilded mirrors in the Louis XV or Chippendale Rococo style, such as the large version shown in **Fig. 3.48**.

A recurring theme in European eighteenth-century Rococo design was the so-called 'Ho-Ho bird', a bird from Chinese mythology said to bring good fortune. Its popularity continued with nineteenth-century reproductions of the Rococo style, particularly as an adornment for mirrors. Such

Fig. 3.40 **A giltwood armchair in the fashionable French Louis XV Rococo style supplied to Raby Castle by Morant in *c*.1848. In the background is a Palladian marble chimney piece added 100 years earlier by Daniel Garrett.** [Raby Castle, County Durham]

Fig. 3.41 **When Raby Castle was remodelled by William Burn in 1848 the furniture in the Octagon Drawing Room was supplied by George Morant, including the extensive suite of giltwood cabriole-leg seat furniture and the porcelain-mounted card tables.** [Raby Castle, County Durham]

Fig. 3.42 **A large painted wardrobe at Bowhill. Expensively lined in mahogany, it was probably made by James Morison of Edinburgh.** [The Buccleuch Collections]

Fig. 3.43a **Inscribed 'Bowhill Commode', this watercolour project for a wardrobe in white and gold was prepared for the Duchess of Buccleuch, probably by James Morison. The detailing on the upper cornice differs on the left- and right-hand sides, which offers the Duchess a choice of style.** [The Buccleuch Collections]

Fig. 3.43b **Described as a 'Pier Commode' with an expensive mahogany-lined interior, this wardrobe is almost identical to the watercolour by James Morison shown in Fig. 3.43a, but without the cypher or coronet.** [The Buccleuch Collections]

Fig. 3.44 **A watercolour, probably by James Morison, dating to *c.*1842 for a white-painted centre table 137cm (4ft 6in) wide with gilt Rococo-style carving. It is not clear if this was ever approved by the 5th Duchess of Buccleuch, or executed.** [The Buccleuch Collections]

mirrors are very difficult to date with any real accuracy. In contrast with the eighteenth-century originals however, the carving on a nineteenth-century mirror has far less of a cutaway on the reverse, resulting in a heavier look when viewed from the front. The same principle also applies to any later carving, for example the splat of a chair in the Chippendale Revival style. The proportions of the mirror (in **Fig. 3.48**) are the most obvious key to a nineteenth-century date – at 170cm it is too wide for an eighteenth-century example in comparison to the 220cm height.

The pair of parcel-gilt pier tables, **Fig. 3.49** are recorded in an invoice from Thomas Fairs of 139 New Bond Street, to Sir William Middleton of Shrubland Hall in 1849. The house, designed by James Paine in the early 1770s, had been remodelled in the 1830s and underwent another phase of remodelling between 1849 and 1855. The invoice **Fig. 3.54**

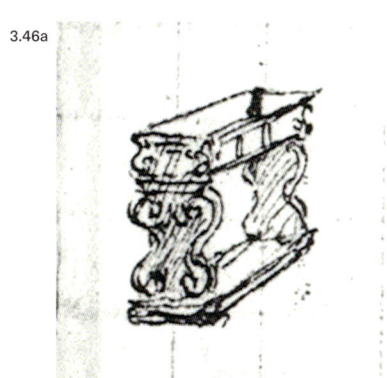

Fig. 3.45 A pen-and-ink sketch from the day books of James Morison. The entry for 2 February 1843 reads 'The Duke of Buccleuch, for Dalkeith' a 'Wardrobe with wings in the French still [sic] finished in White & Gold & varnished for the Queens Room'. The cabinet maker was Veitch, the total cost £52 16s. [Private collection]

Fig. 3.46a The Morison day book entry for '6 Oak Flower Stands' made for the Duke of Buccleuch at a cost of £27 2s 8d for the set. [Private collection]

Fig. 3.46b One of a set of six white painted oak 'flower stands' made for the Duke of Buccleuch in c.1843, each with four white and gold porcelain plaques set in the front. [The Buccleuch Collections]

Fig. 3.47 A charming pencil sketch for the Duke and Duchess of Buccleuch, titled 'cornice of the Window Curtains in the Library'. Under the window is an idea for *jardinières*, possibly an alternative sketch for the set of six, one showing as Fig. 3.46b. [The Buccleuch Collections]

describes work to decorate doors and cornices and also reads: 'To 2 new Boy group pier tables shaped top rails with rich palm dressings gilt in burnished gold parts painted in enamel white_____ £15_10_0'.[28] There is scant record of Thomas Fairs' business and at the seemingly modest cost of £15/10- it is likely that the invoice is for the decoration of the table only. The maker was most probably Morant, who, like Fairs, was based in New Bond Street. Morant supplied a sideboard to the 2nd Earl of Ellesmere as part of a large commission, exhibited at the International Exhibition of 1862, which has striking stylistic similarities to the Middleton tables and the celebrated table designed by the Duchess of Sutherland, also parcel gilt and painted, see **Fig. 4.10**. Morant was not the only firm working in this style; Johnstone & Jeanes exhibited a sideboard with similar 'boys' in 1851. Johnstone & Jeanes worked at Buckingham Palace

BRITISH FURNITURE

3.48

Fig. 3.48 The Drawing Room at Bowhill House. The settee or *confidante* probably supplied by James Morison of Edinburgh. The unusual form lends itself to 'Rococo' design and allows for two people to converse intimately. The design is in a similar style to the Raby Castle seat furniture by Morant, Fig. 3.41. [The Buccleuch Collections]

Fig. 3.49 One of an imposing pair of pier tables described in the invoice, Fig. 3.54, from Thomas Fairs to Sir William Middleton for Shrublands Park in Suffolk in 1849. It is probable that Fairs was the decorator, the maker Morant, also based in New Bond Street. A Thomas Fairs is recorded in the 1840s at 22 and 23 Mortimer St, and 2 Hanover St, listed as 'painter to Her Majesty and sole proprietor of transparent ventilator'. [Butchoff Antiques]

Fig. 3.50 An unusual couch or window seat, possibly by James Morison. A stool in the same vein can be seen beside the Baldock desk in Fig. 2.57. [The Buccleuch Collections]

Fig. 3.51 A distinctive white and gold armchair in the French style, possibly supplied by James Morison. Some furniture in the Buccleuch Collections has a later paper label, perhaps relating to repairs or reupholstery, in this instance printed 'G. Trollope & Sons' and in ink 'Bowhill'.[29] [The Buccleuch Collections]

between 1837 and 1885. In an account of wages between 1845 to 1850, the Lord Chamberlain's accounts show that they charged 7s 2d per day for each cabinet maker, 6s a day for French polishers and 3s for women.[30] The imitation white marble of the 'boy' figures was a recurring theme. A small console table, attributable to a 'Mr Clarke', is illustrated in **Fig. 2.19**, and Clarke also exhibited in a similar style at the Great Exhibition.[31]

By 1850 there were over 100 British marquetry-cutters working in London, and the number of foreign cutters had increased dramatically after the 1848 revolution in France.[32] Amongst the recorded buhl-cutters, the Blake family are the best known of the British craftsmen. As discussed in the previous chapter, their cabinet-making activity – as opposed to marquetry cutting – is not well documented, although Robert Blake styled himself as a cabinet maker in his will (d.1839).[33] It would appear that the business evolved and that Blake made the cabinet work for at least some of their marquetry pieces. The difference between a buhl-cutter and a manufacturer must have been significant at the time but the

3.49

3.50

3.51

Blakes had developed skills for both by the time they made their copies of the Boulle Trianon chests of drawers for the 4th Marquess of Hertford in the 1850s (see **Fig. 4.81a**).

Most of their early work appears to have been in wood marquetry. Attributes that might now be thought of as characteristic include colourful inlaid strapwork and floral and figurative marquetry on a distinctive background veneer, sometimes ebony. It might be supposed that this predates their work in Boulle-style turtle shell and brass. It is difficult to determine their exact date of the wood marquetry,

3.52a

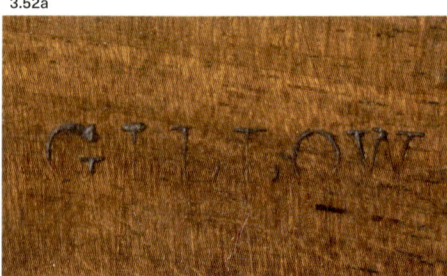

3.52b

Figs 3.52a & b **A pair of walnut display cabinets made by Gillows in the French fashionable taste, veneered in well-figured walnut applied with gilt-bronze mounts cast with musical instruments and a quiver of Cupid's arrows. Each cabinet has the 'Gillow' stamp as shown here. In the 1820s, and again in the later 1850s, the stamp was often 'Gillows'. The use of the stamp shown here suggests a date of the late 1840s or early 1850s, the style of the cabinets is consistent with the pneumatic forms of furniture popularised at the Great Exhibition in 1851.**

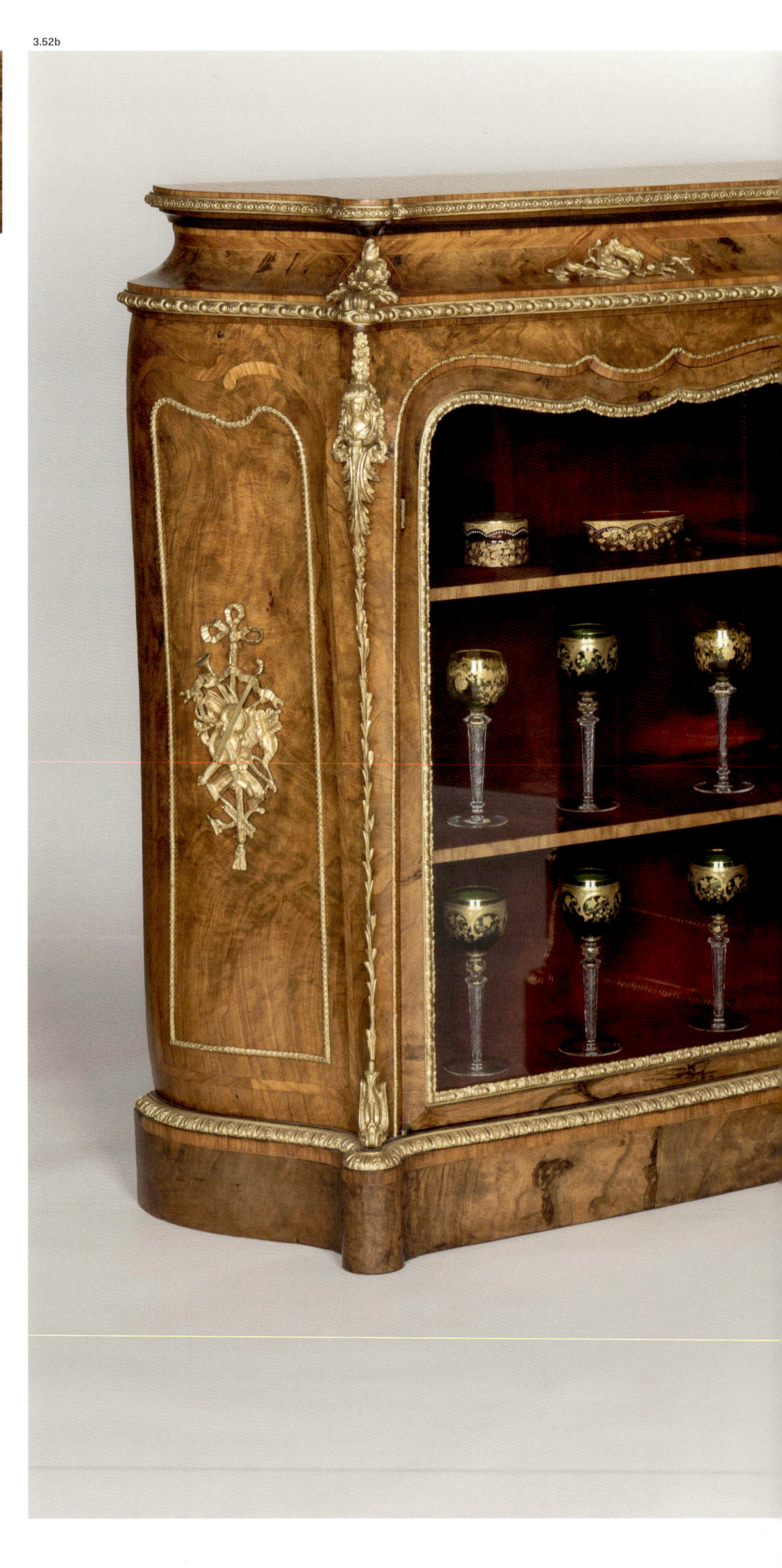

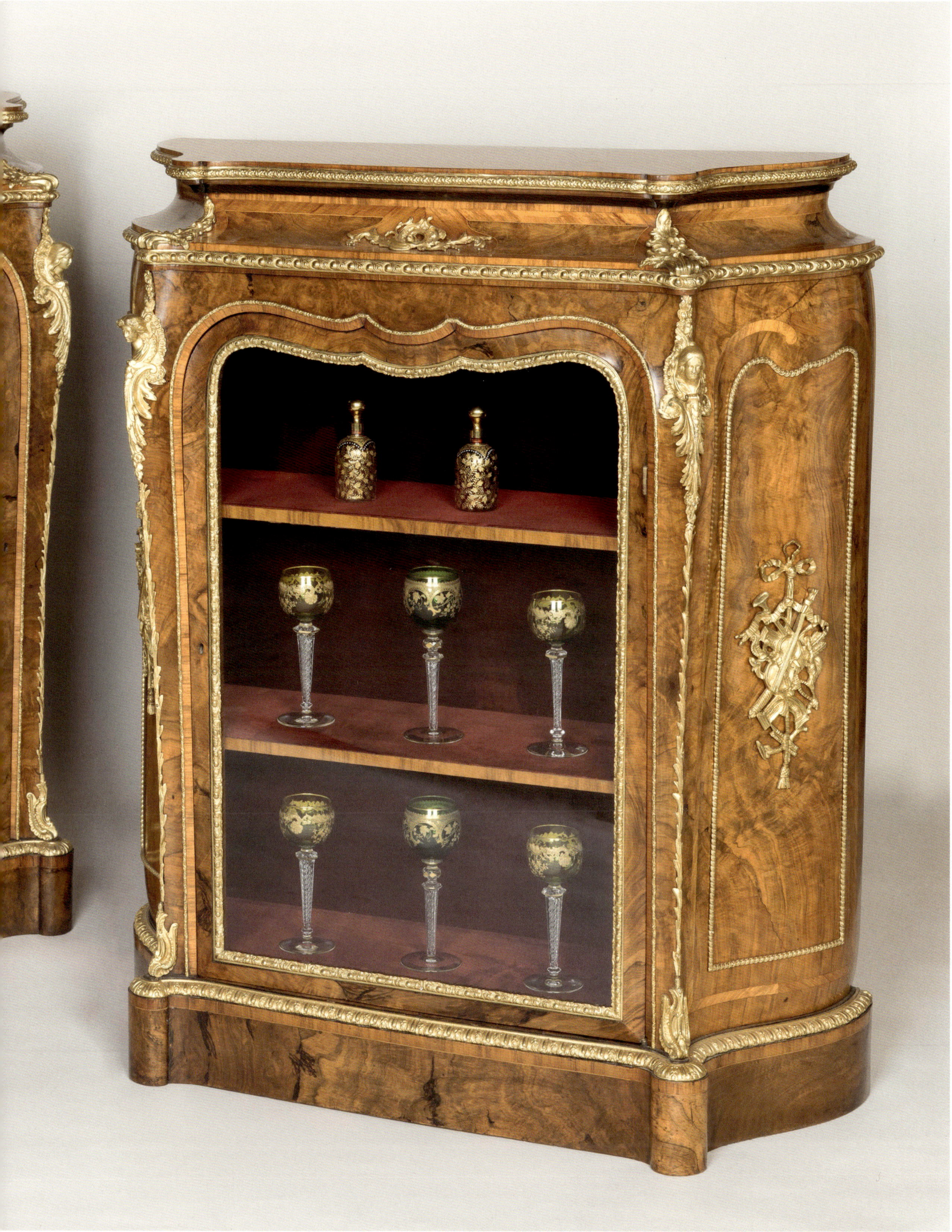

Fig. 3.53 These designs for Chippendale-style girandoles, probably dating from *c.*1840, are inscribed 'Wright P.36 Piccadilly'. [The Buccleuch Collections]

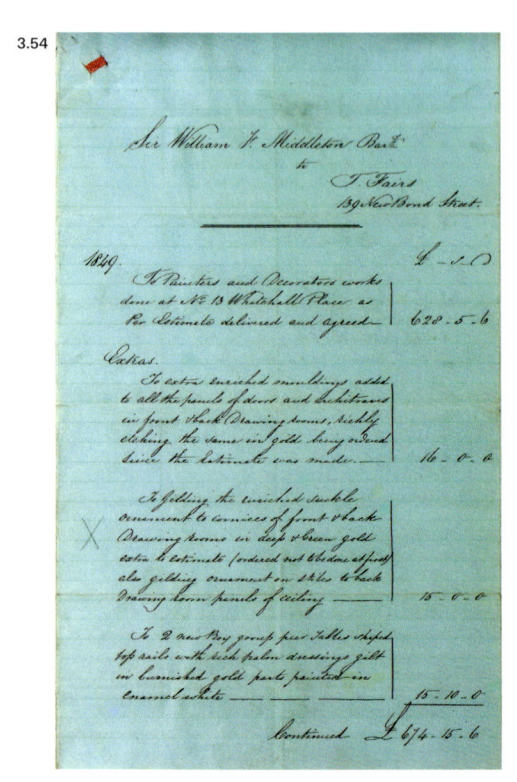

Fig. 3.54 An invoice of 1849 from Thomas Fairs of New Bond Street made out to Sir William Middleton. The last entry reads 'To 2 new Boy group pier Tables shaped top rails with rich palm dressings gilt in burnished gold parts painted in enamel white', at a cost of £15/10/-, almost certainly the pair of tables, one shown in Fig. 3.49. [Butchoff Antiques]

Fig. 3.55 In contrast to the exuberant Rococo mirrors of the mid-eighteenth century, this revival design for a mirror by Charles Hindley & Sons is more restrained and would have been highly fashionable when the firm opened in 1841. [The Metropolitan Museum of Art, New York]

CHAPTER 3: 1840S

3.56

Fig. 3.56 A simple walnut and marquetry table in an eclectic 'Jacobethan' style. It has a rare brass label engraved '*Messrs. Blake, 130 Mount Street, Berkeley Square*', an address used by George Blake from 1846. [© Victoria and Albert Museum, London]

Fig. 3.57 A rare example of a French-style Transitional *guéridon*, the gilt-bronze mounts with Blake's cast signature on the underside in a similar manner to the mounts on the Trianon commodes supplied by Blake to the Marquess of Hertford, Fig. 4.82. [Saltwell Antiques]

Fig. 3.58 A rare example of a card table with a fixed open top. The shape is based on desks by the French eighteenth-century cabinet maker, Joseph Baumhauer, a form that Baldock particularly favoured. The marquetry is a sophisticated reversed floral pattern with different shades on each side. A paper label confirms the master's hand; '*Manufactured by Messrs Blake's, 130 Mount Street, Berkeley Square*'. [Private collection]

3.57

3.58

149

3.59a

3.59b

Fig. 3.59a Arguably the most magnificent marquetry made by the Blake family, this unique piano is the zenith of mid-nineteenth-century revivalist creativity. The case designed and made in London by George Henry Blake for Thomas Henry Foley of Witley Court, fitted with an Érard movement. [The Metropolitan Museum of Art, New York]

Fig. 3.59b The sides of the piano are inlaid in ivory and various woods with scenes of music and merrymaking, held within Régence-style giltwood cartouches. [The Metropolitan Museum of Art, New York]

Fig. 3.59c The elaborate marquetry of the Blake piano case is a reinterpretation of French eighteenth-century designs and marquetry, such as work by Bérain, Oeben and Roger Vandercruse. [The Metropolitan Museum of Art, New York]

Figs 3.59d & e Carved giltwood mask capitals from two of the Érard piano legs. It is not known if the carving was carried out in Blake's workshop or subcontracted. On the right the leering grotesque face of Bacchus is festooned with grapes and entwined with marguerites known as 'The Paris Daisy', on the left Venus with her wreath of roses and flowers. [The Metropolitan Museum of Art, New York]

but there appears to be a distinct progression in the sophistication of the marquetry and the quality of execution, which becomes freer and more assured as the firm passed from Robert Blake to his sons. From the documented pieces the change seems to become increasingly evident around 1840, which might be the impact of the second generation of the firm – George Henry, Charles and James – who continued it after Robert died.[34] After his death, from 1842 the firm was listed as 'Blake, Geo. & Bros' and from 1847 'Blake, Charles, James & Henry'. By 1865, Charles Blake, seemingly alone, was listing himself as a 'manufacturer'.[35] The firm closed in 1879, and the following year an auction of effects was held at Christie's.[36]

Late in the span of the Blake firm, in 1858 and the

BRITISH FURNITURE

Figs 3.60 & 3.61 The corners of two small Louis XV-style writing desks supplied to the 5th Duke of Buccleuch, the marquetry, if not the cabinet work, possibly by Charles and Henry Blake. [Author's photographs]

Fig. 3.62 One of a series of hunting trophies on the legs of a small Louis XV-style desk supplied by Baldock to the Duke of Buccleuch. The style of marquetry is similar to a pair of cabinets at Wrotham Park in c.1843, one signed 'C.H.Blake'. [Author's photograph]

1860s, Charles Blake did extensive work for Lionel de Rothschild, including seemingly simple mahogany pieces and restoration.[37] Two important Blake commissions for marquetry furniture span the period between 1840 and 1865. The first is the magnificent piano case made c.1840, **Fig. 3.59a–e**, the second a circular table for Alnwick Castle completed in 1865, **Fig. 5.92**.[38] The piano case was designed and executed by George Henry Blake and is one of the most exceptional examples of wood marquetry made in the nineteenth century.[39] Commissioned by the 4th Baron Foley from the London branch of the celebrated Parisian firm of Érard, the marquetry is of extraordinary quality and comprises a variety of materials including satinwood, holly, mahogany, tulipwood, ivory and mother-of-pearl. It depicts a diverse range of pictorial subjects, including sheet music, representations of figures from Classical mythology and *singeries*, or anthropomorphic monkeys. The lid, case sides and key flap also feature historical scenes of everyday life: a woman and child warming themselves by a fire, a shepherd boy with a dog, and figures making music or dancing. The piano's decorative scheme was personalised for its owner, bearing the Foley coat of arms in marquetry and the corner masks of Apollo, Bacchus, Diana and Venus, which

Figs 3.63a & 3.63b **Two small writing desks in Louis XV style that have habitually been attributed to Baldock. The marquetry is in the distinctive style of the Blake family who possibly supplied the cabinet work as well.** [James Graham-Stewart]

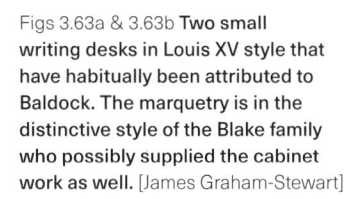

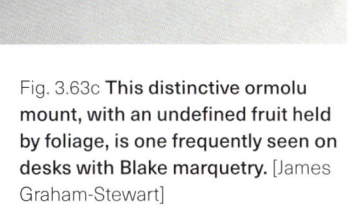

Fig. 3.63c This distinctive ormolu mount, with an undefined fruit held by foliage, is one frequently seen on desks with Blake marquetry. [James Graham-Stewart]

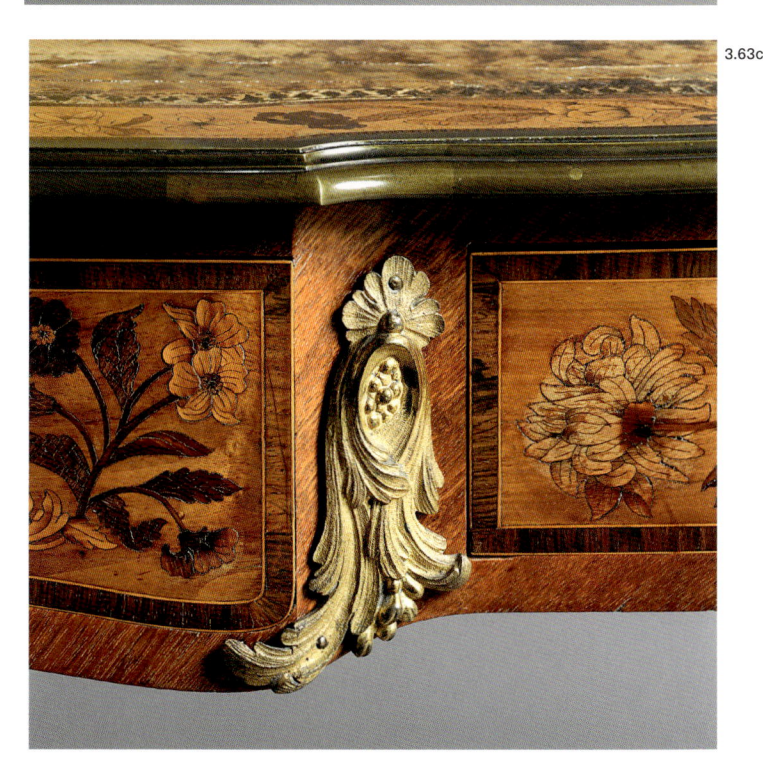

legend relates are said to be modelled on the faces of family members.

The decorative scheme is a fascinating example of a nineteenth-century interpretation of eighteenth-century French references. While on the one hand the marquetry shows a familiarity with the work of Jean-François Oeben and Roger Vandercruse, it also incorporates motifs from early eighteenth-century work in Boulle-style metal marquetry such as the grotesques, birds and animals found on furniture by Bernard I van Risenburgh and Nicolas Sageot, itself often derived from the engravings of Jean Bérain. Despite these disparate stylistic influences, the effect is highly sophisticated and unified, and further enhanced by the fluidity of the gilt-wood mounts which owe their inspiration to eighteenth-century gilt-bronze French furniture mounts from a variety of periods. Whilst a silver plate inset on the lid records George Blake's authorship, another less obtrusive mark records a craftsman responsible for at least part of the woodwork of the piano: the top key lever is stamped 'I. VEITCH'. This may be John Veitch (1809–1878), the son of an Edinburgh cabinet maker who settled in London where his children were born. In 1852 he emigrated to Australia and his occupation was recorded on the Arrivals Register and on his death certificate as 'Carpenter/Piano Forte maker'.[40] Many of Veitch's family were cabinet makers in Scotland and a maker of the same name worked on furniture made in the early 1840s for the Duke of Buccleuch (see **Figs 3.45–3.47**).

While no print sources for the marquetry scenes on the piano have been identified, other marquetry by the Blake family, including a veneered writing desk which was purchased from Baldock in 1841 by the 5th Duke of Buccleuch, can be traced, **Fig. 2.48**.[41] The corner figures

Figs 3.64 **The base of this folio cabinet recalls the form of a seventeenth-century *bureau Mazarin*. It was supplied by Baldock to the 5th Duke of Buccleuch between 1841 and 1843. Baldock's invoice reads:** *'beautifully inlaid portfolio stand in various woods inlaid all over. The interior fitted with frames, ormolu handles'.* [The Buccleuch Collections]

are directly taken from Jacques Callot's celebrated series of engravings, *Varie figure Gobbi* (1616). Such figures, depicting a troupe of grotesque dwarf entertainers at the Medici court, were well-known in England where they seem to have inspired Chelsea/Derby porcelain figures of the second half of the eighteenth century. Baldock, being a porcelain dealer, must be expected to have been familiar with these and it is likely that he was behind the design of the marquetry as well as the form of the table. In 1833 Baldock had supplied the duke with two tables by the Venetian marquetry-cutters Antonio and Lucio de Lucci (*fl.* 1680–1700) on which Callot-inspired figures appear, strengthening the case for Baldock's design input.[42] An interesting feature on these tables is that the de Lucci have used thin strips of pewter or silvered tin in their marquetry to frame the strapwork and Blake, exceptionally amongst his contemporaries, imitated this seventeenth-century technique, using silver wire: as on the Foley piano.[43] A similar technique is evident on the pair of tables illustrated in **Fig. 2.27**.

The output of the Blake firm must have been quite considerable and, by the 1840s, was clearly not confined to the supply of marquetry. Between 1842 and 1843 the Blakes supplied 17 items to the Oxford Street firm of furniture upholders and cabinet makers, Henry Miles and John Edwards, of which eight were circular or octagonal tables; some of these no doubt formed part of the 28 Blake marquetry tables in the Miles & Edwards stock lists from 1843 to 1844.[44] In addition to supplying firms like Morant and Miles & Edwards, Blake also supplied clients directly. There is a bill in the Buccleuch archives showing that Blake supplied the duke directly on at least one occasion in 1844 – 'an inlaid table of elm and ebony', as yet unidentified in the collection.[45]

Small writing desks in the Louis XV style, such as the examples illustrated in **Figs 3.63a & 3.63b**, are often branded with Baldock's 'EHB' mark and veneered in marquetry consistent with documented Blake furniture. The model is based on an eighteenth-century *bureau plat* by Joseph Baumhauer[46] and are similar in outline to the porcelain-mounted tables supplied by Baldock (see below). The cabinet making of the marquetry desks is generally of better quality than that of the porcelain-mounted tables and it is possible that they were produced entirely by Blake – both the marquetry and the cabinet work – and retailed, possibly not exclusively, by Baldock. Early examples of these small desks have distinctive pine muntins under the carcass. Later

CHAPTER 3: 1840S

3.65a

3.65b

3.66a

3.66b

Figs 3.65a & b An unusual shaped centre table, with the 'EHB' brand stamped on the pine underside of the top. Another identical model has been recorded, suggesting that the design was a stock pattern. [Bonhams]

Figs 3.66a & b The top of this folio cabinet has a similar, but slightly less complex, outline to the signed Baldock centre table (Fig. 3.65a, above). The marquetry is confined to the six inset panels, outsourced from a specialist inlayer. [Butchoff Antiques]

155

Fig. 3.67 The familiar shape and scale of small desks habitually attributed to Baldock. This example with porcelain plaques, the flowers possibly painted by William Cook. [Bonhams]

Fig. 3.68 A porcelain-mounted card table of English manufacture, the underside with the G.I. Morant brand mark. [Raby Castle / County Durham]

Fig. 3.69 In contrast with the severe neo-Palladian exterior, Wrotham Park has the distinction of having a fine collection of furniture, much of it in what Davis terms Anglo-Gallic taste, such as the porcelain-mounted desk in the centre of the room, supplied by Baldock in c.1837. [Wrotham Park]

Figs 3.70a & b This style of porcelain-mounted desk, influenced by the Parisian cabinet maker Joseph Baumhauer, is a model often stamped by Baldock. This example has twenty-four Sèvres-style plaques, which were often Sèvres blanks painted in England. The drawers have thin oak linings that show the medullary rays to good effect. A larger version, supplied to Wrotham Park by Baldock, can be seen in Fig. 3.69.[47] [Butchoff Antiques]

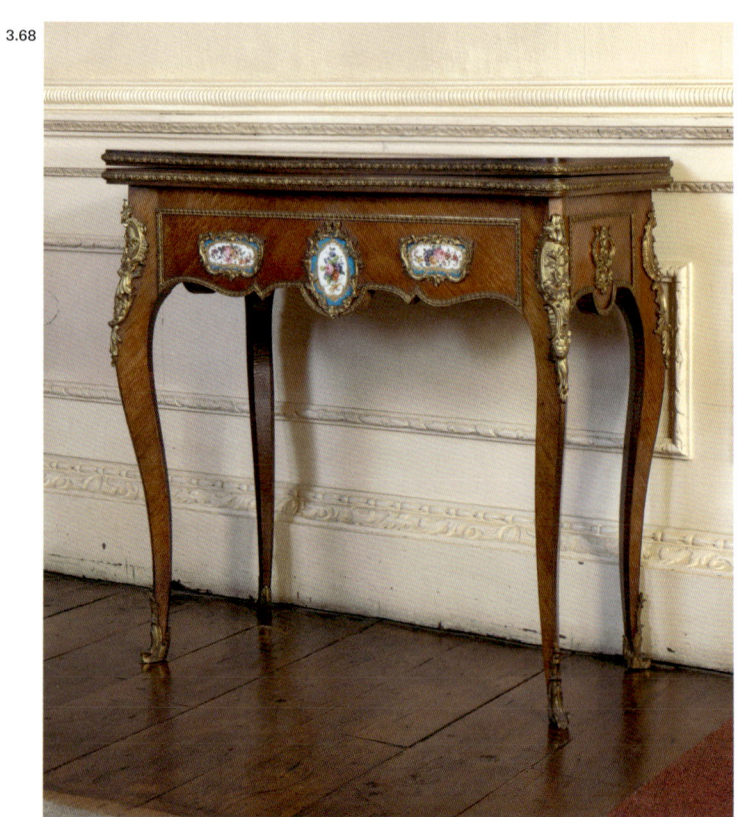

versions are better made; this distinction might be consistent with the Blakes making their own carcasses. It is known that Blake also had access to their own mounts as the firm matured, and the mounts on this type of table are often distinctive, see **Fig. 3.63c**. It is possible that Blake acquired master models and plans from the Baldock workshop sale of 1843. The marquetry on these tables is characteristic Blake work although the designs are varied. Serpents with entwined addorsed bodies and protruding tongues are a recurring theme.[48] They appear on a desk and a table in the Buccleuch Collections as does another distinctive Blake motif – a spray of marquetry flowers in various woods and ivory, both shown in **Figs 2.30a & b**.[49] Confirming the attribution to Blake, a desk with marquetry of this style is at Goodwood House, with a fixed label 'Messrs Blake of 8 Stephen Street, Tottenham Court Road', and another is in a private collection in London. Without the evidence of the labels the attribution would, in the past, have been to Baldock.

During the 1830s and 1840s Baldock sold a number of desks in varying styles with porcelain plaques without any marquetry. Many of the ceramic panels are Sèvres blanks, with flowers and game birds painted in English factories. The decoration is habitually attributed to T.M. Randall for

CHAPTER 3: 1840S

3.69

3.70a

3.71

3.70b

Fig. 3.71 A desk of *c*.1765 made by Joseph Baumhauer, with mid-nineteenth century 'improvements'. This original desk is 35cm (13¾*in*) wider than the nineteenth-century variants. The inverted arc *en arborlette* top is more complex than the Baldock 'copy'. [The Huntington Library / image courtesy of Taylor Fiske]

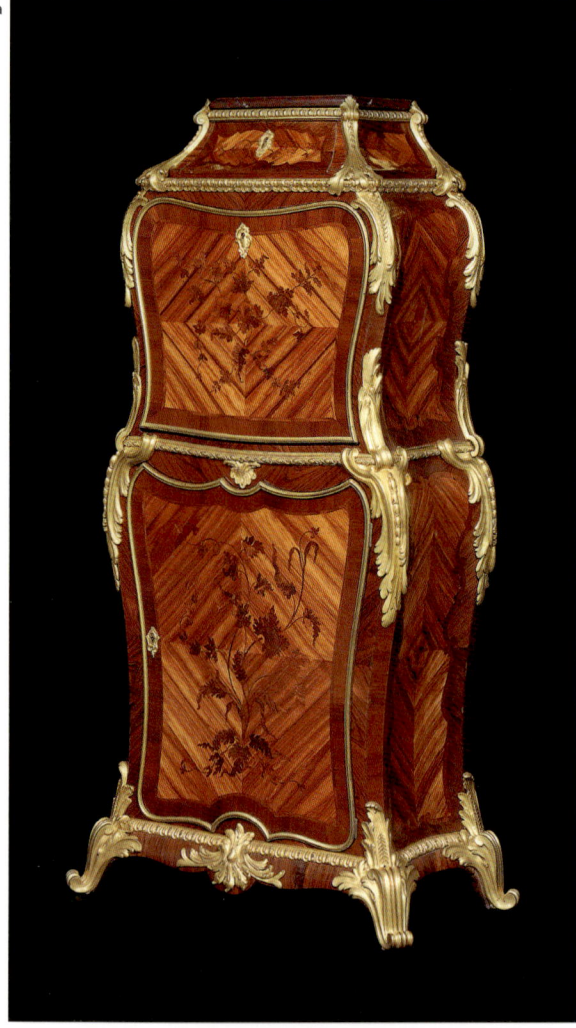

Fig. 3.72a This copy of a fall-front desk, similar to models made c.1760 by Parisian makers such as Dubut and Leleu, has the Baldock 'EHB' brand but may conceivably have been made in France. [Christie's]

Fig. 3.72b The back of the desk in Fig. 3.72a has the brand mark of Baldock and, illustrated here, the later stamp of the dealer Duveen. [Christie's]

Fig. 3.73 A *bonheur-du-jour* in the Metropolitan Museum, made in c.1768, attributed to Martin Carlin. [The Metropolitan Museum of Art, New York]

Fig. 3.74 A writing table by Baldock seemingly inspired by the lower part of the desk by Carlin. [Bonhams]

CHAPTER 3: 1840S

Fig. 3.75a Baldock was effusive in his descriptions to clients. The invoice for this desk, supplied to the 5th Duke of Buccleuch in 1841, reads: 'A beautiful satinwood secretaire richly inlaid and chased mounts, the interior fitted up with drawers'. The desk is of a similar form but more lavish than one he supplied to the duchess in 1838, see Fig. 2.28a. [The Buccleuch Collections]

Fig. 3.75b The desk supplied by Baldock in 1841 to the Duke of Buccleuch has a full-length, custom-made brass hinge to allow for the writing slope to be stable when in use. [The Buccleuch Collections]

Fig. 3.75c Tell-tale sprays of ivory flowers and lavish Sèvres-style mounts, hallmarks of the co-operation between Baldock and Blake. This is a relatively rare example of the use of satinwood at this time. [The Buccleuch Collections]

the game birds, the flowers to William Cook **Fig. 3.67**.[50] The Baldock desks are based on, but smaller than, an original desk of the 1760s by Baumhauer and, as a result, have fewer plaques on the frieze.[51] Compare, for example, the frieze of an eighteenth-century desk now at the Huntington Library (**Fig. 3.71**), with those on a desk by Baldock at Wrotham Park, **Fig. 3.69**. The original Baumhauer desk, illustrated in **Fig. 3.71**, is stamped 'JOSEPH' for Joseph Baumhauer and has a label showing it passed through the dealer Duveen.[52]

Another style of porcelain-mounted writing desk by Baldock is modelled, in a reasonably faithful manner, on the lower part of a small writing desk (only 67cm/26in wide) made by Martin Carlin in c.1768. Baldock supplied an eighteenth-century desk of this model, made by Carlin, to the 5th Duke of Buccleuch in 1830; a similar example can be seen at the Metropolitan Museum of Art, **Fig. 3.73**.[53] Baldock adapted the eighteenth-century design to one that was more to his client's taste, see **Fig. 3.74**. Baldock

159

Fig. 3.76 This rare desk is modelled on French precedents dating to c.1730, by an unknown cabinet maker referred to as 'The Master of the Pagodas'. Veneered in rich red-brown turtle shell this example, of which two are known, was made in England between 1847 and 1848, the date identified by the serial numbers on the Chubb locks. [Private collection / Photograph Careysheffield.com]

Figs 3.77 Attributed to the ever-inventive Levien, and incorporating various New Zealand veneers, this cradle was almost certainly made to celebrate the birth of Princess Helena, Queen Victoria's third daughter, born in 1846. [Terry Green]

altered many pieces for reasons of fashion, for example a *cartonnier* of the 1760s by Jean-François Leleu now in the Wallace Collection.[54] An undated pencil sketch of a porcelain-mounted desk with ink annotations thought to be in Baldock's hand, is at Boughton House, see **Fig. 2.46**. Although clearly based on the Louis XV style, Baldock's drawing is more typical of the second quarter of the nineteenth century in a style often erroneously called 'Napoleon III'. It is similar in manner to the card table stamped by Morant at Raby Castle shown in **Fig. 3.68**.

The fall-front desk, or secretaire, shown in **Fig. 3.72a** is a reasonably faithful copy of a Parisian precedent of the 1760s; examples made by Jean-François Dubut, others by Jean-François Leleu. This copy has Baldock's 'EHB' brand and has the added stamp of the dealer 'Duveen', see **Fig. 3.72b**. The Duveen mark is with a cold metal stamp, whereas Baldock's mark is habitually with a hot branding tool. Similar nineteenth-century copies of this popular model were made in Paris by the firm of Monbro, who later also worked

Figs 3.78a & b **A rare teapoy made by J.M. Levien after he settled in London in c.1843. The distinctive base shows the continuing influence of Richard Bridgens.** [Richard Gardner Antiques]

Fig. 3.79 **James Annear arrived in Wellington, New Zealand in August 1840, and, like Levien, his style of furniture followed London fashions. This table is made entirely from local timbers, such as totara, rewarewa and maire. It is signed and dated** *'October 29 1848 Maker James Annear.'* [Museum of New Zealand Te Papa Tongarewa]

Fig. 3.80 **A rare centre table, dating to between 1846 and 1851, by the Scottish émigré Ralph Turnbull, who worked in Jamaica using rare and exotic tropical hardwoods. The elaborate marquetry includes boats, lighthouses and a letter to Queen Victoria.** [Thomas Coulborn & Sons]

in London. Monbro was both a cabinet maker and retailer of *ancien régime* decorative art, and the fact that both he and Baldock supplied this model begs the question as to whether they had a business association of any sort, something that would be eminently probable considering Baldock's position in the London trade. The first recorded copy of this popular model was supplied by Baldock in 1837. One of Baldock's clients, the wealthy collector Charles Mills, owned an original eighteenth-century example which may have created the opportunity for the copies.[55]

Baldock's interpretations of the eighteenth-century French style are competent pieces of furniture using fine-quality veneers, most fitted with gilt mounts varnished in the English manner, as opposed to highly burnished and mercury-gilded mounts in the eighteenth-century French manner such as the pair of desks he supplied to the Duke of Buccleuch in 1831, mentioned in the previous chapter, **Fig. 2.57**. It was not until the latter years of the 1840s that high-quality English-made reproductions of eighteenth-century French precedents became more mainstream, some preceding the important

Fig. 3.81 A satinwood and kingwood centre table with a 1m (3¼ft) diameter Italian specimen marble top. The base has the brand mark 'G.I. Morant 91 New Bond Street'. The interlaced cypher, 'CC', is discreetly inlaid into the lower part of the support between the legs. [Private collection]

Fig. 3.82 At 1.4m (4½ft) in diameter, this is an unusually large imported marble top attributed to Alfonso Cavamelli of Rome. The parcel-gilt burr walnut base with elaborate Rococo foliage is stamped 'Taprell, Holland & Son, 19 Marylebone Street, St. James' London'. Stephen Taprell retired in 1843, which might suggest an early 1840s date for the table although it is possible the old stamp continued in use for a period of time. [Butchoff Antiques]

Fig. 3.83 Walnut was a veneer that was becoming increasingly popular. The figuring of the top has been dramatically heightened and inlaid with Baroque reserves of Italianate-marquetry hunting scenes in various woods. [Private collection]

and well-documented group made for the 4th Marquess of Hertford discussed in Chapter 4 – 1850s. Between 1847 and 1850, a pair of desks, one of which is illustrated here in **Fig. 3.76**, were made copying a desk by the eighteenth-century maker whose name is lost to us, referred to as 'The Master of the Pagodas', relating to the frequent inclusion of Chinese-inspired decorative motifs on his furniture, particularly gilt-bronze 'pagoda' mounts.[56] Examples of this distinctive mount are on the central drawers of the nineteenth-century desks; the four corner mounts are in the form of stylised Chinese figures. The locks are stamped by Chubb, the serial numbers dating them to circa March 1848.[57] An apparently identical pair of desks, most likely these two, were advertised by the Georgian Galleries in the March 1928 issue of *The Connoisseur* for £200 each. They were described as coming from the collection of the late Lady Wimbourne, née Lady Cornelia Spencer-Churchill, eldest daughter of the 7th Duke of Marlborough, at Merley House. The name of the cabinet maker or the firm who made the desks remains unknown. The construction of their drawer

CHAPTER 3: 1840S

3.84

3.85

Fig. 3.84 An exceptional 'Adelaide Green' porcelain top by Copeland & Garrett dating to 1841. Formerly in the collection of the Goldschmidt-Rothschild family at Villa Grüneburg in Frankfurt, the base has similarities to work by Morel & Seddon. [Carlton Hobbs LLC]

Fig. 3.85 An oval tip-top or 'loo' table in well-figured walnut, the grain highlighted by black staining. This example, applied with ormolu mounts, has scrolled Greek-key toes reminiscent of examples by Holland & Sons. [Nan Xu]

linings, with the quarter mouldings running the length of the drawers, clearly shows that it was a sophisticated English, almost certainly a London, workshop. Like the Buccleuch desks, the constructional details are that of a well-trained English hand, not a French émigré. A third nineteenth-century 'pagoda' desk in Boulle-style marquetry is known but thought to be French-made, and two more of the same size, with identical mounts, were sold at the celebrated Mentmore Towers sale.[58] The Mentmore desks were veneered with a tulipwood trellis in a more conventional mid-eighteenth-century manner.

Elaborate cradles were a traditional way of celebrating the birth of an important child, especially a royal birth. An outstanding cradle by the eminent woodcarver William Gibbs Rogers, shown at the Great Exhibition in 1851, is illustrated in **Fig. 4.13**. The example shown here, **Fig. 3.77**, is by Johann Martin Levien. Believed to have been commissioned by Queen Victoria and Prince Albert, probably for the birth of their fifth child, Princess Helena, in 1846. It is in the royal couple's favoured Cinquecento style and uses English and New Zealand timbers in both solid form and veneers. The main body is in totara knot, the inner headboard and the outer end are veneered in totara, puriri, maire and white pine.

The tripod base of the marquetry teapoy by Levien, **Fig. 3.78b,** is another instance of the influence of the designs of Richard Bridgens and falls into the group so often, possibly erroneously, identified with the Baldock workshops. Stylistically a piece of this type can be categorised as 1840s. German-born Levien experimented with New Zealand woods after a three-year stay in Wellington from 1840. Levien was clearly both a talented craftsman and a designer capable of working in many different styles, and would have required a substantial workshop; he was still making and altering furniture for Baron de Rothschild in Piccadilly in 1865.[59] In complete contrast to the teapoy, his work in the Louis XV style can be seen in Chapter 4. Another maker based in New Zealand, James Annear (1814–1883), worked in a similar but plainer style to Levien, as can be seen in a combined chess and work table, **Fig. 3.79**.

The parquetry table in **Fig. 3.80** made by Ralph Turnbull (1788–1865) is probably unique. A Scot who emigrated to Jamaica, he incorporated many rare and exotic woods, using

163

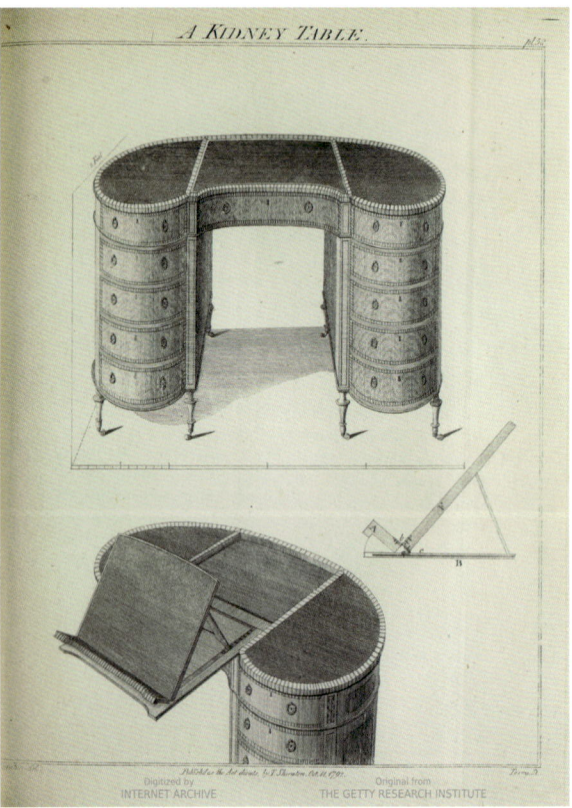

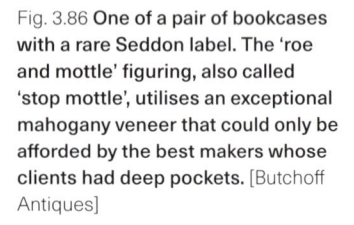

Fig. 3.86 One of a pair of bookcases with a rare Seddon label. The 'roe and mottle' figuring, also called 'stop mottle', utilises an exceptional mahogany veneer that could only be afforded by the best makers whose clients had deep pockets. [Butchoff Antiques]

Fig. 3.87 A kidney-shaped writing table of graceful form. Made in walnut, the lyre supports are a continuation of the late Sheraton and Regency styles. [H. Blairman & Sons]

Fig. 3.88 A design for a kidney-shaped desk in Thomas Sheraton's *The Cabinet-Maker's and Upholsterer's Drawing-Book.* [from Thomas Sheraton, *The Cabinet-Maker and Upholsterer's Drawing-Book*, 1793, pl. 58]

specimens of rosewood, ebony, birds-eye maple, sabicu, satinwood, padouk, lacewood, palm wood, amboyna, yacca, mahoe and mahogany. The overall form of the table is Regency, but it was made by Turnbull between 1846 and 1851. There are similarities to the work of Edmund Nye of Tunbridge Wells, the master of parquetry who exhibited at the 1851 Great Exhibition. Wood mosaic was a popular, specialised craft, made with painstaking detail.

The three centre tables shown here, **Figs 3.81–3.83**, are of a more conventional tripod form than the distinctive Bridgens' pedestals. The example with a veneered marquetry top is more picturesque than refined, **Fig. 3.83**. The top is inlaid with four surrounding panels showing hunting scenes which are set within Baroque-style lambrequin 'curtains' as if part of a theatrical production. The panels are inlaid into walnut, the veneer specially chosen to emphasise the grain. The exceptional and distinctive base of the table by Taprell, Holland & Son, **Fig. 3.82**, with the addition of applied giltwood-carving outlining the legs in the Rococo Revival manner, is unusually grand. The top, although typical of

Figs 3.89a & b **Attributed to Gillows, this fine amboyna-veneered desk has Chubb locks, the serial numbers corresponding to February 1849.** [Private collection]

Fig. 3.89c **Well-figured walnut has always been one of the most popular veneers for this style of kidney desk. This detail shows the locking flap open to allow access to the drawers in the pedestals, in the same manner seen on the so-called 'Wellington' chests.** [Private collection]

expensive keepsakes brought back from excursions to Italy, is a fine example with a mixture of specimen stones and micro mosaics. The Taprell, Holland & Son stamp suggests a date of between 1835 and 1843, the base supplied to complement the top. The choice of burr walnut veneers, while a popular wood at the time, is an unusual choice for the combination of parcel-gilding and marble. The design of the central micro-mosaic roundel is an amalgamation of the Antique *pietre dure* Doves of Pliny in the Capitoline Museums and the floral bouquet on a Roman mosaic floor now in the Pio-Clementino Museum. The Vatican Workshop had been established in the sixteenth century and this distinctive style of micro mosaic was developed there from the 1770s. The overall design and composition of the marble top suggests that it may be the work of Alfonso Cavamelli of Rome.

The ubiquitous circular table, large examples with a fixed top removable for transportation, smaller versions with a tip-top to allow it to stand vertically in the corner of a room, has been a perennial favourite since the late seventeenth century. The top was often highly decorated and would have been a showpiece and talking point amongst those who were wealthy enough to afford such a luxury. The base of the table, **Fig. 3.84**, shares a number of similarities with tables made by Morel & Seddon as part of a commission for Windsor Castle in 1828. The exceptionally large porcelain plaque has the maker's mark of porcelain manufacturer Copeland & Garrett and can be dated precisely as it is recorded in the maker's ledger. A volume in the Copeland archive titled *Fixings Book from October 25th 1839 to May 1841* records the order on 29 March 1841 as follows: 'WG Rich bas relief Victoria scrolls (?) on 391 Green & inner gold border with group in centre & festoons in panels, 1 36 inch Circular Table Top 15gns.' Unfortunately, there is currently archival evidence as to the maker of the base.

The beautifully veneered 'stop mottle' mahogany bookcase, **Fig. 3.86**, bears the label of T. & G. Seddon with their Gray's Inn Road address to which they moved after a fire in 1830. One of a pair of bookcases, the locks are

3.90a

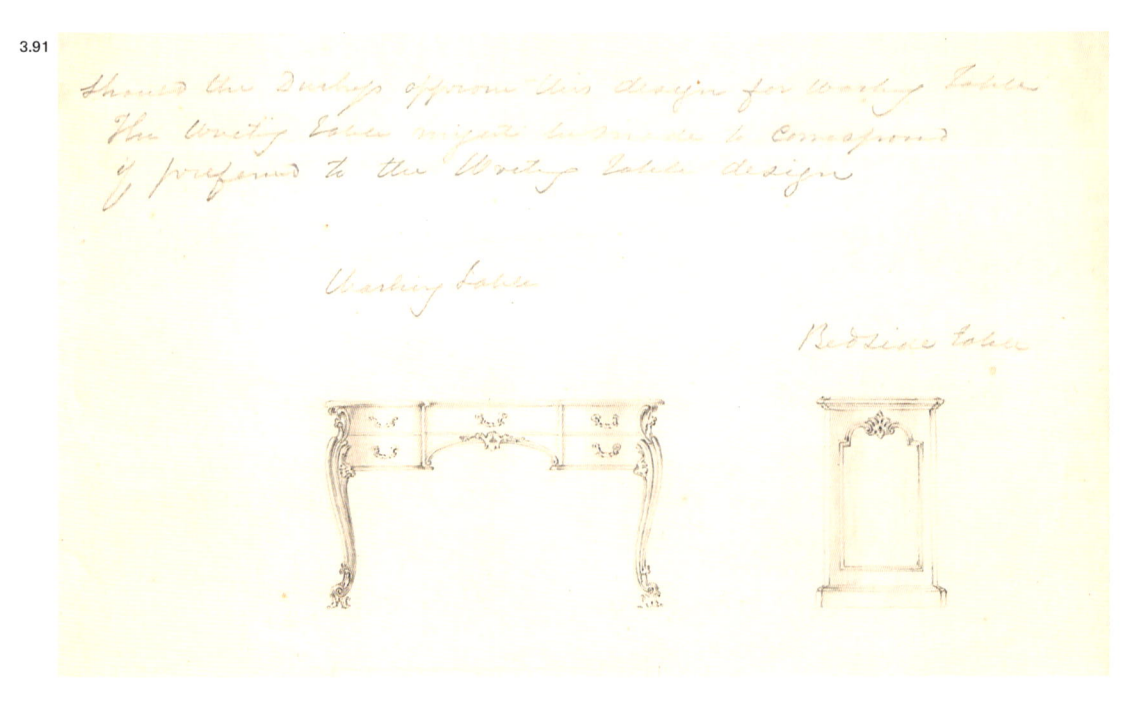

3.90b

3.91

Figs 3.90a & b On the left a 'Monocleid' cabinet with solid and glazed doors by Sopwith & Co. of Newcastle. Probably dating to the mid-1840s, it was available later as shown on the right from the 1851 Great Exhibition. The 1851 engraving suggests that the upper doors could be glazed, and there are numerous variations to the cresting which may be down to artistic licence (see also p.14). [3.90a: Casa-Museu Medeiros e Almeida; 3.90b: *London Illustrated News*, September 6, 1851, p. 308]

Fig. 3.91 Adapted from Chippendale designs of the mid-eighteenth century, this undated and unsigned drawing for a 'Washing Table' for the Duchess of Buccleuch's approval, is annotated to suggest that it could be adapted as a writing table. [The Buccleuch Collections]

3.92a

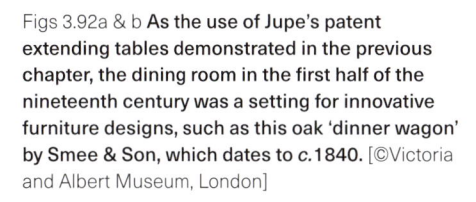

3.92b

Figs 3.92a & b **As the use of Jupe's patent extending tables demonstrated in the previous chapter, the dining room in the first half of the nineteenth century was a setting for innovative furniture designs, such as this oak 'dinner wagon' by Smee & Son, which dates to *c*.1840.** [©Victoria and Albert Museum, London]

stamped 'VR' – are the locks Victorian replacements and the cabinet a decade earlier? The low serial or job number inked in '780' on the label hints that the cabinet might be an earlier piece as it resembles a design in Nicholson's *The Practical Cabinet-Maker, Upholsterer, and Complete Decorator* of 1826 or Ackermann's *Repository* of 1827. A year earlier Smith illustrated a secretaire bookcase with 'curl' or 'flame figured' mahogany in his *Cabinet-Maker and Upholsterer's Guide*. By 1853, Blackie described this highly figured veneer as 'much less popular than formerly'.[60]

The pioneer of the perennially popular kidney-shaped tables and desks was Thomas Sheraton, his design of 1791 from *The Cabinet Maker's and Upholsterer's Drawing-Book*, is shown as **Fig. 3.88**. The form was used again in a myriad of variations from the 1820s onwards and is a model that always crossed the artificial barrier erected by twentieth-century antique dealers in Britain, as it was one of the few items post-1830 that they would stock. **Fig. 3.89a** is a variant of a Gillows design, recorded several times in their archives.[61] The Chubb locks are stamped with the consecutive numbers '196333–7' and marked '57 St Patent / 57 St. Paul's Churchyard / London / Makers to Her Majesty'. As with the

'Master of the Pagodas' writing desk **Fig. 3.76**, the Chubb records are an accurate dating tool and confirm that the locks on this desk were made in February 1849.

A general depression in the British furniture-making trade towards the end of the 1840s was alleviated by a series of exhibitions, culminating in the extraordinary success of the Great Exhibition. The Royal Society of Arts' Exhibition of Manufacturers at Covent Garden in 1845, and a visit by Prince Albert to the Exhibition of the Manufactures of Birmingham and the Midland Counties in 1849, were events that helped provide impetus for Britain to emulate and improve on the French Exposition des produits de l'industrie. The result was the highly successful and profitable Great Exhibition held in London's Hyde Park in 1851. By the end of the 1840s there was already mounting excitement at the prospect of the exhibition. The Birmingham exhibition included a large display by the local firm of *papier-mâché* manufacturers, Jennens & Bettridge. *The Art Journal* termed one *papier-mâché* technique 'gem-enamelling' in reference to the jewel-like studding on some of the raised decoration. The white and red studding imitated oriental pearls and rubies within a gilt foliate ground. At their Belgravia showrooms in London, the Birmingham-based firm proudly exhibited a set of large trays, some 170cm (67in) wide, ordered by Ibrahim Pacha to use as divan tables in Egypt.[62] Still popular in the 1860s, James Bettridge patented a method to inlay aluminium into his furniture to heighten its decorative effect.[63] To this creative industrialist, the use of paper, steamed, pressed and moulded, appeared to have offered a

Fig. 3.93 **The saloon of Dunn's Chinese exhibition, engraved for** *The Illustrated London News* **in 1842, was recorded as being '240 feet long and 50 feet wide'.**[64] [Colin Waters / Alamy Stock Photo]

limitless supply of forms and designs, and the art was at its zenith by the middle of the century. Jennens & Bettridge won a gold Isis Medal at the 1849 Society of Arts Exhibition; other winners included the bronze lamp and furniture-fitting company, Thomas Messenger & Sons of Birmingham, and the Coalbrookdale Iron Company. *The Art Journal* of 1849 is full of praise for Jennens & Bettridge whilst they were at the Society of Arts Exhibition, claiming that 'the compartment occupied (by them) is one of considerable brilliancy'. Nevertheless, the writer was happy to recommend that a 'little less redundancy of ornament might recommend them more strongly to persons of refined taste'.[65]

Another *papier-mâché* maker was George Jackson & Sons of 49–50 Rathbone Place. Established in 1756, they supplied frames to Buckingham Palace in 1840 and in *c.*1849 they published a volume of almost seventy patterns for *papier-mâché* furniture. However, as successors to the firm of Henry Clay, Jennens & Bettridge were the largest manufacturers of *papier-mâché* furniture and decorative objects in the world. Clay had patented his manufacturing process. The complexity of the designs and fragility of the material necessitated resorting to timber supports made by cabinet makers and even, on occasion, metal framing.[66]

Mechanics' institutes became an important method of education for furniture makers; the first started in Edinburgh in 1821 and by the mid-century there were over 700 throughout the country. The northern cities were beginning to develop their own sophisticated industries. Leeds, with a population of 150,000 by 1840, had over seventy cabinet makers recorded in the 1830–40 period. The city staged exhibitions in 1839, 1843 and 1845, including a 'Museum of Antiquities' to stimulate trade, craftsmanship and design.[67]

The Newcastle firm of Thomas Sopwith is one of only a handful of furniture-making firms in Newcastle founded in the eighteenth century that continued well into the twentieth, flourishing from 1769 until 1935. The mahogany cabinet, **Fig. 3.90a**, was made in the mid-1840s and it, or a similar example, was exhibited at the Great Exhibition in 1851. Sopwith's unusual name for the cabinet 'monocleid' was because, despite numerous compartments, it only requires one key. The idea was first used by Sopwith in 1836 or 1837 and used in various guises by the firm throughout the century. The cabinet illustrates the difficulties encountered when dividing furniture into decades. It was first designed in the 1830s, made in the 1840s and exhibited in the 1850s. The example shown here is a clear refence to Chippendale's French style of the previous century. An early client of the firm was the author Robert Louis Stephenson. Thomas and

3.94

Fig. 3.94 Without the evidence of the Blake signature, this pier table, one of a pair, would be considered to be of French. Veneered in thuya, the form is an adaptation of a Louis XVI model; the designer may have been familiar with the work of Claude-Charles Saunier, who became a *maître menuisier en ébène* in 1752. However, when the tables were being conserved and the mounts were removed for cleaning several incised marks were revealed. The mark 'Blake' is on the underside of each of the gilt-bronze pierced galleries, together with traces of serial numbers. One reads 'A Oval £2 149', the costing for this pattern of model, another is incised 'Blake 93', another 'Small Circ'. The diamond lozenges in the centre of each frieze are incised 'Blake'. The wide range of master models available in the Blake workshops, for example the Transitional guéridon, Fig. 3.57, underlines the sophistication of the Blake family workshops by the 1840 to 1850 period. No longer making marquetry for Baldock or Morant, for example, by the mid-century they had been able to expand their output to copies of *ancien régime* furniture, which may answer how they, in conjunction with John Webb, were able to furnish some of the copies made for the Marquess of Hertford discussed in the next chapter.
[Butchoff Antiques]

Jacob Sopwith had substantial showrooms in the centre of Newcastle by 1838. Their nearby 'cabinet manufactory' was a substantial concern, using steam power. An engraving shows the 200-foot-long (61 metres) workshop with over two dozen benches. A Monocleid cabinet is shown against one wall, a craftsman working on French-style cabriole leg seat furniture. The inventive energy of Sopwith, a friend of J.C. Loudon, was summed up as 'one of that exhausting band of prodigiously busy Victorians'.[68]

Chinese influence on British furniture and decorative arts had been apparent sporadically throughout the eighteenth century and again during the Regency period. This was in part caused by a sustained interest in the Chinese furniture exported through Canton (modern day Guangzhou). A collection of this style of black lacquer furniture with gilt highlights is at Burghley House, where some of it was inventoried as early as 1738. The following century the American philanthropist Nathan Dunn (1782–1844) ventured to China to revive his flagging fortunes in 1818 and returned to Philadelphia in 1832, taking with him a large collection of Chinese artistic and cultural objects. In 1838 he exhibited his 'Chinese Museum' in Philadelphia with an accompanying 120-page illustrated catalogue, *Ten Thousand Chinese Things*. Over 100,000 visitors saw the exhibition in Philadelphia and an equal number in London, where the collection was displayed in 1842 in a pagoda-like exhibition hall erected to the west of Albert Gate in Knightsbridge, **Fig. 3.93**. In 1842, between 70,000 and 80,000 of his catalogues were sold in the United States and Britain. Dunn died in 1844 and his partners brought his Chinese collection to London again in 1851, opening it on 1 May to coincide with the Great Exhibition. Although the series of life-size clay figures of Dunn's Chinese acquaintances aroused much interest at the exhibition, the second exhibition had less impact and much of the collection was auctioned at Christie's in December 1851. The auction opened a new chapter in the story of Asian influence in British art. A third of the objects were bought by one London dealer and through his shop the remnants of the collection were disseminated to young British artists and designers ready to transfer global influences into modern design.

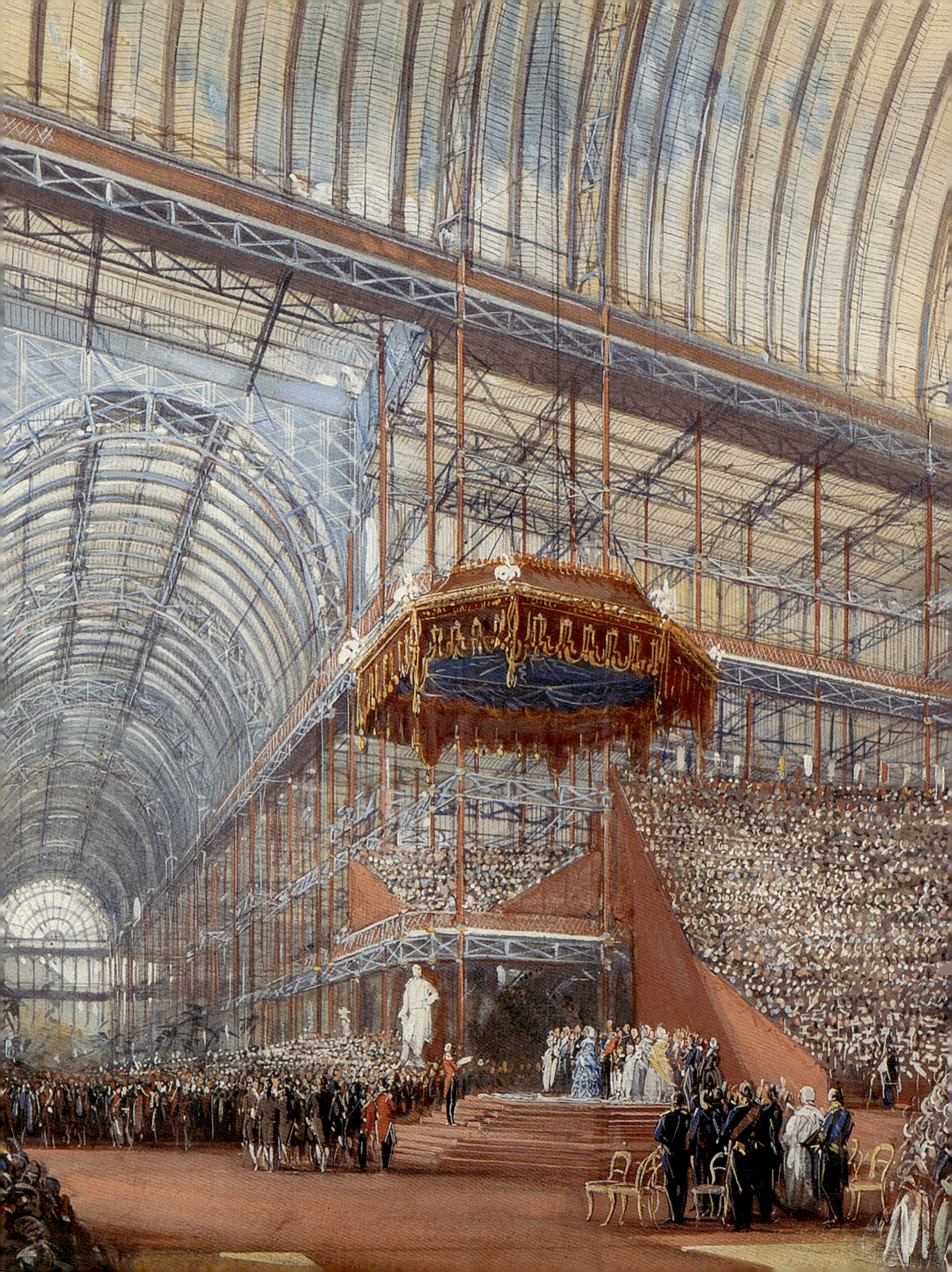

CHAPTER 4

1850s

*'The history of the world, I would venture to say, records no
event comparable in its promotion of human industry…'*
(Henry Cole)

*So let us raise
Victoria's praise,
And Albert's proud condition,
That takes his ayes
As he surveys
This Cristial [sic] Exhibition*
(William Thackeray 1851)

In Britain the decade of the 1850s was dominated by the Great Exhibition of 1851, its full title: The Great Exhibition of the Works of Industry of All Nations. The decade was arguably one of the most eclectic in terms of furniture production, ranging from sophisticated exact reproductions of eighteenth-century royal French furniture supervised by John Webb for the 4th Marquess of Hertford, to wildly imaginative romantic carved furniture by William Cookes of Warwick or the Tyneside school of Thomas Tweedy and Gerrard Robinson.

The advent of the exhibition known universally as 'The Great Exhibition' or more colloquially as 'Crystal Palace' was the British response to the exhibitions that had been held intermittently in Paris between 1798 and 1849 – *Les produits de l'industrie*. Whereas the French exhibitions had been essentially for French produce, the 1851 exhibition in Hyde Park was intended, as the full title suggests, to be an exhibition for all nations, including Asian products, the first truly international exhibition. Britain had been fully aware of the importance of exhibitions for promoting trade; earlier exhibitions at The Society of Arts were a stimulus to manufacture but were not on the scale of the Paris exhibitions.[1]

Fig. 4.1 (opposite) **A watercolour by Joseph Nash recording the re-opening of the exhibition building at Sydenham on 10 June 1854, attended by Queen Victoria and Prince Albert.** [Butchoff Antiques]

It was recognised by the British government that the *Grand National Exposition* in Paris had been 'a powerful agent in the cause of Continental improvement'.[2] The *Art Journal* of 1849 commented on the success and scale of the French exhibition which had 4,494 entries. This and an exhibition in Birmingham the same year were probable stimuli for the 1851 extravaganza. The idea of a British exhibition was suggested by Francis Whishaw, secretary to The Society of Arts, in 1844 at a small exhibition in the Society's rooms. The more positive intent to mount an annual exhibition of select specimens of British manufacturers and decorative art was discussed at a meeting on 3 March 1847. Henry Cole and Prince Albert[3] were the dynamos behind the Society of Arts exhibitions, and recognised the public thirst for such events, with 20,000 visitors flocking to the Society in 1847, 70,000 in the following year, rising to 100,000 in 1849. That year Cole visited the 11th Quinquennial Paris Exhibition and noticed the lack of accessibility to international participants. The able patronage of Prince Albert helped obtain the necessary support and the Royal Commission for the Exhibition announced its plans in February 1850.[4]

A brief summary of the industry involved to build and mount the 1851 exhibition indicates the sheer scale of it. The drive needed was an indication of the strength of British ingenuity and innovation.[5] Covering twenty-six acres (10.4 hectares), the unique purpose-built building enclosed and preserved fully grown trees. The structure of cast iron and

BRITISH FURNITURE

4.2

4.3

4.4

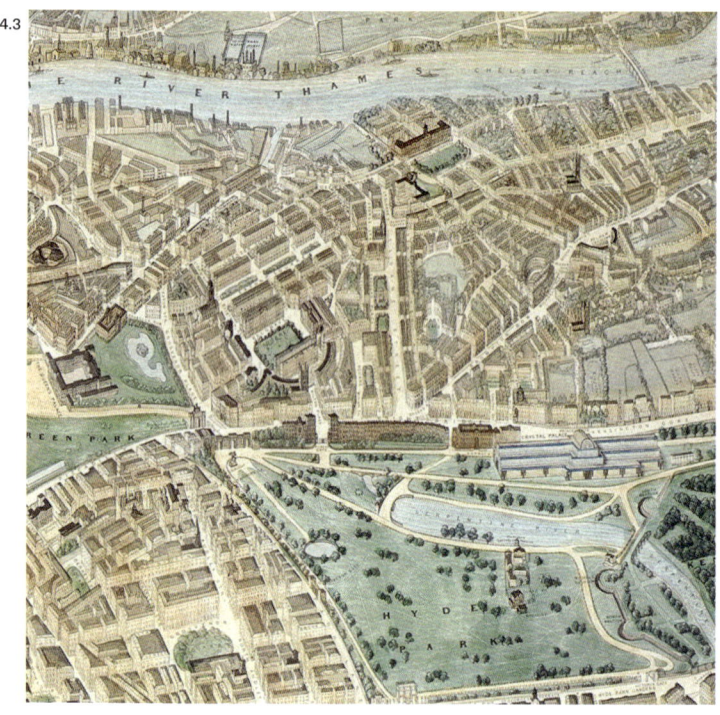

Fig. 4.2 An oil painting by P. Le Bihan of Queen Victoria and Prince Albert arriving in an open carriage at the Crystal Palace for the official opening of the Great Exhibition on 1 May 1851. Albert's prominence underscores the important role he played in organising the event. [Alamy Stock Photo]

Fig. 4.3 The 1851 exhibition was situated just south of Gore House in Kensington, where an influential exhibition of period furniture was to be held in 1853. The ramparts of the South, Middle & North Bastions of the fort built in 1642 are clearly outlined. [Alamy Stock Photo]

Fig. 4.4 The antlers on this mahogany-framed armchair almost 130cm (approx. 50in) wide, are of Scottish origin, from a mature fallow deer buck. Perfect for a hunting lodge, this is a more robust variation of contemporary chairs made entirely of horn by Rampendahl of Hamburg. [Butchoff Antiques]

CHAPTER 4: 1850S

Fig. 4.5 Although not the first exhibition of Chinese decorative art in Britain, the display in this watercolour by Joseph Nash in 1851 introduced the mysteries of the East to a much wider audience. [Getty Research Institute]

Fig. 4.6 In contrast to the Copeland & Garrett porcelain tabletop of 1841, Fig. 3.84, this table is in the Greek Revival style similar to one exhibited in New York in 1853. The design is from a vase in the Sir John Coghill collection, the rosewood base sympathetically adapted to reflect an ancient Greek vase.[6] The applied foliate panels on the baluster and plinth cleverly mirror one of the borders of the ceramic top. [Anthony Outred]

glass, designed by Joseph Paxton,[7] took a mere nine months to build, with an army of over two thousand workers at its peak. The unprecedented 563-metre (1,847-foot) frontage using new techniques and materials, became emblematic of the first international exhibition; one of a series throughout the second half of the nineteenth century with each country vying and competing over scale, design and content. The new building, quickly nicknamed 'The Crystal Palace' or 'The Great Shalimar', had wide, open internal boulevards. Each discipline was divided into separate 'classes' ensuring manufacturers could show their craftsmanship and ingenuity. Furniture was exhibited as Class 26 'Furniture, Upholstery, Paper Hangings, Papier Mâché and Japanned Goods'. The project became a showcase of British industry and, although at first derided, it was a huge financial success, making a

173

4.7a

4.7b

Figs 4.7a & b This model of console table, one of a pair, was awarded a prize at the 1851 exhibition. The polychrome marble tops are by Thomas Woodruff of Bakewell, purchased by Queen Victoria for Osborne House. The bronze lion monopodia was probably designed by Ludwig Grüner, in the manner of another German-born designer, K.F. Schinkel. [Royal Collection Trust / © His Majesty King Charles III 2023]

constructed on 42nd Street for the 1853 World's Fair held in New York. In 1854 in Munich the First General German Industrial Exhibition was held in the specially constructed *Glaspalast*. Both buildings were modelled on the London construction.[9] The original intention was to have an exhibition every five years but the next British exhibition on an international scale was not held until 1862. The next European international fair was held in Paris in 1855, with a host of British manufacturers and furniture makers exhibiting.

Photography was in its infancy, there are few black-and-white images from the Great Exhibition and rarely of individual items of furniture. However, a plethora of engravings exist of the exterior, interior and thousands of the exhibits. The line engravings were made with varying degrees of accuracy. In terms of the British furniture shown there was a wide variety, some that exists today but much of it presumed lost or destroyed. Furniture was widely praised: 'It would have been difficult to select any department of the Great Exhibition which could compare with Class XXVI (Furniture) as an evidence of our national prosperity'.[10] Hunt's *Hand-Book to the Official Catalogues* was available to visitors, who were flocking to see the exhibits. Hunt wrote that there were 536 exhibitors in the furniture section.

Many newspapers and journals commented on the exhibits, often accompanied by high-quality line engravings, some in colour. The first section of this chapter shows a sample of the furniture, including illustrations from the weekly journal, *The Illustrated London News*. The considerable coverage of the exhibition by the *News* continued from the opening to the moving and re-erecting of the building at Sydenham in 1854.[11] With generous attention to furniture, the journal published line engravings of a weird and wonderful array of British furniture, much of which is unknown today and made by little-known or seemingly unrecorded firms. Illustrated here are a few examples: from Ireland, A.J. Jones of Stephen's Green in Dublin exhibited an extensive suite carved in bog yew including an 'Omnium', or *étagère* and chair carved appropriately with a harp and Irish wolfhounds, **Figs 4.12a & b**.[12] In an 1853 dedication to the Duke of Leinster, John Lambert Jones wrote: 'The main characteristic of the collection is wonderful Picturesqueness'. Banting, France & Co. exhibited a sideboard and wine cooler in a modernised Regency manner. Bantings had supplied furniture to the Duke of Sussex, George IV and Queen Victoria at Windsor Castle and Buckingham Palace, and gained an honourable mention for their display. Their exhibits included a circular marquetry table, **Fig. 4.8**, a sideboard made from oak grown in Windsor Forest, a satinwood china cabinet, a kingwood secretaire and an amboyna oval table. Some of these pieces can be traced

surplus of £186,000 – over £20 million in today's values. The surplus was used to found the South Kensington, the Science and the Natural History museums and the legacy of the exhibition dominated the remainder of the century. The exhibition catalogue, lavishly illustrated with fine-quality steel engravings, showed a wide variety of manufacturing and craftsmanship on a worldwide scale. Queen Victoria took a great interest in the project championed by her husband, her diaries recording more than fifty visits, including during the construction, and she performed the opening ceremony on 1 May. Queen Victoria and Prince Albert commissioned a series of forty-nine watercolours of the exhibition, intended to be reproduced as chromolithographs.[8] The exhibition closed on 15 October with more than six million visitors having passed through the doors, an average daily attendance of 42,831. The structure of the huge building was an extraordinary feat of modern engineering and was a bold statement of Britain's place in the world in terms of achievement and manufacturing. In the United States a 'Crystal Palace' was

174

today but many have long since disappeared. John Calder of Bath made an inventive walnut circular table, the centre of which could revolve so that decanters of wine could easily be circulated, a development of the D-shaped so-called hunt or social tables, often made of mahogany, which were placed in front of a fire.[13] Much of the illustrated furniture followed vague principles of the Louis XV period but were adorned with much bolder, almost Baroque carving, such as a tall four-door vitrine by W. & C. Freeman of Norwich. Other examples include a hall table and chair by Mills of Bradford in Yorkshire, and an oak cabinet depicting Pallas wearing her aegis by Hayball of Sheffield. Arthur Hayball, a pupil of the Sheffield School of Design, also exhibited a massive sideboard, all the rage in the mid-century, as did Hoyle of Sheffield and Johnstone & Jeanes of London.

Sir Matthew Digby Wyatt (1820–1877), the art historian and architect, was in the perfect position as a commentator for the exhibition. Over the course of his career, he served as Slade Professor of Fine Art at Cambridge, Honorary Secretary of the Royal Institute of British Architects, Surveyor of the East India Company and Secretary of the exhibition. Wyatt exhibited drawings at the exhibition and reported on the fair, in addition to producing the two-volume *Industrial Arts of the Nineteenth Century*, highlighting pieces of exceptional merit. Another recorder was John Burley Waring (1823–1875), an architect and artist who, in his early years, studied in London, Italy, Spain and Paris, where he refined his skills as a draughtsman and produced works such as *Designs for Civic Architecture* (c.1850) and *The Arts Connected with Architecture in Central Italy* (1858). Waring, in conjunction with Wyatt, produced four guidebooks to the special Courts of the Great Exhibition and served as superintendent of the works of ornamental art and sculpture in the Art Treasures Exhibition in Manchester in 1857.[14] Both Waring's and Wyatt's volumes were published by Day & Son, lithographers to the queen. Their chromolithography display won a prize in the Fine Arts Court at the 1851 exhibition, some of which are reproduced on these pages (see **Figs 4.28, 4.38 & 4.43**).

Day & Son also collaborated with the renowned architect and designer Owen Jones, publishing his seminal work *The Grammar of Ornament* in 1856. In the 1830s Jones had travelled widely in Europe and the Middle East and made a prolific series of drawings of national characteristics of ornamentation.[15] He was responsible for the layout and interior decoration at the exhibition and for arranging the various courts when the Crystal Palace was re-erected at Sydenham in 1854. Jones wrote that his original drawings for the Egyptian Court were made when he visited Egypt 'on the spot in 1833'. For the Greek Court he offered an apology for not showing his thoughts on the rich colours of the marble

Fig. 4.8 A fine centre table by Banting, France & Co., of St James's Street in the heart of London. The centre pedestal looks to Bridgens' designs of the 1820s and the top has beautifully executed marquetry in Elizabethan Revival style. [*The Illustrated London News*, 6 September 1851, p. 312]

but had no such inhibitions with colour in his *Grammar*. Jones had undertaken a series of plaster casts and impressions on paper in 1837, which served as a basis for his Alhambra Court,[16] and he also supervised a Roman Court. Many of the Egyptian, Roman and Greek illustrations inevitably show similarities to earlier furniture of the Regency period but Jones was creating new possibilities with his polychrome illustrations, much in the manner of the Paris architect Jacques Ignace Hittorff. Owen Jones's *Grammar* included Chinese,[17] Elizabethan and even Maori designs. His designs were also an inspiration to the makers of marble furniture in Derbyshire, such as an example now in the Victoria and Albert Museum by Samuel Birley,[18] shown at the 1862 exhibition. Derbyshire became an important centre for inlaid marble items, including many small objects for the tourist trade. Several spectacular pieces of marble furniture are recorded, one being the near pair of console tables by Woodruff of Bakewell, **Figs 4.7a & b**, with cast-iron lion monopodia, probably influenced by Ludwig Grüner; they have clear antecedents in the designs of Karl Schinkel, working in Berlin

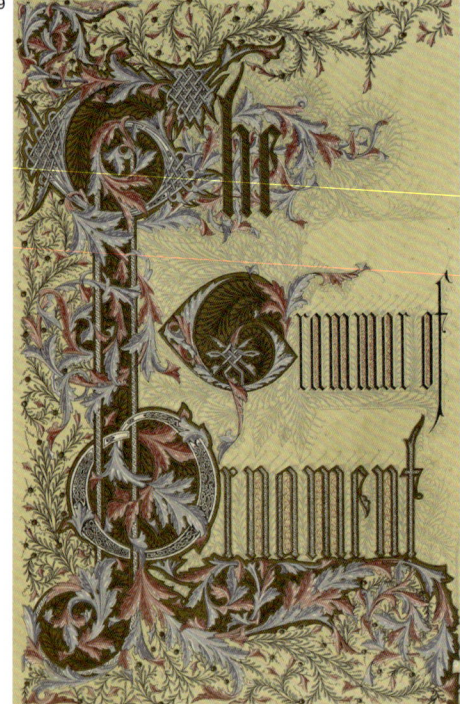

Fig. 4.9 The title page of Owen Jones's seminal *The Grammar of Ornament*, first published in 1856. [The Getty Research Institute]

Fig. 4.10 An elaborately carved table by Morant that typifies the naturalism of the 1851 exhibition; a version may be seen in the bottom right-hand corner of Fig. 4.50a. The design of the base was inspired by the Duchess of Sutherland and an example was delivered to the Duke and Duchess for Stafford House in 1838. A variation of the table, the property of Sir Francis Cook, presumed to have been supplied by Morant, was photographed in c.1905 in the Living Room at Monserrate Palace. On an example in the Victoria and Albert Museum the leaves and flowers are of pressed and moulded leather. [Artokoloro / Alamy Stock Photo]

in the early 1830s. The Woodruff tops include hardstones such as agate, chalcedony, alabaster and lapis inlaid into a local Ashford black marble ground. The Dukes of Cambridge and of Devonshire were patrons of Woodruff and 'Grüner obtained Woodruff's address from the Duke and, having paid a visit to establish that Woodruff would be able to execute "his designs", placed the order for two console tables'.[19]

Much of the furniture shown at the 1851 exhibition was over-elaborate and arguably not representative of furniture either wanted by, or available to, a wider market. The excesses of carving, pneumatic forms and often outrageous designs as portrayed in the catalogues show exotic, very expensive examples better preserved in a museum than an average or even luxurious home. Peter Floud pointed out that '… the exhibition catalogues (especially the illustrations, which were paid for by the exhibitors) give a false impression of the relative importance of the various manufacturers, and in particular greatly exaggerate the real weight of the West End luxury firms…'[20]

Commentators of the exhibition give us much of our information. *Art Industry, Furniture, House Fittings and Decorations* of 1879, edited by George Yapp, who also wrote the 1851 official catalogue, documented a series of exhibitions with illustrations of hitherto unpublished furniture. Examples from 1851 were beds with elaborate half-testers by T. Fox and by Smee & Son, both from London, but the most sumptuous carved items were by the Rogers father-and-son team of William (carver) and Harry (designer). Rogers had worked at Carlton House in 1817, at Brighton Pavilion and the House of Lords.[21] Commissioned by the Queen for the infant Princess Louise, born in 1848, the exquisitely carved cradle, **Fig. 4.13**, is made from Turkish boxwood. The Queen called it 'finer than anything of the kind, either antique or modern'. Litchfield later described it as '…symbolising the union between the British royal household and Saxe-Coburg and Gotha by Harry Rogers' who had '…Introduced his famous boxwood carving about seven years previously'.[22] The fine-quality carving by Rogers was represented in a large body of his work, mainly in boxwood, including a Bible cover and a crozier head. Cinquecento in its purity, this Italianate style was never popular with the wider public and today still does not have the appeal of 'Old French'.

Thomas Wilkinson Wallis exhibited a series of much-admired carved lime wall-hangings of exquisite detail in 1850 and 1851 (see **Figs 4.19, 4.20a & b**). These included a large

Fig. 4.11a Both these chairs were exhibited at the 1851 exhibition. On the left the heraldic chair by G. Shacklock of Bolsover in Derbyshire, the rustic chair on the right by Collinson of Doncaster, reputedly from a 2,000-year-old oak tree, submerged in the bed of the River Dun. [Yapp, *Art Industry, Furniture, House Fittings and Decorations*, 1879, pl. XIII]

Fig. 4.11b The 1851 exhibition chair carved in bog oak by Collinson of Doncaster. [Doncaster Corporation]

Figs 4.12a & b (overleaf) An extraordinary armchair made by Arthur James Jones of Dublin in 1850 and shown at the Great Exhibition. Made from yew wood retrieved from ancient peat bogs, the arms are carved with a recumbent and a baying Irish wolfhound, the collars alternatively carved with the mottos 'Gentle when stroked' and 'Fierce when provoked'. [Butchoff Antiques]

nosegay representing Spring, with a thousand representations of forty-seven varieties of spring flowers in bud. However, the much-vaunted Kenilworth Sideboard by Cookes & Sons of Warwick was 'In some respects the noblest production in the Exhibition', although in the same breath he wrote: 'in others, it is somewhat defective', **Fig. 4.18**.[23] It was almost as if the critics were trying not to show favour lest they be accused of favouritism. Made of oak from a tree on the Kenilworth Estate, the Cookes sideboard was termed a 'buffet' at the exhibition and was carved with a depiction of Elizabeth I entering Kenilworth Castle in 1575. The Earl of Leicester leads her horse on foot, whilst his rival the Earl of Essex is mounted on a charger. Sir Walter Scott was the inspiration, his romantic novel *Kenilworth* first published in 1821, and the sideboard had been nine years in the making. Such was the power of both British tradition and confidence in the future that this huge 'buffet' had been started long before there was any concept of an international exhibition.

This style of carving, creating monumental sideboards laden with game, had emerged in the 1840s with the so-called 'Warwick School', with Cookes the best-known firm, and also T.H. Kendall. Sir Walter Scott was the inspiration for another large carved piece at the exhibition. William King, a carver from Whitehaven, exhibited his 'Aldobrand Cabinet', made of 'British oak', the carving inspired by the description of Oldenbuck's cabinet in Walter Scott's novel of 1816, *The Antiquary*. Cookes exhibited another profusely carved sideboard, the Alscot sideboard, designed by Hugues Protât, dated 1853, first shown at the Manchester Art Treasures Exhibition in 1857. The French designer Protât had worked with Henri-Auguste Fourdinois in Paris and may have sought refuge with him in London as a result of the turmoil in mid-nineteenth-century Paris. This style of naturalistic carving soon spread to the United States, introduced by designers such as the Paris-born Alexander Roux. Roux exhibited carved sideboards of a similar form at the 1853 New York 'Crystal Palace'.[24] These 'Altars of Gastronomy' were overt symbols of wealth and Victorian wellbeing, a reminder of

4.12a

4.12b

4.13

4.14   4.15

Fig. 4.13 Commissioned by Queen Victoria for the infant Princess Louise by W.G. and W.H., this boxwood cradle by Rogers, dated 1850, was shown the following year at the Great Exhibition. [Royal Collection Trust / © His Majesty King Charles III 2023]

Figs 4.14 & 4.15 On the left one of a pair of carved lime wood mirrors tentatively attributed to the Rogers family. The engraving on the right is of a miniature frame by Rogers, carved with pinks in boxwood and shown amongst his exhibits in 1851. [4.14 Butchoff Antiques; 4.15 *The Art Journal Illustrated Catalogue, The Industry of All Nations*, 1851, p. 9]

Fig. 4.16 One of a pair of giltwood console tables with malachite tops of the highest quality bought for 160 guineas by the Duke of Cleveland at the sale of Horatio Walpole, 3rd Earl of Orford, at Wolterton Hall in Norfolk.[25] An annotation on the Raby records states that they were carved and partially restored by William Rogers. However, the style of carving is out of character with Rogers' fine detail and is more in the manner of Clarke, see Fig. 2.19. [Raby Castle, County Durham]

Fig. 4.17 A view of Cookes & Sons workshop from *The Illustrated London News*. The figure wearing a cap is standing beside a pointing machine, an instrument for measurement and scaling of carving – a device already in use in ancient Greece. [*The Illustrated London News*, Vol. XIX, 8 November 1851, supplement]

Fig. 4.18 The Kenilworth Buffet by Cookes & Sons of Warwick, carved with a depiction of the entry of Elizabeth I into Kenilworth Castle in 1575, was variously admired and derided at the 1851 exhibition. [Digital image courtesy of the Getty's Open Content Program]

the large buffets of the seventeenth-century Baroque, used for displaying silver or gold plate and vessels as a sign of the importance of the house to impress and welcome visitors.

Another important carver was James Morris Willcox, who worked for two periods with Cookes. His rare small-scale pollard-oak side table, which may well have been made in the 1840s, **Fig. 4.21**, is complete with not one but two pre-printed paper trade labels or visiting cards nailed to the underside. The 5th Duchess of Buccleuch, taking a rest from her royal duties as Mistress of the Robes, had been much enamoured with her discovery of Willcox when she visited Leamington Spa in 1841. Writing her monthly report to the Duke, 'I write a line Dearest Love to tell you that I went to Mr Willcox yesterday and trust that with Lady M's advice I made a good selection. I spent more than was intended but not much. The brace of partridges were £9'.[26] It might be assumed that the 'brace of partridges' was of carved wood in the Grinling Gibbons manner rather than freshly shot game!

Oak, a relatively difficult wood to carve in fine detail, was used for many of the large sideboards that adorned large country houses. Willcox supplied the celebrated large sideboard in 1858 to George Lucy for the Great Hall at Charlecote Park in Warwickshire, at a cost of £1,600. Many of these large items were made from homegrown oak, in the case of Charlecote, reputedly from Warwick Castle. Willcox's carved sideboard for another great Warwickshire house, made for Lord and Lady Leigh at Stoneleigh Abbey, is a virtuoso performance of the Rococo Revival. Willcox influenced other skilled carvers such as his former apprentice, Thomas Kendall. One of the most

BRITISH FURNITURE

4.19

4.20a

4.20b

182

Fig. 4.19 First modelled in clay, it took Thomas Wallis eight weeks to complete this limewood *nature morte*, similar to the precision of the work of Jean Demontreuil in the 1790s. [*Autobiography of Thomas Wilkinson Wallis*, 1899, plate facing p. 82]

Figs 4.20a & b *Trophy of Spring*, an exquisitely carved foliate trophy by Thomas Wallis. Known as the 'Lincolnshire Gibbons', he submitted seven carvings in 1851 and *Trophy of Spring* was awarded a medal. It was his most intricate carving and took him eight months to complete. [Louth Museum]

gifted woodcarvers, Thomas Wallis of Louth submitted seven items to the exhibition in 1851. His *Trophy of Spring* took eight months to create, and he was awarded a medal for his diligence and skill, **Figs 4.20a & b**. It is an unusual design and stands out from the more familiar and exquisite carvings by Wallis and his peers. Wallis's work took months to complete, starting with making clay models. One of Wallis's admiring clients was G. Tomline who in 1850 paid £100 for a limewood carving. Wallis could only work in natural light and wrote, 'I completed the group – red-legged partridge, woodcock and snipe.... I worked at it for eight weeks, including the modelling in clay', **Fig. 4.19**.[27] In 1850 Wallis was given leave to study carvings by Grinling Gibbons at Chatsworth and 'Burleigh House' [*sic*].[28] Known as the 'Lincolnshire Gibbons',[29] he was gifted and adaptable, making an extraordinary chinoiserie chair to a design by Lady Constable, for Burton Constable Hall, **Fig. 4.22**. Without the archival records it would have seemed a suitable candidate for the Royal Pavilion, Brighton almost fifty years earlier.

The exotically veneered sideboard, **Fig. 4.27**, by Levien, was shown at the 1851 exhibition and purchased by H.S. Westmacott for his house in Penrhyn, North Wales. Levien made a similar example for the King of Prussia ten years later. His variety of designs in different styles appears never-ending. The Prussian-born Johann Martin Levien was clearly a past master at adapting to, and promoting, current taste. Travelling to South America then New Zealand, he set up business in central London, selling New Zealand veneers to such eminent makers as Dowbiggin and Gillows with examples of his work on display at New Zealand House in Broad Street, London.[30] Clients included the Rothschilds, 'for whom Levien fitted out an entire room in totara and kinau'.[31] A polychrome side cabinet designed by Levien, was exhibited by Dowbiggin & Son in 1851, **Fig. 4.31**. Levien's work impressed the royal family and in 1846 the *London Sun* reported:

MR. LEVIEN. HIS SPLENDID WORKMANSHIP FOR THE QUEEN, AND THE FURNITURE WOODS FROM NEW ZEALAND: 'We are happy to announce that her Majesty has been pleased to confer upon Mr Levien the appointment of cabinet-maker to her Majesty, in token of the very elegant specimens of workmanship made by him from the woods of New Zealand. Her Majesty the Queen was the first to patronise him. And he has secured great favour with her Majesty by his workmanship, his skill, and his woods'.[32]

There is an almost never-ending seam of variety, as makers vied to attract the attention of a potential customer. White & Parlby of 49 & 50 Great Marlborough Street, who made elaborate casts in cement for interior use, exhibited a delicate and almost unusable ladies' work table – the carving is so extravagant that it renders the use of the

Fig. 4.21 An unusual tripod console table beautifully carved in pollard oak by James Willcox of Warwick. Underneath are two paper labels stating Willcox was a 'Dealer in Antique Furniture' as well as a carver. [Private collection]

Fig. 4.22 Designed by Lady Constable for Burton Constable Hall, this chinoiserie dragon chair was carved and gilded by Thomas Wilkinson Wallis. [© Burton Constable Foundation]

table all but impossible. At the 1862 exhibition the firm experimented with *carton pierre*, a form of *papier-mâché* – highly decorative but impractical for large items of furniture such as their exhibit of a French-inspired side cabinet with six kneeling putti. Snell & Co., a firm established in 1775,[33] were major exhibitors in 1851. A walnut and parcel-gilt secretaire by Snell looks more like an Italian mirror above a *cartonnier*. Snell also exhibited a carved mahogany sideboard and mirror with figures after models by Queen Victoria's favourite sculptor Carlo Marochetti, **Fig. 4.28**. A 'young working-man' called Henry Hoyle made a distinctive carved walnut sideboard while training at the Sheffield School of Design. Where are these pieces now? Do they even survive? The same goes for a beautiful circular table by Banting, France & Co., who traded from Pall Mall and St James's Street, London between 1811 and 1925, but later examples of their work are scarce. The top and tripod are inlaid with plausible Elizabethan strapwork, **Fig. 4.8**. Another table by Banting, with an oval top, uses a base that looks back to the Bridgens style of tripod of the late 1820s. One of the most surprising engravings in *The Illustrated London News* is a group of *papier-mâché* furniture by Spiers and Son, based in Oxford High Street, 'designed by Mr. Owen Jones'.[34] Active since *c*.1815, William Caldecott of 53 Great Russell Street exhibited an octagonal table inlaid with stylised Elizabethan motifs. The claim by John Webb of Bond Street, celebrated for his series of commissions for the 4th Marquess of Hertford in the mid-1850s, that the table, **Fig. 4.29**, is 'old' and 'Elizabethan' is clearly outrageous – possibly the reporter 'misunderstood'. C.J. Richardson exhibited a table

4.23

Fig. 4.23 A rare 'Buhl' centre table, the brass, pewter, copper and mother-of-pearl inlaid onto a richly figured walnut ground. The six subjects represent The Opening of Pandora's Box, following an earlier design by the sculptor John Flaxman, the table made by Robert W. Herring & Sons of Fleet Street and exhibited on stand 205 at the Great Exhibition. [Bonhams]

4.24

4.25

4.26

and triangular stool in a more faithful but still romanticised manner, **Fig. 4.30**. Richardson was not listed as a furniture maker; his twenty-one engravings in *Studies of Ornamental Design* of 1851 suggest he was solely a designer. A similar style suitably appealed to Scottish taste and J. Wilson & Co. of Ayr represented Scotland at the Dublin exhibition of 1853 with a large Elizabethan-style bookcase emblematic of the United Kingdom. The large amount of furniture made by the Morison family in Ayr and Edinburgh, and Wilson's capable work, show how productive many provincial towns had become. Although synonymous with carved furniture, the Warwickshire firm of William Cookes won the 'small Gold Medal' at the Royal Dublin Society Exhibition of Manufacture, Produce and Invention in 1850 for a 'very beautiful marquetrie [*sic*] loo table, in Amboyna and ebony, which evinced the best taste in the selection of the woods, and great neatness in the fitting'.[35]

The glass fountain designed by Osler, weighing 4 tons, **Fig. 4.33**, was 'perhaps the most striking object in the exhibition'.[36] The exhibition was a golden opportunity for makers to show craftsmanship and ingenuity. The mahogany capstan table, **Figs 4.34a–d**, is a remarkable combination of miniaturisation and engineering. Only 61cm (24in) in diameter fully extended, it is exquisitely made out of

Fig. 4.24 A 'pier table and glass' by Holland & Sons, probably intended for a music room. The profuse carved Rococo decoration is not only gilded but also highlighted with silver and copper colouring. For the 1855 Paris exhibition, Holland produced a more sophisticated cabinet on lion monopodia supports in a Graeco-Roman style. [*The Illustrated London News*, 5 July 1851, p. 28]

Fig. 4.25 A library suite by Gillows, comprising a desk and deeply upholstered couch with an extravagant Rococo armchair, exhibited in 1851. [*The Illustrated London News*, 19 July 1851, p. 93]

Fig. 4.26 A boldly carved oak sideboard and cellaret exhibited by Gillows in 1851, the eagle supports a reinterpretation of William Kent designs over one hundred years previously. [Frederick Litchfield, *Illustrated History of Furniture [...]*, 1907]

Cuban mahogany; the cut-steel mechanism allowing it to be opened and closed by the tiny handle. Exhibited by Samuel Hawkins of 54 Bishopsgate Street Without, London, the four-volume *Official Descriptive and Illustrated Catalogue of the Great Exhibition of 1851* illustrated and discussed the table's mechanism in great and appreciative detail. Cuban mahogany, sometimes called Santo Domingo mahogany, is the much-revered king of mahoganies. With provincial workshops situated in Lancaster, Gillows had a geographical advantage in the choice of timbers imported from the Caribbean. Their display of a portion of a mammoth log of Santo Domingo mahogany illustrated the practical difficulties

Fig. 4.27 Made by the Prussian-born Johann Martin Levien, the main veneer is indigenous New Zealand burr totara, the detailed carving in boxwood was by an Italian named Lavati. [Sotheby's]

Fig. 4.28 The figures flanking the mirror on this 1851 exhibition sideboard exhibited by Snell are after models by the sculptor Baron Marochetti. The lion monopodia are reminiscent of the designs of Karl Schinkel and Ludwig Grüner. [D.M. Wyatt, *The Industrial Arts of the Nineteenth Century*, vol. II, 1851, pl. 125. Courtesy of the Smithsonian Libraries and Archives]

in sourcing, transporting and veneering rare, imported timbers.[37] The south-western gallery of the exhibition had a display of an immense variety of woods that could be used for making and decorating household furniture.

The 1851 exhibition was a watershed of both design and industry. One of the most iconic and lasting images in the realm of furniture is Dr Calvert's Digestive Chair. Made of flat rolled steel, Calvert recommended armless rockers for 'invalids and the weaker sex'. The concept was one from the 1840s, Thomas Webster's *An Encyclopedia of Domestic Economy* (1845) recommending an iron rocking chair for exercise.[38] R.W. Winfield & Co. of Birmingham was one of several tubular chair makers. They had a large stand at the exhibition where they showed a similar chair. The first example was in tubular brass, a material that was used in huge quantities for bed frames. By the 1862 exhibition, Winfield had strengthened his tubular metal chair by substituting rectangular strips or 'straps' of metal.[39] The original strap metal examples are very strong but are outnumbered by twentieth-century copies. In 1844 Charles Dickens rented a house in Devonshire Terrace, London, and the inventory included an iron rocking chair in the dining room.[40] The strap steel chair, **Fig. 4.36**, is a rare example with an illustrious and watertight provenance. It was given to Hans Christian Andersen in 1859 on the occasion of his fifty-fourth birthday.[41] Andersen aptly encapsulated our romanticised thoughts on Victorian comfort – 'At home… my living room was a complete fairy tale…. I thought this evening of writing a tale *from the living room of a confirmed*

Fig. 4.29 **Without the caption in** *The Illustrated London News*, **it would be impossible to attribute these three pieces to the Bond Street dealer John Webb. The caption claims that the table is 'old' and 'Elizabethan'.** [*The Illustrated London News*, 23 August 1851, p. 256]

Fig. 4.30 **An engraving for designs in the idealised Elizabethan style by C.J. Richardson.** [*The Art Journal Illustrated Catalogue, The Industry of All Nations*, 1851, p. 256]

Fig. 4.31 **Shown here only in sepia, this polychrome Italianate side cabinet designed by Ludwig Grüner was exhibited in 1851 by Thomas Dowbiggin & Son whose premises Holland & Sons took over the same year.** [Artokoloro / Alamy Stock Photo]

bachelor and letting the furniture, pictures and knick-knacks tell his story'.[42] The form of such chairs recalls the steamed bentwood chairs made in beech by the Austrian innovator Michael Thonet. One of the first examples of 'tubular' furniture was illustrated by John Porter of London in his wire work and iron furniture trade catalogue of 1840.[43]

The renowned *papier-mâché* firm, Jennens & Bettridge, made a far less practical chair and it is unlikely many were commissioned or have survived. Designed by H. Fitz Cook, it was first exhibited in 1851, aptly termed the 'Day Dreamer' and, like other selective examples of 1851 exhibition furniture, it appears to anticipate the naturalism of art nouveau. *The Illustrated Exhibitor* of 1851 described the decoration: 'The chair is decorated on the top with two winged thoughts… representing happy and joyous dreams.' At the side is a figure of Puck lying asleep… holding a branch of poppies in his hand'.[44] Jennens also exhibited their 'Victoria Regina' cot alongside a pianoforte, the keys of which were constructed of turtle shell and mother-of-pearl in a 'tasteful and novel pattern'. By the time of the 1867 exhibition, the firm had taken the technology further with an upright piano with Islamic-style polychrome decoration made, incredibly, in *papier-mâché*. Another *papier-mâché* furniture maker, Henry Clay of London, exhibited a dressing-table set in 1851 and the plasticity of the medium makes it appear to be, in the exhibition line engraving, almost melting. Another less well-known maker was Lane, possibly Thomas Lane, a japanner of London and Birmingham.

Winfield & Co. are best known for their rocking chairs, one of the most elaborate shown in **Fig. 4.37a**, but the most spectacular exhibit from their Cambridge Street Works was a magnificent four-poster bed in brass cast in a hybrid of Renaissance and Classical styles, **Fig. 4.38**. The exhibition catalogue wrote of Birmingham: 'The *"brass toy trade"*, despite its nominal insignificance, has probably contributed more than any other to the prosperity of that busy town'. In 1866 Aitken noted the consumption of brass in Birmingham had risen from 100 tons in the early eighteenth century to 10,000 tons per annum in 1851, with 7,000 people working in the brass trade.[45] Winfield themselves employed over 600, of whom 150 worked on metal bedsteads.

Examples of the many names of makers and their furniture now lost or buried in archives are the 'Gladiatorial table' by J. Fletcher of Ireland, a *papier-mâché* chair by McCallum & Hodson of Summer Row in Birmingham,[46] and a cheval screen by a T. Nicoll of a form that could have been made by any number of firms. At the higher end of the scale, George Trollope & Sons, who had started out as stationers and paper hangers in 1778 but had become fully fledged cabinet makers by the 1850s, exhibited a tall sideboard with a triple mirror back carved with game similar to many of their peers and of 'rich and elaborate carving'.[47] In contrast they also exhibited a dressing chest influenced by contemporary French forms, see **Fig. 4.43**. Trollope described the dyes on the twenty species of wood of the marquetry as being natural, not artificial; should the colours fade, as they surely would, it was advised that the effect can be restored by 'scraping' (i.e. sanding or scraping off a fine layer of wood to reveal the freshness of the original dyes), and then re-polishing.[49] In 1855 Trollope once again were noted for marquetry furniture of stained woods, and they exhibited a satinwood cabinet in an exaggerated Elizabethan manner with twist-turned columns and knopped spires, designed by R. Beavis, inlaid with tulip and linden woods, **Fig. 4.44**. John Harris Heal, son of the founder of the Heal dynasty, exhibited a Louis XVI-style dressing table in 1851 'tempered with a rumbustious Victorian touch, and made authentic by the medallion of Queen Victoria'.[50] One commentator wrote that Heal's table and mirror were of unusual design, and 'In designing the marquetry, strict botanical accuracy, both in form and colour, ... even the fibres of the leaves, ... are of wood of the necessary colours.'[51]

Much of the exhibition furniture was too grand and expensive to be commercial, such as a large chimney piece

Fig. 4.32 **John Steevens of Taunton has reinterpreted the late seventeenth-century cabinet on stand with this extraordinary example in walnut, profusely inlaid with marquetry and placed on herm supports. The male figures represent Youth, Manhood, Maturity and Old Age, the four female figures are 'The Passions'.** [*The Art Journal Illustrated Catalogue, The Industry of All Nations*, 1851, p. 220]

Fig. 4.33 **The glass fountain by Osler of Birmingham inside the 1851 exhibition hall looking east from the Transept. Osler also exhibited a pair of 8-foot-high (2.4 metres) candelabra made for Osborne House.**[48] [© Victoria and Albert Museum, London]

CHAPTER 4: 1850S

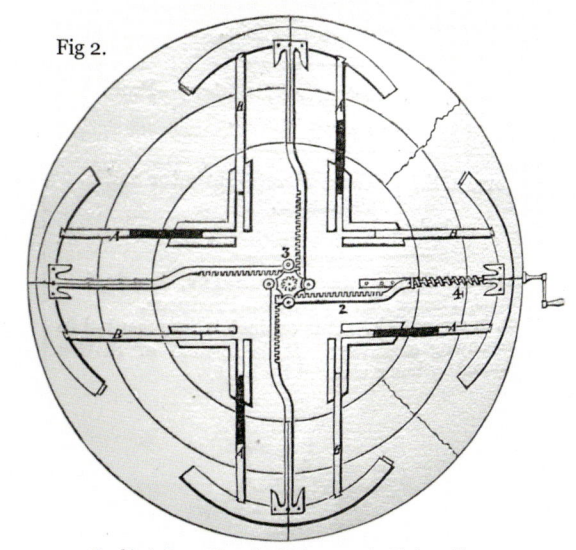

Figs 4.34a–d **This remarkable miniature extending table in Cuban mahogany was exhibited by Samuel Hawkins at the 1851 exhibition.**
[4.34a–c: Butchoff Antiques; 4.34d: from *Official Descriptive and Illustrated Catalogue*, 1851, p. 754, Fig. 2]

Fig. 4.35 **An extravagant Johnstone & Jeanes capstan table exhibited in 1851, an elaborate variation of the 1835 Jupe patent.**[52] [*The Illustrated London News*, 1 November 1851, p. 557]

and bookcase designed by the illustrator Thomas Robert Macquoid and made by Holland & Sons. Carved in walnut with inlaid marble and made in Baroque proportions, it has lost its place in history, unlike the Crace cabinet made in the 'Medieval style' that we would today term Gothic Revival, **Fig. 4.45**.[53] The Medieval Court was a separate display at the exhibition and was centred on a magnificent font towering towards the glass roof. It was described as 'tricked out in gaudy-coloured draperies, and glittering brass…presented a stunning *coup d'oeil*'.[54] The Crace cabinet was made by John Gregory Crace to a design by A.W.N. Pugin and is a relatively rare survivor of the Medieval Court. An early manifestation of this had been a sixteenth-century style cabinet designed by Pugin around 1845 for his own house, The Grange, and possibly made by George Myers at his workshops on Ordnance Wharf in Lambeth. Myers worked with Pugin regularly and was closely associated with the Medieval Court at the Great Exhibition. Crace's work is a dominant feature of the Palace of Westminster, where he

189

worked in collaboration with Pugin. Crace also had worked for the 6th Duke of Devonshire at Devonshire House and at Chatsworth where his distinctive furniture remains to this day, **Fig. 4.46**. In contrast, Hindley exhibited a simplified Gothic cabinet in a style that has more in common with Regency Gothic. Crace regretted the lack of suitable furniture for mansions in the medieval style, advertising in *The Builder* under the heading 'Ancient Furniture' and stating that they had prepared 'appropriate specimens'.[55]

Edward Joy was one of the first furniture historians to publicly lament the lack of appreciation for the humbler firms and, in many if not most cases, the unknown craftsmen and women. He documented the growing number of provincial firms making furniture in the rapidly expanding

Fig. 4.36 **A birthday present to Hans Christian Andersen in 1859, re-upholstered thirteen years later in a William Morris pattern. The stylish form and use of tubular or strap metal paved the way for twentieth-century designs.** [Hans Christian Andersen Museum]

Figs 4.37a & b **An exemplary case of a tubular-brass rocking chair of the type championed by R.W. Winfield.** [Walpole Antiques]

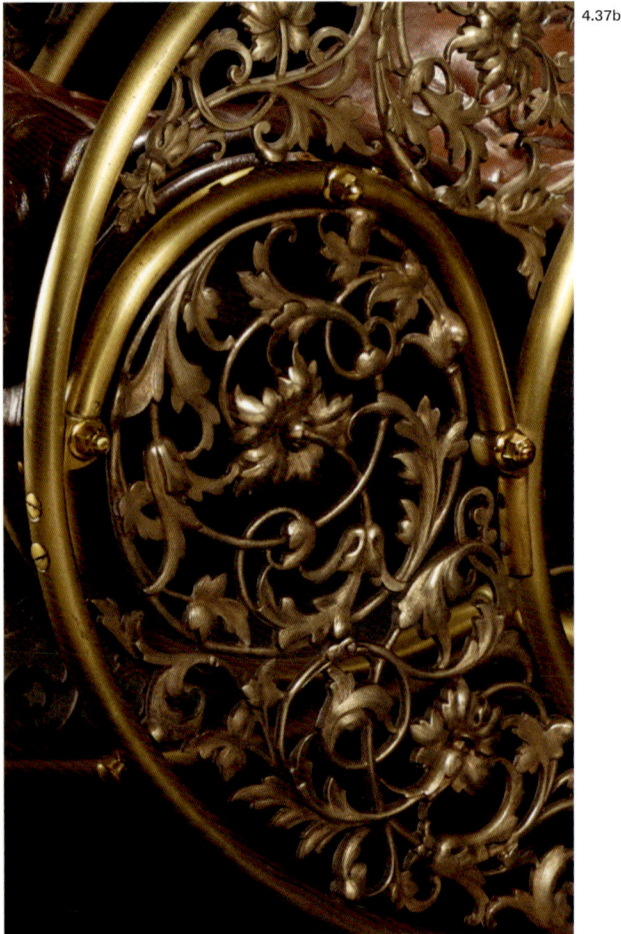

Fig. 4.38 This bed was described by *The Art Journal* as 'one of the best objects of its kind ever brought before our notice'. It was made by the innovative Birmingham firm of R.W. Winfield & Co. who won awards in 1851, 1862 and 1878. [D.M. Wyatt, *The Industrial Arts of the Nineteenth Century*, vol. I, 1851, pl. 43]

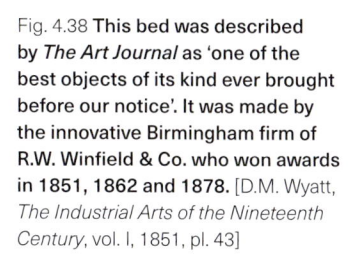

Fig. 4.39 A tripod table, the top and support entwined with serpents. Confusingly and probably in error, *The Illustrated London News* caption cited the firm as Holland & Sons, 'from Warwick'.[56] [*The Illustrated London News*, 1 November 1851, p. 557]

Fig. 4.40 Henry Palmer of Bath is one of many short-lived firms about which we know little. This walnut table is more an exercise in carving than a practical piece of furniture. The tripod base is wider than the top and would be easy to damage. [*The Art Journal Illustrated Catalogue, The Industry of All Nations*, 1851, p. 256]

provincial towns and cities such as Bath, Birmingham, Bristol and Manchester, and other examples such as Bates of St Albans, Abbot of Colchester, and Barrie of Edinburgh. Few of these firms are known today. T.H. Bates was a labourer who made a loo table from four thousand pieces of native English timbers, and J. Barrie 'a ploughman (working) in the evening, by candlelight'.[57] Edmund Nye of Tunbridge Wells is an exception due to the fact that he often labelled the myriad of small treen objects he made inlaid in the now familiar 'Tunbridge Ware' end-grain mosaic.[58] The Star of Brunswick Table by Henry Eyles of Bath, **Fig. 4.49**, demonstrates the ability of provincial makers and is a good example of the inventiveness and technical competence of British firms. The table, exhibited upright at the exhibition to show off the Chamberlain's Worcester plaque, is in walnut with a pollard oak top. Eyles also exhibited a walnut armchair inset with a large Worcester porcelain portrait plaque of Prince Albert and a matching, more dainty, side chair showing Queen Victoria.[59] The design for a more conventional and commercial walnut loo table was patented by another Bath maker, Henry Palmer, in 1849. The table has a delightful exaggerated outset buttress for the tripod support.[60] Palmer went a step too far with impractical tripod supports surmounted by oversize putti, for a table exhibited in 1851, **Fig. 4.40**. Loo tables were perennially popular, one by the hitherto unknown Watson 'in which the bouquets of flowers and groups of figures are shaded almost with the delicacy of a painting'.[61]

BRITISH FURNITURE

4.41

4.42

Fig. 4.41 **A watercolour, *c*.1855 by Samuel Rayner, of a luxurious dressing room, the blue-and-white fabrics complemented by the side table, the form of which is unusual.**
[© Victoria and Albert Museum, London]

Fig. 4.42 **A watercolour from the 1850s by Samuel Rayner of a London town house conspicuously furnished with contemporary French furniture.**
[© Victoria and Albert Museum, London]

192

Fig. 4.43 Exhibited by George Trollope & Sons in 1851, the marquetry of this French-inspired cabinet uses naturally coloured dyes. [D.M. Wyatt, *The Industrial Arts of the Nineteenth Century*, vol. I, 1851, pl. 75]

Fig. 4.44 Designed in an exaggerated Elizabethan manner, with twist-turned columns and knopped spires by R. Beavis, this satinwood cabinet was exhibited by George Trollope & Sons in 1855. [George Wallis, *The Exhibition of Art-industry in Paris*, 1855, p. 10]

Fig. 4.45 Crace made this elaborate and highly praised Gothic-style carved oak 'armoire' with a matching cabinet to a Pugin design for the Medieval Court at the Great Exhibition. [© Victoria and Albert Museum, London]

In the ever-increasing inventiveness of the period, low-relief decoration was created by the use of iron moulds which were heated and applied with enormous pressure to the wood, which was thus carved or, more correctly, 'embossed'. At the Crystal Palace, the London-based Patent Wood Carving Company exhibited an elaborate cabinet that could easily be mistaken for a Flemish example. The wood was shaped – effectively carved, by heating with hot metal dies. The inventive Victorian mind, combined with seemingly endless business opportunities in a thriving marketplace, thought up ingenious methods of making furniture more widely available. *Papier-mâché* was one of the few that appeared to last. Another was the French invention of *bois durci*, patented in France and England in 1855 using sawdust from rosewood and animal blood to make small plaques of a fine and durable detail. As early as 1656 John Tradescant discovered *gutta percha*, a form of latex used widely for domestic items from the 1840s. The Gutta Percha Company was formed in 1845 and exhibited console table and mirror frames made at the Great Exhibition. The London firm of

4.46

4.47

4.48

Fig. 4.46 **A table in the Lower Library at Chatsworth, a room decorated and furnished by J.G. Crace for the 6th Duke of Devonshire in *c*.1840.** [The Devonshire Collections, Chatsworth. Reproduced by permission of Chatsworth Settlement Trustees]

Fig. 4.47 **Made for Francis Barchard at Horstead Place, the design of this oak open bookcase can be attributed to A.W.N. Pugin, the joinery to J.G. Crace.** [James Graham-Stewart]

Fig. 4.48 **Made in oak in the Pugin Gothic manner by Crace with metalwork by Hardman of Birmingham, this sideboard was made for John Naylor at Leighton Hall, in *c*.1855 at a cost of £95 15s.** [Sotheby's]

Fig. 4.49 **The Star of Brunswick Table in walnut and pollard oak made by Henry Eyles of Bath for the 1851 exhibition.** [© Victoria and Albert Museum, London]

4.49

Leake exhibited a chair with leather boiled and pressed to form a decorative, embossed surface. These novel furniture-making ideas were to produce more furniture for less expense to the consumer, and of course increased profitability to the manufacturer.

Since their formation in 1836, the firm of Jackson & Graham had become a major centre for all aspects of household furniture and interior decoration, including paper hanging, and added a carpet department a decade later. They were major contributors to the 1851 exhibition. They had furnished the 'Robing-room' at the exhibition 'for the use of Her Majesty on her frequent visits', the furniture covered with blue silk damask from Spitalfields. Jackson & Graham also showed their prowess with a ceiling cast in *carton pierre* with flowers and animals, the room centred on a *gutta percha* table. Their large sideboard, despite being designed by a French hand, that of Prignot, is patriotically made of British oak, measuring 12 feet high and 10 feet wide (3.7 × 3.1 metres), the figures representing the Seasons, Hunting and Fishing, and is illustrated in *Recollections of the Great Exhibition*, **Fig. 4.53a**.

The English adaptation of the Louis XV genre, easily identified by the use of cabriole legs, is evident in the pair of walnut card tables by John Hicks, a Cambridgeshire carver who initially came to London to work on the reconstruction of the Palace of Westminster (see **Fig. 4.54**). The complex marquetry tops depict virtually identical landscapes of Renaissance-style geographers measuring globes, against

Fig. 4.50a **A view of the Furniture Court at the Great Exhibition, on the left the exhibits of John Webb (the bed hung in blue silk is on the stand of William Smee & Sons). The porcelain-mounted small table and the pair of tall giltwood** *torchères* **may well be those now at Raby Castle. On the right are two variations of the Morant tripod table, Fig. 4.10.**[62] [© Victoria and Albert Museum]

Fig. 4.50b **Another view of John Webb's stand at the 1851 exhibition, showing one of the pair of 36-light** *torchères*. **The small table is typical of porcelain-mounted furniture made in the 1830s and 1840s.** [Album / Alamy Stock Photo]

a Classical background with columns, obelisks, putti, vast flower-filled urns and a sweeping staircase.[63] Hicks joined his father in business as a carver, initially setting up premises of workshop and accommodation in 3–5 Kendal Mews, Blandford Street in Mayfair after his father's death in 1864. He was joined by William Lumbus, his son-in-law, and they produced items in the fashionable French taste. Hicks retired in 1880, Lumbus died in 1885, and the firm traded until 1892.

Johann Martin Levien submitted four Louis XV-style pieces of furniture to the exhibition in 1851, none of which are in a style he is hitherto known to have worked and in a completely different discipline to his recorded work. Most probably purchased at the 1843 Baldock auction, three of these pieces are illustrated in the engraving **Fig. 4.55a**; the porcelain-mounted jewel casket on stand is similar to the example thought to have been purchased in 1846 by Prince Albert for Queen Victoria and still in the Royal Collection, **Fig. 4.55b**. The payment ledger for £25 4s is to 'Mr. Levien Fancy Table', dated 1846, the year Levien obtained a royal warrant.[64] French in style and presentation but with English locks and hinges, variations were made by unidentified makers, such as the one in **Figs 4.56a & b**. A popular model, another example is in the Buccleuch Collection at Bowhill House and may have been supplied by Baldock in the 1840s or possibly ordered from Levien by the 5th Duchess of Buccleuch, who, as Mistress of the Robes, would have been aware of Queen Victoria's example. The royal cabinet has

Fig. 4.51a This *torchère*, with thirteen ormolu candlearms, is one of a set of four. There are three pairs of tall giltwood *torchères* in the Baron's Gallery at Raby Castle. [Raby Castle, County Durham]

Fig. 4.51b A detail from one of the set of four *torchères* at Raby Castle highlighting the two-tone gilding. [Raby Castle, County Durham]

Figs 4.52a & b One of a pair of 36-light *torchères*, which are seemingly the pair exhibited on John Webb's stand, number 171, at the Great Exhibition, the lithograph shown as Fig. 4.50b. [Raby Castle, County Durham]

more lavish porcelain plaques than other known examples. It seems a canny move by Levien to have sold this model to the royal household and then exhibited it five years later at the Great Exhibition, although the continuing popularity of porcelain-mounted furniture is apparent in the lithograph **Fig. 4.50b**, showing a view of John Webb's stand in the Furniture Court at the Great Exhibition; another jewel casket is at Raby Castle, possibly bought by the Duke and Duchess of Cleveland at the exhibition, together with at least one of the three pairs of tall giltwood *torchères* with ormolu candle branches also at Raby Castle, each almost 3 metres tall (approx 9½ft).[65] The exhibition catalogue described a pair on the stand of the Bond Street dealer John Webb 'Pair of candelabra, of sculptured wood, gilt, with or-molu branches carrying 72 lights'. Their ebonised wood triangular concave stands are still in use at Raby, **Figs 4.52a & b**.

The Great Industrial Exhibition in Dublin, held in 1853 had a large furniture section, housing eighty-three exhibitors, few of whom are known today. One sideboard, made by Patrick Beakey & Hugh McDowell of 39 Stafford Street in Dublin should be readily identifiable: 'A large mahogany

197

4.53a

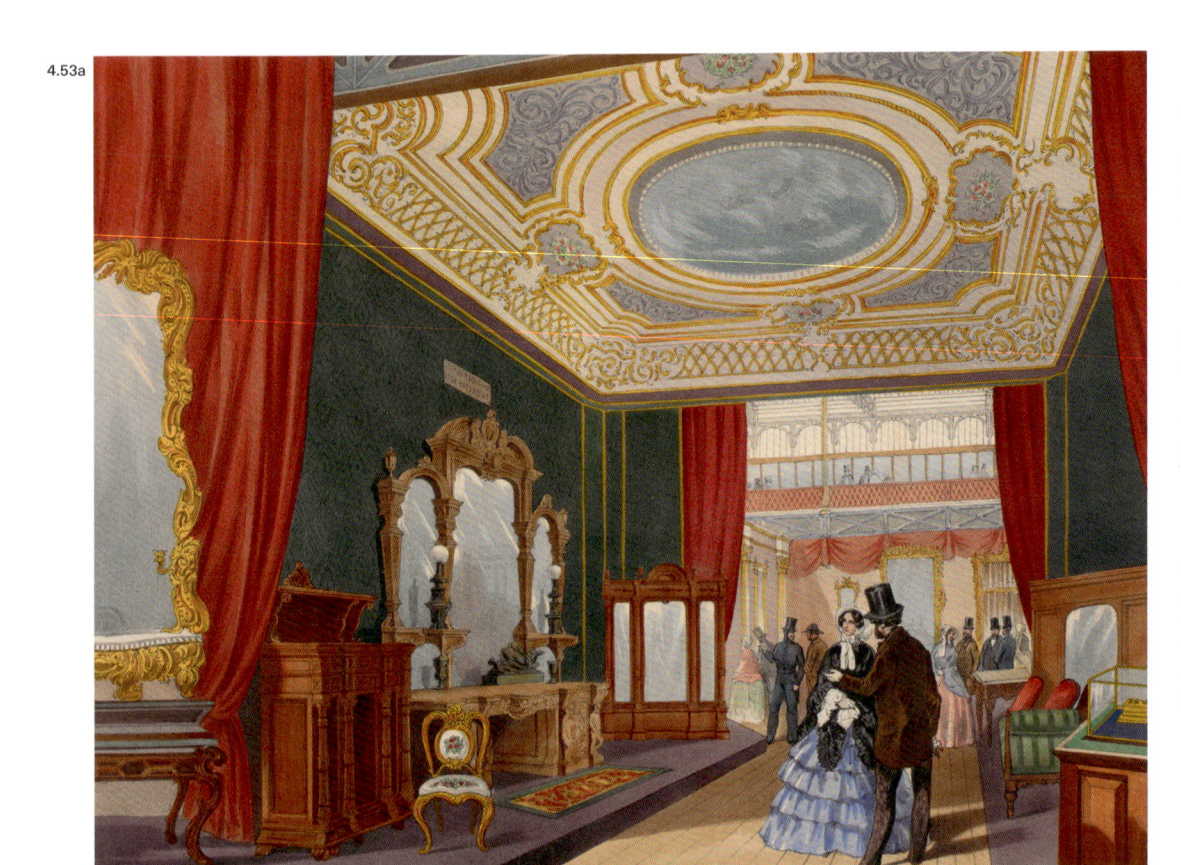

4.53b

Fig. 4.53a The Jackson & Graham stand at the 1851 exhibition. The mirrored sideboard is made from 'British oak' to a design by Alexandre Eugène Prignot. It measures 12 feet high and 10 feet wide (3.7 × 3.1 metres), the figures representing the seasons, hunting and fishing. [Alamy / British Library]

Fig. 4.53b Jackson & Graham had expanded rapidly since their establishment in 1836 and were the exclusive London outlet for the prestigious bronze foundry of F. Barbedienne of Paris whose ebony and bronze cabinet dominated their stand. [© Victoria and Albert Museum, London]

Fig. 4.54 Not as remarkable as mainstream exhibition furniture, this pair of tables in the French Louis XV manner is more typical of English commercial firms. By the little-known maker John Isaac Hicks of Mayfair, the maker could well have remained anonymous except that auction records show that they were acquired direct from Hicks's descendants. [Butchoff Antiques]

Fig. 4.55a This bureau, jewel cabinet and occasional table, made in London in the French style, exhibited by Levien in 1851, are at odds with his more familiar work. All three pieces are of a type supplied to Baldock by George Morant and it is possible Levien had purchased the three pieces from the auctions of Baldock's stock in 1843. [*The Illustrated London News*, 17 May 1851, p. 427]

Fig. 4.55b Similar or identical to Fig. 4.55a, this jewel cabinet in the Royal Collection, veneered in tulip and kingwood, may have been purchased by Prince Albert for Queen Victoria in 1846. [Royal Collection Trust / © His Majesty King Charles III 2023]

4.54

4.55a

4.55b

sideboard… representing Peace and Plenty… a large looking glass at the back, in a carved frame, representing England, Ireland, and Scotland'.[66] Most of the Dublin exhibitors were Irish, including James Egan and Jeremiah O'Connor of Killarney whose arbutus suite, loaned by the Earl of Eglinton, was made from 157,000 pieces and 'executed at his factory'.[67] O'Connor had exhibited at the 1851 exhibition in London and a year later in Cork. In 1858 the Prince of Wales visited Killarney and bought one of O'Connor's tables, and a cabinet and a davenport were presented to Queen Victoria in 1861.[68] Killarney furniture comprises numerous pieces of small parquetry inlay set with images of local flora and fauna. This type of furniture is very distinctive, in many ways similar to Tunbridge Ware from Kent. Arbutus, grown in the Killarney area of south-west Ireland, is a whitish close-grained wood which yellows with age. Killarney furniture is profusely inlaid, often with marquetry of important houses such as Muckross Abbey, Muckross House, Glena Cottage, or Ross Castle. Other local timbers were used, such as holly, sycamore, laburnum, maple and yew.

As well as the quintessential Irish Killarney Ware, other items were shown at the exhibition made of local timbers including bog oak and bog yew. Robert Strahan & Co., self-styled as 'Designers and Manufacturers', of 24 Henry

Figs 4.56a&b A variation of the jewel casket shown in Figs 4.55a & b made by an unknown hand. The chevron-veneered tulipwood, crossbanded in kingwood, is French in style, but the construction and the type of lock confirm the English manufacture.
[Butchoff Antiques]

Fig. 4.57 Queen Victoria's private Retiring Room at the 1851 exhibition, with button-upholstered seat furniture in the 'Old French' style, often used as a term by contemporaries for an eclectic mix of Louis XIV and Louis XV fashions. The sprung chairs have exaggerated 'hips' to the thin cabriole legs.
[© British Library Board. All Rights Reserved / Bridgeman Images]

Street, Dublin, exhibited furniture in walnut as well as in Spanish mahogany, a term used for the larger mahogany logs from Santo Domingo. They also showed a rosewood 'marchioness', a form of furniture presently unknown, presumably a conversation seat for the centre of a drawing room. The firm of Robert Strahan was founded in 1776 (only closing in 1969) and they exhibited in London in 1862 and again in Dublin in 1864. A carved rosewood table by the firm is shown as **Fig. 2.15**. English contributions in Dublin in 1853 included a full suite of drawing room furniture comprising nineteen pieces in walnut from Francis Styan of Chester Street in Birkenhead. Some names are familiar, although contributions from T. Nixon of Kettering and Ruddle of Peterborough, firms now unknown, included deal furniture which cannot now be identified. Better known is Samson Wertheimer of 35 Greek Street in Soho, a maker and dealer who exhibited a range of furniture and objects in the *cinquecento*, Louis XIV and other styles. Wertheimer is credited as a maker of Boulle-style furniture – 'it is costly' and the pieces are 'either copies or imitations of old work'.

The commentator Bevan also noted, not in reference to Wertheimer, that 'A spurious kind of Boulle is made with composition in place of the tortoiseshell'.[69] Jackson & Graham were emerging as regular and much respected exhibitors. In Dublin in 1853 they exhibited a sideboard applied with still life carvings of fish and game and the innovative feature of corbels, to support oil lamps.

Whereas elaborate and monumental furniture as exemplified by the Prignot cabinet, (**Fig. 4.63a**) has come to typify the mid-nineteenth century on both sides of the Channel, it borrowed from the scale and sculptural full-relief wood carving of seventeenth-century Baroque. Cast iron, the material used for the main frame of the 1851 'Crystal Palace', was also used for furniture. The deerhound table, now at the Coalbrookdale Museum of Iron in Shropshire, is the zenith of the genre, **Fig. 4.62a**. Supported by four life-size deerhounds with heads proudly raised, their collars painted with the coat of arms of Hargreaves of Broad Oak, near Blackburn, the table weighs just over 812kg (1,790lb). Designed by John Bell (1811–1895), it was made in 1855 for the Paris Exhibition

Fig. 4.58 **The Great Industrial Exhibition in Dublin opened on 12 May 1853.** [Courtesy of the Wellcome Collection]

Fig. 4.59 **A quintessential piece of Killarney marquetry furniture, the top with a view of Muckross Abbey, inlaid onto an arbutus wood ground.** [Bonhams]

Fig. 4.60 **A mahogany campaign chest by Gregory Kane, a specialist maker working in Dublin between** *c.*1829 **and** *c.*1888. [Christopher Clarke Antiques]

and retains most of its original cold-painted decoration. The top is painted to resemble marble, the deerhounds gilt, their muzzles gently rubbed over the years. Although Coalbrookdale is the best-known cast-iron furniture maker, other foundries tried their hand such as the fire-grate makers Stuart & Smith from Sheffield who exhibited an elaborate cast-iron hall table at the 1862 exhibition in London, cast with putti amongst foliage.

The Morant and Baldock style of porcelain-mounted furniture, inspired by the French fashion of the 1760s and 1770s, was waning in popularity by the 1850s. A more innovative approach can be seen on the cabinet on stand in a Renaissance style made for the 1855 exhibition by Holland & Sons, **Fig. 4.66**. Ebony veneered, it incorporates a brightly coloured contrasting porcelain plaque copying William Mulready's *Crossing the Ford* of 1842, the porcelain painted by George Grey. The cabinet was designed by the Dresden architect Gottfried Semper, who, in 1852, had been appointed by Henry Cole as a lecturer at the Government School of Design at Marlborough House. The stand is supported on lion monopodia similar to the work of the Paris foundry of Ferdinand Barbedienne but by the less well-known but important Paris foundry of Charles Matifat, who charged £75 for the castings. The cabinet, which had cost £237 to make, did not find a buyer at the exhibition and was purchased by the South Kensington Museum in 1860 for £200. Holland's exhibited furniture in various styles in Paris. In a heavy, almost Norman-inspired Elizabethan style, the architect and chromolithographic artist James Kellaway Colling designed a library suite for the firm, comprising a

Fig. 4.61 **The cast-iron table designed by John Bell as exhibited by the Coalbrookdale Iron Company in Paris in 1855.** [© RMN-Grand Palais (domaine de Compiègne) / René-Gabriel Ojéda]

Fig. 4.62a **One of the four life-size cast-iron deerhounds looking up longingly in an obedient stance. Each has a collar painted with the coat of arms granted to John Hargreaves of Broad Oak.** [Ironbridge Gorge Museum Trust]

Fig. 4.62b **Provincial makers were well represented at the exhibitions in the 1850s. The Coalbrookdale Iron Company made the main gates for the 1851 exhibition, and in 1855 in Paris exhibited this cast-iron centre table, weighing 812kg (1,790lb), the painted faux-marble top supported by four life-size deerhounds.**[70] [Ironbridge Gorge Museum Trust]

library or pedestal desk, chairs and bookcase in oak inset with malachite and Irish marble, **Fig. 4.64**.

Although cabinet-making skills were of equal proficiency on both sides of the Channel, in the early exhibition era British furniture makers lacked the necessary design skills. Jackson & Graham were one of the first to recognise this need and employed Alexandre Eugène Prignot as their principal designer from 1849 to 1855. For Prignot, as for his former master Henri-Auguste Fourdinois, London was a safe haven while Paris went through the political upheavals of 1848, which ended the reign of Louis-Philippe. Prignot's career illustrates the international nature of the mid-century furnishing trade as he worked in the United States, Belgium, Russia and Spain as well as Britain. One of the most significant examples of Victorian luxury furniture is the monumental cabinet designed by Prignot for Jackson & Graham, exhibited at the Paris *Exposition Universelle* of 1855 and purchased new by the South Kensington Museum for £2,000, **Fig. 4.63a**.[71] The cabinet was a *tour de force* of production. No less than forty designers, modellers, cabinet makers, carvers, gilders and metal chasers worked on the cabinet. This overtly French taste was a dominant factor in British furniture design from a revival of the elaborate Rococo in the 1820s and the love for the Baroque of 'Louis Quatorze'. The direct purchase of such an important cabinet from exhibition to museum has left a wealth of detail about the piece, which is so often sadly lacking in furniture records. Originally the porcelain plaques were ordered from Sèvres in Paris but 'after a most unbusiness-like delay', Mintons of Stoke-on-Trent were asked to complete the order.[72] The porcelain plaques were painted by a Mr Grey, of Marlborough House,[73] after designs by Messrs Remon and Polish. The castors were by Cope & Collinson, whose stamp is frequently seen on original brass castors throughout the Victorian period. The Birmingham firm of Elkington, Mason & Co. made the mounts, cast in brass and then electro-gilded. Despite being a brass alloy, this type of mount, once gilded and adorning furniture, is universally called 'gilt-bronze'. According to a report, a list of the names, designers, cabinet makers and other crafts people was given to the *Furniture Gazette* in 1886 but the editor seemingly failed to publish them![74]

Fig. 4.63a **The 1855 Paris-exhibition cabinet, made by Jackson & Graham to a design by Alexandre Eugène Prignot, incorporating Minton ceramic plaques, electroplate mounts by Elkington & Co., the castors by Cope & Collinson.** [© Victoria and Albert Museum, London]

Fig. 4.63b **The cabinet at the 1855 exhibition in Paris.** [© Victoria and Albert Museum, London]

4.64

4.65

4.66

Fig. 4.64 One of many exhibits sent to Paris in 1855 by Holland & Sons. This desk and chairs are in an eclectic Norman-inspired Elizabethan style, the design by J.K. Colling. [George Wallis, *The Exhibition of Art-industry in Paris*, 1855, p. 4]

Fig. 4.65 A 'walnut-tree couch' by Jackson & Graham in a fully blown pneumatic Rococo Revival style. [*The Illustrated London News*, 2 August 1851, p. 157]

Fig. 4.66 Made by Holland & Sons for the 1855 Paris exhibition, Professor Semper charged £25 for the design, the Arcadian setting of the porcelain panel painted by George Gray at a cost of £15 15d 0s. [© Victoria and Albert Museum, London]

Such exhibition furniture was (almost) always lavishly praised; Matthew Digby Wyatt described the Jackson & Graham cabinet as, 'good in composition and highly satisfactory in every detail of design... The interior is finished with as much care as the exterior, being of satinwood inlaid with tulipwood and the fronts of the drawers inlaid with ivory and panelled, the panels being fitted with finely-chased and gilded metal-work'. In 1855 Wyatt commented on the firm's use of steam machinery. Other firms using steam-powered saws and veneer cutters included Hollands and Seddon & Co.[75] Prignot published photographic anthologies of his furniture designs which were influential in Europe and Russia as well as in the burgeoning new market of the United States. Unlike many of his contemporaries, Prignot continued to design furniture in the same vein seemingly for the rest of his career, as can be seen in two drawings of attenuated Baroque form in the Cooper Hewitt Museum in New York.[76]

Jackson & Graham also exhibited Rococo-style furniture at the 1855 Paris Exhibition, in contrast to their avant-garde furniture of the late 1860s or early 1870s. An example of a relatively early piece by Jackson & Graham is a 'walnut-tree' three-seater couch, similar in outline to hundreds of extant examples but richly and extravagantly carved, **Fig 4.65**. Another *dressoir* by the firm was praised for being 'a beautiful frame for the potter's art set'.[77] Wyatt considered Jackson & Graham's Louis XVI-style cabinet 'the first really noble piece of cabinet maker's work, the figurative carving by Claudio Colombo'.[78]

Britain's growing global reach, aided by the success of the 1851 exhibition, meant that the demand for British furniture continued to grow at home and abroad. At home, despite the appalling infant mortality rate, the population expanded;

more people were living in towns and the industrial classes were becoming wealthier. Publications of furniture designs were an increasingly useful tool for retailers, to inspire their designers and potential clients. An influential publication was *The Cabinet-Maker's Assistant* published by Blackie & Sons in 1853. With some sixty pages of technical drawings and a comprehensive list of woods commonly used in British cabinet making, there were also a considerable number of line drawings of furniture designs. Many were in the Rococo style, and it would appear that some pre-dated the Great Exhibition, borrowing, for example, from Richard Bridgens and other designers of the previous generation. Helped by the distribution of printed designs, the inventiveness of the mid-century seemed to know no bounds and drew on a wealth of home-grown and international sources. The preface to *The Cabinet-Maker's Assistant* concluded that 'Any workman who would attain to any eminence in his trade ought to possess a competent knowledge of Drawing…' and eighty pages followed on how to achieve such heights.

The design of the so-called credenza shown here, **Fig. 4.70a**, is a development from the French *commode à l'anglaise* or *à encoignures* although this style of cabinet in France in the 1780s was of Neoclassical form, such as those made by Martin Carlin and Claude-Charles Saunier. The unidentified English maker here has followed the prevalent fashion for the Rococo, with a concave top and doors divided by notional cabriole 'legs' adorned with gilt-bronze foliage. This form of cabinet, with many variations, was adapted in France and Britain in the second quarter of the nineteenth century, for example a credenza of exaggerated pneumatic form, exhibited by Smee of Finsbury Pavement in 1851.[79]

Furniture made for Windsor Castle makes a welcome but rare appearance on the open market. The amboyna-veneered tip-top circular table, **Fig. 4.71a**, was originally in one of a suite of bedrooms at Windsor, de-accessioned from the Royal

Fig. 4.67 Dining chairs often had turned legs, the Louis XV-style cabriole leg considered suitable for parlour chairs. This pair, from a set of four, are similar to work by Henry Wood, of Percy Street, London, who styled himself 'a decorative draughtsman'. He illustrates a similar chair in an 1848 Supplement 'Plates for Berlin Woolwork'. [Private collection]

Fig. 4.68 The finely figured walnut of this card table in the Louis XV style is contrasted with the rich green baize when open. The top has beautifully matched blackened grain veneered in two halves, unlike French tops which would more commonly be quarter-veneered. [Butchoff Antiques]

Fig. 4.69 Regularly found on fire and pole screens, it is rare to find Berlin woolwork mounted on case furniture. The form of the cabinet is common enough, the addition of the back panel suggests the piece was specially made to accommodate the lady of the house's needlework. [Tew Archive, Christie's © 1987]

4.70a

Figs 4.70a & b **Veneered primarily in kingwood and Circassian walnut, the top and apron of this so-called credenza are inlaid with foliage using a variety of specimen woods. British designers of the Victorian age had an increasing interest in plant forms and the science of botany was a continuing obsession in the mid-century.** [Butchoff Antiques]

4.70b

Collection in *c.*1953. Stamped 'Holland & Sons', there is also the Windsor brand mark for Room 243 and the inventory date of 1866. Not surprising for a royal purchase, the table displays the finest London cabinet-making skills of the mid-century. The parcel-gilding on the highlights, especially the Vitruvian scroll below the fluted baluster, is of a very high quality and is on wood, despite the appearance of being made of gilt-bronze. By the 1860s, Holland's refined the central fluted baluster support of this model and added a cluster of three or four slender fluted columns.

The use of veneers continued to be an important feature of British furniture making, for example on the kidney-shaped desk, **Fig. 4.74**. Termed 'A Kidney Table' by Sheraton, it has always been a popular model and was revived in the 1830s–1840s. In his 1803 *Cabinet Directory*, Sheraton wrote 'some are made for writing and reading at with piers

BRITISH FURNITURE

4.71a

4.71b

Figs 4.71a & b **Left:** The use of expensive imported amboyna veneer and the parcel-gilt decoration sets this Royal table by Holland & Sons at the top echelon of 1850s furniture. **Right:** The 1866 branded inventory mark on the table. [Private collection]

Fig. 4.72 Elaborately inlaid in trailing flowers on a well-figured walnut ground, this unusual centre table is a rich reimagination of the French Louis XV style as interpreted by British firms. [Raby Castle, County Durham]

Fig. 4.73 The Louis XVI style was becoming popular by the late 1850s. This detail from a library table veneered in walnut with gilt-bronze mounts is in the style of Holland & Sons. [Butchoff Antiques]

Fig. 4.74 An extremely fine kidney desk in carefully chosen, well-figured burr walnut. The addition of gilt-bronze mounts is a passing reference to the popularity of French taste. The reverse with open shelves adds to the sense of luxury. It is stamped by the retailer James Winter but may well have been made at Gillows by John Barrow. [Apter-Fredericks]

Figs 4.75a & b The underside of this ladies' sewing table, of exhibition quality, has the inked stencil mark of Morant & Boyd, a trading name the firm used between 1851 and 1859. [Butchoff Antiques]

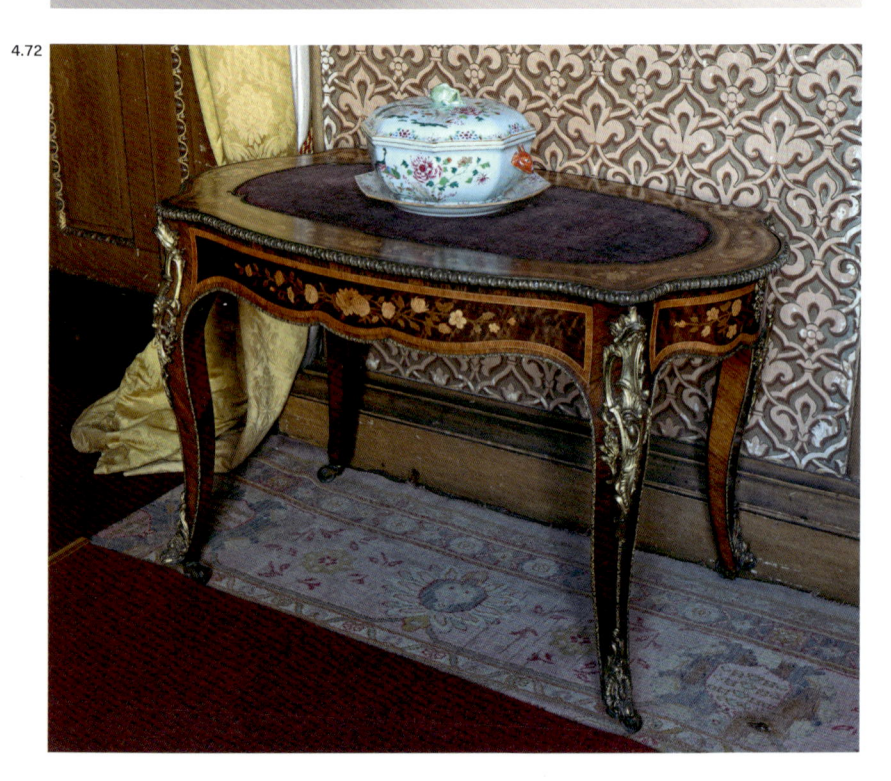

of drawers at either end. Others are made for ladies' work tables with only a shallow drawer at the top'. The shape continued to be popular throughout the nineteenth century, more often in walnut in the mid-century, but by the late 1870s, with an eye to the revival of the Sheraton-style, veneered in satinwood. Although in the style of Gillows, the illustrated example is not signed by the maker. The Chubb locks are an aid to the date of manufacture, beautifully stamped with the consecutive numbers 196333-7, which date the manufacture of the locks to February 1849. The desk is similar to one stamped by Gillows which is fitted with Bramah locks. Under the central drawer is the pencil inscription of John Barrow, the son of a Liverpool cabinet maker. John Barrow's name appears in the Gillows records between 1834 and 1848.[80] Sheraton used the term 'piers' for the stack or tier of five short drawers at either side. Although frustratingly rarely signed, furniture of such exceptional quality can be attributed to a variety of firms. In 1868 Holland & Sons supplied a walnut-veneered desk of similar form, also with a brass gallery, to R.N. Thornton for his house in Sidmouth, at a cost of £27 10s.[81]

Although not signed, the detail of the table legs, **Fig. 4.73**, is typical of the work of Holland, who were beginning to explore the Louis XVI style. In contrast, the pretty and

CHAPTER 4: 1850S

4.73

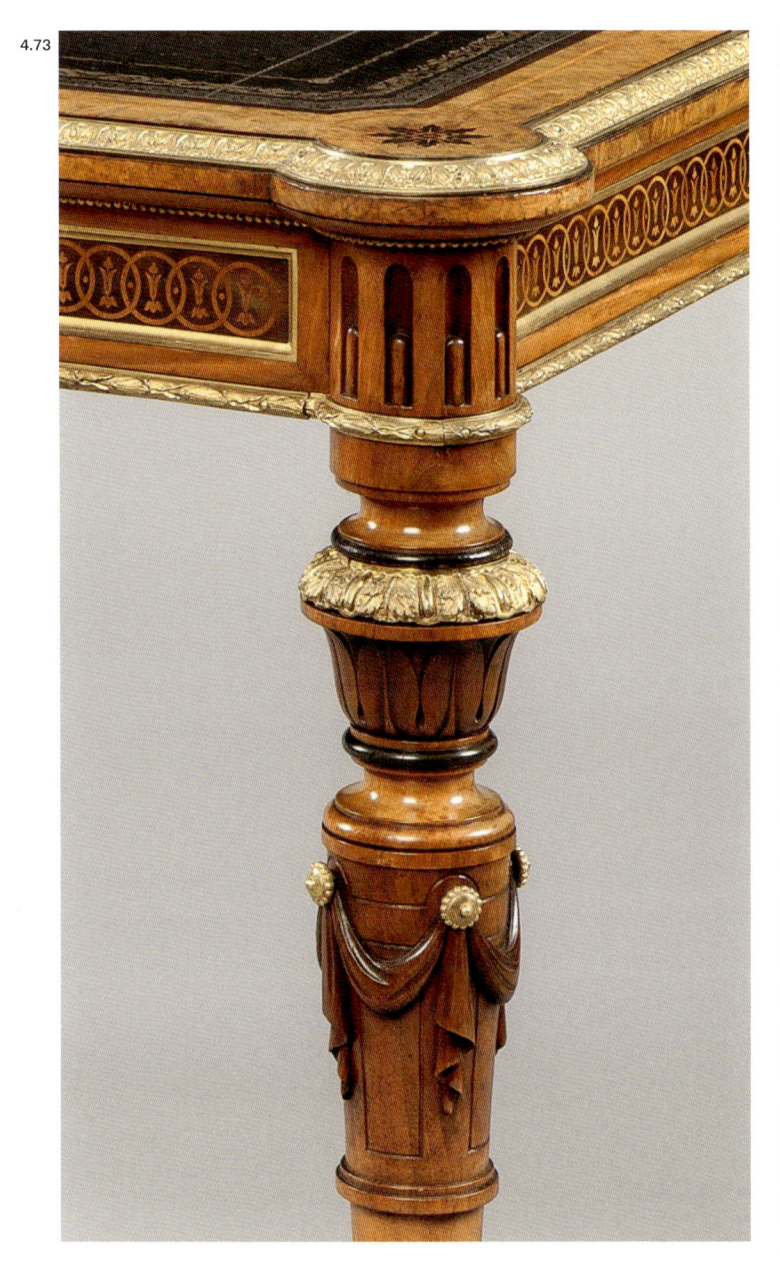

4.75a

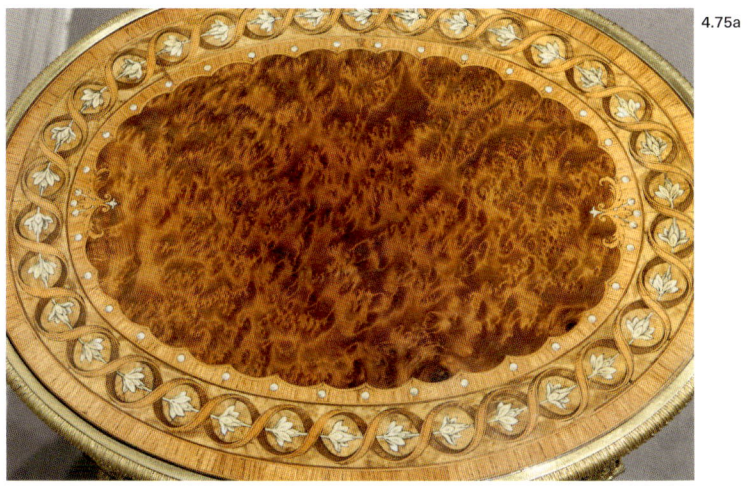

4.75b

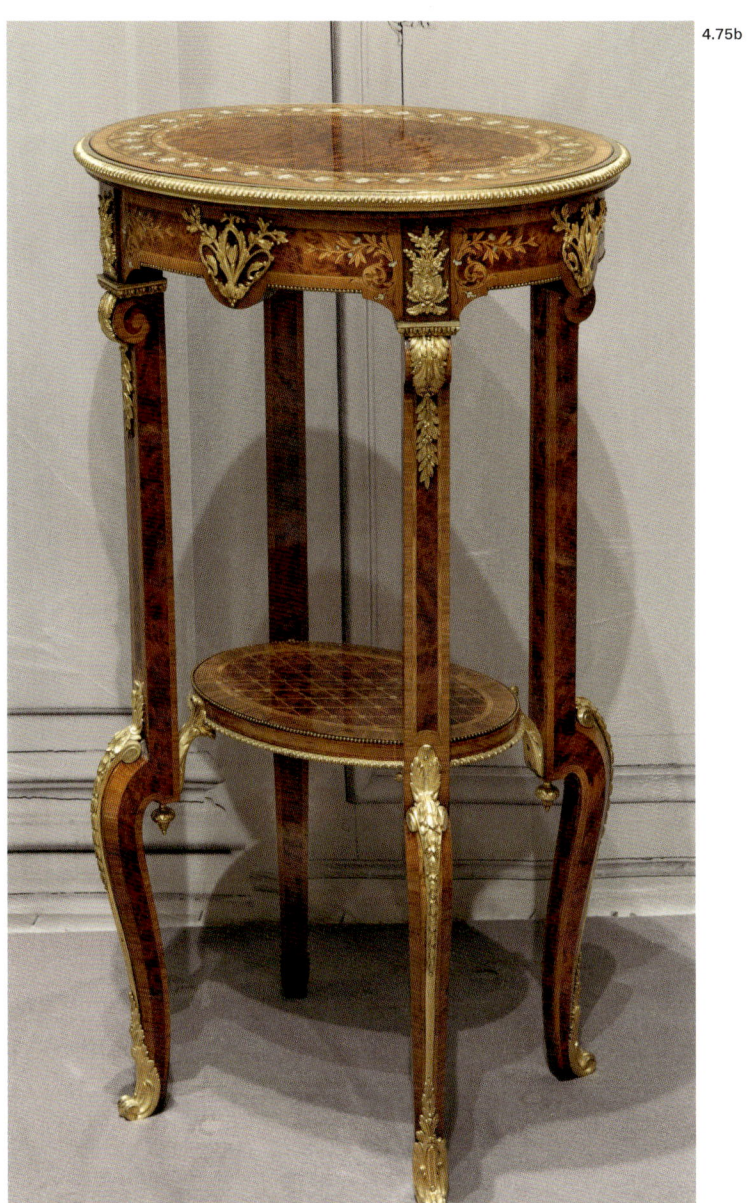

4.74

4.76a

Figs 4.76a & b Musical instruments are inlaid amidst a foliate spray into a veneer of Circassian walnut on this unusual table made in the French Louis XV style. The interior is cedar-lined; the locks simply stamped 'VR' for *Victoria Regina*, little help as to the date of manufacture, or the maker. [Butchoff Antiques]

CHAPTER 4: 1850S

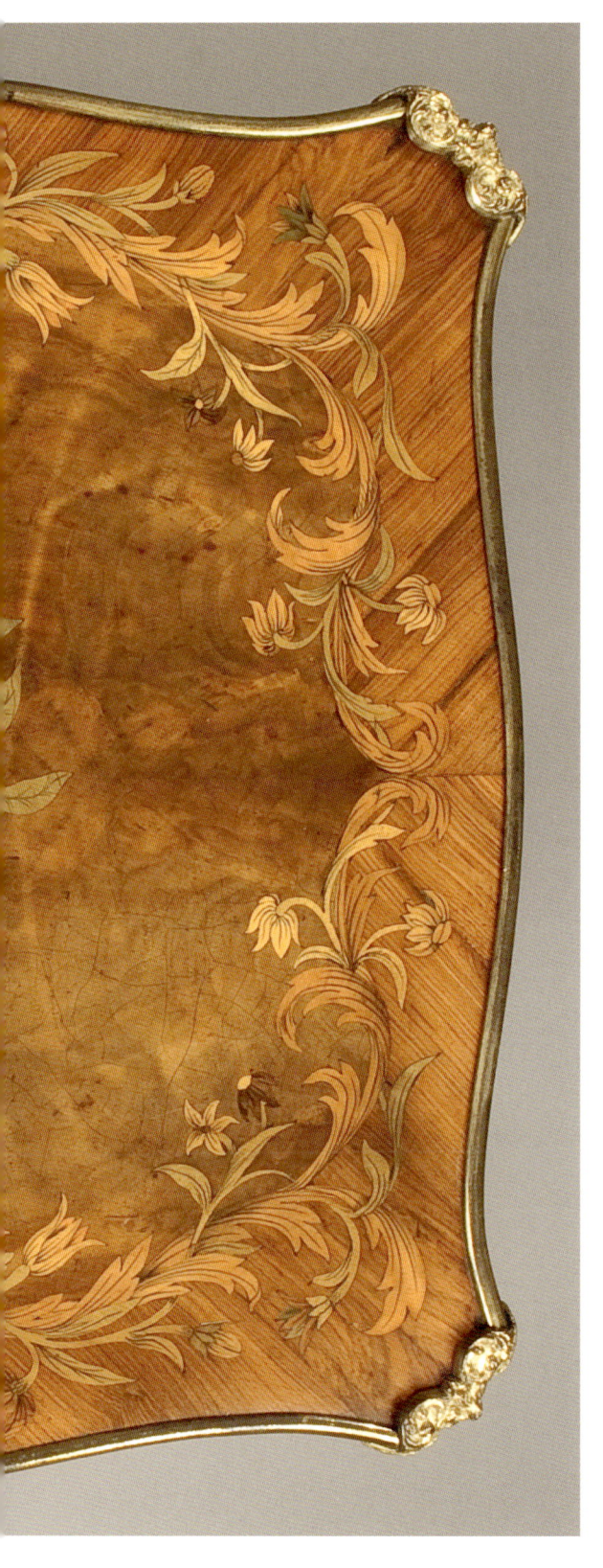

4.76b

211

delicate Louis XV-style ladies' work table, **Fig. 4.76a**, is inlaid with *ancien régime* Rococo-style flowers and musical instruments. The exceptional ladies' sewing table, **Fig. 4.75b**, is a good example of the revival of the French Transitional style, defined by straight upper legs leading to an exaggerated short cabriole lower section. Although at first glance it may appear to be French, the English maker has raised the stretcher to make it 'float'. Of exhibition quality, the construction and marquetry inlays are of the finest that can be found amongst London makers at the time, a quality that would be expected of the eminent royal supplier, Morant & Boyd, whose stamp is underneath. Otherwise difficult to attribute, this specific trading name was used between 1851 and 1859 helping historians and collectors to date the table neatly within the decade.

Simple, robustly made furniture in the Gothic and medieval styles continued to be popular and has always remained a niche market. The oak table designed by A.W.N. Pugin for Horstead Place in Sussex for Francis and Arentina Blanchard, **Fig. 4.78**, is delightful in its simplicity. As a precursor to the techniques of construction adopted by the makers of Arts and Crafts furniture, the distinctive X-frame legs of the table are held together by wooden dowels or pegs which are left in full view, a style of joinery in continuous use since medieval times. Pugin's simple furniture, in the Arts and Crafts ideal showing constructional details, is encapsulated in a simple circular table designed in 1854 by George Edmund Street for Cuddesdon College, near Oxford.[82] Philip Webb

Fig. 4.77 **A chair designed by E.W. Pugin in 1858, this example was made in 1864 for the Pugin family home, The Grange. C. & R. Light reprinted similar designs in 1881.** [© Victoria and Albert Museum, London]

Fig. 4.78 **Designed in the early 1850s by A.W.N. Pugin and made by John Webb during the period 1852–53 for Horstead Place in Sussex, this oak table has structural details that were adopted by the Arts and Crafts makers a generation later.** [© Victoria and Albert Museum, London]

Fig. 4.79 **Horstead Place in *c*.1860, the owners at the time, the Blanchards, turning as they walk towards the front door.** [© Victoria and Albert Museum, London]

Fig. 4.80 **A watercolour by James Roberts of the Drawing Room at Balmoral Castle, dated September 1857.** [Royal Collection Trust / © His Majesty King Charles III 2023]

joined Street's influential architectural practice in 1852 and William Morris joined the practice in 1856.

Pugin's table is similar to those made by John Webb for the House of Lords. Webb, a dealer, was a middleman for J.G. Crace who made many pieces in the Gothic style, to Pugin's designs.[83] The Renaissance was also of interest to the inveterate dealer Webb. He was the driving force for the purchase of the antiquarian collection formed by Jules Soulages in the 1830s and 1840s. Amongst the illustrious subscribers who were willing to guarantee the purchase of the collection in 1856 were several cabinet-making firms, including that of Webb himself, Holland & Sons, Trollope, Jackson & Graham, Crace, Gillows, Johnstone & Jeanes, Morant and Spiers of Oxford.[84]

Still only eighteen, Edward Welby Pugin tried to complete commissions that had been left unfinished after his father's untimely death, aged forty, in 1852. His furniture is more ornate than his father's, more French-influenced and without the effortless architectural strength championed by his father. Various London firms such as Crace, Gillows, Holland & Sons and Howards adapted Pugin furniture designs by father and son, in the late 1850s and early 1860s. Pugin's ubiquitous side chair designed for the House of Commons was made in a variant form from the 1850s by firms such as Hindley & Sons.[85] In 1881 C.R. Light published line engravings of 1850s Pugin-style furniture, perpetuating the Gothic style well into the 1880s.

Luxury furniture of the decade was rich and extravagant with a wide experimentation of forms and styles. In quiet contrast the furniture at Balmoral has a timeless quality with a feeling of comfort and light. Prince Albert bought the estate in 1852 and it only took two years to build and furnish the new castle. On 7 September 1855 Lady Augusta Bruce, lady-in-waiting to the Duchess of Kent, noted work by Hollands in the as yet unfinished castle: 'The general woodwork is light coloured, maple and birch chiefly, with locks and hinges etc. silvered, and the effect is very good…'. The duchess returned later that day to find that Holland's men had finished everything.[86] The watercolour by James Roberts (**Fig. 4.80**) shows a light and airy room with distinctly Scottish overtones. Pale woods and silver-plated mounts were used. The side cabinets were made for Queen Victoria and Prince Albert for the Drawing Room at Balmoral in 1855 by Holland & Sons.[87]

COPIES OF FRENCH FURNITURE COMMISSIONED IN LONDON IN THE 1850S AND 1860S

Nineteenth-century copies of over 120 different models of eighteenth-century French royal and aristocratic furniture have now been recorded, most made in Paris.[88] There were few makers in Britain who undertook such work and English cabinet makers who made direct copies of French furniture are not well documented. Basic differences in construction and metalwork techniques between the two countries were first published in 1981.[89] Paris-made copies are frequently signed but few English copies are attributable with any certainty to an individual firm or maker and it is rare for them to be signed. The term 'English' can be narrowed down, as these copies appear to have only been made in a handful of London workshops that were capable of creating furniture to the high level of elaboration achieved by their Parisian contemporaries. This is not a question of skill. Many makers in British urban centres were highly accomplished and were as skilled as their French counterparts, but few had the correct training or emotional and cultural heritage to copy French models with unfailing exactitude. A few of the top London makers were able to employ French craftsmen; the political uncertainties of the revolutions of 1830 and 1848, as well as the Paris Commune of 1871, ensured a steady supply of skilled French labour seeking security in London.[90]

The most comprehensive group of English copies came about as a result of an extraordinary commission by the 4th Marquess of Hertford, a wealthy English aristocrat and Francophile who lived mainly in Paris.[91] Hertford was a keen buyer of important French *ancien régime* furniture and wanted copies of pieces that were unlikely, or never, going to appear on the art market. There is no known single impetus behind the commission. The exhibition held at Gore House in 1853 appears to have been the ideal opportunity for Hertford to commission replicas. The catalogue which accompanied the exhibition, *Specimens of Cabinet Work*, lists the exhibits and the lenders' names, but without engravings or photographs. It was the first retrospective exhibition of French furniture held in England in the nineteenth century and pre-dated any such retrospective in Paris, for example the *Musée rétrospectif* of 1865.[92] In total, 112 objects were loaned to the exhibition, sourced mainly from eminent collections such as those of Queen Victoria, the dukes of Buccleuch, Northumberland and Hamilton, and the industrialist Sir Charles Mills. The exhibition was clearly intended as an exercise in education: the catalogue preamble stated that 'Persons are privileged to make Drawings and Sketches'. Hertford made good use of this privilege, no doubt primarily intended for the use of students. He wrote to his agent in London, the picture dealer Samuel Mawson, asking him to have accurate and detailed drawings made of a number of pieces of furniture. On 11 June 1853 Hertford

Fig. 4.81a One of the four known copies by Blake of the Duke of Hamilton's Boulle commode, the model that had been delivered for Louis XIV's bedroom at the Trianon in 1708–9. The first recorded copies were by Blake in London, with later examples made by various Paris makers. [Sotheby's]

Fig. 4.81b The name 'Blake' on the underside of one of the paw feet on the copies of the Trianon commodes suggests that the Blakes were responsible for the bronze master models sent to the foundry for casting. [Linke archives]

wrote from Paris: 'You might do me a great service & oblige me very much. You know there is at present an exhibition of works of art at Gore House. I should very much like to have drawings made of some of the principal & the most beautiful articles of furniture not of the middle ages but of the time of Louis XIV, XV & XVI especially the fine Cabinet by Gouthières [sic] sent by the Queen...I should like these drawings to be most accurately made...with exact dimensions. The ornaments very carefully copied...Of course you will not mention that the drawings are for me...large & distinct enough to be...used if I...have anything made from them'.

A postscript asked for confidentiality, the Marquess saying 'I am under the rose'.[93]

In total, Hertford had sixteen replicas of French *ancien régime* furniture made, seven in London and nine in Paris. Not all had been at Gore House. Six were in the Boulle manner, five were copies of Louis XV furniture, four were copies of Louis XVI royal chests of drawers, and one was a copy of the comtesse de Provence's jewel cabinet made by Jean-Henri Riesener, **Fig. 4.83a**. Two comprehensive articles about the commission have been written, one during the period 1910–11, and the other in 1987.[94] Hertford was an intimate of Napoleon III at a time when the French imperial family and the English royal family were in close accord. The relationship between the two men must have been an advantage in getting permissions to measure the furniture from the imperial collection and to make moulds of the bronzes. In 1852 the Minister of State at the Tuileries wrote to the *Intendant* at the Palace of Fontainebleau requiring him to allow the founder Crozatier to 'draw and mould fragments of ornamentation that the Marquess of Hertford wishes to have reproduced for himself alone'.[95]

The most significant of Hertford's copies to be made in Paris was the copy of the *bureau du Roi* from Versailles, which remains in the Wallace Collection.[96] The work on the desk has traditionally been attributed to Carl Dreschler, the master *bronzier* in Charles Crozatier's foundry. Crozatier died in February 1855 and it is unclear exactly when the desk was made. As *bronziers*, Crozatier and Dreschler would have had to employ a highly skilled cabinet maker and marquetry cutter to make furniture to this exemplary standard.[97] A further copy by Henry Dasson was shown at the *Exposition Universelle* of 1878, and several other copies followed. By the 1890s, Hindley & Sons of London were claiming to have made one 'in their own workshops' (see Chapter 8 – 1890s).

Gore House was a golden opportunity to obtain copies of objects in British collections. Hertford was in touch with an English dealer in Paris, Edward Rutter, who in turn passed the English commission to John Webb in London. Webb's account, starting from December 1855, listed seven

Fig. 4.82 **The Front State Room at Hertford House, showing the copy of the Boulle cabinet lent by Sir Charles Mills to Gore House in 1853. This and its companion were probably made by Blake in London.** [Wallace Collection / Bridgeman Images]

copies of pieces from Gore House. Fortnum recorded that Hatfield 'the bronzist' 'made copies for the firm of Webb & Forrest of the Strand' and it is probable that Hatfield's were responsible for most if not all of the bronze mounts for this commission.[98] Four of the replicas were listed on an invoice of 1857, the total cost of all seven pieces, including packing and carriage, coming to £6,340.[99] The most expensive by some margin was the so-called 'Gouthières [sic]' cabinet, **Fig. 4.83a**. At £2,500, it was just over three times the cost of each of the other copies. The relative value in modern-day terms is almost impossible to compute realistically, but it could be estimated to be £2–4 million.[100] An interesting contemporary comparison is with the 13.7 ton bell for Big Ben, which cost £2,401 to make in 1859. In contrast, second-hand or 'antique furniture' often cost significantly less, for example, a small fall-front desk, or secretaire, made in the 1780s by Adam Weisweiler cost Hertford only 400 guineas in 1856.[101]

Whereas Hertford saw the furniture exhibited in Paris at the *Musée rétrospectif* in person, he did not travel to London

Figs 4.83a & b **The unique copy of the jewel cabinet made for the comtesse de Provence by Riesener in 1787. Ordered by the Marquess of Hertford from Rutter in *c.*1853, it was the most expensive of the copies, invoiced by Webb at £2,500. The English cabinet construction combines with the very finest bronze work, virtually indistinguishable from the original.** [Sotheby's]

In January 1854, Rutter wrote to Hertford to inform him of the progress of four of the copies that were being made under Webb's supervision in London: 'I now beg to offer for your inspection 4 (inserted) Photographs taken very cleverly from each of the Originals, two from the Duke of Hamilton's Commode front and back, one from Her Majesty's Cabinet, and one from the Duke of Beccleuch's [*sic*] Bureau'. He added 'and am happy to inform you that they are progressing rapidly'.[104] He anticipated that the pair of chests of drawers, or commodes, after the model Boulle delivered to Trianon in 1708, would be ready 'about the beginning of March next, the pair of Clock Bureaux…about the month of July next', and that the jewel cabinet would be ready 'about the end of the year, there being in the latter a tremendous quantity of most difficult work'. There is no known record of an estimate for the copies and it would appear that Hertford had ordered them regardless of cost since, at the end of the letter, Rutter wrote that he was hoping 'to be able to shortly inform you of what will be about the cost of the five pieces of furniture'.

Hertford had asked for drawings but producing copies in such a manner, however skilled the draughtsman and accurate the work, would not have achieved the required precision. In a significant letter of 11 December 1853, he wrote to Mawson: 'Many thanks for having had the drawings completed…I hope that it [the cost] will not be very considerable for I find, between you & I, that some dealers we know, have had the fine things of this collection *surmoulé* so they will be able to obtain perfect copies & from drawings it is impossible'. To make such complex furniture accurately from drawings alone would seem an improbable task, and five days later Hertford wrote: 'By what I have heard, between you & I, I am certain that complete casts have been taken of some of the things, *shape & all*'.

to see the exhibition at Gore House. Rutter sent him a group of photographs, almost certainly a selection of those taken by the South Kensington Museum's photographer, Charles Thurston Thompson.[102] This is an early and fortuitous use of the new medium of photography; in the 1850s Prince Albert became a keen advocate and collector of photography, and he, along with Queen Victoria, became patrons of the Photographic Society in 1853.[103] Instead of exhibiting the furniture again, the images were used at the Manchester Art Treasures Exhibition, opened by Prince Albert on 5 May 1857. The exhibition attracted more than 1.3 million visitors.

4.83b

Hertford's intelligence was correct. Casts had been taken. In 1854, a report was published by the Department of Science stating that 'seventy casts were taken from the furniture lent to the department last year, and exhibited at Gore House'.[105] This highly significant information, previously unpublished, finally explains the mystery of how these and subsequent copies are as good as they are. To copy the woodwork is a relatively straightforward task for a trained cabinet maker. However, to copy three-dimensional mounts accurately is almost impossible without being able to take them off and make plaster or gelatine moulds. The knowledge that seventy gilt-bronze mounts were removed and casts made explains the extraordinary quality and exactitude of Hertford's copies. Although no record has been found as to who made the casts of the master models, examples inscribed 'Blake' may be the key. However, Blake is unlikely to have had a foundry sophisticated enough to make the finished gilt-bronze mounts. The Hatfield family were a prominent London foundry, brass chasers and ormolu workers. Their connection with John Webb would have made them the natural choice for the Blakes to send their precious master models to for casting.

The 11th Duke of Hamilton loaned to Gore House, along with other furniture, his single example of the Trianon chest of drawers.[106] It is unknown whether Hertford knew that Boulle's chests of drawers were originally made as a pair, but he ordered a pair for himself. A further pair appeared on the market in the twentieth century, **Fig. 4.81a**. They are not recorded as having being ordered by Hertford but are clearly linked to this commission. Each of the four is discreetly signed 'Blake', referring to the family of buhl-cutters and cabinet makers, on the undersides of the single handles fitted to their top drawers. Significantly, the names appear to be engraved after casting, while the letters 'A', 'B', 'C' and 'D' are cast into each handle. These letters correspond to the carcasses of the chests of drawers. Some of the mounts have the Blake script signature on the underside, **Fig. 4.81b**. The construction of all four pieces is unmistakably English, but it includes, unusually, drawer linings in walnut, a wood more commonly used in French eighteenth-century cabinet work.

Most of Hertford's copies were not thought to be an essential part of the Wallace Collection when bequeathed to the nation in 1897. As a result, they became the property of Sir John Murray Scott, secretary and advisor to Sir Richard (heir to Hertford's collection) and Lady Wallace, before being sold at auction in 1913. The catalogue contains two significant entries. Lot 292 was 'A Pair of Boulle Coffres-Forts - 48 in. wide...with two drawers...boldly chased winged female busts...tops of veined red marble slabs'. They were bought by Pawsey & Payne for £147 and were surely the pair made by Blake for Hertford. Lot 294 was 'A Pair of Boulle Cabinets – 50 in. high, 57 in. wide...the centre of each fitted with a door which encloses four drawers and with four drawers on either side...the angles enriched with small panels enamelled in blue, in emulation of lapis-lazuli'.[107] These were the copies of another Boulle piece,

Fig. 4.84a **The companion copy to the Elector of Bavaria's desk in the Wallace Collection is in the Casa-Museu Medeiros e Almeida in Lisbon. Exceptionally, it is stamped 'J. Webb' in large letters on the underside of the apron.**
[Casa-Museu Medeiros e Almeida]

a cabinet on stand exhibited at Gore House, also ordered by Hertford in 1853, **Fig. 4.82**. They were bought by the dealer A. Wertheimer for £199 10s.[108] Much of the Murray Scott legacy, also comprising a substantial part of Hertford's property at 2 rue Laffitte, was bequeathed to Lady Sackville, who subsequently sold it to the dealer Jacques Seligmann. Many of these works of art were sold in the United States by Seligmann during the early years of World War I. According to Seligmann's son, Germain, 'The first private collector to see this collection while it was still at rue Laffitte was Henry C. Frick'.[109]

Two of the Blake copies of the Trianon chests of drawers are now in the Frick Collection.[110] The pair, 'C' and 'D', were bought by Henry Clay Frick through the dealer Joseph Duveen in 1916.[111] 'A' and 'B' sold at auction in London in 1990.[112] The sequential lettering suggests that all four were made at the same time. The detail is such that the walnut drawer linings of all four chests of drawers, on the evidence of visual examination, were all made from the same section of tree.

The pair of copies of 'architectural' Boulle cabinets, one shown in the Front State Room at Hertford House, **Fig. 4.82**, were listed at £1,470 on Webb's invoice to Hertford. The inscription on the Thompson photograph erroneously stated that the original had been lent to Gore House by Queen Victoria but the owner was Sir Charles Mills of Camelford House in Mayfair, a wealthy banker and avid collector of French eighteenth-century furniture. The Hertford copies and subsequent examples are of unusual proportions, copying the low plinth of the Mills cabinet instead of being raised on a stand, as conceived by Boulle. One original Boulle cabinet is in the Hermitage and a second is in the Duke of Buccleuch's collection at Boughton House, and both are on tall, later, stands but a third cabinet with its original stand is in a private collection.[114] Although no Blake signatures have been found on the undersides of the mounts of the Hertford copies, it is probable that the Blakes were involved with them. The model was later reproduced in Paris in 1869 by Charles-Guillaume Winckelsen and again by his sucessor, Henry Dasson, in 1880.[115] It is interesting to note that no nineteenth-century maker appears to have ever made stands in keeping with the Boulle original concept.

Webb continued to supply copies of Boulle furniture after the Hertford commission. Referring to the furniture at Alnwick Castle, the Duchess of Northumberland noted that around 1870 'the four Buhl cabinets in the salon, as well as the 2 marquetrie [sic] cabinets in the drawing room, were made for us in Paris under the instructions of Mr. John Webb of Bond Street', and that 'Mr

Fig. 4.84b **The underside of the apron of the Elector of Bavaria's desk in Lisbon is stamped twice 'J. Webb'.**
[Casa-Museu Medeiros e Almeida]

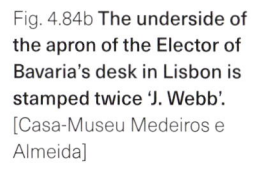

Fig. 4.84c **One of the copies made for the 4th Marquess of Hertford. The reverse of the desk, now in the Casa-Museu Medeiros e Almeida, is a unique variation, being expensively veneered in Boulle marquetry. This example was kept by Hertford in Paris, it is probable that, unlike the Wallace Collection version, it was originally intended to be freestanding.**
[Casa-Museu Medeiros e Almeida]

Webb also undertook the table, which was making for so many years under his supervision' (see **Fig.5.92**). A letter at Alnwick Castle in the Northumberland Archives is another clear link between Blake and Webb.[116]

The Hertford copies that can be directly linked to Webb are described in the all-important account of 1855–1857, sent by Webb from 22 Cork Street to 'The most Honble. The Marquis of Hertford KG': 'To two very fine Commodes in Buhl [sic] and black shell richly mounted with ormoulu [sic] and Griote [sic] Marble slabs for Do. shaped & moulded £650'. These are the Blake Trianon chests of drawers. The marble slabs vary in shape and moulding on the copies from the originals. Another entry on the account describes 'To two fine Boule [sic] Cabinets of Architectural taste of the finest period with drawers on each side and a Door in the Centre enclosing drawers etc etc the whole comprised of black shell & ebony and richly ornamented with finely chased & gilt mounts etc etc £1470', the 'step top' model shown in **Fig. 4.82**.

Three other objects were included on the Webb invoice: two copies of the Elector of Bavaria's writing table, made c.1715 for Maximilian II Emanuel by Bernard I van Risenburgh, and a copy of the comtesse de Provence's jewel cabinet.[117] Webb was still pressing for the balance three years later, writing on 5 July 1858 that 'I am now induced to trouble you with this because at the moment I am rather in a corner for want of some funds'.[118] The Webb invoice shows that Hertford paid £1,650 for the pair of writing tables. Importantly, he chose to have a slight alteration made – he had his own coats of arms set on both copies instead of copying the enamel plaques of the original, which bore the arms of the Elector of Bavaria. The clock movement was made in England, by Peter Saphin of London. Only one copy of the Elector of Bavaria's writing table remains in the Wallace Collection today.[119] The second, now in the Casa-Museu Medeiros e Almeida in Lisbon, **Fig. 4.84a**, is stamped 'J. Webb' in large letters under the apron, **Fig. 4.84b**.[120] The Lisbon example is more elaborate, and certainly would have been more expensive to make, as the back is completely veneered in Boulle marquetry, **Fig. 4.84c**, whereas the Wallace version has a plain oak back, not intended to be seen. Like the Trianon chests of drawers signed by Blake, the drawers are lined with walnut. The writing table now in Lisbon was left to Sir John Murray Scott by Sir Richard Wallace. The original had been in the collection of the dukes of Buccleuch and lent to the Gore House exhibition.[121]

The jewel cabinet copied from the model made by Riesener was by far the most expensive of all the Hertford copies. The original had been made for the comtesse de Provence in 1787, confiscated by the Revolutionary Government in 1793 and later offered to Napoleon

Fig. 4.85 **The Furniture Court at the 1862 International Exhibition, showing on the right a Buhl-marquetry Rococo writing desk, a Boulle side cabinet and a Boulle-style console table commissioned from Toms & Luscombe by the 2nd Earl of Craven. Also visible is a rectangular marquetry centre table exhibited by Litchfield & Radclyff.** [*The Illustrated London News*, 27 September 1862, p. 352]

Fig. 4.86 **Possibly the 'Buhl' desk exhibited at the 1862 International Exhibition in London by Toms & Luscombe, at 230cm wide (90½in), this large desk is one of several that are known of this model, some brass-inlaid, others in wood veneer. Made in the Louis XV Revival manner, it is the same form as the pair supplied by Baldock to the Duke of Buccleuch in 1831, Fig. 2.57, based on a French, or possibly German, eighteenth-century example.** [Butchoff Antiques]

Bonaparte by *Femme* Aulmont in 1809.[122] However, the emperor declined to buy it, as he preferred to buy a new jewel cabinet, and it was sold out of France. It was subsequently purchased by George Watson Taylor, who was forced to sell much of his property, including the cabinet, at auction in 1825, where it was bought for George IV for 400 guineas.[123]

On his invoice, Webb described the copy of the cabinet as 'a magnificent cabinet of Mahogany with stand & stretcher, elegantly and elaborately ornamented with ornate decoration after the one at Windsor Castle…2500'. The construction of the cabinet, as with all the furniture copied for Hertford under Webb's supervision, is typically English and the cabinet maker has not attempted to copy the box-like technique used by Riesener. Similarly, the insides of the drawers show English quarter mouldings and their dovetails are not exact reproductions of the joinery used on the original cabinet. However, the accuracy of the complex gilt-bronze castings is extraordinary and, if indeed the mounts were made in London, shows that London makers were equal to their Parisian counterparts when money was no object. During a recent comparative examination of the original cabinet and the Hertford copy it was possible to measure and compare the mounts; the Hertford mounts are accurate to 0.01 of a millimetre. Even by taking moulds using modern computerised techniques, it would be difficult, due to shrinkage, to achieve such a small reduction in the size of the mounts of a copy. The mahogany veneers on the cabinet are also extraordinary for their close and minutely detailed comparison with the original panels.

Copies from Hertford's collection of French eighteenth-century furniture are known to have been made later in the nineteenth century when loaned by Sir Richard Wallace to an exhibition at the Bethnal Green Museum between 1872 and 1875 (see **Fig. 9.78**).

The first time copies of French *ancien régime* furniture were exhibited was at the 1862 International Exhibition in London; all the examples appear to be London-made. One

4.85

4.86

Fig. 4.87 It is probable that these copies of early eighteenth-century Boulle furniture, both made as pairs and exhibited at the 1862 International Exhibition by Toms & Luscombe, were made in England by émigré craftsmen. [J.B. Waring, *Masterpieces of Industrial Art & Sculpture at the International Exhibition*, 1862, pl. 252]

of the best-documented firms was Toms & Luscombe who exhibited copies of furniture by André-Charles Boulle. Part of their commission from the 2nd Earl of Craven is shown in the engraving, **Fig. 4.85**. The firm had exhibited furniture in the French style at the Great Exhibition of 1851, for example 'A pair pedestals in buhl and ormolu and pair of tulipwood stands and cabinets ornamented with china and ormolu'.[124] The 1852 census recorded that Toms & Luscombe employed in their specialist workforce two buhl-cutters.[125] The firm had written to Lord Hertford in 1857 with a bill for a 'pair of Buhl Cabinets'. Adding no further details, they wrote 'We are sure the Cabinets will be found to be all your Lordship could wish' and that they would keep them for as long as necessary, presumably until he could arrange for their collection.[126] It is possible that the cabinets supplied to Hertford were the same model as those made for Lord Craven and exhibited in 1862. Hertford's pair is most probably the two that are today at Treasurer's House in York,[127] having been sold in the 1913 dispersal sale of part of Sir John Murray Scott's furniture.[128] The model is similar to a French mid-nineteenth-century version by Befort of Paris, again copying the Boulle style. Fine copies of the highest quality, the York examples have mahogany backs and central panelled muntins with beading to hold the panels, suggesting that they were made in England, although elements of the construction suggest a probable émigré hand. A single cabinet was shown by Toms & Luscombe at the International Exhibition, alongside a Boulle-style writing desk, almost certainly the desk shown in **Fig. 4.86**.[129] In 1860, Lord Craven had engaged William Nesfield, a leading Gothic Revival architect, to make substantial alterations to his house at Coombe Abbey. One might ask whether Craven had heard about, or even seen, the pair of cabinets made for Hertford by Toms & Luscombe, and ordered a pair for himself.

Boulle created his oft-copied console table, shown here in a version by Toms & Luscombe, **Fig. 4.87**, in 1701 when he supplied a smaller version to the young Duchesse de Bourgogne at the Château de la Ménagerie. Two similar eighteenth-century tables attributed to Boulle are in the Wallace Collection, dated *c*.1705.[130] The copy is reasonably similar to these.[131] Only if it were possible to examine the drawer construction and substrate timbers of the Toms copies could it be ascertained whether such a piece was made in Paris or London. An unlikely possibility is that Toms & Luscombe were merely retailing the table and cabinets.

Two low side cabinets were exhibited at the International Exhibition by Philippe and Adam Dexheimer, **Fig. 4.88**. The small cabinet featured a marquetry panel, while the larger cabinet was fitted with *pietre dure*. The height of such cabinets became an increasingly important factor for retailers during the mid-nineteenth century, as it was desirable for them to be low enough to allow for paintings to be displayed above. Without inspecting the construction, it would be impossible to be sure if the Dexheimer cabinets were made in London or Paris, as the firm of Dexheimer Frères was based in both cities. The best clue would be the style of locks; in France, they were typically double throw and ran the full height of doors, which was not the case in England.

It is often difficult to be precise as to when exactly competent English copies of French eighteenth-century furniture were made. Often described as 'second half of the nineteenth century', or 'third quarter of the nineteenth century' by dealers and in sale catalogues, much of this furniture could easily have been made at the very end of the 1890s, or even in the early twentieth century.

It is believed that the large Buhl-marquetry desk shown in **Fig. 4.86** was the actual example exhibited by Toms & Luscombe at the 1862 International Exhibition, where the firm was awarded a medal for 'Buhl cabinets and tables for good design and workmanship'.¹³² Variants of the desk appear in the inventories of Clandon Park and Bowhill House. The Bowhill pair are discussed in Chapter 2, **Fig. 2.57**, and, dating from 1831, appear to be the first examples of this model being reproduced.¹³³ A number of examples of this very large desk are known, rarely in Boulle marquetry.¹³⁴ A pair of rosewood-veneered examples are in the collection of the Earls of Normanton at Somerley House, purchased from Toms & Luscombe in 1871. A further example was purchased from Wright & Mansfield by the 7th Viscount Powerscourt for his house in County Wicklow. *The Illustrated London News* was unconvinced about the Toms & Luscombe exhibits but 'The workmanship, however, is in all cases of great excellence; and the ornament, considered part from the work, is of a very high order.'

Fig. 4.88 The Parisian firm of Dexheimer Frères opened a premises at 124 Wardour Street in 1862 and exhibited in London the same year. [J.B. Waring, *Masterpieces of Industrial Art & Sculpture at the International Exhibition*, 1862, pl. 138]

Fig. 4.89 The Rothschild desk, thought to be the original model, first copied with variations by Baldock for the Duke of Buccleuch in 1831. Sold at auction in 1937, titled 'Catalogue of the Magnificent Contents of 148 Piccadilly'. [*Catalogue of the Magnificent Contents of 148 Piccadilly, W.1*, 1937, lot 259, pl. XLI]

CHAPTER 5

1860s

*'Never was there a year...in which so much has been done,
and such vast huge progress made.'*
The Times, 1 January 1861

*Crowds gather round the cabinet-work of a Fourdinois, a
Roux, or a Grohé, a Jackson & Graham, a Crace, or a
Wright & Mansfield.*[1]

As in the 1850s, exhibitions had a profound influence on English furniture design in the 1860s. Two exhibitions in particular, the International Exhibition held in London in 1862 and the *Exposition Universelle* held in Paris in 1867, helped disseminate a wide variety of furniture styles and forms, some old, some new and innovative. The London exhibition was held on the site of what is now the Natural History Museum in South Kensington. The death of Prince Albert in December 1861 cast a shadow over the event and, unlike in 1851, Queen Victoria did not attend the opening ceremony. The building costs were £300,000, paid in part out of profits from the Great Exhibition of 1851, and, despite *The Art Journal* referring to it as 'a wretched shed holding marvels of art', the building and materials were reused to build the Alexandra Palace, which opened in 1873. Although a somewhat underwhelming exhibition in comparison to the 1851 extravaganza, there were many successes in 1862 with over 6 million visitors.[2] The acclaim of the exhibition spurred Eugène Rouher, a prominent French statesman, to form an exhibition committee, Prosper Mérimée believing that 'the results of the Exposition prove, that if rapid progress is not made in France, we will quickly be outstripped by our rivals'.[3]

The catalogue of the British Section of the 1867 exhibition lists the number of manufacturers engaged in London in 'the several branches of the fancy furniture trade':

Cabinet-makers 812
Upholsterers 486
Carvers and gilders 342
French polishers 142
Cabinet carvers, inlayers, and liners 108
Bedstead-makers 43
Chair, sofa and stool-makers 252

In 1865 wood and cabinet wares to the value of £289,887 were exported, against imports of £128,925.[4]

The contrast of furniture styles presented at the exhibition must have been quite startling – a revival of Georgian and painted medieval styles were seen for the first time alongside a continuation of Gothic. Some, such as Crace, exhibited in a Gothic idiom, which, arguably, had not changed since his success at the Crystal Palace in 1851.

In *Our Mutual Friend* (1862), Charles Dickens describes Mr and Mrs Veneering as 'bran-new people in a bran-new house in a bran-new quarter of London. Everything about

Fig. 5.1 (opposite) **Exhibited in 1862, this chromolithic print of a parcel-gilt, home grown pollard oak and Italian walnut cabinet by the Manchester firm of James Lamb shows sculptural figures of Wine and Harvest by Hugues Protât, to a design by W.J. Estall.**
[J.B. Waring, *Masterpieces of Industrial Art & Sculpture at the International Exhibition*, 1862, pl. 243]

Figs 5.2a & b 'Royal clutter' – Two hand-coloured photographic views of the Duchess of Kent's Drawing Room at Frogmore House, taken in 1861. [Royal Collection Trust / © His Majesty King Charles III 2023]

the Veneerings was spick and span new. All their furniture was new…'.[5] Despite Dickens's mockery, the demand for new furniture ensured a steady and ever-increasing trade for cabinet-making firms. As in 1851, exhibitors in 1862 were from all over Britain, many from the industrial north, which had started to flex its financial and manufacturing muscles. An example is Lamb of Manchester, a fast-growing furniture-making enterprise, which had to satisfy rapidly expanding demand. Established by James Lamb around 1840 at 16 John Dalton Street,[6] with workshops a ten-minute walk away in Castle Street, their stand exhibited the sophisticated, but almost outdated, oak, walnut and parcel-gilt cabinet, **Fig. 5.1**. Lamb, certainly aware that Jackson & Graham had employed the French designer Prignot on the cabinet they exhibited in Paris in 1855, turned to the Parisian modeller, Hugues Protât, and the English designer, W.J. Estall, to work on the cabinet.

Far from being provincial, by the end of the decade James Lamb was aware of the designs of other makers such as Charles Bevan and Bruce Talbert. Talbert also designed for the Manchester firm of Dovestone, Bird & Hull between 1862 and 1865, moving to London in 1866 where he worked for Holland & Sons. The following year he was awarded a silver medal for his reformed Gothic furniture, and he subsequently designed for Gillows. Trained as a neo-Gothic architect, Talbert saw 'little difference between interior and exterior architectural décor'.[7] Another northern maker was Marsh, Jones & Cribb. Although not recorded at the 1862 exhibition, the small satinwood side cabinet, **Fig. 5.3**, bearing their pre-printed and handwritten label is of exquisite quality and demonstrates that northern firms were more than capable of making furniture to the highest standards. This appears to be an early revival of the use of plaques, similar to work exhibited by Wright & Mansfield in 1862. The Marsh, Jones & Cribb label states the craftsman's name, 'Nicholson', and the job number, '47963', written in ink. Marsh Jones took over from the Leeds cabinet maker John Kendell in 1863, and records show a Kendell chest of drawers of c.1840 is numbered '16320'. A later Marsh Jones label with the date 1895 is numbered '73195'.[8] Mounting Wedgwood plaques in furniture had a long history. In the 1790s, George Seddon ordered medallions from Wedgwood for furniture decoration, and Sheraton commented on the use of Wedgwood plaques for this purpose: 'In the freeze [sic] part of the commode is a tablet in the center [sic]…These are to be had, of any figure or on any subject, at Mr. Wedgewood's [sic]'.[9]

Thomas Knight of Bath was another firm in the top echelon of provincial makers, showing great flexibility of design and craftsmanship. For the 1862 exhibition, Knight made an oak pedestal desk, the small drawers on the upper part set in the Italianate manner with coloured semi-precious stones, **Fig. 5.5**. It was purchased by William Preston of Ellel Grange, a house largely furnished by Gillows, with Jackson & Graham responsible for much of the interior decoration, including a massive pollard oak buffet, which cost £200 in 1864. A 1979 image shows Gillows' later alterations to the base of the desk, changing the drawers to cupboard doors with the addition of a brass upper gallery.[10] A collection of designs in the Victoria and Albert Museum show that Knight of Bath were not confined to the 'traditional', but also made a robust and unconventional armchair of a distinctive style.[11]

CHAPTER 5: 1860S

Fig. 5.3 **A paper label pre-printed 'MARSH, JONES, AND CRIBB (late Kendell & Co.)', on the back of this side cabinet suggests that it dates to the 1860s, soon after the firm took over from John Kendell. The inclusion of a Wedgwood plaque was most famously used by Wright & Mansfield.** [Nan Xu]

Fig. 5.4a **A polychrome** *pietre dure* **marble table exhibited in 1862 by Samuel Birley of Ashford-in-the-Water, Derbyshire. English makers inlaid the hard stones into a solid marble slab, unlike the Italian makers who cut marble into a thin veneer.** [© Victoria and Albert Museum, London. V&A Museum number 157&A-186]

Fig. 5.4b **The design for the Birley table was by J. Randall.** [© Victoria and Albert Museum, London. V&A Museum number. E.304-2011]

227

BRITISH FURNITURE

Fig. 5.5 **An individually designed oak desk, the central panel set with malachite, cornelian, lapis and serpentine** *pietre dure*, **shown by Knight of Bath at the 1862 exhibition. Two years later, the purchaser, William Preston, had the lower section altered by Gillows.** [*The Art Journal Illustrated Catalogue of the International Exhibition*, 1862, p. 205]

Figs 5.6a & b **The designer of this simple but highly decorative pair of cabinets has contrasted the bright colours of the lithographs with the mellow indigenous timber of solid maple.** [Carlton Hobbs LLC]

The firm made furniture after designs by, amongst others, one of the foremost avant-garde designers, Christopher Dresser. His 1862 publication, *The Art of Decorative Design*, was an important landmark, and he became a highly influential designer of decorative arts.

The prize-winning inlaid marble table exhibited in 1862 by Samuel Birley at the 1862 exhibition is shown alongside the original design by a J. Randall, **Figs 5.4a & b**. It is a fine example of the Derbyshire 'imitations' of Florentine *pietre dure* originally made for the Medici family. The English makers of Derbyshire and Devon inlaid their coloured marble into a solid marble top, akin to the *champlevé* enamel technique, whereas Italian inlaid marble tops were veneered.[12]

Photography played a far greater role in documenting the 1862 exhibition than it had the 1851, with over four hundred stereoscopic black-and-white images taken. However, exhibition publications were still laden with precise engravings, including a limited selection of chromolithographs.[13] The superintendent of several galleries at the exhibition was J.B. Waring. His three-volume commentary, *Masterpieces of Industrial Art & Sculpture at the International Exhibition, 1862*, was printed by Day & Son, who had also published his 1851 catalogue. The deceptively simple maple cabinets, **Figs 5.6a & b**, are lined with colourful lithographs of various decorative items,

Fig. 5.7 This extraordinary and probably unique partners' desk by Howard & Sons in the Pompeiian style 'with winged creatures...in bronze richly gilt' was shown as part of a suite at the 1862 exhibition. [Butchoff Antiques]

Fig. 5.8 An engraving of the 1862 bookcase in the Pompeiian style, part of the Howard & Sons suite of library furniture. [*The Art Journal Illustrated Catalogue of the International Exhibition*, 1862, p. 57]

contained behind panes of glass on both the exterior and interior of the doors. Taken from Waring's *Masterpieces* the colour plates bring to mind the elaborate polychrome themes of the German-born French designer and architect Jacques Ignace Hittorff. The images include porcelain vases and plates by manufacturers such as Meissen, and those from Copenhagen, Berlin, St Petersburg and Paris, as well as English potteries. The grisaille sculptural figures of the interior of one cabinet are taken from Wyatt's *Industrial Arts of the Nineteenth Century* of 1851.[14] A comparison of the lithographs in the published volumes with those on the cabinets suggests that they were produced from the same plates. It is possible, therefore, that the cabinet originally belonged to the offices of Day & Son, who were closely associated with both Waring's and Wyatt's exhibition projects, allowing a practical piece of office furniture also to serve as tribute to the company's graphic output.

The widespread publication of discoveries made in the first properly regulated excavations at Pompeii, which began in 1860, prompted a revival of the Classical theme with a seemingly unique suite of furniture in the Pompeiian style exhibited by Howard & Sons in 1862. The desk is a rare and early example of Pompeiian influence, **Fig. 5.7**. Discreetly monogrammed on one cartouche 'H&S', for Howard & Sons, and with the exhibition date on the opposing side, it was designed by a 'Mr Vandale', described as an 'artist to the firm', as part of a suite of library furniture that incorporates the very latest fashion of 'Pompeiian' art. The *Art Industry* publication, *Furniture Upholstery & House Decoration*, an exegesis of the 1862 exhibition, illustrated and discussed the suite in warmly approving terms. The art critic George Yapp also wrote about the bookcase, admiring its 'mechanical arrangement'.[15]

The 1850s style of large, tall carved sideboards continued into the 1860s, a decade that otherwise was full of promise and innovative excitement. Two examples are shown here: one made in the capital, the other provincial, taken from Warings' *Masterpieces*, **Figs 5.9a & b**. Woodgate, a 'dealer in foreign China, ancient and modern furniture' of High Holborn made or retailed in a similar heavy style in the antiquarian taste.[16] These are seminal works, instantly recognisable as 'Victorian'.

Another continuation from the 1851 exhibition, alongside the Gothic theme, was the idea of the bounty of nature. The romanticised image of 'plenty' was manifested in a wide variation of large, profusely carved sideboards. Exhibiting a heavily carved sideboard decorated with game and/or fruit had seemingly been a rite of passage for British firms during the 1850s, but one that was soon to fade out of fashion. The wider availability and reduction in price of mirror glass allowed for the inclusion of large mirrors, usually held by carved crestings. A typical example can be seen in the line engraving of a light oak sideboard by Clement George & Son of London, the cresting carved with snakes devouring fruit and the lower panel hung with game, **Fig. 5.9b**.[17] An example by Jackson & Graham was a monumental sideboard using quarter-cut and pollard oak, 12 feet (3.6 metres) high and 10 feet (3 metres) wide, with freestanding figures of huntresses and children gathering the harvest. The carvings were later described by *The Furniture Gazette* as 'being emblematic of festal gatherings... attributes of the field, the forest, and the river...surmounted by the head of an otter'.[18] Engravings

Fig. 5.9a A line drawing of a large sideboard by John Steevens of Taunton. The report in *The Art Journal* commented on the fine skill of provincial carvers and described the cabinet as 'a remarkable work, considered as the production of a provincial town'. [*The Art Journal Illustrated Catalogue of the International Exhibition*, 1862, p. 244]

Fig. 5.9b The London firm of Clement George & Son designed this light oak sideboard in-house, 'the whole of their work and carving being executed by their ordinary workmen'. [*The Art Journal Illustrated Catalogue of the International Exhibition*, 1862, p. 276]

in journals such as *The Illustrated News of the World* are a further invaluable source of visual information. Large sideboards were a must for grand and stately houses, the number and height of the shelves a sign of rank in medieval France. George Yapp wrote: 'An ancient dining-hall without some such *dressoir* to show off the family plate…is not half furnished'.[19] Made for the 2nd Marquess of Conyngham at Slane Castle, Fry of Dublin exhibited a mirrored sideboard and a pier-glass of carved and gilt lime wood in the medieval style for the Drawing Room. Lamb of Manchester's contribution was magnificently carved, in oak and walnut, partly gilt, with Classically clad women, representative of wine and the harvest, **Fig. 5.1**.

Very much in the tradition of the Kenilworth Buffet shown in 1851, the 'Robinson Crusoe' sideboard, made by Gerrard Robinson in 1857 and exhibited in 1862, is one of the finest examples of the genre, **Fig. 5.10**. Robinson, an eminent wood sculptor, made at least four large, elaborate oak sideboards and numerous individual panels and figures. He first experimented with the theme of Robinson Crusoe in 1857 with a crudely constructed sideboard, now in the Victoria and Albert Museum.[20] His pictorial sideboards depicted essentially British scenes. For the 4th Duke of Northumberland, he made the Chevy Chase sideboard between 1862 and 1867, **Fig. 5.11**. The carving immortalised Sir Henry Percy (1364–1403), known as Sir Harry Hotspur, in his struggle against the king.[21] Equally exuberant is Robinson's Shakespeare sideboard, also exhibited in 1862.[22] Another large sideboard depicted Derby Day at Epsom. The Laing Art Gallery in Newcastle has panels by Robinson carved with the story of Robert Burns's *Tam o' Shanter*, exhibited in 1862, as well as an intricately carved regal boar hunt. Robinson's employer, the thirty-five-year-old Thomas Tweedy, had been inspired by exhibits at the Crystal Palace in 1851 and exhibited the 'Robinson Crusoe' sideboard at the 1862 exhibition. It is fitting that Robinson, from Newcastle, should choose a subject for the sideboard and also a settee, such as the story of Robinson Crusoe. Sharing a name may have amused him but the Crusoe theme was particularly relevant to a northerner; Daniel Defoe is thought to have based his novel on the survival of Alexander Selkirk of Fife, a castaway from 1704 to 1709.[23] Inspired by Defoe's romantic story first published in 1719 and no doubt encouraged by his foreman at the time, Tweedy also exhibited a set of dining chairs, each with a triangular top-rail and a carved panel detailing part of Crusoe's survival. The suite included

CHAPTER 5: 1860S

Fig. 5.10 The highly acclaimed and popular 'Robinson Crusoe' sideboard made by Gerrard Robinson of Newcastle c.1862. [M.S. Rau Antiques]

Fig. 5.11 According to tradition, Robinson's Chevy Chase sideboard was never sent to Alnwick Castle. In the 1960s, it was at the Grosvenor Hotel in Shaftsbury where this promotional image was taken. [Author's collection]

Figs 5.12a & b Thomas Kendall of Warwick, a pupil of James Willcox, exhibited this Elizabethan-style screen and Louis XIV-style oak table in 1862. [*The Art Journal Illustrated Catalogue of the International Exhibition*, 1862, p. 109]

a companion settee with portrait medallions of both Crusoe and Man Friday, whose figures are used as somewhat unlikely supports for the settee, which is 2 metres (6 feet 5 inches) wide.[24] *The Art Journal* wrote: 'Few objects in the Exhibition attracted more attention than the Robinson Crusoe Sideboard...the carved panels picture leading incidents in the ever-famous story, they are exceedingly well executed and certainly the work merits the very general popularity it undoubtedly obtained'.[25]

Another virtuoso carver, Thomas Kendall, a pupil of James Willcox, took over his master's workshop in Warwick in 1859. His drawings show that he was an accomplished draftsman, favouring the Elizabethan revival. He exhibited an Elizabethan-style screen in 1862, designed for Brooke Evans in the previous year[26] and demonstrated his virtuosity in 1862 exhibiting an oak side or pier table in an overtly French Louis XIV style, **Figs 5.12a & b**. For Sir Charles Mordaunt at Walton Hall in Warwickshire, a house designed by Sir Giles Gilbert Scott, Kendall made a 26-foot-long (approx. 8 metres) dining table.

However, these beautifully made exhibition sideboards were not without their critics. With the benefit of hindsight, J.H. Pollen wrote in 1876: 'Excellent wood sculpture used to

231

be executed in England, from the days of Grinling Gibbon [*sic*] to those of Adam and the Chippendales, suited to the furniture then in fashion. I wish I could say that our furniture makers of today could easily, or did generally, command such talents. Ingeniously carved representations of animals and game on sideboards we sometimes see, but game "dead" in every sense'. Pollen preferred the work of French sculptors but felt that they were insufficiently trained to pass off the animals as 'realistic'. Still-life sculpture was carved by hand, but an increasing number of steam-driven carving machines meant that wood could be carved in low relief or in three dimensions by means of revolving cutters. Machine carving was essentially for repeat work, since once the master model was finished a machine could 'trace' the pattern in wood to make a duplicate. A juror in Dublin in 1865 and again in Paris in 1867, Pollen was '…acquainted with shops and dealers, private collectors, connoisseurs, of all nations; retaining an opinion that London was after all the best place for purchase, if you knew where to go. Hunting here and there, he was able to acquire easily many beautiful and valuable things.'[27]

Sideboards were not the only target for the woodcarver's chisel. Between 1872 and 1875, Robinson supplied a large carved chimney piece to the 3rd Earl Manvers for his Library at Thoresby Hall. Known as the Robin Hood chimney piece, it is carved with a stag at bay, in front of the thousand-

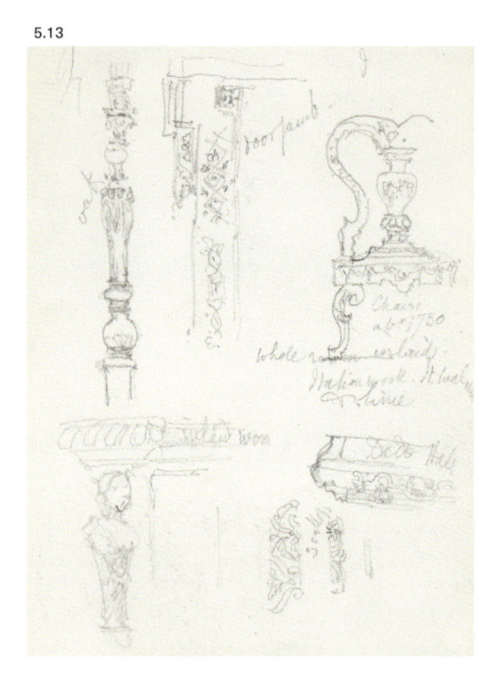

Fig. 5.13 A page from a sketchbook by J.H. Pollen noting eighteenth-century furniture and architectural details. [Bodleian Libraries, Pollen archive, uncatalogued MS.17906/26]

Fig. 5.14a This pair of carved walnut figures of Charles the Bold and John the Fearless were carved in Thomas Tweedy's workshops, possibly by Gerrard Robinson. They are typical of the historic revival in the mid-nineteenth century that was still in demand in the 1880s. [Private collection]

Fig. 5.14b The articulated visor of John the Fearless (Jean Sanspeur) probably carved in the Tweedy workshop by Gerrard Robinson. (Fig. 5.14a). [Private collection]

Fig. 5.15 Elaborately carved with roses, shamrocks and thistles – representing England, Ireland and Scotland – this large library table by an unknown maker, over 6½ ft (2m) wide, is unusual in solid walnut, a wonderful wood for the carver's chisel. The whole frieze is carved with lozenges representing Latin texts including 'fons et origo' (Source and Origin) and 'verb sap' (verbum sapienti, A Word to the Wise is Enough). [Butchoff Antiques]

year-old Major Oak in nearby Sherwood Forest. Robinson proudly printed an image of the chimney piece on his trade card. The walnut figures illustrated here are of two fifteenth-century dukes of Burgundy, John the Fearless and Charles the Bold, carved by Robinson and Thomas Tweedy, **Fig. 5.14a**. They represent a romantic genre greatly in vogue in the mid-nineteenth century, in which the use of idealised historic imagery was an important feature; a typical example is a canterbury made from the celebrated Herne's Oak, a tree felled in Windsor Great Park.[28] By tradition, the canterbury was made by the Hanover-born Heinrich Ludwig Goertz, or his son, who were upholders and cabinet makers to George IV, William IV and subsequently Queen Victoria. The date of 1863, the year the Prince of Wales married, is carved amongst Elizabethan-style strapwork and foliage. The initials 'WS', for William Shakespeare, appear opposite those of Queen Victoria and 'Bertie', the Prince of Wales. As well as making furniture from celebrated oak trees, many objects, mainly small artefacts, are reported to have been made from old buildings or vessels, such as Nelson's flagship HMS *Victory*. Such a provenance is often difficult to substantiate but the 'Windsor oak' event was corroborated in an article in *The Illustrated London News* in 1863.[29]

Design was increasingly the focus of attention. At the closure of the 1862 exhibition, the South Kensington Museum commissioned a survey, which found that '344 students, in the employ of 104 manufacturers, had been engaged on the works exhibited' and were alumni of the innovative South Kensington design school.[30] By 1862, there had been a steady increase in cabinet-making firms employing 'in-house' designers, such as Clement George & Son, who made the large mirrored sideboard shown in **Fig. 5.9b**. Others were better known makers, such as Gillows, Heals, Holland & Sons, Jackson & Graham, Seddon and Trollope.

Many high-quality and inventive items record no definitive maker, so the historian can only date and attribute on stylistic grounds. An example is the pair of cabinets attributed to Gillows, **Fig. 5.16a**. The cabinets, of hybrid Louis XVI shape but with Gothic-style brass fittings, are a true pair, the porcelain plaques are painted with the seasons represented as women in Classical dress, Spring and Winter on one, and Summer and Autumn on the other. Gillows also used large porcelain plaques on a side cabinet shown in 1862, supplied to J.D. Allcroft for his house at Lancaster Gate, **Fig. 5.37**. A physical clue to the maker is the distinctive slots hidden on the underside of the drawers to prevent splitting from shrinkage, a feature often seen on furniture by Gillows. The metalwork, especially the brass grilles, has similarities with work by the Birmingham metalworking firm John Hardman Trading Co. Ltd, which flourished between 1838 and 2008. Birmingham firms, large and small, had been major suppliers of metalwork since the time of Matthew Boulton in the eighteenth century. Hardman supplied metalwork to Crace, to Burges at Cardiff Castle and to many other major projects, including those led by the Pugin family.[31] The attribution to Gillows is strengthened by comparable metalwork being found on documented furniture by that firm.[32] The detailing of the cabinets is exceptional – the foliage on the frieze is in low relief, not marquetry. The parquetry side panels suggest the hand of a German-trained marquetry-cutter.

In 1862, the critic George Yapp described the English Court of the exhibition as 'solid, noble...not garish, not redundant in embellishment' and praised Gillows for their

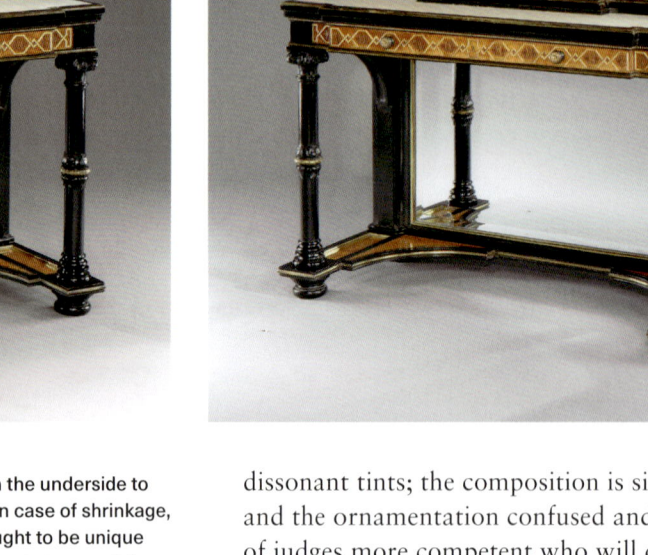

Figs 5.16a & b Although probably by Gillows, a definitive attribution as to the maker of this fine quality pair of cabinets remains unsolved. The drawers have the distinctive feature of slots hidden on the underside to prevent splitting in case of shrinkage, a detail once thought to be unique to Gillows but recorded on work by other makers. [Butchoff Antiques]

leather-backed dining chairs. In 1868 George Sala was less forgiving, describing a cabinet made by Holland & Sons as:

'a large dressoir, or sideboard, in wainscot oak, magnificent in carving, in brass work, in picked-out bits of colour, and draped, even in front, with some most medievally figured hangings. It is Gothic — domestic Gothic — to the core; Gothic in every crocket, and rib. The late Mr. Pugin would have clapped his hands over it. Mr. Ruskin might weep over it, M. Viollet-le-Duc go into ecstasies over it. I am ignorant and tasteless enough to think it exceedingly ugly. It is pure Gothic, no doubt; but its beauties must be appreciated by the Goths. It is glaring and inharmonious in colour — a very "warden-pie" of dissonant tints; the composition is singularly undignified, and the ornamentation confused and...there are hundreds of judges more competent who will declare this work a masterpiece. I daresay it is; but I don't see it. It is to me devoid of meaning and purpose, and, with its crowd of ledges, shelves, and pigeonholes, looks as though it had not made up its mind whether to be a sideboard or a bureau. The green mediaeval hangings are especially unsightly'.[33]

Despite the perceived lacklustre appearance in the eyes of some critics, there were many fine pieces exhibited in 1862 by new and established firms. Notable newcomers were William Burges and William Morris. Morris, who, with Edward Burne-Jones, Dante Gabriel Rossetti, Philip Webb and others, such as William Watt, founded Morris, Marshall, Faulkner & Co. in 1861. Others were Thomas Seddon, who had trained in Paris in 1841, and Norman Shaw, who championed the so-called Queen Anne style. The Medieval Court at the 1862 exhibition contained the familiar theme of the fourteenth

Fig. 5.17 **This panelling, in a colourful Renaissance style, was exhibited by Crace & Son in 1862 and contrasts somewhat with the plainer, but nonetheless extravagant, central cabinet and ebonised cabinets on either side, also produced by Crace. Crace used this style of grotesque decoration in the Lower Library at Chatsworth in c.1840, Fig. 4.46.** [J.B. Waring, *Masterpieces of Industrial Art & Sculpture at the International Exhibition*, 1862, pl. 247]

Fig. 5.18 **Exhibited by Crace at the Paris exhibition in 1867, this finely executed cabinet is in the firm's Italian Renaissance style, which the firm was to perfect in the decoration of Longleat House a decade later.** [G. W. Yapp, *Art Industry, Furniture, Upholstery, and House Decoration*, 1879, pl. XCLIII]

and fifteenth centuries, as in 1851. This by now often heavy, ornate style was termed either 'Gothic', 'Medieval' or 'Henry VIII'. E.W. Pugin continued and amended his father's style. Supervised by J.B. Waring and J.D. Crace, the Medieval Court housed four spectacular cabinets designed and painted by William Burges and William Morris. Burges wrote that 'medievalism...has become a national style'.[34]

The coved overhang of the cabinet exhibited by Crace in 1862 (**Fig. 5.21**) had an enduring influence on designers such as Norman Shaw. The Crace family had a long and lasting impact on furniture and interior design, having worked for a prestigious group of clients, including the Crown, from George III to Queen Victoria, the 4th Marquess of Bath at Longleat, the dukes of Devonshire at Chatsworth, and, in the 1890s, the 1st Viscount Astor at Cliveden and Hever Castle.

The ever-widening variation of styles produced in the mid-nineteenth century meant that designers had to keep up to date and constantly reinvent their designs. This must have created an enormous challenge for foremen and traditionally trained cabinet makers. Even the larger London firms would be hard pressed to keep producing new cutting plans for the timber and new formes for mouldings. These pressures were compounded by the ever-present threat of workshop fires. Holland & Sons had a series of fires over the decades. The firm spent £1,250 in 1857 on steam-powered machinery. It seems miraculous that a fire in their Ranelagh Street workshops in November 1861, with considerable loss of stock timbers and tools valued at over £5,000, did not necessitate their withdrawal from the exhibition the following spring.

In contrast to the avant-garde, traditional influences continued. With the conference table, **Fig. 5.33a**, Johnstone & Jeanes have cleverly adapted the eighteenth-century form of a pedestal or partners' desk to allow four people to sit at it at the same time. Veneered in pollard oak, it makes striking use of British timber, lightly inlaid with stylised ebony stringing and roundels. The gadrooned handles can be interpreted as East Asian flowerheads or Japanese *mon*, the ebony stringing painstakingly inlaid into the turning. The use of well-figured native oak is similar to furniture of the Regency period, for example that of George Bullock, while the stringing is comparable to contemporary designs by Charles Bevan for the furniture made by Marsh, Jones & Cribb for Titus Salt.

The cabinet with a glazed central door was exhibited by Gillows in 1862, **Fig. 5.37**. The step-top is in the

Fig. 5.19 **A 'Geometric Gothic' inlaid walnut card table designed by John Dibblee Crace. One of a pair supplied to William Gibbs of Tyntesfield House in 1867.** [Trustees of the Cecil Higgins Art Gallery (The Higgins Bedford)]

Fig. 5.20 **A stereoscopic image of the Medieval Court at the 1862 exhibition, showing two cabinets made by Harland and Fisher in 1858 to a design by William Burges. The armchair is by Seddon & Sons, reputedly painted by Dante Gabriel Rossetti.**[35] [Digital image courtesy of the Getty's Open Content Program]

Figs 5.21 & 5.22 **Gothic versus medieval: Both of these cabinets were exhibited at the 1862 exhibition. 5.21: An imposing sideboard designed by Crace in the 'Pugin' style at Scarisbrick Hall. The coved overhanging cornice became a recurring theme of the Gothic Revival. 5.22: A polychrome cabinet in a medieval style, designed by William Burges, made by Harland & Fisher, and painted by E.J. Poynter.** [Both from J.B. Waring, *Masterpieces of Industrial Art & Sculpture at the International Exhibition*, 1862, pl. 205 (5.21) and pl. 155 (5.22)]

Fig. 5.23 **The Gothic library in the Palace of Monserrate near Sintra in Portugal. The prominent X-frame chair was probably designed by J.G. Crace and inspired by designs from Crispijn de Passe's *Oficina Arcularia* (1590–1612). The partners' desk is a more conventional form, also supplied by Crace.** [© PSML]

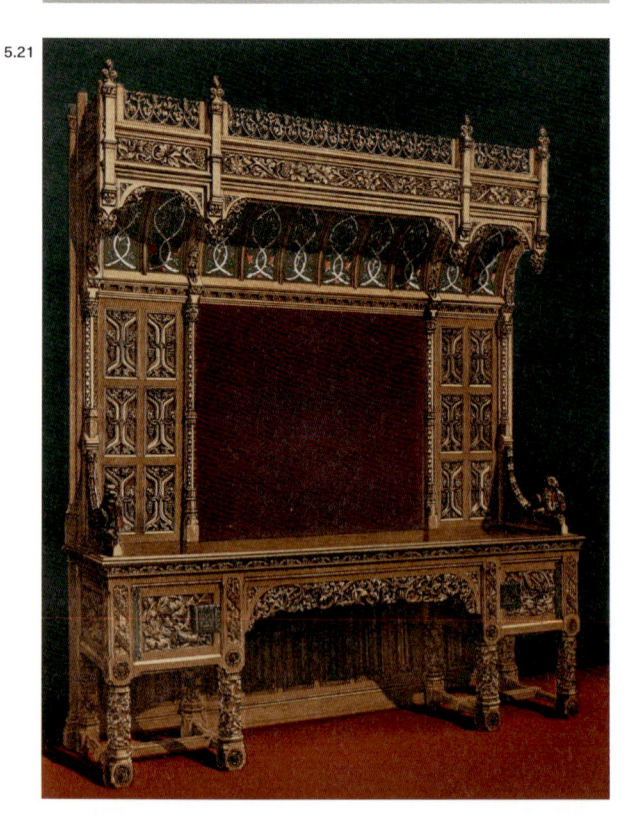

same eclectic French genre as an example by James and Thomas Scott of Edinburgh, who must have been aware of Eugène Prignot's designs, or were at least up to date with contemporary French fashion, **Fig. 5.50**. The step top is a mid-nineteenth-century invention, which was not in common use until the 1860s. The Gillows cabinet, one of the objects published as a chromolithograph by Day & Son, was purchased by the glove manufacturer John Derby-Allcroft for his London house.[36] The overall breakfront form, with curved glazed ends and a centre panel, suitable for plain glass, a mirror or a medallion, is essentially still in the form of a Louis XVI *commode à l'anglaise*, popularised in France in the late 1770s by cabinet makers such as Martin Carlin and Claude-Charles Saunier. This form of cabinet was

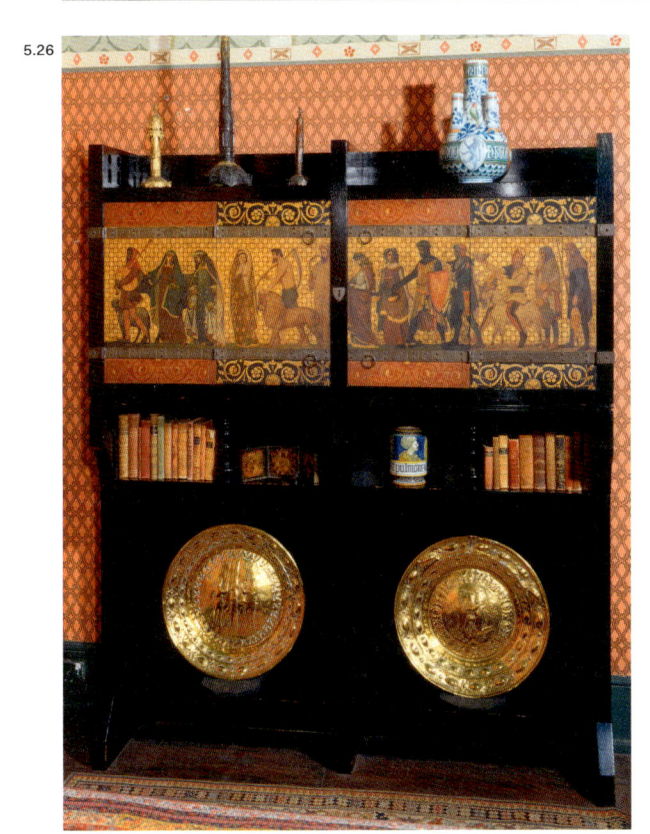

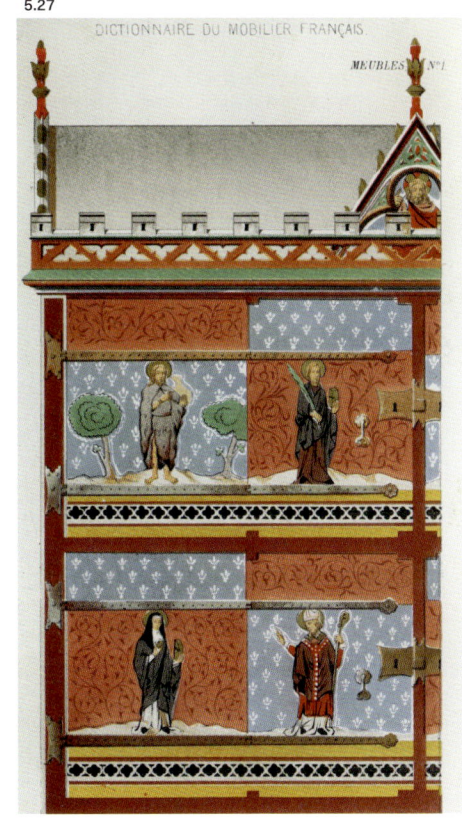

Figs 5.24 **William Burges's office at his architectural practice on 15 Buckingham Street, photographed by Francis Bedford in 1876. Burges himself decorated his chambers, which were located in a seventeenth-century riverside building in an area of London popular with architects, artists and engineers. The armchair is a Burges design. The Japanese cabinet and the Classical figure are evidence of Burges's wide-ranging interests, many of which fed into his designs.** [Trustees of the Cecil Higgins Art Gallery (The Higgins Bedford)]

Fig. 5.25 **The Drawing Room of Burges's home, Tower House, Melbury Road, Kensington, photographed in the late 1870s.** [Trustees of the Cecil Higgins Art Gallery (The Higgins Bedford)]

Fig. 5.26 **The colour scheme of this bookcase, designed by William Burges and painted by Dante Gabriel Rossetti *c.*1862–3 for Alphonso Warrington Taylor, the business manager of Morris, Marshall, Faulkner and Co., is dramatically contrasted against an ebony carcass.** [Trustees of the Cecil Higgins Art Gallery (The Higgins Bedford)]

Fig. 5.27 **Burges interpreted features from thirteenth-century polychrome *armoires*, this example from Noyon Cathedral, another at Bayeux.** [M. Viollet-le-Duc, *Dictionnaire raisonné du mobilier français...*, 1858, no. 1]

adapted variously in France and Britain during the second quarter of the nineteenth century, as in **Fig. 5.36**.[37] Yapp recorded that the main veneers on the Scott cabinet were, unusually, made of lancewood (*horoeka*) from New Zealand. Such furniture was almost certainly inspired by knowledge of the timbers imported by Levien. Another Edinburgh maker, Richard Whytock & Co., was the only Scottish cabinet maker represented at the Paris *Exposition Universelle* in 1867. Made in the Classical style, their ebony bookcase was praised by *The Art Journal* for being 'less costly' than other exhibits and they were awarded their third exhibition medal.[38]

Levien imported exotic woodworking timbers from New Zealand as early as the 1840s. After settling in London, he developed a successful cabinet-making career with a wide range of designs. His Pompeiian-style cabinet shown in the chromolithograph is a magnificent display of polychrome inlay that appears to be painted, **Fig. 5.44**. However, it is a complex marquetry design consisting of fourteen different timbers, including amboyna, coconut, ebony, maple, harewood, holly, orange, pear oak, purpleheart, sandalwood and walnut. The sculptural figures on the doors are inlaid with engraved ivory. The chromolithograph may be a reasonably accurate rendition of how the colours

Fig. 5.28 **Burges's 'Crocker Dresser' at 15 Buckingham Street, photographed in the 1860s.** [Trustees of the Cecil Higgins Art Gallery (The Higgins Bedford)]

Fig. 5.29 **Burges's bedroom at 15 Buckingham Street, photographed *c*.1876, featuring his 'Sleeping Beauty Bed' painted by Henry Holiday in 1867.** [Trustees of the Cecil Higgins Art Gallery (The Higgins Bedford)]

Fig. 5.30a **The Narcissus Washstand, designed by Burges for 15 Buckingham Street, photographed in the 1860s and shown in colour opposite.** [Trustees of the Cecil Higgins Art Gallery (The Higgins Bedford)]

might have appeared and it gives a useful insight into bright nineteenth-century colour schemes which vied with the vivid medieval hues championed by Burges. The bright tones would perhaps be too garish for modern taste and, if the cabinet has survived, it would appear very different and faded in colour but having accumulated a rich patination through time and polish. It must have been marquetry in its most stunning hue, even if exaggerated by the lithographic artist. The incorporation of the words 'Art Furniture' in Levien's publication in 1861, *The Woods of New Zealand*,

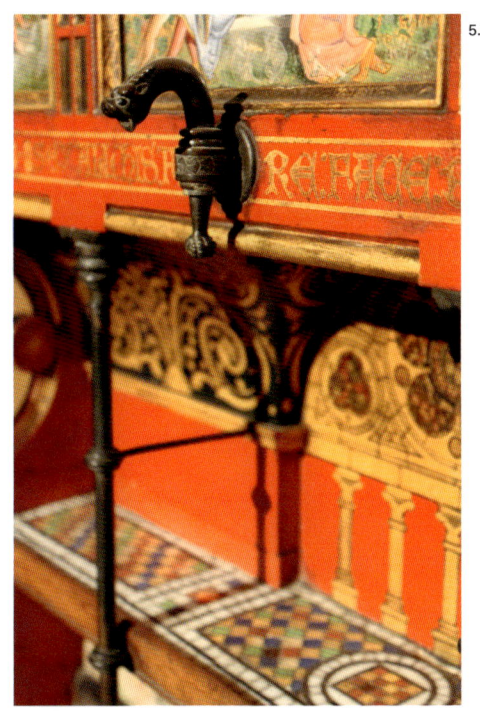

Figs 5.30b–d The wonderful polychromatic painted 'Narcissus Washstand' was designed by William Burges between 1865 and 1867 for his personal use at 15 Buckingham Street and subsequently used at Tower House, his house in Melbury Road, Kensington. [Trustees of the Cecil Higgins Art Gallery (The Higgins Bedford)]

and their Adaptability to Art Furniture, may have been one of the first references to what was to become a catchphrase for a modern, aesthetic style of furniture and design. 'Art Furniture' was the title given to a series of designs by the architects Walford & Donkin, but their work on 'Fret carved Chairs' and sideboards was in a fussy Reformed Gothic manner.[39] The Art Furniture Company was formed in 1867 and closed the following year but the term is forever associated with designers such as Godwin or makers such as Collinson & Lock. By 1880 the term was commonplace and covered a wide range of furniture in a style that might have been approved by Levien, though not by Godwin or his followers, and was incorporated in the title of the newly launched review *The Cabinet Maker and Art Furnisher*.

The problem of attribution is a constant preoccupation for historians as comparatively little English furniture of any period is signed. However, stamps and labels became more common by the mid-nineteenth century. The exquisite pair of stands, **Figs 5.43a–c**, is typical of this dilemma. The marquetry is the very best that the mid-nineteenth century

5.31

5.32

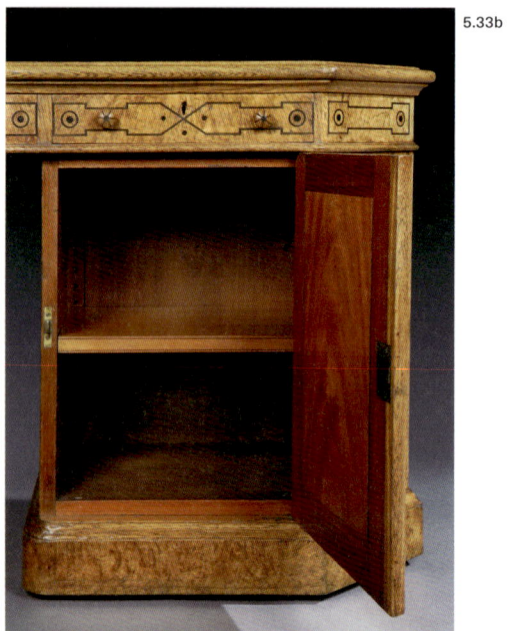

5.33a

5.33b

Figs 5.31 & 5.32 In contrasting styles, both these tables are stamped 'Johnstone & Jeanes 67, New Bond St. London'. 5.31: A walnut-veneered, kidney-shaped table formerly in the Handley-Read Collection.[40] 5.32: A parcel-gilt amboyna table, with an eye on the designs of Owen Jones of the previous decade. The trestle ends are of a type also used by Trollope & Sons. [5.31: Trustees of the Cecil Higgins Art Gallery (The Higgins Bedford). 5.32: Butchoff Antiques]

Fig. 5.33a Stamped 'Johnstone & Jeanes 67, New Bond St London', this pedestal desk is of unusual form, able to sit four people at a time, more a conference table than a partners' desk. The desk is a modernised version of an early George III 'four-way' desk illustrated in Cescinsky.[41]

Fig. 5.33b The open door and single multi-adjustable shelf of this compartment in the Johnstone & Jeanes desk demonstrate the simplicity of well-made British cabinet work, with no expense spared on the solid mahogany interior. The figuring of the oak veneer is exceptional; the ebony stringing has parallels with Charles Bevan's designs of the 1860s.
[Private collection]

Figs 5.34 & 5.35 **The drawing room at Whitbourne Hall, a Greek Revival house built in 1862. The centre table was probably the one described in an invoice from Cowtan in March 1866. Possibly made by Holland & Sons, the detail [Fig. 5.35] shows the well-figured walnut top. The overall form is similar to Parisian centre tables.** [5.34: Author's Image. 5.35: Butchoff Antiques]

Fig. 5.36 **This superb quality side cabinet was supplied by Cowtan to Edward Bickerton Evans at Whitbourne Hall between 1866 and 1872 and can be seen in situ in Fig. 5.34. It is probable that Cowtan sourced the cabinet and other furniture from Holland & Sons.** [Christie's]

could produce and has distinct similarities with that of the recorded work of the Blake family. It is possible that the Blakes made the stands as well as the marquetry; if not, the quality and workmanship suggest one of the very top London firms and another candidate may be Holland & Sons. Their form is taken from late seventeenth-century English examples of *torchères* by makers such as Gerrit Jensen, often accompanied by a mirror on a side table or mounted to a wall.[42] Examples can be seen at Boughton House. An unusual revival of the 1860s, the illustrated pair is of the finest quality satinwood, while the marquetry is in mother-of-pearl, ivory and exotic imported woods. The foliage is intensely observed, with bellflowers and botanical specimens; one shows a cabbage rose mounted by a butterfly, the other, a bouquet of asters. The underside of one of the bases bears an old label: 'Heirloom 1889'. This is tantalising but not enough to attribute their ownership to a particular house or family. Family archives may, one day, reveal the maker. The two *bonheurs du jour*, **Figs 5.47a & b**, are stylistically similar to the work of Holland & Sons, but like so much furniture of exemplary quality, if unsigned or undocumented only an attribution can be made. The centre table and side cabinet, **Figs 5.34, 5.35 & 5.36**, can be attributed to Hollands on slightly firmer ground. Between 1860 and 1862, Edward Evans built Whitbourne Hall in an imposing Greek Revival style combined with elements of the work of

Fig. 5.37 Exhibited in London in 1862, this step-top cabinet is a *tour de force* by Gillows and shows their familiarity with the Pompeiian style. The ceramic tiles are painted *en camaieu* with Roman Classical portraits, Venus and cupids studying the Arts. It was purchased by John Derby Allcroft for his house in Lancaster Gate and subsequently removed to his country house, Stokesay Court in Shropshire. [*Country Life*, 1994]

Fig. 5.38 One of a set of satinwood chairs made by Gillows to accompany the cabinet Fig. 5.37 at the 1862 exhibition. Purchased by J.D. Allcroft for his house in Lancaster Gate, removed to Stokesay Court in Shropshire. [Sotheby's]

Fig. 5.39 A rare painted and parcel-gilt mirror in the Adam Revival style purchased by J.D. Allcroft for Lancaster Gate, subsequently removed to Stokesay. It was almost certainly made by Charles Nosotti and may well have been purchased with the Howard & Sons cabinet and table in *c*.1862, Figs 5.41 & 5.42. [Sotheby's]

Fig. 5.40 A cabinet, partly carved in boxwood, exhibited by Gillows in 1867 when it was described as a combination of a console, cabinet and *étagère*. A mixture of contemporary French *goût grec* in the style of Guillaume Diehl, the panels represent Art on the left, Architecture on the right. [G.W. Yapp, *Art Industry, Furniture, Upholstery, and House Decoration*, 1879, pl. CXIII]

Robert Adam. However, the drawing room furniture was of French inspiration and was supplied, along with the interior decoration, by Cowtan & Sons between 1866 and 1872.⁴³ The firm almost certainly contracted out their cabinet-making commissions, in this case probably to Holland & Sons. The invoice from Cowtan relating to **Figs 5.34 & 5.36** reads:

'A very handsome Marqueterie and inlaid Cabinet in Thuya, Walnut and purple woods richly mouted with gilt ormolu, plate glass in doors, inside lined with Utrecht velvet £145.' *The centre table* 'An Occasional Table en suite £45 10'.

Figures 5.47a & b, are an adaptation of the French style, but the cabinet making is clearly by an English hand. When the gilt-bronze mounts were removed for cleaning on one of the desks, the incised mark 'MB' was evident on the reverse of some, indicating that the mounts were from the established Paris firm of Maison Millet. The suggestion is that the maker, possibly Holland & Sons, was anxious to establish

Figs 5.41 & 5.42 Two pieces of furniture in the Pompeiian manner by Howard & Sons, purchased by J.D. Allcroft and possibly shown at the 1862 exhibition. Both pieces have a printed Howard & Sons label, the side cabinet with a brass label embossed below the royal coat of arms 'C. Nosotti, Carver and Gilder, Upholsterers'. The table has the Howard stamp and is numbered 2218 and 1037. [Sotheby's]

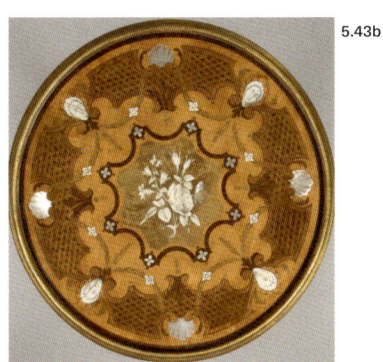

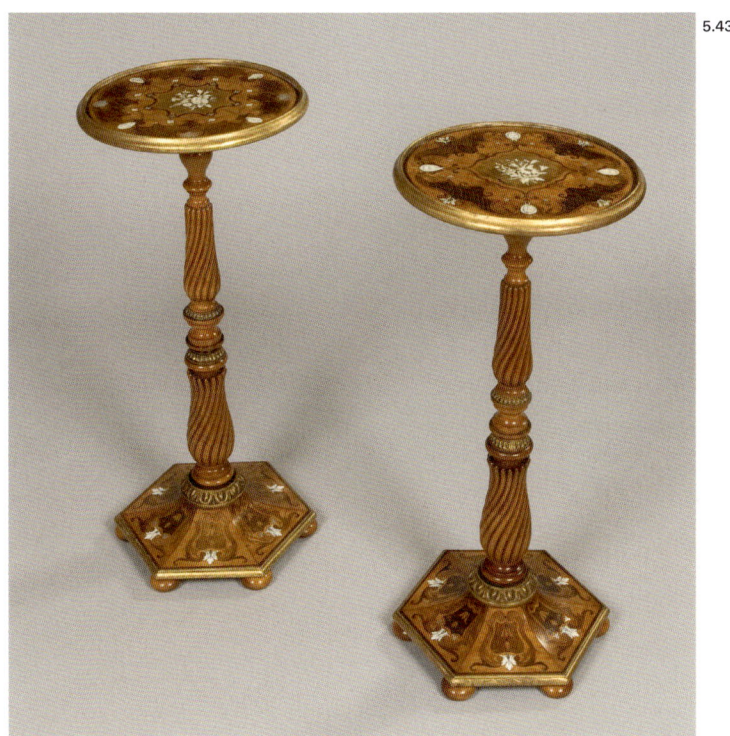

Figs 5.43a–c The intensity and style of the marquetry tops and quality of this pair of stands might be enough to suggest the work of the Blake family. Drawing on late seventeenth-century precedents, the pair are in an overtly French style but they are mainly veneered in satinwood, not commonly used in Paris. [Private collection]

5.44

Fig. 5.44 French in form, with Pompeiian-style motifs, the exotic polychrome colour decoration of this cabinet, exhibited in 1862 by Levien, is not painted but marquetry with fourteen different coloured and stained woods, with ivory figures. [J.B. Waring, *Masterpieces of Industrial Art & Sculpture at the International Exhibition*, 1862, pl. 120]

Figs 5.45a & b The quality of the marquetry is confirmed by the Blake signature on the bronze border of this table, similar to one by J.F. Oeben made in the 1760s. The marquetry is fine but Blake has copied Oeben's style, so is less effusive than their normal output. The table was formerly owned by the Hope-Edwards family. [Private collection]

Fig. 5.45c The gilt-bronze border surrounding the top of the Oeben-style table. The incision 'Blake' is an indication that the mount was modelled by the Blake firm and cast either by them or in a foundry on their behalf. [Private collection]

5.45a

5.45b

5.45c

credentials as makers of 'French' furniture, so ordered the mounts directly from Paris and fashioned the form of the timbers, especially the legs, to fit. Both desks are in beautifully coloured satinwood outlined in purpleheart – the contrast when new would have been quite startling. The carcass and construction of each is identical, as are the mounts, although the Sèvres-style painted panels differ in shape and topic. The complex interiors have a series of drawers and cupboards held by a subtle series of secret catches that are difficult to find without prior instruction. The main group of small drawers in the centre is opened by pushing down on a central gilt-bronze foliate device. The canted sides on the inside are opened by pushing gently on a piece of thin, unpolished moulding inside the large cupboards, reminiscent of the 'hidden' compartments found in bureau bookcases of the early to mid-eighteenth century. What was the purpose of these secret compartments? Are they for the owner to hide his financial affairs, or affairs of a romantic nature?

Fig. 5.46a & b The unusual design of this table, stamped by Charles Blake, looks back to the firm's copies of the 1708 Trianon commodes by Boulle seen in the previous chapter (Fig. 4.81a). The outswept leg at either end replicates that on a commode illustrated in plate III of Mariette's engravings of c.1709. The central masked vase repeats one found on a pair of nineteenth-century Boulle-marquetry coffers in the Wallace Collection.[44] The underside has a rare C. Blake stamp. [Butchoff Antiques]

Fig. 5.46c Once in the Hope-Edwards family, the marquetry on the top of the table (above) is inlaid loosely in the style of J.F. Oeben of the 1760s. [Butchoff Antiques]

BRITISH FURNITURE

The prestigious firm of Thomas Dowbiggin was absorbed by Holland & Sons, who flourished for almost a century, from 1843 to 1942. Hollands made a distinctive series of circular centre tables, the first recorded version seen in a chromolithograph of 'A Marqueterie Table' designed by a 'Mr Rosenberg', **Fig. 5.53**. Waring praised the work, 'for fineness of execution colour and good taste, is far beyond that which is usual in such work'.[45] The marquetry is of the highest quality, as would be expected from a royal maker at an international exhibition. In the design, Hollands used the familiar flared fluted leg of Classical form. This form of support became common in the late 1850s, either with four or three columns. When new, the marquetry would have been in an array of colours and tones which, within a relatively short period of time, would have faded considerably. The thuya-veneered example, **Fig. 5.51a**, has elaborately worked gilt-bronze mounts, the base applied with three rams heads, while the base of the walnut example, **Fig. 5.52**, has female masks. It would appear that all three examples were cut from the same cabinet maker's plans, albeit with tops of differing diameter. The marquetry varies considerably in detail but is always of a consistently high quality. A further example in thuya, with rams' heads mounts and lily of the valley marquetry with ivory petals, was made for Richard Napoleon Thornton in 1868.[46] Thornton ordered a number of pieces of furniture from Hollands in 1868, including a variation of the circular tip-top table, for his house in Sidmouth. When Symonds and Whineray first published in 1962, Holland & Sons were still in business and many of the entries for the Thornton commission are recorded in the day books, which are now in the National Archives.[47] Another variation in the Victoria and Albert Museum, with the same basic form of base, but with four instead of the more habitual three legs, also uses thuya as the main veneer.[48] An octagonal table veneered in amboyna, **Fig. 5.108**, uses the same form of leg, but the design of the marquetry is influenced by Owen Jones's publication *The Grammar of Ornament*. The overall form suggests the maker was George Trollope & Sons, their showroom, grandly titled 'The Museum of Decorative Art', was on Halkin Street, Belgravia. Gillows and other makers also used the four-leg columnar support. A popular model of this form, by Gillows, with a chessboard and folding top, called a 'Princess's Table' or a 'Prince's Table', is shown here, **Fig. 5.61**. On an 1866 invoice for a walnut 'Loo Table' priced at £33, Gillows described this form of support as 'a cluster of carved pillars and claws'. The invoice also named and priced two models of easy chair made by Gillows – a 'Demidoff' at £12 8s and a 'Lucan' at £6 6s.[49]

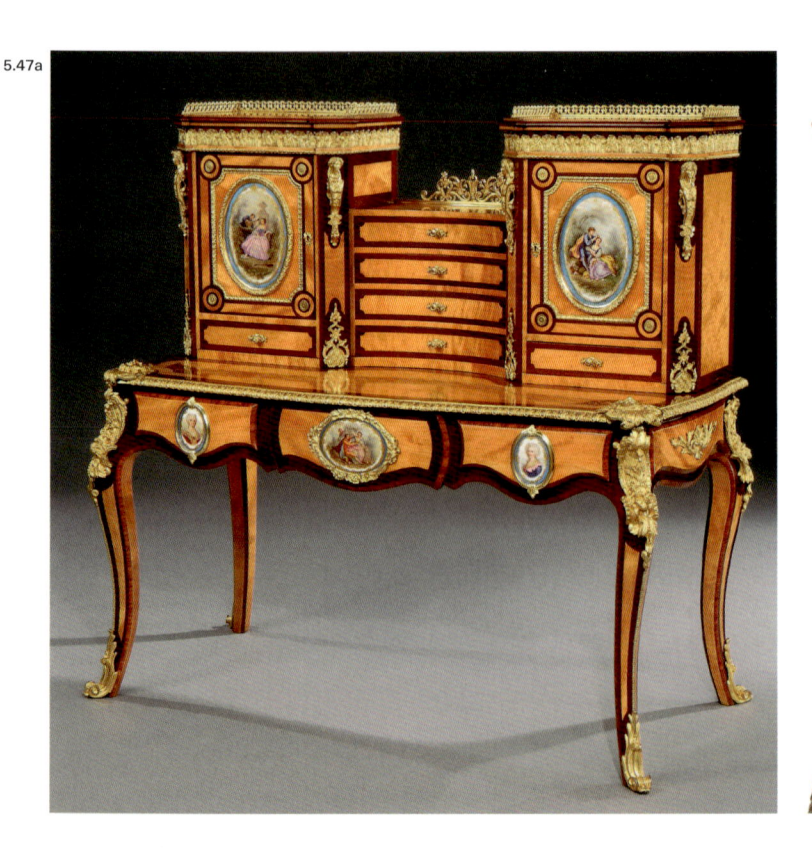

Figs 5.47a & b The construction of these satinwood *bonheurs du jour* is English, but when the mounts of one of the pair were removed for cleaning two showed the cast marks 'MB', indicating that they were sourced from the well-established Parisian firm of Maison Millet. The carcass and construction of each is identical, as are the mounts, although the Sèvres-style painted panels differ in shape and topic. [Butchoff Antiques]

Fig. 5.48 **A cabinet exhibited by Jackson & Graham in 1862, the overall form pre-dates their work in the Owen Jones style of the late 1860s and early 1870s. This rare French-inspired example has a newly fashionable Algerian onyx marble slab top with twist-turned columns and complex and intricate bronze mounts and plaques.** [J.B. Waring, *Masterpieces of Industrial Art & Sculpture at the International Exhibition*, 1862, pl. 111]

Fig. 5.49 **Charles Ingledew of Berners Street exhibited a variety of French-inspired chairs in 1862. According to Yapp they were 'covered with richly decorated morocco leather'.**[50] [*The Art Journal Illustrated Catalogue of the International Exhibition*, 1862, p. 280]

Fig. 5.50 **Shown at the 1862 exhibition, this step-top cabinet by James & Thomas Scott of Edinburgh must surely have been designed by a French hand such as that of Eugène Prignot.** [J.B. Waring, *Masterpieces of Industrial Art & Sculpture at the International Exhibition*, 1862, pl. 191]

The davenport remained a popular and useful small desk in the mid-nineteenth century and appeared in a wide range of variations. For example, one was exhibited in *papier-mâché* by Jennens & Bettridge in Paris in 1855, and others were drawn by King, Smee or later Wyman in 1886. Two illustrated examples show the imaginative variations to a well-tried format, **Figs 5.54a & 5.59**. They are far removed from the comparatively simple and practical form of desk thought to have been invented by Gillows and promoted by Loudon decades earlier. Although they continued to be made in large numbers in various woods, walnut and burr walnut being perennially popular, some were made as showpieces. The two illustrated are exemplary, both with French-influenced floral marquetry. One is a rare and exotic desk of English influence, but it is not known exactly where it was made or by whom. The main veneer is ash, while the upper part is of amboyna, banded in ebony. The marquetry suggests the influence of Tunbridge Ware and Japanese designs, **Fig. 5.59**. The other, **Figs 5.54a–d**, is veneered in West Indian satinwood, harewood, kingwood and a multitude of specimen woods. The central marquetry panel of the davenport, **Fig. 5.54d**, has the initials 'AE' for Alice Ernestine Hawker. Alice was betrothed to Alfred James Thornton, son of the barrister R.N. Thornton of Knowle Cottage, Sidmouth, for whom Holland & Sons supplied furniture.[51] It is part of an extensive suite combining Louis XV and XVI sources including the *bureau en pente* engraved with the date of the commission, 1868, **Fig. 5.55**.[52]

The torsade leg seen on the table, **Fig. 5.57b**, is another feature inspired by eighteenth-century France. The tapering, twisting form was used on the lower halves of columns flanking furniture by Adam Weisweiler and others in the 1780s. Whereas Weisweiler often entwined his columns with gilt-bronze, a demanding and expensive technique, the bronzed effect on the legs of the English table is not gilded, nor is it metal; the maker has used copper sulphate to stain sycamore. The hand-painted plaques, held within gilt-bronze frames on the frieze, depict the arts of Literature, Music, Painting and Sculpture, the latter in the form of the bust of the Venus de Milo, along with portraits of Prince Albert and Queen Victoria. It is conceivable that the same French influence has inspired the maker of the *étagère*, **Fig. 5.58a**. Less

Figs 5.51a & b Veneered in thuya and crossbanded in satinwood and tulipwood, this table is not signed but has close similarities to one supplied by Holland & Sons in a well-documented commission by R.N. Thornton. [Butchoff Antiques]

Fig. 5.52 Produced with slight variations throughout the decade, this one has female masks to the base. Another is in the Royal Collection. (RCIN 39521). [Butchoff Antiques]

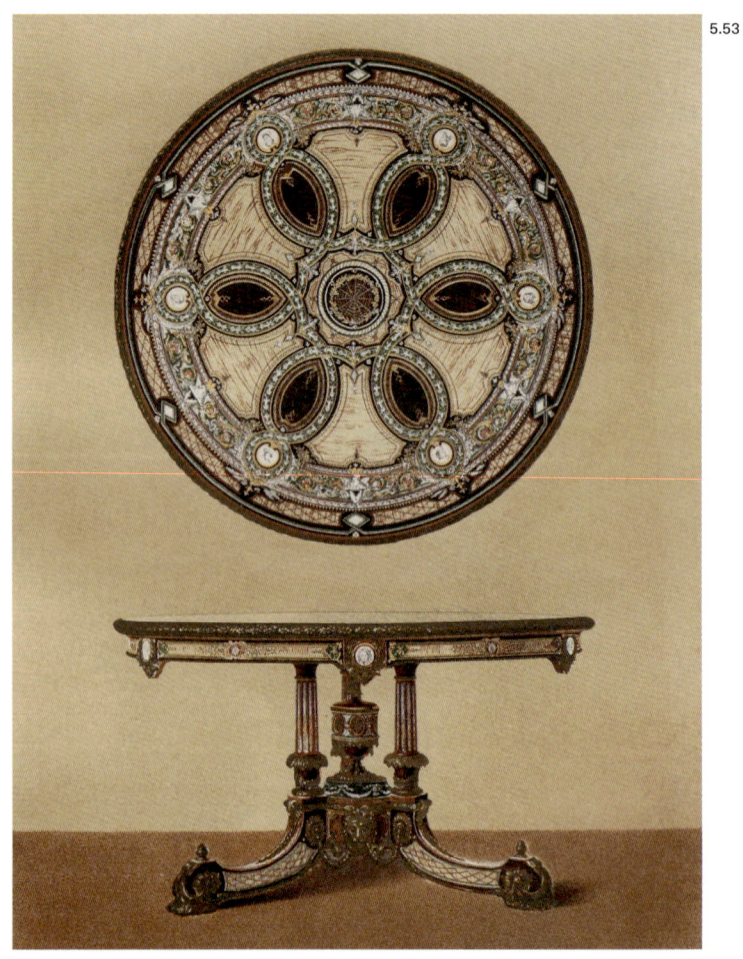

Fig. 5.53 A 'Marqueterie Table' exhibited in 1862 by Holland & Sons. Designed by a Mr Rosenberg, the base is of a distinctive form used by Hollands in the mid-nineteenth century. The marquetry is of the highest quality – the nearest rival being a circular table exhibited in 1872 by Jackson & Graham with Etruscan-style inlays (see 1870s chapter). [J.B. Waring, *Masterpieces of Industrial Art & Sculpture at the International Exhibition*, 1862, pl. 40]

CHAPTER 5: 1860S

5.54a

5.54b

5.54c

5.54d

Figs 5.54a–d **Part of an extensive range of furniture made for the Thornton family by Holland & Sons. The central marquetry cartouche of the desk has the initials 'AE' for Alice Ernestine Hawker, the wife-to-be of Alfred, son of R.N. Thornton, of Sidmouth.** [Private collection]

Fig. 5.55 **Part of an extensive commission made by Holland & Sons in 1868 for R.N. Thornton of Sidmouth. This French-inspired *bureau en pente* inlaid with a purpleheart trellis on satinwood, cost £64 10s.** [Private collection]

5.55

sophisticated than the use of stained sycamore to simulate bronze, here the maker has wrapped a bronze beading around the columnar supports.

A distinctive group of French-style inlaid furniture is habitually attributed to Donald Ross. Once based in Ealing, Ross started a workshop on Denmark Street in Soho, close to many of his contemporaries. His trellis marquetry, highlighted with small ebony dots, was a constant theme and became the workshop's speciality. This distinctive trellis, apparent in all Ross-style furniture, is drawn from Parisian marquetry of the late 1780s and 1790s. For many years the design source was wrongly thought to have been inspired by the work of Pierre Garnier, a highly esteemed Parisian cabinet maker. The most frequently seen Ross pieces are small

249

BRITISH FURNITURE

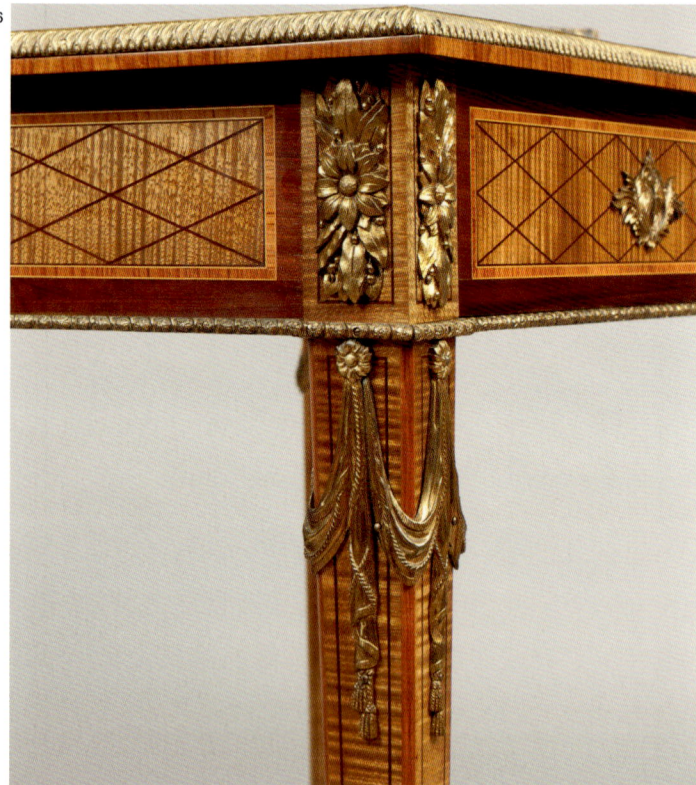

5.56

5.57a

5.57b

occasional tables that appear singly or often as a matched pair; it is possible that Ross never intended them to be a true pair, **Fig. 5.66**. Once considered to be of French eighteenth-century manufacture, in the late 1970s Clive Wainwright discovered information in the Victoria and Albert Museum archives that showed that a pair of tables in the museum, acquired in a bequest from Captain H.B. Murray in 1911, were in fact made by Ross.[53] A note of 1928 showed that Ross's son had visited the museum and identified the tables as his father's work. Donald Ross, known as 'Thomas Henry Gallic Ross',[54] was first recorded exhibiting a drawing room suite at the 1851 Crystal Palace exhibition. It is not easy to date his distinctive furniture with any certainty, but the bulk of his work was probably made between the 1860s and 1880s. The similarity of the 'dotted marquetry trellis' suggests that most of these pieces are from the same workshop but other makers may have also adopted it; see **Fig. 5.70a**. The trellis, distinctive legs in purpleheart or mahogany, together with an unusual gilt-brass capital, are often enough to validate an attribution to Ross. Ross does not appear to have signed his furniture, but many of the items, especially his small occasional tables, are stamped with a retailer's name, frequently Edwards & Roberts, but also Gillows and the little-known John Watson. The printed paper label on a *bonheur du jour* attributed to Ross stylistically suggests that it was retailed by Lane, formerly a carver and gilder, citing the Sloane Street address he used

Fig. 5.56 Possibly by Holland & Sons, this fine table is influenced by French eighteenth-century precedents such as the work of Jean-François Leleu.[55] The capitals of the legs have a gilt-bronze swag in the style of Philippe-Claude Montigny of the 1770s, as does the smaller table, Fig. 5.57b. [Butchoff Antiques]

Figs 5.57a & b This rare table is unsigned but was surely made by Holland & Sons. Traces of labels on the piece show that it was once owned by Lord Cornwallis of Linton Park. It is decorated in a rich variety of woods, including harewood, boxwood, kingwood and stained sycamore, alongside engraved ivory inlay. The torsade legs are inspired by French precedents. [Butchoff Antiques]

Figs 5.58a & b An unusual *étagère* in the French manner, the marquetry inlaid into a mahogany ground, incorporates a stylised auricular 'Green Man' mask. The supports, with applied spiral beadings, are unusual. The maker has used high-quality cedar for the two narrow drawer linings. [Private collection]

Fig. 5.59 Using ebony, amboyna and ash, this davenport with cedar-lined drawers has highly individualistic detailing. It has no obvious precedent although it might be presumed to be British made. The parquetry suggests the influence of Tunbridge Ware and Japanese design. [Private collection]

from 1866, **Fig. 5.68**.[56]

French styles of furniture predated the seeds of a revival of the George III style by several decades. First apparent in the early 1860s, the Georgian Revival continued unabated and remained perennially popular. One of the earliest documented examples is an important suite, which included two low side cabinets and a pair of candelabra stands, exhibited by Wright & Mansfield in London in 1862. As a form of furniture, the cabinet was, like its French counterparts, a late eighteenth-century development, low enough for pictures to be hung above. The cabinet, **Fig. 5.76**, is not signed but has attributes which suggest the work of Wright & Mansfield. In addition, it has two sage-green Wedgwood plaques of frolicking putti and Cupid which are the same pattern as their exhibition cabinet bought by the South Kensington Museum in 1868, **Fig. 5.122**. Two other cabinets exhibited by Wright & Mansfield, were made of 'richly gilt' gean wood, and appear to have been based on the same cabinet maker's plan, **Figs 5.77 & 5.78**. Whilst both are mounted with familiar Wright & Mansfield-style plaques by Wedgwood, the prospective

Fig. 5.60 One of a pair of *commodes à l'anglaise* adapted from the French model, Gillows design number 14176. Gillows have used electroplate panels, which were probably supplied by the Parisian firm of Christofle. [Sotheby's]

Fig. 5.61 Styled a 'Prince's Table', this drop-leaf games table is similar to one in an 1869 Gillows order book, design number 7585. Each flap has a swivelling tray for gaming tokens. The concept of a four-leg support became popular in the 1860s, as demonstrated by the group of Holland tables shown in this chapter. A table of similar design is in the Abbot Hall Art Gallery and Museum. [Christie's]

Figs 5.62a & b Made in an anglicised Louis XV/XVI transitional style, this table is attributed to Holland & Sons due to the fine quality. The top is veneered in book-matched Circassian walnut, outlined in tulipwood and green-stained sycamore or 'harewood'. [Private collection]

client was given the choice between cupboards flanking open shelves, or glazed side cupboards. The George III-style satinwood furniture exhibited by Wright & Mansfield in 1862 was almost revolutionary in its Neoclassical refinement. Commenting on the exhibition stand, George Sala described the Adam Revival cabinet in glowing terms:

'Messrs. Wright & Mansfield have a very sumptuous armoire cabinet in the English Louis Seize style, of satinwood, elaborately inlaid with coloured woods, and panelled with delicious little slabs of Wedgwood ware in pale blue and white. The cabinet is the sunniest and gracefullest thing imaginable; but it is just the shadow of a shade too light and jocund. It looks as though it had been made to be eaten; and although it may contain some day "sugar and spice, and all that's nice," you don't want to eat your cup-board'.[57]

What Sala described as satinwood was 'ginn' or 'gean' wood, a wild highland black cherry or bird cherry (*Prunus avium*), which thrives in Scotland and the north of England. The veneers were from the estate of the commissioning client, Sir Dudley Coutts Marjoribanks, an early patron of Wright & Mansfield. He commissioned the firm to refurbish Guisachan, which he acquired in 1856,[58] and to furnish his London residence, Brook House on Park Lane,

Fig. 5.63 The use of thuya as the principal veneer on this pair of French-influenced side cabinets, with a contrasting kingwood crossbanding, sets off the 'Watteau-esque' painted porcelain plaques. [Butchoff Antiques]

Fig. 5.64 Retailed by Hall of Manchester, this games compendium veneered in coromandel was probably made in a specialist London workshop and similar or identical examples may have other retailers' labels. [Private collection]

Fig. 5.65 The desk is in an overtly French but eclectic Louis XVI style complete with Sèvres-style porcelain plaques. The lock on the long single drawer is stamped 'VR Patent' and 'C&T London' for the lockmaker Cope & Timmins. The cabinet maker has used amboyna, which at first glance is similar to the thuya used by contemporary French makers. [Private collection]

between 1867 and 1869. The use of gean in furniture commissioned by a prominent Scottish client followed a well-established tradition. In the eighteenth century, gean furniture had often been advertised by Scottish makers as an alternative to walnut and mahogany and, being a local product, was cheaper.[59] The 4th Duke of Atholl (1755–1830), the 'planting' duke, had planted 25 million trees over the course of his lifetime, some of which he had made into furniture.[60] Marjoribanks may well have been aware of this and suggested the use of gean to Wright & Mansfield. A common woodland and hedgerow tree, Marjoribanks would have had access to a plentiful supply of gean on his estates in Inverness-shire. It is likely to have been used for reasons of economy and as a tribute to what was available in Scotland, and doubtless specified in the Wright & Mansfield commission. Between 1854 and 1869, several pieces of furniture were made for Marjoribanks's London and Scottish homes by Wright & Mansfield. No other prominent London cabinet maker is known to have used gean, which gives Marjoribanks's commissions a unique place in English furniture making. The suite also included a chimney piece mounted with Wedgwood medallions, which was exhibited in 1862, **Fig. 5.79**.

Marjoribanks was a Liberal MP, elevated to the peerage in 1880 as the 1st Baron Tweedmouth. An avid collector of Wedgwood and the work of the British Neoclassical

5.66

Fig. 5.66 These small tables are one of the most common forms of the output of Donald Ross. They were probably made as individual examples but sold 'as pairs' if required. They are, to all intents and purposes, identical to a pair in the Victoria and Albert Museum, once thought to be genuine eighteenth-century examples.[61] [Private collection]

Fig. 5.67 Made in England, possibly by Ross, this type of light and portable work table – variously named a *vide poche* or *tricoteuse* (from the French verb *tricoter* to knit) – was used as a lady's table on which to place pieces of sewing, stitching and embroidery. This model is based on a group attributed to Jean-Henri Riesener and Martin Carlin. The first version was thought to have been made by Riesener for Marie-Antoinette to celebrate the birth of her first son, the *dauphin*, in 1781. [Butchoff Antiques]

Fig. 5.68 A paper label, probably dating to the end of the nineteenth century, from a *bonheur du jour* attributed to Donald Ross, reads 'To H.S.H. The Prince & Princess of Teck, JOHN LANE, 174 Sloane Street, Knightsbridge. Carver & Gilder, Dealer in Antique China, Furniture & Works of Art'. [Bonhams]

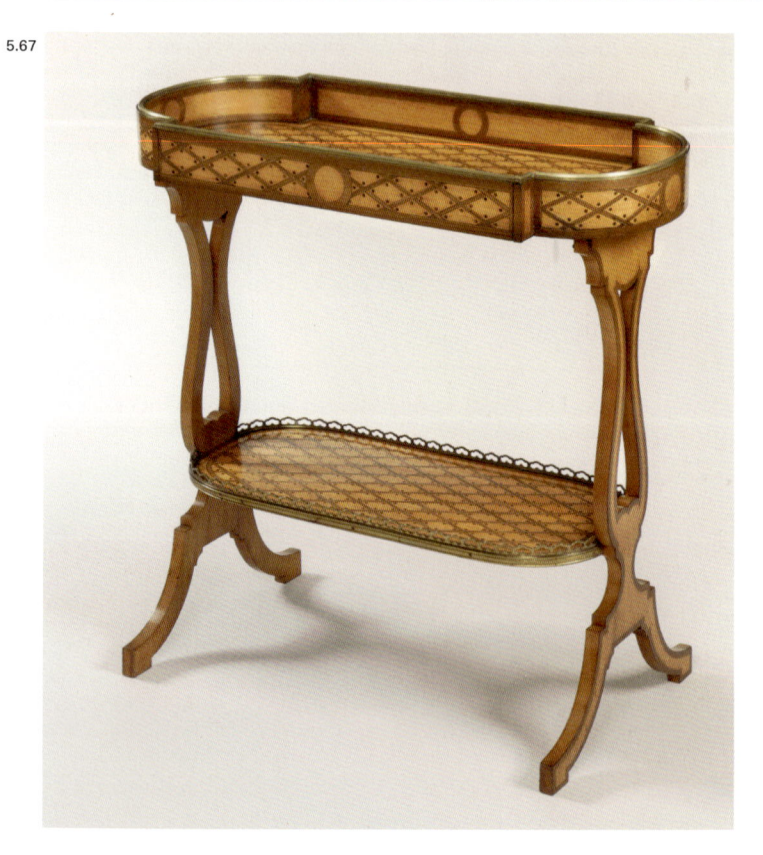

5.67

5.68

254

CHAPTER 5: 1860s

5.69

5.70a

5.71

5.70b

Fig. 5.69 The 'dot and trellis' inlay again indicative of Ross's work. One drawer of this pair of centre tables is stamped by Edwards & Roberts and once again the veneer is principally in *citronnier*, with Sèvres-style porcelain plaques. The maker has used the same cabinet makers' plan as the desk shown in Fig. 5.71. [Butchoff Antiques]

Fig. 5.70a Copying the early Louis XVI period design of Neoclassical cylinder-top desks, the English maker has incorporated the 'dotted marquetry trellis' veneer hitherto attributed to Donald Ross. However, the constructional differences, especially the legs, suggest another maker, possibly Bertram & Son. [Mayfair Gallery]

Fig. 5.70b An open, well-made drawer with mahogany linings from a writing table probably by Ross but with less elaborate mounts to the legs. [Mayfair Gallery]

Fig. 5.71 Stamped 'Edwards & Roberts', in their capacity as retailers, this desk has all the characteristics of the work of Donald Ross, notably the dotted marquetry trellis and the framing of the tapering legs in gilt bronze with a distinctive foliate capital. [Private collection]

255

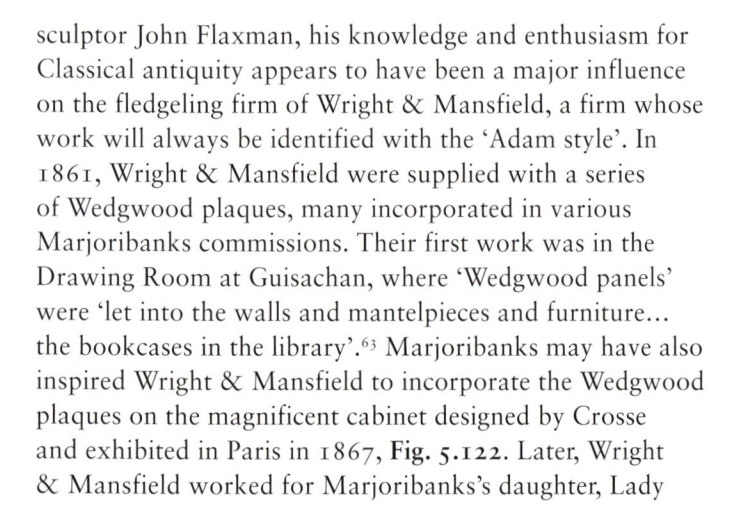

Fig. 5.72 Although this pedestal desk in coromandel veneer is unsigned, a virtually identical desk was made in satinwood, stamped Wright & Mansfield. [Butchoff Antiques]

Fig. 5.73 The central drawer on this partners' desk made in the George III manner, veneered in fine mahogany, is stamped Holland & Sons. The desk has the traditional arrangement of drawers in each pedestal with panelled doors to the back. The handles are inspired by Robert Adam and similar handles are used on the cabinet, Fig. 5.74. [Butchoff Antiques]

Fig. 5.74 The elegance and comparative simplicity of this inlaid side cabinet in the Adam Revival manner is of a style associated with, but not exclusive to, Wright & Mansfield. The richly figured satinwood veneers and the finely chased handles are exceptional. [Private collection]

Fig. 5.75 A marquetry longcase or 'Grandfather' clock attributed to Holland & Sons. The movement is by C.J. Klaftenberger, President of the British Horological Institute.[62] Held in high esteem by Queen Victoria and Prince Albert, Klaftenberger received regular orders for clocks and watches from the royal couple for them to present as gifts. The pendulum is mercury compensated to allow for accurate timekeeping. [Private collection]

Fig. 5.76 A satinwood cabinet inset with jasper Wedgwood plaques in the manner of Wright & Mansfield with delicate, now faded, foliate Neoclassical marquetry. Many makers used fashionable green jasper Wedgwood plaques, such as Lamb of Manchester on their Etruscan Revival cabinet exhibited in Paris in 1867, Fig. 5.125. [Private collection]

sculptor John Flaxman, his knowledge and enthusiasm for Classical antiquity appears to have been a major influence on the fledgeling firm of Wright & Mansfield, a firm whose work will always be identified with the 'Adam style'. In 1861, Wright & Mansfield were supplied with a series of Wedgwood plaques, many incorporated in various Marjoribanks commissions. Their first work was in the Drawing Room at Guisachan, where 'Wedgwood panels' were 'let into the walls and mantelpieces and furniture… the bookcases in the library'.[63] Marjoribanks may have also inspired Wright & Mansfield to incorporate the Wedgwood plaques on the magnificent cabinet designed by Crosse and exhibited in Paris in 1867, **Fig. 5.122**. Later, Wright & Mansfield worked for Marjoribanks's daughter, Lady Aberdeen, at Haddo House, a magnificent Palladian building designed by William Adam in 1732 (see Chapter 6 – 1870s).

In a different but still Neoclassical style, an upright piano was also made for Marjoribanks by Wright & Mansfield, **Fig. 5.80**. It was fitted with an Érard movement, number 5862, and painted with Neoclassical designs in the manner of George Brookshaw (*fl.* 1783–8) by Messrs Pincon & Prolisch, the carving by R.W. Godfrey. Contemporary commentary compared the London firm's work favourably to the eighteenth-century creations of the 'Adelphi' Adams. As nineteenth-century designers looked back to earlier precedents, it was inevitable that they should refer to the designs of Robert and James Adam. It appears that Wright & Mansfield were the first to revive and reinterpret the

CHAPTER 5: 1860s

5.75

5.76

Georgian Neoclassical style. However, they also made 'exact' copies of eighteenth-century furniture, such as a Pembroke table (**Fig. 5.81**) and a painted satinwood armchair in the 1790s style of Seddon & Sons, which were bought by the South Kensington Museum at the Wright & Mansfield stock auction in 1886.[64]

Alfred Thomas Wright and George Needham Mansfield had traded with Samuel Hanson until 1861. According to Litchfield, whose father's cabinet-making firm of Litchfield & Radclyff had also exhibited in 1862, both Wright and Mansfield had previously worked as assistants at Jackson & Graham.[65] The auction of Wright & Mansfield stock, after the partnership's dissolution in 1886, was divided into three sections. The second category included 'Old English, Chippendale & Sheraton Furniture' and also 'Boule [sic] Clocks'. The third comprised 'many costly and beautiful Specimens of Cabinet Work… designed and manufactured, regardless of cost, specially for various exhibitions'.[66] It was a marquetry piano with an Érard movement that received the most attention at the auction, *The Times* reporting that: 'there is nothing in the rooms which does more credit to English art workmen…than the piano which is really quite equal in the exquisite finish of the inlay work and splendid colour of the different patterned tulip and king woods to any of the Marie-Antoinette furniture which sold for thousands of pounds in the Hamilton Palace and Blenheim sales'.[67]

The remaining stock and a confirming comment in *The Cabinet Maker and Art Furnisher* showed that Wright & Mansfield had been investing heavily in antique furniture, which was fast becoming more expensive. Presumably these objects were used as a basis for the firm's copies.

The increasing scarcity of old models was evidence of the growing popularity of Georgian furniture in the 1870s and 1880s. Wright & Mansfield were acknowledged to have been important players in the taste for Georgian reproductions. In July 1886, *The Cabinet Maker and Art Furnisher* wrote that the firm 'must be accounted the leaders of that passing fashion which has happily brought back into our houses many of the charming shapes of the renowned eighteenth-century cabinet makers...the best forms of Chippendale, Hepplewhite and particularly Sheraton have been made to live again under the renovating influence of these able manufacturers'.[68]

The illustrated George III-style painted satinwood dressing table is, to all intents and purposes, identical to one in the Victoria and Albert Museum, **Figs 5.85 & 5.86**.[69] The museum example had belonged to a collector of satinwood furniture, John James (1818–1879). James lent the table and a chest of drawers to the South Kensington Museum in 1860 and, ten years later, the museum purchased both items for £200 each. It might reasonably be assumed that the handful of recorded copies were made from 1860 onwards, when the original was on public display, and not before. Both Hindley & Wilkinson and Maples advertised examples as their own, but it is probable that the copies were made by a specialist maker who sold them to the larger London houses. A similar dressing table was at a loan exhibition of English furniture held at the Bethnal Green Museum in 1896.[70] The recorded copies are thus difficult to date.

The Victoria and Albert Museum example has always been a conundrum. First exhibited as 'period', i.e., c.1790, by the 1960s it was deemed to be a 'Victorian' copy, and later was given the unlikely date of between 1820 and 1835. Traditionally called 'Sheraton', it is in a style not popular in the 1820s and 1830s. The basis for the dating was the fact that the dressing table has oval Sheffield-plate handles, 'a technique that fell out of use in the mid-1830s'.[71] In this author's opinion, formed after close inspection, the upper part is undoubtedly by a late eighteenth-century hand.[72]

Figs 5.77 & 5.78 Variations of the Adam style, made from Scottish gean wood, exhibited by Wright & Mansfield in 1862. One of the tripod stands can be seen in a painting by Alfred Emslie (Fig. 7.1). [5.77: from *The Art Journal Illustrated Catalogue of the International Exhibition*, 1862, p. 12. 5.78: *The Illustrated London News*, 21 June 1862, p. 646]

Fig. 5.79 An *Art Journal* illustration of Wright & Mansfield Georgian Revival pieces exhibited in 1862: a gilt candelabrum and a clock and bracket above a girandole mirror flank a chimney piece in gean wood with Wedgwood plaques. The accompanying grate and fender were by Feetham of Clifford Street who, by coincidence or design, exhibited in close proximity to Wright & Mansfield at the 1876 Centennial Exhibition (see Chapter 6 – 1870s). [*The Art Journal Illustrated Catalogue of the International Exhibition*, 1862, p. 104]

Fig. 5.80 **A painted piano with an Érard movement, supplied with a chair en suite. Commissioned by Sir Dudley Coutts Marjoribanks and exhibited in 1862, it formed part of Wright & Mansfield's prize-winning stand.**[76] [Butchoff Antiques]

Fig. 5.81 **On display today at the Cannon Hall Museum, this satinwood and marquetry Pembroke table was acquired by the Victoria and Albert Museum at the auction of Wright & Mansfield's effects in 1886.** [© Victoria and Albert Museum, London]

However, the delicate turned legs and hipped stretcher appear to have been replaced at some time, presumably prior to 1860, although the small fitted oval box on the stretcher is also clearly from the late Georgian period. The assumption might be that the delicate base was damaged and rebuilt, possibly by a hopeful dealer who knew that James was an avid collector. The grisaille oval panels on the upper part are also of the Sheraton period, but all the polychrome foliate painting and painted white 'stringing' has been added, presumably at the time the piece was rebuilt.[73] Edwin Foley, in his 1910 *The Book of Decorative Furniture*, includes a commentary alongside a stylised watercolour of an identical table, noting that it was the property of Thomas Kirkley of Cleadon Park, dating the table to the late eighteenth century. He writes that the Cleadon table is the sister piece to the one in the South Kensington Museum but is missing the oval workbox on the stretchers.[74] Although there is no documentary evidence as to the original designer, in 1892 Litchfield tentatively attributed the table to Seddon & Shackleton, a more likely source than Sheraton.[75]

Another model made several times in the 1860s is a Pembroke table based on a design by Sheraton from *The Cabinet-Maker and Upholsterer's Drawing-Book* of 1792,

Fig. 5.81. Sheraton called the table 'A Harlequin Pembroke Table' and wrote that 'This piece serves not only as a breakfast, but also as a writing table, very suitable for a lady'.[77] Painted with allegories of the Arts, Painting, Writing, Music and Drama, it is one of several metamorphic pieces designed by Sheraton which were published in 1792 and 1802. The style of painting and gilt gesso foliage and husk decoration are similar to work by Wright & Mansfield but no signed examples are known. A further example of the revival of the Adam style in the 1860s is a Classically inspired satinwood upright piano, with an Érard movement, designed by Leonard William Collman (1816–1881) and exhibited in 1862.[78] Further to the purchase of the spectacular cabinet exhibited by Wright & Mansfield in 1868, **Fig. 5.122**, the South Kensington Museum bought, for £11, a pair of Adam-style knife-urns from the London dealer, Murray Marks, under the impression that they were made in c.1780, **Fig. 5.87**. Recent examination shows that the urns were made in the mid-nineteenth century and were virtually new when purchased by the museum, the maker unknown. Are the urns fakes or are they perfectly innocent copies made, for example, by Wright & Mansfield? The purchase was on the advice of Sir Mathew Digby Wyatt, the museum keen to extend its collection of rare 'Georgian' artefacts. Wyatt regarded the pair as 'very elegant in all respects, difficult and good in workmanship'.[79] Today they are more interesting as copies after an unidentified model. This type of knife case, with a rising lid, was used in the second half of the eighteenth century, normally standing on a pair of pedestals housing plate warmers, placed either side of a sideboard or a side table. The dealer Murray Marks (1840–1918), a friend of Dante Gabriel Rossetti and William Morris, took over his father's premises at 395 Oxford Street in 1875 and commissioned Norman Shaw to re-design the façade in the fashionable Queen Anne style. In a reaction to expanses of 'large panes of glass', the new façade was decidedly 'quaint', with a window divided by carved wood into small square panels.[80] In his search for Georgian furniture, Rossetti commissioned Marks to find a table for Kelmscott Manor: 'It should be of the Pembroke kind' and 'two square tables, one mahogany and one satin wood'[sic].[81]

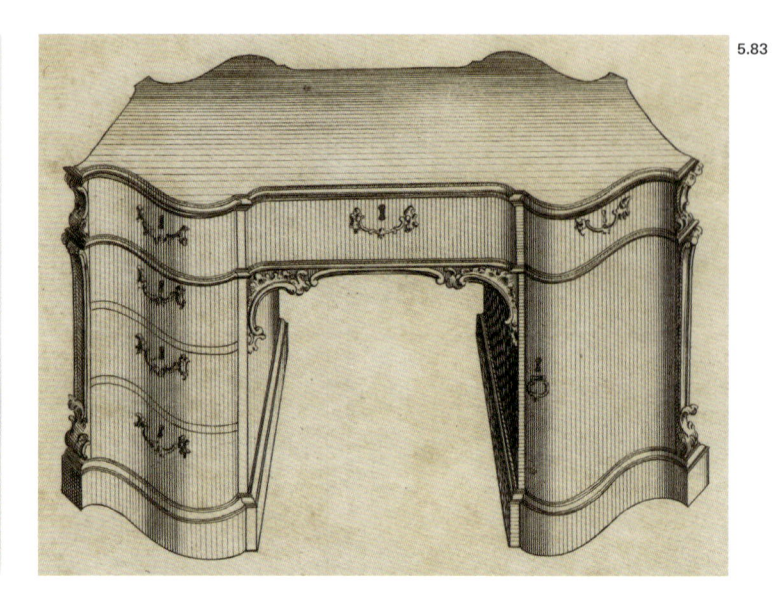

Unexpected champions of the Georgian era were Dante Gabriel Rossetti and Edward William Godwin. Collard noted that when Godwin could not find what he wanted he decided 'to hunt up second-hand shops, for eighteenth-century mahogany work inlaid with strips of satinwood…the eighteenth century won the competition, and my dining room was furnished with a bow-fronted sideboard, Chippendale chairs, flap tables…all of admirable colour, design, and workmanship'.[82] In 1867, Rossetti asked his friend Murray Marks to look out for Chinese furniture when searching for goods in Brighton.[83] With influential figures such as Rossetti and Godwin and indeed William Morris looking for Georgian furniture as a plentiful and cheap commodity, it is not surprising that mainstream makers like Wright & Mansfield looked back to the same period to influence their furniture designs.

Fig. 5.82 This beautifully grained oak pedestal desk is inspired by a Chippendale design. The silver-plated drawer handles are highly stylised. [Butchoff Antiques]

Fig. 5.83 The design for the oak desk is similar to plate 10 in *Household Furniture in Genteel Taste*, published in 1760 by Roger Sayer for the 'Society of Upholsterers, Cabinet-makers etc.'. A drawing by Thomas Chippendale, published the same year, shows an almost identical desk without the carved spandrels to the kneehole, included in the third edition of *The Gentleman and Cabinet-Maker's Directory*, 1762, plate 82. [Robert Sayer, *Genteel Household Furniture in the Present Taste*, 1760, pl. 10]

Rossetti moved into his Georgian house in Chelsea in 1862 where he had two Sheraton-style settees, a modern example for a bedroom, a period model for his sitting room. Henry Treffry Dunn, an artist and friend of Rossetti, wrote that it was 'one of the most curiously-furnished and old-fashioned sitting-rooms that it had ever been my lot to see'.[84] Georgian furniture in the 1860s was reasonably priced on the second-hand market, and the eclectic mix suited Rossetti, Morris and their circle. Rossetti 'delighted to take an evening's walk through Leicester Square, visiting the various curiosity shops…or through Hammersmith, a district where many a Chippendale chair or table could be then met with and bought for nothing'.[85] Between 1861 and 1862 Rossetti painted and probably designed the settee for a bedroom in his Chelsea house which, without the ebonising, could be mistaken for a late Sheraton design, **Fig. 5.91**. Made by Morris & Company, the medallions of Amor, Amans and Amata were painted by Rossetti. The Georgian settee of the late 1790s with a trellis back was in Rossetti's sitting room, and Rossetti is seated reading the proofs of his *Ballads and Sonnets* to Theodore Watts-Dunton in the gouache by Treffry Dunn, **Figs 5.89 & 5.90**. For their innovative and simple designs, Messrs Morris & Company won two gold medals at the 1862 exhibition.

5.84

Fig. 5.84 **Richly figured mahogany was a popular choice for a gentleman's pedestal desk. This example, with boldly carved fruit applied to the canted sides, is fitted with Hobbs & Co. locks. It is in a similar but reduced form to a 'four-way' desk of the mid-eighteenth century. The central drawer bears an inset circular plaque indicating that it was made or supplied by Hamptons of Pall Mall.** [Butchoff Antiques]

The period between the London exhibition of 1862 and the Paris fair of 1867 was one of incredible achievement and workmanship. An exemplary example from this time is a circular table showing an 'Allegory of the Senses', made by Charles and Henry Blake for the 4th Duke of Northumberland, in situ still at Alnwick Castle, **Fig. 5.92**. Although the initial watercolour design was drawn by Charles Philip Slocombe in June 1853[86] the table was not delivered until twelve years later, in part due to the death of the marquetry-cutter Henry Blake.[87] The presumption is that the work was then supervised by his brother Charles Blake, but Yapp records that it was finished by a Mr Vert, thought to be a Spanish craftsman. On seven sheets, the design is now in the Victoria and Albert Museum, the complex marquetry using a countless number of wood species.[88] Clive Wainwright discovered a note in the Alnwick Castle archive linking the table to 'the Blakes, the great makers of Marquetrie in London'.[89] A further letter in the Alnwick archives, dated 10 February 1865, links the work of Blake to the dealer John Webb.[90] Yapp described the table as 'the most remarkable example of marquetry produced in this country'; possibly he had not seen the Blake piano illustrated in **Fig. 3.59a**.[91]

'…*everything in Marlborough House may broadly speaking be said to be of British make*'.[92] One of the most remarkable commissions of the decade was a suite of furniture made by Holland & Sons for the Prince and Princess of Wales at Marlborough House, part of which is shown here, **Figs 5.95, 5.96a–c**. In his publication, Beavan described the cabinets and the quality of their execution, noting that 'Quite the most beautiful objects in the room are two Louis XVI cabinets mounted in ormolu, with ivory plaques in centre panels and inlaid with various woods. They cost £300 a-piece the occasional tables and writing-tables, matching this exquisite pair of cabinets, are also very handsome'.[93] Although the cabinets are overtly French in form, their overall decoration suggests an English designer's hand. Their style would seem to suggest that they were supplied to Marlborough House when the prince and princess were married in 1863. The architect Sir James Pennethorne supervised an extensive remodelling of the house for the royal couple, including the creation of a series of sumptuous state rooms. Much of this refurbishment was undertaken by Holland & Sons.[94] It would appear that the side cabinets were made for the most important room, the Great Drawing Room, which was decorated in white and gold stucco. Whilst occupied by the royal couple, the house became a glittering venue for high society and foreign dignitaries, and a showcase for British craftsmanship. One contemporary commentator wrote: 'in connection with furniture…both the Prince and Princess have…done their utmost to encourage home manufacturers in every department'.[95] Both the cabinets are stamped with the inventory mark for Marlborough House; the doors have inset ivorine name plaques and are stamped 'Holland & Sons'. The design of the cabinets represents the height of Victorian eclecticism, featuring a melody of exotic timbers as well as Circassian walnut, which was widely used in British furniture

5.85

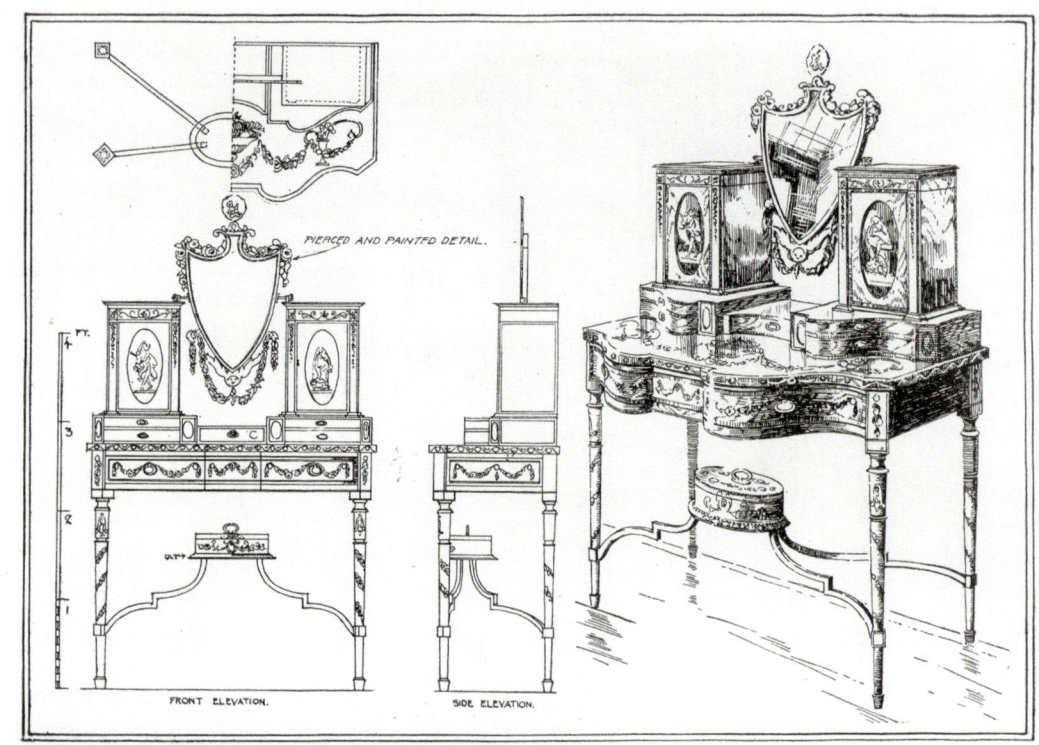

Fig. 5.85 The popularity of the Victoria and Albert Museum dressing table, similar to Fig. 5.86, continued in 1920 when *The Cabinet Maker* published this scale drawing. [*The Cabinet Maker*, 28 February 1920, p. 462]

Fig. 5.86 An example of a dressing table in the so-called Sheraton manner, of which several examples were made. The model features in a later (post-1887) Hindley & Wilkinson catalogue and appears to have been popular with American clients. Another example which has been in the Victoria and Albert Museum since 1860, appears to be eighteenth century, the base rebuilt in the 1850s. [Private collection]

Fig. 5.87 A pair of knife urns purchased for the South Kensington Museum in 1870 as eighteenth-century originals. Were they made with intent to deceive or simply high-quality copies? [© Victoria and Albert Museum, London]

5.86

5.87

262

CHAPTER 5: 1860S

Fig. 5.88 The Whistler-painted settee is against the wall in this nineteenth-century photograph of the Morning Room at Old Swan House. The circular table was designed by Philip Webb and probably made by Morris, Marshall, Faulkner & Co. It is similar to one formerly in the Ionides Collection in the 1880s chapter. [Historic England (Bedford Lemere)]

Fig. 5.89 When Treffry Dunn painted this gouache at Rossetti's house in 1882, he described the original George III-period settee in the sitting room as 'the only comfortable piece of furniture visible'. The settee was later purchased by Wickham Flower for Old Swan House in Chelsea before being offered for sale in New York in 1910. [© National Portrait Gallery, London]

Fig. 5.90 The sitting-room settee from Rossetti's Chelsea house which featured in Treffry Dunn's 1882 gouache, Fig. 5.89. Part of a suite with six side- and two armchairs, the settee was later exhibited by the London dealers, Partridge, Lewis & Simmons at the Plaza Hotel, New York, in 1910. The painted panels were thought to have been added by James McNeill Whistler, who was a neighbour and friend of Rossetti in Chelsea. [Private collection]

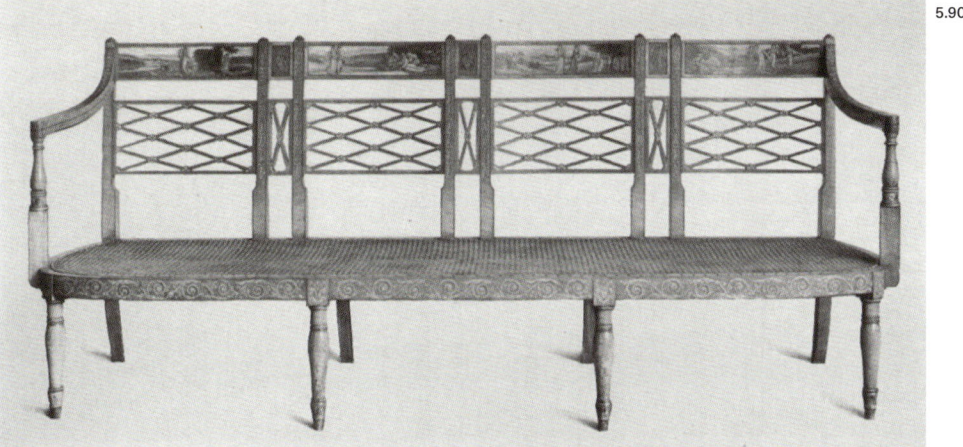

5.88

5.89

5.90

Fig. 5.91 **Rossetti's Sheraton-inspired settee made between 1861 and 1863 by Morris & Co, for the bedroom at 16 Cheyne Walk, Chelsea. Rossetti painted the three top-rail panels himself.** [© The Fitzwilliam Museum, Cambridge]

of the period. The surfaces are enriched with ivory-inlaid drapery, paterae, turtle doves, lovers' bows, garlands, martial trophies and lambrequins. Portraits of John Milton, John Keats, Geoffrey Chaucer and William Shakespeare refer to British literary heritage. The porcelain roundels are in a technique known as *camaïeu*, a development of the *pâte-sur-pâte* process, involving the layering of tints of a single colour to create an illusion of high relief. The shape of the cabinets followed contemporary Parisian forms, which were based on late eighteenth-century models. These were revisited in the nineteenth century by, for example, Grohé Frères in the 1860s and Henry Dasson in the 1880s. However, Hollands created something far more elaborate than most French designs. Both cabinets have gilt-bronze mounts of a higher quality than that typically seen on English furniture, being mercury gilt rather than gilt lacquer.

A similar cabinet, formerly part of Charles Handley-Read's collection, is in the Victoria and Albert Museum, **Fig. 5.98**.[96] It has been speculated that this cabinet was also made for Marlborough House.[97] Although not signed, the museum's example bears many hallmarks of being made by Holland & Sons in the 1860s and a table *en suite* with it bore their stamp.[98] However, the marquetry, although similar in some respects, is of a different design to the cabinets from Marlborough House. The execution is of the same high quality and may well be by the same marquetry-cutter, but it is by no means *en suite* with the Marlborough House furniture, nor does it have the exuberant, high-quality ormolu of the royal furniture. The female figures in the oval panels are comparable to influential designs by Thomas Hope, first published in 1809 and republished in 1841.[99]

Beavan describes that in the Main Dining Room of Marlborough House was 'a remarkably handsome sideboard by Holland & Sons. Like the rest of the furniture, it was made of mahogany and gold'.[100] On state occasions, the back of the sideboard was removed and a buffet added to display plate. Holland held a warrant for upholstery for the prince and princess and Beavan noted that 'their beautiful cabinet-work can more than hold sway with anything made abroad'.[101] The Dining Room was 'of handsome mahogany, plain in design…made entirely in London workshops'.[102] The princess's boudoir was considered the prettiest room in the house: 'some of the furniture is modern and some antique; but it is all marqueterie'.[103] Her bedroom was furnished with 'beautiful light Hungarian oak inlaid with purple wood and slightly gilded', while the dressing room had inlaid mahogany furniture with pretty chintz covers.[104] Other bedrooms were furnished with pieces in maple and inlaid with 'purple wood'.[105] Bamboo-style furniture adorned some of the royal visitors' bedrooms, the sitting rooms furnished with inlaid ebonised wood and Miss Knollys, the Lady of the Bedchamber, had black and gold furniture in her apartment.

The marriage of the Prince of Wales to Princess Alexandra of Denmark in 1863 was a popular royal wedding celebrated throughout Britain, with many gifts and presentations. One of the most idiosyncratic was a large writing table, an idea initiated by the 'Ladies of Bath', **Fig. 5.100**. The desk is a Louis XV-inspired writing table, or *bureau plat*, with an upper tier, or *gradin*. It was made by Thomas Knight of Bath to a design by C.E. Davis. Entitled *'The Ecritoire'*, a small volume by the seven-times mayor of Bath, Sir Jerom Murch, explained that the Worcester porcelain plaques, designed by Arthur Murch, were made by Thomas Bott, a decorator much favoured by Queen Victoria. The plaques commemorated monarchs of Britain from *c*.500 BCE to 1860. What the royal couple thought of the gift is unrecorded, but it is certainly a *tour de force* in craftsmanship. Eight cherubs sculpted in limewood hover around massive peacock legs in contrasting dark rosewood, each set with the arms of the four British nations. The impetus was to show the royal couple that Bath could achieve the heights of cabinet making

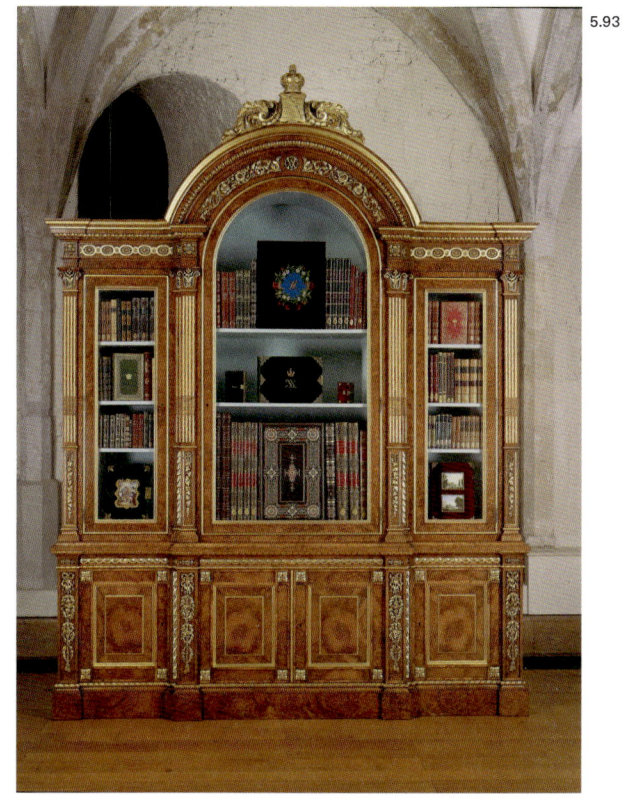

Fig. 5.92 'The Senses' – a marquetry table designed in 1853 by Charles Slocombe for the 4th Duke of Northumberland. Made in London by the Blake family firm, it was finally delivered in 1865. [The Northumberland Collection]

Fig. 5.93 A magnificent amboyna-veneered display cabinet, made by Holland & Sons for Queen Victoria in 1864 to hold mementos of the late Prince Albert, at a cost of £259 2s 8d. The arched top has Prince Albert's arms above the 'VA' cypher. [Royal Collection Trust / © His Majesty King Charles III 2023]

Fig. 5.94 The Drawing Room at Alnwick Castle, photographed in 1929. The centre table by Blake, delivered in 1865, is still in situ today. [*Country Life*, 1929]

5.95

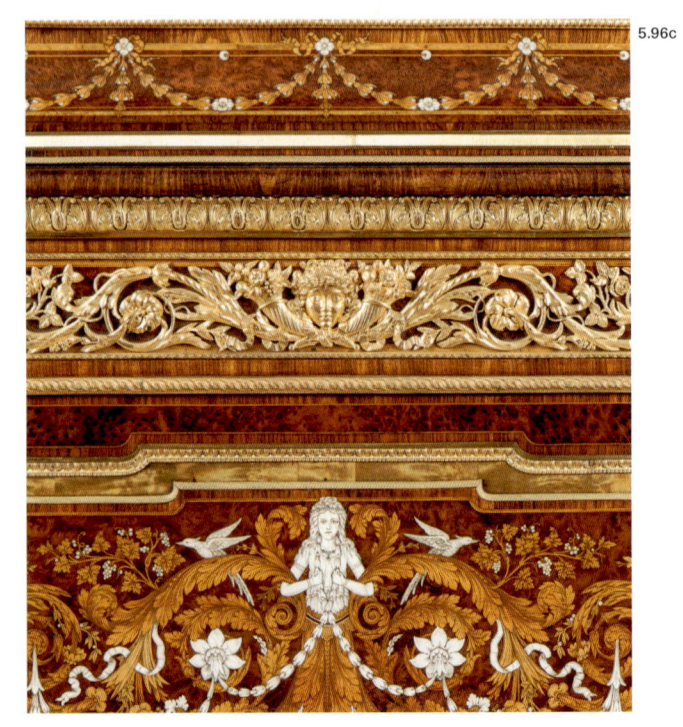

5.96b

5.96a

5.96c

Figs 5.95, 5.96a & b **Two cabinets by Holland & Sons made for Marlborough House. Each intricate and complex cabinet door, executed in marquetry in various woods and ivory, is identical except for the engraved ivory portrait medallions in profile. The large cabinet depicts Chaucer and Shakespeare, the smaller cabinet Milton and Keats.** [Butchoff Antiques]

Fig. 5.96c **The side of the Chaucer and Shakespeare cabinet highlighting the complex veneering and crossbanding in thuya, Circassian walnut and rare specimen woods, set with attributes of summer in gilt-bronze.** [Butchoff Antiques]

Fig. 5.96d **The back of the Chaucer and Shakespeare cabinet stamped with the Marlborough House inventory mark.** [Butchoff Antiques]

Fig. 5.97 **The Great Drawing Room at Marlborough House, a photograph taken in *c*.1896, showing a similar cabinet to the ones delivered by Holland & Sons.** [A.H. Beavan, *Marlborough House and Its Occupants, Present and Past*, 1896]

Fig. 5.98 **Similar but not identical to the Marlborough House cabinets, this cabinet is unsigned but was sold at auction with a table *en suite* stamped Holland & Sons.** [© Victoria and Albert Museum, London]

and technical ability, reported in an elaborate presentation folder as: 'the skill of the artists and artisans of the city'.[106] Technical delays meant that the desk was not presented to the royal couple until 1870 in a ceremony at Marlborough House. In 1896, Beavan wrote that there was 'an ebony table of rare workmanship, mounted in ormolu' in the Tapestry Room which may possibly be a reference to this desk. He also described how 'the room is crowded with pretty furniture'.[107] After the death of Edward VII in 1910, the desk entered the possession of Queen Alexandra's favourite brother-in-law, the Duke of Connaught, and remained with him until his death in 1940.

By the time of the 1867 exhibition in Paris, George Trollope & Sons were at the height of their powers as furniture makers and decorators. An 1864 extract from the diary of Lady Frederick Cavendish underlines the standing of the company among many of its clients: 'Thence to our splendid mansion No 21 Carlton House Terrace, where we met Mr. Talbot and Mr. Trollope, the builder and furnisher's man. And we have settled the whole painting of the house, chosen all the papers and the principal grates and discussed many other points'.[108] The amboyna-veneered octagonal table was of a form favoured by the firm, **Fig. 5.107**. The buttress supports are similar to a design used by Crace & Son.

Experimentation with different timbers and techniques continued, partly to be 'new' and 'up to date', partly to save costs. In 1861 John Dyer patented a process of imitation marquetry by stencilling onto veneers.[109] The side cabinet in **Fig. 5.110a** and the detail in **Fig. 5.110b** are a rare example of this technique, the cabinet unsigned but attributable to

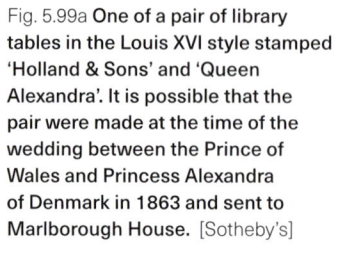

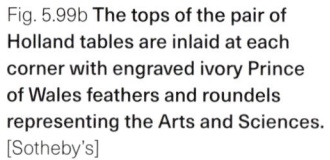

Fig. 5.99a One of a pair of library tables in the Louis XVI style stamped 'Holland & Sons' and 'Queen Alexandra'. It is possible that the pair were made at the time of the wedding between the Prince of Wales and Princess Alexandra of Denmark in 1863 and sent to Marlborough House. [Sotheby's]

Fig. 5.99b The tops of the pair of Holland tables are inlaid at each corner with engraved ivory Prince of Wales feathers and roundels representing the Arts and Sciences. [Sotheby's]

Fig. 5.100 An undated image of an idiosyncratic royal presentation desk, possibly taken at the Knight of Bath workshops on completion. [John Evan Bedford Library of Furniture History]

Fig. 5.101 Bruce Talbert designed this walnut cabinet in the Reformed Gothic style for Holland & Sons for the 1867 exhibition in Paris. Described by Hollands as 'An inlaid walnut wood Cabinet suited for Gothic furnishing — relieved by enamelled discs and subjects in silver deposit modelled from Tennyson's Day-dream'. The centrepiece of the Holland display in 1867 was a more imposing cabinet with references to Shakespeare, including Macbeth and Pericles, the Prince of Tyre.[110] [© Victoria and Albert Museum, London]

Fig. 5.102 The paper label printed 'G. TROLLOPE & SONS' on the back of this amboyna-veneered cabinet applied with Wedgwood plaques might suggest that it was retailed rather than made by them. A pencilled '3799' may one day be traced to an order book. Trollope also used Copeland porcelain plaques. [Christie's]

Dyer & Watts. The company exhibited a stencilled maple wardrobe at the Paris exhibition of 1867, which was later bought by Empress Eugénie. The firm was praised for its use of highly polished pitch pine used for bedroom furniture: 'It is clean, with neat lines of red, grey, and black, some of the lines imitative of inlaid wood'.[111] Jackson & Graham, Holland & Sons and others were also selling pine furniture, probably made for them by other workshops. A commercial reaction to the perceived excesses of the period was the use of so-called Hungarian Ash. Inspired by the simplicity of early nineteenth-century Biedermeier furniture from central Europe, ash became a popular wood which, despite its trade name, was mostly imported from North America. From a commercial point of view, ash had many benefits: it could be felled when young; it had straight grain, which was useful for drawer linings; and could offer highly figured almost

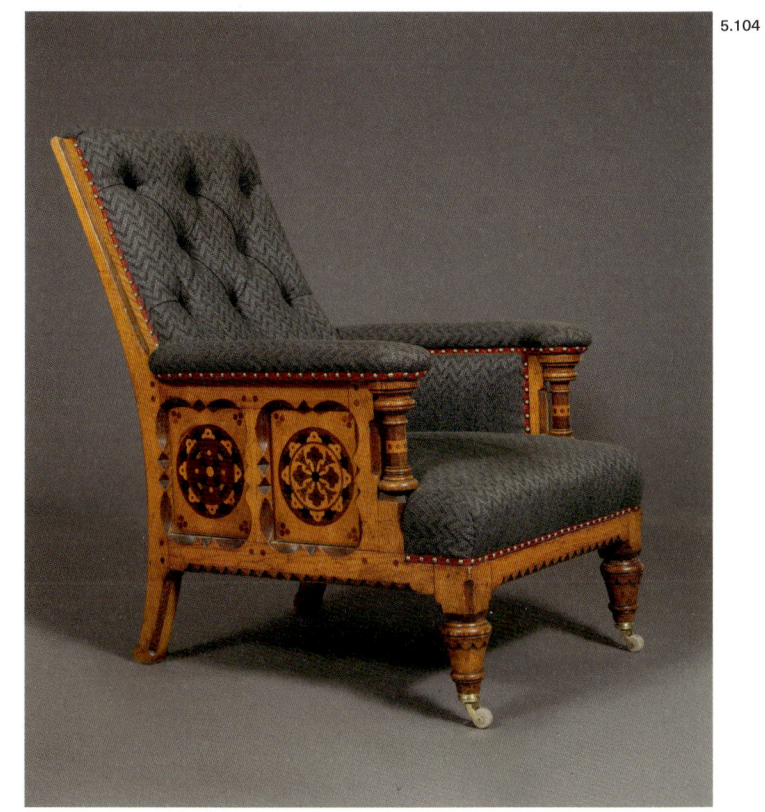

Fig. 5.103 The British furniture section in Paris at the 1867 exhibition. The stand of Jackson & Graham can be seen on the right with George Trollope & Sons on the left. [*The Illustrated London News*, 21 June 1862, p. 576]

Fig. 5.104 One of a pair of inlaid oak armchairs possibly designed by Charles Bevan and made by Marsh, Jones & Cribb for Titus Salt. [Carlton Hobbs LLC]

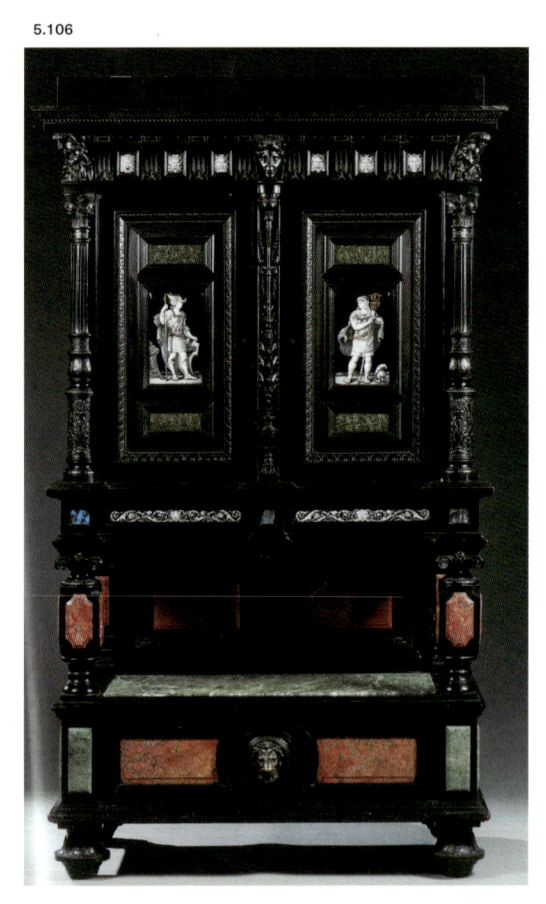

Fig. 5.105 Reputedly once owned by Lord Egremont, this large display cabinet was exhibited by Trollope in London in 1862. Designed by Richard Bevis, the carving was by Mark Rogers. The English porcelain plaques are a celebration of the Italian Renaissance, depicting Cellini and Michelangelo. [Sotheby's]

Fig. 5.106 Exhibited first at the Dublin Exhibition in 1865 and again in Paris in 1867 by Trollope, the bronze lion mask on the drawer uses the same casting as used by Trollope in 1862. The high-quality enamel plaques painted with Roman soldiers are initialled 'P.S.', possibly for the Sollier brothers.[112] [Sotheby's]

Fig. 5.107 An amboyna-veneered octagonal table by Trollope & Sons, exhibited in Paris in 1867 alongside a centre table in the same style. The radical design of the base is at odds with the Grecian decoration of the octagonal top, which is more typical of London makers of the 1860s. It is comparable to the top of the table in Fig. 5.108. [Sotheby's]

CHAPTER 5: 1860S

5.108

5.109

5.110a

5.110b

Fig. 5.108 The richly inlaid laurel and paterae border of this amboyna octagonal table suggests the influence of Owen Jones. The maker was possibly Holland, or Trollope of Halkin Street. [Private collection]

Figs 5.109 The use of well-figured Hungarian Ash is a feature often used by Holland & Sons in the 1860s. [Wick Antiques]

Figs 5.110a & b Dyer & Watts patented a method to stencil decoration onto timber, in this instance maple. Fig. 5.110a is probably the prototype in marquetry. In what is otherwise an identical cabinet down to every detail, the close-up of coloured foliage is another cabinet showing their method of stencilling. Unlike marquetry, the colours have remained remarkably fresh. [Wick Antiques]

zigzag-like figuring, which could be used in solid form, especially for bedroom furniture. Hollands as well as Gillows took advantage of this highly decorative wood, on occasion outlining it with purpleheart crossbandings.

A new aesthetic emerged in the 1860s, described in 1872 by the French art critic and collector Philippe Burty as 'Japonisme'. It was to have a lasting influence for the remainder of the century. In this emerging style the names of Christopher Dresser (1834–1904) and Edward William Godwin (1833–1866) appear for the first time, as well as other influential designers, such as Charles Locke Eastlake (1836–1906) and Thomas Jeckyll (1827–1881). Less well known are the designs of Richard Charles (dates unknown), published in 1868 in *The Cabinet Maker*. The designs of Charles, Talbert and Eastlake appear similar at first glance (all three worked in a strong architectural form), but Charles's extant designs are more delicate. After having published a series of articles anonymously Eastlake published his seminal *Hints on Household Taste in Furniture, Upholstery and Other Details*, richly illustrated with line drawings, in 1868. The work was internationally popular and was reprinted in the United States in 1872.[113] Although Eastlake's influence was wide ranging, relatively few of his furniture designs were executed; most of those that appear are thought to have been made by Jackson & Graham. Advocating the use of solid wood and traditional construction methods, Eastlake championed Morris as one of the first 'Arts and Crafts' makers.

The entry of the United States commodore, Matthew C. Perry, into Japanese waters in 1853–4 had resulted in the United States and Great Britain signing treaties with Japan. These were followed by Japanese treaties with Russia, Holland and France in 1858. An exhibition of Japanese goods at the International Exhibition in London in 1862, based on a collection formed by Sir Rutherford Alcock, the British Consul in Tokyo, created great interest amongst designers and consumers.[114] The young Arthur Lasenby

Fig. 5.111 'The Bloomfield Cabinet' by Charles Locke Eastlake, its uncompromising form underlines his dislike of fussy exhibition furniture as outlined in his *Hints on Household Taste in Furniture, Upholstery and other Details* of 1868. [Oscar Graf]

Fig. 5.112 By 1867 James Shoolbred of Tottenham Court Road was advertising simulated bamboo furniture, in this instance bedroom furniture, in what was described as 'In the Japanese Style'. [The Stapleton Collection / Bridgeman Images]

Fig. 5.113 A fine music cabinet, inlaid with ebony and ivory, possibly designed by Owen Jones, made *c*.1863 probably by Jackson & Graham. [Anthony Outred]

5.113

Liberty (1843–1917) managed the dispersal of some of the 1862 exhibition merchandise, opening his eponymous store in 1875, which continues today.

The Japanese Court at the London exhibition was seen as an exotic novelty, although the subtle difference between the mixed Sino-Japanese display in 1851 and the purity of the Japanese stand of 1862, with items from the collection of Alcock, may have been lost on the general public. Asian influence had an immediate impact on furniture design,

and by 1867 the enterprising firm of James Shoolbred was advertising a bamboo-style, aesthetic bedroom suite, **Fig. 5.112**. Bamboo turnings became commonplace, and complete pieces of furniture were made from imported bamboo by over 250 manufacturers established mainly in London and Birmingham.

As early as 1859, William Burges had copied a trellis from a Japanese cabinet in his own collection for decoration on a 'Wines & Beers Sideboard'.[115] It was not until 1867

Fig. 5.114 An ivory-inlaid display cabinet designed by Owen Jones in the cinquecento style, made in the Jackson & Graham workshop. A series of eight identical sections were made by the firm for an apse at Fonthill, c.1865. The discreetly hidden cabinet maker's stamp 'R Robinson', a name previously unrecorded, has been discovered on this cabinet. [H. Blairman & Sons]

Fig. 5.115a An ebonised display cabinet with ivory inlay, possibly designed by Owen Jones. It is the only piece of Jackson & Graham furniture on record with the unique signature of Peter and Forster Graham, partners in the firm. Part of the Jackson & Graham commission from Alfred Morrison, it is, uniquely, dated '1866'. [Trustees of the Cecil Higgins Art Gallery (The Higgins Bedford)]

Fig. 5.115b The only known signed piece of furniture by Jackson & Graham, detail from the vitrine, Fig. 5.115a. [Trustees of the Cecil Higgins Art Gallery (The Higgins Bedford)]

that Godwin designed his iconic Anglo-Japanese sideboard, some made of ebonised mahogany by William Watt & Co.; ebonised pine examples were also produced until *c*.1880.[116] Godwin's dramatically innovative design was immensely practical and stylish and could not be in sharper contrast to the heavily carved sideboards produced by the Warwick School. In the words of Kenneth Ames, 'The Battle of the Sideboards' had truly begun.[117]

Figure 5.113 shows an ebony and ivory music cabinet that has all the hallmarks of a relatively early collaboration between Owen Jones and Jackson & Graham. The central section has five divisions for music folios above a fall-front with shelves for sheet music with leather edges. An ivory-inlaid monogram on the front incorporates two 'G's. It is tempting to speculate that Jones designed the cabinet for George Eliot and G.H. Lewes as part of the new decorative scheme for their house, The Priory, Regent's Park, incorporating their first initials in the monogram.[118]

Owen Jones's influence on furniture design grew throughout the 1860s, fuelled by his publication of *The Grammar of Chinese Ornament* in 1867. In the late 1860s, Jackson & Graham fitted out a new room added to Alfred Morrison's country house, Fonthill. The room was lined in ebony-veneered, ivory-inlaid panelling and fitted with a fire surround and overmantel designed by Jones. The intricate detail of the design was meticulously executed by Jackson & Graham; the minute ivory foliage inlaid into hard ebony demonstrating a high degree of skill, **Fig. 5.114**. Jones also designed the tall cabinet supplied by Jackson & Graham to Morrison at 16 Carlton House Terrace, **Fig. 5.120**. In 1870, Henry Cole described the house as 'filled with marquetrie [*sic*] designed by Owen Jones...mixture of Greek & Moorish, perfect mechanical work'.[119] Jones had access to the extensive collection of works of art amassed by Morrison and realised that he had not given enough thought in his 1856 *The Grammar of Ornament* to the Moorish and Islamic influence on Chinese decoration. His new publication coincided with a heightened interest in Asia and the dawn of the European Aesthetic movement.

The signature, **Fig. 5.115b**, on the Jackson & Graham vitrine, **Fig. 5.115a**, is the only known signature of the partners in the firm. Possibly significantly, it is made of individual letters and not a one-piece stamp as one might expect, such as 'Jackson & Graham' but reads 'Peter & Forster Graham London 1866'. The vitrine was part of the firm's commission from Alfred Morrison and is an important indication as to the date of this style of very high-quality furniture with engraved ivory marquetry inlaid into ebony. It is a useful contribution when considering the maker of such furniture, habitually attributed to Jackson & Graham by style and quality but without actual documentation.

Another piece which must be from the same workshops is the little ebony and ivory-inlaid writing table, one of the most fascinating examples of British furniture made in the French idiom, **Fig. 5.117a**. It is a Victorian updating of the *chiffonnière* supplied by Jean-Henri Riesener to Marie Antoinette in *c*.1781 and later acquired by the 10th Duke of Hamilton. The lock is simply stamped 'VR' for Victoria Regina which is little help as to the date of manufacture. There were two public opportunities for copying the French design: the first and most probable was when the original desk was shown at the South Kensington Loan Exhibition in June 1862;[120] the second was when it was offered at the auction of the contents of Hamilton Palace by the 12th Duke of Hamilton twenty years later.[121] Although the dimensions differ, the shape of the 'copy' is clearly the same as the original, but less complex, with only a writing slide above the drawer. It has been made in a modern and innovative manner, using the decorative contrast of ebony and ivory instead of the original more familiar concept of gilt bronze, *satiné* and stained woods. The unknown designer and maker have echoed the 'ormolu' of the original in two-dimensional form, with beautiful and striking inlaid and engraved ivory interpreting the original marquetry. Even the pierced ebony gallery meticulously copies the original, but in ebony. The

Fig. 5.116 **The catalogue of the Hamilton Palace sale illustrated the original table supplied by Riesener to Marie-Antoinette in *c*.1781, purchased by the dealer Samson Wertheimer for Baron Ferdinand de Rothschild in 1882 for £6,000 and now at Waddesdon Manor.** [Author's image]

5.117a

Fig. 5.117a A rare and innovative ebony and ivory-inlaid writing table, a two-dimensional exercise inspired by a *chiffonnière* supplied by Jean-Henri Riesener to Marie-Antoinette in *c*.1781. [Private collection]

Fig. 5.117b A detail of the front of the work table inspired by the *chiffonnière* supplied by Jean-Henri Riesener to Marie Antoinette. At a time when other London makers were making exact copies of French royal furniture, this appears to be a unique example of a maker, almost certainly Jackson & Graham, using an innovative technique of *trompe l'oeil* in ivory to simulate not only marquetry but also the highly complex three-dimensional gilt-bronze mounts. [Private collection]

5.117b

Fig. 5.118 **A centre table designed by Owen Jones and made by Jackson & Graham between 1867 and 1870 for Alfred Morrison at 16 Carlton House Terrace.** [H. Blairman & Sons]

Fig. 5.119 **An extraordinarily inventive armchair in a modernised Georgian form. One of a pair made by Jackson & Graham to a design by Owen Jones for Alfred Morrison at 16 Carlton House Terrace,** *c.*1867–70, it is veneered in mahogany, purpleheart, ebony, harewood and holly with parcel-gilt highlights.[122] A small table, inlaid in satinwood, almost certainly from the same commission is shown on p. 565. [Art Institute of Chicago]

drawer is of solid mahogany with a quarter moulding typical of the best English makers.

The centre table and one of a pair of armchairs, originally with a sofa, designed by Owen Jones and made by Jackson & Graham for Morrison's house at 16 Carlton House Terrace, **Figs 5.118 & 5.119**, are in a highly inventive style. The pierced back of the chair has a similar feel to the legs of the table, both unusual and inventive with conforming swirling foliage. The large cabinet, **Fig. 5.120**, about 10ft high (over 3m), was also made for the house and is inlaid with a variety of woods, including ebony, purpleheart, holly and sycamore. The glazing of the central upper part is framed in gilt bronze.

Two magnificent cabinets exhibited by Jackson & Graham and Wright & Mansfield at the 1867 Paris exhibition could hardly be of greater contrast, **Figs 5.121 & 5.122**. Jackson & Graham chose the High Renaissance style for a hardstone encrusted cabinet. Engravings from 1867[123] show the lower portion with different side doors to the finished cabinet. The cabinet was not ready in time for the exhibition, did not find a buyer and four years later was shown in completed form at the 1871 International Exhibition in London. George Wallis, the Keeper of the Art Collections at the South Kensington Museum, wrote that 'The CABINET…will be classed amongst the most admirable specimens of its class: perhaps no country, in our time, has produced a work so perfect'.[124] However, it again failed to find a buyer, probably because of a combination of two factors: cost and a waning British interest in large Renaissance-style cabinets. Sent abroad again, this time to Vienna for the 1873 World's Fair, it was eventually returned to Jackson & Graham in London. Intriguingly, for such a fine piece that would have taken countless hours to make with a considerable outlay of materials and time, the precise circumstances surrounding the commission are uncertain. An unsubstantiated rumour, reported in *The Furniture*

Gazette, was that it was commissioned by the future Earl of Bective (1844–1893) to celebrate his marriage to Lady Alice Maria Hill in 1867.[125] The cost of the cabinet is seemingly unparalleled at £4,000, the equivalent of close to £5 million today. However, this does not square with the fact that the cabinet was shown again in London and Vienna over the next six years, and eventually sold at auction for 500 guineas.[126] *The Furniture Gazette*'s report on the demise of one of Jackson & Graham's craftsmen, Ole Petersen, a name hitherto unknown, showed he was the cabinet maker who executed this piece. He died aged thirty-nine and had 'for many years past been almost exclusively engaged upon the exhibition work of Messrs. Jackson & Graham'.[127] Another of the firm's craftsmen was named as Andersen, once again, a Danish name. Might it be presumed that there was a certain influx of Danes into England as a result of the trauma of the Second Schleswig War in 1863–1864?

Hungerford Pollen became Assistant Keeper of the South Kensington Museum in 1863 and, working in his early years with such luminaries as Dante Gabriel Rossetti, William Morris and Edward Burne-Jones, was aware of progressive design. His legacy is a fascinating collection of furniture acquired for the museum through the exhibition era. Perhaps unusually for an upper-middle-class man, educated at Eton and Oxford, he was interested in the *craft* of furniture making, not simply the outer surface; he recognised the superb skills of the men and women who worked in the myriad of cabinet-making workshops throughout Britain.[128] His comments on the Jackson & Graham cabinet designed by Lormier, **Fig. 5.121**, when shown at the World's Fair in 1873 underline his grasp of detail and understanding of the mysteries of veneering. He noted the '…great mechanical skill in a modern piece of very difficult execution…The little columns of an inch and a half diameter were entirely covered with reticulated pattern in different woods…The marquetry in the instance of these columns had to be wrapped round each circular shaft'.[129] George Sala had also commented on the cabinet at the 1867 exhibition, noting that it had been impossible to finish the last three marquetry panels of the cabinet in time, so a photographic print was displayed under glass at the exhibition, which was later replaced by marquetry panels after they were completed. Sala continued 'the workman…has laid in the ivory morsel by morsel, strip by strip, curve by curve. The result is most perfect unity, solidity, and natural grace. You might pass your finger — as connoisseurs try fine porcelain'.[130]

Sala gives a frustratingly incomplete account of a group of 170 British 'working tourists' subsidised to visit the exhibition in Paris. In typical Sala humour, he gives two fictious names, 'John Bradawl' and 'Timothy Teesquare' with little or no detail. Intriguingly he suggests that they might 'peep into a few French workshops, and shake hands…with a few shop-mates'.[131]

The enlightened director of the South Kensington Museum, Henry Cole, was far-sighted enough to purchase exhibition pieces in the full knowledge of their importance as a record of design history and the extraordinary skills needed to produce such works of art. The exhibition items that are seen on the market today are few and far between and offer a rare opportunity to see, observe and collect. One of the most significant purchases of furniture was the magnificent 'Adam' cabinet set with Wedgwood plaques and exhibited by Wright & Mansfield in Paris in 1867, **Fig. 5.122**. A complete

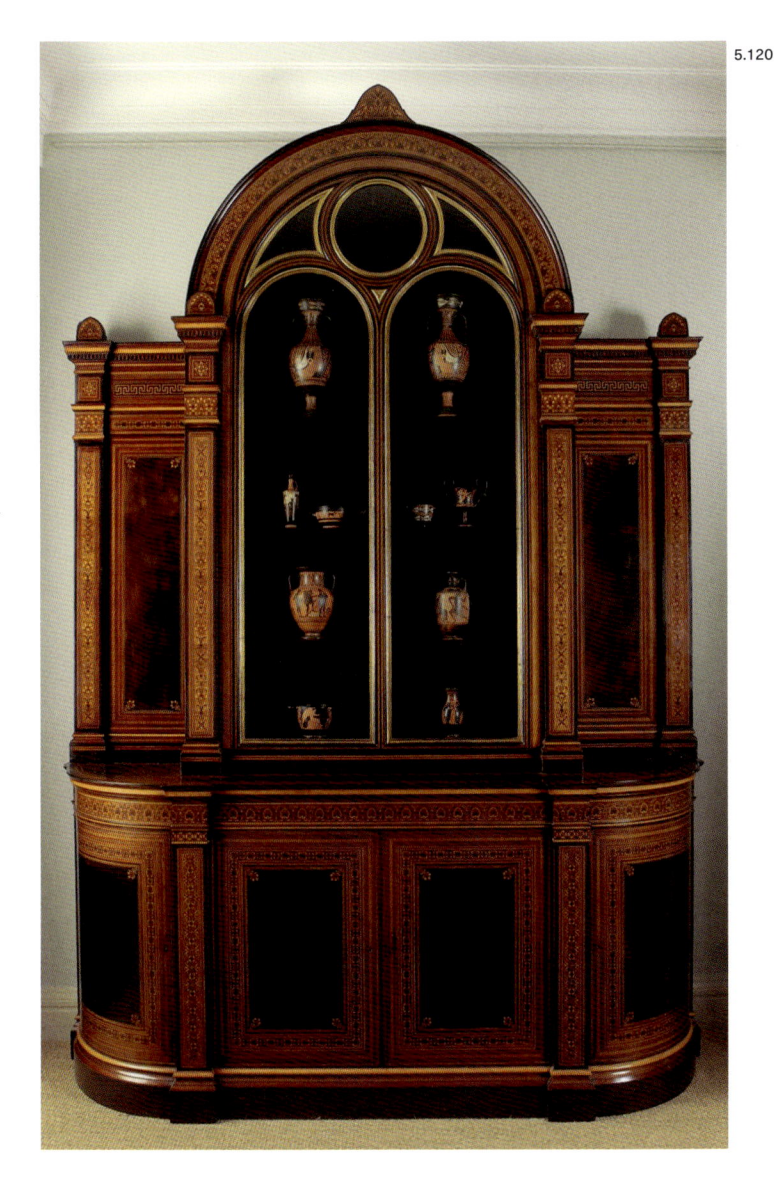

Fig. 5.120 **Exhibited in Paris in 1867, this cabinet was made *c*.1865 by Jackson & Graham for Alfred Morrison at 16 Carlton House Terrace. The woods used include ebony, purpleheart, holly and sycamore. The glazing of the central upper part is framed in gilt-bronze.** [Harris Lindsay]

5.121

Fig. 5.121 Designed by Alfred Lormier and made by Ole Petersen for Jackson & Graham, this cabinet in ivory and ebony is a masterpiece of design and execution. Only the lower part was ready to exhibit at the 1867 Paris exhibition, but when completed was shown in its entirety in London in 1871 and again in Vienna in 1873. The locks are stamped 'Chubb & Co., Makers to Her Majesty, No. 596210'.[132] [Galerie Neuse]

Fig. 5.122 Designed by the unheralded 'Mr Crosse' and made by Wright & Mansfield, this satinwood veneered cabinet, over three metres (10ft) high, was the only piece of British furniture to be awarded a gold medal in Paris in 1867. Originally valued at £1,400, it remained unsold at the exhibition and was purchased the following year by the South Kensington Museum for £800. [© Victoria and Albert Museum, London]

contrast to Jackson & Graham's Renaissance-stye offering, it was the second international airing of the Georgian Revival style, with the designs of Robert Adam used as a base. Pollen admired it greatly: 'I must not pass over in silence a beautiful kind of furniture which was in fashion a century since, and has been revived by Messrs. Wright & Mansfield, and other firms, viz. satin-wood furniture'.[133] Wright & Mansfield were awarded a gold medal for the cabinet, the only time such an honour was given to an English cabinet maker. The judges were presided over by Alexandre du Sommerard, director of the Cluny Museum, and M. Wilkinson, *Administrateur de Mobilier de la Couronne*, the medal was presented personally by Napoleon III. For their efforts, however, Wright & Mansfield suffered a similar fate to that of Jackson & Graham. Their cabinet, originally priced at £1,400, was eventually purchased by the South Kensington Museum for £800.[134] Even at that reduced figure, it was still an extraordinarily large sum.

Despite the high quality, it is surprising that the gilt decoration is not bronze but gilded wood over a white bole, burnished to an astonishing hue. The normally unseen back panels are of mahogany, while the husks or swags round the necks of the sphinxes are, somewhat unusually, made of a type of composition material made using a similar technique

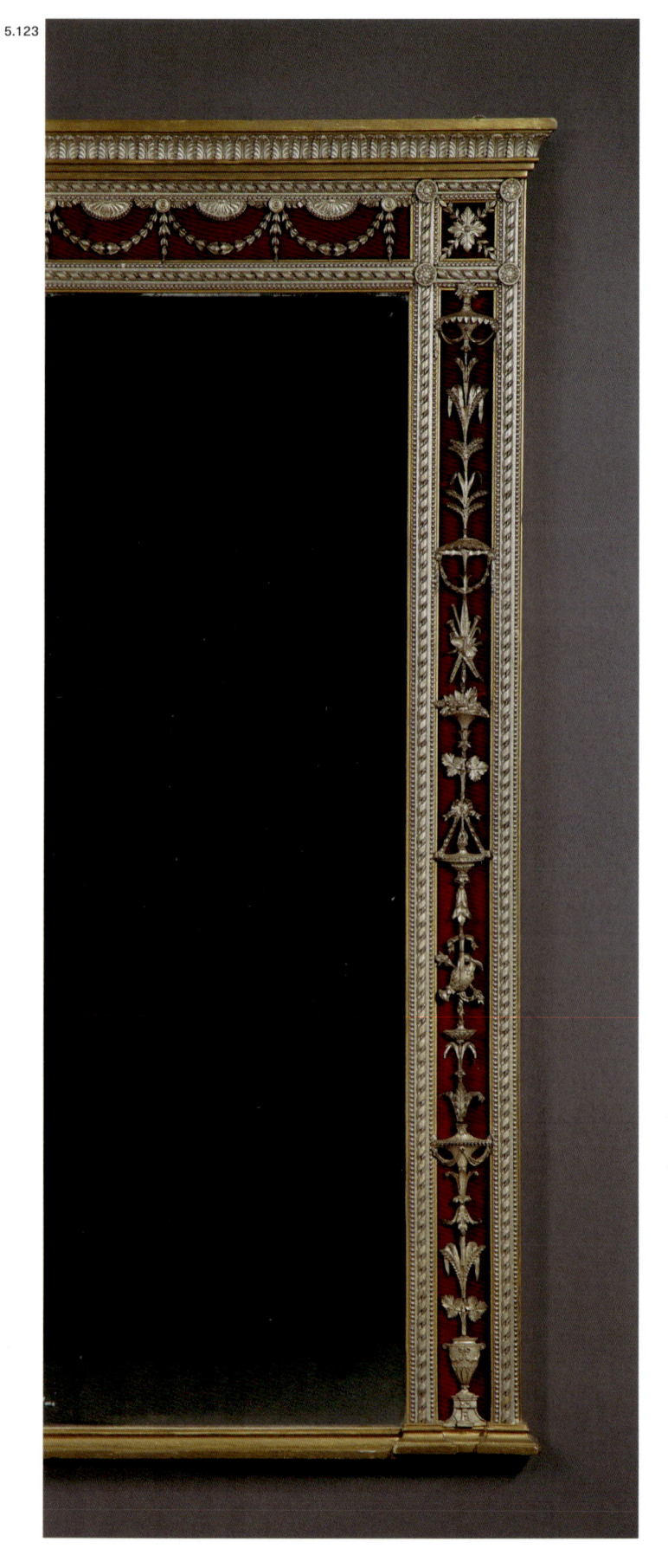

Fig. 5.123 The unknown maker of this mirror, an exercise in rectilinear Neoclassical design, has overlaid silver-gilt decoration on a luxurious red velvet ground. [Carlton Hobbs LLC]

Fig. 5.124 Robert Strahan & Co. sent a variety of furniture to the Dublin exhibition in 1865. The mirrored cabinet was in rosewood, the cresting carved with birds and fruit in sycamore. [*The Art Journal Illustrated Catalogue of the International Exhibition*, 1862, p. 104]

Fig. 5.125 A Wedgwood, ivory, amboyna and ebony cabinet exhibited in Paris in 1867. Made in the Etruscan style, the locks are stamped 'J. Lamb, Manchester, Secure Patent'. Lamb's name 'was a synonym for the best in everything he did from 1850 to 1885…'.[135] [Sotheby's]

Fig. 5.126 The maker of this ivory-inlaid satinwood cabinet from the 1862 to 1867 exhibition era remains a mystery. The form of the cabinet and Etruscan-style inlay has similarities with cabinet shown on the left by Lamb of Manchester exhibited in Paris in 1867. Jackson & Graham, Holland & Sons or Trollope & Sons are also contenders. [MS Rau Antiques]

to that used by the Booker family of Dublin, who wrapped mirror columns with composite swags. By 1867, Wright & Mansfield had firmly established themselves as London's foremost exponents of the Adam Revival style in furniture.

Following on from the success of the Great Industrial Exhibition held in Dublin in 1853, the Guinness family of brewers financed a second exhibition in the city in 1865. One exhibitor was the Dublin firm of Fry with forty craftsmen on their payroll including marquetry inlayers and gilders. Robert Strahan & Co. exhibited the Rococo Revival mirrored sideboard (**Fig. 5.124**) and an oak centre table supported by recumbent winged beasts, the same piece they had exhibited in London three years earlier. English makers such as Crace and Howard & Sons were also represented; Gillows sent a 'walnut sideboard, carved and inlaid with marbles'. J. Eagan of Killarney had a stand showing arbutus wood furniture, an essentially Irish style. Patrick Beakey of Dublin, active between 1825 and 1900, had exhibited in Dublin in 1853 and returned in 1865, under the name of Beakey & McDowell, with a suite of Gothic-inspired furniture.

The looking-glass maker, George Sims of London and Manchester began silvering mirrors in 1818. By the mid-1860s the firm was silvering over eleven acres of glass every year, as well as making furniture.[136] In 1878, Sims registered an Adam-style design for a pair of large mirrors. It was more elaborate than the unusual silver-gilt example of the 1860s shown here with decoration overlaid onto red velvet, **Fig. 5.123**.

In the 1860s, firms such as Hampton & Sons emerged as makers and retailers on a large scale. The firm's 200-page catalogue, published in 1869, was crammed with engravings in a wide variety of styles, with furniture to suit most pockets. By this time, more and more steam machinery was being used, even by firms supplying the luxury market. Increasingly only the most delicate operations were executed by hand. This set the scene for the development of the next decade and the increasing rise of the middle-class consumer.

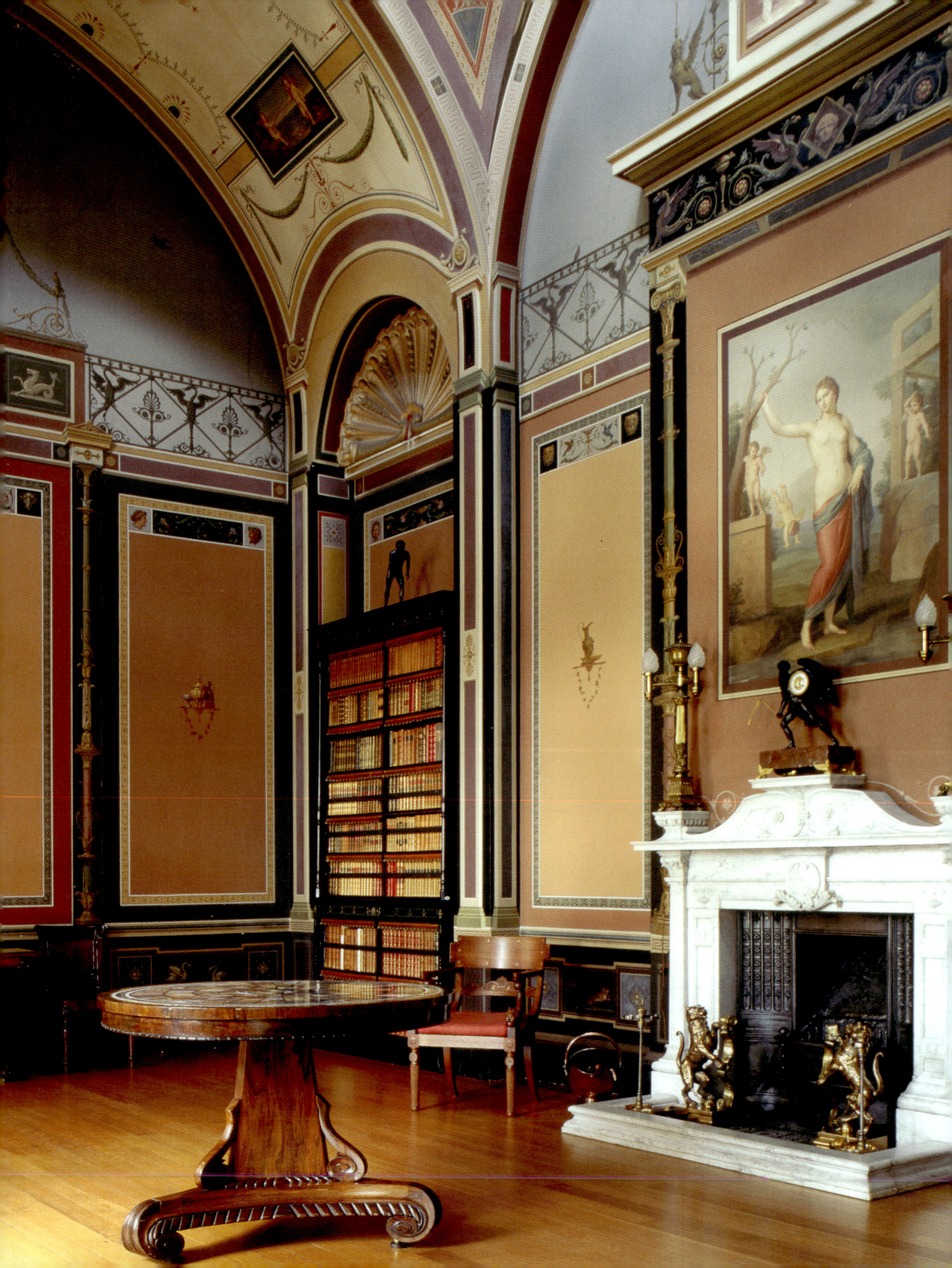

CHAPTER 6

1870s

'Our millionaires are maniacs for collecting things.'[1]

Publications throughout the nineteenth century allow contemporary insights into furniture and decoration, of which *The Furniture Gazette*, first published in 1872, is a prime example.[2] Each issue offered a wealth of interesting information to the furniture historian and collector. It was the first journal dedicated to furniture and the associated trades and is a rich seam of informative detail. Other publications included *The Cabinetmaker & Art Furnisher* (1880), *The Building News*, *The House-Furnisher and Decorator* (1871) and *The Art-Workman* (1873). Although the weekly reports and advertisements are somewhat repetitive, *The Furniture Gazette* is full of interesting snippets; recently digitalised they are easily searched.[3] Larger mainstream firms, such as Jackson & Graham (amongst others) are mentioned, but it was mainly the smaller firms who advertised in what was essentially a trade magazine. Comments were on both a practical and informative basis. On a practical level, such reports can give us an understanding of specific marketing techniques of the furniture trade. The weekly reports also served to educate, frequently discussing previous styles of furniture and decoration. Although it seems surprising to our modern views of marketing, the more established firms such as Gillows, Morant and Dowbiggin did not deign to have a window display. Competition from new large stores, such as that of James Shoolbred, forced makers to change this strategy, and it was reported that Jackson & Graham would 'place one choice item in their window'.[5]

Comprehensive furniture catalogues were produced by retailers; one by James Shoolbred in 1874 shows the wide variety of goods available at the time. Following a relatively new trend, Shoolbreds was a complete house furnisher, down to bedding, pots and pans. Advertising over four hundred pieces of furniture, their 1874 catalogue contained numerous line engravings of complete rooms, ranging from the Medieval Revival style through Louis XVI Neoclassicism to *Japonisme*. A popular model was the small oak bench in the Aesthetic manner with a brass chrysanthemum flowerhead in the form of a Japanese *mon* applied at either side, **Fig. 6.5**, some stamped with the 'Kite' registration mark from the British Patent Office from which the year of the patent can be read. A range of hall stands and seat furniture in the *Japonisme* and 'Art Botanical' taste espoused by Christopher Dresser appeared in the 1875 and 1876 Shoolbred catalogues. As well as the more utilitarian, the firm provided furniture made to the highest standards. A prime example was a stunning upright piano designed by H.W. Batley, housing a Collard & Collard movement, the first example exhibited in Paris in 1878, **Fig. 6.6**. The satinwood case is in the Aesthetic style of 'Art Furniture', luxuriously carved with Chinese-style fretwork and sunflowers in solid boxwood.

Fig. 6.1 (opposite) **The Pompeian Room at Ickworth House completed in 1879 by F.C. Penrose and J.D. Crace would have been the ideal location for the suite of library furniture exhibited by Howard & Sons in 1862, Fig 5.7.**[4] [*Country Life*, 1993]

285

Fig. 6.2 **The cosy style of the Victorian era was captured in 1872 by the *Punch* cartoonist John Tenniel in Lewis Carroll's *Through the Looking-Glass* and *What Alice Found There*.** [Ivy Close Images / Alamy Stock Photo]

Fig. 6.3 **Queen Victoria's Private Dining and Lunch Room at Buckingham Palace, photographed in 1873. The George IV chinoiserie side tables and many of the fittings were originally made for Brighton Pavilion. In the centre is a late variation of a Jupe-style extending table.** [Royal Collection Trust / © His Majesty King Charles III 2023]

Fig. 6.4 **The Drawing Room at Tyntesfield, with painted decoration by John Crace, photographed by Bedford Lemere in 1878. The pair of cabinets are presently unattributed but have similarities with a cabinet by Lamb of Manchester and a satinwood cabinet in the previous chapter, Fig. 5.125.** [Historic England (Bedford Lemere)]

Shoolbred made an iconic sideboard, later termed the 'Pet' sideboard, designed by Bruce Talbert and exhibited by Gillows at the 1871 International Exhibition. Similar designs by Talbert are illustrated in his 1876 publication, *Examples of Ancient and Modern Furniture*.

Each issue of *The Furniture Gazette* gave an exhaustive list of imported timbers and kept a watchful eye on the rapidly developing timber and furniture-making industry in the United States. Subsequent years devoted much comment to concerns about the increasing competition from the United States, especially the threat of medium-priced and lower range furniture. The journal reported on the inventiveness of American woodworking machinery and the quality of their hand tools. In 1878, British furniture exports exceeded those of the United States by £50,000,[6] but there was considerable concern about the decrease in the export activity from British furniture firms: 'In London the trade is far from brisk'.[7] American, notably Chicago, furniture makers were providing fierce competition. By 1879, the highest quantity by value of British furniture exports was to Britain's various territories in South Africa; the not inconsiderable sum of £88,932. France was next at £52,670, followed by the Channel Islands at £20,640.[8] W.C. Wigg, an East End furniture maker and dealer, had the innovative idea of publishing a catalogue in Portuguese in an attempt to tap into the growing wealth of South America.[9] The import duty however could be punitive. For example, in Uruguay the duty on furniture was set at 37 per cent.[10]

Books on furniture abounded. The bookseller Bernard Quaritch, who set up his own business in London in 1847,

Fig. 6.5 A walnut 'Aesthetic' hall bench retailed by James Shoolbred. Each side is applied with a brass Japanese-style sixteen-petal chrysanthemum *mon*. It was a popular model and continued to be made in walnut or in oak well into the 1880s and later, some with the diamond-shaped 'Kitemark' registration. [Private collection]

Fig. 6.6 James Shoolbred & Co. employed Henry Batley to furnish their exhibition house on the Street of Nations at the Paris Exhibition of 1878. Batley's designs included suites of satinwood and boxwood furniture and a piano of the same design as this example. The slender ring turned legs were used by Shoolbred on their more commercial furniture. [© Victoria and Albert Museum, London]

advertised new and second-hand books in *The Furniture Gazette* in 1876, the year that the journal commenced an ever-expanding bibliography of furniture and decoration publications. By 1876, the typeface of its title page was changed, bringing its look more in line with current Aesthetic trends in the decorative arts.

Inspired by the enthusiasm and drive of luminaries such as Henry Cole, education was the key to success. The 1st Duke of Westminster began allowing limited access to his collection at Grosvenor House, restricted to four hours, and only on Sunday afternoons. Tickets were limited to artisans and people in the trade, clearly intended as an opportunity for them to learn, but a further restriction was that it was weather dependent – the duke did not want visitors 'on wet afternoons'. Entry tickets could be applied for from larger furniture makers or retailers such as Crace, Jackson & Graham or Gillows.[11] Training was all-important and recognised as essential to the success of the industry. In July 1872, with Queen Victoria's third son, Prince Arthur, Duke

Fig. 6.7 **A Dining Room by Gillows at the Prince of Wales's Pavilion at the 1878 exhibition. Gillows also created a 'Modern Jacobean' hall for the exhibition and an elaborate boudoir in the Adam style for the Princess of Wales.** [Look & Learn]

DINING-ROOM AT THE PRINCE OF WALES'S PAVILION—PARIS EXHIBITION, 1878.

of Connaught and Strathearn, in the chair, a report noted: 'It has long been acknowledged that if this country is efficiently to maintain its manufacturing supremacy in the markets of the world, the technical education of our artisans must be improved'.[12] Training of personnel from the provinces was equally as important. Examples included John Manuel junior, who received training at the Sheffield Art School, one of whose examiners was no less than Edward Poynter R.A.,[13] and Christopher Dresser, born in Glasgow to a Yorkshire family, who attended the Government School of Design at Somerset House at the age of thirteen.

Information in contemporary trade journals for historians today is limited by the comparative rarity of signed or fully attributable examples of furniture. Extensive lists of makers ranged from Wallace of Curtain Road in London to Payne & Co. of Cardiff, and from 'The Golden Chair' in Manchester to Symon of Aberdeen. The lists show the enormous number of firms involved in the furniture and associated trades, many of whom are unknown today, their furniture, if still in existence, unidentifiable. The furniture industry in London was slowly spreading to the east. In 1846 there were fifty-nine furniture workshops recorded in the East End, eighty-nine by 1859.[14] By the mid-1870s, *The Furniture Gazette*'s listing of cabinet makers was expanded to cover the whole of Britain, not just London.

The journal estimated that there were some 5 million houses to be furnished in Britain. Few could afford furniture at the top end of the market but there was an inevitable growth of demand at home as well as abroad. In 1890 it was estimated that 57,000 people were employed as cabinet makers, including approximately 9,000 women, with a further 7,500 employed as carvers and gilders and 7,000 French polishers. There were over 12,000 furniture workers in London, more than 1,800 in the Birmingham area, 795 in Manchester, 610 in Leeds, 454 in Bradford and 454 in West Derby. By this time increasing trade union activity was also beginning to benefit the conditions of the working population.[15]

As demand for furniture boomed in the 1870s, the Leeds firm of Jones & Cribb, advertising in the first of the new series of *The Furniture Gazette* as 'late Kendall & Co.', promised 'constant employment and good wages for good workmen'. Underlying the rapid growth of provincial firms, in the same issue the little-known 'Punch Brothers of Middlesbrough [sic]' were looking for 'twenty good cabinet-makers...five polishers and four good deal hands'.[16] Shortages of manpower were reported in May 1873 with an increasing demand for cabinet makers in London. In June 1877, the journal published comparative wages of the cabinet trade in seventy-five English towns. The average hours

Fig. 6.8 **Robinson & Son of Rochdale, initially timber merchants and joiners, started making machinery in 1848. This advertisement for an 'endless band sawing machine' for cutting shapes is from their 1873 catalogue after they had exhibited at the Vienna Exhibition.** [Robinson catalogue]

Fig. 6.9 **Established prior to 1845, the Birmingham firm of Udal & Sons produced a familiar array of medieval and Gothic-style brass fittings for furniture, as can be seen in this advertisement.** [*The Furniture Gazette*, 12 July 1879]

worked per week were fifty-five. Lancaster workers earned 30s a week, Londoners up to £2, whilst Taunton wages were 22–26s per week and York 26–28s. A week later a report on the state of many workshops made depressing reading. Titled 'Cheerless Workshops' the reporter wrote that 'many of them are dark, crowded, dreary places...workshops that were dark and damp'.[17] Workshop conditions appear to be at odds with the extraordinary high quality of the work that we see and treasure today. A report on Foster & Cooper shows that many firms were buying in wholesale furniture, whilst pointing out that they also made items in-house. With two warehouses in the city and a sawmill, the Nottingham firm was clearly an important manufacturer and employer. Their new premises used machinery made by Robinsons of Rochdale for sawing timber, as well as Armstrong's patent machine for making dovetails and a 135-foot-long (41 metres) machining room for planing.[18] The band saw was an essential machine for any workshop and Robinsons constantly improved their design to try to stop blades breaking. Advertising in *The Furniture Gazette* often brought about a visit from the journal's reporters, usually to good effect. Peter Lironi, a frequent advertiser based in Worship Street near Finsbury Square, known for mirror frames, was described in August 1877 as an important wholesale cabinet maker to the trade. *The Furniture Gazette* is full of references to a plethora of makers about whom we know basic facts such as work addresses but without evidence of exactly what they made.[19] A reporter visiting William Waines of Newington Butts, who had started modestly in 1848 and whose premises had grown to a two-acre site, wrote, 'There are also workshops in which every process of furniture is going on; in one, cabinet and chair makers are busily plying their tools; in others, inlayers and artists are employed in the decorative portions; polishers, couch and chair stuffers

Fig. 6.10 Made in ash, this bedside table, seemingly simple but made to the highest standard and inlaid with foliate marquetry, stamped 'GILLOW & CO. L6009', was supplied to Joseph Shuttleworth at Old Warden, c.1878. [Christie's]

Fig. 6.11 An engraving of the façade of the 1871 Annual International Exhibition in London. As with previous exhibitions, the decorative arts, although they had a significant presence, were dwarfed by engineering and scientific innovations. [*International Exhibition*, engraved by J.T. Wood]

and bed and mattress makers; while elsewhere may be heard the unceasing click of sewing machine, and women be seen actively sewing together breadths of carpet and fashioning into shape all sorts of material for curtains'.[20]

The cabinet-making trade expanded dramatically in the East End, especially in the Curtain Road area. Many makers, such as Cohen or William Walker & Sons, advertised as 'Wholesale & Export Cabinet-makers'. Some of Walkers' work, made in their 'Steam Cabinet Works', is stamped with their name. Most East End makers sold to middlemen and, as their work is often not signed, the actual maker may never be correctly identified. In September 1879, *The Furniture Gazette* gave a long description of Walkers' premises: 'floor after floor of artistic furniture'.[21] There were 'satinwood sets' inspired by makers and designers from the second half of the eighteenth century, such as Chippendale, Adam and Sir William Chambers. In Paris, Walker displayed a large cabinet by R. Davey, one of their in-house designers, made of brown oak inlaid with pear and ebony, the decoration and carving in the Moorish style. A frequent advertiser was William Oliver & Sons, 'Fancy Wood Merchants', who were adjacent to Walkers' premises.

The Furniture Gazette published an increasing number of line drawings of furniture, almost all unattributed. The designs represent a familiar style of furniture typical of the 1870s, often incorporating the ubiquitous turned spindles seen, for example, on furniture designed by Thomas Collcutt and furniture made for Shoolbred & Co., or Collinson & Lock. *The Cabinet-makers' Pattern Book*, first published in 1875 by Wyman, repeated many designs from *The Furniture Gazette*, which they also owned.[22] Amongst many contributors to more than 1,000 designs in the *Pattern Book* was the firm of Child & Hinde, innovative cabinet makers based on Euston Road in London. In 1872, the firm had installed steam power, including a lift for moving materials and the finished articles.[23] Cabinet-making machinery was becoming more sophisticated and more widespread. The same year, John Richards published *A Treatise on the Construction and Operation of Wood-working Machines*.[24]

Weekly reports of timber imports give an impression of the sheer quantity of exotic woods brought into the main ports of Britain. Mahogany, mainly sourced from the Caribbean but also Surinam, was the most desirable timber for furniture, with an annual value of £680,000 prior to 1873. Walnut was 'the next favourite...about one-seventh that of Mahogany'. Virtually no rosewood was imported at this time.[25] A single auction in Liverpool in April 1873 advertised almost 170,000 feet (51,816 metres) of mahogany, the ship *Clementine* alone bringing some 48,000 feet (14,630 metres) from Honduras. Logs of mahogany, sometimes 3 feet (1 metre) square, had a value of £1,000 or more.[26] Mahogany imports from Tabasco in Mexico were causing a negative effect on the price of the better Honduran and Cuban varieties.[27] By contrast, only 10,950 feet (3,337 metres) of Circassian walnut imported from Poti on the eastern coast of the Caspian Sea was available at the Liverpool auction. Walnut was also imported from Italy and, increasingly, the United States. British colonies were a new source of cabinet woods, with £80,000 worth of timber imported from Tasmania.[28] A considerable quantity of cane, for the bamboo-furniture industry, was imported from Tonkin in Northern Vietnam. Firms such as Ewart & Son of Euston Road in London, or J.S. Barton of Eton, made relatively cheap bamboo furniture, with Shoolbreds at the higher end of the scale. Bamboo is durable and strong, with straight halms, and was an obvious and cheap wood for the new vogue for all things Asian.

By July 1877, a downturn was reported in the availability of mahogany, with the imported volume much reduced.[29] Figured logs in satinwood were scarce and 'saleable at high prices', whereas 'small plain logs are plentiful and almost unsaleable'.[30] Walnut remained readily available, to the extent that prices eased off, but maple and ebony 'seem to lack buyers'.[31] Ebony is one of the hardest woods to work, and Owen Jones actively sought out a company that could work with ebony to his satisfaction: 'Mr. Morrison found that no house out of London was prepared to undertake a task that necessitated importations of select woods from all parts of the world. In Mr. Forster Graham, Owen Jones found a man able to enter into his ideas and to give practical

Fig. 6.12 An ebonised and painted 'Art cabinet' designed by Thomas Collcutt, made without the maker's signature by Collinson & Lock in 1871. It was bought for the Bethnal Green Museum using part of the fund held by the Commissioners of the 1851 exhibition. Other versions were displayed in Vienna in 1873 and in Philadelphia in 1876. [© Victoria and Albert Museum, London]

Figs 6.13a & b The ivory stringing inlaid into ebony may point to work by Jackson & Graham. The top is set with *pietre dure* marble samples, including lapis lazuli, malachite, Siena rosso, Algerian onyx and Sicilian jasper. The border is inlaid with ivory palmettes in the style of Owen Jones. [Private collection]

Fig. 6.14 Exhibited at the Annual International Exhibition in London in 1872 by Jackson & Graham, the top of this striking table is of the highest quality London-produced marquetry. Decorative medallions, inlaid with Classical lyres, are inlaid into a light wood, possibly Scottish cherry. [Courtesy of the Minneapolis Institute of Art]

Fig. 6.15 The complex marquetry on the top of this Jackson & Graham table is subtly different to one designed by Alfred Lormier shown at the Paris Exhibition in 1867, and possibly again in 1874. Veneered in amboyna, the base – with a central column and four flanking columns – has a Greek key pattern and a Vitruvian scroll more in keeping with the Etruscan Revival. [Private collection]

Figs 6.16a & b The central expanse of Macassar ebony veneer on this table attributed to Jackson & Graham is in striking contrast to the amboyna panels outlined with delicate foliage of mistletoe and asters. [Butchoff Antiques]

effect to them'.[32] In contrast, pine was increasingly used for furniture as a show wood, especially for light-coloured Aesthetic bedroom suites, such as those produced by Shoolbred.[33] Ash and pine furniture was always on display at Jackson & Graham, and Hollands, 'though they do not profess to make any of it'.[34]

Although Caribbean timbers were precious commodities at the time, space had to be cleared for the cultivation of food. An article lamented that in Jamaica some '30,000 acres of forest are cleared every year for (the) cultivation'. The writer continued, 'Little, if any, of the timber…is utilized, but is invariably burnt on the spot' and that 'the waste is enormous. I have seen fully £1,200 worth of beautiful mahogany and Santa Maria cut down…to plant an acre of yams, and the wood burnt as it lay'.[35]

The 1871 Annual International Exhibition in London was on a smaller scale to previous exhibitions and was less successful, but it still drew over 1 million visitors and made a profit. Henry Cole had devised a ten-year exhibition plan, but after three years, in 1874, he curtailed the project due to lack of enthusiasm and disappointing attendance figures. There were, however, outstanding furniture exhibits. Trollope & Sons exhibited a cabinet, the overall form with a hint of Owen Jones design, using the novel technique of

6.16b

'xylotechnography', a method of staining wood to simulate marquetry, particularly effective when used as a substitute for ivory inlay in ebony.[36] A bedroom suite purchased from Maples, now at 18 Stafford Terrace, the home of Linley Sambourne, has white painted stringing in the manner of Jackson & Graham. The foliage is similar to the ivory inlay on the table, **Fig. 6.13b**.

The Commissioners of the 1851 exhibition used profits to purchase the cabinet shown here, **Fig. 6.12**, with the ubiquitous ring-turned legs. Exhibited in 1871 by Collinson & Lock and made to a design by Thomas Collcutt it was presented to the newly built Bethnal Green Museum.[37] In 1870, the enterprising Frank Collinson and George Lock had bought their employer's company, the old established

6.17a

Fig. 6.17a One of a pair of ivory-inlaid ebony display cabinets of exhibition quality attributable to Jackson & Graham on the basis of style and quality, the ivory inlay possibly by Ole Petersen. [Butchoff Antiques]

Figs 6.17b & c The pair of display cabinets are identical except that the designer has, in a romantic gesture, placed the two carved ivory heads facing each other. The heads are probably intended to represent the medieval logician and theologian Peter Abelard and his love affair with the language scholar Héloïse d'Argenteuil.

Fig. 6.18 **In 1886, over ten years after his design for a serving table, Fig. 6.19a, Aitchison was still advocating the use of ivory inlaid into ebony. In this instance for a 'small drawing room or entrance hall' for Sir Wilfred Lawson MP at 1 Grosvenor Square.** [RIBA]

firm of Herring & Co., and formed a successful partnership the following year.[38] In 1871, they published their *Artistic Furniture Catalogue*, with designs by Moyr Smith, one of Christopher Dresser's assistants, and Collcutt. The firm continued until 1897, when they were absorbed by Gillows and were leading makers of 'Art Furniture'. In 1885, Collinson & Lock bought the celebrated firm of Jackson & Graham, where both men had also previously worked. Their 1871 exhibition cabinet, of Aesthetic design in ebonised wood with contrasting polychrome decoration, was a major influence on contemporary furniture. Collinson & Lock exhibited another version at the 1873 Vienna World's Fair, which incorporated a painted panel by Burne-Jones.[39] A third cabinet, with a panel painted by Charles Fairfax Murray, was exhibited at the Philadelphia Centennial International Exhibition in 1876.[40] Design was the key to the firm's success. Between 1872 and 1876 Godwin worked for Collinson & Lock while at the same time contributing designs in his less well-known Jacobean style to *The Furniture Gazette*, published under the banner 'Old English Furniture', see **Fig. 6.85b**.[41] Other designers working for Collinson & Lock included Bruce Talbert and Henry W. Batley. Similar to the interior settings of the New York firm of Kimbel & Cabus, Collinson & Lock's stand at the 1876 Centennial International Exhibition in Philadelphia was neatly divided into rooms, and it was this innovation that helped increase their reputation and secure business in the United States. A black-and-white photograph of their 1876 exhibition stand illustrates the range of their furniture, **Fig. 6.100**. The firm continued successfully with Godwin-designed Anglo-Japanese furniture at the Paris *Exposition Universelle* in 1878, where their work was highly regarded. They were awarded two gold medals, exhibiting an interior for a house designed by Collcutt in the William III style of the 1690s and a rosewood cabinet.[42] In contrast, they made an upright piano, elaborately carved in a Mannerist style, for a member of the Rothschild family. The firm's reputation was held in sufficient regard that, as early as 1879, the title pages of an auction catalogue advertised 'Handsome furniture, Designed in the early English style by Messrs. Collinson & Lock'. One lot was described as 'A very fine Rosewood cabinet, inlaid with various woods and ivory, with figure subjects by Rooke painted on the panels'.[43] This may be one of the first references to the elaborate ivory-inlaid furniture designed by Stephen Webb, examples of which are illustrated in the following chapter.

Jackson & Graham's style of the late 1860s and early 1870s changed radically, becoming distinctive and instantly recognisable. In 1872, the critic Yapp commented on the beauty of the design of the marquetry on a circular table exhibited by them, lamenting that it was only reproduced 'in poor black and white'.[44] Shown here in colour, **Fig. 6.14**, the top, designed by Prignot, is magnificent and highly elaborate, the border in the manner of Owen Jones. The

6.19a

Fig. 6.19a A rare engraving of an ebony and ivory-inlaid serving table, designed by George Aitchison, installed at Frederick Lehmann's house, 15 Berkeley Square. [Moncure D. Conway's *Travels in South Kensington*, 1882]

Fig. 6.19b The original plan and top of the Lehmann serving table by the architect, George Aitchison, dated 1874. [RIBA]

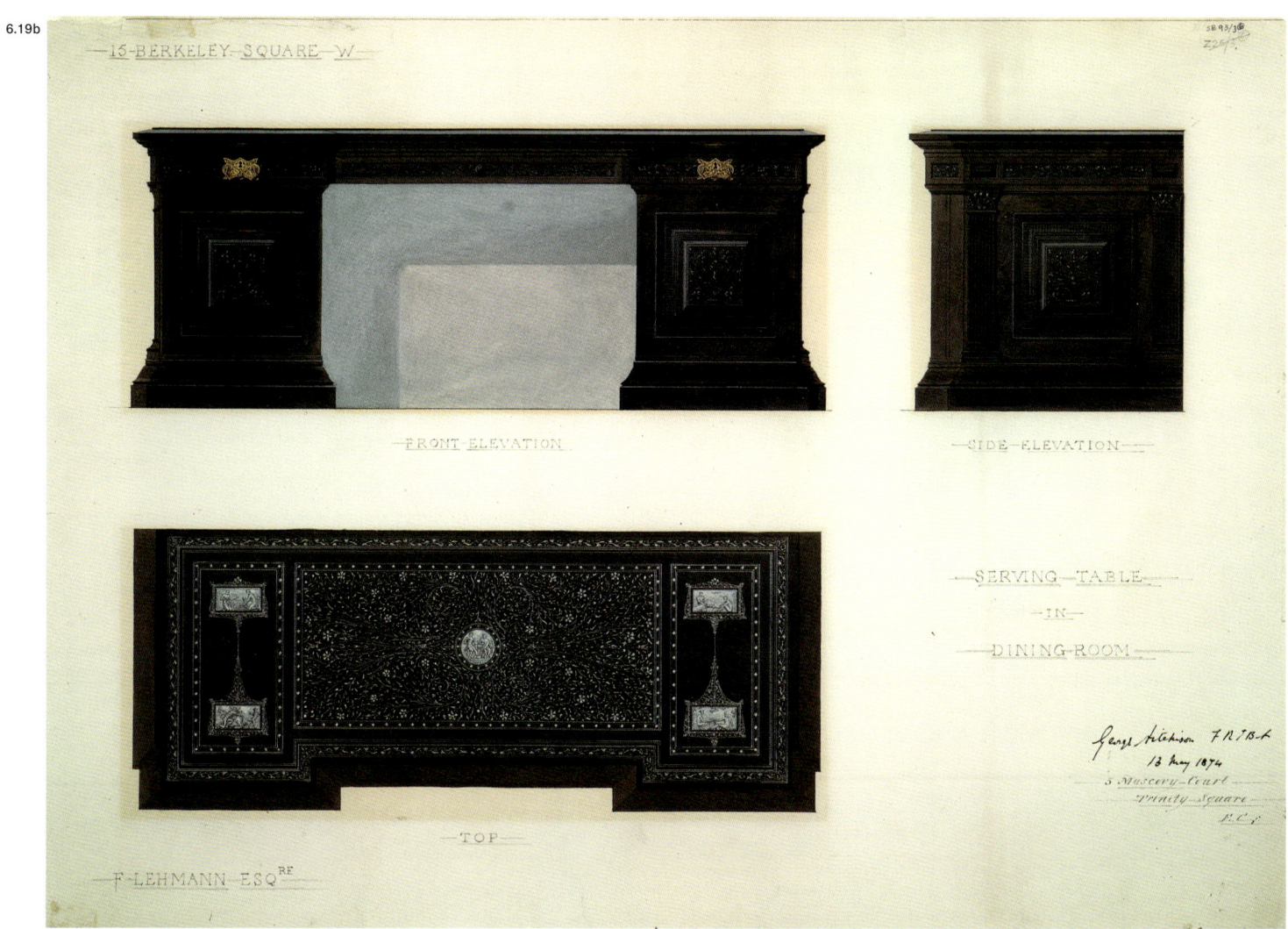

6.19b

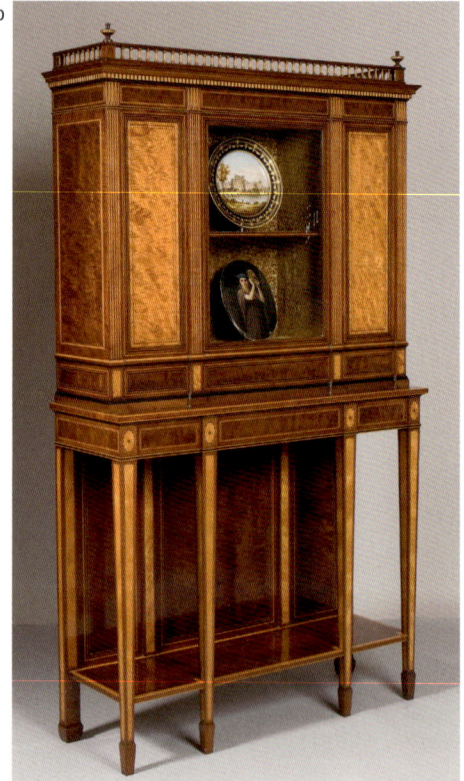

Fig. 6.20 Using fiddle-back mahogany veneers contrasting with satinwood, this cabinet compares with one of similar dimensions designed by Bruce Talbert and made by Jackson & Graham, exhibited in Paris in 1878. The Chubb locks are numbered consecutively 819933/4/5, dating them to the year after the exhibition, to May 1879. [Private collection]

Figs 6.21a–c One of a pair of amboyna-veneered cabinets in an eclectic design which borrows from earlier Boulle and Levasseur cabinets. Possibly by Jackson & Graham, the number 630262 on the Chubb locks date them to between 1871 and 1874, the same date as a cabinet by Jackson & Graham designed by Owen Jones for Henry Brassey, Fig. 6.22.[45] The mark on the key is a reminder that Chubb had opened a shop at 57 St Paul's Churchyard in 1827.[46] [Private collection]

marquetry references the contemporary taste for Classical antiquity, as in the wildly extravagant *Maison pompéienne* built in Paris between 1856 and 1860 for the mistress of Prince Napoleon Bonaparte, Napoleon III's cousin.[47] Inlaid in a fully fledged Etruscan style, the decoration is more profuse than two other examples in **Figs 6.15 & 6.16a**. **Figure 6.16a** has a dramatic Macassar ebony centre panel in striking contrast to the amboyna outline that is decorated with delicate foliage of mistletoe and asters, probably taken from *The Grammar of Ornament*.[48] The elliptical table in **Fig. 6.15**, with a primary veneer of amboyna, was almost certainly designed by Alfred Lormier. It also has similarities to a table commissioned by Alfred Morrison for either 16 Carlton House Terrace or Fonthill House, shown by Jackson & Graham at the 1867 Paris Exhibition. The inlay around the border is beautifully worked with acanthus foliage inlaid into end-grain palm wood, the Morrison example easily identified by an 'AM' monogrammed cartouche. *The Magazine of Art* in its review of the 1867 Paris Exhibition described the Morrison table as 'Composed of the Choicest materials and exhibiting the perfect workmanship'.[49] It is likely that the three tables used the same cabinet maker's pattern for the four flanking columns and central stem. The ebony and ivory-inlaid display cabinets attributed to Jackson & Graham, **Fig. 6.17a**, are a true pair, the romanticised male and female carved ivory heads centring the cornices are different portraits and face each other. Unsigned, the sophisticated design and high quality of workmanship, especially the distinctive ivory inlay, point to the workshops of Jackson & Graham.[50] The ebony veneer is laid onto a mahogany ground for stability, an expensive practice; a luxury that points to one of the top firms. Furniture of this style does not conveniently fit into decades, and it is impossible without specific evidence to decide if they were made in the late 1860s or early 1870s. As well as Lormier and Prignot, Jackson & Graham employed another French designer, Thomas Jacob, in the 1870s. The three designers were each earning the not insignificant sum of £700 per annum.[51]

John Hungerford Pollen had worked with Rossetti, Morris and Burne-Jones and subsequently, in 1863, became an assistant keeper at the South Kensington Museum,

6.22

6.23

Fig. 6.22 **Richly inlaid in purpleheart, palmwood, thuya and ivory, this is the largest recorded version of a series of side cabinets in Macassar ebony by Jackson & Graham. The monogram is for Henry Brassey, the Chubb locks stamped with serial numbers for between 1871 and 1874.** [Fitzwilliam Museum, M.15–1980]

Fig. 6.23 **One of a pair of Macassar ebony side cabinets with similar marquetry details found on attributed Jackson & Graham furniture, presumably based on Owen Jones's designs. The outset columns are inlaid with intricate ivory stringing.** [Butchoff Antiques]

resigning in 1876 to work as private secretary to Lord Ripon. A juror at the Dublin Exhibition in 1865 and again in Paris two years later, Pollen had a good knowledge of furniture and the skills needed to produce the intricate exhibition pieces. He recognised the exceptional skills of the Jackson & Graham craftsmen.

> 'I might call attention to Messrs. Jackson & Graham's elaborate cabinet of marquetry, in patterns of Oriental character, after designs by the late Mr. Owen Jones (sent to the Vienna Exhibition by Messrs. Jackson & Graham)…

The little columns of an inch and a half diameter were entirely covered with reticulated pattern in different woods. As the shafts were tapering, so the reticulated patterns had to be graduated in size from top to bottom. This was a feat of most difficult execution…The marquetry in the instance of these columns had to be wrapped round each circular shaft; and each edge, therefore, of every portion of pattern and groundwork had to be sawn out with bevelled edges, so that when rolled, the inner edges might meet and the outer edges remain in contact…a most laborious and costly operation'.[52]

Writing about Frederick Lehmann's house at 15 Berkeley Square in 1882, Moncure Conway noted tantalisingly, 'George Aitchison, architect of Leighton House redesigned the drawing-room…The chief ornament is a large cabinet, reaching nearly to the cornice — ebony and ivory — recently brought from the Vienna Exhibition'.[53] Aitchison had designed a serving table for Lehmann in 1874 in an uncompromising and distinctive form, the ivory inlay on ebony veneer depicting various fruits, **Fig. 6.19a**. Italianate, ivory-inlaid ebony furniture 'in the Greek style' was still being illustrated in trade journals in 1884.[54] It might be assumed that the sideboard was made by Jackson & Graham. A distinctive feature of their furniture is the exceptional quality of execution and design of the marquetry, either in various woods or in ivory, such as that attributed to Ole Petersen. Also used extensively by Collinson & Lock, ivory had been greatly prized since the sixteenth century as a material for fine, precise inlay. The use of ivory in a black ground by Jackson & Graham might refer back to the ivory stringing and stylised foliage on a pair of ebony open bookcases made in 1806 by Marsh & Tatham, altered by Nicholas Morel and George Seddon for George IV in c.1828.[55]

The shape of the pair of small side cabinets, **Fig. 6.21a**, is derived from a form popular in France during Louis XIV's reign and revived under Louis XVI in reverence to Boulle and the *Grand Siècle*. Veneered in amboyna, and

Fig. 6.24 **A monumental cabinet, almost 3 metres (over 9 ½ft) high, signed by Charles Toft the chief modeller at the Wedgwood factory, dated 1878. The cabinet was the focal point of the company's installation at the Paris *Exposition Universelle*. The plaques were custom made with no expense spared and feature portraits of Chaucer, Milton and Shakespeare as well as scenes from their plays.**
[Carlton Hobbs LLC]

Fig. 6.25 The **Palais du Trocadéro at the Paris *Exposition Universelle* held between May and November 1878. At 67 acres (270,000m^2), the site was larger than any previous exhibition.**
[Alamy Stock Photo]

Fig. 6.26 A pair of cabinets, in painted satinwood, stamped 'Gillow & Co 3677' and '3678', which dates them to between 1875 and 1876.

Fig. 6.27 With slight differences to the pair above, only one of this pair of cabinets with painted ivorine panels, is stamped by Gillows; the number '3175' indicates the date of manufacture was 1875. [Private collection]

Fig. 6.28 A pair veneered in amboyna, with the 'Gillow & Co.' stamp, the numbers '8265' and '8266', dating them to between 1879 and 1880.

possibly made by Jackson & Graham, the numbers on the Chubb locks allow precise dating to 1871. Alongside their Classically inspired furniture, Jackson & Graham was also still exhibiting in the Gothic style in 1874, which was not to the liking of *The Furniture Gazette*, whose reporter found it 'faulty'.[56] Nevertheless, the firm won the *Grand Prix d'Honneur* in Paris in 1878 for their maintenance of standards and progress in thirty years of art workmanship, one reviewer noting that '…the workmanship is so perfect that even with the aid of a powerful magnifying glass scarcely the slightest imperfection is to be found anywhere'.[57]

The two cabinets, **Figs. 6.22 & 6.23**, a form of side cabinet commonly called a 'credenza' are part of a series of differing sizes and detail veneered in Macassar ebony and although undocumented were certainly made by Jackson & Graham to designs by Owen Jones. The sizes vary between 6 and 8 feet (1.8–2.4 metres). Records show that the largest example, **Fig. 6.22**, was made by Ole Petersen, the talented Danish-born cabinet maker and inlayer who worked on most of Jackson & Graham's exhibition pieces. Petersen died at the age of thirty-nine but had 'for many years past been almost exclusively engaged upon the exhibition work of Messrs. Jackson & Graham'.[58] This example has four pilasters (there exists a further smaller variation with only two pilasters), the central door inlaid with the monogram 'JSS', in this instance with a Chubb lock numbered '632202', dating it precisely to 21 April 1871. The number on the Chubb lock fitted to **Fig. 6.22**, gives a less precise date range of between 1871 and 1874.

6.29a

6.30

6.29b

Figs 6.29a & b **A side cabinet or 'credenza' by Gillows with similarities to their drawing dated March 1867 shown below. The number 1225 below the Gillows stamp places the date of manufacture to between 1871 and 1872.** [Butchoff Antiques & City of Westminster Archive Centre]

Fig. 6.30 **On this small box stool by Gillows, the stamp and number 2701 sets the date of manufacture between 1874 and 1875.** [Private collection]

Henry Brassey was a member of the general committee that organised the Owen Jones memorial exhibition at the London International Exhibition in 1874 with a catalogue illustrated with designs for, amongst others, Alfred Morrison. Exhibition number 185 included '*Forty Drawings, in Three Portfolios. Exhibited by Messrs. Jackson & Graham*'. The selection committee for the memorial exhibition was a roll call of furniture grandees. Meeting at Morrison's house, 16 Carlton House Terrace, it included William Burges, Crace and Christopher Dresser.

Despite the comprehensive detail of the Gillow archives, there are no drawings for three pairs of unusual cabinets, **Figs 6.26, 6.27 & 6.28**; two pairs are in satinwood, another pair veneered in amboyna. The two satinwood examples appear almost identical in form but the slight differences, for example to the outer frame of the doors, suggest they were not made as a set of four. The painted ivorine panels under the cornice are the same but reversed. The four roundels on the doors are different but of a similar theme of frolicking cherubs. Noticeably, there are slight differences to the gilt-bronze roundels on the frieze and to the decoration of the stretcher. Although it might be assumed that Gillows used the same cabinet-maker's plan for all three pairs, the amboyna cabinets are slightly different in size, less elaborate and presumably cheaper to produce. All are in the new Etruscan style, with an eye on the popularity of Adam design, adapted to a modern aesthetic. The use of ivorine shows that the maker was familiar with new materials, not surprising for

302

6.31 A pair of carved oak library armchairs from the Naval and Military Club in St James's. Founded in 1862, the club was formerly based at Cambridge House, 94 Piccadilly, affectionately known as the 'In and Out', due to the prominent entry and exit signs for carriages on the gateposts.[59] [Butchoff Antiques]

Fig. 6.32 Designed by G.W. Fairbank and shown by W. & J.R. Hunter at the Annual International Exhibition in London in 1872, this dressing table has Wedgwood plaques set into what was reported as a ground of Hungarian oak, though was most probably Hungarian ash, showing off the highly figured natural grain, a feature of ash that was becoming increasingly popular. [G.W. Yapp, *Art industry, furniture, upholstery, and house decoration*, 1879, pl. CXLII]

Figs 6.33 & 6.34 Both of these cabinets are in the Neoclassical style popularised by Wright & Mansfield. The cabinet on the left (Fig. 6.33), however, was designed by R. Charles and made in the East End steam works of William Walker. On the right (Fig. 6.34) is a satinwood cabinet by Johnstone, Jeanes & Co., highly praised by reporters at the 1878 exhibition. The form of the Johnstone cabinet, with a mirrored upper part flanked by display cabinets, is now a familiar shape seen as typically 'Victorian'. The Adam influence is reflected in rich, highly coloured marquetry, a more accurate rendition of the George III era than the overall design of the cabinet. [6.33: G.W. Yapp, *Art industry, furniture, upholstery, and house decoration*, 1879, pl. CXLV. 6.34: *The Illustrated Catalogue of the Paris International Exhibition*, 1878, p. 139]

one of the largest furniture firms. Discovered by chance in 1869, ivorine, also known as cellulose nitrate or xylonite, was used in many forms but is particularly familiar when used on the small plaques stamped with a maker's or retailer's details, often affixed to the underside of a piece of furniture, or inside a drawer, from the 1870s. One of the most familiar is that of S. & H. Jewell, who used ivorine to replace their earlier oval stamped-brass name tags.[60]

The Gillows side cabinet, **Fig. 6.29a**, is of a conventional form but with highly refined marquetry and the added expense of serpentine glazed doors at the side – a more complicated form than normal convex glass. The mirrored upper part was not fashionable during the twentieth century, and many have been removed. The Gillows archive shows that the poorly struck number '1225' stamped on the illustrated example dates its manufacture to 1871 or 1872.[61] Another example, almost identical but with more gilded mounts, has a brass gallery instead of the mirrored upper part.[62] The cabinet-maker's plan and style of these cabinets is typical of Gillow; another, varying only in the inlay of the central panels, was sold from Ellel Grange, a house in Lancashire, described as 'A Mini Mentmore'.[63] The 1866 invoice reveals that it retailed for £90 5s. Built in 1860 in the style of Osborne House, the contents of Ellel remained largely untouched until dispersal.[64] Documentation of the major items of furniture made or supplied to the house indicated that most of the furniture was made by Gillows (see **Fig. 5.5**). Also by Gillows, a small box-like stool is stamped '2701', a job number which dates it to between 1874 and 1875, **Fig. 6.30**. Here, Gillows used a medley of veneers, including mahogany, amboyna, kingwood and thuya. The Neo-Grec stringing around the portrait plaque suggests a somewhat weakened influence of Owen Jones's *Grammar of Ornament*. The additions of Louis XIV-style gadrooned feet and Louis XVI-style Classical columns are a sign of typical Victorian eclecticism.

Figure 6.38a is an unusual desk of outstanding quality made from light-coloured satin birch, each niche with a gilt-bronze owl, **Fig. 6.38b**. The breakfront style of the writing surface, with Gothic-inspired supports combined with a padded footrest, could point to a date of manufacture in the 1860s, though the provenance might indicate that it

Fig. 6.35 **With several of the London makers reviving the Adam style in marquetry and painted decoration, it is difficult without documentation to be sure of an attribution to a specific maker of this fine cabinet, one of a pair.** [Private collection]

Fig. 6.36 **Cooper & Holt of Bunhill Row exhibited this oak sideboard at the Vienna Exhibition in 1873. Designed in a medieval style similar to that of Seddon or Bevan, three years later in Philadelphia the firm had turned to a more modern, Aesthetic style.** [G.W. Yapp, *Art industry, furniture, upholstery, and house decoration*, 1879, pl. CXLVI]

Fig. 6.37 **By 1871, Arthur Foley of the Fisherton Machine Cabinet Works in Salisbury employed over twenty men and women to support his furniture and decorating business.[65] This somewhat eccentric dressing table is heavily influenced by French styles and not at all sure of its antecedents.** [G.W. Yapp, *Art industry, furniture, upholstery, and house decoration*, 1879, pl. XLVII]

was made as late as the early 1880s. The desk was in the collection of the industrialist Sir William Armstrong, created 1st Baron Armstrong in 1887; documents indicate that it was once at his house at Cragside and then at Bamburgh Castle. Norman Shaw created a suite of rooms at Cragside, 'The Owl Suite', for a visit by the Prince and Princess of Wales in 1884. The idea of the top housing a tambour cupboard is of French inspiration, as is the rather idiosyncratic copper-electrotype plaque of frolicking putti on the frieze, reminiscent of gilt-bronze mounts designed by Jean-Henri Riesener in the 1770s.

The Vienna World's Fair of 1873, dominated by the huge rotunda designed by Karl Freiherr von Hasenauer with the structural engineer John Scott Russell from Glasgow,[66] was a showcase for the Aesthetic movement. Greatly influenced by art from Asia, British exhibitors included Gillows, Holland & Sons, Morant and the newly established firm of Collinson & Lock. Baird noted that Christopher Dresser 'was instrumental in negotiating the sale of the Shinto "Hall of Dance"', part of the Japanese exhibits by the Alexandra Park Company, together with other pieces to be sent to London.[67]

The 'world' in the title of the exhibition was no exaggeration. China was well represented, exhibiting Cantonese furniture that competed with black lacquer furniture with gilt highlights, a fashion popular in Britain. In the same vein, Gillows exhibited 'Black and Gold cabinets', designed by C.J. Henry. S.J. Nicholl exhibited an ebonised cabinet 'the most original piece of furniture

Figs 6.38a & b **The gilt-bronze owls on this desk, made for the industrialist Sir William Armstrong, are inkwells. The heads, with glass bead eyes, revolve to open a 'hidden' compartment.** [Private collection]

Fig. 6.39 **Made by Gregory & Co. of London in 1877 for Chateau-sur-Mer, Newport, Rhode Island, this rosewood desk is typical of commercial 'artistic' furniture.** [Philadelphia Museum of Art]

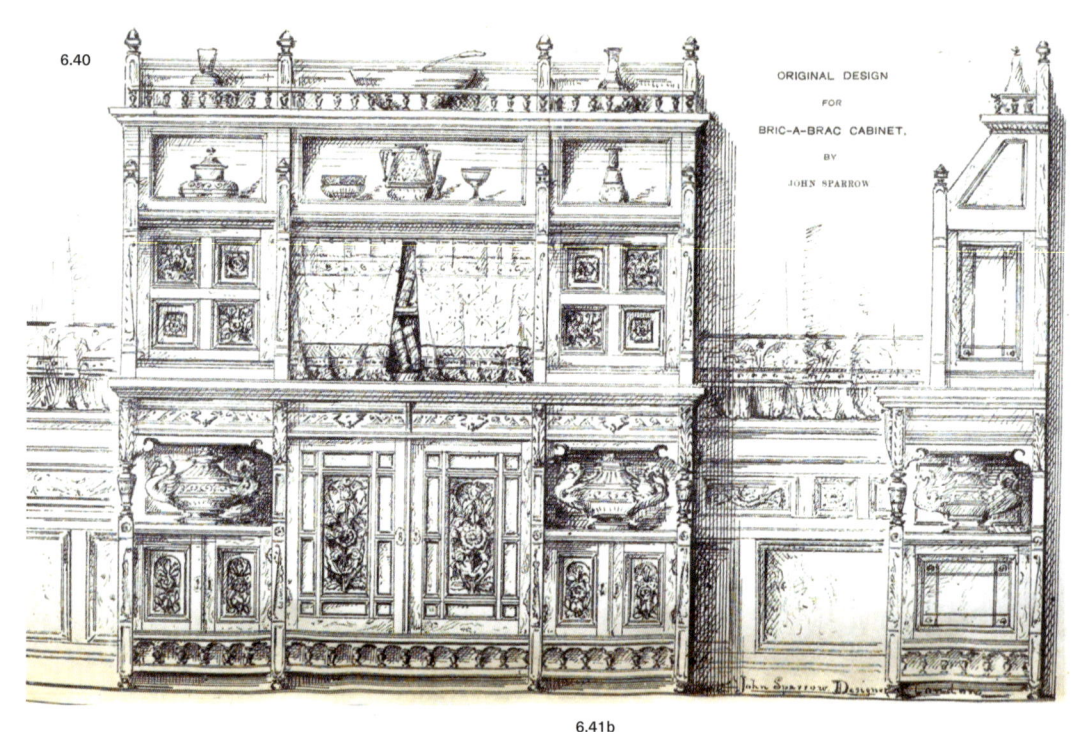

Fig. 6.40 John Sparrow published this 'original design' entitled a 'bric-a-brac' cabinet in 1877. [*The Furniture Gazette*, 3 March 1877, p. 131]

Figs 6.41a & b A glass armchair by Osler of Birmingham, the chromed leg collar stamped 'F&C Osler', upholstered in pale blue velvet. The accompanying watercolour (Fig. 6.41b) shows the original suggestion for upholstery, in a vivid red. [6.41a: Christies. 6.41b: Photo by Birmingham Museums Trust]

Fig. 6.42 An intricate and highly detailed design for the production of a glass double chair back settee by F. & C. Osler. The finished product is shown in the top right corner. [Photo by Birmingham Museums Trust]

6.43 An *étagère* by F. & C. Osler, the legs held by iron rods, the three mirrored shelves with a revival of Neoclassical motifs. [Photo by Birmingham Museums Trust]

Fig. 6.44 A preparatory drawing for a glass table by Osler showing facetted apron panels and thistle legs housing iron retaining rods. [Photo by Birmingham Museums Trust]

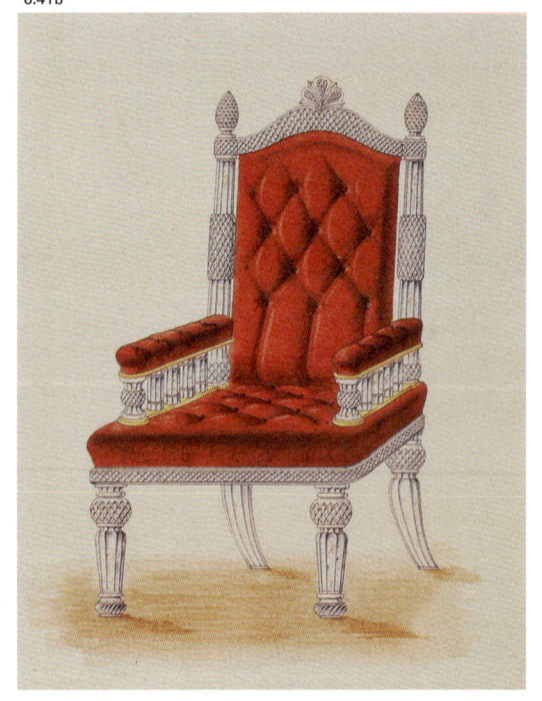

design exhibited'.[68] One example of the Japanese style was an ebonised cabinet by Cox, also designed by Nicholl (exhibition number 2630). To make sure the general public understood the origins of the design, a small Japanese object was placed on the top for good measure. A Japanese-influenced cabinet by Watt (exhibition number 2642) was described, presumably due to its simplicity, as 'almost quakerish'.[69] Two weeks later, a 'Mr. B. Charles' wrote to complain that his name as designer had been left out of the report. A more authentic style of Chinese furniture, not borrowing from British forms, was a selection of carved furniture from Ningbo, a port south of Shanghai.

Although makers of furniture in this new aesthetic (see the delicate desk in **Fig. 6.39**), Gregory & Co., founded in 1859, also exhibited a medieval-style sideboard, almost 11 feet (3.3 metres) in height, at the Vienna Exhibition. Gregory's were typical in catering for all tastes and styles, later employing Charles Bevan as a designer for a rosewood drawing room suite shown in Paris in 1878. A little-known designer, John Sparrow, designed a 'bric-a-brac' cabinet in the same genre,

6.42

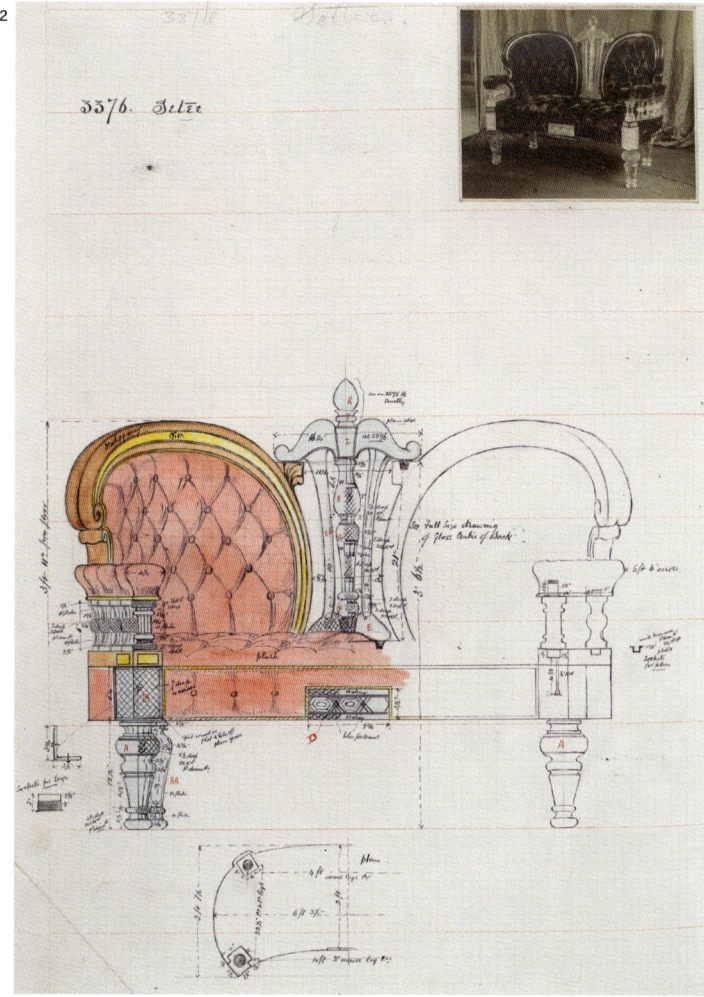

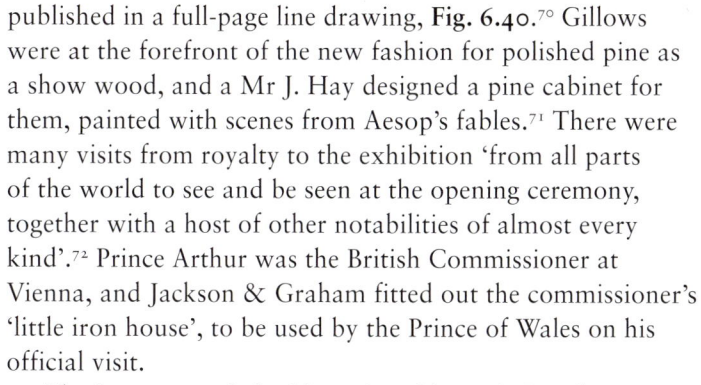

6.43

6.44

published in a full-page line drawing, **Fig. 6.40**.[70] Gillows were at the forefront of the new fashion for polished pine as a show wood, and a Mr J. Hay designed a pine cabinet for them, painted with scenes from Aesop's fables.[71] There were many visits from royalty to the exhibition 'from all parts of the world to see and be seen at the opening ceremony, together with a host of other notabilities of almost every kind'.[72] Prince Arthur was the British Commissioner at Vienna, and Jackson & Graham fitted out the commissioner's 'little iron house', to be used by the Prince of Wales on his official visit.

The Japanese style had been in evidence in London at the Annual International Exhibition of 1874. Christopher Dresser was commissioned by the United States government to write a report on the design of household goods, and he visited the Centennial International Exhibition in Philadelphia in 1876 en route to a four-month tour of Japan. In Japan, he was able to present the emperor with artefacts made in Britain. In 1882, his publication *Japan, Its Architecture, Art, and Art Manufactures*, demonstrated his early insight into the sophistication of Japanese culture.

Later, the influential magazine *The Studio* praised the influence of Dresser, describing him as 'perhaps the greatest of commercial designers, imposing his fantasy and invention upon the ordinary output of British industry'.[73]

Although a limited amount of glass furniture was made early in the nineteenth century, innovative commercial glass furniture was exhibited for the first time in Paris in 1878.[74] Thomas Osler of Birmingham, established in 1807, opened an Oxford Street branch in 1845, becoming F. & C. Osler in 1852. In competition with French firms such as Baccarat or

Fig. 6.45 **Glass chairs, tables, beds and whatnots, as well as this tall Gothic-style side cabinet, were shown by Osler at the 1878 Paris Exhibition.** [*The Illustrated Catalogue of the Paris International Exhibition*, 1878, p. 142]

Fig. 6.46 **In 1878, Jackson & Graham exhibited several similar Italian Renaissance-style, ivory-inlaid cabinets. This model, with an arched, swan neck cresting, is similar to one bought by Henry Brassey. The cabinets appear to be slightly different sizes, but possibly used the same cabinet maker's pattern.** [*The Illustrated London News*, 16 November 1878]

Fig. 6.47 **An exhibition cabinet in an adapted Louis XVI manner by Jackson & Graham, with applied *pâte-sur-pâte* porcelain panels in the style of Marc-Louis Solon, a French émigré who arrived in Stoke-on-Trent in 1870. The exquisite, engraved ivory marquetry had become a Jackson & Graham speciality by the mid-1860s.** [G. W. Yapp, *Art industry, furniture, upholstery, and house decoration*, 1879, pl. XLIV]

Fig. 6.48 **The Juno Cabinet, designed by Bruce Talbert and exhibited by Jackson & Graham in Paris in 1878.** [© Victoria and Albert Museum, London]

Pantin, they had exhibited their four-ton glass fountain and candelabra in 1851 and 1862, adding furniture in 1878. A Society of Arts report summed up this splendour and luxury:

'There is a splendid crystal chair of state and footstool. The framework is of cut glass, arranged in skilfully devised patterns, glittering like a mass of gems, which will attract the notice of many of the Eastern potentates who visit the Exhibition. At the back of the court is a cabinet, which is a truly magnificent piece of workmanship of pure Gothic design. The back, which is formed by a large pier glass [mirror], is without spot or blemish. The body of the cabinet, composed of cut-glass pillars and panels, is one mass of engraving and cutting. Although a very large number of pieces have been used, the nicety with which they are joined is such that the keenest eye is unable to detect the points of union; while the refined taste with which this cabinet is executed is worthy of the old masters…The combination of the darkened woodwork, ormolu work, and gilt carvings make up a whole, which for beauty of design and boldness of execution

Fig. 6.49 **An ebonised and gilt corner cabinet, designed by Bruce Talbert stamped 'Gillows & Co., 5647', dating it to between 1877 and 1878. The panels are painted with a young boy in Elizabethan breeches and a girl in contemporary dress.** [Oscar Graf]

Fig. 6.50 **The Octagon Boudoir made by Gillows for the Princess of Wales at the 1878 Paris Exhibition.** [Robert W. Edis, *Decoration & furniture of town houses*, 1881]

Fig. 6.51 **Side cabinet. The top of the right-hand door is stamped 'LAMB MANCHESTER'. The stamped serial number 33011, as with similar numbers by Gillows, almost certainly refers to a design or a commission and may help to indicate the date of manufacture. Once in the collection formed by Charles Handley-Read, the foliate inlays show the influence of Bruce Talbert.** [The Higgins Bedford]

Fig. 6.52 **Dated 1876, this extraordinary oak and marquetry cabinet, titled the 'Croydon Cabinet', is carved with the signs of the Zodiac, the Elements, and figures emblematic of the Arts. It was sent to Paris by the Croydon firm of A.C. Ebbutt, and 1878 was the last International Exhibition to show eclectic medieval/ Gothic cabinets sporting overhanging cornices.** [*The illustrated catalogue of the Paris International Exhibition*, 1878, p. 42]

is unsurpassed, and will do not a little to enhance the reputation already gained by Messrs. Osler for their manufacture of glass'.[75]

Despite being made of glass, the sections joined by metal rods, such furniture was remarkably strong. Taking advantage of its popularity amongst the upper echelons of the Indian market, Osler opened showrooms in Bombay and Calcutta. Queen Victoria was made Empress of India in 1876, and designs from the subcontinent had already featured in exhibitions of the 1850s and 1860s, including an Indian tent and a magnificent silver-veneered throne chair of a type seen at the Delhi Durbars of 1877, 1903 and 1911.

Jackson & Graham's last gasp on the international stage was in Paris in 1878, their efforts rewarded with the *Grand Prix d'Honneur* for the celebrated Juno Cabinet designed by Bruce Talbert, **Fig. 6.48**, purchased for the khedive of Egypt at a cost of £2,000.[76] Owen Jones designed a delightful summer palace for the khedive[77] and, in Talbert's obituary, it was reported that he had been commissioned to supply a room en suite with the Juno Cabinet at a cost of £6,000. *The Cabinetmaker* described the Juno Cabinet as 'showing the versatility of Talbert's genius, and his power to grasp Classicism with the same success as Gothic and

BRITISH FURNITURE

Figs 6.53a–j The suite exhibited by Holland & Sons in Paris in 1878 purchased by Sir Richard Wallace. Neoclassical sphinxes are painted on the 'Arabian bedstead' in satinwood, Fig. 6.53b. The detail of the richly carved sphinxes that flank the mirror on the dressing table, Figs 6.53c & d, shows the gilt headdresses and wings, their plaits carved out of solid satinwood. [Sotheby's]

CHAPTER 6: 1870S

6.53e

6.53f

6.53g

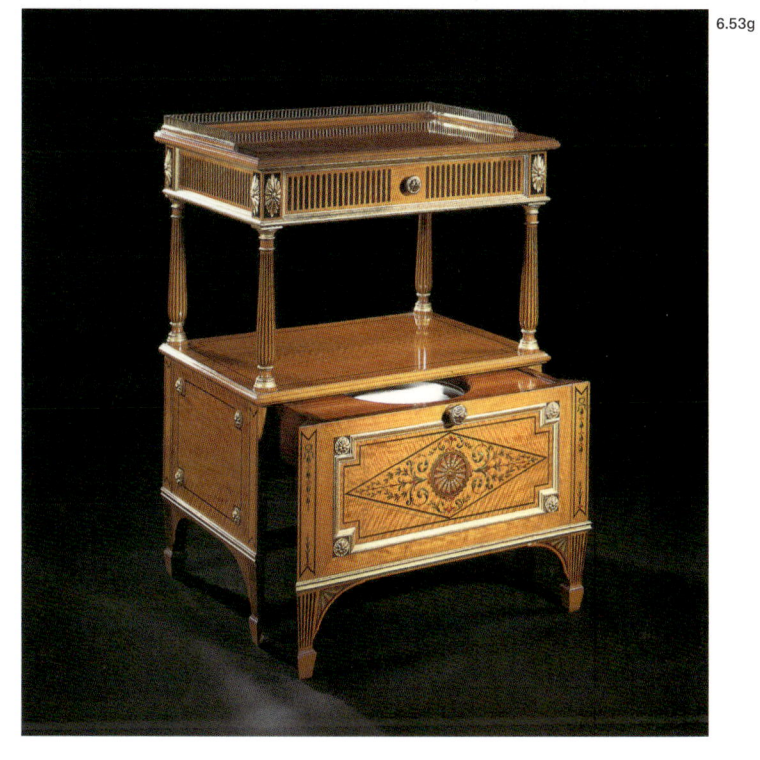

311

BRITISH FURNITURE

6.53h

6.53i

6.53j

Old English'.[78] Jackson & Graham furnished three rooms for the exhibition jurors in the 'Street of Nations', the furniture made in padouk, rosewood and American walnut designed by J.S. Henry. They also exhibited an exquisitely inlaid cabinet designed by Talbert, 'touched up here and there…with mother-of-pearl'.[79] The wealthy son of a railway magnate, Henry Brassey purchased a Renaissance-style cabinet by Jackson & Graham, similar to the one shown in **Fig. 6.46**. To show their awareness of new trends, the firm also exhibited Chippendale-style furniture.

Exhibition catalogues are a useful source of otherwise unheralded makers. Alfred Charles Ebbutt of Croydon was a successful cabinet maker and upholsterer who sent his extraordinarily large and eclectic medieval/Gothic oak cabinet, inlaid with the Elements, the Arts and the Zodiac, to Paris in 1878, **Fig. 6.52**. A similar, but more restrained cabinet was sent by Smee of Finsbury likewise a contribution from Julius Jacoby who expanded his business from provincial Nottingham to London's fashionable Regent Street. It would be interesting to know if such displays had been cost-effective. In an era of so-called 'Jacobethan' furniture, the Edinburgh firm of Thomas Hall picked up the theme of romantic imagery fostered by William Morris and his circle in a room exhibited at the 1878 exhibition depicting the life of Mary Queen of Scots. In a typical misunderstanding of stylistic development, the designer had revisited the 1660s Charles II-style of 'S' scroll supports for chair backs and block-fronted cabinet doors to depict a scene that had taken place in 1548. Another Edinburgh firm, Brown Brothers, also exhibited in 1878. Their mahogany sideboard was in the 'Adam' style, the term based, like that of the Johnstone & Jeanes cabinet in **Fig 6.33**, on the style

312

of marquetry rather than the form of the cabinet. Awarded a silver medal, Henry Ogden of Manchester sent a cabinet designed by H.W. Batty, subtly incorporating Charles II-style mouldings. More obscure makers were George Sealy Lucraft & Son, with three premises at and around 79 City Road in the East End of London. Listed in the 1882 *Trades' Directory* as 'Artistic Furniture Manufactr', they exhibited chairs and tables, two of which caught the eye of Princess Mathilde. They were awarded a medal for a tall, mirrored cabinet in satinwood; the marquetry, but not the style of the cabinet, was in the 'Adam' style.[80] Listed alongside Lucraft in 1882 were Samuel Litchfield in both Bruton Street and Hanway Street, Charles Nosotti, Collinson & Lock and William Watt.

The Adam or 'Adams' style gained popularity in the 1870s. Reflecting the increasing interest in the late Georgian period, throughout the 1870s *The Furniture Gazette* intermittently published detailed line drawings of furniture purporting to be from the second half of the eighteenth century; however, an image of a sideboard by Shoolbred in the 'Adam' style is so profusely inlaid that it could only be 'Victorian'. Shoolbred were reproducing the Adam style in the modern manner by the mid-1870s, following close on the heels of firms such as Wright & Mansfield.[81] At the Paris Exhibition in 1878, Gillows designed an Octagon Boudoir for the Princess of Wales in the 'Adams' Style, **Fig. 6.50**.

Fig. 6.54 Veneered in the finest well-figured satinwood, this wardrobe, no doubt once part of a complete bedroom suite, is inset with Wedgwood plaques and beautifully inlaid marquetry in the Adam manner, as revived by firms such as Wright & Mansfield, Johnstone, Jeanes & Co., and Whytock of Edinburgh. [Private collection]

Fig. 6.55 Trollope & Sons sent this delicately carved limewood mirror to Paris in 1878, which rivals, or is inspired by, an example by the Paris foundry of Barbedienne cast in gilt bronze, exhibited in 1867. Trollope has oddly juxtaposed the mirror with an inlaid satinwood side cabinet and an armchair in the late George III style, flanked by amphora on tripod stands in the Graeco-Roman manner. [*The illustrated catalogue of the Paris International Exhibition*, 1878, p. 129]

In 1995, an important and extensive bedroom suite made by Holland & Sons for the 1878 Paris Exhibition came up for auction, **Fig. 6.53a–j**.[82] The suite had only been in two houses and as a result was in virtually untouched condition. It comprised an 'Arabian' bed, a side cabinet, dressing table, writing table, six side chairs, a night table, a pair of bedside cupboards, a bidet, a side table, a toilet mirror, a washstand and a breakfront wardrobe. The epitome of the Victorian interpretation of the 'Adams' style, Holland made it as a speculative venture, sending it to Paris for the 1878 exhibition. It was expensively made from the best West Indian satinwood, with finely carved details and exquisitely painted polychrome Neoclassical foliage imitating marquetry.

Figs 6.56a One of this suite of finely inlaid satinwood cabinets has the applied label 'Edwards & Roberts, Wardour Street, London'. It is probable that they were acting as retailers, not makers. The quality suggests it was made by one of the top London firms. [Private collection]

Fig. 6.56b The vibrancy of the top of the three cabinets has hardly faded and is a rare reminder of the original hues of Georgian marquetry and Victorian copies. [Private collection]

Contemporary critics were impressed, *The Illustrated London News* reporting: 'The style of the work is that of the Brothers Adam, and the decoration in the manner of Cipriani and Angelica Kauffman. The effect is magnificent, without the slightest tawdriness; nothing to weary the eye on long acquaintance. It is a complete and highly satisfactory show'.[83]

Added excitement for the contemporary press was the fact that the suite was so admired by the renowned collector Sir Richard Wallace that he purchased it at the exhibition for £1,599 16s. Gonse wrote that the purchase of such a suite, the style of which must have been anathema to French commentators, underlined the good taste of the makers: '*Cette chambre à coucher a été acheté tout entière par Sir Richard Wallace. Ce choix est un excellent certificat de bon goût*' ('This entire bedroom was bought by Sir Richard Wallace. This choice is an excellent certificate of good taste').⁸⁴ The Society of Arts concurred: 'Messrs Holland & Sons have a bedroom completely finished in satin-wood in the Adams style...the marqueterie is painted instead of being inlaid...The workmanship is of the best, and nothing could say more for its artistic merit than the circumstance that the whole has been purchased by the distinguished art critic, Sir Richard Wallace'.⁸⁵ Sir Richard had the suite sent to his country house, Sudbourne Hall,⁸⁶ which he had renovated for an anticipated visit by The Prince of Wales. Such a purchase by Sir Richard was unusual, not in character with the rest of the collection he was steadfastly augmenting. A dedicated Francophile like his father, he travelled to his house in France in 1887 never to return to England. The bedroom suite was put into storage at Hollands' premises in Mount Street, together with the drapery. Although the bed hangings, bolsters and pillows do not survive, they were light-blue satin.⁸⁷ Hollands clearly took great care of their charge; records show that once or twice a year the suite was unpacked, dusted down and re-wrapped. In 1893, the suite was returned to Hertford House on the orders of Sir Richard's widow, Lady Wallace.⁸⁸ It was subsequently acquired by the diamond magnate Sir Julius Wernher for Bath House in Piccadilly, which he bought in 1896. Lady Wernher remarried after her husband's death in 1912; three years after she died in 1945 the suite was inventoried at Luton Hoo, a house purchased by the Wernhers in 1903 and refurbished by Mewès & Davis.

In an early report of the increasing love of antique furniture, in 1875 *The Cornhill Magazine* noted 'the art of furnishing must for the present moment be closely connected with the judicious buying of old furniture'.⁸⁹ Whether the bargain hunters of eighteenth-century furniture, such as William Morris and his circle, sparked a revival of interest for the commercial production of eighteenth-century or Adam-style furniture is difficult to ascertain. There is no doubt that the 1870s saw a wider popularity for a reinterpretation of the Georgian style. English pieces were unlikely to be exact copies during this period; unlike furniture in the eighteenth-century style made by their Parisian counterparts, British makers found it hard to resist alterations and 'improvements'. Usually, it is the difference in proportion that gives the period away, enabling a judgement to be made from a reasonable photograph. Various clues can also identify nineteenth-century pieces, such as machine carving. Dovetails were still hand cut in a traditional manner and standards of carcass work in the Victorian era for the best pieces were extremely high. Castors are another identifying factor. The leather-bound castor of the eighteenth century was not used in the nineteenth. By the mid-nineteenth century, white, brown or black ceramic castors, or those made in solid brass were bought in by furniture makers, often with the name of the maker, such as Comyn Ching or more commonly Cope & Collinson, stamped in tiny letters around the collar. Like castors, locks can always be replaced but most Victorian locks are of brass, not iron, and machined, not handmade. Many locks have makers' stamps such as those by Bramah, Sampson Mordan, Comyn Ching or Hobbs, or simply the 'VR' monogram. There are several examples in this and other chapters of Chubb locks with a serial number, which is a helpful tool for precise dating, for example **Fig. 6.21c**.

The large desk by Wright & Mansfield, commissioned by Sir Dudley Coutts Marjoribanks, is one of the most magnificent pedestal desks made during the nineteenth century, **Fig. 6.57a**. As a devotee of the Adam period, and a Neoclassical connoisseur, Sir Dudley had amassed an important collection of early Wedgwood pottery and used the supply of gean wood from his Scottish estates to commission furniture and panelling for his London house. The outline of the desk was designed to mirror the floor plan of Brook House in Park Lane, the exact date of the desk commission uncertain. Exceptionally large and imposing, the drawers are in cedar and mahogany, and no expense has been spared. A seemingly unnecessary but exquisite detail on the small patera on the drawer handles is that, inexplicably, they unscrew. The profusion of sixty-seven Wedgwood panels in black basalt with Classical portrait busts is a novel feature reflecting the client's taste and knowledge. Each plaque is incised on the reverse with the name of the portrait, with a range of Roman emperors depicted, including Julius Caesar, Nero and Vespasian, as well as rulers such as Lycurgus of Sparta and Cyrus, the founder of the Achaemenid Empire. Lady Aberdeen, Sir Dudley's daughter, ordered a version from Wright & Mansfield for Haddo House, **Fig. 6.59**. Less richly embellished, and with fewer plaques, it is still in situ. As a teenager, she was expected by her father to have top marks in every subject, and he would extract a 'trinket' from the unusually long side drawer as her reward for success. The three individually numbered locks are by J.T. Needs, who took over from Bramah in 1871. The carcass of Sir Dudley's desk is stamped 'Hinton' in three places.⁹⁰ The use of Wedgwood plaques in furniture by Wright & Mansfield was described by a contemporary as being comparable 'to the use of plates, medallions and cameos of Wedgwood, or Sèvres ware, which were frequently inlaid by Chippendale, and by the great French furniture makers, or *ébénistes*, of the last century. These are now used in the modern satinwood furniture of Messrs. Wright and Mansfield'.⁹¹ Although critical of the Greek style of the Regency period of the 1820s, *The Furniture Gazette* admired the new Adam style of Wright & Mansfield, noting of the firm's premises that 'we shall find there the most charming specimens of modern furniture

BRITISH FURNITURE

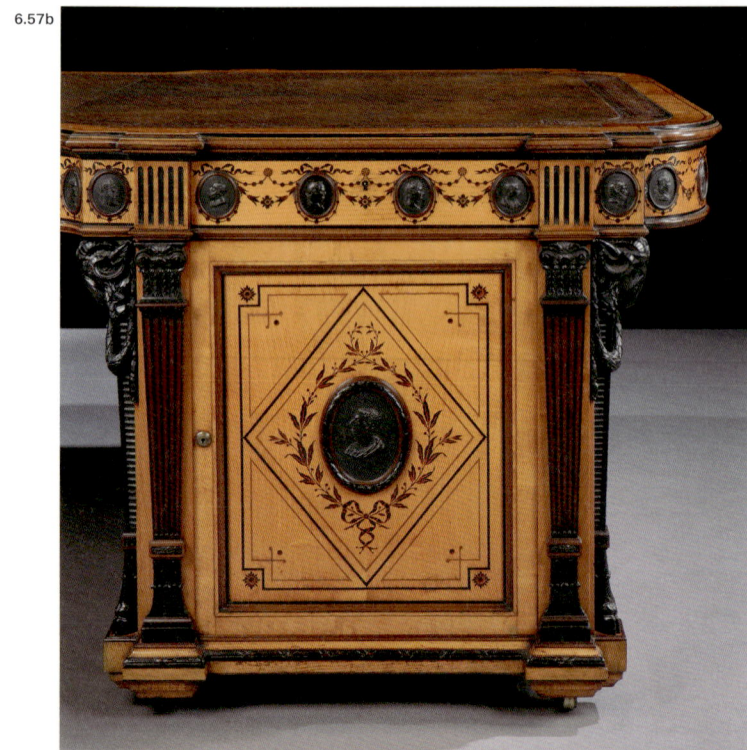

6.57a

6.57b

6.57c

Fig. 6.57a The Brook House desk or library table, almost 8 feet (2.5 metres) wide, commissioned by Sir Dudley Coutts Marjoribanks from Wright & Mansfield. The unusual shape was specifically designed to reflect the floor plan of Brook House in Mayfair built for Sir Dudley between 1867 and 1869. [Butchoff Antiques]

Figs 6.57b & c The trails of festooned laurel, representing Peace, are inlaid in ebony, which has been engraved and highlighted in Pompeiian terracotta red as a foil for the veneers of gean wood, or Highland black cherry. Each corner has an ebonised carved pear wood ram's head in the Adam Classical tradition. [Butchoff Antiques]

CHAPTER 6: 1870S

6.57d

Fig. 6.57d **The generously proportioned Brook House desk has a folio flap in the drawer at one end. There are sixty-seven Wedgwood black basalt plaques of emperors, philosophers, and Flaxman-inspired dancers. The large oval medallions depict Orpheus, holding a lute, and a female figure holding the Pipes of Pan.** [Butchoff Antiques]

Fig. 6.57e **Opposing the reading flap, the desk commissioned by Marjoribanks has an extraordinarily long drawer, a feature that fascinated his daughter Ishbel, the future Lady Aberdeen, as a child. Typically for the nineteenth century, the grain of the bottom of the drawer runs from side to side, unlike front to back construction in smaller drawers of the eighteenth century. Wright & Mansfield have inserted a transverse muntin in the centre to allow for shrinkage to the well-seasoned cedar and mahogany linings.** [Butchoff Antiques]

6.57e

copied from old designs, but always with a view to modern requirements'. The reporter found the compositions of, amongst others, Angelica Kauffman, Cipriani and Hamilton 'of great assistance in the production of furniture'.[92] A plentiful timber on the east coast of Scotland, gean was cited in 1844 as 'being susceptible of receiving a fine polish'.[93] It was used in 1889 for an elegant display cabinet at Cowden Castle in Falkirk.[94]

In her memoirs, Lady Aberdeen, wrote that the decoration of the two desks (c.1878) 'was placed in the hands of Messrs. Wright & Mansfield...who had decorated Brook House and Guisachan for my father, and whose taste and knowledge of the Adams period was unrivalled'. She added that 'the commission was carried out with great skill and perfection, and whilst the price charged at the time was scandalously high, yet the fact remains that these same decorations remain marvellously fresh after a lapse of nearly forty-five years'.[95]

The kidney desk, named no doubt for the shape of its outline, was first designed by Thomas Sheraton in the late eighteenth century and is one of the most popular forms of small writing table; examples continued to be made

317

6.58

Fig. 6.58 A similar outline of desk to the Marjoribanks example was made from the timbers of the Artic explorer HMS *Resolute* and given by the British Government in 1880 to President Hayes of the United States. Three desks using timbers from the *Resolute* were made by cabinet makers at the Joiner's Shop at Chatham Dockyard. An example of reclamation work exhibited at the 1876 *Centennial* was a 5-foot-long (1.5 metres) oak chest made of 600-year-old beams from Salisbury Cathedral sent by Harry Herns of Bristol. [*Frank Leslie's Illustrated Newspaper*, 11 December 1880]

Fig. 6.59 Lady Aberdeen's full-scale version of the Marjoribanks desk, made by Wright & Mansfield for Haddo House in Aberdeenshire, is less richly embellished than her father's example at Brook House. Lined in mahogany and cedar, it still has the unusual long drawer to one side. [Private collection]

6.59

throughout the Victorian era. A typical high-quality version in mahogany by Gillows from the 1870s, illustrated here, has a pierced brass gallery, **Fig. 6.61**. A rare, specially commissioned model was made by Wright & Mansfield for Fetteresso Castle, **Fig. 6.60**; it has Wedgwood plaques like the two partners' desks made for Marjoribanks and his daughter.

Wright & Mansfield continued to exhibit in their by now trademark, Adam style, exhibiting several items at the Philadelphia Centennial International Exhibition in 1876. One of their exhibits 'a restored eighteenth century piece' is otherwise unspecified but we know they were buying period furniture for study purposes and seemingly restoring Georgian examples.[96] One exhibit was the small sideboard in inlaid satinwood, in an easily identifiable George III manner, **Fig. 6.64**. In **Fig. 6.66**, Wright & Mansfield have varied the design by using oval not circular painted door panels. It appears that only one example of this model was exhibited in 1876 but they were made as a pair or possibly a series were made.[97] The firm also sent to Philadelphia a more complex cabinet, **Fig. 6.67**, a form of sideboard similar to one purchased by the Victoria and Albert Museum a century later.[98] The museum's model is a variation of the sideboard illustrated in *The Art Journal* and in *The Cabinetmaker and Art Furnisher* ten years later (**Fig. 6.65**).[99] It has oval panels painted *en grisaille* in the Neoclassical style, surrounded by Classical marquetry and a pair of wooden vases placed on the bowed cupboards of the top. The construction is typical of London cabinet making, the drawers, three of which are stamped with Wright & Mansfield's Bond Street address, have five dovetails at the front and four at the rear, as practised by metropolitan cabinet makers.[100] The carcass is of oak and mahogany, with beautifully figured veneers in the interior. Some economy has been made by using pine for the base of the narrow drawers. The drawers have slots on the underside at the back, a feature often associated with Gillows. The model in **Fig. 6.67** is much closer to the exhibition engraving and is probably the actual piece shown in 1876.[101] In 1886 *The Cabinetmaker and*

Fig. 6.60 **Made by Wright & Mansfield for Fetteresso Castle near Stonehaven in *c.*1878, this gean wood kidney desk is set with large Wedgwood plaques on all sides, in a similar manner to the Marjoribanks and Lady Aberdeen desks.** [Private collection]

Fig. 6.61 **A kidney desk stamped 'Gillows' on the middle drawer. The fine quality Honduras mahogany has now faded. A well-tried model from previous decades, it has been updated by ebonised stringing influenced by Owen Jones. The banks of drawers lock in the same manner as the so-called Wellington chests popular in the 1830s and 1840s.** [Private collection]

6.62

6.63

6.64

6.65

Cabinet-Work, by Messrs. Wright and Mansfield, London.

Cabinet-Work, by Messrs. Wright and Mansfield, London.

Art Furnisher cited Wright & Mansfield as the pre-eminent firm for the Sheraton style: 'They must be accounted the leaders of that pleasing fashion which has happily brought back into our houses many of the charming shapes of the renowned eighteenth-century cabinetmakers'.[102] The piano and the sideboard were described as the *chefs-d'œuvre* of the collection.[103]

Much unsigned furniture in this late Adam or early Sheraton manner is attributed to Wright & Mansfield today, more in hope than judgement. As can be seen in this and the following chapter, other firms such as Johnstone & Jeanes also made furniture in the Neoclassical Revival style.[104]

Another group of furniture was bought directly by the South Kensington Museum from the Wright & Mansfield stock auction in 1887. The partnership had closed in 1884 and the remaining stock was dispersed in 1886 and 1887. A 'cottage piano' realised £220 10s, a sideboard £175. For the purposes of education, the museum acquired a pair of armchairs, a Pembroke table **Fig. 5.81** and a selection of unused marquetry panels, **Figs 6.70–6.72**.[105] The shield back of the chairs is commonly associated with the designs of George Hepplewhite, published in *The Cabinet-Maker and Upholsterer's Guide* of 1788, although the Wright & Mansfield version is after a model by George Seddon. All the copies are finely made, and it is difficult to tell from a photograph whether they were made in the eighteenth century or are copies. However, when the chairs are compared side by side with an eighteenth-century pair in the Victoria and Albert Museum, the proportions of the copies are noticeably less generous. The Wright & Mansfield copies, and a similar suite of the 1870s, **Fig. 6.68**, comprising a pair of armchairs and a chair-back settee, are copied from the set of eighteen chairs supplied in *c.*1790 by Seddon, Sons & Shackleton to D. Tupper of Hauteville House, Guernsey.[106] If

CHAPTER 6: 1870S

Fig. 6.62 A corner of a small writing table possibly by Gillows; the use of well-figured thuya is relatively uncommon at this date. [Butchoff Antiques]

Fig. 6.63 A burr walnut desk stamped 'Gillows'. Although of a 'kidney' type, the block fronted drawers are unusual and the angular aspect of the rear is uncompromising, possibly indicating that it was intended for commercial or estate office use. [Sotheby's]

Fig. 6.64 A small sideboard in an update of the George III style, exhibited by Wright & Mansfield at the Philadelphia Centennial Exhibition in 1876. The coloured marquetry is inlaid into a satinwood ground. The circular door panels are also in marquetry. [*The Art Journal*, 1876, p.165]

Fig. 6.65 A more dramatic adaptation of the Adam Neoclassical style also exhibited by Wright & Mansfield in Philadelphia in 1876 with an asking price of £400. [*The Art Journal*, 1876, p.165]

Fig. 6.66 A rare marquetry small sideboard, identical in form and size to the pair exhibited at the 1876 Centennial Exhibition by Wright & Mansfield. The main difference is the use of oval painted door panels, not circular and inlaid as drawn in the exhibition example, Fig. 6.64. [Wick Antiques]

Fig. 6.67 Probably the version of the cabinet exhibited by Wright & Mansfield at the Philadelphia Centennial International Exhibition in 1876, this example is stamped 'WRIGHT & MANSFIELD, 104 BOND ST. LONDON'. It is much closer to *The Art Journal* exhibition engraving (Fig. 6.65) than the one in the Victoria and Albert Museum.[107] [Heritage Auctions]

6.66

6.67

BRITISH FURNITURE

Fig. 6.68 A settee by Wright & Mansfield, from a suite that includes armchairs. The design is similar to the suite supplied by Seddon, Sons & Shackleton to D. Tupper of Hauteville House, Guernsey, in 1790. A pair of similar chairs by Wright & Mansfield was purchased by the South Kensington Museum in 1887 as examples of fine reproductions,[108] but when placed alongside models of *c.*1790 subtle differences can be observed. [Wick Antiques]

Fig. 6.69 An armchair by Gillows, stamped 'I. Bradley L3425' and 'Gillow' The shield back of this chair and the settee opposite is inspired by Hepplewhite's *'Cabinet Maker and Upholsterer's Guide'*. [Wick Antiques]

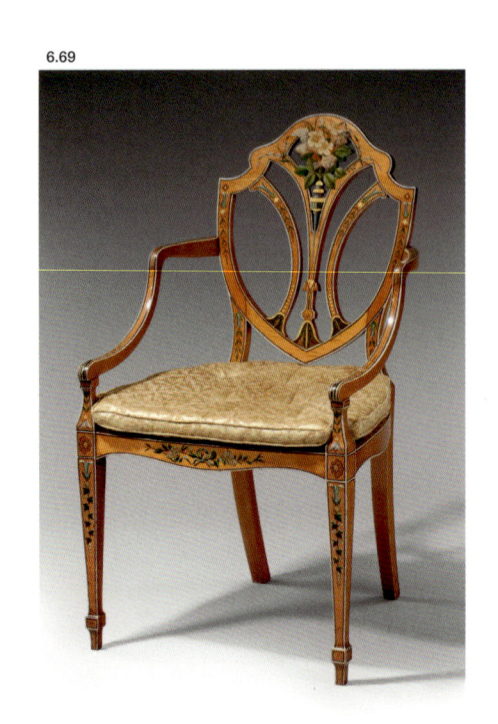

proof were ever needed that it is easy to mistakenly attribute furniture to one particular maker simply on the evidence of known examples, an almost identical armchair was made by Gillows, **Fig. 6.69**. As noted by Litchfield, this revival of Sheraton and Hepplewhite designs was apparent from the end of the 1860s, and Wright & Mansfield made a speciality of reproducing this type of furniture.[109]

The marquetry panels from the Wright & Mansfield auction are more typically nineteenth century, albeit in a quasi-eighteenth-century manner. One was made by a French hand. Quarter-veneered in *satiné*, the reverse has a Wright & Mansfield label and a stock number, **Fig. 6.72**.[110] The panel has the traditional backing of an old French newspaper as part of the marquetry packet. Was it purchased as a sample from Paris, or was it a French craftsman working in London, reading a newspaper imported from home? Another sample, stock number 4310, is dated 19 April 1879.[111] Other small fragments of marquetry show fine craftsmanship, but the very thin veneers, measuring under 1mm, were evidently machine-cut with a bandsaw, **Figs 6.70 & 6.71**. It is often not possible to date these panels accurately. They could have been made in the 1860s or '70s or, less likely, in the early 1880s.

British makers were less enthusiastic about the Renaissance Revival than their Parisian or Milanese counterparts. In Britain, the full Italianate style is seen mainly in the third quarter of the century; the designs of Alfred Lormier for Jackson & Graham were pre-eminent in the field, **Fig. 5.121**. Less satisfactory, but more inventive, were attempts by Gillows, such as the cabinet shown here in walnut with grisaille panels, **Fig. 6.75**. The unusual table, **Fig. 6.73**, is an innovative design by the French-born Charles Mellier. Naturalised in 1871, Mellier was one of the finest makers working in London. He took over the London arm of the Parisian maker Georges-Alphonse-Bonifacio Monbro in 1868.[112] For this table, Mellier has adopted the manner of fifteenth-century Florentine architect Filippo Brunelleschi. The design incorporates a geometric pattern of perspective; the cruciform structure of the base emphasises the light, see-through tracery. Each outer support is made up of a carved lion monopodium that can be compared to François Ier prototypes at the Château de Fontainebleau. The table formerly belonged to the collection at Minley Manor, a French Renaissance-style house, partly copied from the Louis XII element of the Château de Blois. Built between 1858 and 1860 for Raikes Currie, a partner in Curries & Co. bank, almost all the interior decoration of the principal rooms at Minley was carried out by Mellier, **Fig. 6.74**.[113] Elsewhere, in an unexplained relationship with Wright & Mansfield, Mellier made a music cabinet to match an upright piano and stool painted with George III-style Neoclassical figures.[114]

Alongside the emerging commercial adaptation of the eighteenth-century styles was a vogue for all things Aesthetic, with its eclectic design sources, a movement gaining popularity in Britain and the United States. Rediscovered in the 1860s, the fascination with Asia continued, running its course, in furniture manufacturing terms, by the mid-1880s. The intellectual inspiration for such a movement came from many quarters, not least from Oscar Wilde whose

Fig. 6.70: A marquetry sample from the 1887 Wright & Mansfield auction (Victoria and Albert Museum, 235-1887). [© Victoria and Albert Museum]

Fig. 6.71: Another marquetry panel bought from the 1887 auction. (Victoria and Albert Museum, 234-1887). [© Victoria and Albert Museum]

Fig. 6.72 A third panel bought from the 1887 auction, bearing the Wright & Mansfield stock number 4588; this marquetry sample is by a French hand. [© Victoria and Albert Museum]

rooms in Magdalen College, Oxford in the mid-1870s were appropriately filled with blue-and-white china. Wilde wrote of people hurling their parents' mahogany furniture into the streets, paradoxically at a time when the contemporary Georgian style was also gaining ground commercially and was sought after by luminaries such as Rossetti. Diverse cultures were explored for design inspiration by the Aesthetic movement designers, and it was perhaps inevitable that the ancient Egyptian style would appeal again, as it had in the early part of the nineteenth century. In 1863, W.E. Nesfield had included an Egyptian stool on the title page of his *Specimens of Mediaeval Architecture*. Artists were once again at the forefront of this revival. Holman Hunt's sitter in *Il Dolce far Niente* (1866) is lounging on an Egyptian-inspired chair, **Fig. 6.76**. Hunt wrote in his autobiography: 'a young lady sat to me, and I commenced a picture…I made use of the Egyptian chairs, which, having been borrowed and painted by other artists, were no longer attractive to me for Oriental subjects'.[115] Lawrence Alma-Tadema, who obtained a knighthood in 1899, had experimented with furniture designs in the 1860s, looking afresh at Egyptian themes and making sketches at the British Museum.[116] In 1872 Alma-Tadema included an Egyptian-style stool in his painting *The Death of the Pharaoh's Firstborn Son*; the stool

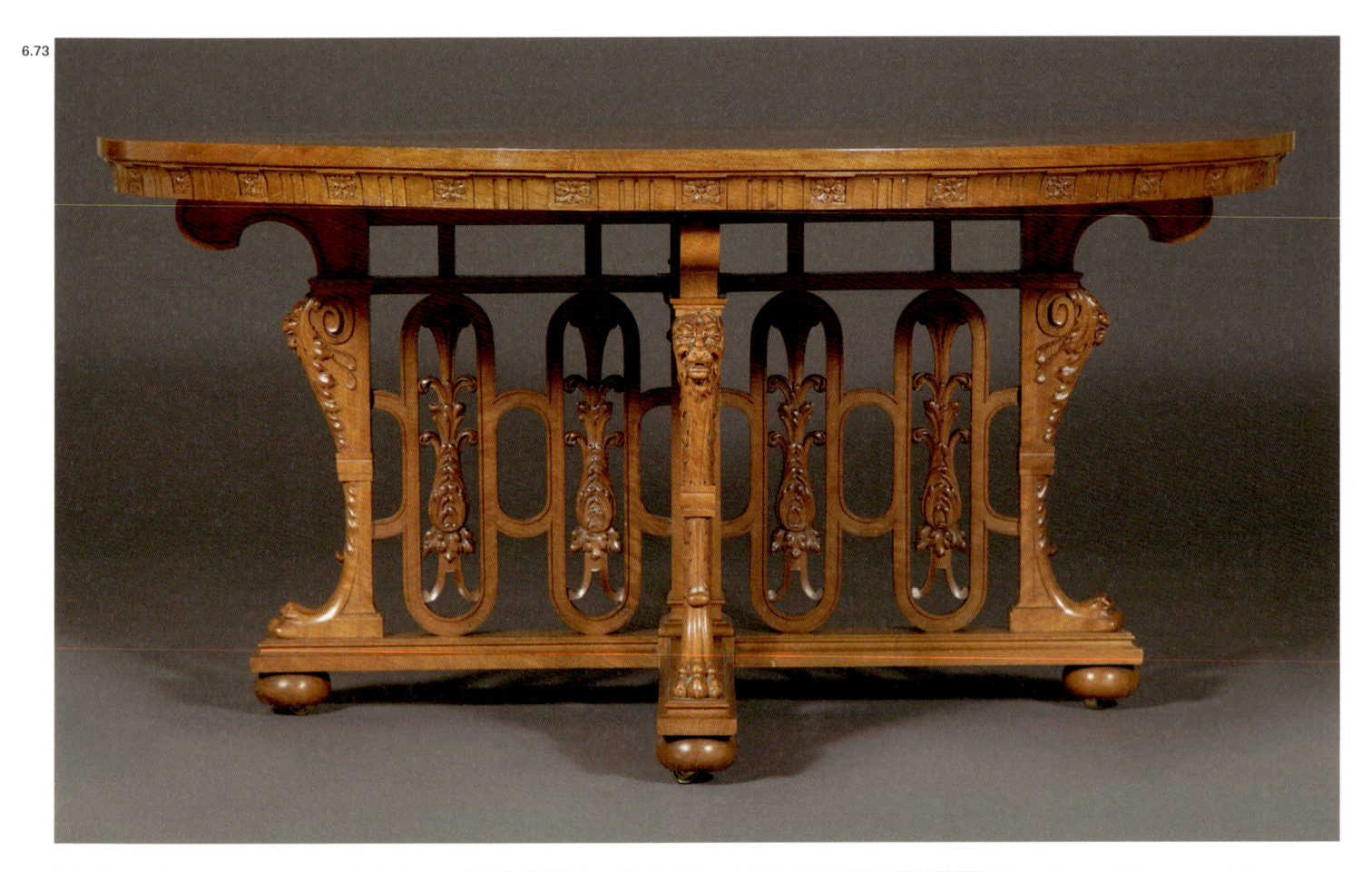

Fig. 6.73 With echoes of 1560s designs by Du Cerceau, this unusual table in walnut was supplied to Minley Manor by Charles Mellier & Co., who worked extensively at the house. It is stamped twice on the underside 'C. MELLIER LONDON'. [Carlton Hobbs LLC]

Fig. 6.74 The walnut table by Mellier in situ in the Drawing Room, illustrated in a privately published catalogue of the collections at Minley Manor, a collection formed by Bertram Wodehouse between 1866 and 1896. [Historic England (Bedford Lemere)]

was soon adapted commercially by Liberty's. Christopher Dresser and E.W. Godwin were both entranced by the simplicity of Egyptian furniture. In 1867, Godwin designed furniture for his personal use based on the Egyptian style. His design for a side table, based on a four-legged stool, became popular when manufactured by Collinson & Lock and was subsequently illustrated in 1877 in *Art Furniture: from Designs by E.W. Godwin, F.S.A., and others, with Hints and Suggestions on Domestic Furniture and Decoration* by William Watt. *The Building News* regularly reported on furniture designs and published engravings by John Moyr Smith in *Ancient Egyptian Furniture* in the British Museum's collection in 1875. A design by Godwin, dated as early as *c*.1860, showed 'Anglo-Japanese designs', including a table clearly inspired by an Egyptian stool.[117]

The term 'Art Furniture' had appeared in *The Building News* in December 1868, the same year Eastlake referred to the 'Art Furniture Company'. William Burges, E.W. Godwin, William Morris, Thomas Seddon (nephew of George Seddon), Bruce Talbert and Philip Webb all designed furniture that could be grouped under this umbrella, but it was Godwin, inspired by the simple designs of furniture made for his own personal use in 1862, who adapted the Japanese style to British furniture in the early stages of the Aesthetic movement.

The sparing use of detail and the simplicity of the Japanese aesthetic appealed to progressive designers and was a fresh approach, in contrast to the often-muddled designs borrowed from an earlier era. This type of furniture was easier to keep dust-free at a time when designers were becoming more aware of the importance of personal health and hygiene.[118] The sunflower became a recurring emblem of the British Aesthetic style and can be seen in the architectural detail on many Queen Anne-style houses of this period, often cast in red brick. Possibly inspired by William Makepeace Thackeray's *The History of Henry Esmond*, a novel about an officer in the service of Queen Anne, published in 1852, an eclectic, romanticised version of the so-called Queen Anne style in furniture had emerged by the 1870s. In 1881, Mrs H.R. Haweis, the influential author, wrote that all furniture was called Queen Anne, even if in reality it was English Chippendale or French Empire.[119] The relative simplicity of the Queen Anne style can be seen as a reaction to the fussy opulence of furniture of the mid-nineteenth century and, combined with the popularity of Asian forms, a new form of Aesthetic was born. Designers frequently incorporated lilies and peacock feathers in their Aesthetic versions of Queen Anne. It might seem incongruous that a revival style from the early eighteenth century should be mixed with the Asian aesthetic, but the two became intertwined in a search for a new Victorian style.[120] The concept of the cabriole leg, an

Fig. 6.75 **The top edge of the drawer of this Renaissance-style cabinet has the Gillow stamp and '2029' dating it to between 1874 and 1875.** The plaques are painted *en grisaille* with Mercury, Cupid, Psyche, Neptune, Tritons and Hippocampi. [Private collection]

essential feature of the Queen Anne period and its revival, was, however, somewhat frowned upon. *The Furniture Gazette* wrote about 'Bow-legged Furniture', criticising the cutting of wood against the grain: 'since abortions of this character were general in the days of Queen Anne, and this Queen Anne revival has bought them again into use'. Not a true reflection of the Queen Anne period, the Queen Anne style was said to be 'a poet's dream – a painter's craze – William Morris, and Dante Rossetti, and their school have

Fig. 6.76 *Il Dolce Far Niente*, a painting by William Holman Hunt started in 1859 but not exhibited until 1867. The sitter is shown lounging dreamily on an Egyptian-style chair similar to the one in Fig. 6.81. [Christie's]

Fig. 6.77 Made by Collinson & Lock or William Watt & Co. in *c.*1876, this ebonised wood table with brass feet compares to a design by Godwin published in *Art Furniture* in 1877. A less refined variant was still available in the 1912 Morris & Company catalogue. [© Victoria and Albert Museum, London]

Fig. 6.78 An ebonised and parcel-gilt 'Aegyptian' low chair designed by the Glasgow-born Daniel Cottier for his successful eponymous firm, which advertised as 'art furniture makers, mural decorators, and glass and tile painters', and also dealt in antiques.[121] [Oscar Graf]

Fig. 6.79 Based on Godwin's 1872 design and known as the 'Smallhythe' table, this example in mahogany is difficult to date with certainty. It was probably made by Collinson & Lock. [The Huntington Library, Art Museum, and Botanical Gardens]

devised it between them'.[122] Some of the main proponents were Batley, Collcutt, Collinson & Lock, Godwin and Shaw. *The Furniture Gazette* credited Shaw as the leading light of modern Queen Anne, commenting that he was previously 'a master in Gothic design'.[123] *The Furniture Gazette* reproduced simple line drawings by Godwin 'specially designed for this journal',[124] see **Fig. 6.85a**, and many of his designs were imitated by commercial makers. Between 1872 and 1874, Godwin had an arrangement with Collinson & Lock for them to use his designs; these were later commercialised, possibly without Godwin's agreement. Godwin's historic designs of furniture for Dromore Castle were made by Watt between 1867 and 1870. Although world renowned for his Aesthetic designs, Godwin designed 'Old English' and Jacobean-style furniture for *The Furniture Gazette* in 1876, **Fig. 6.85b**. A rare example of a press or 'court' cupboard by him is shown as **Fig. 6.87**.

A relatively unknown Aesthetic designer was O.W. Davis, whose design for an extensive dining room suite was made by Shoolbred for the Lord Mayor of London. Despite numerous designs published in contemporary magazines, comparatively little Aesthetic furniture is recorded. One example is an Aesthetic-inspired library suite by Audas & Leggott, cabinet and art furniture makers of Hull. There were designs by R. Hunter, a maker in Eden Street, Hampstead; another designer was Charles Leggott, possibly connected with the Hull workshop and others by a 'Mr A. Lackenby'.[125] In the 1870s, Rottmann, Strome & Co. imported, with resounding success, imitation leather paper from Japan, so often seen applied to British-made commercial Aesthetic furniture. Embossed and lacquered, *kinkarakawakami* paper used tinfoil to create the effect of gilding, inspired by leather wall-hangings of the late seventeenth and early eighteenth centuries. Demand was so great that in the 1880s the firm opened a factory in Yokohama to make wallpaper for export. By 1886 Rottmann was also importing Moorish furniture.

The architectural practice of George Edmund Street was a productive environment for a host of aspiring designers, such as Morris, Shaw and Collcutt. Strong contrasting colours popular during the early nineteenth century and the polychrome decoration of the 1860s gave way to more subtle hues in the Aesthetic movement of the 1870s. The colour scheme in the Peacock Room, designed by James McNeill Whistler and Thomas Jeckyll between 1876 and 1877 for the London home of the wealthy Liverpool ship-owner Frederick Leyland, is subtle, exhilarating and was definitively 'new'.[126] Despite the invigorating Aesthetic design, the walls were covered with sixteenth-century leather from a house in Norfolk.[127] The square supports designed by Jeckyll for the shelves to hold the extensive collection of blue-and-white Chinese porcelain have similarities with structural details used by Godwin. However, elsewhere both designers continued to use turned supports derived from Jacobean and Georgian forms, the latter a style of turning also favoured by commercial makers such as Collinson & Lock or James Shoolbred & Co.

6.80 **A group of designs of 'Ancient Egyptian Furniture' by John Moyr Smith.** [*The Building News*, 5 November 1875]

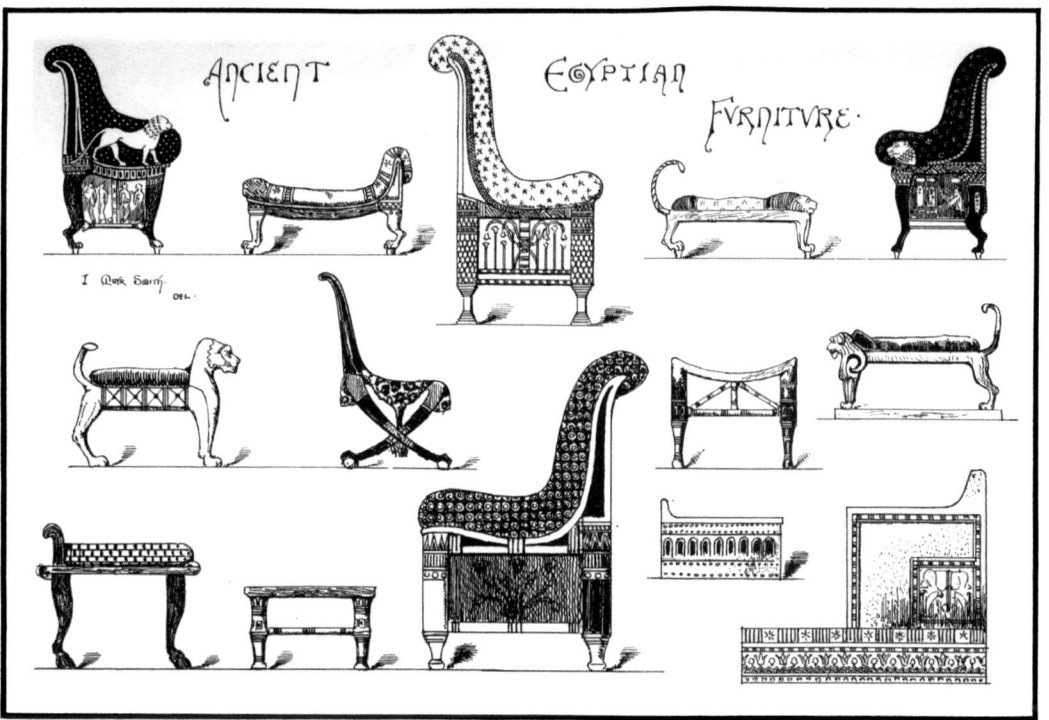

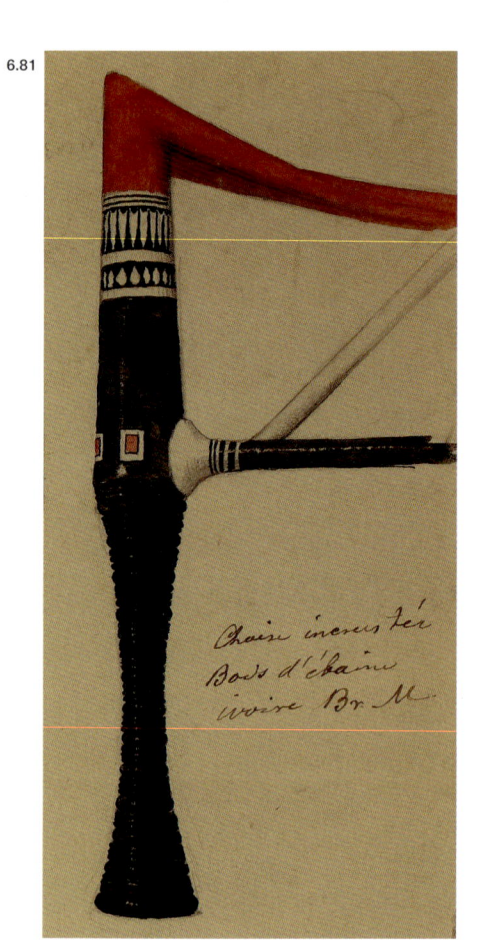

Fig. 6.81 One of a series of studies made in *c*.1870 by Lawrence Alma-Tadema of an ebony and painted Egyptian stool in the British Museum, the caption written in French, *c*.1870. [Cadbury Research Library]

Fig. 6.82 A delightful sketch for a chess table, one of a series of drawings by E.W. Godwin made between 1872 and 1883. [© Victoria and Albert Museum, London]

Fig. 6.83 A series of sketches for dining room furniture in the Jacobean manner by E.W. Godwin, 1872–83. Studies for Plate 7 of *Art Furniture from Designs by E.W. Godwin*, by W. Watt, London. [© Victoria and Albert Museum, London]

By June 1873, Shoolbred had enlarged their already substantial premises with a new department devoted to furniture and decoration.[128] Growth of department store trade was exponential; Shoolbred's first catalogue, published in 1874, was thirty-eight pages in length, expanded to eighty-four pages in 1876 and over 400 pages by 1884. Like many of their contemporaries, Shoolbred offered a complete house-furnishing service. They exhibited two black-and-gold cabinets in Paris in 1878, one a corner cabinet, the other a three-tier sideboard, both commercial versions of Aesthetic-style furniture. At the same time, they also produced satinwood furniture of a similar style to that of Collinson

Fig. 6.84 A wardrobe in beautifully figured ash made by William Watt in c.1878 after designs by E.W. Godwin. It is an inventive form that may well have been the forerunner for the space-saving 'Compactum' wardrobes that became popular in the early twentieth century. [© Victoria and Albert Museum, London]

& Lock, which, without name stamps, would be difficult to attribute to a specific maker. Ring-turning on the upright supports and legs of Shoolbred furniture was seemingly influenced by the designs of Collcutt or the architect Alfred Waterhouse. What little documented furniture designed by Waterhouse that survives has a light Gothic and Aesthetic mix with a twist of Godwin's Jacobean that is hard to define. Godwin exhibited his distinctive Aesthetic style in Vienna in 1873, in Philadelphia with Collinson & Lock in 1876, and on the William Watt stand in Paris in 1878, the same year that he designed a studio for Princess Louise at Kensington Palace.[129] George Gilbert Scott (Junior) was another designer who adapted the Jacobean form in the 1870s, his furniture also made by Watt, **Fig. 6.90**.

The contents of 18 Stafford Terrace in 1877, the home of the *Punch* cartoonist Linley Sambourne, are a good indication of comfortable, contemporary fashion; his house is an invaluable record of 'Victorian clutter', **Figs 6.91a–c**. These late nineteenth-century photographs show, for example, a pair of satinwood display cabinets in an up-to-the minute Adam revival style – a commercial diminution of the prize-winning satinwood cabinet exhibited by Wright

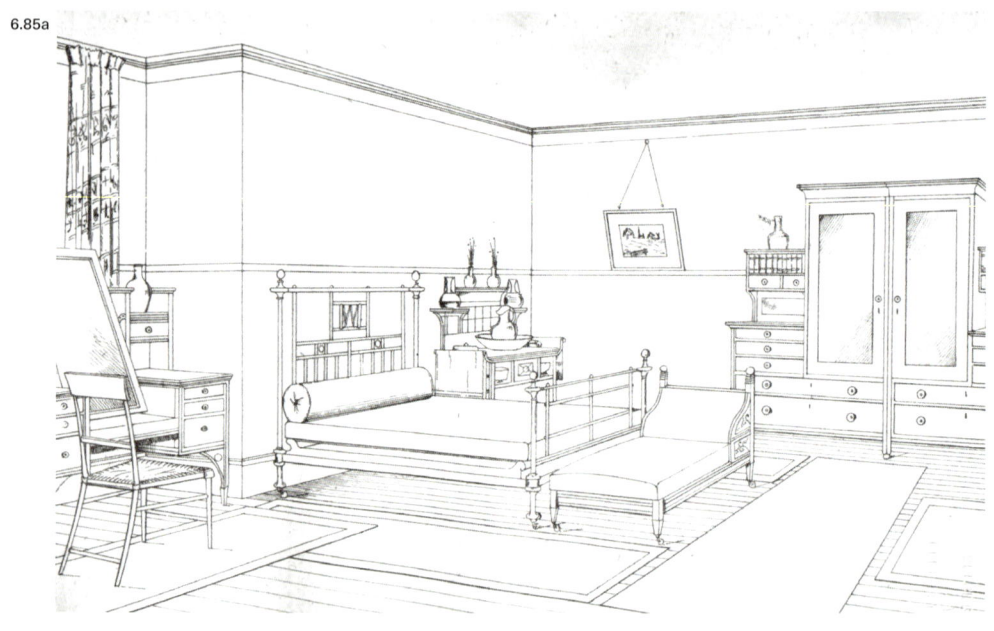

Fig. 6.85a **Bedroom furniture illustrated in** *The Furniture Gazette*, designed by E.W. Godwin in an 'aesthetic' style with clean, symmetrical lines, the bedstead of tubular brass. [*The Furniture Gazette*, 23 September 1876, p.187]

Fig. 6.85b **'Old English' or 'Jacobean Furniture'** drawn by Godwin for *The Furniture Gazette* in 1876. Godwin has modernised the seventeenth-century style without any pretence at making copies. [*The Furniture Gazette*, 19 August 1876]

Fig. 6.86 **An oak armchair in the Queen Anne style**, originally for the Tabard Inn in Bedford Park, a public house designed by Norman Shaw between 1879 and 1880.[130] A popular model, it was probably made by William Birch and there were also variations by Morris & Co. [H. Blairman & Sons]

& Mansfield in Paris in 1867. The settee and chairs in the Morning Room were of the same revival style, not exact copies or reproductions. Also in the Morning Room, but not illustrated here, was a mahogany low or 'dwarf' cabinet of breakfront form with an ivorine label of Edwards & Roberts. The dining room sideboard was a combination of the Gothic and Aesthetic styles, a blending between the two seemingly opposing concepts. Influenced by Eastlake, it reflected furniture made by Gillows to Talbert's designs that was shown at the 1872 London Exhibition. Talbert wrote frequently to *The Furniture Gazette*; in May 1873 he complained that his designs had been poorly copied or changed without his permission.[131] Although provincial by comparison, there are traces of Talbert's ideas in furniture supplied to Manchester Town Hall, a neo-Gothic municipal building designed by Alfred Waterhouse between 1876 and 1877; some of the furniture was made by the Manchester firm of Dovestone, Bird & Hull.[132]

Furniture made by Gillows to Talbert's designs featured at numerous international exhibitions, including the International Exhibition of 1873. Gillows exhibited in both the medieval and Jacobean styles, their designs imitated by other firms. Highly detailed, Talbert designs included bold geometric inlaid patterns, intricately carved squares of boxwood and rows of small turned spindles. His *Gothic Forms Applied to Furniture, Metal Work, and Decoration for Domestic Purposes* was published in London in 1868 and in the United States in 1873, followed by *Examples of Ancient*

Fig. 6.87 **The 'Shakespeare' sideboard**, designed by Godwin, the design patented by William Watt in 1881. Godwin has subtly updated the mid-seventeenth-century form of a north country press cupboard as part of a dining set, using wooden dowels in period fashion but adding a mirror to the recessed back panel. [H. Blairman & Sons]

Fig. 6.88 **Possibly supplied by James Capel between 1872 and 1873**, this oak armchair has similarities to a set designed by Alfred Waterhouse for the 1st Earl of Selbourne. [Tew Archive © Christies 1987]

Fig. 6.89 **Henry Capel's Art Furniture showrooms** of 'Artistic furniture' at Great Titchfield Street. Capel exhibited 'Art piano music stools' at the 1878 Paris Exhibition. [© Victoria and Albert Museum, London]

& Modern: Furniture, Metal Work, Tapestries, Decoration in 1876.[133] His third book, *Fashionable Furniture: A Collection of Three Hundred and Fifty Original Designs, Representing Cabinet Work, Upholstery and Decoration*, was published posthumously in 1881. Talbert's influence in the United States was immediate – a cabinet, dated between 1877 and 1880, attributed to Daniel Pabst and made to a design by the architect Frank Furness, is clearly of American design but with Reformed Gothic overtones that are unmistakably British.[134] In *Examples of Ancient & Modern Furniture*, Talbert wrote about the confusion of terminology at the

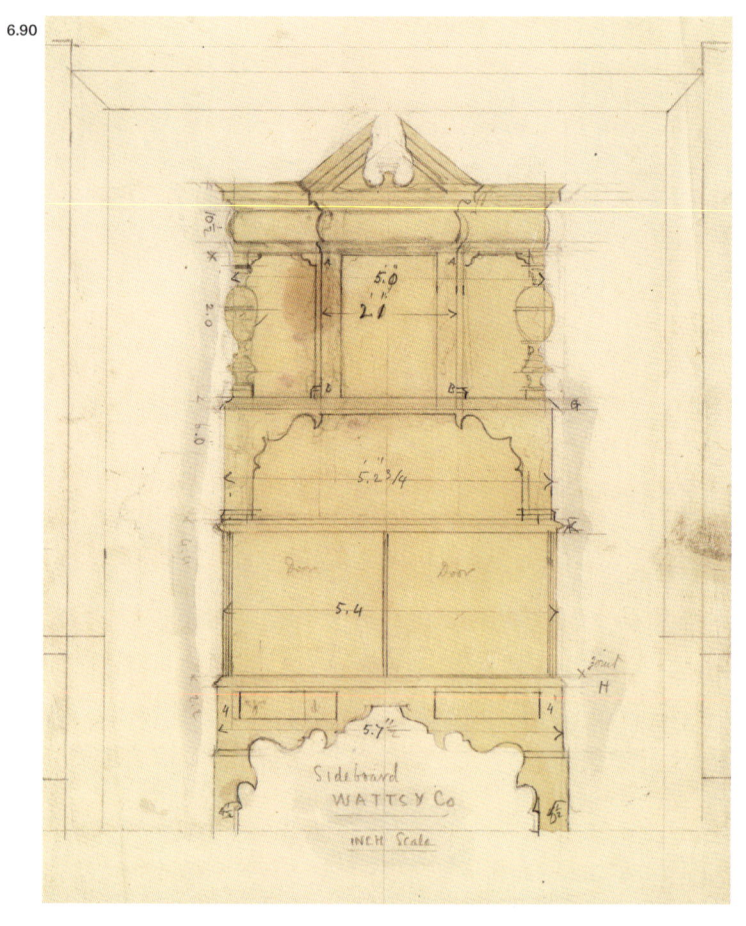

Fig. 6.90 'Jacobeathan' with a touch of 'Queen Anne', this elevation for a sideboard designed in 1874 by George Gilbert Scott junior includes detailed measurements for the maker, Watts & Co., with instructions to use English walnut. [RIBA]

Figs 6.91a–c Three views of 18 Stafford Terrace, home of Linley and Marion Sambourne. Above the Talbert-style sideboard is a large convex mirror. Either side of the fireplace are a pair of marquetry cabinets in satinwood and elsewhere painted shield back chairs similar to sets made by Wright & Mansfield and Gillows. A more recent colour image of the house is shown in Chapter 8, Fig. 8.30. [Courtesy the Countess of Rosse]

time: 'It is a common current mistake to name modern black and gold painted furniture "Gothic" or "Old English". Both terms are very wide'.[135]

Alongside the reinterpretations of British style and the Aesthetic, furniture in the French manner was perennially popular and always of exceptional quality. The marquetry on the centre table by the short-lived partnership of Morant, Boyd & Blanford is exceptional, the standard of craftsmanship suggesting a royal commission or an exhibition piece, **Fig. 6.98**. The partnership – based at 91 New Bond Street, with workshops just behind in Haunch of Venison Yard and a 'Steamworks' in Hammersmith – was formed in 1870 and lasted until 1884. Love is the theme of the marquetry on the table; the central panel shows Cupid wooing Knowledge and the Arts, the corner spandrels are inlaid in ivory with billing doves. The wide crossbanding is, unusually, in plane tree, the wood cut at an angle to set off the medullary rays. The pair of light and portable occasional tables, **Fig. 6.95**, are similar in outline to a model of *c*.1879 by Henry Dasson of Paris.[136] Veneered in plum-pudding mahogany, they are stamped 'Morant & Co.'; imitating the Louis XV/XVI transitional style, they are however almost certainly French imports.

Figure 6.96 illustrates a cabinet in the French Louis XVI style by Gillows. Up to date with contemporary fashion, it is veneered in coromandel with a European imitation of Chinese lacquer on the door. The interior is beautifully panelled in mahogany in an expensive manner to be expected from the upper echelon of London makers. Without the evidence of the Gillows stamp and serial number, and the

Figs 6.92 & 6.93 Details of two tables veneered in coromandel, the one on the left (6.92) stamped by Holland & Sons. The example on the right (6.93) is not signed but the ivory inlay on the drawers is the same as the signed table, enough for a firm attribution to Hollands. The leg capitals are similar to those on the Dowbiggin cabinet Fig. 6.97. Although the standard of British cabinet making was very high by the mid-century, there were only a few firms that could achieve this quality of craftsmanship. [Private collection]

British-made Comyn Ching lock, it would be difficult to identify the nationality of the cabinet. The design of the gilt-bronze screw feet, sometimes referred to as 'Thor's thunderbolts', is taken directly from the designs of André-Charles Boulle of *c*.1700. The lower, more squat style of cabinet is, however, more typical of the late eighteenth-century Boulle revival by makers such as Étienne Levasseur. This later Boulle style was revived by Paris makers from the 1850s to 1870s, and it is interesting to find an English piece in the same genre. The gilt-bronze apron mount, for example, is typical of Henry Dasson, who made a similar cabinet with Japanese *hiramaki-e* lacquer.[137] The top of the door is stamped 'Gillows 1866', which relates not to the year of manufacture but to the workshop numbering system, dating it to 1874. Gillows claimed to be meticulous in only stamping furniture made by them in their own workshops. In 1888, Thomas Clarke, a partner of the firm, under oath to a Select Committee at the House of Lords, stated: 'We occasionally buy some fine examples of French furniture, and most of these examples we are repeating ourselves in this country, examples beautifully made. We never put our name

BRITISH FURNITURE

on goods unless we manufacture them ourselves'.[138] This is slightly at odds with a statement given by an independent cabinet maker, William Parnell, 'a firm like Messrs. Gillow, for instance will receive an order, and it will probably be made in some sub-contractor's shop'.[139]

The Centennial International Exhibition of 1876 was the first official World's Fair in the United States. Held in Philadelphia from May to November, it was a celebration of the 100th anniversary of the signing of the Declaration of Independence. Like the European exhibition venues, the main exhibition building was a temporary structure, albeit at the time the largest building in the world, enclosing 21.5 acres (87,000m²).[140] The exhibition occurred at a time when American visitors were beginning to travel more frequently to Europe and attend design schools. A large British presence included furniture makers, notably Collinson & Lock, and comprehensive photographs of their stand and others' survive, such as those shown here, **Figs 6.100, 6.102, 6.104, 6.105, 6.106a & 6.106b.** Collinson & Lock's exhibit was well received and included furniture designed by both Godwin and Talbert.

Praise for Wright & Mansfield at the Centennial International Exhibition was profuse, with one publication even going so far as to describe how they 'have been long known as among the most artistic furniture-makers in the world'.[141] Two of the pieces sent by them were illustrated in *The Art Journal* under 'Gems of the Centennial Exhibition', **Figs 6.64 & 6.65.** The epitome of the Sheraton revival in satinwood with delicate Neoclassical inlay and female figures swathed in Classical dress, the comparison with solid oak

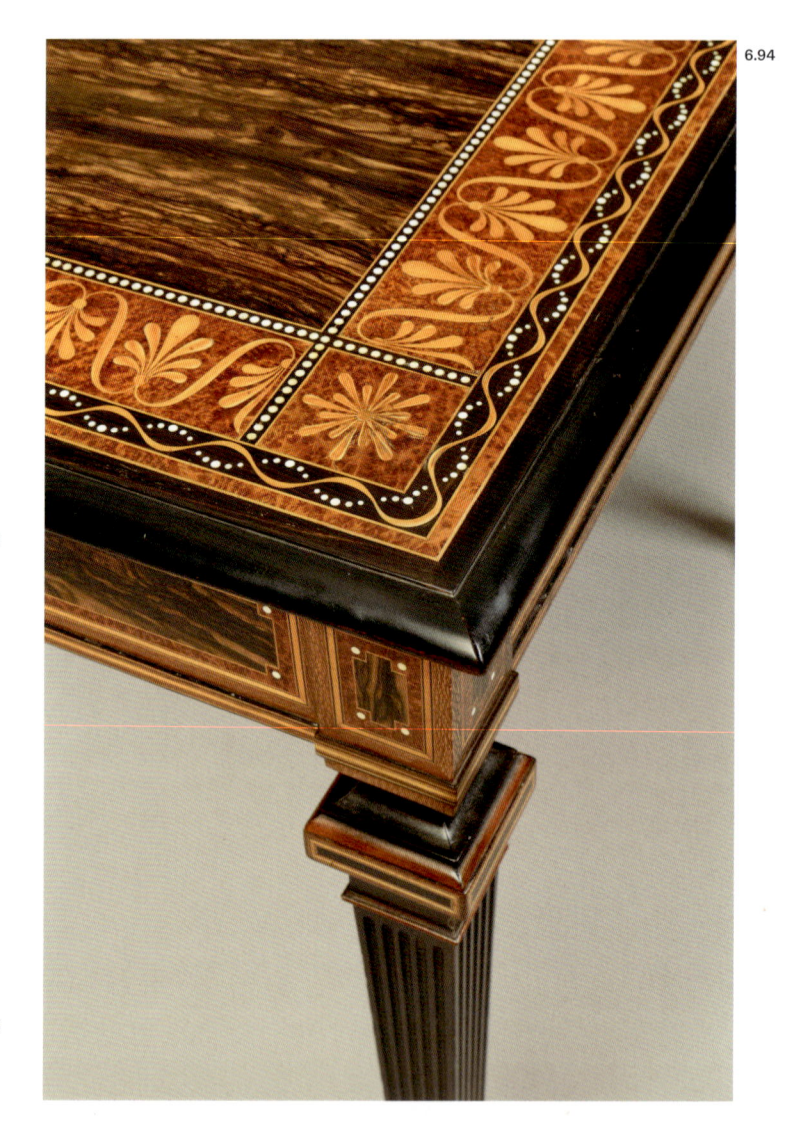

6.94

6.95

6.96

334

CHAPTER 6: 1870S

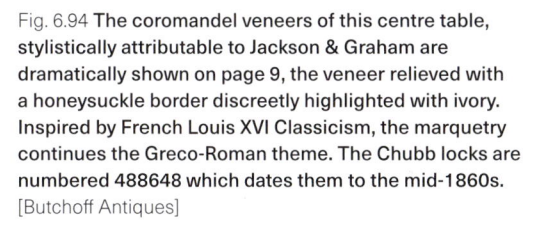

Fig. 6.94 The coromandel veneers of this centre table, stylistically attributable to Jackson & Graham are dramatically shown on page 9, the veneer relieved with a honeysuckle border discreetly highlighted with ivory. Inspired by French Louis XVI Classicism, the marquetry continues the Greco-Roman theme. The Chubb locks are numbered 488648 which dates them to the mid-1860s. [Butchoff Antiques]

Fig. 6.95 Although stamped 'Morant & Co.' on the edge of the drawers, these delicate tables in the Louis XV/XVI transitional style, veneered in plum-pudding mahogany, were probably imported from Dasson of Paris. [Private collection]

Fig. 6.96 Confusingly stamped 'Gillows 1866', the number relates to designs produced in 1874. The lacquer is English, japanning, imitating Chinese lacquer. [Butchoff Antiques]

Fig. 6.97 Made for Queen Victoria by Dowbiggin & Son in 1871 for Osborne House at a cost of £85. The porcelain plaques are German set in rosewood, ebony and mahogany. The floral marquetry on the leg capitals is similar to the Holland capital seen in Fig. 6.92. [Royal Collection Trust, RCIN 41237/© His Majesty King Charles III 2022]

Fig. 6.98 The top of a table by Morant, Boyd & Blanford, designed in the French manner. The corner spandrels and wide crossbanding are, unusually, veneered in plane tree, cut to show off the decorative effects of the medullary rays. The centre panel is of thuya, outlined in stained holly and inlaid with ivory. [Private collection]

Figs 6.99a & b This elaborately adorned marquetry centre table, in the French style, has the precious remnants of the maker's label: Howard & Sons. [Private collection]

335

Fig. 6.100 **A view of the Collinson & Lock stand at the 1876 Centennial International Exhibition. The contemporary 'Art Furniture' was displayed below a reproduction of a Dutch seventeenth-century brass chandelier.** [The Free Library of Philadelphia]

Fig. 6.101 **Praised by Charles Eastlake, Collinson & Lock had great success at the International Exhibitions. These two cabinets, described as 'parlor-cabinets' in a restrained Aesthetic style, were shown in Philadelphia. The smaller, corner cabinet, was offered at £90; the side cabinet in satinwood with ivory marquetry and parcel-gilding was offered at £150.** [George T. Ferris, *Gems of the Centennial Exhibition*, 1877]

furniture in the 'Eastlake style' shown at the exhibition by the Mitchell & Rammelsberg Furniture Co. of Cincinnati could not have been more of a contrast. Nevertheless, Eastlake's honest and rugged Gothic style was highly influential and much appreciated in the United States. The photograph of the Wright & Mansfield stand at the exhibition, taken from an upper gallery, **Fig. 6.102**, renders the furniture diminutive compared to the scale of the building. A side cabinet can just be discerned, possibly that in **Fig. 6.67**. Not visible in this image, on the back of the George III-style breakfront wardrobe was a mirror that closely resembles the Adam-style giltwood mirror in **Fig. 6.103**. To the left of the stand is that of Cooper & Holt, with Feetham, the chimney-piece fitters, just behind.

The contrast between furniture on the Howard & Sons stand at the 1876 Centennial International Exhibition in Philadelphia, **Fig. 6.104**, and their Louis XVI-style centre table, **Fig. 6.99b**, could not be more marked. It shows the diversity of the large London firms, who catered for all tastes, and all pockets. Perhaps Howard felt that the North American taste at the time was for plainer pieces with an emphasis on upholstery. **Figure 6.99** is a highly sophisticated centre table in the French manner, with elaborate marquetry, probably intended for the domestic or European market. The legs have a skilfully matched chevron veneer, the gilt-bronze swags a conceit reminiscent of the eighteenth-century Parisian cabinet maker, Philippe-Claude Montigny. Howards arranged thin slices of veneer in geometric large patterns that they called 'wood tapestry'; they patented a method of inlaying thin veneers, the patterns being punched out by a zinc plate pressed by a heavy roller.[142] Fine hand cutting was still traditionally done by hand with a coping saw, the saw's teeth were hand cut in the workshop by the cutter and the blade would require constant replacement. Recently found documentation and watercolours of furniture supplied to St Petersburg by Howard & Sons show that this comprised more conventional pieces, not dissimilar to those exhibited at the 1876 Centennial.[143]

CHAPTER 6: 1870S

Fig. 6.102 The tall wardrobe on the Wright & Mansfield stand at the 1876 Centennial International Exhibition looks diminutive in the vast exhibition space. The firm also exhibited a Regency-style convex mirror and one in the Adam style similar to that shown in Fig 6.103. [© Free Library of Philadelphia / Bridgeman Images]

Fig. 6.103 A mirror in the Adam manner close in design to one exhibited on the Wright & Mansfield stand. Next to the Adam mirror on the stand was an early example of a Regency Revival circular convex mirror in giltwood with an eagle or similar cresting. [Butchoff Antiques]

Fig. 6.104 The Howard & Sons stand at the 1876 Centennial International Exhibition. Most pieces are Aesthetic-influenced, but the cloth on the central table, like the seat furniture, is hung with the ubiquitous fringes and tassels that define the 'Victorian' era. The table is similar to one by Howard at Raby Castle, Fig. 3.39b. [The Free Library of Philadelphia]

BRITISH FURNITURE

6.105

6.106a

6.106b

Fig. 6.105 *The Furniture Gazette* reporter called the style of this sideboard, exhibited by Scott Morton & Co., 'Queen Anne', despite the carved portraits of Rembrandt, Rubens, Dante and Shakespeare.
[The Free Library of Philadelphia]

Figs 6.106a & b Two views of the Shoolbred stand at the 1876 Centennial International Exhibition. The firm exhibited a wide variety of furniture, ranging from an expensive Gothic Reform cabinet to more sedate bedroom and seat furniture.
[The Free Library of Philadelphia]

Cox & Son, with a workshop in Lambeth and a showroom in the Strand, were leading makers of fittings for churches, and made good use of architect designers, putting together a room setting for the 1876 exhibition with an Eastlake-influenced Gothic bureau bookcase and 'matching' chimney piece. To Americans, retail prices must have seemed high – much of the furniture from Britain was essentially handmade and more expensive than the factory-made furniture produced in the United States. Imports for the purposes of display were tariff free but if sold, a tariff of 35 per cent was imposed. Nevertheless, British exhibitors fared well, and the American commentator Walter Smith noted that many British firms used an innovative design for their stands – simply by building cordoned-off room settings.[144]

The range of furniture exhibited was varied in an attempt to account for all tastes and was doubtless an exploratory exercise to assess the potential for a new market. The award-winning Edinburgh firm of William Scott Morton & Co. exhibited an uncompromising sideboard in stained wainscot oak carved with portraits of Rembrandt, Rubens, Dante

338

and Shakespeare, and with panels of embossed leather, **Fig. 6.105**. In the 1860s, William Scott Morton had worked for Johnstone & Jeanes in London, returning to Scotland in 1867. His firm subsequently supplied a dining room suite for Frank Jay Gould at his villa at Maisons-Laffitte and, from 1903, worked in association with Robert Lorimer. Other furniture to Morton's designs had been made or exhibited by Kendal, Milne & Co. of Manchester. The firm had a stand at the Manchester Exhibition of 1857 on which they showed an inventive spider-leg table that anticipated the Art Nouveau style. The report on a carved sideboard in Italian walnut, sent by the furniture maker and author Miss Emma Phipson of Basingstoke, highlights the enormous quantity of furniture made in Britain, which cannot easily be traced today.[145] Scotland was seen as having potential for both creativity and commercial opportunity. In 1873, a committee had been formed for an exhibition in Aberdeen, including somewhat mysteriously 'furniture of artistic design, antique'.

The British commissioner's headquarters and St George's House at the Centennial International Exhibition were decorated by Cooper & Holt, for which they were awarded two diplomas. They were praised by the jurors as 'among the very finest pieces of work contributed by England', adding somewhat naively that the cabinet was 'probably a copy of an old model'.[146] The engraving, **Fig. 6.107**, of their large side cabinet shows a familiarity with the modern aesthetic, not dissimilar to designs of Collinson & Lock. Other awards were made to Bradley Barnard and Leonard Collman [*sic*] of London, Scott Morton & Co., and others less well known today. The large stand of James Shoolbred & Co. was, like that of Collinson & Lock, divided into room settings, exhibiting expensive and more functional furniture, **Figs 6.106a & b**.

Fig. 6.107 **Cooper & Holt were awarded two diplomas when they exhibited this cabinet in 1876. With Aesthetic style overtones it incorporated silver-plated glass plaques on an ebonised cherry ground.** [Walter Smith, *Masterpieces of the Centennial International Exhibition Illustrated, II: Industrial Art*, 1876, CXLIX]

Fig. 6.108 **A sheet music cover of 1881 for *My Aesthetic Love*, the woman's dress and furniture an interpretation of the Aesthetic movement.** [© Victoria and Albert Museum, London]

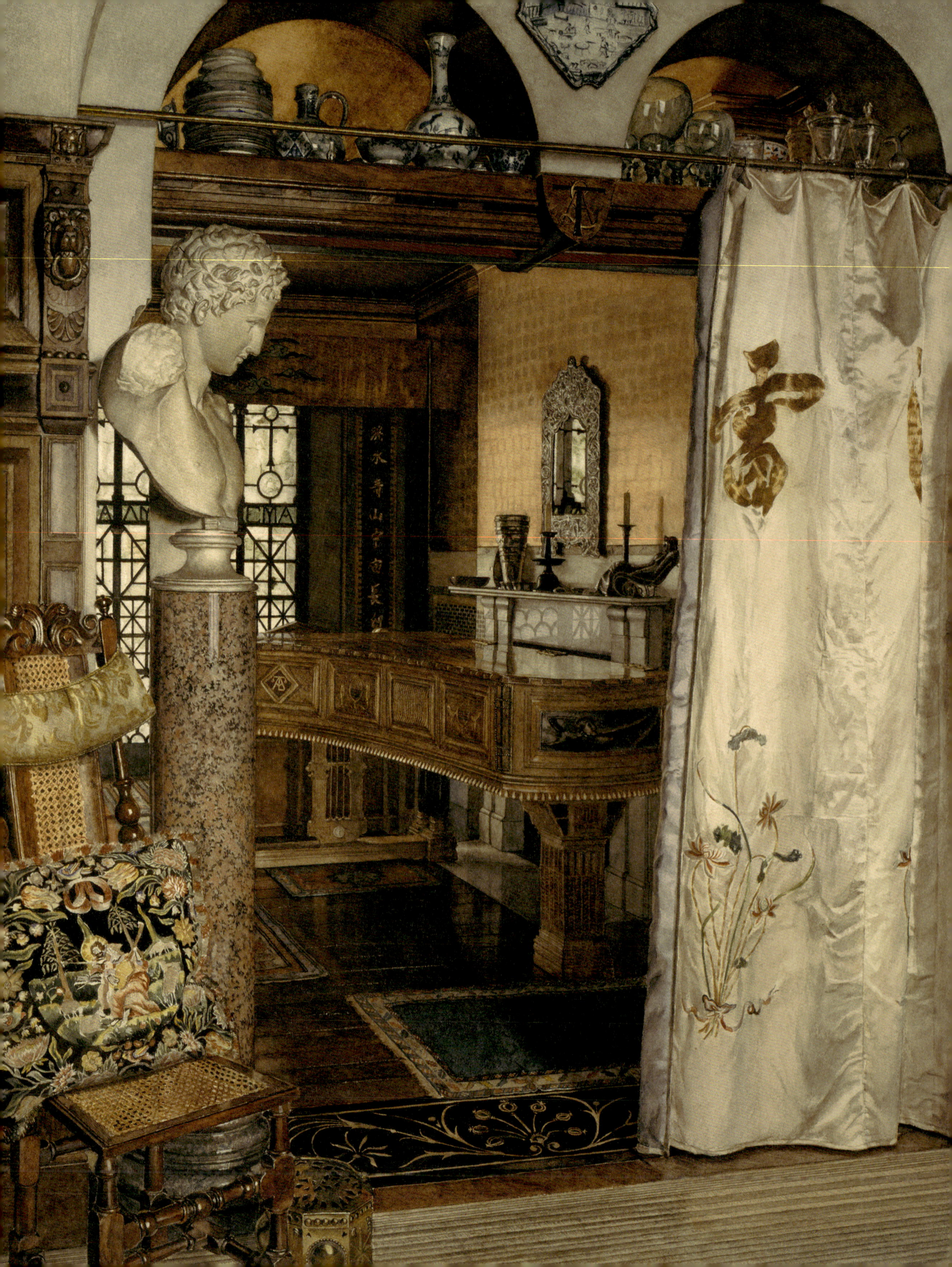

CHAPTER 7

1880s

'The chief object of rich and accomplished men in most ages of luxury and refinement has been, to make the house, its walls, ceilings or floors, and necessary of useful furniture, costly and beautiful.'[1]

In literature, art and society, Britain in the 1880s was transitioning from the strict Victorianism of the mid-nineteenth century to the Belle Époque of the period 1890 to 1914. The decorative arts were no exception, and the result is a decade difficult to define, especially in furniture design and production.

Moncure D. Conway, an American preacher, writer and abolitionist, published a helpful guide to the interiors that he saw in his *Travels in South Kensington* of 1882.[2] As well as the table shown as **Fig. 6.19a** in the previous chapter, Conway's book contained two illustrations of Belle Vue House, a Georgian building overlooking the Thames in Chelsea, **Figs 7.4 & 7.5**. The rooms have a more conventional approach to furnishing than today's isolated examples of avant-garde 1880s pieces in museums suggest. Both the Library and the Drawing Room have modern interpretations, not copies, of mid-eighteenth-century drop-leaf tables; the example in the Drawing Room is in a style still popular between 1910 and 1930. There is an overall feeling of relaxed comfort, apparent also in an engraving of the Drawing Room at Townsend House, the home of Lawrence Alma-Tadema, and a watercolour of the Gold Room, **Figs 7.1 & 7.7**. The furniture is upholstered and cosy, the curtained doorway flanked by side chairs in the Carolean manner. Medieval, Gothic and Renaissance forms were less in evidence than in previous decades, replaced by forms of the mixed Jacobean and Elizabethan, the 'Jacobethan' style, which grew in popularity over the next thirty years. Reproductions of Georgian furniture, some accurate, others fanciful, began to dominate and, unless we look at specific commissions or dated furniture, notably that in the emerging Arts and Crafts manner, dating specifically to the 1880s is often simply subjective.

The enfilade at Cliffe Castle, Yorkshire, completed in 1883 for Henry Butterfield, **Fig. 7.3**, was the height of comfort and luxury, and demonstrates the increasing importance of the upholsterer. Heavily upholstered armchairs and sofas often demanded the skills of the London firms.

The painting by Alfred Emslie of an intimate dinner at Haddo House is of a more formal but similarly eclectic interior, **Fig. 7.2**. The painting shows an evening hosted by the 1st Marquess of Aberdeen in honour of Prime Minister William Gladstone on his tour of Scotland. Lady Aberdeen is seen turning to Gladstone; to her left is the 5th Earl of Rosebery, who succeeded Gladstone as prime minister in 1894.[4] The overall feeling is of unabashed luxury, wealth and comfort. The dining chairs are heavily padded, the entrance of the serving staff is hidden by a folding screen of Chinese or Japanese inspiration in the Aesthetic manner. The *torchère*

Fig. 7.1 **An extraordinarily precise watercolour by Anna Alma-Tadema of the Gold Room in Alma-Tadema's home at Townshend House in c.1883. The Byzantine styling of the Broadwood piano was designed by George Fox.**[3] **The unusual head cushion on the Charles II chair suggests regular occupancy, the transverse silk curtain in an up to the minute Aesthetic fashion.** [Nelson-Atkins Museum of Art, 81-30/86]

Fig. 7.2 *Dinner at Haddo House* painted by Alfred Emslie in 1884. A giltwood *torchère* by Wright & Mansfield, similar to the pair they exhibited at the 1862 International Exhibition, can be seen to the far right of the kilted piper. [National Portrait Gallery, London]

Fig. 7.3 The luxuriously upholstered enfilade at Cliffe Castle, Yorkshire, completed in 1883 for Henry Butterfield. The swagged drapery, trimmed with heavy fringes and tassels, matches the silk damask wall panels and deeply sprung and padded armchairs, with a carpet specially imported from France. [Cliffe Castle, Bradford Museums & Galleries]

Fig. 7.4 **The Library at Belle Vue House in Chelsea,** *c.*1880, the well-used desk probably made in the 1860s. The armchair is a reproduction of Georgian examples, and the gateleg table with a narrow top is similar in form to a 'spider-leg' table, a version of which was designed by Godwin in 1877. [Butchoff archive]

Fig. 7.5 **The Drawing Room at Belle Vue House in Chelsea.** The gateleg table, with a shaped gadrooned top, is a contemporary affectation of the late Jacobean style. [Butchoff archive]

Fig. 7.6 **A view of the Japanese Drawing Room at 14 De Vere Gardens,** photographed by Bedford Lemere in 1887, the ceiling suitably in keeping. The bamboo chairs were probably made by Peter Bastendorff & Co. or W.T. Ellmore of Leicester who made a wide range of bamboo furniture, from cabinets to seat furniture.[5] [Historic England, Bedford Lemere Collection]

Fig. 7.7 **The comfortable Drawing Room in Townsend House, Chelsea,** *c.*1882, the home of the artist, Lawrence Alma-Tadema. [Butchoff archive]

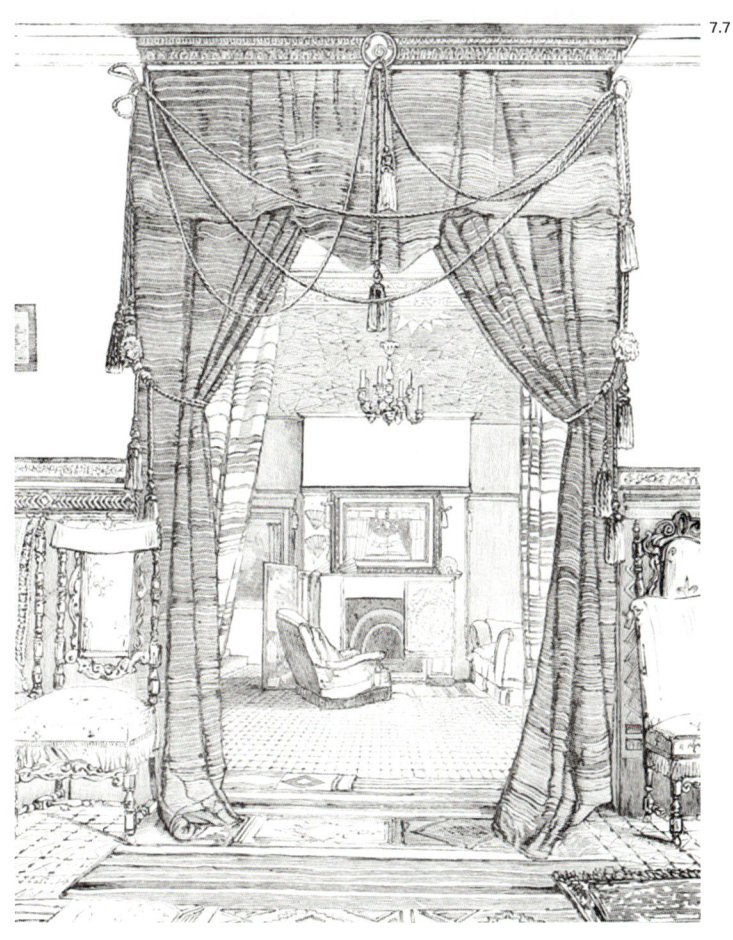

Fig. 7.8 **Louis XV meets mahogany.** Holland & Sons have spared no expense for this wine cooler – the contents protected by a high-quality Bramah lock. The *bombé* top and sides are extravagantly cut from solid mahogany, not veneered. [Butchoff Antiques]

Fig. 7.9 **Traditionally called a silver table, this mahogany example is in the Chippendale 'Chinese Gothick' style.** The firm who made it is unknown, and it could have been made by any number of manufacturers. Whoever it was, they have fastidiously pierced both the gallery and the legs. As with mid-eighteenth-century fretwork in this manner and better-quality copies, the fretwork is made up of a three-piece cross-grained laminate for strength. See **Fig. 1.48** for a silver table by Gillows. [Butchoff Antiques]

Fig. 7.10 **Stamped by Collinson & Lock but without a serial number,** this ivory-inlaid rosewood cabinet has an Aesthetic purity of line mixed with a hybrid 'Chinese Chippendale' gallery and doors. [Christie's images]

shown to the right of the standing piper is most probably one of the pair exhibited by Wright & Mansfield at the 1862 International Exhibition and almost certainly bought by the hostess's father, Sir Dudley Coutts Marjoribanks (see **Fig. 5.79**).

In 1880, the architect Colonel Sir Robert Edis delivered a series of six Cantor Lectures at the Royal Society, in which he argued virulently against many designs, especially those of the previous twenty years. Edis was a committee member for the National School of Woodcarving, together with the Royal Academician, Edward J. Poynter, when the school opened in January 1879. The publication of his lectures, *Decoration and Furniture of Town Houses* (1881), was a comprehensive look at the complete home and its furnishings. An enthusiast for the Queen Anne style, Edis praised Holland & Sons, illustrating a sideboard in Spanish mahogany as 'an exceedingly good specimen of modern work after Sheraton', **Fig. 7.22**, thus also putting his imprimatur on the now established Georgian Revival.[6] Designs by the great English furniture designers, Chippendale, Adam and Sheraton were in demand; the simplified lines having a cleaner, more refreshing look compared with the heaviness of earlier decades. As in the previous decade, *The Furniture Gazette* continued to give advice on design, and by the mid-1880s was illustrating Adam-style marquetry in more accurate detail, demonstrating a return to the commercial appreciation of the clean lines

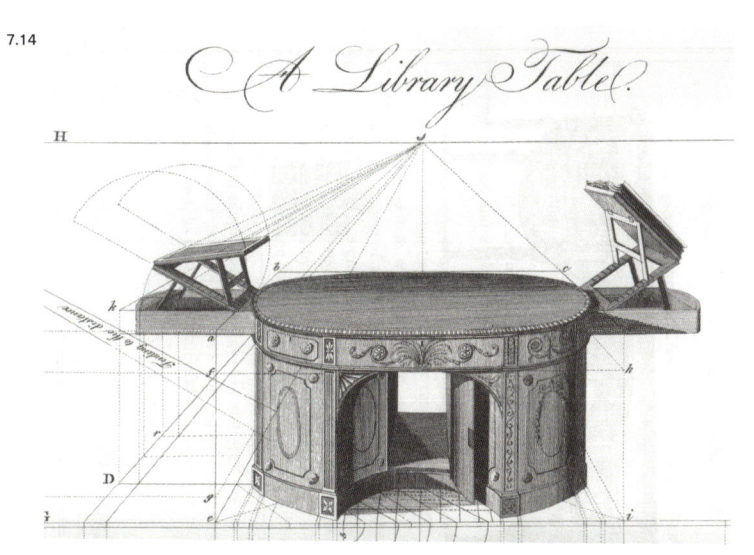

Figs 7.11– 7.14 These two oval desks in mahogany from *c.*1880 are in the style of Sheraton, but without the marquetry that is seen in his *Cabinet-Maker & Upholsterer's Drawing-Book* of 1791, Fig. 7.14. [Butchoff Antiques]

Fig. 7.15 An 1828 engraving of the Duke of Wellington at a period desk in the library at Apsley House, Hyde Park Corner. [Butchoff archive]

seen during the third quarter of the eighteenth century.

Royal pavilions at British and international exhibitions were a chance for makers to show off their prowess. Royal commissions were keenly sought-after and hard won. They also indicated current fashions. On open days for the trade or the general public, the opportunity to view the royal sitting and dining rooms could help influence contemporary taste and was of clear commercial benefit to the suppliers. The royal pavilion at the popular International Fisheries Exhibition in 1883, furnished by Gillows, was 'open to visitors on presentation of their cards on Wednesdays'; the Boudoir of the Princess of Wales was 'decorated in the

Fig. 7.16 Despite having Hepplewhite overtones and Adam-style marquetry, the central display sections of this rare pair of cabinets are out of proportion and too attenuated to be of eighteenth-century design. [Private collection]

Fig. 7.17 Consciously imitating the style of Robert Adam, this pair of side cabinets makes no pretence to be eighteenth century. The style of painted decoration suggests a date before the 1890s. [Private collection]

Adam style, the furniture of satinwood', **Fig. 7.20**.[7] Possibly inspired by Gillows' Octagon Room in Paris in 1878, Liley & Wood of Radnor House furnished the royal pavilion at the 1884 Norwich Festival in the 'Adam style', although in reality it was a simplified Queen Anne style. The Prince and Princess of Wales commissioned a local cabinet-making firm for their suite at the Norwich Festival. Trevor, Page & Co., the 'well-known firm of cabinet-makers and house-furnishers of Norwich', made a fumigated-oak dining room suite, the chairs covered in alligator morocco.[8] Fumigation using ammonia rendered the wood a darker hue and highlighted the grain pattern; it was a popular technique amongst Arts and Crafts makers. It appears that the royal couple was subjected to all the new styles; at the 1886 Colonial and Indian Exhibition their rooms were decorated in the Chinese fashion but furnished with so-called Sheraton furniture, uncharacteristically veneered in rosewood and inlaid with ivory. In 1884, the Princess of Wales appointed Henry and John Cooper of Great Pulteney Street as her furnishers. Coopers, who had exhibited a rosewood cabinet at the 1878 *Exposition Universelle* carved with scenes from Tennyson's poem *The Princess*, showed their versatility at the International Health Exhibition of 1884: they, like Gillows, exhibited ancient and modern Cairene woodwork, **Fig. 7.21**. Government contracts were an increasingly important source of work. In 1885, *The Furniture Gazette* computed that £350,000 had been spent by the British government on furniture for St James's Palace, museums and Parliament amongst others.[9] Having gained a reputation for good-quality household furnishings, Shoolbred & Co. received a royal warrant in the mid-1880s for the supply of furniture to Queen Victoria. By now the firm was supplying high-quality furniture to clients throughout the Empire, and to grand houses in Scotland such as Kinloch Castle, the home of Sir George Bullough on the Isle of Rùm.

Scottish demand for luxury furniture was growing, fuelled by the prosperity of cities such as Glasgow, with its natural harbour and growing ship-building trade. Wylie & Lochhead, a firm started by an upholsterer, Robert Wylie, and William Lochhead, who worked in a cabinet-making business, was highly successful. In 1829, the partnership had opened premises in the East End of Glasgow.[10] By 1883, it had a flourishing department store and was the largest furniture-making business north of the border, with outlets in London and Manchester. In November 1883, it suffered a disastrous fire which destroyed the buildings to a value of £100,000. *The Furniture Gazette* reported that 'the warehouses contained, perhaps, the largest stock of the kind in Scotland' but this did not stop the firm's growth.[11] They bought

Fig. 7.18 **By the time this bedroom was furnished by Jackson & Graham to the design of Robert Edis at the International Health Exhibition in 1884, the firm was making more run-of-the mill furniture than at previous exhibitions and advertised 'completely fitted rooms'.**[12] [Look & Learn]

Fig. 7.19 **It is possible that the designer of this inventive fire screen had read Bevan's dictum at the opening of this chapter. The upper section opens to reveal a baize-lined card and writing table. A suitable piece for a small room, it is veneered in rosewood with a highly individual foliate and vine marquetry. The shield is embroidered with flowers, possibly worked by the lady of the house.** [John Garner]

up various properties, demolishing them to make new, modern department stores. In April 1885, Wylie's opened a 20-metre (approx. 65 feet) frontage on Glasgow's Buchanan Street running to Mitchell Street at the back.[13] In 1888, the firm was awarded a royal warrant as cabinet makers and upholsterers. It is interesting to observe how many furniture-making firms and department stores, established in a modest manner in the first half of the nineteenth century, started out as drapers or upholsterers: Heals, Shoolbred and Comyn Ching, for example.[14]

Glasgow shipbuilding brought work for furniture makers. In London, Gillows, no strangers to royal and aristocratic commissions, exhibited samples of the specialised furniture they had made to fit out *Livadia*, Alexander II of Russia's ill-fated new steam yacht, launched in 1880 from the Govan shipyard of John Elder and Co. The Gillows furniture, written up by *The Furniture Gazette* under the heading 'Sumptuous Furniture', was 'of mahogany, richly carved, enamelled white and relieved with colours and gold'.[15] Other furniture suppliers were the little-known maker and designer Robert Christie[16] and also Jackson & Graham and Shoolbred. The fixtures and fittings for the yacht cost over £500,000, including a fountain amongst other luxuries. A series of photographs of the interiors by Bedford Lemere shows a range of furniture which, although clearly 'of the period', is not furniture commonly seen today. The State Dining Room by Robert Christie had white-painted furniture adapted from the Louis XVI style, using chairs with straight rear legs, a feature suggesting that they were possibly imported from France, **Fig. 7.25**.

During this period, Gillow & Co. continued to win important contracts. In 1881 they supplied furniture to a Bradford mill owner, John Foster, for the new wing at Hornby Castle, situated only a few miles from their Lancaster workshop. Gillows' varied commissions included a contract to furnish the South African parliament and the royal pavilion at the International Fisheries Exhibition, **Fig. 7.20**.

Edis's *Decoration and Furniture of Town Houses* included information and exemplars from Jackson & Graham as well as Holland & Sons, utilising Edis's own designs, one of which shows how he curtained off his own 'ordinary Grate & Mantel'.[17] In line with Godwin's beliefs, there was an increasing understanding of the health benefits of being able to keep furniture dust-free. Edis's concerns over dust led him to design furniture for the 1884 International Health Exhibition. Fitted furniture was deemed healthier and Jackson & Graham were awarded a Gold Medal for their fitted pieces. The first manual vacuum cleaners had been invented in the United States in the 1860s, and the plinths of cabinets, such as a credenza, no longer rested on the floor; space was allowed for cleaning underneath.[18] The engraving

347

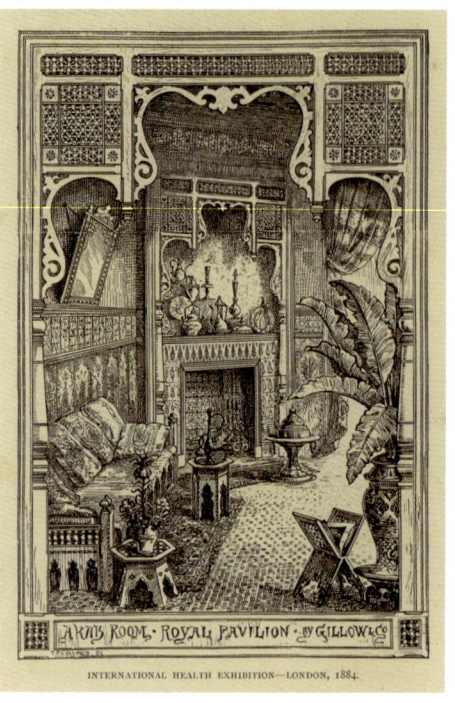

Fig. 7.20 **The Boudoir in the Pavilion of the Prince and Princess of Wales** at the highly successful International Fisheries Exhibition of 1883. The room was provided by Gillows but the oval table in the foreground is possibly a Maples model. [Look & Learn]

Fig. 7.21 **The 'Arab Room'**, part of the royal pavilion by Gillows at the International Health Exhibition, 1884. Every element is in an adopted Moorish style. [Look & Learn]

in **Fig. 7.23** from *Decoration and Furniture of Town Houses* illustrated a 'Sussex' armchair and a modern side cabinet by Jackson & Graham in the style of Collinson & Lock. The two companies merged in 1885, opening the following year at Jackson & Graham's Oxford Street premises.[19] Edis had praised Jackson & Graham and Gillows at the 1884 exhibition 'for the loan of some exceedingly good examples of modern, so-called Chippendale, Adams and Sheraton work'.[20] A refreshing Georgian Revival style had by now been established, one that was to dominate the 1885 to 1920 period of British furniture making.

From the mid-nineteenth century upholstered furniture had claimed an important place in the domestic interior and was a feature in every household by the 1880s. Chairs were no longer always formal objects, although they remained so in the dining room, but instead were comfortable, relaxed and above all, plush. Even without the elaborate fringes that are such a feature of the Victorian era, upholstery was expensive and was rarely of simple design. The introduction of the Pullman coach from the United States heightened comfort for travellers. Trains were furnished with *bergère* chairs and settees that would have been perfectly suited to a living room. Different forms of chair were given a variety of popular names for easy identification. Oetzmann & Co., whose extensive works and showrooms stretched from 67 to 79 Hampstead Road in London, offered a 'Prince of Wales' chair designed for women, with a back in the form of a plume of the Prince of Wales's feathers, and another called 'The Wolsey'.

A characteristic feature of chairs for the late 1870s and 1880s was the use of short, squat turned spindles. Some have a spiral twist, cut with increasingly complex mechanical

Fig. 7.22 Plate VI of Edis's 1881 publication with furniture by Holland & Sons. On the right is an 'Escritoir' [*sic*] of a type that was becoming fashionable and continued to be popular up to the 1920s. The desk and the Spanish mahogany sideboard are modernised 'Adam'. [Private collection]

Fig. 7.23 A drawing room by Jackson & Graham of an 'aesthetic' nature that is far removed from the grandeur of their exhibition work. The side cabinet, designed by R.W. Edis in 1881 for Jackson & Graham, was available in walnut or mahogany with 'Chinese' paintings at a cost of £16. The simple armchair and the occasional table retailed at about 30 shillings each (compared with the 'Sussex' armchair by William Morris on the left, which was only 9 shillings). [*The Art Journal*, 1880, vol. 6]

Fig. 7.24 A photograph by Bedford Lemere of the Tsar's Sitting Room on *Livadia*, as furnished by Gillows. [Private collection]

Fig. 7.25 The cabinet maker and decorator Robert Christie supplied the furniture for the State Salon on *Livadia*. [Private collection]

lathes. Such supports and similarly turned legs were often a feature of Shoolbred designs but became a common feature of the commercial application of the Aesthetic style mingled with Queen Anne. It is difficult, however, to discern a distinct pattern of designer or maker for the vast number of these chairs as the decade evolved, the wide variety of different styles ebbed and flowed. Richard D'Oyly Carte wrote in praise of the new Savoy Theatre and praised this mixed aesthetic: 'The decorations are by Messrs. Collinson & Lock…Without adopting…the…"Queen Anne", and "Early English" or entering upon the so-called "aesthetic" manner, a result has now been produced which…will be appreciated by all persons of taste.'[21] The Aesthetic also became a feature of American furniture. A mahogany and teak cabinet of the mid-1880s, designed by the American designer Lockwood de Forest, has a Japanese aesthetic of which Godwin would have approved, combined with a *mistri*-style Indian carving.[22]

The exponential growth of municipal buildings was the perfect opportunity for furniture makers to show off their ability. Active in Ireland, Brew & Claris were commissioned to supply mid-range furnishings of polished oak with green-upholstered morocco for the Town Hall and Municipal Buildings in Victoria Street, Belfast, in 1880. They also received a substantial commission for the dining, sitting and refreshment rooms of Alexandra Palace in London. The furniture included seven buffets ranging in size from 2.4m

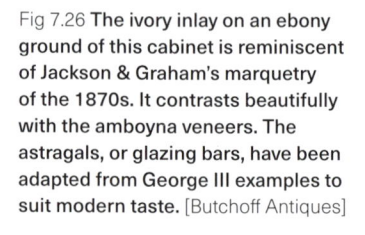

Fig. 7.26 The ivory inlay on an ebony ground of this cabinet is reminiscent of Jackson & Graham's marquetry of the 1870s. It contrasts beautifully with the amboyna veneers. The astragals, or glazing bars, have been adapted from George III examples to suit modern taste. [Butchoff Antiques]

Figs 7.27a & b The haphazard stylistic attributions of the time were not as we interpret them today. In September 1885, *The Furniture Gazette* called both tables 'furniture in the Louis XVI style'; they look more like Holland & Sons of the 1860s. [*The Furniture Gazette*, September 1885]

Fig. 7.28 A ladies' chair of low proportions with a wide seat to accommodate women's fashions. Exhibited in 1882 by Dovestone, Davey, Hull & Co. in Manchester, the back anticipates the fluidity of Art Nouveau. [*The Furniture Gazette*, 4 November 1882, p. 306]

to 3m (8–10ft) in a variety of styles, including Renaissance, Early English and 'Domestic Gothic'. Their chairs, dinner-wagons, dining tables and bookcases were described as of serviceable, fine workmanship. Of particular note was a Gothic buffet over 3m (approx. 10ft) high, made in 'antique oak' lined with Cordoba leather and with an Aesthetic, lightly incised decoration highlighted with gilding.[23] *The Furniture Gazette* reported on the impressive 70-foot-wide (21 metres) store frontage of Brew & Claris, the offices 'nicely fitted up in Spanish mahogany and oak'.[24] The firm's premises at Finsbury Pavement had 'floor after floor filled with furniture of such excellent design and superior finish that even the most fastidious of customers is likely to be non-plussed by an *embarrass de richesses*'.[25] There are tantalising snippets in the various reports of the firm such as – 'Brew & Claris…have supplied the furniture and fittings for Messrs. R. Etzensberger & Co.'s New Model Coffee House'.[26] Much of this type of furniture must have long been destroyed

CHAPTER 7: 1880S

7.29

7.30

7.31

7.32

Fig. 7.29 Using the finest, beautifully matched East Indian satinwood, this tea table, its pair baize-lined for card playing, is George III in style. The contrasting ebonising is a Victorian conceit, one not used in the 1770s. [Nan Xu]

Fig. 7.30 Although based on late eighteenth-century principles of Sheraton's influence, this fine, delightfully designed satinwood table makes no pretence at being a period piece. The oddly proportioned stretcher and the hipped example, as with the table shown in the engraving of the Boudoir in the Pavilion of the Prince and Princess of Wales at the *International Fisheries Exhibition* of 1883, Fig. 7.20 immediately suggest a Victorian interpretation of Georgian models. [Private collection]

Fig. 7.31 This type of *bergère* chair is inspired by, but not copied from, Sheraton. To suggest age, the decoration is painted with an exaggerated *craquelure*. The invention of hole-boring machines meant that caned panels became fashionable again in the late 1880s, and by the early twentieth century double caning was used for the more substantial so-called *bergère* suites which included a settee. [Private collection]

Fig. 7.32 Possibly supplied by Maples, the richly painted Neoclassical-style foliage contrasts with the bright yellow of the satinwood veneer. The decoration is so well painted as to suggest a professional artist, possibly not a full-time employee of the furniture workshop. The overall '*semainier*' form is a mixture of eighteenth-century Irish and French Empire. [Private collection]

or dispersed into anonymity. The pavilion of the Prince of Wales furnished by Brew & Claris at the Colonial and Indian Exhibition in 1886 included a vestibule fitted up with bamboo furniture in the Chinese style. The reception room included 'a cabinet in the Anglo-Japanese style…A Chinese couch…and a small octagonal table, Inlaid with mother-of-pearl, tortoiseshell, and ivory'. The boudoir was in the style of Sheraton, and the dining room included 'various chairs in the Chinese style, inlaid with ivory'.[27] Over-ambitious expansion and stiff competition resulted in the Brew & Claris partnership being dissolved in June 1886; their final bankruptcy sales were held in 1888.

In a departure from the high standards set by the firm in earlier decades, Jackson & Graham exhibited at a wholesale exhibition in 1881, showing pine furniture of a design associated with Charles Bevan a decade or more earlier. In contrast, the firm also won an urgent commission to furnish the King of Siam's new palace in Bangkok, the furniture constructed to withstand the climate. The commission included 104 side chairs for a 30m-long (approx. 98ft) dining table, and a 5m (16½ft) dining table made of a single slab of mahogany. They also made the king an oak desk, with one key fitting all the drawers.[28]

Whereas French and Italian furniture and decorative arts for the so-called cottages in Newport on Rhode Island are well documented, work sent from Britain is less well known.[29] The runic-style table and coffer made in well-figured oak are rare examples of work commissioned from

351

Fig. 7.33 In an interesting re-interpretation of the late seventeenth-century aesthetic, Gillows have incorporated a pair of Japanese export ivory-mounted panels into a cabinet on stand of Flemish inspiration. The lock was supplied by Comyn Ching, the drawer is stamped 'Gillows 1882', most probably the serial number.[30] [Sotheby's]

Fig. 7.34 The Long Drawing Room at Old Swan House, Chelsea, designed by Norman Shaw for Wickham Flower. The room contains a mixture of seventeenth-, eighteenth- and nineteenth-century furniture; the oval table is an interpretation of Chippendale in a form that did not exist in the eighteenth century. A Morris & Co. 'Rossetti' armchair is in front of the Morris table with, in the background, a Broadwood piano featuring painted decoration to a design exhibited by Burne-Jones at the Arts and Crafts exhibition in 1888. [Historic England, Bedford Lemere Collection]

Morris & Co. for the United States, **Figs 7.35 & 7.36**. In September 1883, Miss Catherine L. Wolfe opened the gates of her new house on Ochre Point, the house aptly named Vinland in testament to the legend that it was the location where Vikings first landed in North America. Morris & Co. supplied carpets and other decorations, and, at Morris's suggestion, work was executed by Walter Crane and Edward Burne-Jones.

Exhibitions were by now a proven method of advertising the range and quality of London and provincial furniture makers. In contrast to his advocacy in 1882 of simple, well-made 'good citizen's furniture', William Morris's first exhibition outside his own London showrooms was at the Manchester Fine Art and Industrial Exhibition in October 1882, where Gillows exhibited rosewood bedroom furniture with 'silver' handles. In an unlikely combination, Morris & Co. exhibited alongside Jackson & Graham in Bristol at the Industrial and Fine Art Exhibition in February 1884. Bertram, presumably William Bertram of Dean Street, also exhibited, as did Watts & Co. As a seaport, Bristol manufacturers were able to source exotic timbers direct from the Americas and the city contained several steam-powered furniture factories. Leading Bristol firms in the mid-1880s were Uriah Alsop, Laverton & Co., Smiths, and Trapnell & Gane, all keen to supply a growing population and take advantage of improved rail links, especially to the industrial north. Trapnell & Gane presented a marriage chest to Princess Henry of Battenberg on the occasion of her marriage in 1885, the carved decoration alluding to Bristol's illustrious past. Following on from the well-received novelty of the divided room settings of Collinson & Lock at the 1876 exhibition in Philadelphia, Dovestone, Davey, Hull & Co. copied the concept at the Manchester Fine Art and Industrial Exhibition in 1882. They exhibited a modernised ladder-back armchair, and their small ladies' chair (**Fig. 7.28**) could well be dated, without evidence of the catalogue, twenty years later as 'commercial art nouveau'.[31]

Notwithstanding Edis's enthusiasm for the Queen Anne genre in 1881, as early as 1875 *The Furniture Gazette* had ventured the opinion that the rage for the so-called 'Queen Anne style' was over 'so far as the more educated portion of the community and the great West-end manufacturers are concerned'.[32] The article admitted that this misnamed style included Chippendale, Adam, Sheraton and indeed Baroque motifs, all of which were mainstream by the 1880s. In

August 1880, Edwin Foley illustrated a Queen Anne chimney piece with Baroque and Elizabethan-style 'jewels' added for good measure. Foley, who by the late 1890s was designing in an angular Art Nouveau manner, wrote about early forms of furniture, and one of the most identifiable and endearing motifs of Chippendale designs was his interpretation of Chinese-style blind fretwork.[33] Chinese-style open fretwork, perhaps partly inspired by balconies and bridge parapets in the landscaped parks of the Summer Palace in Beijing, was illustrated in 1889 by Rupert Brook in *Original Designs for Writing Tables*, **Fig. 7.39a & b**. Brook's comprehensive work included a chronology of line drawings of 'period' furniture 'for the use of Architects, Furniture Designers, Cabinet makers [sic] and Others'.[34] The Chippendale aspect of these designs is unmistakably an 1880s interpretation; unsatisfactory to purists, these pieces could never be termed 'copies'. *The Furniture Gazette* illustrated a bedroom suite with these features, wrongly described as being made and designed by Barnett Moss of Great Eastern Street in London; Barnett Moss had simply purchased the suite from Longstaff & Pitcher of Hampstead Road.[35] The line between maker and retailer, especially at the wholesale level, was a fine one and often misrepresented by firms about whom we know little today.

The term 'Queen Anne' remained in use in the 1880s, although was increasingly recognised as having little historical accuracy. Sewell & Sewell, with newly enlarged premises and showrooms in the East End, produced cabinets described as being Queen Anne without any features that the modern connoisseur would recognise as being from the period of her reign. Some critics laid the blame for the term 'Queen Anne' firmly on the shoulders of artists: 'It was a poet's dream — a painter's craze — William Morris, and Dante Rossetti, and their school between them'.[36] John Ward, in *How to Furnish a House*, tried to correct the misnomer, describing 'an inlaid bedroom suite in the modern Classical style, or so-called "Queen Anne"'.[37] In a public lecture, Oscar Wilde pointed out that 'the Queen Anne style…was by no means specially connected with the name or reign of that sovereign'.[38]

The Jacobethan style was another favourite ripe for plunder, sometimes relatively 'pure' in interpretation but without any attempt to deceive, **Fig. 7.40**. Cawley & Co. of New Inn Yard, just off Great Eastern Street, designed an oak bookcase with a distinctly Charles II style of carving, correctly incorporating Moorish-inspired geometric applied mouldings that were popular between the 1660s and 1680s.[39] Showing their versatility, Cawley, under the name of the Antique & Foreign Furniture Co., also supplied bamboo furniture. Bamboo furniture remained popular and the material was adaptable to a host of different types of furniture, often incorporating lacquer panels.[40]

Fig. 7.35 Displaying the rugged characteristics of Philip Webb's designs, Morris & Co. made this runic-influenced oak centre table in 1883 for Catherine Lorillard Wolfe's new house, Vinland, in Newport, Rhode Island. [Newport Historical Society]

Fig. 7.36 A runic- or Nordic-style oak coffer made by the Morris workshops for Vinland in 1883. [Newport Historical Society]

No historic style escaped the hand of the new influx of designers. A firm called Sewell, possibly Sewell & Sewell, exhibited at the Third Annual Furniture Exhibition at the Agricultural Hall in London in 1883, alongside firms such as Debenham & Hewitt of Cheltenham, showing a Spanish mahogany bedroom suite in a modernised Hepplewhite manner.[41] Also in the spring of 1883, the maker or retailer R. Hunter of Cardington Street, Euston, exhibited in the Chippendale and Adam styles at Humphrey's Hall near Albert Gate. Descriptions of smaller exhibitions in the press, unless accompanied by line engravings, render the finished items untraceable. Engravings and detailed descriptions of furniture from a wide variety of firms, about which we know relatively little, from all parts of Britain (although dominated by the London trade), underline the vast size of the Victorian furniture industry. Will we ever trace a curious-

Fig. 7.37 A walnut writing table by Howard & Sons, who have adapted a mid-nineteenth-century desk to the 'modern' style by adding simulated bamboo legs, the turned stretcher adding stability and a 'footrest'. [Tew Archive, Christie's © 1987]

Fig. 7.38 An advertisement by the London maker Model & Co. With a plentiful supply from Asia, much of it from Vietnam, bamboo furniture was cheap and easy to make. [*The Cabinet Maker*, 1 November 1880, p. 98]

Figs 7.39a & b Incorporating numerous elements from the previous century, this design by Rupert Brook for a cylinder bureau, illustrated in *The Furniture Gazette* in 1881, has an impractical arrangement of Chinoiserie and Aesthetic joining the legs. [*The Furniture Gazette*, 2 April 1881, p. 219]

sounding music canterbury with springless locks and flower stands, exhibited by Ernest H. Maplesden of Henley Cottage, Battersea, at the Third Annual Furniture Exhibition? Despite the ever-growing volume of trade, there was only a slight change in the number of cabinet makers. Circa 1870, there were 48,333 men and 8,612 women working in the cabinet and upholstery business, compared with 51,761 and 7,985 respectively in the census of 1881.[42]

It might be assumed that the comparatively small fluctuation of craftspeople in the intervening decade was due to a more extensive use of machinery. Reports of what are today little-known makers underline our ignorance of even some of the seemingly larger firms, for example Moore & Hunton, which had nearly 4,000 square metres (approximately an acre) of floor space and had been in business for over a century by October 1885.

Fig. 7.40 Tudor House in Hampstead, built in 1883 for William Goode, was furnished in the eclectic 'Jacobethan' manner that remained popular well into the twentieth century.

Fig. 7.41 An imaginative cabinet or buffet by Windle; honestly captioned as being 'Designed and made up from old material'. Made in Nottingham, this is an elaborate type of made-up furniture that was popular in the large houses in the Midlands known as 'The Dukeries'. [*The Furniture Gazette*, 1 October 1885]

From 1880, as art editor of *The Furniture Gazette*, Christopher Dresser was able to illustrate pieces made and/or imported by his own short-lived company. Formed with Charles Holme in 1879, Dresser & Holme of Farringdon Road made furniture to Dresser's designs, not all of it particularly creative, such as his modernisation of the chaise longue, **Fig. 7.43**. Perhaps not surprisingly, almost every edition of the journal under Dresser's editorship had long essays on Japanese art, together with exhaustive treatises on design. The Art Furnishers' Alliance, established in 1880 by Dresser to promote his work, was also short-lived; it closed in 1883. The intention at the premises in New Bond Street had been to furnish a complete home in Dresser's inimitable style, with furniture possibly exclusively made by Thomas Knight of Bath. Chubb & Son of Queen Victoria Street made similar chairs with a quasi-Egypto-Arabian look, **Figs 7.42 & 7.44**. In December 1882, the British Museum had placed its collection of Egyptian furniture in a more prominent position, coinciding with a revival of interest in the Egyptian aesthetic, and *The Furniture Gazette* introduced its own small logo in an Egyptian style based on the wings of Isis.[43] The three- and four-legged 'Thebes' stools designed by Leonard Wyburd and patented by Liberty & Co., were made from 1884 until about 1919, **Fig. 7.46**. An engraving from c.1889 of Alma-Tadema's studio shows a similar Egyptian-style stool to that in **Fig. 7.47**.[44]

The circular extending dining table patented by Robert Jupe in 1835 was revived by Johnstone & Jeanes at the Paris exhibition in 1878.[45] *The Daily Telegraph* was fulsome in its praise of its complexity, describing how 'the whole table, indeed, is a puzzle'. It also commented how 'circular dining-tables are just now much more fashionable than the old "telescopic" tables'.[46] Two are shown here, one with four outset columnar legs, an invention of the 1880s, **Fig. 7.49a**. The self-tapering centre support of one stamped by Maple & Co., **Fig. 7.50**, is at first glance closer to Regency tables and is indicative of the revival of interest in that period. In 1889 Johnstone, Norman & Co. refurnished part of Windsor Castle, and supplied a set of circular extending dining tables to the castle in 1891, see also **Fig. 6.3**.[47] T.H. Filmer of Berners Street in the 1840s and Collinson & Lock in the 1880s retailed their own variations, each with a different and distinctive metal operating system.[48] The Collinson variant is stamped with the company name but no design or stock number, which might suggest that it was bought in from another firm. Like Collinson, Gillows, Maples and other firms were buying in furniture and, unless the stamp is accompanied by the serial or design number, it is probable that the item was not made in-house.

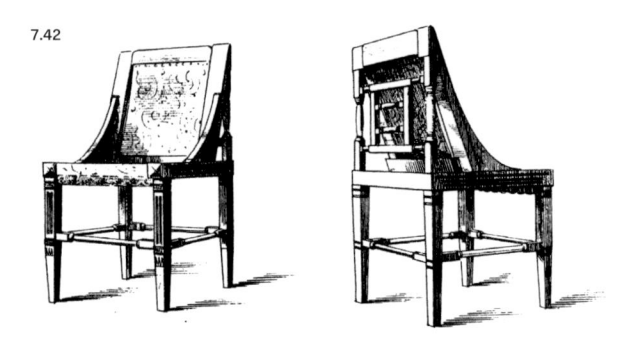

Fig. 7.42 **Four designs for chairs of ancient Egyptian inspiration by Chubb & Sons, made for the Art Furnishers' Alliance. Dresser designed similar chairs in 1873, illustrated in** Principles of decorative Design. [The Furniture Gazette 8 July 1880, p. 306]

Fig. 7.43 **As editor of** The Furniture Gazette, **Christopher Dresser was able to publish his own designs, including this modernised Regency chaise longue, with appropriate upholstery.** [The Furniture Gazette, 24 July 1880]

Fig. 7.44 **A mahogany and gilt chair in the Egyptian manner designed by Dresser, made by Chubb or Thomas Knight. It has Dresser's distinctive foliate quadrants on the side supports and pierced latticework of a type seen in** mashrabiyan **architecture.** [Image © National Museums of Scotland]

Fig. 7.45 **An Art Furnishers' Alliance parcel-gilt low chair by Chubb or Thomas Knight to a Dresser design.** [Oscar Graf]

Fig. 7.46 **A three-legged 'Thebes' stool, a model designed by Leonard Wyburd and patented by Liberty & Co. in 1884, based on an ancient prototype in the British Museum which dates to 1550–1300 BCE.**[49] **This example bears the Liberty's original applied label.** [Royal House Antiques]

Fig. 7.47 **A mahogany stool made in the ancient Egyptian style for Liberty & Co., who patented the design in 1884. This example was probably by William Birch or by North & Sons, both of High Wycombe. The design was by Leonard Wyburd, Director of Liberty's Furnishing and Decoration Studio, established in 1883. Wyburd also added a back to this design so that it could function as a 'corner' chair.** [Victoria and Albert Museum, CIRC.439-1965]

Fig. 7.48. **A bedside cabinet, probably made by Knight of Bath. Dresser has redesigned a ubiquitous, functional cabinet and heightened the simplicity of its Egyptian-style foliage by using an ebonised ground; it has similarities to a wardrobe made for Hiram Owston at Bushloe House near Leicester, in 1874.** [Oscar Graf]

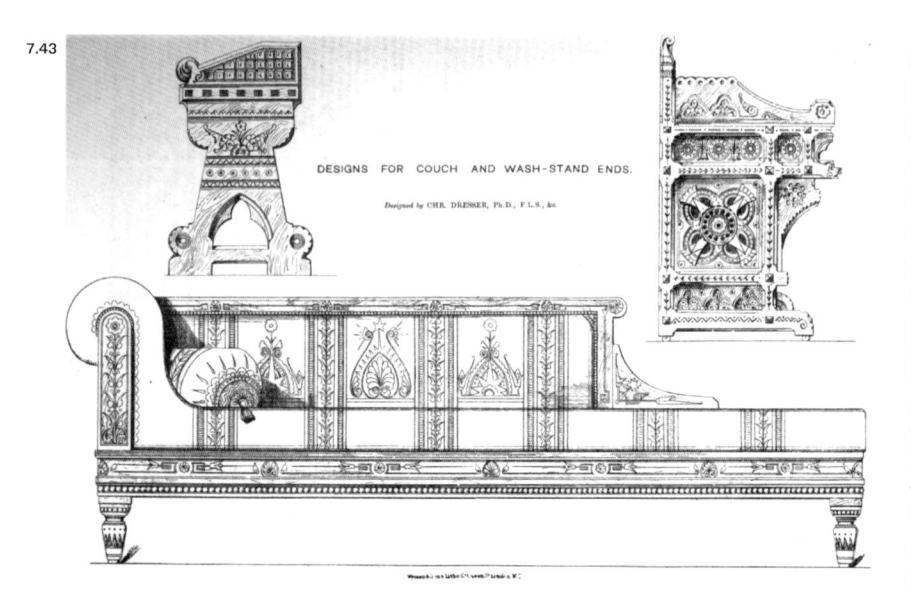

The handsome mahogany armchair by an unknown maker is a good example of the Regency Revival, **Fig. 7.54**, made to a design by Thomas Hope c.1807 for use in the breakfast room at his house in Duchess Street. Hope described the model as 'after the manner of ancient *curule* chairs'.[50] The curule chair, or *sella curulis,* was an X-frame chair or armchair used in ancient Rome by high-ranking dignitaries. The illustrated chairs are an accurate interpretation of Hope's design; another version in his line engraving of The Aurora Room has an anthemion-carved back, **Fig. 7.53**.[51] William Beckford of Fonthill appears to have owned a set of six such chairs inspired by the Hope design.[52] Later variations, variously dated as '1870', '1880' or 'late nineteenth century', are stamped by firms such as Gregory & Co. of Regent Street in London. A simplified version with a padded curved back support was found to have a paper label on the underside inscribed 'MARSH, JONES, & CRIBB' (Late 'Kendell & Co.'), dated 4 February 1890.[53] Less refined but more comfortable versions were produced featuring upholstered backs, and turned 'H' spindle stretchers with rear stretchers for extra strength, making them suitable for meeting rooms or gentlemen's clubs; an example by Jackson & Graham is illustrated in Edis, see **Fig. 7.52**.[54]

Suspicions about furniture authenticity were aroused in the 1880s. In 1883, the *Magazine of Art* noted: 'In recent years a fashion for Sheraton's furniture has sprung up and has so widely spread that modern cabinet makers have found

7.44

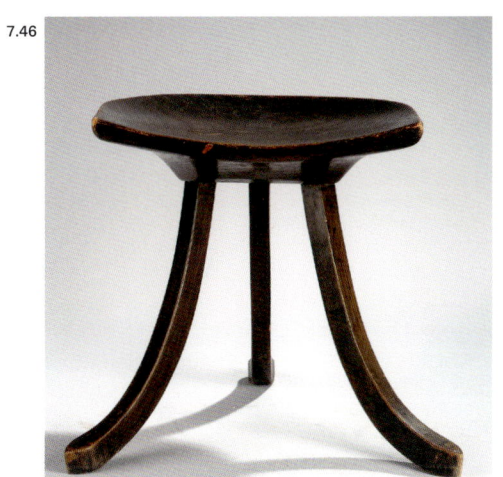

7.45

7.46

7.47

7.48

it worth their while to reproduce many specimens and even to attempt original work in the same style'.[55] Writing in 1931, the celebrated furniture historian Herbert Cescinsky summarised the Sheraton period in *The Gentle Art of Faking Furniture*: 'The distinctions between the original Sheraton of 1790–1800 and the copies of 1840–1880 are often very fine indeed, and cannot be explained in a book. After all, many of these 1880 copies are very antique by now'. Today we must add another 100 years to the aging process. Cescinsky added that 'later copies [of Sheraton designs] are plentiful. Gillow of Lancaster, the Seddons, Edwards & Roberts, Wright & Mansfield, Jackson & Graham, Johnson & Jeans [*sic*], and Cooper & Holt, of Bunhill Row, all specialised in "Sheraton" until about 1880.'[56] Before Cescinsky, Litchfield had noted that 'with the wear and tear of a household this furniture has acquired a tone or "patina" which renders its resemblance to its prototype very close'.[57]

The trade press gave detailed statistical commentary on tonnage, value and types of timbers and exports of furniture. The quantity of timber imported into British ports in the 1880s is a guide to fluctuations in trade and the prosperity of furniture makers. In London alone, 5.6 million bales of timber were imported in 1881, a decrease of over 10 per cent from 1880, demand inevitably increasing dockside prices. A year later there were 6.3 million bales of timber imported. Over 1.2 million bales of mahogany were imported into Liverpool alone each year between 1880 and 1883.[58] Not all these imports were for making furniture; the building of

BRITISH FURNITURE

Figs 7.49a & b Johnstone & Jeanes made capstan tables from the reign of William IV until 1904. This variation of the Jupe patent expanding table is signed on the brass mechanism 'Maple & Cº., London & Paris'. When fully opened the diameter extends from 168 to 244cm (approx. 66–96in). The outset supporting columns set it aside from the earlier models, dating it to from c.1880 onwards. [Butchoff Antiques]

Fig. 7.50 This superb capstan table, in solid *pau rosa,* was made by Maple & Co. some fifty years after Jupe's patent was taken out. The pedestal base reflects the 1880s revival of interest in Regency forms. [Private collection, Photograph by Ken Adlard]

Fig. 7.51 An advertisement placed by Wright & Mansfield in 1883 in *The Building News*.[61] Although similar to the firm's output, none of the illustrated items appear to be recorded with their stamp. In April 1883 the journal likened the firm's work in the Chippendale style to that of Jenks & Wood, a little-known firm declared bankrupt in 1891. [St Croix Architecture]

ships, trains, hotels and municipal buildings all increased the need for imported hardwoods. The amount of imported precious timbers in the 1880s might suggest that demand for luxury furniture was improving but for the upholsterers at Gillows in 1888, 'most of the men have been on half time for a year'.[59] In an era of plush upholstered furniture this is surprising; other large London firms were now employing far fewer upholsterers. Holland & Sons in the early 1870s employed seventy to eighty upholsterers and in 1888, six; Bantings went from thirty to forty down to two; Crace from twenty down to eight.[60] The East End was fast becoming increasingly active at the expense of the West End makers. Business activity varied across the nation. Trade was slow in Birmingham, Bradford, Leicester, Manchester and Sheffield, whereas in Bath, Barrow-in-Furness, Bristol, Exeter, Liverpool, Northampton, Oldham and Torquay, along with 'several minor places', trade blossomed.[62] Makers had to put up with the erratic availability of wood being shipped across the Atlantic Ocean in all weathers, resulting in fluctuations in prices. However, the use of steamers, especially for the trade from the Baltic to Hull and Grimsby, made crossings more reliable and shortened journey times which helped contain costs. The extensive use of American 'black' walnut over the previous two decades caused concern – prices were rising, and the Indiana forests, one of the main areas of supply, were rapidly being depleted. By August 1884 American black walnut was in less demand, which begs an interesting question: was the drop-off in the use of walnut driven by fashion or lack of supply? Did the furniture makers adapt and change and thus dictate 'fashion' when they could not

7.51

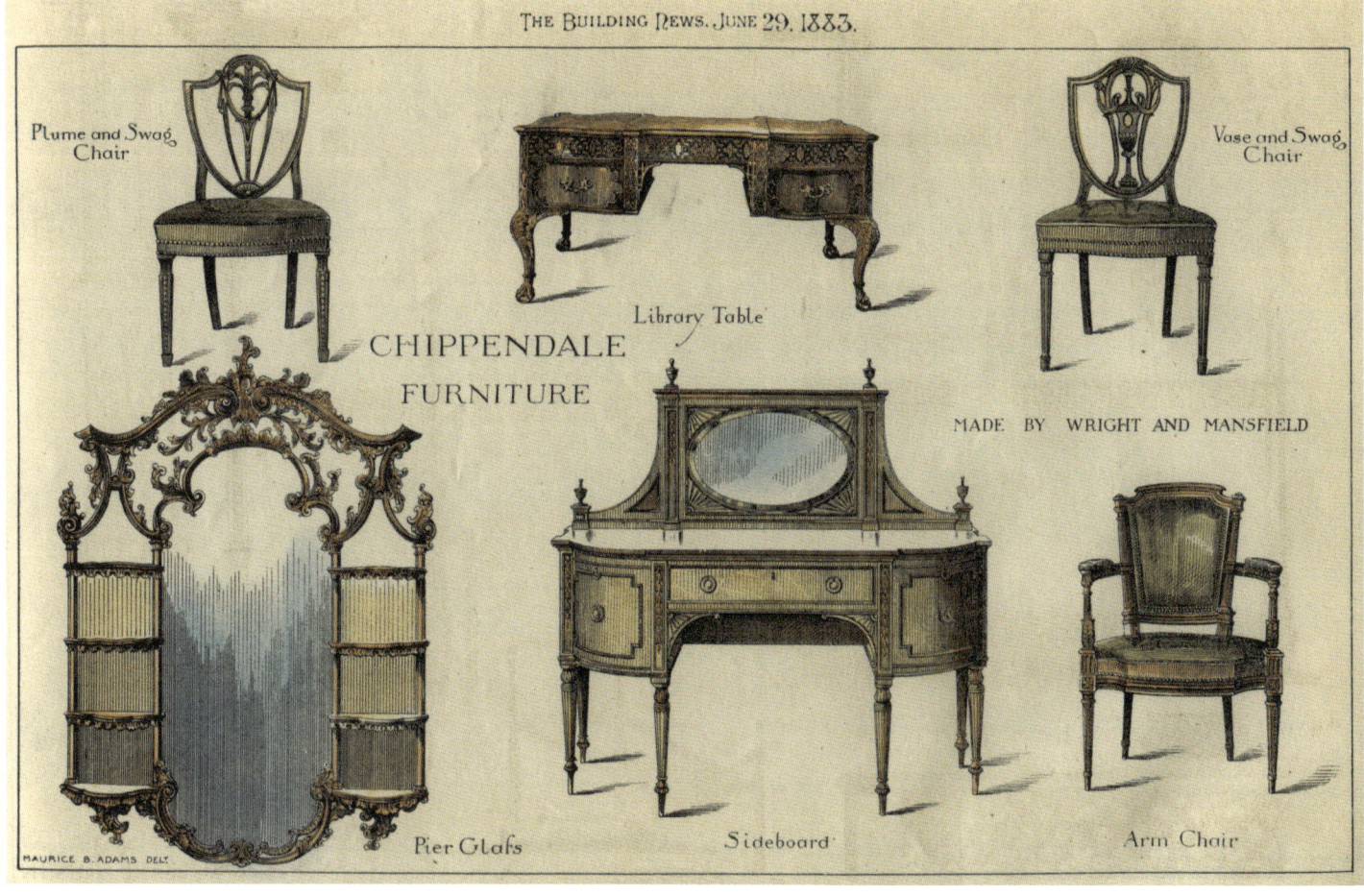

CHIPPENDALE FURNITURE MADE BY WRIGHT AND MANSFIELD
The Building News, June 29, 1883.
Plume and Swag Chair; Library Table; Vase and Swag Chair; Pier Glass; Sideboard; Arm Chair.

find enough of a product, in this instance commercially available walnut? The rising population inevitably increased demand. The need for mid-range furniture was growing, the luxury market was less stable. The population of London now exceeded 3.5 million, with approximately 400,000 people in Birmingham. Leeds, Manchester and Liverpool each housed well over 300,000 people. Despite this growth, *The Furniture Gazette* reported 215 cabinet makers and upholsterers failing in 1879, and 146 failures the following year.[63]

London-made furniture was popular but expensive, the better firms, especially those participating in the international exhibitions, were hard pressed to balance their books. Other closures were due to the failure to find a successor to the business. The partnership of Wright & Mansfield, formed in 1861, was dissolved in 1886, Mansfield continuing the business alone. The firm's unwanted stock was sold at auction in 1886 and 1887,[64] some items were purchased by the South Kensington Museum, including chairs, a Pembroke table, a card table and interesting samples of marquetry, bought for study purposes (see Chapter 6 – 1870s). As well as their own in-house copies, there were original eighteenth-century Chippendale and Sheraton pieces in the auction, much of it highly praised.[65] The auction also included French-style pieces, for example a mahogany cylinder desk.

A victim of their own desire to make furniture of the very highest quality, in 1882 Jackson & Graham suffered a spectacular financial failure.[66] They had invested heavily in machinery and there were a total of 465 creditors. By far the largest was Mrs E. Graham, presumably of the same Graham family, who was owed £52,600, almost £4 million in today's terms. Many well-known firms were listed as creditors, including the hardware suppliers Comyn Ching as well as Cope, Coalbrookdale and also Feetham. The Parisian firms of Barbedienne, Charbonne, and Guéret Frères also suffered from the bankruptcy. It is interesting that all seven of these companies were involved in the metal or casting trade, three of them French. This opens up the tantalising question – how many of the high-quality gilt-bronze mounts on English furniture were made in France to order (see, for example the desk, **Fig. 5.47**)? Other British furniture makers were owed many thousands of pounds, including Oliver & Sons, Hewett, and Humphrey, the latter two owed over £5,000 each. Recapitalisation revived Jackson & Graham for a few years, and they were able to exhibit at the International Exhibition at the Crystal Palace in 1884

Fig. 7.52 Edis published this Jackson & Graham room setting in 1881. The canopy above the sideboard is of the type criticised for being 'large and heavy', while Edis thought the carving expensive and a dust trap.[67] Variations of the curule armchair, after a Hope design, were popular and offered by several manufacturers. [Butchoff archive]

Fig. 7.53 The 'Aurora Room', plate 7 of Thomas Hope's *Household Furniture & Interior Decoration* showing four curule armchairs. [Butchoff archive]

Fig. 7.54 Inspired by ancient Rome, this handsome curule armchair model was designed by Thomas Hope. Examples by Gregory & Co. are known, one shown at the Chicago Exhibition in 1893. [Christie's Images]

with a show of 'high class furniture.' However, disaster struck the newly reconstituted company when a fire occurred in their warehouse in June 1885, although the firm's showrooms and shops in Oxford Street escaped. What remained of the company was taken over by Collinson & Lock in 1885; they immediately redecorated the old showrooms, exhibiting furniture in all the popular and current styles to much acclaim: 'These rooms have been entirely remodelled and decorated, and are filled with choice examples of cabinet work of a very high character'.[68] Both Frank Collinson and George Lock had trained with Jackson & Graham. They 'were both brought up in the house [of Jackson & Graham] as young men, and, left some forty or fifty years ago for Herrings, of Fleet Street, whom they succeeded about 1870'.[69]

The potentially lethal combination of shavings, sawdust and chemicals in cabinet makers' workshops, many now with gas lighting, made fire a constant threat. The Birmingham firm of Marris & Norton was one of many such casualties, their 'gigantic cabinet-making and upholstering establishment…was last month totally destroyed by fire'.[70] Of the many bankruptcies reported during the 1880s, some cabinet makers, with surprisingly high debts are names almost unknown today.[71] In an attempt to grow their business, by the mid-1880s there was a marked increase in the number of makers operating both as retail and wholesale dealers. Marris was one such firm. They participated in the Exhibition of Birmingham Manufacturers, exhibiting a dining room in pollard oak, and drawing room and bedroom furniture in rosewood.[72]

The London firm of Nosotti & Co., with showrooms stretching from 93 to 97 Oxford Street, took a full-page advertisement in the back of the 1882 Hamilton Palace Collection auction catalogue when it was reprinted with the results immediately following the auction, **Fig. 7.56**.[73] Calling themselves 'Manufacturers of High Class Furniture', Nosotti offered a copy of a small Boulle cabinet with a plaque of Louis XIV (lot 174 in the auction) for 250 guineas; the original had realised £2,310. The firm had almost certainly not made the copy in-house; it was most likely Paris made, for example by Henry Fourdinois, Charles Winckelsen or his successor Henry Dasson.[74] Charles Mellier & Co. are another familiar modern cabinetmaking firm who bought at the auction. Acting as agents for Sir Richard Wallace, they purchased a pair of 'Buhl' cabinets by Levasseur for £3,150.[75] Nosotti & Co., founded by the Milan-born Charles Andrea Nosotti in 1822, are mainly known now as one of carvers and gilders but it also offered a wide range of household furniture and goods of a far more modest style than the Boulle copy. The attempt to move into the upper echelons of the trade clearly failed and by 1885 Oetzmann & Co. were advertising Nosotti's stock at 'Greatly Reduced prices', **Fig. 7.57**. Oetzmann continued to thrive, advertising the bankrupt stock of Brew & Claris in 1888 and that of Frank Giles & Co. in 1896. The will of J.R. Oetzmann was published in 1886, showing a personal fortune of over £40,000.[76]

An exhibition of antique and modern furniture held in Leeds in March 1881 separated the numerous loans of antique pieces, mainly seventeenth century, in the upper gallery from the modern furniture on the ground floor. The local firm of Marsh, Jones & Cribb exhibited a complete modern bedroom made in sequoia, a softwood, its warm cedar-like colouring better suited to drawer-linings. It is interesting to note that timber from California at this point had become available in Britain. At the Forestry International Exhibition in 1884, the Edinburgh firm W.S. Brown used sequoia, as did the California Redwood Company; Maple & Co. advertised its use in 1886.[77] The transcontinental railroad, from the east to the west coast of the United States, had opened as early as 1869; the Panama Canal opened much later, in 1914. Churchill & Sim exhibited 'foreign hardwoods, admirably adapted for cabinet-making purposes'. Marsh Jones won a contract for the Leeds Public Library making bookcases and counters in American walnut. Library furniture was the subject of a special conference and exhibition in Plymouth in September 1885, suggesting that some firms were beginning to specialise, a sensible way to contain costs. Supporting 'local firms', much of the New Town Hall in Westminster was lavishly veneered with imported American walnut by J.A. Jones & Co. of Old Street in the East End. An Anglo-Japanese drawing room suite by Hummerston Brothers of Leeds, shown at the 1881 exhibition, also made use of American walnut.[78] The firm employed thirty craftsmen and made all their own furniture, for which they were awarded medals at various exhibitions,

and supplied Aesthetic furniture to local clients such as the Earl of Harewood as well as furniture and decorations to Temple Newsam. Fortuitously, a large collection of drawings by the firm has survived.[79] Another suite of American walnut, inlaid with ivory, was made by John Reid & Sons of Leeds, a firm still working in 1900.[80]

The new wealth being generated in Yorkshire resulted in a growing demand for furniture. This meant that high-quality craftsmen and women were drawn to the area; the lower costs of rent and labour in the north of the country must surely have been a concern to London makers. The fact that Joseph Nutter, a cabinet maker from Halifax in Yorkshire, could leave £40,000 in his will in 1884 is perhaps a testament to the canny nature of the inhabitants of the county. Other Yorkshire makers were represented at the Leeds exhibition in 1881, such as Samuel Holdsworth of Wakefield, Philips

Fig. 7.55 The simulated bamboo gilt-metal columnar supports of this table are inspired by a series made by Adam Weisweiler c.1790. This example by Johnstone & Norman, made between 1880 and 1900, is unusual as there are three 'bamboo' columns in each group, unlike the Weisweiler originals. Wright & Mansfield also made this model in various sizes but, distinctively, with only two columns to each cluster. In the 1750s, English mahogany tables for displaying silver used triple cluster columnar legs for added strength and stability. [Butchoff Antiques]

Fig. 7.56 Nosotti & Co.'s advertisement in the Hamilton Palace sale catalogue reprint offering a facsimile of lot 174, a small Boulle side cabinet. [Author's collection]

Fig. 7.57 An advertisement by Oetzmann in *The Graphic*, 30 May 1885, selling off Nosotti stock at 'GREATLY REDUCED PRICES'. The enterprising Oetzmann later advertised a 'handsome inlaid walnut davenport' in the 1891 edition of the American publication *London of To-day*.[81] [Author's collection]

Figs 7.58 & 7.59 By no means confined to ivory-inlaid marquetry, the wide range of Collinson & Lock's output included this matched pair of rosewood and turtle shell *bureaux Mazarin*, one in *première*, the other in *contre, partie*. [Carlton Hobbs LLC]

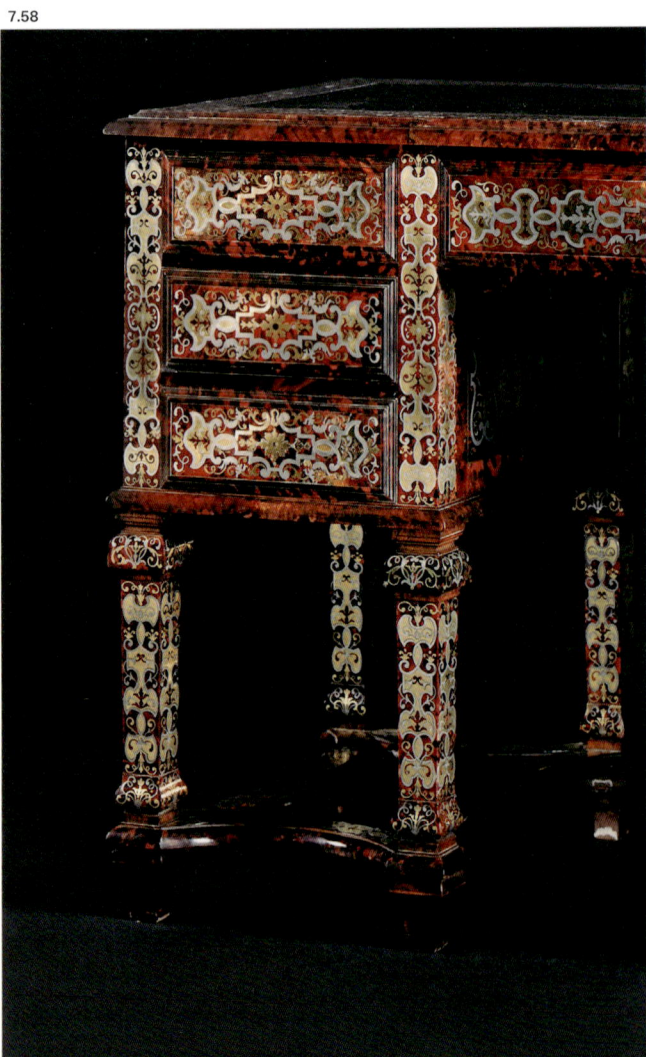

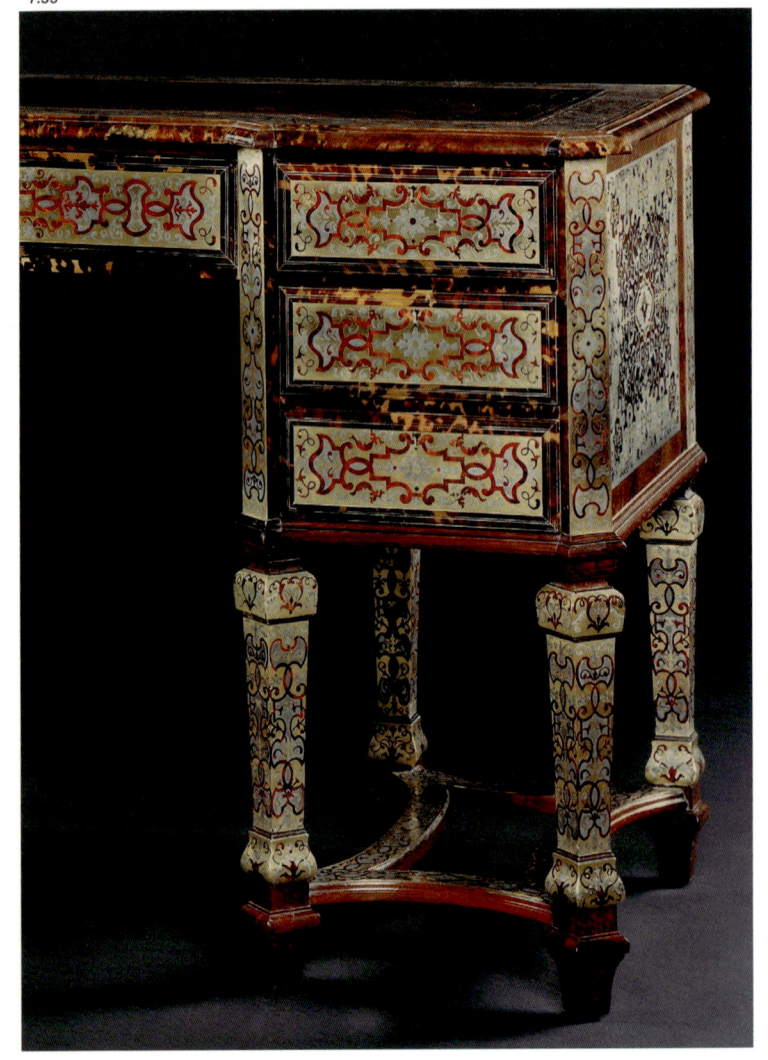

of Otley (Chippendale's birthplace) and Charles Mills of Bradford. Two London exhibitors were also noted – the London-based American importer William Angus & Co., and Collinson & Lock. Since the late 1870s, the Scottish-born Angus had imported furniture direct from American factories, taking advantage of American technical ability in the use of machines to set up a company in London in 1879.[82] Angus sourced his furniture from different American manufacturers, importing it to London for assembly. His business grew rapidly in the 1880s. *The Illustrated Guide to the First Annual Furniture Trade Exhibition*, recorded that the Angus firm had a stock of up to 20,000 chairs.[83] The number of advertisements for woodworking machines made in the north of England and the United States underlines the amount of machine work carried out at the time.

Not to the taste of the aesthete Oscar Wilde, American imports of sturdy and practical furniture were often cheaper than their British counterparts due to the increased use of machinery, and it was imported in large quantities. Not one to hold back, during a lecture tour of the United States Wilde spoke scathingly about American design and lifestyle in general. He specifically castigated 'American houses, ill-designed, decorated shabbily and in bad taste…filled with furniture that was not honestly made and was out of character'.[84]

Furniture was still being made in dark, sombre tones in the 1880s, but simplicity of design became increasingly important. A series of hall furniture made in locally sourced dark oak from the old Caledonian Forest at Dalkeith by W.S. Brown of Howe Street, Edinburgh,[85] was in contrast with the simplicity soon taken up by another Scottish designer, Sir Robert Lorimer (1864–1929) much of it made by the established Edinburgh firm of Morison. In 1884, the First International Forestry Exhibition in Edinburgh included a reception room furnished by another Scottish company, Cranston & Elliot, who, like their countryman, simplified design and decoration. The popularity of such exhibitions can be judged by the number of visitors: some 500,000 went to the Edinburgh show. The Victoria Cabinet and Chair factory of Beith, some twenty miles south-west of Glasgow, was just one of the Scottish firms that was gaining a reputation for high-end furniture.[86] Despite the increased trade, or possibly as a result of general prosperity, this did not stop craftsmen from three Beith factories organising a strike to try and reduce working hours from fifty-seven to fifty-one hours a week.[87]

In Ireland, there were two furniture makers exhibiting from the north of the country at the Dublin exhibition in September 1882 – Park & Cunningham of Belfast and McGowan Brothers of Coleraine. The number of Irish cabinet makers and upholsterers in the 1880s had declined, nevertheless the 1883 Industrial Exhibition in Cork showed that the Irish trade was still able to produce good furniture, with firms such as John Daly, Grants and the looking-glass manufacturer, Burrowes & Son of Cork, amongst the makers who were represented.

The advent of photography in trade magazines and catalogues helped to determine accurate images of furniture. Some of the most useful photographs are those taken by the firm of Bedford Lemere. Establishing his eponymous firm in London *c.*1865 with a studio on the Strand, Lemere (1839–1911) undertook commissions from architects, builders, owners, interior decorators and furnishers. Lemere's son, Henry (Harry) Bedford Lemere (1865–1944), joined the firm in 1881 and his work sealed the company's reputation as the foremost architectural photographers of the period. Employing at its peak four photographers and covering the work of many leading architects, the firm's photographs have done the most to mould our image of late Victorian and Edwardian architecture and interiors. The Historic England Archive holds around 23,000 of their glass-plate negatives and over 4,000 prints, as well as other archive items. The endless, rather badly delineated drawings in magazines and journals such as *The Furniture Gazette*, *The Cabinet Maker* or *The Builder* had often given furniture unsatisfactory spindly or splayed legs and had been an unfortunate influence on poorly informed, commercial makers. The increasing use of photography enabled designers to see an exact image, one they could copy, resulting in more accurate renditions of eighteenth-century styles.

Catalogues of furniture designs, famously used by Thomas Chippendale in the 1750s, were an ever increasing and important business tool. Popular in the early years of the nineteenth century, the international exhibitions perpetuated their use, and by the 1880s copious line engravings were beginning to be supplanted by actual photographs. In 1881,

Fig. 7.60 **The Scottish-born William Angus imported large quantities of sturdy, American machine-made furniture into Britain.** [*The Furniture Gazette*, 1 October 1886, p. xii]

Fig. 7.61 A satinwood cabinet in the 'Queen Anne' style that has similarities with drawings by Waring. The maker is not recorded but Henry Ogden of Manchester is a possibility.
[Butchoff Antiques]

C. & R. Light published their comprehensive 435-page catalogue, *Registered Designs of Cabinet Furniture*, compiled as a guide to prospective buyers with over 2,000 household items available.[88] The same year, W. Walker of Bunhill Row issued a catalogue with a wide range of furniture to suit every pocket. The catalogues are not always dated and often only the approximate date of publication can be determined. This is true, for example, of a catalogue by Hindley & Wilkinson, whose richly illustrated but undated publication entitled *Architectural Decorators, Designers, Upholsterers & Manufacturers of High-Class Furniture* can only be pinned down to a date of post-1887, **Fig. 7.65**. The firm had two central London showrooms, one in Old Bond Street, another in Welbeck Street, with a manufactory at Upper Charlton Street in Marylebone. They appear to have made, or at least retailed, a very wide style of furniture, including a version of the so-called Sheraton toilet table shown in **Fig. 5.86**, noting that 'This beautiful example of fine cabinet work is an exact reproduction by Messrs. Hindley & Wilkinson of the original in the South Kensington Museum'.[89] Interestingly, the Hindley catalogue also included a photograph of a copy of the celebrated *bureau du Roi* 'recently executed by them to a special commission'. It is inconceivable that Hindleys had actually *made* a copy of the Oeben/Riesener desk delivered to Louis XV in 1769, they most probably commissioned or bought it directly from a Paris maker. This opens the question as to who was responsible for the commissioning of the 1878 Paris exhibition example, reportedly made for Lord Ashburton by Henry Dasson of Paris.[90] The dating of the Hindley catalogue suggests that the model of the *bureau du Roi* it advertised could have been ordered from Dasson or possibly Beurdeley. The early 1880s was the beginning of a forty-year period in which the larger London firms illustrated furniture in their catalogues that was clearly made in Paris, for example by François Linke or the Sormani firm. Some suppliers, such as Kahn, advertised correctly that these pieces were French imports; others were less open, with the inference being, as in the Hindley catalogue, that they were made 'in their own workshops'.

As well as being an important decade for the growth of catalogues, the 1880s saw the growing significance of large, well-marketed furniture emporia which catered for both the middle and luxury markets. Furniture by Maples in the later years of the century is frequently, but not always, labelled or stamped but it is difficult to pin down the firm's early work. Founded as a drapery firm in 1841, by 1857 John Maple began to sell furniture with his half-brother, Henry Adams, and also James Cook, trading as Maple & Company. In 1870, prior to his retirement in 1891, John Maple had made his sons, John Blundell and Harry, partners. John was the driving force, and by 1880 Maple & Co. described themselves as 'The Largest and Most Convenient Furnishing Establishment in the World'. The stock advertised in their catalogues was not always in the luxury bracket but contained a wide array of furniture, including 'Art Furniture' with 'a most wonderful assortment of NEW and ARTISTIC FURNITURE on SHOW'.[91] Working and business practice by Maples came under close scrutiny by the House of Lords select committee and both John Blundell Maple and a junior partner, Horace Regnart, underwent incisive questioning from Lord Rothschild and other members of the committee. 'Once you got into the power of Maples…it is impossible to open an account with other houses.'[92] Harris Lebus was questioned, stating that he worked exclusively for Maples, all the work was completed in Lebus's own premises.[93] One

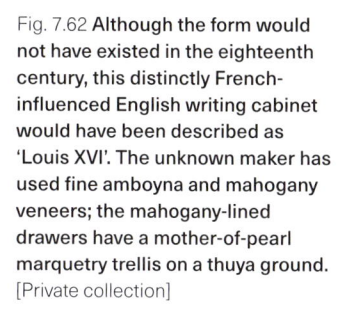

Fig. 7.62 Although the form would not have existed in the eighteenth century, this distinctly French-influenced English writing cabinet would have been described as 'Louis XVI'. The unknown maker has used fine amboyna and mahogany veneers; the mahogany-lined drawers have a mother-of-pearl marquetry trellis on a thuya ground. [Private collection]

Figs 7.63 & 7.64 Two unusual commodes, or side cabinets, of French influence, drawing from the Transitional style. Both veneered in *Gonçalo alves*, the doors are painted with Classical motifs on a gold ground reminiscent of first-century Roman decoration. The two-door cabinet is stamped 'J^{as} Shoolbred & Co 8344', the firm's numbering system yet to be identified, the other unsigned. [Private collection]

witness, John Richards, a maker of high-class furniture and art furniture with 35 years' experience, stated that Maples pressed him to take a larger workshop to do more work for them and he 'expended a lot of money laying down plant and machinery'. Richards became so dependent on business from Maples that he was forced to give them a charge on his premises. In his answers to the committee, Richards stated that he had made furniture for firms such as Hewetson & Milner, Hindley's, Smee, Hewson & Hornby of High Holborn as well as Jenks & Holt (exhibitors at the Third Annual Furniture Exhibition in London in 1883), Hunter of Moorgate Street, Taylor, Fisher & Blunt and many others. By 1888, Richards was specialising in 'ash inlaid work', and 'had a complete monopoly' ... 'this was very saleable ... and [Richards] did very well at it'. For a very large furniture firm, Maples had a surprisingly small team of seven designers and three draughtsmen.[94] Does this underline that they were indeed buying in a large proportion of their furniture?

Part of the company's success was the export of furniture and household goods to Paris and Buenos Aires. With retail outlets in both cities as well as London, Maples furnished many hotels, initially working in Argentina with Thompson

& Co., establishing their own premises in the capital from 1906.[95] In 1884, Maples were appointed upholsterers and cabinet makers to the court of Spain. An engraving in 1893 showing the Maples corner property on Tottenham Court Road gives an impression of the vast size of the store; like competitors such as Shoolbred they were 'complete house furnishers'.[96]

In a comprehensive catalogue printed in 1876, Shoolbred boasted that the illustrated items were 'specially designed for the company' and could be sent 'to any part of the Kingdom'. Making use of modern communications, and in an effort to compete commercially, the catalogue also stated, 'The Carriage of All Goods paid to any Railway Station in the United Kingdom'. The Shoolbred catalogue was illustrated with engravings of complete rooms, including a 'Bed-Chamber in the "Adams" Style', an eclectic mix of Adam Classicism with French Louis XVI overtones. A bedroom suite in a modernised Gothic style could enterprisingly be redesigned for a drawing room or dining room.

Furniture makers continued to benefit from global trade, with Australia becoming an increasingly important export market. English-made furniture had been exhibited in Melbourne and Sydney, and by 1882 Australia had become the largest recipient of British furniture exports, followed by America. In 1881, Walker of Bunhill Row exhibited (and won the First Order of Merit prize) in Melbourne alongside less well-known dealers, such as the firm run by Henry, William and Arthur Arrowsmith of New Bond Street, and Frederick Conrath & Sons of North Audley Street. In 1883, Walkers, which had been operating for nearly fifty years, opened a second building to accommodate their expanding business.[97] *The Furniture Gazette* itself won a prize at both the Melbourne and Sydney exhibitions. Great Britain was still by far the largest exporter to the United States, and India was an increasingly important destination for British furniture. Import duties to India had been relaxed in 1878, and as a result exports increased from £19,233 in 1879 to £50,276 in 1883.[98] To protect their own industry, France increased import tariffs for furniture by approximately 10 per cent.

British firms began to turn away from French designers such as Prignot and Lormier, the Jackson & Graham in-house designers, and were keen to continue the gains they had made over their French competitors. In an interesting co-operation of May 1881, the Art Workmanship Exhibition, also called the Exhibition of Works of Art Applied to Furniture, was held at the Albert Hall. Leading firms were encouraged to set up stands for other exhibitors to display smaller accessories. The more established firms included: Crace; Morant, Boyd & Blandford; Jackson & Graham; Gillow; Holland; Howard & Sons; Wright & Mansfield; Collinson & Lock; Gregory; Shoolbred; and Johnstone &

Fig. 7.65 The cover of an early Hindley & Wilkinson catalogue, produced sometime after 1887. The gilded cherubs are doubtless a reference to their reproductions of furniture from the Carolean period. [Butchoff archive]

Fig. 7.66 A china cabinet exhibited by Graham & Biddle at the Paris exhibition in 1889. Based at Graham House, 463 Oxford Street, they advertised as 'Art Furnishers' proudly pointing out that they had formerly been partners with Jackson & Graham. Little is known of their furniture, either as retailers or makers, although several items are recorded with the Graham & Biddle stamp, Fig. 8.22.[99] [*The Furniture Gazette*, 1 July 1889, p. 3]

Fig. 7.67 One of a pair of oak tables stamped by Howard of Berners Street, one with traces of the firm's paper label. The sturdy Gothic appearance is relieved by an intricate geometric parquetry design on the top. [Carlton Hobbs LLC]

Fig. 7.68 Plans for a breakfast table in 'hard mahogany' designed by Maurice Adams, placed by Thomas Robertson & Son of Alnwick in an 1883 issue of *The Building News*. The thriving firm supplied furniture to the Duke of Northumberland and also had a London outlet. [St Croix Architecture]

Jeanes. Gregory & Co. of Regent Street exhibited drawing room furniture in rosewood; Jackson & Graham's work was described as being 'of exceptional interest'; and Wright & Mansfield exhibited in the Adam and the Chippendale styles. An exhibition, with the unlikely title of the Wool Exhibition, held at the Crystal Palace in May 1881, was the venue for Maples' innovative display in which they set up an entire house, decorated and furnished throughout. The drawing room furniture was in satinwood, the dining room in walnut and the morning room in mahogany.[100] Once again showing their innovation, Maples furnished the capacious and fashionable Holborn Restaurant, completed towards the end of 1883. The designs were based on illustrations of French furniture in the 1882 Jones Bequest to the South Kensington Museum. This refurbishment and associated publicity heightened the growing interest in a stricter interpretation of the 'Louis' styles and added yet another layer of decorative features alongside the now familiar Aesthetic style and the

CHAPTER 7: 1880S

7.66

7.67

7.68

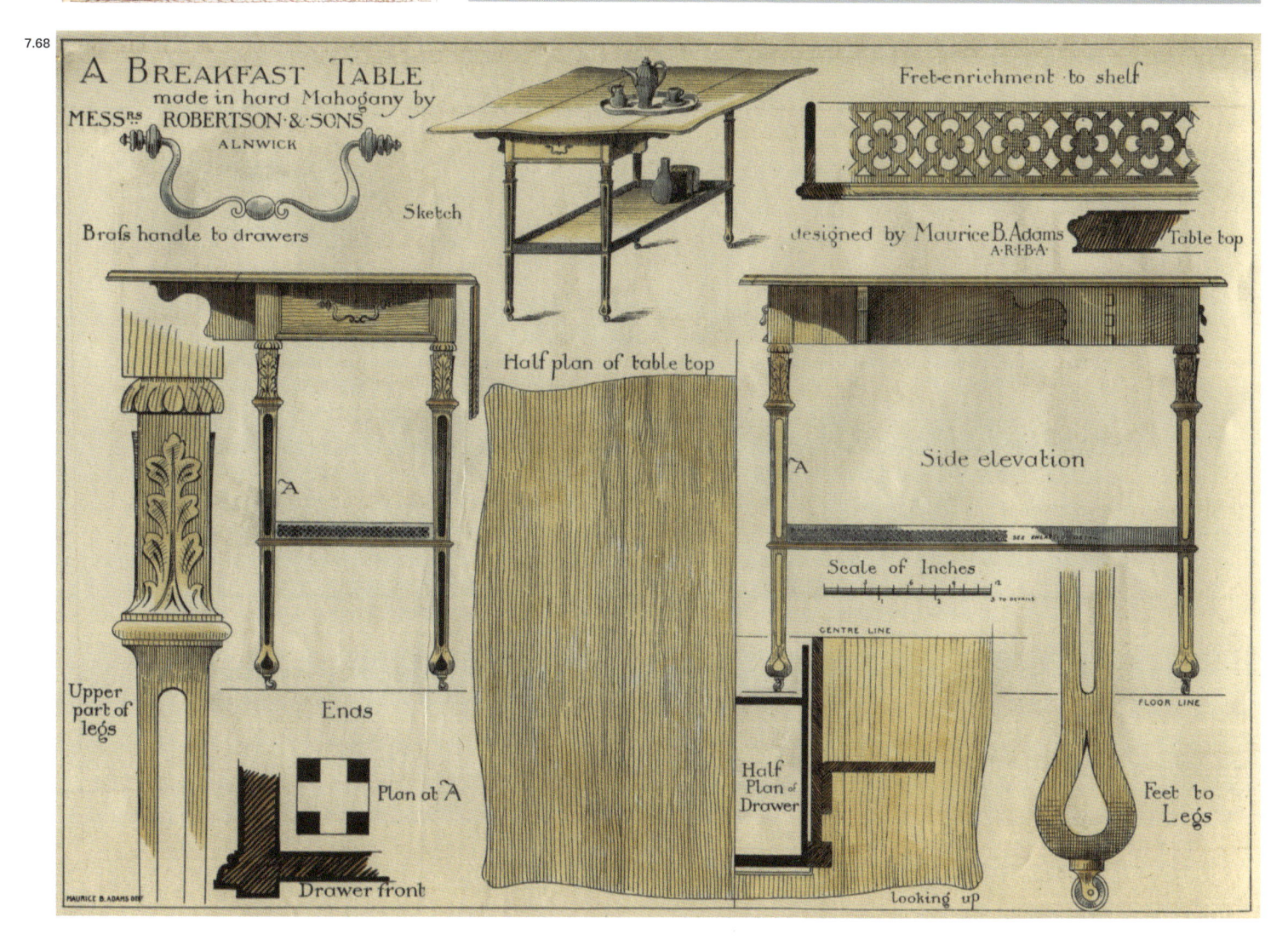

revived interest in Chippendale, Adam and Sheraton. Writing in the *Magazine of Art* in 1883, Eustace Balfour identified the differences between the styles of Chippendale and Sheraton. However, the illustrations (for example a 'Sheraton Desk and Bookcase') show that contemporary interpretations were still favoured over exact or near exact reproductions.[101] Line drawings of eighteenth-century Adam period furniture started to appear in *The Furniture Gazette* in the 1880s, some drawn by the Bristol firm of Wood & Hemmons, who mixed antique pieces with reproductions of their own manufacture.[102]

Contemporary commentators helped to promote the larger makers. Charles Pascoe named Johnstone, Norman & Co.'s New Bond Street showroom as 'no better place for buying English furniture of the best workmanship', describing Gillows, Collinson & Lock, Gregory, Hamptons and Morris & Co. also 'of the first rank'; less costly were Maple, Oetzmann and Atkinson & Co.[103] *The Illustrated London News* published an extended article about Howard & Sons in 1878, stating that 'none stands out more pre-eminently than the well-known house of Howard & Sons, of Berners-Street, whose exquisitely appointed dining-room furniture was one of the chief attractions of the Paris Exhibition'. Their wares were 'admirable designs in antique and modern styles carried out to perfection'.[104] Howard still made Gothic Revival furniture in a style that Bruce Talbert had been designing in the late 1860s. A 'Talbertian' side cabinet, which would be difficult to date accurately within a twenty-year period, was exhibited by Howard in Paris at the 1889 exhibition. The firm made some interesting, relatively plain but subtly designed furniture in oak such as the table shown in **Fig. 7.67**.

Foreign competition was relentless. Van Mol of Great Eastern Street, with a steam manufactory in Mechelen, Belgium, suggested they were making their furniture in London, although it is more likely that this was a ploy to

Fig. 7.69 An 1887 Bedford Lemere photograph of a room in Croxteth Lodge, Liverpool, furnished by Waring & Sons. The architectural fitted screen was to keep out excessive heat and sunlight in the summer and keep the room warm in the winter. [Historic England, Bedford Lemere Collection BL08473]

Fig. 7.70 A mahogany writing desk in the Drawing Room at Standen. The wide satinwood banding is more typical of reinvented Georgian furniture of the late nineteenth century. Probably designed by George Jack for Morris & Co., an example advertised in an engraving by Goodall & Co. is profusely inlaid with marquetry. [National Trust]

appear 'British'. Despite foreign competition, the output of the large London firms was astounding. Maples announced in August 1882 that they were just completing the furnishing of one hundred rooms at the Grand Hotel in London and other hotels as far afield as Newcastle, Preston, Birmingham, Glasgow, the Isle of Wight and Pangbourne, as well as the Royal London Yacht Club in Cowes and the Hotel Carol I in Romania. The East End of London was increasingly important for the huge volume of shipping using the London docks, and new hotels were needed to house the traders and businessmen. Blyth & Sons of Chiswell Street, a firm that had been established for almost seventy years, furnished the Galleons Hotel in the Royal Albert Docks with walnut dining room furniture. Maples were not averse to using illustrations in their catalogues adapted from catalogues of other firms, a contentious point of copyright, subsequently there was a move to copyright designs. In 1883 Maple & Co. won a successful court case protecting the copyright of images in their catalogues but not all judges were of the same opinion; in other cases, copyright claims were denied.[105]

The increased demand for furniture pushed the furniture trade into the East End of London, where rents were cheaper and labour plentiful. Garret-masters organised small workshops, some simply in a lean-to at the rear of a dwelling, where the small workforce would make repeated quantities of one particular item, be it a sideboard or much needed bedroom furniture, with a concentration on wardrobes rather than chests of drawers. The 1881 census recorded over 12,000 men employed in the East End furniture or allied trades, with another 2,200 young men and boys. Curtain Road was the central area with showrooms in and around the adjacent streets. A large quantity of furniture made in the East End was exported to the colonies, and British provincial dealers also bought from the East End. The bulk of this trade supplied larger stores such as Shoolbred, but much was made speculatively without a specific commission, making craftsmen vulnerable to 'hawking' their produce and forced to sell it at a disadvantageous price. This was not confined to middle market furniture but, perhaps surprisingly, also included luxury products. Charles Booth wrote tellingly about potential fakes: 'From the East End workshops… produce goes of every description, from the richly inlaid cabinet that may be sold for £100, or the carved chair that can be made to pass as rare "antique" workmanship'.[106] Much of the sawing, turning, fretwork and even polishing would be carried out by specific trades. Booth noted that

Fig. 7.71 **An iconic mahogany chair, designed by Mackmurdo in 1881, a year before he founded the Century Guild, made by Collinson & Lock in 1883, the painted pierced splat is an early foray into Art Nouveau.** [The Huntington, 2009:16]

Fig. 7.72 **The tall back of this chair was possibly inspired by caned chairs popular during the Restoration period in the 1660s. Made by either Collinson & Lock or Goodall & Co., a similar example was exhibited as part of a music room designed by the Century Guild in 1886.** [Victoria and Albert Museum, W.74-1975]

Fig. 7.73 **Designed by Mackmurdo and possibly Herbert Horne, under the banner of the Century Guild, this fall-front writing desk, looking back to French *sécretaires* of the Empire period, was made for Pownall Hall by Goodall & Co.** [Saint Louis Art Museum, 87:1990]

there were about twenty veneer dealers in the East End producing knife-cut veneers on a roller with up to sixty per inch but some machines could cut between eight and one hundred or even more veneers to the inch at a rate of seven to ten veneers per minute.[107] Booth, a fellow of the Statistical Society, was called to give evidence to the House of Lords Select Committee on the Sweating System of labour, an inquiry into manufacturing as a whole, not just furniture. Booth realised that provincial makers had healthier working conditions and that the tendency in London was distinctly away from large factories and in favour of home work and small workshops. Arnold White stated that 'Some large houses stamp as their own manufacturing goods not made by them, but which are made in garrets, or in the workman's home'. He added, 'The articles are sent to the customer as the work of a great shop, and often bear the stamp of the great shop as being their own manufacture'. Should there be a problem with the article, the men sent to rectify it 'have to bear out the statement that the furniture was made at the great shop'. White mentioned that even such a house as Collinson & Lock, by then amalgamated with Jackson & Graham, might stamp with their name furniture that was made in Curtain Road.[108] It is probable that some plain, unadorned furniture with the Collinson & Lock stamp was outsourced, including some of their quasi-Italo-Flemish plain carved furniture or the exotic pair of Boulle-style writing desks shown in **Fig. 7.58 & 7.59**.

'Antique' is a word much misused in the furniture trade but some designers were honest, at least at the time of manufacture. For example, the architectural firm of Wadmore & Baker designed a buffet for a Mr Beeching of Ferox Hall in Tonbridge. Of imposing proportions, it was made by Harry Helms of Exeter to incorporate five late sixteenth-century carved panels and made as a vehicle to display the earlier panels with no pretence that the whole cabinet was 'old'. By the mid-1880s, designers were incorporating original carved panels from the late sixteenth and early seventeenth centuries into new creations; for example, a massive buffet by the Nottingham maker W. Windle, assembled with three tiers of shelves, made as if wanting to convey an image of the owner's wealth with a show of silver, **Fig. 7.41**. Despite continued interest in the Baroque, the extravagant style of woodcarving, so popular at the Great Exhibition, was on the wane by the 1880s. In 1880, George A. Rogers, continuing in his father William's career, organised an exhibition of Ancient and Modern Carving at the newly built Albert Hall.[109] The hall was home to the School of Woodcarving, originally founded by Gillows.

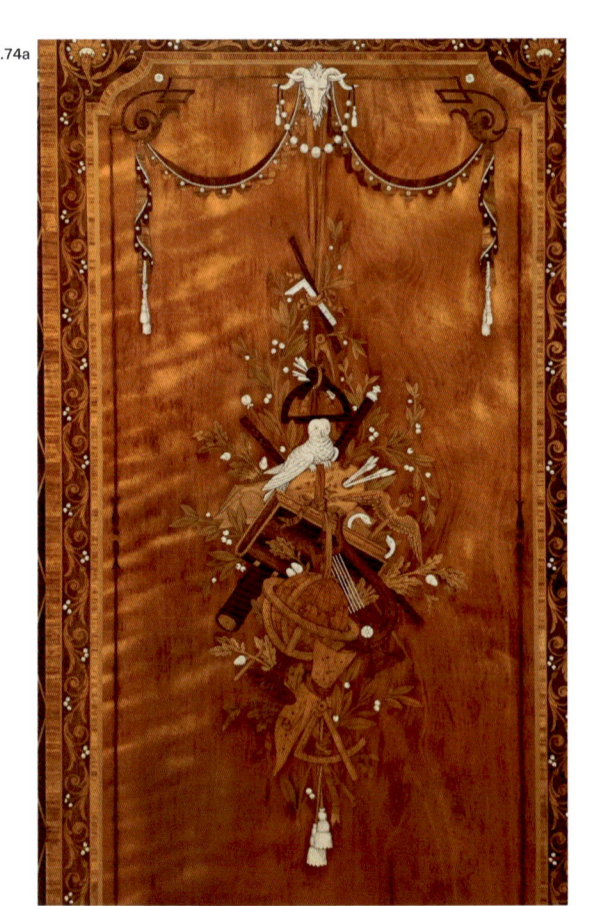

Figs 7.74a & b **A pair of fine-quality side cabinets or chiffoniers attributable to Lamb of Manchester on the basis of the distinctive columns and capitals. The cabinets were separated for many years until recently and have aged differently. The doors are inlaid with attributes of Music and Science.** [Private collection]

CHAPTER 7: 1880s

7.75

Although carving by hand continued to be a popular pastime for individuals as a means of relaxation, machines could carry out carved decoration at a greatly reduced cost, albeit mainly in a two-dimensional plane.[110] Many large buffets were made in the third quarter of the nineteenth century, often of carved, dark-stained oak. It was a style particularly fashionable in the grand houses of the Nottinghamshire 'Dukeries', and they often incorporated earlier panels, with spurious dates to give them 'authenticity'.[111] One of the originators of this style of fake oak furniture was the Yorkshire-born George Shaw (1810–1876), who had been making and 'improving' oak furniture in the Tudor style since the 1830s, notoriously his 'Paradise' beds.[112] George Elcock, one-time president of the West End Cabinet-makers' Society made carved oak cabinet furniture, supplying Edwards & Roberts from the early 1870s.[113]

In 1887 *The Art Journal* illustrated a sideboard and chair in the Charles II style by Kendal, Milne & Co. of Manchester. The concept of a sideboard had reverted from the essentially flat-top versions of the George III era to large buffets in a seventeenth-century manner for displaying *bric-à-brac*. As with many successful furniture suppliers of the latter years of the nineteenth century, the firm had been established as drapers, in 1796. From 1862, their department store traded as Kendal, Milne & Co., opening cabinet showrooms in fashionable Deansgate in 1870, as well as cabinet-making

7.76

Fig. 7.75 **Designed by W.J. Estall, this ebonised Aesthetic movement corner chair is stamped 'Lamb Manchester'. This popular model was used in the consulting room of Sigmund Freud, another in the London home of the actress and theatre producer Edith Woodworth.** [Private collection]

Fig. 7.76 **Photographed in 1888, this room in St Margaret's Mansions in Westminster is furnished entirely in the Moorish taste by Collinson & Lock. In contrast, the desk chair is in the aesthetic manner similar to the example shown above by Lamb of Manchester (Fig. 7.75).** [Historic England / Bedford Lemere]

371

Fig. 7.77 A coromandel side cabinet, based on a Louis XVI *commode à l'anglaise* but with an open front, is inlaid with ivory, harewood and boxwood stringing, the frieze with ivory Neoclassical griffins. It is not signed but the distinctive columns and capitals suggest that it may have been made by Lamb of Manchester. [Private collection]

Fig. 7.78 Made *c.*1880, this Macassar ebony canterbury with satinwood crossbanding is not signed but also in the style of Lamb of Manchester. [Private collection]

workshops to the east of the city. The impetus of local schools of design, and the urgent need to furnish the growing population, meant the establishment of more provincial firms making furniture, much of their work unsigned. *The Furniture Gazette* and *The Art Journal* give the researcher many names to conjure with, such as a Mr Milne of the Lancaster School of Art. Could he be James Milne of Kendal, Milne & Co.? Without a maker's stamp or extant design, these firms have faded into oblivion.

One of the celebrations for Queen Victoria's Golden Jubilee in 1887 was the Royal Jubilee Exhibition, held in Manchester. The enormous site befitted the rapid expansion of the industrial north and was visited by more than 4.5 million people over 166 days. The exhibition provided the Century Guild of Artists the opportunity to show their designs.[114] The locally based firm of Edward Goodall & Co. of King Street[115] exhibited what would be described today as 'quaint' furniture in a Georgian style; their range included a reinvention of an eighteenth-century writing cabinet similar to a design once attributed to T.E. Collcutt.

A plainer example probably by George Jack is at Standen House in Sussex, **Fig. 7.70**. Another version is in the Victoria and Albert Museum.[116] The Standen example is in plain mahogany, the Goodall engraving shows profuse marquetry, both without a swan neck cresting. Aslin illustrates a marquetry example with an elaborate upper section with swan-neck cresting.[117] The unconventional form has a similarity to the style of furniture by George Jack who also designed for Standen. Goodall's furnished rooms at the Manchester Town Hall opened in September 1887, 'the [furniture] designs were prepared by Mr. Waterhouse'.[118]

The Century Guild, formed in 1882 by the architect and designer Arthur Heygate Mackmurdo, was not a commercial success and was forced to close ten years later. However short-lived, some of the Guild's designs, for example high-back dining chairs made *c.*1886 by Goodall & Co. for Pownall Hall in Cheshire, are some of the most sophisticated items of furniture of the *fin de siècle*, **Fig. 7.72**. A chair of this pattern was exhibited by the Century Guild at the International Exhibition of Navigation, Travelling,

Commerce and Manufactures in Liverpool in 1886. However, it is Mackmurdo's mahogany chair, designed a year before he founded the Century Guild and made by Collinson & Lock, that is one of the most iconic furniture designs, **Fig. 7.71**. The swirling pierced fretwork back, painted to heighten the plant form, takes the naturalism seen at the Great Exhibition of 1851 into a new era of asymmetry which anticipates Art Nouveau. Mackmurdo was a friend of John Ruskin and William Morris. He had studied cabinet making and actually *made* some of the furniture he designed. The Century Guild also exhibited furniture designed by Mackmurdo at the International Health Exhibition of 1884.

The continued popularity of the *credenza* was partly due to the fashion for the Victorian household to display an ever-increasing number of objects. *The Furniture Gazette* illustrated such a cabinet, remarking that buyers wanted furniture that was useful not merely ornamental: 'Give us shelves upon which we can display our nick-nacs [sic]. We have sufficient flat surfaces upon the walls of our rooms'.[119] The coromandel-veneered cabinet or *commode à l'anglaise*

Fig. 7.79 Like many of his contemporaries, Lamb has used the French eighteenth-century form of a *commode à l'anglaise* for this coromandel veneered cabinet, the engraved ivory plaques representing Arcadian harmony. One door bears the stamp 'LAMB MANCHESTER' and the unidentified number '12 10 7'. [Butchoff Antiques]

by Lamb of Manchester, **Fig. 7.79**, is testament to the high standards provincial makers had reached by the third quarter of the nineteenth century. James Lamb founded the firm in 1843 and became one of the most successful nineteenth-century regional British cabinet makers. At its height, Lamb had a workforce of almost 200 and employed highly regarded designers such as Hughes Protât, Bruce Talbert and Alfred Waterhouse, the latter the architect of Manchester Town Hall and the Natural History Museum in London. The quality of the firm's work was consistently high, receiving the judges' commendation for their 'Art Furniture' in London in 1862, along with awards at other major international exhibitions. Judging by the repeated use of a distinctive ormolu capital on the columns and the same

Fig. 7.80 **Started in 1887 for John Allcroft, the central hall of Stokesay Court has fine Elizabethan Revival panelling. Much of the original furniture was supplied by Hamptons of Pall Mall. The table in the centre is of the Bridgens ilk, such as those by Morant (see Chapter 3 – 1840s).** [Country Life Picture Library/Future PLC]

Fig. 7.81 A portable coromandel-veneered drinks cabinet, made by George Betjemann & Sons, once owned by General Sir Walter Norris Congreve (1862–1927), who, as a captain, was awarded the Victoria Cross in the Second Boer War for his actions at Colenso. He subsequently served in World War I. [Nan Xu]

Fig. 7.82 An advertisement in *The Graphic* placed by Hampton & Sons in 1882, exhibiting an 'Adam' style bedroom suite at their Suffolk Street Galleries. [Look & Learn]

Fig. 7.83 Using the finest ebony veneers, this music cabinet, stamped 'Lamb' in large capitals and 'Manchester' in a smaller typeface, incorporates a Wedgwood-style basalt plaque. [Butchoff Antiques]

Figs 7.84a & b (overleaf) Stamped 'Hampton & Sons' with the serial number '1771',[120] the plum-pudding mahogany veneer on this cabinet is inlaid with ivory and satinwood in the Renaissance Revival manner. The detail image shows addorsed fabulous mythological dragons highlighted with ivory flowers. The style of the inlay is similar to that seen on Collinson & Lock cabinets, but also appears in a Hamptons illustrated catalogue, Fig. 9.69. [Butchoff Antiques]

CHAPTER 7: 1880S

7.81

7.82

7.83

375

7.84a

7.84b

Fig. 7.85 Although of Louis XVI-style outline, this rare rosewood cabinet is inlaid in the Renaissance style. The ivory figure of Harvest suggests that it might have been one of a series of cabinets illustrating the Seasons. A brass plaque inside the door is engraved '1883 Jetley, 8 North Audley Street London Designers Upholsterers and Cabinet Makers'.[121]
[Private collection]

style of simulated fluting, it is probable that furniture with the same device is also by the Manchester firm, **Figs 7.77 & 7.78**. Lamb's work is well represented in many museums both in Britain and internationally; the Manchester City Art Gallery has several examples, ranging from their exhibition-quality work to fine but more humble furniture in oak or walnut. The firm clearly had the means and access to the finest imported veneers, and much of their luxury furniture was veneered in coromandel (**Figs 7.79 & 7.83**), here with the added expense of a Wedgwood panel.

An expensive and exotic veneer, coromandel was normally used in limited quantities. Due to its expense, it was often used on luxurious, richly fitted small writing slopes, dressing cases and travelling boxes of all shapes and sizes. An elaborate example is a drinks cabinet made by George Betjemann & Sons, **Fig. 7.81**. The Betjemann name is seen on many of the better fitted boxes and dressing tables, such as the one in **Fig. 10.112b**.

Aesthetic furniture illustrated in the *Artistic Furniture Catalogue* by Collinson & Lock was produced by the firm from 1871. In the 1880s and 1890s they made a series of ivory-inlaid pieces of furniture, mainly cabinets and small tables, the marquetry in a Renaissance style. George Lock, a direct descendant of Matthias Lock, the celebrated furniture designer during George III's reign, was one of the principals of the firm and is believed to have drawn the cabinet maker's plans. Stephen Webb designed the intricate marquetry and was possibly responsible for at least some of the actual hand work. A distinctive feature of the Collinson & Lock ivory marquetry is the delicacy of the engraving, adding another layer of skill, and cost. Webb's work is immediately recognisable with its individual interpretation

CHAPTER 7: 1880S

Figs 7.86 & 7.87 This style of ivory-inlaid low cabinet by Collinson & Lock was available with a glazed or solid central door. The left-hand example is stamped 'Collinson & Lock London 580', on the right simply 'Collinson & Lock',[122] in each case the stamp is on the top of the central drawer. A museum example was reputedly purchased by the original owner from Maple & Co. in Paris.[123] [Butchoff Antiques]

of Renaissance forms, profusely and delicately inlaid with scrolling arabesques and languishing putti. Webb designed for Collinson & Lock between 1885 and 1896 and it would seem that he continued working in some capacity with Gillows after the Gillows takeover of Collinson & Lock in 1897. He was a member of the Art Workers' Guild between 1887 and 1902, exhibiting as a member of the Arts and Crafts Exhibition Society from 1888 to 1906. Webb was Collinson & Lock's chief designer during this period. Most of his Renaissance-style inlay was in ivory, the work cut in a somewhat mechanical manner but nevertheless highly skilled and delicate. The marquetry-cutting machines at Collinson & Lock were operated by women, each paid £2.50 per week.[124] Similar designs were used in wood marquetry by the firm, presumably such work was cheaper, the overall design lacking the finesse of their ivory-inlaid work. Webb wrote extensively on ivory inlay in art periodicals, including the *Art Workers' Quarterly*, which published some of his designs in 1902; designs that are arguably somewhat at odds with his membership of the Arts and Crafts movement.[125] The Victoria and Albert Museum ascribes his interpretation of the Renaissance arabesque to the impact of the teaching at the School of Art at South Kensington. There are undoubted similarities to the designs of Walter Crane, specifically the cover for his publication *The Baby's Bouquet*, of c.1878. However, the popularity of the Renaissance as a design source grew unabated and various publications may have contributed to Webb's ideas. One, G.J. Oakeshott's *Detail and Ornament of the Italian Renaissance* of 1888, may well have been a prompt for the fashion for his ivory inlay. An example of this style by Gillows is a cabinet stamped with the number 16321, which dates it to between 1884 and 1885, i.e., before the takeover.[126] Gillows continued the popular Collinson & Lock theme of the Renaissance-style cabinet with Webb's inimitable style of delicate ivory inlay. Collinson & Lock made a range of variations, for example their seminal cabinets, such as **Figs 7.86 & 7.87**. The marquetry designs were adapted to different types of furniture such as the cabinet in **Fig. 7.88**. A version of the octagonal table in **Fig. 7.90** was exhibited in Chicago in 1893.[127]

The large ivory-inlaid cabinets of the type seen in **Fig. 7.91** may originally have been a Collinson & Lock concept, but extant examples were made and signed by Gillows. A seemingly identical example, design number 18578, is in the Gillows design books for November 1889. The same design appeared in *The Art Journal* two years earlier. It is possible that the example illustrated is the cabinet numbered

7.88

7.90

7.89

Fig. 7.88 **An ivory-inlaid rosewood and marquetry fall-front writing desk. The design is attributed to G.J. Lock and Stephen Webb, manufactured by Collinson & Lock, numbered 8727, the lock is by Cope & Collinson. The marquetry panels in ivory have similarities with those in Fig. 7.87 and are probably cut from the same pattern.** [Christie's images]

Fig. 7.89 **A thuya-veneered and ebonised canterbury, the style and execution of the engraved ivory marquetry in the manner of Collinson & Lock.** [Casa-Museu Medeiros e Almeida]

Fig. 7.90 **A photograph taken c.1898 of a Gillows showroom, arranging three ivory-inlaid pieces of old Collinson & Lock stock designed by Stephen Webb in the 1880s, offered in the Collinson & Lock/Gillows dispersal catalogue of c.1898. See also Fig. 8.26.** [Clive Edwards]

'Gillows, 16575',[128] suggesting that the firm had produced 2,000 pieces of furniture in the intervening two years. The model is shown in *Examples of Furniture and Decoration by Gillows*, where it is described as 'A Rosewood cabinet, carved and richly inlaid with ivory and pearl in the style of the Italian Renaissance'.[129] Gillows illustrated the same style of cabinet as late as 1904, and similar furniture was still being advertised in a later, undated Hamptons catalogue of 1910–1920.

Sensitivity to the use of ivory is well understood today but it should not be assumed that this style of marquetry was always executed in elephant ivory. Synthetic materials were often used as a substitute.[130] One design by Stephen Webb that has remained very popular, and is relatively practical even today, is a small table in a reinterpretation of the Queen Anne style of c.1710. Examples were in the collection of the Duke of Connaught, Edward VII's brother.[131] Two ivory-inlaid tables in this genre are shown in the illustration of a Gillows showroom of c.1898, after Gillows had taken over Collinson & Lock in 1897, **Fig. 7.90**.

The painting of Mrs Luke Ionides, **Fig. 7.96**, by William Blake Richmond, shows a small inlaid polygonal table made in North Africa, probably in a small artisanal workshop in the bazaars of Cairo, or in the further reaches of the Ottoman Empire, such as Syria. These tables are seen frequently today, all with individual variations. Many were imported by Liberty's or Rottman & Stone in a form that today would be called 'flat pack', some delivered directly to the British customer for self-assembly. 'Moorish' taste

CHAPTER 7: 1880S

had become a pan-European phenomenon by the 1860s; a 'Moorish' pavilion had been exhibited by Prussia as part of its contribution to the 1867 *Exposition Universelle* in Paris.¹³²

Like those of China and Japan, the visual culture of the Middle East and North Africa provided a rich source of decorative vocabulary that Western artists and designers could draw on, and the improvement of international transport widened access. Victor Hugo, widely read in Britain, wrote about the Alhambra Palace in Spain and, with the opening of the Suez Canal in November 1869, Cairo was now en route to India and the East. The publication of the *Rubáiyát of Omar Khayyám* in 1859 fuelled interest in the Middle East and the romanticised vision of the Islamic world that came to be reflected in painting, decorative art and architecture, including the designs of William Burges. Burges was also influenced by the publication of *L'Art Arabe* by Prisse d'Avennes in 1877.

Smoking rooms with hookah pipes were all the rage. Burges created the magnificent Arab Room at Cardiff Castle between 1880 and 1881, and an Arabian-style smoking 'eyrie' within the Château de Chillon-like exterior of Castell

Fig. 7.91 **This model of cabinet was illustrated in *The Art Journal* in 1887 and appears to be identical to an 1889 drawing from the Gillow records. It was featured in the 1904 Gillows catalogue as item number 3368.** [Trustees of the Cecil Higgins Art Gallery]

Fig. 7.92 **An unsigned cabinet inlaid with panels of brass marquetry on a rosewood ground. The use of brass imitates the 'Buhl' style, but the design is more like Webb's Renaissance ivory inlay.** [Sotheby's]

Coch in 1879, both built for the 3rd Marquess of Bute. At Castell Coch, Burges followed close on the heels of George Aitchison, whose Arab Hall at Leighton House in London was one of the earliest manifestations of Islamic Revivalism in Britain.¹³³ Twenty years later, Warings merged the 'Arabian' style with Art Nouveau for the Smoking Room at the Berkeley Hotel in London (**Fig. 8.21**) and subsequent publications continued to reflect an appreciation for Islamic Revivalism well into the twentieth century.

Liberty & Co. quickly picked up this trend, making and importing furniture in an 'Arabic style' and popularising the complex woodturning seen on *mashrabiya* screens used in Islamic architecture. It is often difficult to distinguish

7.93

7.94

7.95

Fig. 7.93 This delicate, inlaid satinwood tripod table has all the modern elements of the 1870s and 1880s, including the stylised hipped legs that are reminiscent of Godwin's elegant curves. [Nan Xu]

Fig. 7.94 An oak table inspired by the designs of Philip Webb, and formerly in the Ionides Collection. Also available in rosewood, the inspiration for the design is a group of medieval-style tables emanating from the Morris circle during the 1850s, one of which is shown in a *c.*1900 photograph by Bedford Lemere of Rosetti's house in Chelsea (Swan House), Fig. 5.88. [Oscar Graf]

Fig. 7.95 Although Leighton House had been commissioned in 1866, it was only completed thirty years later, the Arab Hall started in 1877. According to George Aitchison and Walter Crane, the design was based on the twelfth-century palace of La Zisa in Palermo, and included seventeenth-century tiles and Damascus-carved wooden lattice-work. [Royal Borough of Kensington and Chelsea archive]

the country of origin of such 'Moorish' furniture, and Liberty's, for example, applied their label to pieces of their own manufacture and outsourced furniture, whether made in Britain or in the Middle East. The acquisition of the St Maurice and Purdon Clarke collections by the South Kensington Museum in 1883, and the increasing number of British visitors to Egypt, heightened the interest in Islamic motifs, which Liberty's exploited so ably in their furniture designs.

Gillows picked up on the 'oriental' style at the Royal Pavilion of the International Inventions Exhibition in the summer of 1885. At Marlborough House, the Prince of Wales displayed 'chairs of carved English oak, upholstered in cloth of gold, brought by the Prince from India', which he visited in 1874.[134] Indian taste was reflected in the extraordinary interior of Elveden Hall, designed for Maharaja Duleep Singh, as early as 1871. At the Third Annual Furniture Exhibition in the Agricultural Hall in the spring of 1883, Charles Holme & Co., no longer working in direct association with Christopher Dresser but still on Farringdon Road, exhibited two rooms from Damascus. The eighteen sections of the Oriental Court furnished by Holme 'contributed what is undoubtedly one of the greatest charms in the whole Exhibition'.[135] By 1885, Holme had been taken over by Mawe & Co., who exhibited imported Middle Eastern and Asian furniture at the 1885 *Exposition Internationale d'Anvers*. These objects, which were considered 'exotic', were exhibited alongside a more typical

Fig. 7.96 **Painted in 1882, this portrait of Mrs Luke Ionides, by William Blake Richmond, encapsulates the exoticism of the 1880s. The screen is made from Japanese kimono silk and the octagonal table in the foreground is North African, of a type imported in a variety of forms and in large numbers.** [Victoria and Albert Museum, E.1062:1, 2-2003].

Figs 7.97a & b **A chair design published in *The Cabinet Maker* in 1883. The model was created in walnut for the Fine Art Society by George Faulkner Armitage in *c.*1880 and is based on corner chairs of the George II era from the 1740s, the attenuated back reminiscent of the so-called 'barber's chair', a feature adopted by Voysey and Mackintosh in subsequent decades.** [7.97a *The Cabinet Maker*, 1 September 1883, p. 41. 7.97b: Sotheby's]

7.98

7.99

7.100

Fig. 7.98 **The ivory and ebony decoration applied onto the cedar veneer of the back of one of the Grecian-style music room chairs designed by Alma-Tadema for Henry Marquand. Made in 1885 in London by Johnstone, Norman & Co. The suite is now dispersed across various museums in London, New York, Norfolk VA, and Melbourne.** [Victoria and Albert Museum, W.25.12-1980]

Fig. 7.99 **An ivory-inlaid bench borrowing from ancient Egyptian motifs. Once wrongly attributed to Christopher Dresser, its origins are unknown. Although there are some similarities with the work of Giuseppe Parvis of Cairo, the use of mahogany suggests it was made in Europe, possibly Britain. The back swivels, allowing it to be used from either side; possibly it may have been intended for use in a museum gallery.** [Victoria and Albert Museum, CIRC.511-1965]

Fig. 7.100 **Designed by Leonard Wyburd and made by Liberty & Co. between 1883 and 1888, this oak armchair has a matching settle, with the same Egyptian-style pierced *mashrabiya* back.** [Trustees of the Cecil Higgins Art Gallery]

English look, one of numerous examples provided by the London maker Blyth & Sons, who exhibited a brown oak sideboard, or Sewell & Sewell, whose walnut sideboard was in the Queen Anne style.[136] The Colonial and Indian Exhibition at the Albert Hall in 1886 was visited by more than five million people, demonstrating a fascination for, and the widespread popularity of, imported styles. Lampooned as the 'Colinderies' the exhibition was organised under the active patronage of the Prince of Wales.

In contrast to period revivals and with little reference to mainstream developments, or even the group of designers producing English Gothic or Aesthetic ideas, furniture designed by the Dutch-born artist Lawrence Alma-Tadema was of a unique flavour, much of it made for his house in St John's Wood Grove in London. The most extraordinary example of his designs is a suite for a music room, centred around a Steinway piano, designed for Henry Gurdon Marquand, President of the Metropolitan Museum in New York. Made by Johnstone, Norman & Co., the suite was first exhibited in London in 1885 to rapturous acclaim from the press. The total cost was £25,000; the piano was said to be £5,000, the easy chairs £600 each and the smaller chairs £400.[137] Alma-Tadema also designed furniture in the Egyptian and Roman styles, seen in his paintings.

The second half of the decade continued to be a time of intellectual activity for architects and designers alike, with various societies formed to promote the decorative arts. The best-known movement is the 'Arts and Crafts', which has been extensively documented and published. Although such furniture when new was often expensive, it does not in the main form a part of the luxury market addressed in this book. Indeed, the movement's founders may have abhorred any such link. With its roots embedded in the spirit of Pugin, often with plain simple constructional details, the movement was born out of an exhibition promoted by the Art Workers' Guild in 1884, with Charles Francis Annesley Voysey as a founder member. William Morris took over as president in 1891 until his death in 1896. The ethos was to celebrate the individual craftsmen, not the company or its owner. To avoid the strain of repetitive piecework, the ideal was for one person to make an entire item, using the skill of colleagues for various disciplines such as metalwork or upholstery. The craftsman would thus no longer have to stand on a production line, repetitively handling one part of the work, such as turning or cutting out timbers. To satisfy the Ionides family's taste for modernity, Morris & Co. were commissioned to make an oak grand piano, to a design by Burne-Jones with lavish gilt gesso applied foliage decorated by Kate Faulkner, in 1883. The piano was exhibited five years later at the Arts and Crafts Exhibition Society at the New Gallery. In keeping with Arts and Crafts philosophy, the ten craftsmen involved in the work, which included the five cabinet makers, were credited in the exhibition catalogue.[138] Men such as Ruskin and Morris were inspirational in promoting the ideal of small workshops, simple design and

7.101

7.102

Fig. 7.101 Exhibited at the Arts and Crafts exhibition in 1889, this mahogany cabinet is one of a series on the theme of the charms of Orpheus. Designed by W.A.S. Benson, the contrasting incised decoration on a pale beech ground was by his brother-in-law, Heywood Sumner. [National Museum of Stockholm]

Fig. 7.102 The original version of this cabinet, now at Waddesdon Manor, was made by René Dubois in c.1774. This extraordinary and unique copy, made with the same dimensions as the original at almost 4 metres (13 feet) high, was made in England for Milton Hall in the late 1880s. [Private collection. Photograph: Christopher Payne]

construction, which became hallmarks of the movement. The term 'Arts and Crafts' was coined by the bookbinder T.J. Cobden-Sanderson for the Arts and Crafts Exhibition Society, an offshoot of the Art Workers' Guild. The society was founded in 1887, holding its first exhibition at the 'New Gallery' in Regent Street in May 1888.

The mahogany cabinet by William Benson and his brother-in-law, Heywood Sumner, **Fig 7.101**, is one of a series celebrating the charms of Orpheus. Initially exhibited at the Arts and Crafts exhibition in 1889, the cabinet has an important place in the development of the Arts and Crafts movement. Cobden-Sanderson's phrase 'Arts and Crafts' became a banner with which to teach a wider audience about aspects of furniture making and other skills. The Home Arts and Industries Association, for example, founded in 1884, staged exhibitions of 'Arts and Crafts' at the Royal Albert Hall until 1913 in an attempt to broaden the skills of working people. By 1889, it had 450 classes, 1,000 teachers and 5,000 students.[139] Benson, his name always recorded as 'W.A.S. Benson', known for his metalwork, was encouraged by Morris to make furniture. Benson opened the Eyot Works in Hammersmith in 1880 and later a retail outlet in New Bond Street, becoming a director of Morris & Co. in 1896. The Morris firm did not adhere to the fundamental principles of the cause, and their furniture became more derivative and dependent on Georgian designs as the century closed, such as the designs of George Jack shown in the following chapter.

As a postscript to the decade, and in complete contrast to the increasing popularity and influence of the Arts and Crafts style, copies of French furniture remained in fashion. An extraordinary commission, both in terms of magnitude and circumstance, was the unique copy made in the 1880s of a

Fig. 7.103 **In July 1883, under the title 'Modern Art Furniture',** *The Furniture Gazette* **published a 'Large Bookcase for Library'. Extracted from** *How to Furnish a House***, by John Ward, the design is in what, although fanciful, is a reasonably accurate rendition of the George III style of the 1780s.** [*The Furniture Gazette*, 14 July 1883, p. 25]

Fig. 7.104 **A 'ribband back' armchair in a Hindley & Wilkinson catalogue taken directly from a side chair in Chippendale's** *Director* **of 1754, plate XVI.** [Butchoff archive]

monumental fall-front desk and cabinet made in *c.*1774, with bronze mounts by Jean Goyer, the cabinet making by René Dubois. Tradition has it that the owner of the eighteenth-century cabinet guaranteed the gambling debts of a fellow officer and, to pay off the debt, sold the original to Ferdinand de Rothschild, and it is still at Waddesdon Manor. Geoffrey de Bellaigue cited an announcement in the *Bucks Herald* in 1890, stating that the original 'has just been disposed of to a representative of the Rothschild family for £30,000' – an incredible sum at the time.[140] A condition of sale was that an exact copy should be made in such a way that visitors to the original house would not realise it was a replacement. There is no known record of where the copy was made, in England or France. Close inspection shows that it has English cabinet-making construction, mostly of mahogany, and the likelihood is that the fine bronze mounts were commissioned from the Hatfield family, who worked in both London and Paris.[141] Such a copy would have been made in a sophisticated workshop; the bronzes removed from the original to be copied *surmoulé*. If the clients' pockets were deep enough, the high quality of such copies continued well into the twentieth century, see **Fig. 9.78**.

7.105

7.106

7.107

Fig. 7.105 A pedestal sideboard of a style introduced in the Hepplewhite era with a pair of large knife boxes and a matching wine cooler. The Neoclassical-style marquetry is too rigid to be mistaken for the eighteenth-century furniture that it purports to imitate. [Private collection]

Fig. 7.106 The narrow proportions of this Neoclassical-style inlaid bookcase are typical of reproductions of the 1880–1910 period. [Butchoff Antiques]

Fig. 7.107 One of a pair of commodes profusely painted with a heavy *craquelure* in the Neoclassical 'Adam' manner, each door with a different representation of motherhood. [Private collection]

7.108

Fig. 7.108 A fine marquetry *demi-lune* cabinet with all the attributes of Neoclassicism, but instantly recognisable as a Victorian interpretation of the genre. The marquetry is too thin, almost inhibited in comparison, especially the somewhat oddly draped swags on the drawers and upper part of the doors. [Private collection]

The enthusiasm for the Georgian styles, encouraged amongst others by the interests of Rossetti, Morris and the intellectual circle of the 1860s in their frustration at the lack of good contemporary design, became the mainstay of British furniture production in the last decades of the nineteenth century. By the 1890s the modified Georgian styles of the previous century became more noticeably what is now termed 'Edwardian', even if pre-dating 1901. As the population grew in the larger towns and cities, there was a premium on space for housing. Quite simply, smaller houses meant smaller rooms. Proportions of furniture were reduced; accordingly, legs became thinner and more spindly, and one glance at the overall look shows that, although based on eighteenth-century forms, an armchair such as **Fig. 7.104** was obviously not a period piece. Unless the item is documented with a known provenance or, on even rarer occasions, dated, eighteenth-century revival pieces are notoriously difficult to date accurately. Despite the vogue for the so-called Queen Anne style of the late 1870s and 1880s, much of the furniture that truly owes its design to the very early years of the eighteenth century was produced in the period from around 1900. The design for a Neoclassical bookcase, **Fig. 7.103**, appeared in *The Furniture Gazette* in 1883; yet at the same time there were the first hints of the development of a style that would be later called 'Art Nouveau', such as the Mackmurdo side chair, **Fig. 7.71**.

The last six images in this chapter are a type of furniture difficult to date within a period of twenty years. All are inspired by late eighteenth-century Neoclassicism, but the proportions and details show clearly that they are not 'of the period'. Proportions are the key, be it the overall scale of the piece or the decoration, whether marquetry or painted. The shape of the sideboard in **Fig. 7.105** is convincing at first glance but the knife urns on each pedestal are exaggerated and out of proportion. The mahogany crossbandings are too wide and the marquetry inhibited. The small display cabinet in **Fig. 7.106** is elegant but too tall and thin, the marquetry too fussy. **Fig. 7.107**, one of a pair of commodes, is beautifully painted in what is often termed the Angelica Kauffman style, but the scale of the D-shape is wrong, too narrow to be a period example, and the turned legs too tall. The marquetry *demi-lune* cabinet, **Fig. 7.108**, is much closer in proportion to the George III period as is the marquetry. However, the marquetry is too thin and rigid in comparison with eighteenth-century work, especially the somewhat oddly draped swags on the drawers and upper part of the doors.

7.109

Fig. 7.109 A kidney-shaped desk in the Sheraton manner. Stamped by Edwards & Roberts, it is difficult to date this popular style of decoration more accurately than to the 1880s or 1890s. The original design appears in Sheraton's *The Cabinet-Maker and Upholsterer's Drawing-Book*, 1791. [Private collection]

7.110

Fig. 7.110 The central drawer of this painted mahogany kidney-shaped desk has an applied brass plaque stamped 'Druce & Co, Baker Street & Portman Square'. The firm is listed in *Kelly's Directory* in 1871 as upholsterers; they probably did not make the desk but sold it as retailers. [Butchoff Antiques]

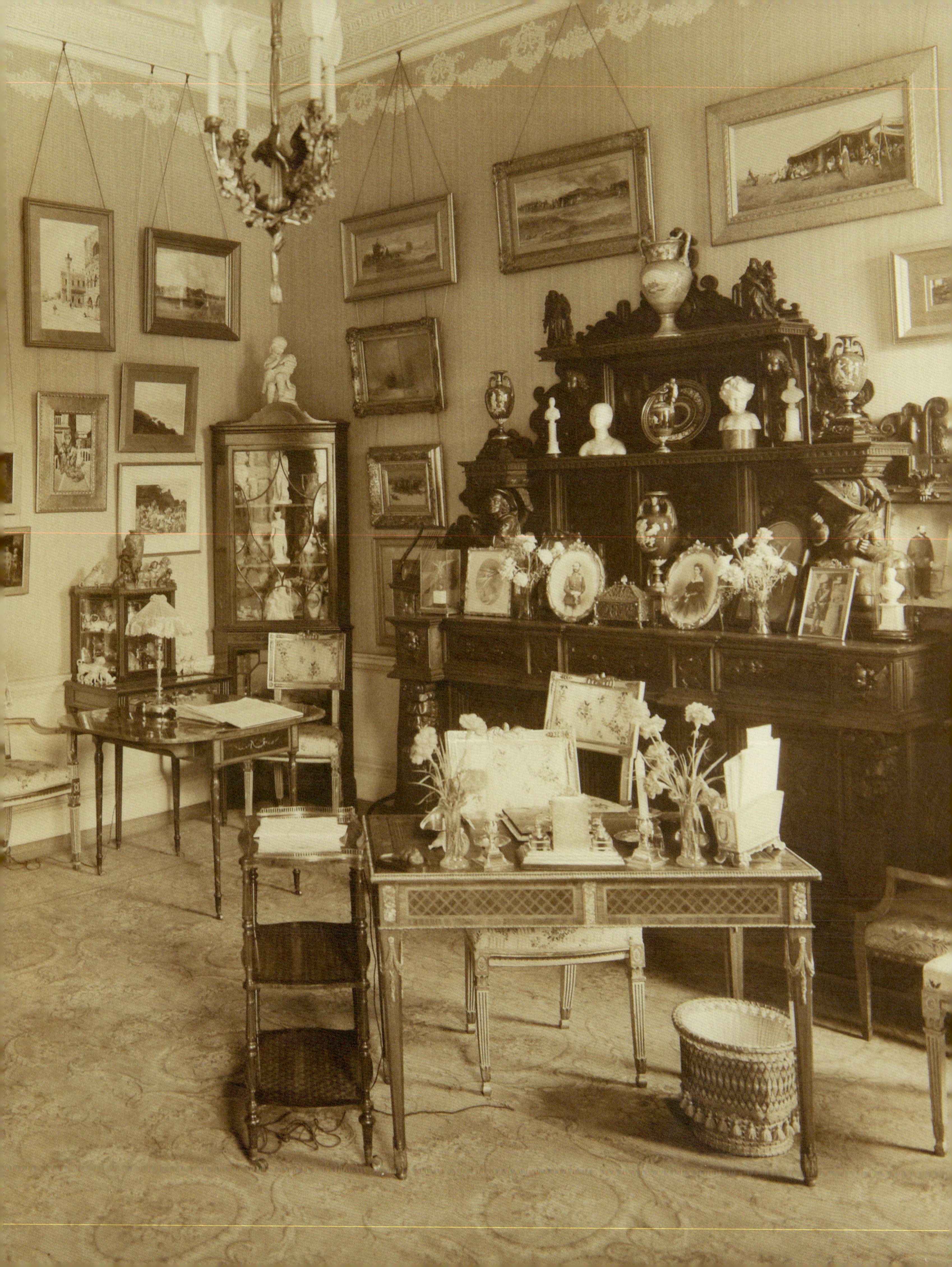

CHAPTER 8

1890s

'We have lived in this house ever since we were married and it has taken years to accumulate whatever treasures we possess. What you see is the very best. That has been my principle throughout; not to buy anything but what was really good. But it has taken time to accumulate. There has not been an unlimited exchequer to draw upon.'[1]

Unless examining the Arts and Crafts movement, or the development of Art Nouveau, the 1890s are, like the 1880s, difficult years to define in furniture design. Texts about furniture in most modern publications, if indeed they discuss and illustrate any furniture from the late nineteenth century, rarely include mainstream or reproduction furniture. There is a mass of well-documented trenchant information published about the Arts and Crafts movement but surprisingly little about the continuation of old designs, copies or the luxury market. Apart from rare exceptions such as the Museum of the Home, well-spaced museum settings show off handsome designer furniture but usually out of context.[2] The black-and-white photographs illustrated here, **Figs 8.1–8.4**, show domestic settings crammed with furniture, including dealers' showrooms, such as those of Atkinson & Co. In 1892, an article in the perennially popular *The Lady* advocated what might be taken for 'Victorian clutter': 'The secret of a pretty room is to break up the straightness... and to arrange the chairs so that they look as if a merry party of gossips had just vacated them'.[3] More enlightened firms such as Shoolbred were starting to exhibit in a cleaner, less fussy style as they and other suppliers advocated a return to Georgian simplicity, **Fig. 8.6**.

The cabinet-making trade throughout Britain at the dawn of the new decade was brisk, with few men out of work. Grievances over wages in Glasgow and nearby Beith were settled by the reduction to a fifty-one-hour working week north of the border. Surprisingly, English firms worked longer hours, for less recompense; between 4 and 6 shillings a week less than their Scottish counterparts. Notwithstanding the apparent air of prosperity, there was a steady flow of furniture makers and associated trades closing down, mainly due to bankruptcy, and partnerships were wound up on a regular basis. These were mostly small firms whose names have long since been forgotten and no doubt much of their furniture was unsigned, their history lost forever. *The Furnisher and Decorator* recorded that out of fifty branches of the Alliance Cabinet Makers' Association, twenty-six reported good or very good business, thirteen as fair or very fair, and five as 'quiet'.[4] There were fewer than one per cent of London members out of employment, less good in Manchester but good in Sheffield.

The 1890s was an era of new and emerging styles co-existing alongside period revivals and foreign influences. Atkinson & Co.'s vast showrooms on Westminster Bridge Road were crowded with large display cabinets and seat furniture in the emerging 'Quaint style', **Fig. 8.5**.[5] Sophisticated showrooms such as Shoolbred or Gillows were more akin to a comfortably furnished domestic interior than

Fig. 8.1 **Queen Alexandra's Writing or Sitting Room at Marlborough House, photographed in 1912. The glazed corner cabinet probably dates to the late 1890s, other furniture is earlier – the desk is similar to one by Holland of *c*.1870, Fig. 6.99b.** [Royal Collection Trust / © His Majesty King Charles III 2023, RCIN 2102011]

391

8.2

Fig. 8.2 'Victorian clutter' in Queen Victoria's Sitting Room at Osborne House, photographed in 1897. The tripod table draped with a cloth to the left of the desk was almost certainly made by Johann Levien in the 1850s.[6] [Royal Collection Trust / © His Majesty King Charles III 2023, RCIN 2300722]

8.3

Fig. 8.3 Every piece of furniture has a covering in this seemingly random distribution of chairs. The cluttered Drawing Room at Wickham Hall, photographed by Harold Palmer in 1897, has a French mid-nineteenth century Boulle Revival table from the 1850s on the left. [Bridgeman BAL43948]

CHAPTER 8: 1890S

Fig. 8.4 The theatre designer C.J. Phipps created the interiors of 7 Chesterfield Gardens in 1893 for Rachel Beer, Siegfried Sassoon's aunt. The room is crammed with Japanese and Chinese objects, augmented by European-made bamboo chairs; the bench on the left is by Viardot of Paris. [Bedford Lemere, 1893]

Fig. 8.5 A photograph of one of the many showrooms of Atkinson & Co. of Westminster Bridge Road, London. The drawing room furniture is in solid or veneered mahogany, whilst other photographs show their white-painted bedroom furniture, often termed 'enamelled'. [*The Opulent Eye* (Cooper), p. 68, pl. 16, Butchoff archive]

Fig. 8.6 A showroom at James Shoolbred & Co.'s Tottenham Court Road headquarters. The photograph, taken in the 1890s, shows a sophisticated display of modern interpretations of the Georgian style. [Historic England BL15582]

a crowded showroom, **Fig. 8.6**. Gillows also displayed what they termed as 'New Art', furniture which was produced in quantity but is little in demand today. For the next decade Gillows continued to thrive, refurnishing the Adelphi Hotel in Liverpool 'in the most luxurious and artistic style'.[7] Continuing a trend of previous decades, many established firms sold furniture under their own names claiming exclusive designs, although a considerable portion of their stock was made by wholesalers in the East End of London. Many firms carried a vast stock, even in central London, such as Thomas Halse of Marshall's Yard, near St Pancras church, who specialised, in 1892, in 'light easily moved tables of which he has over one thousand in stock', as well as 'a large stock of seasoned timber of every description'.[8]

The eclectic mix of designs in the line drawing in **Fig. 8.8** includes a hanging cabinet of Georgian influence in a style similar to the pair of satinwood examples in **Fig. 8.7**. Bottom left of the engraving is Moorish-inspired furniture either made in Britain or imported from the Ottoman Empire. Opposite is a Louis XV-inspired 'Quaint' corner cabinet

393

Fig. 8.7 **By the end of the century the simplicity of Georgian designs had become more popular. The thirteen-pane glass panels of this pair of satinwood hanging cabinets featured in the design for a bookcase, plate LXIII in Chippendale's *Director*. The attenuated swan neck cornices,** almost forming a heart shape, typify late nineteenth-century adaptations of Georgian scale. [Rau Antiques]

Fig. 8.8 **'A Darby & Joan Chair', drawn by Robert Coxon in the 'Quaint style'.** [*The Furniture Gazette,* 15 September 1891]

of a type that would sit happily in Atkinson's showrooms, **Fig. 8.5**. The draughtsman and designer, Robert Coxon also shows a 'Darby & Joan' settee, seemingly embracing William and Mary designs with Sheraton and a hint of Art Nouveau. Is it possible that Coxon was aware that John Darby and his wife Joan were first mentioned in a poem by Henry Woodfall, published in *The Gentleman's Magazine* in the early Georgian era in 1735?[9] His drawing of a hanging cabinet owes much to the designs of Godwin while the Moorish table by the 1890s had become a 'must have' for any fashionable household. The furniture trade was quick to capitalise on the Middle Eastern style. The popularity of exotic, Eastern style of comfort was slow to wane, *The Cabinet Maker* still promoting 'Arab' interiors as late as 1918.[10] Most 'comfortable' homes continued an eclectic mix of inherited and new furniture, special purchases, and selected treasures. In 1940 Lady Alexandra 'Baba' Metcalfe had 'brought a walnut wing-chair from Kedleston…' from 'Montacute, pieces of lacquer furniture. She had mingled Regency and Victorian with Oriental, and pinned up a Bedouin style tent over her bed…'.[11] Like Rottman & Stone, Shoolbred and Liberty imported bone-inlaid Islamic-style furniture, the best-quality pieces probably made in Cairo.

Just as distance was no longer problematic for imports, sales at home and abroad were facilitated by modern forms of transport. Like their contemporaries, Shoolbred supplied clients all over the British Isles – one of its many substantial commissions in the late 1890s were the furnishings supplied to Sir George Bullough for the newly built Kinloch Castle on the Isle of Rùm.[12] On occasion, Shoolbred furniture has an applied label which states 'From Shoolbred', suggesting that the firm had not actually made the item in its own workshops but had bought it in from the wholesale trade. Mainstream furniture for a wider public was made in commercial quantities and retailed by many different firms, such as Heals, Hindley & Wilkinson, and Maples, as well as Shoolbred.

The simplicity of Georgian design was reflected by Arts and Crafts makers who re-interpreted seventeenth- and eighteenth-century forms, underlined by honest construction.

Veneers were eschewed and dovetails and joints were celebrated and in full view. Commercial enterprises also looked to the past, with designers adapting the Georgian style by adding a modern twist of Art Nouveau or craft design. W.R. Lethaby's (1857–1931) charming seventeenth-century-style coffer inlaid with marquetry sheep, **Fig. 8.10**, made in *c.*1892, is a typical example of the honest craftsmanship of the Arts and Crafts movement; the dovetails meant to be seen and admired in a more sophisticated way than seventeenth-century examples. The coffer by Lethaby, and the cabinet by George Jack of 1893, **Fig. 8.11**, do not hide their respect for seventeenth-century models. Contemporary reviews of Jack's cabinet were mixed, one comment was that it looked like an 'exaggerated inlaid tea-caddy on a clumsy stand'.[13] Innovative when first shown at the Arts and Crafts Exhibition in 1889, the cabinet was still available in the illustrated Morris & Co. catalogue of 1912. The most elaborate of these cabinets, with profuse marquetry on all four sides, was priced at 98 guineas, with a plainer version available at 60 guineas. In 1906 other versions were sold by Morris & Co. to Stanmore Hall and to Ickworth. The hybrid

Fig. 8.9 'A Georgian Dining Room' in one of Hindley & Wilkinson's extensive showrooms, illustrated in an undated catalogue published after 1887. [Butchoff archive]

Fig. 8.10 In form this oak coffer is in seventeenth-century style albeit with Georgian-style bracket feet. Designed by William Lethaby and made by Kenton & Co., the closely dovetailed front panel is inlaid with marquetry sheep in a charming and bucolic English manner, the perfection of the Arts and Crafts idiom. [Paul Reeves]

Fig. 8.11 Revered today, George Jack's writing cabinet was criticised at its first showing at the Arts and Crafts Exhibition of 1889. [Victoria and Albert Museum, CIRC.40:1 to 10-1953]

BRITISH FURNITURE

8.12

8.13

8.14

8.15

Fig. 8.12 A dresser designed by Philip Webb for Morris & Co., a model still available in the company's 1912 catalogue. Inspired by the traditional provincial high dressers of the eighteenth century, the most easily recognisable 'modernisation' is the upper tier with a sloping top borrowed from the Reform Gothic of previous decades. [Lyon & Turnbull]

Fig. 8.13 A comfortable Saville 'easy chair' made by Morris & Co., probably designed by George Jack. The square-cut legs are a recurring feature of Jack's designs. [Victoria and Albert Museum, CIRC.401.1960]

Fig. 8.14 Designed by Gimson and made by Bowen for Kenton & Co., this writing cabinet, based on a Spanish seventeenth-century *vargueño*, was purchased from the Kenton & Co. Exhibition in 1891 by the architect and designer Allan F. Vigers. [Victoria and Albert Museum, CIRC.404:1 to 4-1964]

Fig. 8.15 Designed, or more correctly re-discovered, by George Jack and made by Morris & Co. *c.*1893–95, this Regency-style *bergère* is typical of the type of reproduction furniture made by Morris & Co., a popular model still available in their 1912 catalogue. [Victoria and Albert Museum, CIRC.249 to B-1961]

display cabinet, **Fig. 8.16**, is also by Jack. An eclectic mix of medieval, Carolean and Georgian styles, it is a wonderful and beautifully made, innovative piece. Although marquetry became less evident in his designs, possibly due to commercial considerations, Jack almost always managed to incorporate an element of inlay, such as the repeated use of a chequer banding on, for example, the cabinet, **Fig. 9.17**.

In the commercial world, Morris & Co. needed to make a profit and turned to more derivative furniture based mainly on the Georgian period. Possibly facilitated by their purchase of the Holland & Sons Pimlico workshops in 1887, Morris was able to produce more intricate furniture, eschewing the basic down-to-earth nature of the Arts and Crafts movement. Jack supplied many designs to Morris, succeeding Philip Webb as the company's chief designer in 1890. Jack's later designs for Morris were inspired by the eighteenth century and have a distinctive and highly individual charm. The Regency-style *bergère*, or caned armchair, designed by Jack, **Fig. 8.15**, was a popular model manufactured by Morris from c.1893, still available in the 1912 catalogue. Made in mahogany, the loose cushions in the illustrated example are upholstered in Morris & Co.'s Tulip chintz. Deceptively 'Regency' in appearance, a clue to the revived design is that the legs are a little too high, a detail accentuated by the brown ceramic castors. Similarly, the spade feet are too heavy: solid, practical differences that help to indicate that such pieces are later examples. Shoolbred also made a Regency-style library armchair, or *bergère*, with caned back and sides, often mistakenly thought to be eighteenth century. More refreshing is the innovative Saville mahogany easy chair made by Morris & Co., thought to have been designed by Jack, **Fig. 8.13**. The waved outlines of the rails under the arms can be compared to work on a sideboard by Jack, which was displayed by Morris & Co. at the Manchester Royal Jubilee Exhibition in 1887. The square-cut baluster legs and arm supports of the Saville chair are a distinctive style exclusive to the late Victorian era and were used frequently by Jack.

Following on from the third Arts and Crafts Exhibition in 1890, Ernest Gimson set up Kenton & Co., together with William Lethaby and Detmar Blow; Blow was soon replaced by Sidney Barnsley. The firm comprised a syndicate of architects who refused to follow the rules of the Royal Institute of British Architects. All were members of the Society for the Protection of Ancient Buildings and designed in a style sympathetic to their own ideals. Gimson wrote: 'We are going to take a shop in Bloomsbury for the sale of furniture of our own design and make'.[14] The overriding principle was that the designers were architects and that each piece was made by one artisan from start to finish. This was in stark contrast to factory workers who were often repeating the same aspect of cabinet work, no individual ever acknowledged as the actual maker. As with previous Arts and Crafts exhibitions, in 1890 individual craftspeople were recognised and celebrated, such as the Kenton foreman William Hall, who also made furniture for Voysey, and Augustus Mason, who made a cabinet for Gimson and C.R. Ashbee. Despite initial success, Kenton was

Fig. 8.16 George Jack has combined medieval-style marquetry with an oversize seventeenth-century-inspired cabinet with Georgian glazing bars. [Victoria and Albert Museum, W.42:1 to 8-1929]

Fig. 8.17 The sparse, functional workshop at Pinbury, shared by Ernest and Sidney Barnsley with Ernest Gimson, photographed c.1895. The no-nonsense, practical nature of the space was repeated in many small provincial workshops. [© Edward Barnsley Educational Trust]

Fig. 8.18 'The public will have quaintness' – *The Cabinet Maker and Art Furnisher*.[15] A high-backed chair designed by Punnett, made by Birch of High Wycombe. [Lyon & Turnbull]

wound up only two years later. Moving to the Cotswolds, Sidney and Ernest Barnsley, with Gimson and C.R. Ashbee, inadvertently started the 'Cotswold School', which carried independent furniture craftsmanship well into the twentieth century.[16] In the wake of Ashbee, more than one hundred craftspeople settled in the Chipping Campden area from 1902. The Cotswold makers became a beacon of design and construction that inherited the traditions of 'craft' furniture, soundly made and of 'simple' honesty.

The inspirational designer Charles Annesley Voysey rejected the Gothic roots of his grandfather's architectural practice and, after training with J.P. Seddon, developed a novel eye for detail. Preferring oak, his furniture is deceptively simple, its subtlety lost on commercial designers who tried to emulate his distinctive style. Unlike the Cotswold School, the legacy of the iconic work of designers like Voysey, and Walter Cave and Frank Brangwyn, has no convenient moniker for their style of design. The 1890s saw the emergence of 'The Four', the Glasgow School of designers, which included the celebrated Charles Rennie Mackintosh whose career is the subject of many books.[17] A comprehensive study of Voysey shows his breadth and skill as a designer in an Arts and Crafts genre.[18] Furniture by these gifted and innovative designers was expensive thus in a sense 'luxury', but the contemporary traditionalist or commercial maker would have scoffed at the simple outlines. In 1891, Denning encapsulated the concept of handcrafts in the title of his book, *The Art and Craft of Cabinet-Making*. This was in contrast to the more general magazines and trade catalogues, which promoted the 'Quaint' or 'Fanciful' style. It was firms such as Liberty & Co. that carried the commercial combination of Arts and Crafts and Art Nouveau into the new century, selling, for example, pieces made by the Pyghtle Works of Bedford who also made furniture for Baillie Scott and, by 1900, Voysey. Furniture magazines promoted and perpetuated a myriad of furniture styles, but it was the publication of *The Studio* from 1893 that offered an inspirational source for new designs.

In an attempt to modernise eighteenth-century French and English furniture, the English 'Quaint' style had a slender, spindly look to it. Cabriole legs lost their voluptuous nature and appeared to be almost too weak to support the weight of a cabinet, or the sitter on a chair. This type of furniture was often made of satin birch, limed or green-stained oak, or rosewood, inlaid with beech or boxwood foliage, the more expensive pieces with a smattering of mother-of-pearl or ivory inlay. Precious ivory was cut into very thin stringing and bent to follow, for example, the curved back of a chair, or a cabriole leg. There was less emphasis on deep carving than in previous decades; machine-carved panels in low relief were cheaper to produce. The heaviness of the Gothic had disappeared, and the attenuated verticality of the Art Nouveau style became more apparent. Chairs were made in considerable quantities by firms such as William Birch of High Wycombe. Birch also had cabinet-making workshops supplying, amongst others, Liberty's. E.G. Punnett's designs for the Birch firm are in an iconic English 'Quaint' style, with a flourish of Art Nouveau, **Fig. 8.18**. Although some of his furniture is substantial in nature, many of the designs of G.M. Ellwood are another hallmark of the 'Quaint' style.[19] Ellwood was a founder member of the Guild of Art Craftsmen. Both Ellwood and Punnett designed for J.S. Henry, often in a highly stylised English Art Nouveau manner with tall backs to chairs and vertical 'supports' that have more to do with style than function. 'Quaint' became a mixture of late eighteenth century with a pinch of Aesthetic, Arts and Crafts and Art Nouveau. It dominated the main trade from *c*.1890, diminishing in popularity towards 1914. Ellwood also designed for the Bath Cabinet Makers Company and the long-established Trapnell & Gane of

Fig. 8.19 George Walton designed the new Eastman Photographic Materials building and furnishings in Regent Street in 1898, shown here. The Kodak building in Glasgow followed two years later. [*The Building News*; RIBA11158]

Bristol. Three such 'Quaint' side cabinets by the Bath Cabinet Makers Company were exhibited in Paris in 1900, each having attenuated supports that give an impression of height, with unmistakable Art Nouveau overtones.[20]

The distinctive style of Heals can be attributed to Ambrose Heal, who trained in the cabinet workshops of Collier & Plucknett of Warwick. He then spent six months with Graham & Biddle, joining his eponymous family firm in 1893. Heal published *Plain Oak Furniture* in 1898, exhibiting an oak bureau, a cottage chest of drawers and a mahogany wardrobe a year later at the sixth Arts and Crafts Exhibition. Preferring to use oak, Heals exhibited an oak and ebony bedroom suite with pewter inlay, designed by Cecil Brewer, at the 1900 *Exposition Universelle* in Paris, and was awarded two silver medals.[21] By this time the Heals shop front stretched from 195 to 198 Tottenham Court Road, part of which had been used by the firm since 1840.[22] In 1915, Ambrose Heal was involved in the Design and Industries Association, whose slogan was 'Nothing Need Be Ugly'. His simple, somewhat stark furniture was at odds with Heals' earlier 'Quaint' style. At the 1900 *Exposition Universelle* in Paris and the 1901 International Exhibition in Glasgow, the firm exhibited furniture in a highly distinctive style that was far removed from designs promulgated by other mainstream makers. Ambrose Heal became a member of the Arts and Crafts Exhibition Society in 1906, joined the Art Workers' Guild in 1910 and was knighted in 1933 for his services to design. There are a host of names associated with these modern movements: Mackmurdo, Ashbee, George Walton and, not least, Charles Rennie Mackintosh, all of whom worked at the turn of the century.

A restrained designer, Walton, like many of his peers, 'modernised' eighteenth-century furniture for contemporary use. Moving to London in 1897, he created a subtle update of the late eighteenth-century style. He had worked with Mackintosh in 1896 on designs for the Buchanan Street Tea Rooms in Glasgow and, whereas Mackintosh's designs are immediately recognisable today, Walton's work is at first glance less obvious. His caned chairs, designed for the Glasgow tea rooms, are unapologetically 'Regency', **Fig. 8.20**. Walton's most distinctive designs are the solid oak benches produced by William Birch, distinguished by stylised pierced hearts in the backs. Retaining the heart motif, Walton's Brussels chair of 1901 was essentially Queen Anne in inspiration, the immediate difference being that the front legs are rounded: the use of a round, tapering leg was a novelty for this style, a feature not seen in the early eighteenth century. Walton's light, attractive tables also borrow from the eighteenth century, looking back beyond Sheraton to the George II/III era, often with Voysey-like details. As well as the Eastman building, **Fig. 8.19**, major commissions for Walton were Wern Fawr in Harlech in 1906, and between 1907 and 1910, the White House in Shiplake, both houses designed for the millionaire George Davidson.

Two Centuries of Soho gives the reader glimpses of the furniture trade of the 1890s.[23] For example, Arthur Cribb & Son, established in 1770 in Soho Square, was by the 1890s producing furniture in the Chippendale, Adam and Sheraton styles. The firm operated according to the dictum of John Ruskin – the first condition of a work of art is that it should be conceived and carried out by one person. This made Cribb's work more expensive than machine-assisted equivalents but secured them royal and aristocratic patronage.[24] *Two Centuries* commented on the extensive library devoted to George III furniture designers owned by the firm of Edwards & Roberts, managed by E. Liobl at Carlisle House in Soho Square, their premises from 1873.[25] The spectre of faking must have been apparent, and a spokesman for the firm was quoted as saying that, despite the popularity for Georgian and French Louis styles of the eighteenth century, 'very little fraud was practised'.[26] However, the evidence of the Jones Collection donated to the Victoria and Albert Museum in 1882, a collection highly praised by contemporaries, illustrates that the difference between old and new was difficult to distinguish. Modern scholarship has shown that several pieces of furniture in the Jones Collection had been altered, and in some cases considerably enhanced, and even made entirely from new. C.R. Ashbee was only too aware of the duplicity involved in some of the copies being made of period furniture. During a lecture at High Wycombe in 1892, he criticised makers for copying 'old styles well enough — even to the worm holes'.[27] The Sinclair Galleries of 55 Shaftesbury Avenue, known for their selection of Georgian marble fireplaces, decorated their showrooms with modern and antique furniture in the French and English styles in a fashion that would have rendered it difficult for the amateur buyer to be certain of the date of origin. The Sinclair Galleries were acquired in 1895 by Frederick Litchfield, son of the dealer Samuel Litchfield who had taken over Baldock's business in 1838. In his book *Antiques: Genuine and Spurious*, Litchfield wrote, '…some forty or fifty years ago the firm of Wright and Mansfield made a speciality of the reproduction of this class of furniture, and time and household wear have given their work a good tone'.[28]

Inspired by 'Arab' smoking rooms such as those made for Lord Leighton and William Burges, commercial makers saw

Fig. 8.20 A classic Regency-inspired armchair designed in 1896 by George Walton, made by Walton & Co. for Catherine Cranston's Buchanan Street Luncheon Room in Glasgow. Walton chose this ubiquitous model for his own house in London. [Lyon & Turnbull]

Fig. 8.21 The Smoking-room at the Berkeley Hotel, fitted out by S.J. Waring in 1897. Warings have combined Art Nouveau with bamboo and rattan furniture similar to work attributed to Jean-Baptiste Kohn.[29] The couch is upholstered with a flat weave or kilim carpet, of a type imported in large numbers from Turkey and Asia.

the benefits of making furniture in a similar style. Warings' smoking room, **Fig. 8.21**, mixed bamboo with kilim weaves. Hampton & Sons' room settings were less homely. Some had strong ideas about furniture for such rooms: 'I do hope I am in time to prevent you buying light oak furniture for your smoking-room; it never looks well for the "cosy semi-oriental room"'.[30] The Alhambra Room at Rhinefield House in Hampshire, a Christmas present from Mabel Walker-Munro to her husband, is another fine example.[31] So-called 'Arab' rooms left no surface untouched by Islamic mashrabiya carving and ornamentation, with imported Cairene furniture mixed with British renditions.

Hamptons also sold old furniture in their 'Galleries for Antiques' in Pall Mall, advertising 'French Furniture from Famous Collections', which included Napoleon III-period 'Buhl' furniture.[32] However, their main business was new furniture based on the traditional styles of the seventeenth and eighteenth centuries, both French and English. Advertising in *Country Life* in June 1898, Hamptons

CHAPTER 8: 1890S

8.22

8.24

8.23

Fig. 8.22 The parcel gilding on the doors of this mahogany cabinet is in a Renaissance style reminiscent of ivory marquetry by Stephen Webb. This cabinet is stamped on the drawers 'Graham & Biddle, London', either as retailers or manufacturers. [Bonhams]

Fig. 8.23 Three 'Drawing Room Cabinets' illustrated in a Hampton's catalogue show ivory-inlaid panels most probably designed by Stephen Webb. Hampton's possibly were able to acquire them when Collinson's was amalgamated by Waring & Gillow in 1897. [Butchoff archive]

Fig. 8.24 A rosewood dressing table with satinwood marquetry, part of a seven-piece bedroom suite supplied by Collinson & Lock to Standen in West Sussex in 1896.[33] The marquetry is far less detailed than the firm's ivory-inlaid furniture of the previous decade and has more in common with that of Shapland & Petter, see Chapter 9, Fig. 9.18. [© NTPL]

illustrated a comprehensively furnished 'modern dining room' in what is now somewhat irreverently termed the 'Jacobethan' style, an eclectic mix derived from the period c.1550 to 1700. Two weeks later, their advertisement for 'a modern drawing room' illustrated furniture in the French style, some pieces clearly of Parisian manufacture. In 1890 a fire in Hamptons' offices destroyed the firm's records but extant, undated catalogues show the enormous breadth of their furniture range. Like most contemporary catalogues they include retail prices. A reproduction Sheraton sideboard cost £13 10s but an oak sideboard of Art Nouveau influence was more than 20 per cent more expensive at £16 10s. The Sheraton-style sideboard was complete with a brass rail for hanging a fabric splashback, a regular feature in the eighteenth century, although few with racks survive today.

401

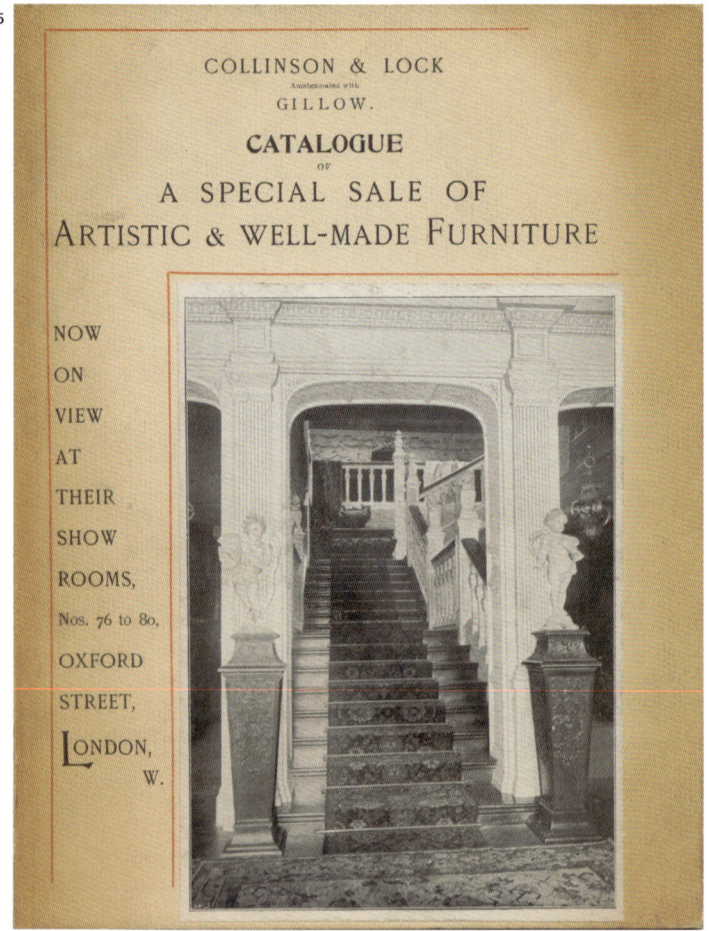

Fig. 8.25 The imposing staircase of Collinson & Lock's Oxford Street showrooms in c.1897. The catalogue was produced by Gillows to advertise their 'Special Sale of Artistic & Well-Made Furniture', to sell the old stock of Collinson & Lock. [Clive Edwards]

Fig. 8.26 A photograph of a Collinson & Lock/Gillows showroom with surplus furniture from Collinson & Lock including their 'Priscilla' armchair. The display cabinet is a contemporary French form, its complex ivory-inlaid ogee trellis marquetry copied from the work of Paris makers of the 1760s. [Clive Edwards]

Fig. 8.27 Part of a commission to furnish the royal pavilion at the Royal Agricultural Show in Warwick in 1892. Made in satinwood with fruitwood marquetry it was commissioned from James Plucknett of Warwick in 1892 by the Urquhart family of Leamington Spa. [Sotheby's]

8.28a

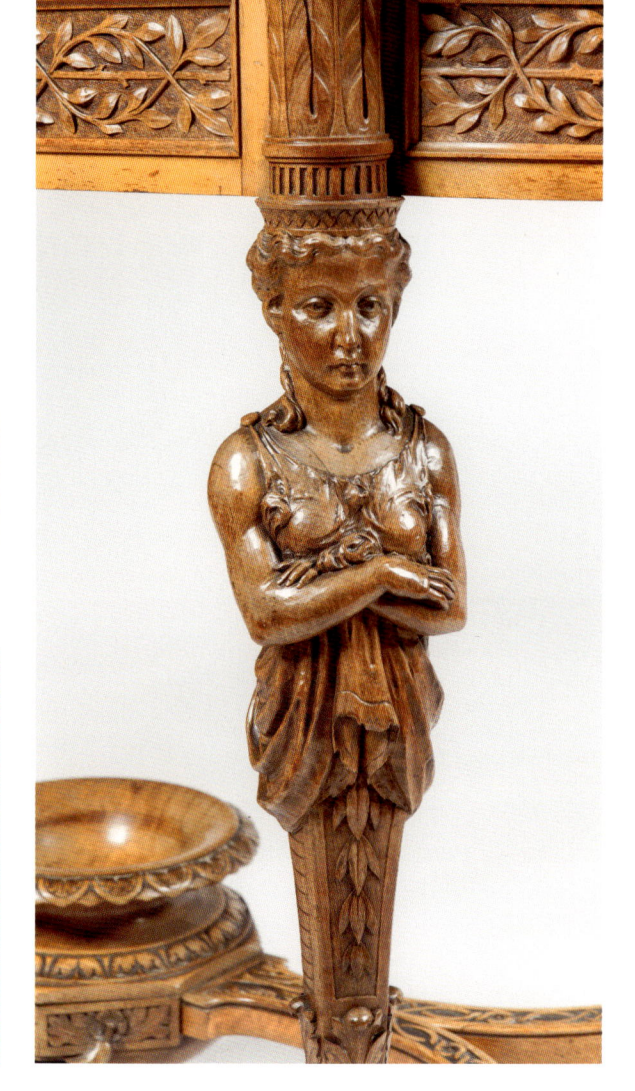

8.28c

8.28b

Figs 8.28a–c This unusual satinwood centre table with a specimen marquetry top has the ivorine label of James Plucknett of Warwick. The extraordinary sophistication of the design of the marquetry underlines Plucknett's ability as a draughtsman. [Butchoff Antiques]

Possibly reusing their display from the World's Columbian Exposition of 1893, Hamptons exhibited at the *Exposition Internationale d'Anvers* in 1894, where they installed a reproduction of the Banqueting Hall at Hatfield House in the Grand Central Gallery of the exhibition hall. Complete with a beamed ceiling and minstrels' gallery, the attention to detail was minute and 'in all respects excellent, and our national reputation for thoroughness…is thereby amply maintained by this enterprising and capable firm'.[34] The firm continued to grow despite the fire in 1890 and, registering as Hampton & Sons in 1897 they acquired James Coulson & Co. in Lisburn, Northern Ireland the following year with 'A Great Inaugural Sale' advertised in January 1898.

The cabinet stamped Graham & Biddle, **Fig. 8.22**, is similar at first glance to one made to a Gillows design of 1887 shown in the previous chapter, **Fig. 7.91**. Instead of the more familiar Webb-style ivory marquetry, the doors are in a Renaissance style, almost replicating Spanish embossed leather. Embossed leather was still fashionable, the panels often accompanied by a dubious historic provenance. Linley Sambourne had replaced his Morris wallpaper with Spanish leather in the 1880s and the Cleves Room at Preston Manor in Brighton still demonstrates the warmth and intimacy of leather panelling.[35] It is not clear if the illustrated Graham & Biddle cabinet was made or simply retailed by the firm. Likewise, an ivory-inlaid version of a more familiar Webb

Fig. 8.29 **Not an inch is undecorated in the cluttered drawing room at Haymount, Holcombe Brook in Greater Manchester. The ivory-inlaid stringing on the table in the foreground was popular on all types of furniture, especially chairs. Next to the grandiose 'Adams' fireplace is the ubiquitous Moorish table, so popular from the 1880s and beyond.** [RIBA7548 RIBA Collections]

design was purchased from Maple & Co. in Paris, the firm acting in this instance as retailers, asking £500 for it.[36] The ivory-inlaid cabinets advertised by Hamptons, **Fig. 8.23**, were almost certainly old Collinson & Lock stock.

The absorption of Collinson & Lock into Gillows in 1897 prompted 'A Special Sale of Artistic & Well-Made Furniture at Prices Considerably Under the Cost of Production' from their premises at 76–80 Oxford Street, prior to being removed to the newly enlarged premises at number 406. In an attempt to lighten the newly acquired stock, the catalogue contained 558 pieces of furniture and decorative items, **Fig. 8.25**.[37] Like other large London stores, the breadth of Gillows stock was enormous, and the showrooms had furniture ranging from well-made but simple bedroom pieces to *meubles de luxe* made in Paris by, for example, François Linke. The image, **Fig. 8.26**, of one of the Gillows rooms shows an ivory-inlaid display cabinet in an English interpretation of a form made in Paris in the 1880–1910 period. Most unusually, the ivory inlay is a complex ogee trellis, apparently inspired by Parisian wood marquetry of the 1760s. The two 'Priscilla' chairs flanking the cabinet would have been termed 'Sheraton' by Gillows, although Sheraton never advocated the cabriole leg. The legs are too thin to be anything but late nineteenth century.

Operating from 1886 to 1905, James Plucknett of Warwick continued the local tradition of finely carved furniture, the company advertising as 'Manufacturers of Rich Carved Furniture'. Plucknett's career as a furniture maker must be one of the most unusual recorded – he trained as a doctor and then as an architect, his first drawing lesson given by no less than Charles Kingsley, author of *Westward-Ho!* and *The Water Babies*. He later styled himself as an 'Art Furniture Manufacturer', a title which was presumably to show that he was up to date with contemporary terminology, although the table in **Fig. 8.28a** is French in style, somewhat old fashioned and influenced by mid-nineteenth-century Paris. In keeping with the grandeur of the large exhibitions of the period, Plucknett furnished the royal pavilion for the Royal Warwick Show held in the grounds of Warwick Castle of 1892. 'The furniture, generally, is of satin-wood [*sic*], inlaid with delicately-tinted woods…the cabinet and chimney-piece form part of a commission and are exhibited by permission of the owner'.[38] The owners were Mrs Urquhart and her daughter Mary for whom Plucknett fitted rooms in their house in Leamington Spa between 1892 and 1895, **Fig. 8.27**. The commission is recorded in detail, with photographs that illustrate similarities between the caryatids of the table, **Fig. 8.28c**, and the Urquhart chimney piece.[39]

In 1888, the businessman William Knox D'Arcy bought Stanmore Hall, adding a Flemish Renaissance-style east front to the existing Gothic architecture, commissioning Howard & Sons to decorate the interior. The large refectory table in the Entrance Hall, **Fig. 8.31**, was a simplified variation of one made by Morris & Co. for Catherine Wolfe at Vinland in Newport Rhode Island in 1883. Between 1891 and 1894 William Morris and Edward Burne-Jones created a suite of tapestries for Stanmore on the theme of the Quest for the Holy Grail. The largest of the tapestries, *The Summons*, shows a mixed series of high-back chairs that, like the Stanmore table's simple unadorned construction, are in a true Arts and Crafts tradition that inspired the Cotswold School and designers well into the twentieth century.

Original hand-drawn designs for furniture-making firms of the last decades of the nineteenth century exist but are not plentiful; many were probably discarded after they had served their purpose. A collection of 114 Hindley & Sons drawings and watercolours offers an interesting insight into the firm's work.[40] A stamp at the bottom of the drawing in **Fig. 8.33** shows the company's Oxford Street address, dating it to 1892 or later. Hindley has adapted a Hepplewhite model, simplifying the central section, probably to reduce production costs. The collection of Hindley designs shows the range of the firm's output from the 1840s to the 1890s. The highly individual 'Reading Station', **Fig. 8.32**, was ordered direct from Hindley's by the Bishop of Ely, Lord Alwyne Compton (incumbent 1885–1905). It allowed for

CHAPTER 8: 1890S

Fig. 8.30 **A room in the house of the cartoonist Edward Linley Sambourne at 18 Stafford Terrace in Kensington. The extract from an interview with Sambourne in 1893 at the opening of this chapter could describe any typical middle-class house at the closing years of the nineteenth century. 'Victorian clutter' is a well-used but apposite term for rooms that slowly and gradually accumulated furniture,** *bric-à-brac* **and** *objets d'art***. In what would seem criminal today, during a general redecoration in the 1880s the Sambournes replaced the William Morris 'Larkspur' wallpaper in the drawing room with imitation Spanish leather. See also Figs 6.91a–c.** [© The Royal Borough of Kensington and Chelsea. Image courtesy of Justin Barton]

Fig. 8.31: **The Entrance Hall at Stanmore Hall in 1892, extravagantly decorated by William Morris. The refectory table retains the solid proportions of Philip Webb's designs.** [London Offices of *The Studio*, London, 1893. The Print Collector / Alamy Stock Photo]

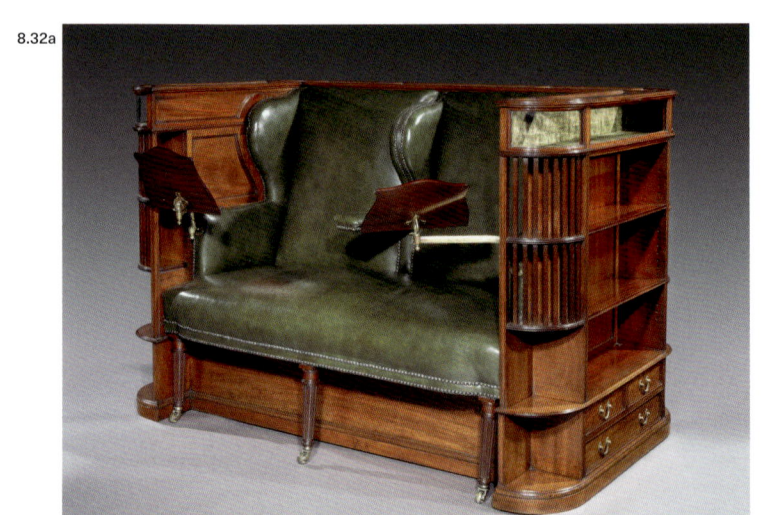

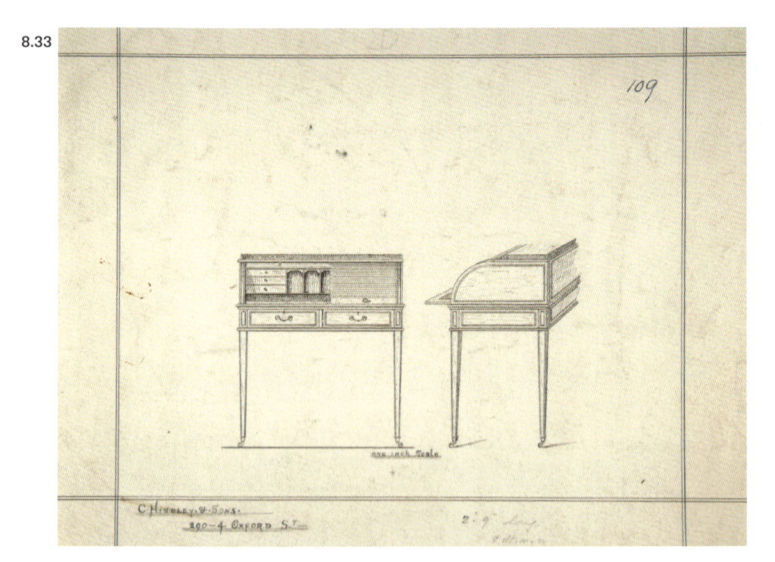

Figs 8.32a & b Dating from *c*.1892, this individually designed 'Reading Station', stamped 'Charles Hindley, Welbeck Street', was ordered direct from Hindley's by the Bishop of Ely. [Private collection]

Fig. 8.33 A drawing in black ink by Charles Hindley & Sons for a cylinder desk in the Hepplewhite style, dating to between 1883 and 1892. [Metropolitan Museum of Art, Harris Brisbane Dick Fund, 1946]

two scholars to sit together at close quarters, each with their own reading stand and small display cabinet above fitted with shelves and drawers. It is possible that Compton was familiar with the neat precision of the fitted furniture made for Sir John Soane some seventy years earlier, such as a drop-leaf table attributed to John Robins.[41] Like many of their contemporaries, Hindley's also supplied fitted furniture such as inglenooks and fireplace surrounds. British furniture makers realised the potential of Russia as a marketplace, and although there is no record of the Empress of Russia ordering furniture from Hindley's, the Court Journal of 22 June 1893 noted an order for fabric sent by them to her at the Alexander Palace in St Petersburg. Charles Hindley was granted an entry visa but there is no known record of him visiting Russia.

Illustrations in weekly journals of the early 1890s, such as the *The Cabinet Maker and Art Furnisher*, show the dominance of the early Chippendale style, and of French furniture, both of which usually manifest themselves as an unsatisfactory interpretation of Rococo. The weekly issues of *The Furniture Gazette* contained numerous line drawings and designs, the outlines of which are familiar today, but they rarely exactly correspond to extant examples of furniture. Most of the artists or designers appear to have been in the regular employ of the journal; in addition to their work in a vaguely eighteenth-century manner there was an increasing interest in the Italian Renaissance and a smattering of Gothic. The numerous line drawings in each edition create a solid picture of the trade at the time with a dazzling array of styles adapted from previous centuries without an attempt to deceive. Designers and manufacturers were keen to point out their 'improvements' in both design and comfort. One of the most prolific in-house artists for *The Furniture Gazette* was James Barr Angus, whose work, unfortunately somewhat uninspiring, is nevertheless a good indication of the slow pace of mainstream furniture design and decoration between the 1870s and 1900. Elsewhere, a long-running series of illustrations was entitled, rather optimistically, 'Original Designs for Furniture', **Fig. 8.34**, another 'Suggestive Sketches of a Cozy Corner'. By the 1890s, however, accurate designs from eighteenth-century pattern books were published, with Georgian makers such as Mayhew and Ince being introduced alongside more familiar names of Chippendale and Sheraton.[42] Good reproductions of Sheraton small tables and cabinets were very popular. *The Cabinet Maker and Art Furnisher* had a distinctive house style of

Fig. 8.34 **A line drawing in the distinctive hand of Henry Pringuer Benn, one of several published in** *The Cabinet Maker and Art Furnisher.* [*The Cabinet Maker and Art Furnisher*, 1892]

line-drawings, possibly all from the same hand. They include drawings by Henry Pringuer of the Benn publishing family which show a sinuosity and lightness of form that define the decade. Probably not intended for the luxury market, they are more appropriate for the middle-class buyer. From 1897 lavish colour supplements were introduced, and a variety of colourful reproduction styles are shown in Chapter 9.

Joseph Crouch was clearly familiar with all the prevalent fashions. His designs for *Apartments of the House* ranged from Shakespearean figures to commercial Arts and Crafts, and to a cosy corner with a wing armchair next to a 'grandfather clock', with a pair of slippers ready for the wearer, **Fig. 8.38**. Correctly termed a longcase clock, the term 'grandfather clock' probably came into common usage at the time of the popular 1876 song 'My Grandfather's Clock'. Crouch's eclectic collection of pencil, ink and wash drawings included a Hepplewhite or Sheraton-inspired shield-back settee, **Fig. 8.35**, with a similar look to the Darby and Joan chair in **Fig. 8.8**. The legs on Crouch's settee are too thin in comparison to the generous size of the shield-shaped back to be anything but a late nineteenth-century interpretation. In keeping with the nineteenth-century's love of nostalgia, one of his drawings included a Shakespearean figure seated at a refectory table, **Fig. 8.36**, while his interpretation of a cabinet in *Apartments of the House* has become almost Islamic in manner, **Fig. 8.39**.

Advertisements in contemporary journals are an indication of the size and complexity of the East End furniture trade but also show that throughout Britain provincial makers were increasingly important. Exhibitions continued to be a valuable venue for makers in both London and the regions. The National Electrical Exhibition, held at the Crystal Palace in 1892, hosted a plethora of furniture makers and retailers, their work in an eclectic mixture of styles, such as a Jacobean-style dining room by Allen & Manooch and a fashionable 'Eastern Boudoir' by J. & H. Cooper of Bath. In common with some but not all exhibitions, admission was restricted to those presenting a visiting card.[43] There were also smaller exhibitions, for example the Art Furniture Exhibition in Shoreditch in June 1898. George Lock, who had withdrawn his capital from Collinson & Lock in 1896, supervised the choice of furniture for the Shoreditch exhibition, his reputation a guarantee that the period furniture on display was genuine. A contemporary journalist remarked that there had not been such a display of old furniture in the East End since the closure of the Bethnal Green exhibition in 1875, which had included important loans of historic furniture from Sir Richard Wallace.[44]

Established in *c.*1880, the wholesale East End manufacturers J.S. Henry advertised in February 1893 as being an 'Originator and Manufacturer' with 'Art Furniture Novelties', and as a 'Designer of Quaint and Artistic Furniture'. The extent of Henry's trade was reported as: 'a name well-known…throughout…the United Kingdom, but also in many parts of our British possessions abroad'.[45] By the time of the 1900 *Exposition Universelle*, where they exhibited through a Paris retailer, the firm's previously simple Art Nouveau-inspired furniture had become more sophisticated, often incorporating decorative inlays, and they were awarded two silver medals. Three years later, at the Arts and Crafts Exhibition Society, most of their designs were by George Montague Ellwood, but Henry also absorbed design features of others, such as W.J. Neatby, E.G. Punnett and Voysey. By 1903, Henry's output included furniture to

Fig. 8.35 **A Joseph Crouch pen, ink and wash drawing of a shield-back settee or 'Darby and Joan' chair of Hepplewhite inspiration.** [Victoria and Albert Museum, E.682-2005]

Fig. 8.36 **A Shakespearean figure as imagined by Crouch, seated at a refectory table.** [© Victoria and Albert Museum, E.674-2005]

Fig. 8.37 **A stylised cabinet drawn by Joseph Crouch combining Arts and Crafts with Art Nouveau.** [© Victoria and Albert Museum, E.656-2005]

Fig. 8.38 **Joseph Crouch's design in *Apartments of the House* for a cosy corner with a wing armchair similar to examples by Birch & Co., next to a 'grandfather' clock, slippers at the ready.** [© Victoria and Albert Museum, E.662-2005]

designs by not only Ellwood but also George Walton and W.A.S. Benson and they exhibited at the Dublin Museum, moving away from simple 'Quaint' furniture and closer to Art Nouveau. As early as 1893 the Henry telegraphic address was 'Meuble, London', the firm clearly aware of the fashion for French design.

Searches of Kelly's Street Directories and trade journals throw up numerous names of furniture makers and retailers, but knowledge of their production is lost today. There are hundreds of examples, such as G. Chant (wholesale cabinet makers), William Bailey & Co., or Law Brothers (East End wholesalers), whose work may never be identified. Others

CHAPTER 8: 1890S

Fig. 8.39 **A cabinet of eclectic Chippendale and Moorish influence by Joseph Crouch illustrated in** *Apartments of the House c.*1890. [© Victoria and Albert Museum]

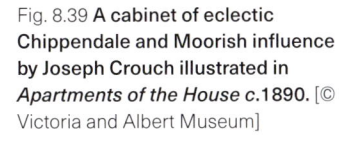

Fig. 8.40a **An extravagant, part-glazed mahogany display cabinet by Morant & Co. in the Chippendale revival manner, the cresting flanked by a pair of Chinese-inspired figures, each with a long Manchurian-style queue. The signature, 'Morant & Co, 91 New Bond Street' is with a die-cast cold metal stamp. Neatly alongside the stamp the date '1898' has been added by hand with an incising tool.** [Wick Antiques]

Fig. 8.40b **The complex eclectic fretwork in a mix of Gothic and Rococo on Morant's display cabinet is made in the traditional manner, with several layers of cross-grained lamination, as used for example on the gallery of so-called silver tables in the mid-eighteenth century for extra strength.** [Wick Antiques]

such as Harper, Osmond, Pateman and Perrin, are presently recorded in name only with little or no detail. In a detailed and thorough account of many of the East End makers, Kirkham (1987) published considerable information but only a small amount of these firms' work can be identified, in part from advertisements and catalogues but rarely with a maker's mark. East End production was not restricted to the wholesale market. Canny buyers sourced everyday furniture from East End firms such as those of William Wallace & Co. of Curtain Road and B. Cohen & Sons, who were able to supply furniture as good as 'aristocratic Bond Street'.[46]

409

Fig. 8.41 **Two designs for a popular style of large side cabinet made with endless variations of form and detail by a wide range of London and provincial makers.** [Supplement to *The Furniture Gazette*, May 1893]

Fig. 8.42 **A 'Chippendale' bookcase in carved mahogany at Edmond Kahn's showrooms in 1892.** [*The Furniture Gazette*, 15 October 1892, p. 198]

Fig. 8.43 **Entitled somewhat hopefully 'A Pompadour Cabinet', the legs of this 'Original Design of a French Music cabinet' are typical of the decade immediately prior to the Edwardian era.** [*The Furniture Gazette*, 16 January 1893, p. 247]

An exhibition in 1893, one of many held at the Royal Agricultural Hall in Islington, showed side cabinets by H.L. Benjamin (working near Curtain Road), made in a style that is seen today in every second-hand shop (**Fig. 8.41**), many now with the superstructure and mirror long since separated. This type of cabinet was made by countless East End makers, such as The Hackney Furnishing Company, but most are unsigned. Mirror glass had slowly become less expensive over the course of the nineteenth century, the costs falling with the repeal of duty in 1845 and by the end of the century it was used in ever-increasing quantities.[47] Victorian mirror glass is much thicker than that used in eighteenth-century mirrors and the distinct bevel is more pronounced. Bedroom suites, such as those by J.J. Child at their Eagle Works, included a dressing table with a fixed swing mirror and wardrobe doors with a bevelled mirror. This had obvious advantages for vanity purposes and also for reflecting light. Much of the glass was made in Yorkshire and Lancashire but despite transport costs, French and Belgian producers were able to produce purer glass at competitive prices.[48]

The economic benefits of the 'showroom-warehouse' are self-evident and gained in popularity in the latter years

8.44

Fig. 8.44 A copy of Riesener's 'Fontainebleau' commode made entirely by British workmen in 1903 to match one made in Paris by François Linke purchased through Johnstone, Norman & Co in 1893. The Linke version had been offered by Queen Victoria's household to the Duke of York and Princess Mary of Teck as a wedding present. Both are now in the Throne Room at Hillsborough Castle. [Royal Collection Trust / © His Majesty King Charles III 2023]

Fig. 8.45 An illustration from a Hindley & Wilkinson catalogue of a lavish furniture showroom at 8 Old Bond Street exclusively devoted to Paris-made furniture, including pieces by leading makers such as Linke and Sormani. [Butchoff archives]

8.45

of the century, often comprising an impressive entrance to ground-floor showrooms below purpose-built workshops. The rapid development of Edmond Kahn's business in Holborn and their Curtain Road warehouse in the East End drew special attention. Their business was evidently large with a comprehensive stock. Some showrooms were dedicated to imported French furniture that 'reminds one of the historian's descriptions of the Palace of St. Cloud'; another room was 'filled with copies of old Chippendale, Sheraton and Hepplewhite furniture'.[49] Kahn had retired as a director of the influential interior furnishing firm of Carlhian & Beaumetz in 1886, and set up his own business importing French furniture. He used the occasion of the extension of his showrooms at 117 Curtain Road to promote the importance of his imported luxury furniture from Paris, notably that of François Linke.[50] French influence can be seen in much of the furniture produced in Britain at this time, although it seems that all that an object needed to be described as 'French' were slender cabriole legs. One such piece, **Fig. 8.43**, was optimistically termed 'A Pompadour Cabinet' but is of a design that would have been abhorrent to a French maker. The opulence of the French style was thought suitable for the royal family. A copy of a commode by J.-H. Riesener, the original made in *c.*1785, was given by the Queen's household as a wedding present to the Duke of York and Princess Victoria Mary of Teck, who were married in July 1893. The supplier was Johnstone, Norman & Co. using their 67 New Bond Street address, the year before they merged with Morant at number 91.[51] Examination of the commode shows that it was made in Paris, almost certainly an unsigned model by François Linke.[52] Another version was ordered by the Princess of Wales ten years later. According to a brass label on the back, the later example was made entirely by British workmen for the Princess of Wales and intended for use at Marlborough House, **Fig. 8.44**.

On the retirement of Charles Hindley, his sons Charles and Edward amalgamated with Wilkinson & Sons soon after

Fig. 8.46 One of a series of highly ornate designs for French rooms by James Barr Angus. The cabinet has more in common with the output of numerous East End makers. [*The Furniture Gazette*, 1 April 1889, pl. 2]

Fig. 8.47 L. & E. Levasseur made cabinet furniture in the French manner as well as this accomplished reproduction of a Chippendale armchair. [*The Furniture Gazette*, 6 April 1893, p. 306]

Wilkinson exhibited at the 1890 Arts & Crafts Exhibition. Much of the old stock was sold at auction in June 1892 'at a considerable reduction'. Despite the amalgamation with the long-established Wilkinson, the *Furniture Gazette* wrote: 'One by one the genuine old firms are dropping out'.[53] As Hindley & Wilkinson, the firm produced a catalogue with rooms lavishly furnished in the French style with furniture by Linke, Sormani and other leading Paris makers, **Fig. 8.45**. A typewritten price list included a Louis XV-style chest of drawers by Sormani, the retail price marked at £220. A Sormani-style dressing table retailed at £150, the cost price to Hindley & Wilkinson being £100. The cost price of the copy of the celebrated Louis XV *bureau du Roi* after Oeben and Riesener was £1,530, retailing at £2,800. Unfortunately, the list does not state the maker's name, although the catalogue boasted, somewhat hopefully, that it was recently executed by them 'to a special commission'.

The ever-increasing popularity of French furniture, both reproduction and innovative, continued throughout the 1890s alongside British period styles and well into the twentieth century. Commenting on the 1893 Furniture Trades Exhibition held at the Islington Agricultural Hall, *The Furniture Gazette* admired the Levasseur family's 'splendid assortment of French cabinet work (of English manufacture, bye-the bye) in the popular Louis Quinze and Louis Seize periods'. E. Levasseur Junior, of Portland Mews in London, was clearly a gifted carver, and his large workshop was capable of reproducing French chairs in the Louis XV and XVI styles.[54] The engraving of an armchair by Levasseur, **Fig. 8.47**, showed the firm was also producing furniture in the English manner, the armchair being an accomplished interpretation of the Chippendale style of the 1750s and 1760s. It is however, like many extant copies from the late nineteenth century, too 'thin' and 'mean' to be anything other than a late Victorian interpretation. Few images survive of documented furniture made by the London firm of S. Trier & Co. who sold reproductions of English and continental-style furniture. Also antique dealers, they described themselves as 'Specialists in the Reproduction of Antique Furniture… the choicest pieces selected from Continental Museums (by special permission)'.[55] It would be interesting to learn more of these 'special permissions' and how the work was copied, by measured drawings or simply photographs. At the 1893 Furniture Trades Exhibition, Trier was marked out for praise: 'their reproductions from the antique are conspicuous for the high order of their workmanship'.[56]

The East End makers Henry and Alfred Vaughan had a flourishing enterprise with a large showroom. 'Old English and Medieval styles are Mr. Vaughan's specialities'. Some of their designs were continued by H.L. Benjamin.[57] Curtain Road in Shoreditch, north of Liverpool Street station, will be forever associated with the British furniture-making industry, a rare survival in the twenty-first century being the showroom of SCP Ltd, still with its late-Victorian sprinkler system.[58] Furniture by provincial makers such as Hutchins & Sons of Weymouth appears to be unrecorded whereas W. Bartlett & Sons of High Wycombe are well known for the chairs they exhibited. At the Furniture Trades Exhibition, the aptly named Mikado Company of Birmingham put

In 1893, to celebrate the 400th anniversary of Christopher Columbus's 'discovery' of the 'New World', the United States mounted the largest international exhibition of the decade in Chicago, the World's Columbian Exposition. The scale was vast, the technology employed cutting edge: the 'Great Wharf' or 'Moving Sidewalk' seven years ahead of the *trottoir roulant* installed at the Paris *Exposition Universelle* of 1900. Britain and its colonies had a space of approximately 46,500 square metre (500,000 square feet) at the exhibition, twice the space allotted to them in Paris in 1889. Exhibiting 'Furniture of Interiors, Upholstery, and Artistic Decoration', British firms won a variety of awards, amongst them Collinson & Lock, whose display of a dining room and a bedroom included furniture incorporating ivory-inlaid marquetry designed by Stephen Webb. The interior decoration and furniture in Victoria House, the headquarters of the Royal Commission at the Chicago fair, was supplied by Johnstone, Norman & Co., which included 'some of the finest reproductions of XVIth and XVIIth Century work from well-known English Mansions and Collections'.[61] Notably the firm was still exhibiting variations of its expanding tables, the invention patented by Robert Jupe in 1836 and revived at the Paris exhibition in 1878.[62] As well as numerous exhibitors of brass bedsteads and billiard tables, the following major furniture makers were listed with examples of their production:[63]

'330 Collinson & Lock, 76-80 Oxford Street, London, W. 'Specimens of dining- and bed-room fitted up with suitable hangings and appropriate furniture, china, art objects, and watercolours; furniture of various descriptions, examples of marqueterie [*sic*], ivory inlaying, carving; repoussé work, including electrical fittings.'

'331 Elliott, James, 54 Brook Street, London, W. Decorative hangings and furniture of interiors, lustra painting; bossa facilis [a method of embossing and decorating metal].'

'332 Gregory & Co., 212, 214, 216 Regent Street, also King Street, London, W. Carved walnut sideboard, side table, chimney piece and overmantel, chairs, settee, and decorations in Italian style, carved mahogany Chippendale bookcase, chairs, tables and decorations.'

'333 Hampton & Sons, Pall Mall East and Cockspur Street, Charing Cross, London, S. W. Works, 43 Belvedere Road, London, S.E.. Facsimile reproduction of the banqueting hall of Hatfield House, England, the seat of the Marquess of Salisbury.'

Fig. 8.48 A showroom of Mavers of Old Broad Street illustrated in 1892, the advertisement somewhat optimistically entitled 'Old Examples of Chippendale, Sheraton Queen Anne & Jacobean Furniture etc.'. [*The Furniture Gazette*, 15 February 1892, p. 37]

Fig. 8.49 Looking west from the Peristyle, Court of Honor and Grand Basin of the 1893 *World's Columbian Exposition* in Chicago, where British interests were allotted an area of approximately 46,500 square metres (500,000 square feet). [Chicago History Museum © Chicago Historical Society]

on a large display of bamboo furniture with suites named 'Sandringham' and 'Empress'.[59] William Ellmore & Son of Leicester also supplied a wide range of bamboo furniture, from cabinets to seat furniture, closing in 1914. Opening a large showroom in London in 1887, they exhibited furniture in bamboo, willow, cane and rush.[60] Also at the exhibition were Frank P. Levi of Crowndale Works, Bayham Street in Camden who purported to make first-class Chippendale furniture, but as was common at the time, for 'Chippendale' read 'Pompadour'.

413

'335 Johnstone, Norman & Co., 67 New Bond Street, London, W. Patent circular expanding dining table, patent circular expanding and extending dining table; a collection of inlaid and carved panels in a variety of woods and metals, illustrating their adaptation to cabinet work.'

'340 Roberts, Geo., 379 Bramall Lane, Sheffield. Antique carved oak and decorative furniture.'

The reports in the *Furniture Gazette* of January 1890 are a useful contemporary source of information on industry practice. A visit to the William Angus & Co. East End workshops in Tabernacle Street showed that, with a branch in the United States, Angus was able to cut costs by buying ready-sawn timber from the Americas, the rough machining already completed. The easier access to suitable timbers by United States manufacturers, and their advanced use of machinery, was a threat to British trade at a commercial level, but their furniture was generally not of a quality or sophistication to concern British luxury makers. Another American manufacturer, Henry Herrmann, had set up business in London in 1877 and boasted a large frontage on Dod Street in Limehouse, which backed onto the River Lea canal with direct access to the docks, greatly facilitating the transport of imported timbers shipped up the Thames, **Fig. 8.50**.[64] Many of the larger firms had their own timber mills and continued to buy their wood for veneers as logs, delivered to main ports such as London, Liverpool and Bristol. The same cities were the point of export for furniture, no doubt some of the imported raw timber going back in finished form to the country of origin. This is especially so with the high demand in cities in Australia, such as Melbourne. Published monthly reports recording the value of furniture exported around the globe. Not all of the destinations are immediately obvious: in January 1893 an incredible £139,925 worth of furniture was sent to Lyttelton in New Zealand, compared to £23,000 to New York.[65] In the United States, the Tariff Act became law on 1 October 1890, raising the duty on many imports to almost 50 per cent, enough to slow down demand for luxury goods into the United States. The act, commonly called the 'McKinley Tariff', required goods to have their country of origin marked on them. Between 1890 and 1902, furniture imported into the United States was stamped with the name of the country of origin, and from 1902 'Made in' was added, a useful dating aid. In the third quarter of the twentieth century, some dealers removed these stamps as it made it too obvious that the piece was, at the time, under one hundred years old and therefore did not qualify as 'antique'.[66]

Despite the growth of the export industry and with the increased use of machinery, in the early years of the decade there was only a slight increase in the number of cabinet makers in employment. Booth lists a count of 29,617 across the country, an 1891 census shows that over 4,000 of these were women, most under the age of twenty-five.[67]

By 1908 the Nottingham firm of Foster & Cooper, cabinet makers and art furniture manufacturers, were styling themselves as 'one of the Largest Manufacturing Firms in the Kingdom'. They frequently commissioned Maurice B. Adams,

Fig. 8.50 **The generous frontage of Herrmann's workshops, Dod Street, in Limehouse, conveniently near the dock.** [Butchoff archive]

Figs 8.51 & 8.52 On the left, a stylised Windsor armchair made by J. Britnell, designed by Ernest Gimson and shown at the third exhibition of the Society of Arts and Crafts in 1890. It was described as being up to date in the 'Quaint Style'.[68] On the right, a more conventional Windsor armchair from Laycock Abbey, drawn by Joseph Crouch for *Apartments of the House*, c.1890. There are a pair of dark-stained armchairs of a similar design at 18 Stafford Terrace, the home of Linley Sambourne. [8.51: *The Furniture Gazette*, 15 November 1890, p. 297. 8.52: Victoria and Albert Museum, E.691-2005]

a major proponent of the Arts and Crafts style, as a designer. Adams lived and worked in the Bedford Park development in West London, the world's first garden suburb. Illustrations of furniture shown at the third exhibition at the Society of the Arts and Crafts in the autumn of 1890 show pieces that would not be grouped under the banner of Arts and Crafts today. A significant curiosity at the exhibition is the drawing of a Windsor armchair by Ernest Gimson, **Fig. 8.51**. Without the accompanying text in the *Gazette*, it would be impossible to attribute such a design in the Quaint style to Gimson, who was described by Pevsner as 'the greatest of the English architect-designers'.[69] A possible explanation is that at the time of publication Gimson was a young man of twenty-five and had not yet developed his distinctive brand of Arts and Crafts.

The Ladies' Work Society was established in 1875 to aid gentlewomen in financial hardship. Mainly known for their textiles, they exhibited widely and, at the Society of the Arts and Crafts exhibition of 1890, exhibited a painted mahogany table in the eighteenth-century tradition, designed and made by M** Shoesmith, **Fig. 8.53**. The engraving also shows an octagonal table in satinwood by Wilkinson & Son, soon to become Hindley & Wilkinson. Other commercial firms seemingly exhibited alongside 'crafts' makers, such as Howard & Sons who exhibited a sideboard, **Fig. 8.55**. The aims of the exhibition, promoted by William Morris, were 'to supply furniture of such excellent manufacture that the name of the workman shall in time be more necessary than its style. When completed is to be stamped with the name of the workman. All machinery is to be religiously boycotted.'[70]

Exhibiting at the Newcastle Royal Jubilee Exhibition, Robson & Sons of Newcastle-upon-Tyne, 'were the largest and most complete house furnishing establishment in the North of England' and were one of many northern firms making and retailing fine-quality furniture.[71] They experimented with Art Nouveau-style foliage, albeit in a somewhat self-conscious manner. A well-made mahogany and marquetry cabinet bearing the firm's label was designed in a thoroughly modern style, the innovative effect somewhat diluted by short ogee bracket feet reminiscent of the George II period, in a manner reminiscent of George Jack's designs.[72] The appearance of an applied label raises the question as to whether it was made or simply retailed by Robsons.

The nineteenth-century revival of mid- to late eighteenth-century Georgian furniture produced many copies which are notoriously difficult to date. A prime example is a 'Salisbury Antique Table' shown in Chapter 1 – 1820s, **Fig. 1.48**. In the twentieth century, dating of reproduction pieces was often wildly optimistic with, for example, 1920s copies catalogued as late Victorian; research is needed to establish more precise dating. Many such pieces exist, especially in the Chippendale style, often with little or no provenance, not attributable with certainty to any specific cabinet maker's workshop. For example, the firm of Henry Samuel of Oxford Street, listed in *Kelly's Directory* in 1891 as 'Dealers in Works of Art', produced good-quality furniture in the George II style, emulating the period of the 1740s to 1760s in a quasi-Chippendale manner, or sometimes direct copies. A good example is the pair of elegant armchairs, **Fig. 8.57**, chairs

415

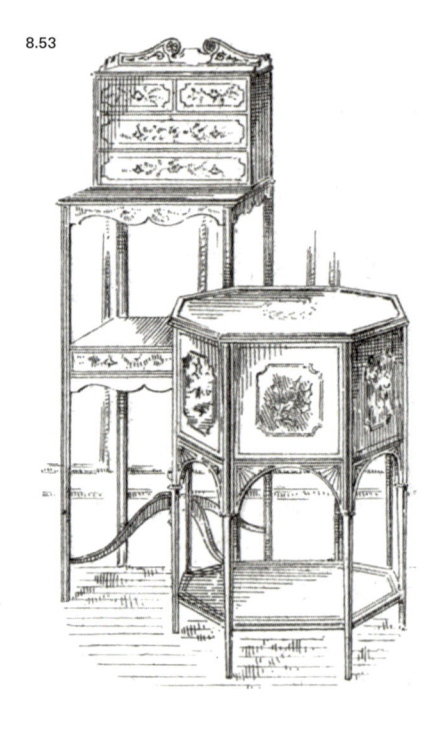

Figs 8.53 & 8.54 Two engravings of contrasting exhibits at the 1890 Arts and Crafts Exhibition Society. LEFT: A painted mahogany table in late George III style exhibited by the Ladies' Work Society. Alongside it is an inlaid satinwood octagonal table by Wilkinson & Son. RIGHT: A more innovative exhibit based on ancient Egyptian models, designed by Leonard Wyburd. [*The Furniture Gazette*, 15 November 1890, p. 298]

Fig. 8.55 A cabinet exhibited by Howard & Sons at the third exhibition of the Society of the Arts and Crafts in 1890. It is difficult to believe that pieces such as this boycotted machinery, as advocated by William Morris. [*The Furniture Gazette*, 15 November 1890, p. 298]

which have in the past been considered to be eighteenth century.

Another group of furniture by H. Samuel, based in Oxford Street, is at first glance of a similar style but, shows the firm's diversity and may be only the tip of the iceberg in understanding the range of the furniture produced by the firm.[73] The group consists of four items formerly at Shottesbrooke Park, a Tudor house in Berkshire, the furniture almost certainly acquired by Guy or Rose Smith prior to 1913 when the house featured in *Country Life*.[74] Some of the work is typical of Samuel's known output in the George II style. Less familiar is work in the Hepplewhite style such as the set of dining chairs in **Fig. 8.58**. The curious, somewhat idiosyncratic, cabinet on stand, **Fig. 8.56a**, is charmingly inventive, reflecting the continuing fashion for the Chinese taste; here the interior is red and gilt-japanned, an adaptation of the early eighteenth-century cabinet on stand. It is not clear if the firm had its own workshops. The likelihood is yes; if not, it used the same subcontractors throughout as there is a consistent theme and handling, especially in their renditions of the early Chippendale style. One fascinating example of Samuel's ability to adapt is a *commode à l'anglaise*, with two doors made from exquisite chinoiserie marquetry panels which must have once adorned a cabinet made by the Roentgen family in the 1770s.[75]

Henry Samuel's furniture stamp included the 484 Oxford Street address. On occasion the firm added a four-figure number in a similar manner, for example, to Gillows, Collinson & Lock or Wright & Mansfield. It is not presently known whether these numbers are serial numbers for identifying designs or cabinet maker's plans, or whether they relate to commission numbers. If the numbers started at zero, the number '8280' on the bookcase in **Fig. 8.61** suggests the Samuel enterprise was substantial. Most of the firm's identified furniture is in the mid-eighteenth-century style, made of mahogany, but a few satinwood pieces are recorded. Samuel, like many of the larger contemporary firms, had an antique furniture department. An early George III-style supper table with chinoiserie open fret sides is known as incorporating earlier elements, suggesting that the antique department was not particularly discerning.[76] The sumptuous octagonal partners' desk in a George II style, **Fig. 8.60**, is an interesting and unusual copy of a desk acquired by George IV for the Octagon Library at Buckingham Palace (then known as Buckingham House), shown in a watercolour of 1818, **Fig. 8.59**. It is difficult to know the exact date of manufacture of the copy. The drawer linings, with a slight blackish stain – a

CHAPTER 8: 1890S

8.56a

8.57

Figs 8.56a & b (overleaf) An individual interpretation of a cabinet on stand by Henry Samuel. The mahogany base is an adaptation of the George II 'Chippendale' style and supports a cabinet of a style that had been popular in the late seventeenth century. The cabinet is shown open overleaf revealing a stunning scarlet red japanned interior contrasting with the solid mahogany doors. The drawers follow a traditional arrangement of Chinese original box cabinet interiors imported into Western collections. The copper cabinet clasps, drawer handles and escutcheons also follow Asian designs. The raised gesso japanning of figures in mountain landscapes with an arched bridge is a hectic Western interpretation, including a ubiquitous bridge. [Both images: Sotheby's]

Fig 8.57 A pair of open armchairs by Henry Samuel in the Chippendale style, once thought to be mid-eighteenth century.[77] To add confusion or 'authenticity', the seats are covered with remnants of eighteenth-century needlework. [Sotheby's]

characteristic of Samuel's furniture – are quite thin, with one less dovetail at the rear of each drawer in the typical manner of large urban firms. The desk has small locks which have no maker's name and are not of the quality seen a generation earlier. The carved foliate decoration is applied, not carved out of the solid mahogany carcass. Might this suggest a later date, perhaps creeping into the twentieth century? Samuel also made a slightly smaller model of the octagonal desk, the applied carved mouldings of which are different, which shows Samuels were adaptable to a client's demands and altered decorative features in a cost-effective manner to create variety.[78] In addition to the Buckingham House desk, another original, mid-eighteenth-century example is known, with the Samuel name and address stamped five times. The assumption is that this original desk was part of the firm's stock as retailers of period furniture and was probably the model for their copies.[79] The carcass of the copies is similar to the cabinet maker's plan of the original but, almost 150 years later, Samuel added extra decorative features, most notably large scallop shells, to suit modern taste. If the Samuel business was founded as early as the 1790s, is it possible that the original desk was supplied by them to George IV and they still held the cabinet maker's plans?

The *bonheur du jour*, cylinder bureau and green-painted bookcase, **Figs 8.65–8.67**, show that the Samuel enterprise was also well versed in the later George III style. The satinwood desks with inlaid stringing and painted Neoclassical decoration, one with oval silver-plated handles, are unusual models for Samuels but the cabinet making is to the very high standards of their more commonly seen reproductions. The lower part of the bookcase has turned tapering legs in the antique fashion as advocated by Thomas Sheraton in plate 20 of *The Cabinet-Maker and Upholsterer's Drawing-Book*. The *Drawing-Book* was reprinted in 1895 and its popularity ensured a renewed interest in Sheraton designs, especially for bedrooms and drawing room furniture. The arabesque decoration of the bookcase (**Fig. 8.67**), painted in the French manner, relates to a late eighteenth-century cabinet made for the 3rd Baron Monson (d. 1806) by George Brookshaw (d. 1823), a *peintre ébéniste* and author of *A New Treatise on Flower Painting*, published in 1797. Also painted in the style of George Brookshaw, the bedroom suite, **Figs 8.68a–e**, has a Harrods label, the actual maker unknown.

417

8.56b

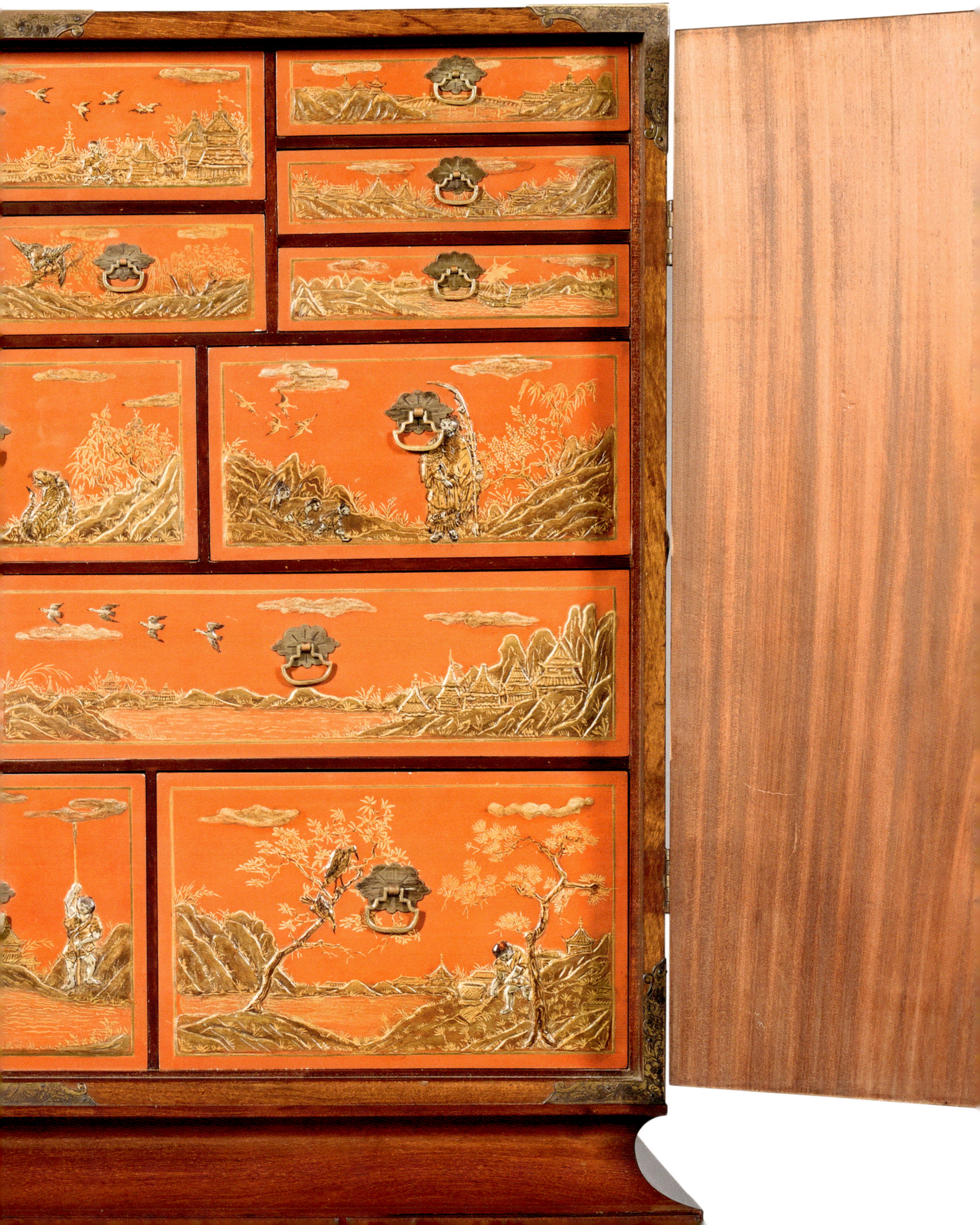

Fig. 8.58 **The shield back chair, always associated with the designs of Hepplewhite, continues to be one of the most popular forms of dining chair. This set of six by Henry Samuel was valued at £200 in a 1927 inventory.** [Sotheby's]

The Maples stamp on the rare pair of cabinets, **Fig. 8.69a**, dates them to after 1895, but the continuation of popular models in trade catalogues could mean they were made as late as 1910 or 1914. Veneered with the finest quality satinwood and mahogany, the columns and frieze are inlaid with harewood characteristic of Maples' output at the height of the company's success, the cornice is inlaid with marquetry swags of foliage in the Adam classical revival style that had re-emerged in the 1860s. To give a more realistic effect of 'Adam' colouration, the background to the frieze is on green-stained sycamore, or harewood, and the faded colours of the eighteenth-century pieces with which they were familiar have been replicated, rather than the original vibrant 'Adam' colours. The two cabinets are the same except that the oval panels on the lower parts of the doors, which show the Four Seasons in marquetry, have been reversed. If, for example, they were on opposing sides of a corridor or enfilade the ovals would be 'read' at the same time, making a true pair. The style of leg used on the cabinets is a variation of one often seen on furniture by Maples and might be a useful indication for attribution. The details of the legs are similar to the desk in **Fig. 8.70**. A small satinwood table with similar legs and engraved decoration was made for the firm by the otherwise unrecorded cabinet maker Bernard Nienhaus.[80] Over many years, Maples used a variety of stamps and applied metal or ivorine labels. English furniture in their Paris showrooms often had the company name followed by 'Paris' stamped on the drawer. The lock supplier for Maples was often Hobbs & Co.

In 1891 Maple & Company was valued at £1 million

CHAPTER 8: 1890S

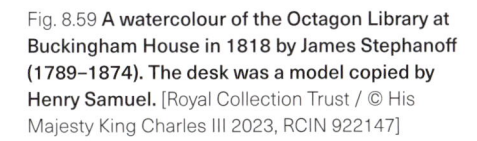

Fig. 8.59 A watercolour of the Octagon Library at Buckingham House in 1818 by James Stephanoff (1789–1874). The desk was a model copied by Henry Samuel. [Royal Collection Trust / © His Majesty King Charles III 2023, RCIN 922147]

Fig. 8.60 An octagonal partners' desk, one of two recorded variations by Henry Samuel, in well-figured mahogany. It is stamped on one of the pedestals 'H. Samuel, 484 Oxford Street, London'. The desk is similar to the one acquired by George IV for the Octagon Library at Buckingham House, above. [Butchoff Antiques]

Fig. 8.61 Numbered '8280' on one of the drawers, the back of this unusual George II-style mahogany bookcase is stamped by Samuel of Oxford Street. [Sotheby's L19356: 8782]

Fig. 8.62 A hall bench enthusiastically stamped 'H. Samuel' four times. The model is adapted from an eighteenth-century design by John Linnell, which in turn was influenced by William Kent's designs of 1744. Smaller versions, more akin to Linnell's work, are also known.[81] [Bonhams]

421

Figs 8.63a & b Stamped 'H Samuel 484 Oxford Street London', the design is taken from one in the 3rd edition of Thomas Chippendale's *The Gentlemen's & Cabinet-Maker's Director* published in 1762, pl. LXXX. Samuels have used fine quality mahogany and have paid attention to the graceful hour-glass form and floral carving of the original design. As with the desk opposite, Chippendale has only drawn the side with cupboard doors, the opposing side has four graduated drawers in each pedestal partly visible in the detail on pp. 554–55. Each oval section has four castors hidden by the plinth; the makers' stamp is set, unusually, underneath the drawer edge. Most makers stamp their name clearly on the top of the leading edge of a drawer. Was this a mistake by the foreman or was it a commission from another furniture firm who wished to disguise their source?

making the Maple family, owners and directors very wealthy; it is unlikely that any other British furniture-making firm would have come close to this level of commercial success.[82] John Blundell Maple was knighted in 1892, the company by then holding a royal warrant. Three years later the company became Maple & Company Limited, changing their stamp to reflect the new incorporation, **Fig. 8.69b**. By 1893 the company employed over 700 people, including 130 joiners, 60 cabinet makers and 105 polishers which, considering the amount of furniture they bought in from smaller firms, indicates that they were still making much in-house. Possibly, however, some of the skilled workers were making and assembling room and hotel fittings.[83]

The name of Thomas Sheraton is quite correctly lauded alongside that of Thomas Chippendale and George Hepplewhite, but another less well-known but important designer was the cabinet maker Thomas Shearer. His *Cabinet-Makers' London Book of Prices and Designs of Cabinet Work* was published in 1788 for the London Society of Cabinet Makers, and reprinted as *The Cabinet-Makers' London Book of Prices* in 1793. Shearer's designs are often more complex than Sheraton's although the two are difficult to distinguish, but Sheraton's name was better known and generally cited regardless in the late nineteenth century. The

CHAPTER 8: 1890S

8.64a

8.64b

thin but elegant reeded legs and outset corners of the pair of writing tables, **Fig. 8.75**, would have almost certainly been sold by Bertram & Son as 'Sheraton style' but may have been adapted from a Shearer design.

The roll-top desk, perfected by the French royal cabinet maker Jean-François Oeben in the 1760s, was popular in the latter part of the nineteenth century in both England and France. The example in **Fig. 8.80a** has inlaid, not painted, foliage in the Adam revival style. Some models of this type have a solid cylindrical top, but this example is more complex with a slatted tambour which opens in conjunction with the leather-lined writing slide. Another popular form of eighteenth-century desk revived in the latter years of the nineteenth century was the Carlton House desk, **Figs 8.77a–c**. Hepplewhite and Sheraton both produced line drawings of this type of desk in their respective publications of 1792 and 1793. Hepplewhite called his table a 'Gentleman's Writing Table'. Sheraton's more elegant drawing in *The Cabinet-Maker and Upholsterer's Drawing-Book*, plate 60, is titled 'A Ladys [*sic*] Drawing and Writing Table', **Fig. 8.77a**.

The first desk of this form was made in 1790 by John Kerr. The term 'Carlton House' desk is only recorded in 1814 by Ackermann in *The Repository of Arts* 'from having been first made for the august personage whose correct taste

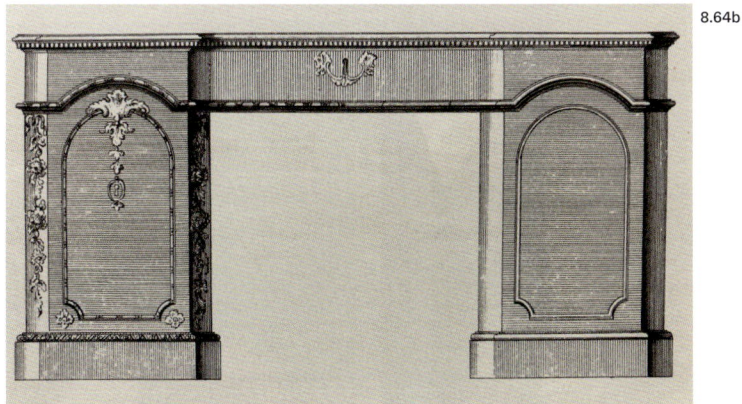

Figs 8.64a & b This example is not signed but is similar in quality to the desk opposite, which might be enough for a tentative attribution to H. Samuel. Once again Chippendale has only drawn one side, showing cupboard doors, the opposing side has four graduated drawers in each pedestal. The accompanying design is pl. LXXVII, also from the 1762 edition of *The Gentlemen's & Cabinet-Maker's Director*. To facilitate easy manoeuvrability, the castors are again neatly concealed under the plinth of each pedestal.

BRITISH FURNITURE

8.65

8.66

8.67

Fig. 8.65 The drawer of this painted satinwood *bonheur du jour*, in a quasi-late Georgian style, is stamped by H. Samuel and, typically, has the 484 Oxford Street address. [Bonhams]

Fig. 8.66 An unusual variation of a Sheraton-revival satinwood cylinder bureau with the H. Samuel stamp and address. [Saltwell Antiques]

Fig. 8.67 A late nineteenth-century polychrome painted breakfront bookcase made or retailed by H. Samuel. The decoration and bow-fronted lower part are characteristic of work by George Brookshaw from *c.*1790.[84] [Christie's Images]

Figs 8.68a–e A brightly painted bedroom suite imitating furniture made in the 1780s by George Brookshaw. One piece has a Harrods label, and the high standard of finish suggests that it was made for them by an unknown specialist workshop. [Butchoff Antiques]

CHAPTER 8: 1890S

8.68a

8.68b

8.68c

8.68d

8.68e

425

8.69a

CHAPTER 8: 1890S

Fig. 8.69a **Two marquetry cabinets in mahogany and satinwood by Maples, probably conceived as a true pair. They are made to the high standards that cemented the firm's global reputation. Maples priced this model at £52 10s.** [Private collection]

Fig. 8.69b **This 'Maple & Cº Lᴅ' stamp was used after 1895, when the firm was incorporated as a limited company.**

8.69b

427

BRITISH FURNITURE

8.70

8.71

912 E Mahogany Inlaid Cabinet £40 0 0
4 ft wide, 7 ft high

913 E China Cabinet
With exceptionally fine satinwood inlaid panels, columns and
frieze harewood inlaid, back and shelves lined silk ; £52 10 0
5 ft wide, 6 ft high

Fig. 8.70 Similar to a desk at Balmoral Castle, the upper-right drawer on this small desk is stamped 'Maple & Cº Lᴅ'. Inlaid onto satinwood with engraved marquetry, the sides have Classical scenes of Diana the Huntress and Leda and the Swan. The oval silver-plated handles are unusual and distinctive. [Private collection]

Fig. 8.71 It is interesting to compare the prices of these two cabinets in a Maple & Co. 650-page catalogue of c.1892. The profusion of inlay and the use of serpentine glass makes the right-hand model, also shown as Fig. 8.69a, some 25 per cent more expensive. [Butchoff archive]

Figs 8.72a & b Almost certainly by Maples, this unusual table of fine quality has the signs of the zodiac inlaid in mahogany and a floral border inlaid in specimen woods. The top is directly influenced by the designs of the eighteenth-century architect Robert Adam. [Butchoff Antiques]

Fig. 8.73a & b An unusual centre table, stamped by Maples. The top is beautifully veneered with a radiating dodecagonal fan medallion in satinwood with etched harewood and kingwood marquetry. The overall form of the table is more commonly seen as an 'envelope' card table, with four triangular flaps opening to reveal a baize-lined playing surface. The accentuated hipped stretcher may well be a Maples 'speciality'. [Private collection]

CHAPTER 8: 1890S

8.72a

8.73a

8.72b

8.73b

429

has so classically embellished that beautiful palace'.⁸⁵ The distinctive 'U' shape of the top and curved back allows the user both convenience and privacy, with numerous drawers and covered compartments for writing paraphernalia, implements and papers. The example in **Fig. 8.77c** has fine, elegant and unfussy stringing and silvered metal handles and, more unusually, silvered castors. It is interesting to compare the handles with the copy of the so-called dressing table, **Fig. 5.86**. The similarities suggest that they are by the same maker, possibly Morant & Co.

The *demi-lune* commode, or half-moon-shaped cabinet, was a much-admired form published by Hepplewhite and was popular again in the latter years of the nineteenth century and well into the twentieth. As with the eighteenth-

Fig. 8.74 **A satinwood display cabinet, possibly by Maple & Co., with painted polychrome which alludes to the muses Terpsichore, goddess of music, and Polyhymnia, goddess of poetry and dance.** [Private collection]

Fig. 8.75 **A fine pair of writing tables from the Savoy Hotel, which opened in 1889. Stamped by Bertram & Son of 100 Dean Street, Soho, the style is in the manner of Thomas Shearer, an eighteenth-century designer who influenced Hepplewhite's designs and was admired by Thomas Sheraton.** [Butchoff Antiques]

Fig. 8.76 **A satinwood breakfront side cabinet with painted polychrome floral decoration outlined in inlaid ebony and purpleheart. Whilst the decoration is more in the eighteenth-century manner of Robert Adam and Angelica Kauffman, the breakfront form and simulated fluting on the legs are Sheraton in style, more commonly seen from the early 1800s.** [Private collection]

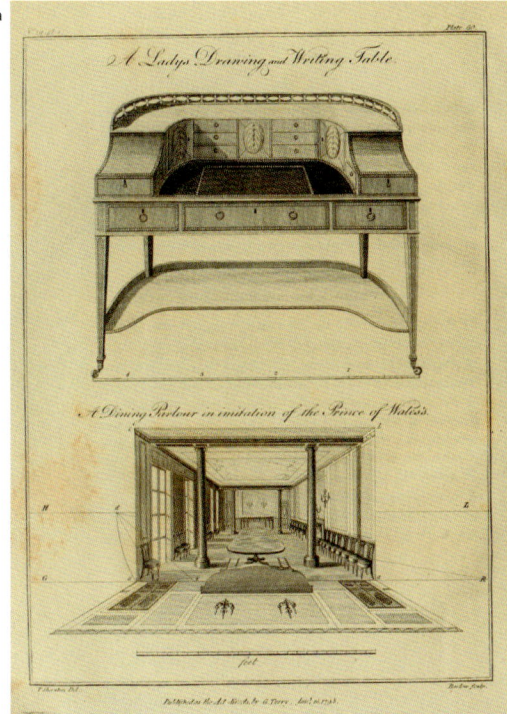

Fig. 8.77a Known today as a 'Carlton House' desk, Hepplewhite's term was a 'Gentleman's Writing Table'. In this engraving of 1793, Sheraton's title is 'A Ladys [sic] Drawing and Writing Table'. [*The Cabinet-Maker and Upholsterer's Drawing-Book*, pl. 60]

Figs 8.77b & c The quality of construction and the beautifully figured satinwood veneers of this so-called Carlton House writing table suggest that it has come from one of the top makers, probably a London firm. [Butchoff Antiques]

Fig. 8.78 A fine-quality marquetry corner cabinet, unsigned but almost certainly by Maple & Co. The satinwood veneers have been carefully selected in a triangular quarter veneer, with an inlaid panel depicting Cupid meeting Euterpe, the muse of lyric poetry. The distinctive short legs are the same as on the cabinets in Fig. 8.69a. [Butchoff Antiques]

century precedents, later versions were often veneered with satinwood. The decoration varies between inlaid and painted foliage, with romanticised interpretations of Angelica Kauffman's or the Irish neoclassical artist, Adam Buck. The doors in **Fig. 8.81** are fine examples of nineteenth-century marquetry, inlaid in a formal Neoclassical style with a central sunburst within a fan medallion. To complete the Classical references, the outer borders are inlaid with trailing anthemion decoration. In contrast, the decoration on the pair of cabinets in **Fig. 8.82** is painted. At the time, the work of the artist was more expensive than the wages of the marquetry cutter. In these examples, the painted version retains the original fresh colours, whilst the inlays have faded considerably. The pair of cabinets also has the more unusual feature of concave central doors rather than the more customary convex doors.[86] The painted panels

8.79

Fig. 8.79 A mahogany side cabinet attributed to Maples on the basis of similar signed examples. The top is inlaid with the figure of Ares in his chariot riding through the skies presaging the Trojan War, the doors with engraved figures of Paris and Helen. The distinctive short legs are the same model as on Figs 8.69a & 8.78, and are a recurring feature of furniture attributable to Maples.
[Private collection]

Figs 8.80a & b The roll-top desk was popular in the latter part of the nineteenth century. This example is similar to a model published by Hepplewhite in 1787. The slatted tambour top opens in conjunction with the leather-lined writing slide.
[Private collection]

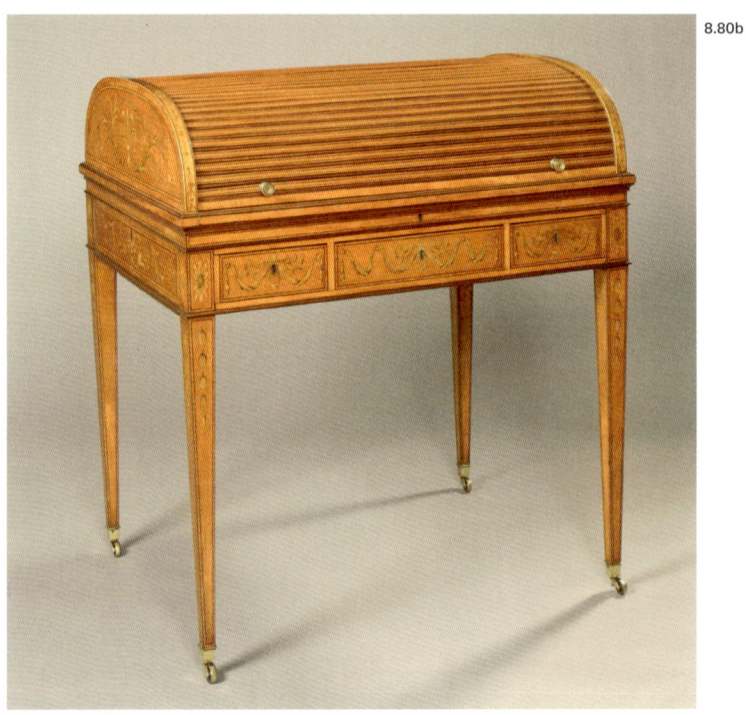

8.80a

8.80b

Fig. 8.81 The maker of this cabinet is unknown, but the influence can be traced to designs by Linnell and also Hepplewhite. The original colours of the marquetry have faded considerably and are now more in keeping with period examples. [Private collection]

Fig. 8.82 A pair of demi-lune commodes or cabinets, with unusual concave central doors. They are decorated in an eclectic Adam manner, which combines a medley of elements familiar from eighteenth-century examples. [Private collection]

8.83

8.84

8.85

Fig. 8.83 Inspired by the work of Adam and his contemporaries, but with no attempt to create anything other than a modern version, this satinwood cellarette, one of a pair, is painted with romanticised cartouches influenced by Angelica Kauffman. [Private collection]

Fig. 8.84 A light and easily moveable satinwood table for the display of treasured items. Although partly inspired by Thomas Shearer's designs and clearly not of eighteenth century form, it would have been termed 'Sheraton' when made in the closing years of the nineteenth century. The glass panels are expensively bevel-glazed. [Private collection]

Fig. 8.85 The back of this satinwood open bookcase has traces of the maker's label, 'Morant & Co. 91 New Bond Street' and the number 145 in ink. [Private collection]

are again influenced by the perennially popular Kauffman. The overall design of the decoration appears to be fanciful, although there are similarities with a marquetry design on an eighteenth-century cabinet formerly in the Lever Collection, which has similarities to the work of Ince & Mayhew.

In the 1970s, suspicions were aroused at the Victoria and Albert Museum about several pieces of fine-quality furniture believed to be from the Regency period.[87] Close examination showed that a number were late nineteenth

Fig. 8.86 One of a pair of chests of drawers with satinwood bandings deliberately contrasted against the mahogany veneer, of a style often seen with the Edwards & Roberts stamp or label. Possibly the firm contracted the manufacture to an East End workshop. The design elements are drawn from Hepplewhite's *The Cabinet-Maker and Upholsterer's Guide*. [Private collection]

Fig. 8.87 One of a rare pair of mahogany wine coolers, a variation of one advertised by Conrath & Sons in 1895. [Adrian Alan Ltd]

Fig. 8.88 A display cabinet by Edwards & Roberts with distinctive marquetry in their house style but possibly made elsewhere to their design, or to order in an East End workshop. [Saltwell Antiques]

century and they were subsequently relabelled. One, a mahogany and brass-inlaid chair, **Fig. 8.93**, is close to a design of 1807 published by the *éminence grise* of Regency design, Thomas Hope.[88] It bears an imitation-ivory label bearing the name of Edwards & Roberts, with the Wardour Street address they used between 1892 and 1895. Edwards & Roberts may have repaired or re-upholstered the chair, but it was concluded that it was made by them, or to their order, in the 1890s. The chair is similar to a pier table with an Edwards & Roberts ivorine label, again thought, when acquired in 1964, to have been of the French Empire period, not of late nineteenth-century English manufacture. Edwards & Roberts sold whole suites in this style, based on Hope's

Fig. 8.89 A 'very large rich Commode' was supplied by Thomas Chippendale to Harewood House in 1773. At £86, it was the most expensive item recorded in Chippendale's bills. This reproduction of the 'Diana and Minerva' commode is smaller than the original; the marble top would have been anathema to Chippendale. [Wick Antiques]

Fig. 8.90 Sir George Sitwell and family at home at Renishaw Hall, painted by John Singer Sargent in 1900. Standing in front of a celebrated commode made in c.1775 by Chippendale, Lady Ida is arranging flowers on an Empire Revival table, the two very different furniture styles living in harmony.[89] [Wikipedia / private collection]

Fig. 8.91 A giltwood octagonal table designed by Robert Christie for Buscot Park. [Windsor House Antiques]

Fig. 8.92 Two designs for furniture in a revived French Empire style, designed and made by Robert Christie for Alexander Henderson of Buscot Park. [*The Cabinet Maker* 1891, author's photograph]

Fig. 8.93 Based on a design of 1807 by Thomas Hope, this brass-inlaid mahogany chair was made or retailed by Edwards & Roberts between 1892 and 1895. [Victoria and Albert Museum, W.29-1976]

8.91

8.92

8.93

8.94

Fig. 8.94 A pencil drawing, c.1892, by John Dibblee Crace for the library of Astor House, the 1st Viscount Astor's London office and apartment.[90] The house is fitted with extravagant panelling and carving reminiscent of the late Tudor style. One frieze by Thomas Nicholls is dominated by a host of carved romantic characters, including the Three Musketeers. Crace also designed furniture for Astor at Carlton House Terrace and Cliveden. [© Victoria and Albert Museum]

Figs 8.95a & b Four Shakespearean figures – Othello, Richard III, Hamlet and Shylock – support this late flowering of the Warwick School and Newcastle style of carving. The table, probably intended for a library, is signed by Gerrard Robinson of Newcastle, dated 1890. [Butchoff Antiques]

8.95a

8.95b

designs, incorporating antique motifs which included lyres, anthemion and honeysuckle, Greek key and star decoration. A rosewood side cabinet in the same Regency style and stamped by Edwards & Roberts completes this interesting group.[91] It is increasingly unclear how much furniture was actually made by the firm. The wine cooler, **Fig. 8.87**, is a model thought by English commentators in the 1890s to have been c.1810, but the design is earlier, more in the style of Robert Adam. The illustrated piece is similar to a line drawing of a wine cooler in *The Cabinet Maker*, made by Conrath & Sons of North Audley Street, their workshops in the Uxbridge Road. One of a pair, it has honeysuckle mounts whereas the Conrath line drawing has rams' heads. Close examination of the line drawing shows other subtle variations to the mounts and the gadrooned knop at the top.[92]

In 1892, Frederick Litchfield commented on the growing demand in New York and London for French Empire furniture. He noted that 'the French dealers have bought up some of the old undecorated pieces and by ornamenting

438

Fig. 8.96 **A rare plaque in carved limewood of great quality, signed by the London carver and gilder James Peake, dated 1895. Peake, described as the modern Grinling Gibbons,**[94] **won a bronze medal in Paris in 1900.** [Wick Antiques]

them with gilt-bronze mounts cast from good old patterns have sold them as original examples.'[93] Although his remark was made in relation to French Empire furniture, it illustrates a renewed interest generally in the decorative style of the early years of the nineteenth century. In an astute observation, Mary Haweis in *Beautiful Houses*, believed the term 'Queen Anne' to be debased, adding it 'means almost anything just now, but is more often applied to the pseudo-classic fashions of the First Empire'.[95] However the quintessentially English Queen Anne vernacular continued to be favoured by architects and their patrons throughout the Edwardian era, ensuring the continuity of the style in furniture production.

Following an editorial in *The Cabinet Maker* in 1884 drawing attention to the Regency and Empire styles, the Bethnal Green cabinet makers M.A. Harper & Sons illustrated an Empire-style chair. Seven years later the journal published furniture sketches by Robert Christie, drawn in an unambiguous revival style to complement the original Thomas Hope furniture at Buscot Park, **Fig. 8.92**.[96] Christie's idiosyncratic octagonal table has recently been rediscovered; the winged female torsos, **Fig. 8.91**, are not cast in bronze but are of carved and gilded wood. As with this 'Empire' table, and his furniture for the Imperial Yacht *Livadia* (**Figs 7.24 & 7.25**), Robert Christie's designs are French influenced, not 'Regency' in style. In 1889 attention had been drawn to the original Empire furniture at Madame Tussaud's waxworks.[97] During the 1890s this Empire revival style, often termed 'Regency', became popular with decorators, especially for use in public spaces such as hotels. One example was the Hotel Cecil in London, with magnificent reception rooms fitted in the Empire manner by Maples in 1896, the furniture possibly sourced by them in Paris. The Waldorf Hotel in New York and the Carlton Hotel in London were both furnished with reproduction Empire furniture, the latter by Warings around 1900. In *The Thirty-five Styles of Furniture* (1904), Timms & Webb published and illustrated a comprehensive study that included Empire designs. However, undated catalogues such as those by Hampton & Sons can be misleading as they show thousands of photographs in a myriad of styles including 'Empire' and the furniture would have been available to order over many years. The comparative simplicity of French Empire style furniture made it cheaper to produce than more complex marquetry furniture in the style of Collinson & Lock that Hamptons also kept in stock.[98]

Amongst a mélange of new ideas and ideals, a few craftsmen managed to keep their businesses viable by simply repeating their old themes and styles. Alongside early nineteenth-century revivals, other older-period revivals were themselves revisited, and the styles co-existed. One such example is the so-called Warwick School of carving, which had been fashionable from the 1840s through to the 1860s, the tradition continuing into the 1890s. Woodcarving

8.97

Fig. 8.97 **A corner of a full-size billiard table made for James Blyth, 1st Baron Blyth by Cox & Yemen. The table is veneered in ebony and, surprisingly the gilt foliage and strapwork are of carved wood, not bronze.** [Nan Xu]

CHAPTER 8: 1890S

Fig. 8.98 The Great Chamber at Chequers Court some thirty years before the house was made available to British prime ministers by Arthur and Ruth Lee in 1921. The cluttered 'diagonalisation' of the room has everything for the period – ancestors on the wall, French furniture, comfortable sofas and a touch of exoticism. In the centre of the photograph is an unusual ebony and amaranth table that had been in the room since before the 1850s.
[Chequers Trust]

had always remained in demand for ecclesiastical use but Gerrard Robinson, whose work was first exhibited in the 1850s, managed to keep his Newcastle workshop open until shortly before he died in 1891. His oak library table, **Fig. 8.95b**, was made in 1890 for a Tyneside butter merchant at a cost of £20. With a resolutely British theme, the table carved by Robinson, with cabinet work by George Bennett, is supported by four Shakespearean characters: Othello, Shylock, Hamlet and Richard III. Three years earlier, Robinson carved panels for Queen Victoria's Diamond Jubilee sideboard, illustrating scenes from her life. Robinson's carving is rustic in comparison to the Grinling Gibbons-like quality of James Peake (c.1839–1918), who had various premises in Westminster throughout his career, **Fig.8.96**. The botanical realism and accuracy of his work is exceptional, winning him a bronze medal in Paris at the 1900 *Exposition Universelle*.[99]

By the end of the decade, it was already clear that the tide was turning against the heavy curtaining and over-upholstered seat furniture of the Victorian era. The American novelist Edith Wharton (1862–1937) in *The Decoration of Houses* (1897) advocated a return to Classical lines and decoration; her work was to become a major influence.

"House Furnisher." July 27th 1907

A CORNER OF A CHIPPENDALE INTERIOR

CHAPTER 9

1900–1909

'This is the age of old furniture. It is the pride and joy of the fortunate possessor, and is secretly desired by the many who have none. For even the man who lacks interest in it for artistic or sentimental reasons can appreciate its solid financial worth.'[1]

The dawn of a new century was not a catalyst for great change in the luxury furniture market. Alongside well-established and now better understood British designs, copies and reproductions of French furniture increased in popularity, mainly in the Louis XIV, XV and XVI styles of the *ancien régime*. A large quantity of new French furniture was imported directly from Paris by dealers, some describing their wares as 'English' or 'Made in our own Workshops'. Whereas in the previous decade reproductions were mainly confined to the so-called Chippendale and the Neoclassical styles, there was an increasing interest in a wider range of styles dating back to the period of Charles II of the 1660s, to a more genuine appreciation of Queen Anne designs and the Regency style. Much reproduction furniture that continued to be made well into the first half of the twentieth century is often difficult to date. With efficiently run workshops, the better-known makers such as Lebus overshadowed a plethora of others large and small; much of this type of reproduction furniture was commissioned by larger retailers who sold it under their own name.

A third category now assumed an important place in the world of furnishing – antique pieces. Duncan's comment at the opening of this chapter summarised the increased interest in buying and selling antique furniture, especially traditional furniture influenced by the big four: Chippendale, Adam, Hepplewhite and Sheraton. As outlined in Chapter 5, firms such as Wright & Mansfield had bought antique, mainly Georgian, furniture for study purposes as early as the 1860s, helping their craftsmen understand eighteenth-century cabinet-making techniques and designs in order to facilitate the making of reproductions. Other makers such as Frederick Parker also bought antique furniture for study purposes, as did Edwards & Roberts. By *c.*1900, large and small furniture makers and suppliers, such as John Barker & Co., Hampton & Sons, Story & Co., Story Bros. & Trigg and Edwards & Roberts, had their own antique departments offering an array of period English furniture from the late seventeenth to the early nineteenth centuries. The long-established firm Bartholomew & Fletcher continued into the 1930s on the Tottenham Court Road, selling well-made reproduction furniture alongside antiques. Frederick Parker & Sons, incorporated as a limited company in 1904, are well known for the collection of antique chairs that they bought to study and copy, but they also made case furniture to a high standard, often indistinguishable from that of rival firms, a sample of which is shown in the following chapter.[2] Demand was also strong for Italian Renaissance furniture, some from the dubious output of the Florentine 'factory'

Fig. 9.1 (opposite) 'A Corner of a Chippendale Interior', the first of a series published by *The Cabinet Maker* in 1907. The armchair might just pass for an artist's impression of an early George III chair, but the side chair is too thin and attenuated, typical of the 1890–1910 revivals. The bureau cabinet is romanticised Chippendale. Rooms from the same series in the Hepplewhite, Sheraton and other styles are illustrated in Figs 9.4 & 9.5a–e.
[*The Cabinet Maker*, 27 June 1907]

of Stefano Bardini.³ Such firms inevitably repaired antique furniture for resale, some were more than minor changes and involved considerable transformation. Today the modern furniture restorer prefers to title himself a conservator, rightly preserving as much of the original form and patination as possible, but such sensibilities were not so apparent in the Victorian and Edwardian eras.

Alongside the demand for copies of Chippendale furniture, the Edwardian era saw increased interest in the later Neoclassical style. The *demi-lune* cabinet in **Figs 9.7a & b** is stamped on the back panel 'Graham & Banks, 445 Oxford Street', although, as is so often the case, it is not clear if this is as makers or retailers. The cabinet, or commode, has the appearance of an accurate copy of a design by Robert Adam of 1774, made by Mayhew & Ince for the dressing room of the Countess of Derby at Derby House in Grosvenor Square.⁴ The copy is in richly coloured fiddle-back satinwood, the central panel painted with Cupid and the Three Graces. Another similar example is of a slightly different size, the quality of both is superb. Were they made

Fig. 9.2 'Victorian Clutter'. Despite the seemingly bourgeois interior, these are the comfortable surroundings of the Princess of Wales's boudoir in York House, St James's Palace, photographed in 1903. The furniture is typical of the early Edwardian period, with an array of small pieces. The almost new, probably German, large vase, on the bookcase looks particularly precarious. [Royal Collection Trust © His Majesty King Charles III 2023, RCIN 2301756)]

Fig. 9.3 Maples and Heals furnished small rooms in a simple neo-Georgian style. This Warings showroom, illustrated in *Our Homes, and How to Beautify Them*, is described as an 'Adams Drawing Room'.⁵

Fig. 9.4 'A Sheraton Interior' with a compilation of pieces based on the designer's engravings in the various editions of *The Cabinet-Maker and Upholsterer's Drawing-Book*. The partially obscured commode on the left, the candelabrum and the patterned carpet and curtaining are taken directly from a Sheraton engraving of 1794. The card table showing in the foreground was published by Sheraton in his 1802 edition. [*The Cabinet Maker*, 1907]

Fig. 9.5a–d A series of plates from *The Cabinet Maker* published in 1907, illustrating a series of rooms in idealised Jacobean, Queen Anne, Chippendale and Hepplewhite styles. See also 9.5e overleaf. [*The Cabinet Maker*, 1907]

9.5a

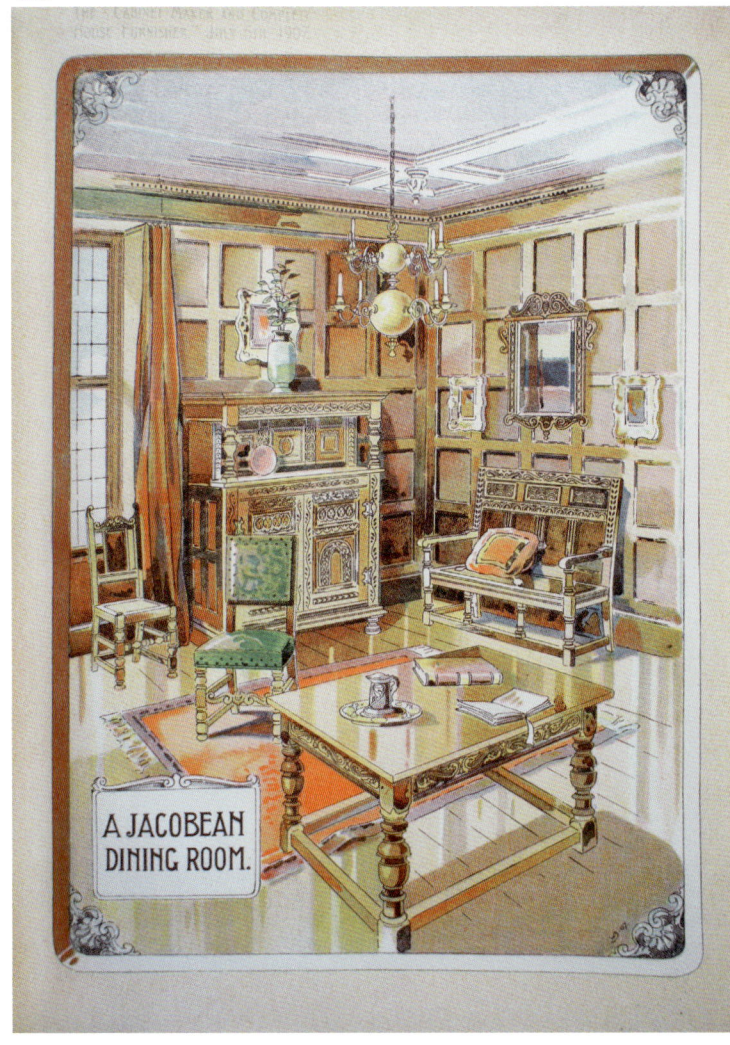

A JACOBEAN DINING ROOM.

9.5b

A QUEEN ANNE RECEPTION ROOM.

9.5c

A CHIPPENDALE BEDROOM

9.5d

A HEPPELWHITE CORNER

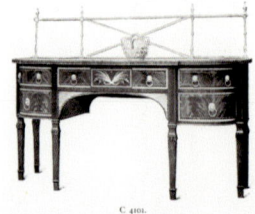

Fig. 9.5e *The Cabinet Maker's* suggestion for a 'Hepplewhite Dining Room'. The Hepplewhite style, deemed suitable for both the drawing and the dining room, was advocated by the makers and showrooms since its comparative simplicity made it more economic to produce. [*The Cabinet Maker*]

Fig. 9.6a The interpretation of the Chippendale style was much abused. The upper sideboard in this image retailed at £34 10*s*, the lower extravaganza of 'best manufacture' cost £53 10*s*. [Butchoff archive]

Fig. 9.6b The lower photograph shows a more traditional sideboard with a brass rail for a curtain to avoid splashing the wall when serving. The marquetry is typical of reproduction pieces. Both are labelled by Hamptons as 'Sheraton', retailing at £16 10*s* and £24 10*s* respectively. [Butchoff archive]

Fig. 9.7a & b **A D-shaped side cabinet or commode dated to** *c.*1900, incorporating painted panels in a style reminiscent of one designed by Robert Adam in 1774 and made by Mayhew & Ince for the Countess of Derby in 1775. Stamped 'Graham & Banks, 445 Oxford St.', it is not clear if the firm made or simply retailed it. See also 9.7c overleaf. [Butchoff Antiques]

in the same workshop, or does the difference in size suggest rival establishments?[6] Full of Neoclassical references, the main, central painted roundel depicts Diana, goddess of the Hunt, holding her bow, eager hounds at her feet. The rings around the painted panels are in a fine harewood marquetry of sunflowers and bellflower husks, with Palmyrene sunbursts in the corners. Also represented are Hebe, goddess of youth, and Flora, goddess of flowers and spring. The top, still in remarkable condition, is painted with images of Venus and Psyche. This popular decorative style on eighteenth-century furniture is habitually, and often inaccurately, attributed to the hand of the Swiss Neoclassical artist, Angelica Kauffman, or Michelangelo Pergolesi, attributions which were much vaunted in describing reproduction pieces.

The *demi-lune* pier table in **Fig. 9.8a&b** is one of a pair by James Hicks of Dublin. Hicks made traditional carved mahogany furniture similar to the work of his fellow countryman Michael Butler, but also copied the Georgian Neoclassical style of William Moore of Dublin. Moore had set up his own workshop in Dublin in 1782 after an

BRITISH FURNITURE

Fig. 9.7c An engraving of the original design for the *demi-lune* commode in the Etruscan manner, Fig. 9.7b, designed by Robert Adam in 1774. [Butchoff archive]

Figs 9.8a & b A pier table inspired by the work of Robert Adam, one of a pair in satinwood by James Hicks of Dublin in *c.*1900. One of the tables is stamped on the reverse 'J. Hicks 5 Lr. Pembroke Street'. [Butchoff Antiques]

Fig. 9.9 A child-size painted satinwood bureau in the George III style, only 76cm high and 43cm wide (29⅞in × 16⅞in). It would have been a suitable contender for the Hampton & Sons 'Antique Furniture' department and is on the same scale as a miniature cylinder bureau also offered by Hamptons, Fig. 9.10. [Private collection]

apprenticship with Ince & Mayhew in London and their influence is evident in the illustrated Hicks table. Hicks's letterhead described the firm as a 'Cabinet Manufacturer, Collector and Restorer of Chippendale, Adam and Sheraton furniture'.[7] Like Moore 100 years earlier, Hicks trained in London, in workshops on Tottenham Court Road. On his return to Dublin in 1894 he set up business at 5 Lower Pembroke Street with a showroom, calling himself an 'Antique Dealer' from 1933. A room in the National Museum of Ireland is dedicated to his work, ranging from mid-eighteenth-century-style traditional Irish mahogany to satinwood and marquetry. This includes a complete range of furniture, from giltwood mirrors to luggage racks and

448

Fig. 9.10 **One of twelve pages titled 'Antique Furniture' in the 1903–1910 Hampton & Sons catalogue. Much of the furniture is of dubious antiquity with somewhat quaint descriptions that linger to the present day, such as the 'Adams' cabinet number O.21, and 'subjects after Angelica Kauffmann [*sic*]', O.22.** [Butchoff archive]

staircases. Lady Fingall referred to Hicks possessing 'an untidy workshop in Pembroke Street, where many great people visited him. His firm employed some 24 cabinet-makers and artisans'.[8] Three marquetry cutters were named as Harry Hicks, Thomas Lennon and Michael Murray, with James Levins specialising in carving. Exhibiting intermittently at the Arts and Crafts Society of Ireland from 1895 to 1917, an early observation was one that characterises the misnomer 'Arts and Crafts' – 'the cabinet-making section, though small is strong, the only regret is that most of the exhibits are obviously reminiscent'.[9] The firm's client list included Princess Victoria, the Crown Princess of Sweden, and Edward VII. After James's death in 1936, his son Henry continued the business, often using walnut with a high-gloss polish in a finish also used by Charles Tozer. A comprehensive dissertation 'James Hicks, Cabinet-Maker 1894–1936' by Fiona Eastwood gives a detailed and informative appreciation of the firm's work.[10]

Today the term 'Edwardian' is often used to describe furniture from the period spanning *c.*1890 to *c.*1915. There

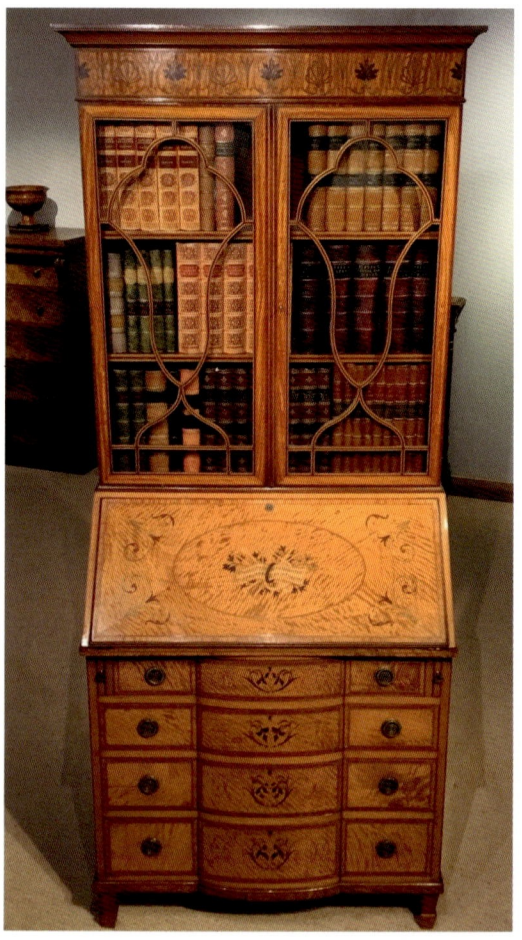

Fig. 9.11 **A well-figured satinwood and marquetry bureau cabinet** influenced by furniture designs of the second half of the eighteenth century. Although a pleasing shape, the proportions and configuration are incorrect for a period piece. The distinctive glazing bars are an innovative, elegant and delicate design. [Christian Davies Antiques]

Fig. 9.12 **A satinwood cabinet stamped Holland & Sons,** made to the high standard typical of the work of top London firms. It incorporates Adam-style Neoclassical marquetry with an earlier style of glazing bars. Unusually, the glazing bars are repeated on the inside, so that no putty is visible when the doors are open, a feature that may well be an aid to the attribution of Holland's later work. [Nan Xu]

Fig. 9.13 **The reduced proportions of furniture** made in the late nineteenth and early twentieth centuries are a factor that can help date these later pieces. Despite the introduction of ogee astragals, the maker almost certainly would have described this bookcase as 'Adam'. [Butchoff Antiques]

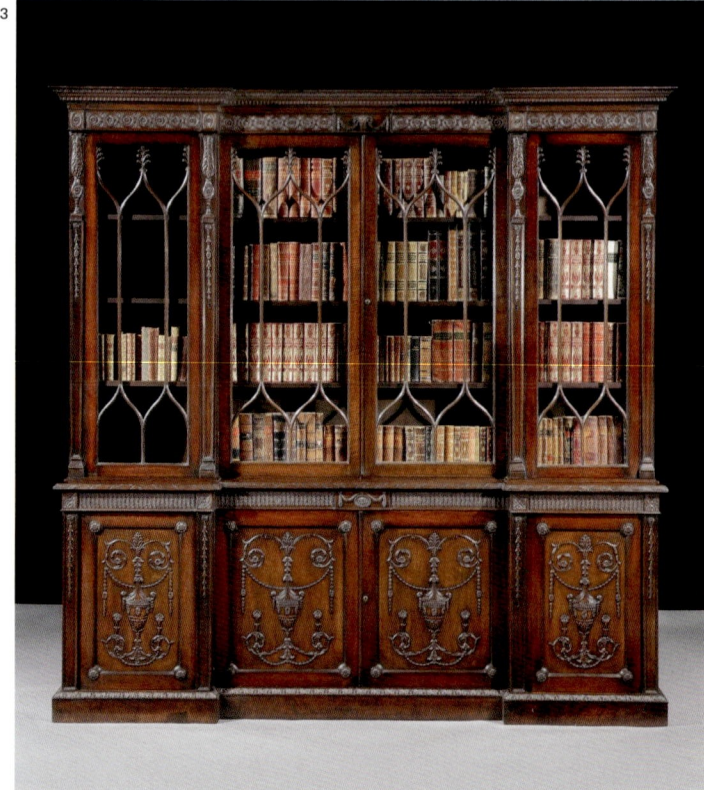

is a general misconception that from 1900 most British furniture became delicate and made of satinwood, frequently with Kauffman-esque Neoclassical paintings, and all such furniture is immediately labelled as 'Edwardian', but it is often difficult if not impossible to know whether it was made in the latter years of Queen Victoria's reign, the reign of Edward VII or that of George V. 'Edwardian' is a loose description of a style which covers furniture such as the satinwood bureau bookcase in **Fig. 9.11**, and the satinwood display cabinet in **Fig. 9.12**, an unusual and late piece by Holland & Sons. The cabinet is designed with well-spaced astragals in a honeycomb-pattern glazing, ideal for displaying porcelain. Making such complex glazing bars in the eighteenth-century manner was time consuming and required great skill as each astragal had to be made separately and each glass panel puttied into place. Manufacturers soon economised by using one sheet of glass for each door, which was placed behind the glazing bars, instead of using individual glass panes.

During the first two decades of the twentieth century, there was a growing divergence between the increasing industrialisation of British furniture and the hand work of Arts and Crafts furniture, termed 'New Art', which became more widespread in the early 1900s. Such furniture by Charles Francis Annesley Voysey and his peers was expensive; it catered to the 'luxury' market despite its apparent simplicity. Only a small group of connoisseurs with pockets deep enough were able to afford such designs, often made as one-off commissions. The Arts and Crafts principle was for one craftsman to make a piece from start to finish, thus giving him the satisfaction of his own, complete production.[11] The romanticised image was of the maker working in a small workshop tucked away in a rural area such as the workshop, **Fig. 8.17**. Craft furniture makers could not, and did not want to, compete with or be compared to the production of the large London or provincial firms. Small workshops with little or no machinery, such as those run by Ernest Gimson, a disciple of William Morris, or the two Barnsley brothers, Ernest and Sidney, produced furniture made to a high standard that referenced earlier designs of the seventeenth and eighteenth centuries. Visible joints, such as dovetails and cleats, combined with natural, often unstained, just lightly waxed, indigenous woods were made in the distinctive style of each maker/designer. These craftsmen have a long and noble history which has been the subject of much detailed discussion, research and publication. Gimson and the Barnsleys set up a workshop in the Cotswolds in 1893, following a maxim of honest craftsmanship. The father of another maker, Gordon Russell, had anticipated the impact of the motor car on trade and tourism and in 1904 purchased

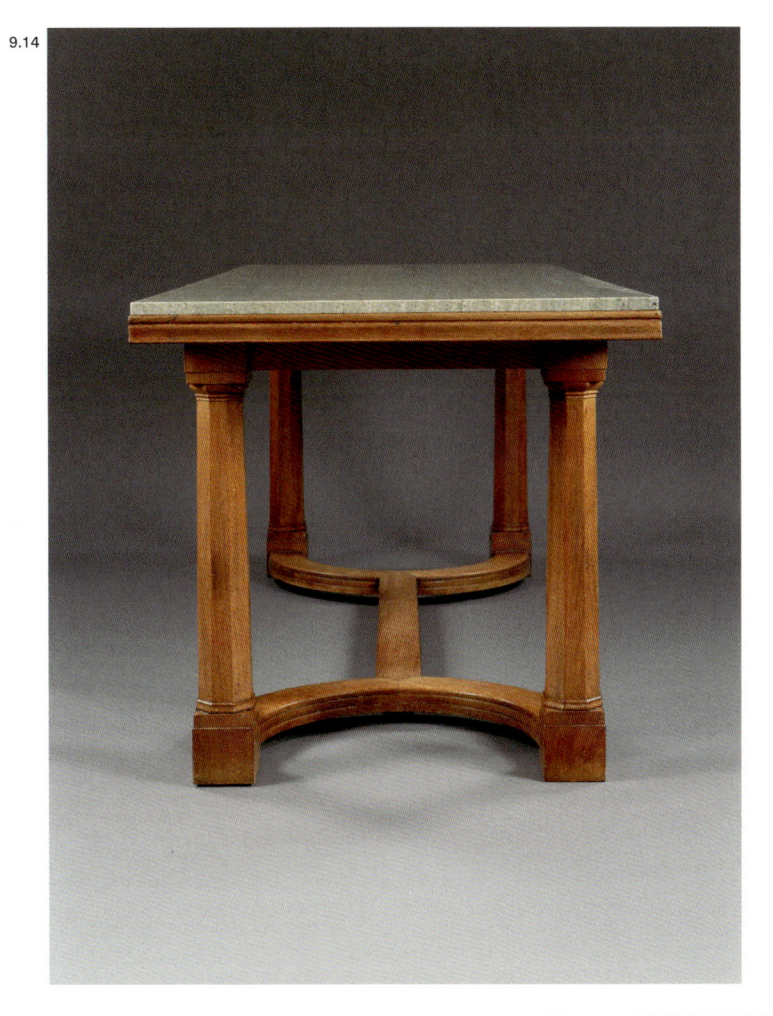

Fig. 9.14 **Attributable to Edwin Lutyens, the distinctive stretchers are similar to a suite of tables made between 1901 and 1905 for Marsh Court. Almost 2 metres (6½ feet) long, this centre table, the legs in the form of Doric columns, would traditionally have been made of oak, but this rare example is walnut with a 'Swedish Green' marble top.** [Carlton Hobbs LLC]

Fig. 9.15 **The close confines of a cabinet maker's workshop in *c*.1900 at the Shapland & Petter factory in Barnstable, *c*.1900.** [Museum of Barnstable & North Devon]

The Lygon Arms in Broadway, Worcestershire. He furnished the hostelry with antiques, establishing a workshop nearby to effect repairs. This was the ideal environment for the young Gordon to learn his craft, and the firm he established in the aftermath of World War I is still designing and making furniture today.

Not all innovative furniture was made to the highest standards. Far be it for any author to criticise Charles Rennie Mackintosh, but his interest was in design, which was seen as paramount, with a new and fresh approach breaking away from the repetition of 'derivative' furniture. Simple designs by Mackintosh were even executed by prisoners of war on the Isle of Man, such as a towel rail from a suite made for Mr and Mrs Horstman in 1917.[12] Nevertheless, a merging of design and quality can be seen in the furniture made for Liberty's or Maples in London, or made in the increasingly important industrial north, such as Pratts of Bradford, a firm that had been established by Christopher Pratt in 1845.[13] In an attempt to be 'modern' and 'innovative', designs of specialised furniture in the Arts and Crafts and Art Nouveau styles were slowly absorbed into mainstream furniture catalogues, but few of these interpretations were successful.

Edwin Lutyens, knighted in 1918, was one of the most exciting architect/designers of the early twentieth century,

Fig. 9.16 A patriotic detail of a mahogany table by George Jack made for Melsetter House, Orkney, the house designed by W.R. Lethaby. [National Museum of Scotland]

Fig. 9.17 A mahogany display cabinet designed by George Jack, a similar one was exhibited by Morris & Co. at the Decorative Arts Building at the Franco-British Exhibition in 1908, Fig. 9.55 and, at £102 18s, still available in the Morris & Co. 1912 catalogue. [Christian Davis Antiques]

his furniture in a simple, strong and highly individualistic Arts and Crafts style based on solid seventeenth-century forms. Whereas refectory tables are usually made of oak, the example in **Fig. 9.14** is made of walnut with a 'Swedish Green' marble top. The strong simplicity of form echoes Lutyens's furniture designs for Marsh Court in Hampshire, a house faced with local chalk stone and built between 1901 and 1905. In a review of the *Exposition Universelle* in 1900, *Country Life* described Lutyens as 'a young architect of conspicuous ability'.[14] Aged only thirty, Lutyens was responsible for the design of the English pavilion at the exhibition, the rooms executed in his inimitable and unmistakable style based on traditional principles. There he exhibited a Broadwood piano standing on fourteen spindle legs with turning that imitated the turning used in the second half of the seventeenth century. Ten variations of this model

CHAPTER 9: 1900–1909

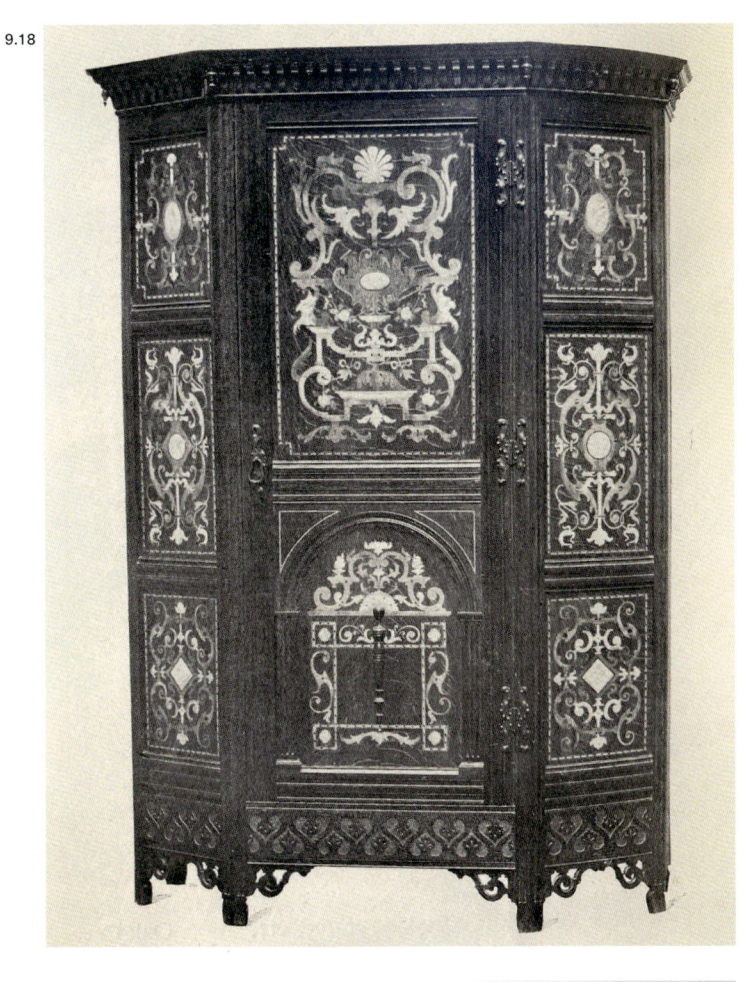

Fig. 9.18 **A coat cabinet in a Hampton's catalogue, identical to one made by Shapland & Petter, with Renaissance-style marquetry and distinctive copper mounts. Available in oak or mahogany, inlaid or plain according to choice. The Shapland version in oak retailed at £21 7s 6p in a Shapland catalogue, whereas Hamptons only charged £17 for the same finish.** [Butchoff archive]

Fig. 9.19 **Although unsigned, this mahogany display cabinet with mother-of-pearl and marquetry lilies, with distinctive copper repoussé mounts is typical of the style and high quality of Shapland & Petter's output.** [Nan Xu]

Fig. 9.20 **An iconic chair, in ebonised oak with its simple attenuated ladderback, designed by Mackintosh for the Willow Tea Rooms in Glasgow c.1903.** [Huntington Library]

of piano were made by John Broadwood & Sons, retailing at £350 each. Over a period of years, the High Wycombe firm Nicholls & Janes carried out work for Lutyens, Janes writing that despite his eminence, the renowned architect was always willing to consult with a craftsman to get the best results.[15] Another High Wycombe maker used by Lutyens was Walter Skull & Son, who had also built up a study collection of antique furniture in the 1880s. Skull's established a reputation for high-quality reproductions, their work well known and in demand in the United States.

Although seemingly very different, the historicist demand for reproduction furniture merged frequently with the

BRITISH FURNITURE

9.21a

THE LATEST STYLE OF ROOM DECORATION. THE HOME MADE BEAUTIFUL.
According to the "Arts and Crafts."

9.21b

Figs 9.21a & b The popular magazine *Punch* lampooned the new 'Arty and Crafty' style. These two engravings give a good impression of the 'Quaint' style with a nod to the designs of Voysey as realised by commercial makers. [Private collection; *Punch*, 1903]

Fig. 9.22 Although clearly not a period piece, this walnut writing desk with a drop front would have been termed 'William and Mary' when sold by Maples in *c*.1910. [Private collection]

Fig. 9.23 An innovative and refreshing walnut and ebony cabinet of *c*.1905 by Ernest Gimson. Its seventeenth-century antecedents are evident in the block-fronted drawers, a recurring theme from the Daneway House workshop. [National Trust/Denis Madge]

9.22

WILLIAM AND MARY WALNUT DROP-FRONT SECRETARY WITH SINGLE HOOD TOP
By Courtesy of Messrs. Maple & Co., Tottenham Court Road, London
PLATE III

9.23

principles of the Arts and Crafts movement. Furthering the principle of home crafts, in 1903 the American-born designer of Scottish parentage, George Jack, who had joined the office of Philip Webb in 1880, published a small volume with detailed instructions on how to hand-carve woodwork. Edited by another celebrated designer/maker, W.R. Lethaby, the book is one of a series of 'Handbooks on the Artistic Crafts'.[16] Lethaby, a co-founder of the Art Workers' Guild in 1884, became professor of design at the Royal College of Art in 1901. He had worked for a short time with the architect Reginald Blomfield, who was a critic of the new passion for collecting 'old', i.e., antique, furniture although paradoxically he championed Chippendale, Hepplewhite and Sheraton. By 1904 Jack had modernised the Georgian theme in a personalised and recognisable eclectic manner, as seen in the combined writing and display cabinet in **Fig. 9.17**. Designed

Figs 9.24a & b **A large carved giltwood overmantel looking glass, almost 3 metres (10 feet) high based on a design by Thomas Johnson published in his *Collection of Designs*, 1758, repeated in *One Hundred and Fifty New Designs* three years later. The animal motifs, characteristic of many of Johnson's designs, derive from Francis Barlow's illustrations of *Aesop's Fables*, published in 1678.** [Butchoff Antiques]

for Morris & Co., Jack made use of a delicate, traditional barber's pole stringing to outline the mahogany panels. The glazing bars at first glance are also 'Georgian' with a modern twist to facilitate the display of porcelain; the cornice and upper shelf perfectly suited to displaying contemporary studio pottery. Illustrated in *The Art Journal* in 1905 and priced at over £100, it was an expensive item, but not 'Arts and Crafts'. Described as 'of highest Sheraton finish', it has little to do with the late-eighteenth-century Sheraton period and is inspired by the middle years of the late George II and early George III era.

By c.1900 Shapland & Petter, the subject of an important monograph, were one of the largest furniture manufacturers.[17] Based in Devon, they were able to take advantage of more space, and lower rent and wages. Working almost exclusively in their own idiom, much of their production has been wrongly attributed to other firms. One example is **Fig. 9.18** appearing in a Hampton & Sons catalogue but identical to one by Shapland & Petter.[18] Unsigned furniture by Shapland that combines Arts and Crafts with Art Nouveau styles is frequently mis-attributed to other makers such as Liberty's, but Bennett's trenchant publication shows that much of the furniture in this style was made for other retailers by the Devon firm. Henry Shapland, a cabinet maker, had travelled to the United States in 1847, where he had witnessed the advantages of machine tools for furniture making. By the 1880s, his firm employed hundreds of workers in the Devon area.[19] Shapland's training as a cabinet maker, combined with Henry Petter's marketing skills, were to prove a winning combination in an increasingly commercial and competitive world. Shapland's ability to adapt and use machinery alongside more traditional hand techniques was supported by Petter's business acumen. Through marketing and extensive catalogues, the firm supplied other 'makers', such as Waring & Gillow and Liberty in London, or Wylie & Lochhead in Glasgow, and numerous smaller firms throughout the British Isles. Due to their network as wholesalers, it can be hard to distinguish the work of Shapland & Petter from furniture sold by firms such as Norman & Stacey of Tottenham Court Road, Goodyer of Regent Street or Christopher Pratt of Bradford. An advertisement in 1902 for Norman & Stacey on the Tottenham Court Road, is titled 'Art Furnishers' with 'A Large Stock of Antique & Modern Furniture on View'.[20]

A characteristic of Shapland & Petter is their so-called 'quaint', 'artistic', attenuated motifs. These include lilies, lotus blossom or peacock feathers in marquetry, often combined with copper repoussé or stained-glass panels. A recurring feature is a stylised rose – the 'Glasgow Rose' similar to the work of Mackintosh or E.A. Taylor. Much of the firm's marquetry has a distinctly Germanic feel, in the style of Buchschmid & Gretaux, with town and landscapes that draw on seventeenth-century designs and stylised figures in a homely Dutch style. The marquetry in **Fig. 9.18**, is less distinctive and can be compared to the Renaissance designs of Stephen Webb; it has similarities with the inlays on a bedroom suite possibly supplied by Collinson & Lock in 1896 for Standen in West Sussex (see Chapter 8, **Fig. 8.24**). Expanding rapidly, Shaplands set up a showroom in London in 1893 on Berners Street, the same street as another provincial firm, the Bath Cabinet Makers company, where they offered a wide range of furniture alongside their

9.25a

Fig. 9.25a A preparatory drawing in Chippendale's own hand for plate XVI in the 1754 edition of *The Gentleman & Cabinetmaker's Director*. Chippendale was justly proud of these designs for 'Ribband Back chairs'. Chippendale's contemporaries rarely copied his designs faithfully, whereas late nineteenth-century makers followed published designs more closely.
[Metropolitan Museum of Art, 1972.581]

Fig. 9.25b Variously stamped 'Hindley & Wilkinson', or simply 'Wilkinson', this Chippendale copy from a set of two armchairs and ten side chairs is in a richly coloured and well-carved mahogany. In comparison to the original 1754 drawing above, the legs of this copy are heavier. A matching armchair was illustrated in a Hindley & Wilkinson catalogue of c.1887.[21]
[Butchoff archive]

9.25b

more familiar Art Nouveau designs. Supplying furniture to Waring & Gillow branches in Europe, in Paris and Madrid, Shapland exhibited under their own name in Budapest in 1902.[22] Shapland himself was responsible for a number of the designs, although the bulk of the design work was by William Cowie, and he published *Style Schemes in Antique Furnishing* in 1909. Much of the firm's output bears one of a variety of ivorine or brass name labels and a tell-tale stamp 'S&PB' on the brass locks. Shapland's book included two advertisements: one by Warings for their 'Faithful copies of the best models of Chippendale, Hepplewhite, Sheraton, and Adams, and their fine reproductions of Louise [*sic*] Quinze and Louis Seize' and one by Gill & Reigate 'Antique Connoisseurs and Experts in Restorations'.

Traditional furniture makers were wary of the fad for 'Quaint' furniture and the unnecessary attenuation of uprights with no structural merit. Ralph Janes was particularly critical. He wrote: 'About 1902, after the Boer War, there came a craze for what was called L'Art Nouveau, which usually meant taking quite a good design, reversing all the nice lines…and piercing it with holes to represent such things as lilies, pomegranates…or inlaying it with crude designs in pewter, ebony or sycamore'.[23] Trade journals played an important role in promoting the Quaint style. Journals such as *The Furniture Gazette* and *The Cabinet Maker* are full of naïve line drawings in the so-called 'Quaint style' which had been adopted by many of the larger firms throughout Britain. In the 1880s and 1890s, the illustrations of W. Baldock had taken Louis Sullivan's wispy 'tangle of tendrils…and tortuous marine growths' to new heights, **Figs 9.21a&b**.

Rural workshops such as Simpson's of Kendal[24] benefitted from the increasing ease and possibilities of travel, facilitating new opportunities to acquire training. Simpson first learned his trade locally with Gillows in Lancaster, moved south to join the Leicester stonemason Samuel Barfield, and then to George Faulkner Armitage in London, whose Stamford Works followed principles of craftsmanship advocated by

CHAPTER 9: 1900–1909

Fig. 9.26 A sideboard and sarcophagus wine cooler advertised by Maple & Co. in *The Illustrated London News*, 5 July 1902. The designer has mixed Chippendale-style applied carving to a sideboard with tapering pedestal cupboards that has more in common with the Regency period. [Look & Learn]

Fig. 9.27 A pedestal desk in the 'Chippendale' manner, traditionally arranged with drawers on the front and cupboard doors on the back. The complex carved ogee bracket foot was adapted by Chippendale from earlier designs. It is easily recognised as a copy by the use of well-figured walnut veneers, whereas mahogany would have been used in the mid-eighteenth century. [Private collection]

Ruskin and Morris. On returning to his native Westmorland in 1885, Simpson established 'The Handicrafts' workshop and exhibited one piece in lightly oiled and polished English oak, the finish a hallmark of crafts furniture, at the Arts and Crafts Society in London in 1889. The simplicity of his work, with Scottish overtones, appealed to local buyers and his furniture enjoys a dedicated following today. With over sixty timber merchants locally from whom to source his wood, his business flourished, enabling him to employ no less than architect than Voysey to design his new house in 1908.

The Chippendale name had become universally synonymous with the abundant style known as Rococo to the extent that in much of the nineteenth century his contemporaries were largely ignored. In c.1834 John Weale reproduced a series of eighteenth-century engravings, misleadingly calling them 'chiefly after Thos. Chippendale', whereas they were by Matthias Lock, François Vivares and Anthony Walker.[25] In 1883 *The Magazine of Art* commented on what today are obvious differences between Chippendale and neoclassical designs by Sheraton, noting that Chippendale worked in mahogany and 'used deep undercut carving and pierced work'.[26] The dining chair in **Fig. 9.25b** is based on plate 16 in Chippendale's 1754 *Director*, entitled 'Ribband Back chairs'. This type of reproduction chair could have been made in the late 1890s or well into the twentieth century. Without the evidence of a maker's stamp, dating in such instances is difficult, subjective, and often decided by quality on the false assumption that the better the quality the earlier the workmanship. However, this example is not only signed but features in a Hindley & Wilkinson catalogue, believed to be post 1887. Deeply carved in solid mahogany, the chair is a close but not exact copy of the original drawing. It follows the spirit of Chippendale but is a late Victorian interpretation, like the drawing of a chair by Levasseur in the previous chapter, **Fig. 8.47**. A sign of attention to detail is the considerable emphasis on the undercutting of the ribbon-tied splats, giving a lighter, three-dimensional air. The apron and legs are too uncertain, too squashed, to be Chippendale 'of the period'. Proud of this imaginative model, Chippendale wrote, 'if I may speak without vanity, [these] are the best I have ever seen (or perhaps have ever been made)'.[28]

Dining chairs in the Chippendale style, and reproductions of chairs that just pre-date Chippendale's *Director* of 1754, are notoriously difficult to date. The beautifully carved mahogany single armchair is a case in point, **Fig. 9.28a**. As a copy it is almost impossible to ascertain in which decade it was made and could be from the late 1880s or well into the 1920s. The long set of twelve dining chairs in **Fig. 9.29a** poses the same difficulty.[29] The slight differences in carving indicate that they are hand carved and there is a heaviness to the carving that is often described for convenience but not necessarily accuracy, as 'Irish'. A similar set from Westwood Park, illustrated both by Cescinsky

Fig. 9.28a & b Chippendale in all but date, this richly carved mahogany armchair is difficult to date precisely, but close inspection of the under frame suggests a post-1900 hand from an unknown but gifted maker. [Private collection]

Fig. 9.29a Invariably termed 'Chippendale', this style of dining chair owes more to Robert Manwaring, who wrote that his designs of 1765 'may be easily executed by the hands of a tolerable skilful Workman'. However, the original designer is unknown, as is the maker of these two from a set of twelve reproductions of c.1900. The claw foot with a distinctive web is a feature often used by Irish makers. [Private collection]

Fig. 9.29b & c Two details from the crisply carved set of chairs in Fig. 9.29a. The virtuoso carving is often termed 'Irish'. The canted terminals have an exaggerated paper scroll. [Private collection]

Fig. 9.30 Two of the long set of chairs shown in Figs 9.29a–c, shown in situ at Westwood Park, Worcestershire. In 1931 this set was illustrated and described by Cescinsky as being eighteenth century.[27] [*Country Life*/Future Publishing Ltd]

9.29a

9.29b

9.29c

9.30

and Macquoid as original, was given to the Metropolitan Museum of Art between 1951 and 1964 but deaccessioned later when it was realised the chairs were not eighteenth century.[30] Records over the last fifty years show that at least twenty-four of these chairs were made. Part of the set at Westwood can be seen in an illustration in *Country Life*, **Fig. 9.30**. Westwood was purchased by the industrialist Edward Partington, 1st Baron Doverdale, in 1896 and it would seem likely that the set was supplied new for him. The Metropolitan Museum noted that the chairs were 'probably Cuban mahogany' and 'evidently made for great durability'. The clue to the fact that the set was out of period was suggested by the statement that 'after many years of use the frames show only the slightest indication of wear'.[31] Often it is the lack of depth of colour of later mahogany which is a clue to the date; the deep hues of a reproduction are from staining, the timber comparatively light coloured where the stain has worn away. In *The Cabinet Directory* of 1803,

BRITISH FURNITURE

9.31

9.32

9.33

Fig. 9.31 Two mahogany armchairs, based on early George III prototypes, from a set of twelve by Bertram of Dean Street. The delicate backs are a honeysuckle pattern of Classical influence. [Butchoff Antiques]

Fig. 9.32 The Bedford Lemere day book records the commissioning client for this photograph as the furniture maker J.S. Henry, raising the probablity that it illustrates their prestigious Mayfair showroom in New Burlington Steet. The armchair on the left appears to be identical to the model supplied by Bertram & Son, see Fig. 9.31. [Historic England BL20435]

Fig. 9.33 Three from a set of twelve armchairs similar to those in Fig. 9.31. This set is not signed and, unusually, the maker has provided two of the chairs in a larger size, 8cm (3⅛in) higher and 9cm (3½in) wider than the guest chairs. [Butchoff Antiques]

Sheraton wrote, 'the kind of mahogany employed in chair making ought to be Spanish or Cuban, of a clean straight grain. Wood of this quality will rub bright and keep cleaner than any Honduras wood'.[32]

Bertram & Son, established in 1830, supplied furniture in the early twentieth century in a variety of styles such as Georgian-style sideboards 'improved' with florid marquetry. Two urn stands with their label are similarly over-endowed with marquetry whereas the original George III examples would have been plain.[33] Many dining chairs reproduced by Bertram are mid-eighteenth century in manner, their repertoire including painted and parcel-gilt chairs and small tables. Such furniture is difficult to pin down to a particular decade, but much of it probably dates between c.1890 and the takeover in 1909 by Charles Bessant, a firm which continued into the 1930s, situated near Bertram's in the heart of London. Bessant consolidated the old Bertram stock, selling off 220 lots of 'Old English Furniture and Modern Furniture of Old French and Old English Designs'.[34] The set of twelve mahogany dining chairs in the Hepplewhite style all stamped by Bertram, **Fig. 9.31**, are unusual not only for the length of the set but for being exclusively armchairs. A similar design dating from the 1770s is on the trade card of Vickers & Rutledge (active 1775–1780), and comparable examples are illustrated in eighteenth-century reference books. There is a variation in the Victoria and Albert Museum[35] and a similar sketch, dated March 1785, in the Gillow archive. The pierced anthemion splat is a particularly sophisticated design; and the chairs are solidly made, the legs morticed into the apron so as not to need stretchers. In order to have a more 'country', Chippendale-style look, Bertrams incorporated stretchers on the long set of twenty-two side chairs, **Fig. 9.34**. Four chairs from this set were made later and, although additional chairs in such sets are usually easy enough to identify, it can be difficult if not impossible to date when later examples were added. Dining chairs were in constant demand. Copies of a set of Georgian dining chairs were made by Greenwood & Sons of Tudor House in York for the Duke of Norfolk at Carlton Towers. From c.1890 to the present day, copies of Regency dining chairs have been made in large quantities, but the most popular and frequently seen models are reproductions of 'Chippendale' chairs. One expert collector, the Dutch-born dealer Murray Marks appreciated the Regency style; retiring to a Regency house in Brighton he 'fitted it up with Georgian furniture and equipment, so that it resembled…the best period of the Regency'.[36]

Furniture by Butler of Dublin epitomises the early twentieth-century adaptation of the late George II and early George III period (c.1740 to 1770). One of the better known and best workshops, Michael Butler established an antique business in Dublin in 1868. Able to source a

Fig. 9.34 **A near set of twenty-two side chairs, three stamped 'BERTRAM & SON, DEAN ST., OXFORD ST., W.' and three numbered '03011'. Four are very slightly different, which suggests that they were added at a later date.** [Private collection]

Figs 9.35 & 9.36 **The twentieth-century Adam-style armchair on the right, one of a pair, is similar to a set pictured in the dining room at Syon House in the 1920s, a room decorated by Robert Adam between 1762 and 1769. The Victoria and Albert Museum has a set of comparable eighteenth-century chairs, the example shown on the left described as exemplifying the 'Adam' style but similar to designs by John Linnell. It was made between 1775 and 1780.**[37] [Left: Victoria and Albert Museum, W.35-1919; Right: Butchoff Antiques]

wide variety of antiques from large Irish houses, his success later allowed him to expand to South Molton Street in the heart of London's Mayfair. As well as making high-quality reproductions, the Butler workshops repaired antique furniture and the firm capitalised on the demand for the Georgian styles, employing forty craftsmen between 1905 and 1910 to make reproduction furniture. Amongst Butler's clients were European aristocrats and wealthy industrialists. In 1903 the firm furnished the Viceregal Lodge in Dublin in conjunction with Strahan & Co. in preparation for a state visit.[38] Macquoid illustrated a mid-eighteenth-century Irish side table of a type copied later by Butler, citing the owner as 'Messrs. Morant'.[39] It begs the question as to whether Morant of London also copied this style of popular Irish furniture or simply sold it in their antique department.

The linen press by Butler, **Fig. 9.39a**, with a low stand on cabriole legs, is typical of Irish makers' adaptations of mid-eighteenth-century designs, colloquially know as 'Irish Chippendale'.[40] The well-carved mask on the apron represents a 'Green Man', a legendary symbol of rebirth and seasonal new growth. The quality of the mahogany is usually very high in Butler's and other Irish makers' furniture. The celebrated dealer Duveen stocked high-quality carved

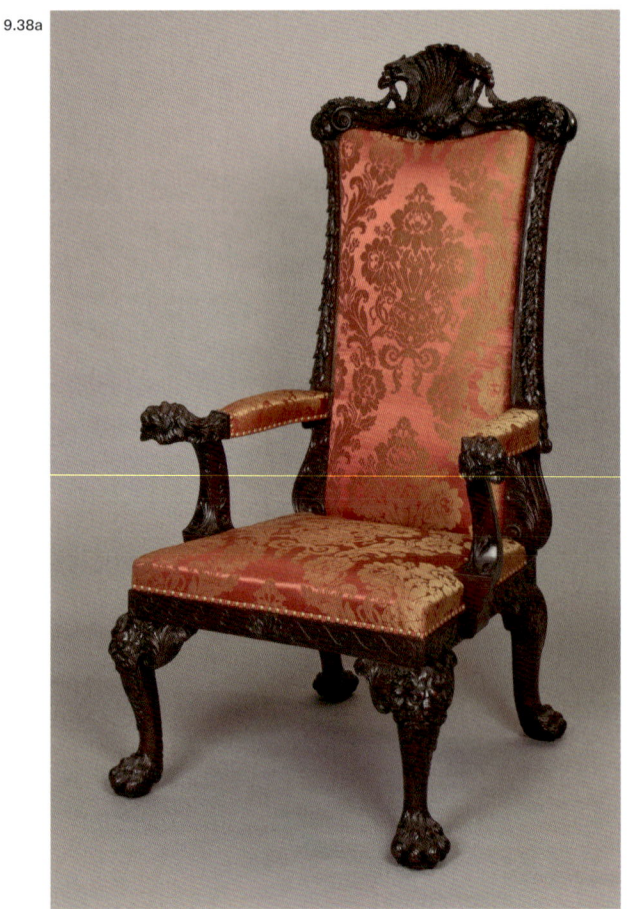

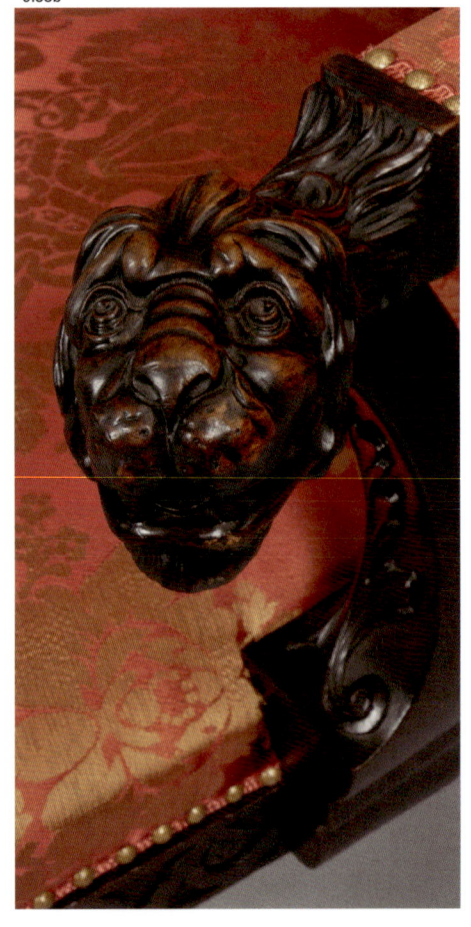

Fig. 9.37 & 9.38a An armchair, referred to as a 'French chair' in the eighteenth century, today known as a 'Gainsborough' chair in Britain or a 'Martha Washington' chair in the United States. Beneath is a 'Master's' chair with a ceremonial high back. Both have the exuberant carving and generous use of fine-quality mahogany that suggests the work of Butler of Dublin. [Private collection]

Fig. 9.38b As a symbol of power, a roaring lion's or leopard's head was a popular arm terminal in the mid-eighteenth century and for later copies. [Private collection]

CHAPTER 9: 1900–1909

9.39a

9.39b

9.39c

Fig. 9.39a & c The low stand of this cabinet, on short cabriole legs centred by a grotesque mask, is typical of Irish copies in the Chippendale style, in this instance with a label printed 'M. Butler, Chippendale, Adam and Sheraton Furniture. etc... 126/127 Upper Abbey Street, Dublin'. A possible eighteenth-century source for Butler may have been a clothes press attributed to the workshop of Giles Grendey now in the Victoria and Albert Museum.[41] [Private collection]

Fig. 9.39b A Green Man mask on the apron of the Butler cabinet on stand. The webbed talon of the foot is a recurring feature of Irish furniture. [Butchoff Antiques]

reproduction 'Chippendale' seat furniture which has the quality of carving and timber that suggest the source may have been Dublin makers.[42]

Many Butler pieces are stamped or bear a label. There is a certain consistency and quality about the firm's work which makes it somewhat difficult to date but the probability is that most reproduction pieces are from c.1900 to 1912, when the firm closed due to the 'weight of [Butler's] gambling debts'.[43]

Master's chairs made for livery companies are a late seventeenth-century concept. To emphasise the importance of the occupants they are made as armchairs and of generous,

if not exaggerated, proportions with a high, throne-like back. Copies were often made as replacements for livery or boardroom use and would not normally be used in a domestic environment. The large mahogany chair in **Fig. 9.38** is one of a pair, the imposing high back carved with a shell supported by eagles' heads holding a swag of laurel in their beaks, the same Classical reference as the giltwood eagles on the table in **Fig. 9.40a**. This style of chair and the pair of pier tables are illustrative of the revived interest in the principles of design employed by the Palladian architect William Kent. The pier tables are similar to an eighteenth-century pair at Longford Castle, home to the Earls of Radnor. An almost identical table was designed by Kent for the Blue Room of Chiswick House, commissioned by the 'Architect Earl', the 3rd Earl of Burlington, c.1727–32.[44]

As the largest furniture retailer and manufacturer in the world, Maple & Co.'s warehouse was one of the sights of London. How much of the furniture with Maple & Co. labels or stamps was made in their own workshops is open to conjecture. One estimate is that, as early as the 1880s, Maples were making less than ten per cent of the furniture that they retailed.[45] From the late nineteenth century,

9.40a

Figs 9.40a & b One of a pair of tables with generous *rouge royale* marble tops that could have been made by any number of the top London firms in the early twentieth century and are as difficult to date accurately as they are to attribute to a specific maker. An almost identical console was designed by William Kent in c.1727–1732 for the Blue Room of Chiswick House, commissioned by the 3rd Earl of Burlington. A similar eighteenth-century pair is at Longford Castle. [Butchoff Antiques]

manufactures in the East End of London were the main producers of furniture, selling wholesale to larger retailers, establishing their own outlets in the Curtain Road area of London. One such firm was that of Louis and Harris Lebus who were a major supplier of bedroom and dining room furniture to Maples. Louis Lebus had emigrated from Breslau in Poland, setting up business in Hull in the 1840s and moving to London by 1857. In 1900, working with his two sons, he built a large factory in Tabernacle Street, moving to a 13½-acre (5.5-hectare) site in Tottenham in 1900. Lebus sent his two sons to the Grand Rapids factories in Michigan, and the Lebus enterprise made good use of machinery for many aspects of manufacturing, including the sophisticated American 'Moores Carving Machines'. The firm proudly became one of the largest furniture manufactories in the world, employing a workforce of almost 1,000 by the 1890s.[46]

Maples had huge buying power; one of its advertisements illustrates 'skyscrapers', cribs of stacked timber at its timber-drying yards on Euston Road and by the Grand Union Canal in Kentish Town, **Fig. 9.42**. Such an engraving may appear to be the fanciful imaginings of an able marketing manager, but the size of the company's timber store was noted in 1893 by *The Illustrated London News*: 'great yards, where huge stacks of timber are ripening for use'. A flyer from Maples, dating to c.1900, stated that the firm used American hazelwood for bedroom suites.[47] They claimed that they imported 'immense quantities [of hazelwood] nearly three

9.40b

Fig. 9.41 **An early twentieth-century photograph showing logs and planks being unloaded at Bridge Wharf on the River Taw in Barnstaple.** [Museum of Barnstaple & North Devon]

Fig. 9.42 **An advertisement showing large cribs of stacked timber at Maples warehouses in Kentish Town situated alongside the Grand Union Canal – fanciful in scale, or reality?** [Private collection]

Fig. 9.43 **An advertisement for Brownlee & Co.'s City Saw Mills on the Clyde Canal in Glasgow. The entrepreneur James Brownlee invented highly efficient sawing machines for his mills, preparing timber imported from all over the world.** [Glasgow Museum]

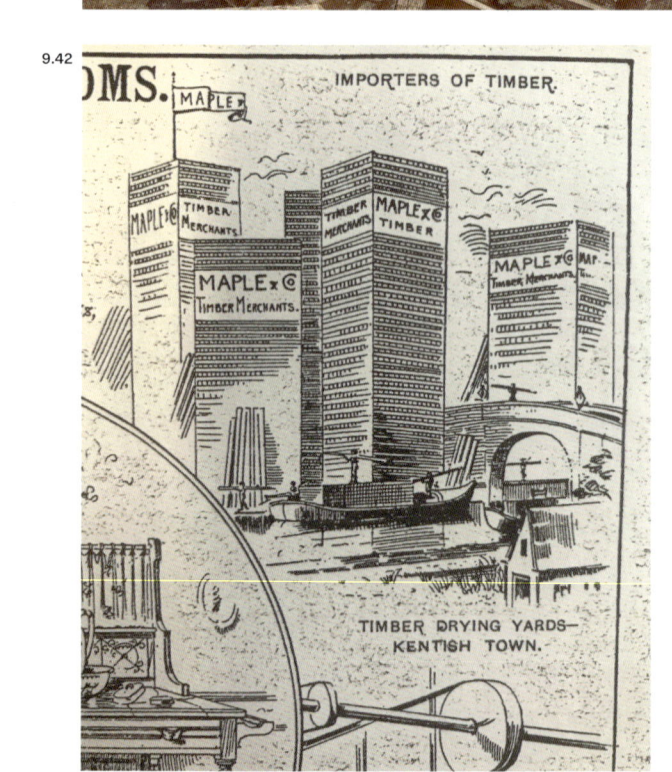

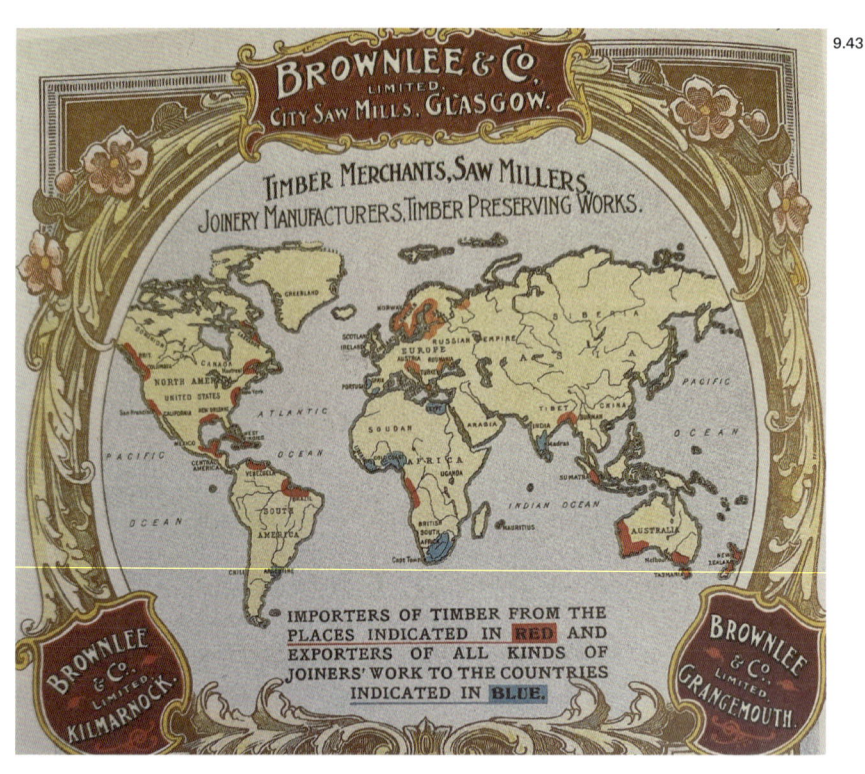

years ago', its 'fine smooth grain' when polished 'comes out a rich golden colour'.[48] Further evidence of the vast stock of timber owned by the company was confirmed by John Maple's own evidence to the Select Committee on the Sweating System in 1888. Maple reported to the House of Lords 'that we hold, of hard woods, 4,476 logs and 3,507 planks'. The stock of deal was over 130,000 planks and an astonishing '37,076 pieces ready cut for legs, in ash, mahogany, and walnut…'.[49] The huge quantity of timber ready-cut for legs would appear to be a contradiction to the suggestion that Maples made less than ten per cent of their stock. Possibly the cut timber was to ensure smaller manufacturers could readily use Maples stock to complete rapidly the increasingly large orders for the firm. The precise knowledge of such a vast stock is an insight into the business acumen of Maple himself, and his management style must have been a major contribution to the firm's success. In the following decade the reach of Maples was captured by a photographer in the Sudan, between Wadi Halfa and Khartoum, who photographed a wall sign reading: 'High Class Furniture, Maple & Co, London, Paris'.[50]

The amount of timber needed for the huge production of British firms for furniture, fittings and boatbuilding in the late Victorian era and up to the Great War was vast. In 1914 William Bullock recorded the increasing importation of African mahoganies. He noted that in 1891, in Liverpool alone, 3,207 tons of African mahogany were imported, rising to an astounding 77,377 tons by 1914.[51] Early twentieth-century images of timber yards and timber being unloaded at docksides, such as in Barnstable in Devon, **Fig. 9.41**, are a reminder of the huge amount of wood, precious or less exotic, imported into Britain to satisfy worldwide demand.

The Jacobean and Elizabethan styles were considered to be suitably 'British', and reproductions were made well into the twentieth century. The copies often lacked the deep patination of Tudor and Stuart examples. In 1902, Story & Co. of High Street Kensington advertised furniture in the Elizabethan style and yet much of this and other firms' furniture could easily be mistaken as having been made in the interwar period, post 1918, **Fig. 9.44**. In a complete stylistic contrast, Story's also made rush-seated chairs adapted from Voysey designs. The simplicity of the pierced heart used in Voysey designs was an attractive and popular motif. Commercial makers regularly reduced architect-designed furniture to popular derivatives, especially when reproducing Voysey's exquisite and innovative style. Similarities of simple, easy to copy designs can be seen in Walter Cave's rare examples of furniture, mainly chairs. Although Heal's simpler Arts and Crafts furniture was initially somewhat scorned, the firm's exhibits at the 1900 Paris fair were highly praised as 'not wanting in refinement, thoughtfulness, and originality' and 'a triumph of craftsmanship'.[52] In a reversal of the doctrine of William Morris, Ambrose Heal, on joining the family firm, designed furniture to be made with machine tools whilst retaining the quality of handmade furniture at a more accessible price.[53]

In an advertisement in 1893, the East End firm of J.S. Henry had styled itself as 'Originator' and 'Manufacturer', selling the 'Latest Novelty. Convertable Cozy [sic] Corners'.[54] A decade later, Henry's was one of the commercial manufacturers who embraced the simpler lines of a new style of furniture, part Arts and Crafts, part Art

Fig. 9.44 Story & Co., first recorded in *c*.1854, advertised their newly redecorated showrooms in 1902, stating that this Elizabethan Revival dining room was designed in their own studios. [Butchoff archive]

Fig. 9.45 Elizabethan-style furniture in one of the James Plucknett Warwickshire showrooms, photographed at the firm's closing-down auction in 1908. [Butchoff archive]

9.46

9.47

Nouveau. George Montague Ellwood, as well as designing for the Bath Cabinet Makers Company, designed a suite of highly acclaimed furniture for Henry which they exhibited at the 1900 *Exposition Universelle* in Paris. Alongside this however, Henry continued to offer reproduction furniture, and the interior photograph, **Fig. 9.32**, is likely to be one of their new showrooms in New Burlington Street. Awarded a gold medal at the 1900 Paris exhibition, the Bath Cabinet Makers Company exhibited four sideboards designed by one of the two brothers who founded the firm in 1892, Charles Richter. Their creative furniture was in sharp contrast to a more traditional display of a study by Howard & Sons.[55] The British Pavilion in 1900 was in an eclectic 'Jacobethan' manner. The Dining Room was supplied by Bertram & Son, the Drawing Room fitted by Collinson & Lock in conjunction with their new owners, Gillows.

At the beginning of the twentieth century, the furniture in, or thought to be in, the Palladian style of William Kent was one of the most copied, and reproductions are still being made today. The most popular model was a console table with a single eagle support, made in natural wood with a waxed, painted or gesso finish. There is no documentation for Kent's involvement in the design of these tables. Generally smaller than the larger slab-top tables of the 1730s, the reproduction model was eminently suitable for the reduced proportions of modern houses and apartments. Kent would have been familiar with eagles as architectural features in Rome and, strikingly, the entrance to the Villa Borghese. Each gate post at the villa is surmounted by a similar eagle in the pose adopted on English tables, facing each other as a true pair. The popular twentieth century model is similar, for example, to a pair of eighteenth-century tables now in the Ionic Temple at Rievaulx Terrace in Yorkshire.[56]

At the Franco-British Exhibition in 1908 the decorating firm of White Allom & Co., established by Charles Allom in 1905, exhibited three giltwood console tables, one with an eagle support, see **Fig 9.51**. A photograph in the Duveen Archives shows one of a pair of tables of a similar model, with a note explaining that one is a genuine example with the possibility of making a new one to make a pair. The Duveen annotation reads: 'A pair of finely carved & gilt Eagle Console tables, one old & one modern…£300 pair In stock'. This compares to a single genuine example priced by Duveen at £288.[57] A pair of eagle console tables flanked the library fireplace at Whitemarsh Hall, the home of Edward Stotesbury at Wyndmoor, Pennsylvania, furnished extensively by Duveen. The ever-popular reproduction of the eighteenth-century mahogany partners' desk was another White Allom & Co. favourite. Charles Allom became chairman of the British section of the Decorative Arts Committee in 1908 and was knighted in 1913 for his design work at Buckingham Palace, see **Fig. 10.97**. Amongst many commissions, he decorated the Henry Clay Frick House on Fifth Avenue.[58]

The international exhibitions became a platform to promote the British ability to supply well-made and expensive copies of antique furniture and fittings, and continued to be a major driver for the furniture trade. *Paris in London*, an exhibition held at Earl's Court in 1902, was a venue for many items of British furniture originally shown at the Paris *Exposition Universelle* in 1900. Six British firms

Fig. 9.46 **Gregory & Co. were established in London's prestigious Regent Street in 1861. In this image, probably dating to *c*.1910, the overall feel is fashionably French, the small centre table made in Paris by François Linke, design number 916.** [Historic England]

Fig. 9.47 **White Allom offered this type of reproduction mirror, somewhat optimistically described as 'Chippendale', for £65.** [Metropolitan Museum]

Fig. 9.48 **One of a set of Queen Anne chairs offered by White Allom for £600. They sold reproductions 'toned down to look old' for £11 10*s* per chair.** [Metropolitan Museum]

Fig. 9.49 **A reproduction chair upholstered in green morocco leather, available from White Allom at £26 10*s* each.** [Metropolitan Museum]

Fig. 9.50 **This style of reproduction Charles II chair, of a type made by Ralph Janes and other High Wycombe makers, was available from White Allom for £7 15*s*.** [Metropolitan Museum]

Fig. 9.51 **The perennially popular Palladian style habitually attributed to William Kent was favoured by the top London makers. This console table with an eagle support was available from White Allom for £75. A similar model was available through Duveen.** [Metropolitan Museum]

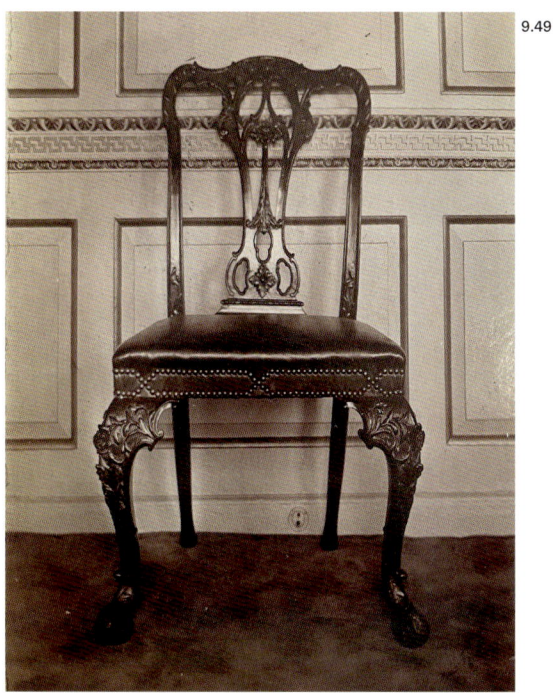

exhibited at the Louisiana Purchase Exposition (informally known as the St Louis World's Fair) in 1904, **Fig. 9.52**. Whereas France and Germany exhibited highly finished furniture in a richly mounted, modernised Louis XV style by Linke of Paris and Zwiener of Berlin, Britain's furniture was more traditional, although alongside the 'old' styles there was furniture with a certain lightness of form, influenced by the Arts and Crafts movement. The rooms of the royal pavilion at St Louis were set out in period fashion with reproductions copied from stately homes. At the centre of the Elizabethan Dining Room was a refectory table, the thin proportion of the baluster legs a clear indication that it was a reproduction. The Georgian Room was furnished with a mixture of what appears to have been period pieces and 'adaptations from a fine Chippendale model'.[59] The sparsely furnished Queen Anne Room housed 'either old or replicas of historical specimens'.[60] The furniture of the so-called 'Adams Room' was distinctly Sheraton in manner, **Fig. 9.58b**.

The decoration and fixed furniture in St Louis included work by Mellier & Co. and William Birch Ltd. 'Grand prizes' were awarded to Waring & Gillow, also Trollope & Sons. Intriguingly, Trollope exhibited a 'few specimens of genuine old furniture...and pieces...made to harmonise with them'.[61] Mellier exhibited in the French style with Louis XVI reproductions, Litchfield remarking that their work was 'quite equal to that of French firms'.[62] Since such furniture was likely made for or by Mellier in Paris for sale in London, Litchfield was close to the mark. William Birch, who started out around 1840 in High Wycombe as solely a chair maker was, by the turn of the century, exhibiting copies of case furniture in Chippendale, Hepplewhite and Sheraton styles. In stark contrast the firm also made their 'Quaint'

Fig. 9.52 The St Louis World's Fair of 1904, correctly titled the *Louisiana Purchase Exposition*, organised to celebrate the anniversary of the purchase of Louisiana in 1803, housed a small section of British furniture makers. This room by Waring & Gillow is a copy of one in an old house at Epsom, with painted panelling and modern adaptations of mid-eighteenth-century furniture. [Butchoff archive]

Fig. 9.53 Linke of Paris was a major contributor to the Franco-British Exhibition held at Shepherd's Bush in 1908 and exhibited several items of furniture in the English style, such as this 'Chippendale' display cabinet. [Linke Archives]

Fig. 9.54 A project by Linke of Paris for a drawing room in the English style. To be made in satinwood with 'Adam' marquetry. [Linke Archives]

seminal rush-seated oak armchair designed by E.G. Punnett, **Fig. 9.61**.[63] Waring & Gillow created a balcony effect for their stand in 1904, with small paned windows enticing the viewer inside. The dining room was dark and imposing with late seventeenth-century style applied carving in the manner of Grinling Gibbons on the walls and imitations of Queen Anne and George I period furniture. In contrast, the drawing room was set out as a French salon, probably with imported Parisian furniture in a conventional reproduction style.

Subsequently, to celebrate the political *Entente Cordiale*, an exhibition hall housing the Franco-British Exhibition was built in 1908 on a new site at Shepherd's Bush. Almost half of the space was devoted to French products and the event welcomed over eight million visitors. By this time the Paris

9.55

Fig. 9.55 Morris & Co. had a large stand in the Decorative Arts Building at the Franco-British Exhibition in 1908. On the left is a 'Solid Mahogany Drawing Room Cabinet by George Jack (see also Fig. 9.17), on the right a cabinet by W.A.S. Benson, both designed in the 1890s. [Private collection]

Fig. 9.56 A cabinet in the 'Queen Anne' style exhibited by Morris & Co. at the Franco-British Exhibition in 1908, made from Italian walnut to a design by M.E. Macartney. [Private collection]

Fig. 9.57 At the Franco-British Exhibition in 1908 there was a loan exhibition of British furniture, in this instance the so-called 'Queen Anne' room which had a mixture of styles from *c.*1660 to 1760. [Private collection]

9.56

9.57

BRITISH FURNITURE

The country was resting on its stylistic laurels and there was disappointment that there was not more innovative British furniture at the 1908 Franco-British Exhibition. However, a contribution from Godfrey Giles & Co. showed 'a little room simply and inexpensively fitted up' and 'a speciality of ingenious furniture…a settee that comes apart in the middle and forms two corner chairs'.[66] As well as a reproduction of the Great Hall at Hatfield, scaled down to two-thirds of the original size, Hamptons exhibited two small rooms of modern reproduction furniture, one in the Chippendale style, the other Adam. A notable contribution to the exhibition was the 7.62m-wide (25ft) stand of Morris & Co., **Fig. 9.55**, which exhibited a wide range of contemporary furniture in a mixture of styles, some modern, other items of a derivative nature such as a Queen Anne-style, Dutch-influenced display cabinet made of Italian walnut to a design by the architect/designer Mervyn E. Macartney, **Fig. 9.56**. Italian walnut was also used for a secretaire cabinet designed by W.A.S. Benson and made by the Morris firm. Morris & Co. was credited as showing the only specimens of living British creative art.

The 1908 exhibition boasted a loan exhibition of period rooms all with what was intended to be genuine antique furniture. Described as a 'William and Mary Room', a 'Queen Anne Room', a 'Chippendale Room', and a 'Georgian Room', to our modern eye the styles were confused and some of the pieces were on the wrong stand, such as a William and Mary table and a George II armchair in the 'Queen Anne Room', **Fig. 9.57**. Mallett, founded by John Mallett in Bath in 1865 as jewellers and silversmiths, exhibited antique furniture, including a two-chair back settee and a magnificent Chippendale bookcase; Mallett's success encouraged them to set up in London at 40 New Bond Street. They made an exact copy of a late seventeenth-century walnut writing table for £200 – the antique original had been bought for £336 60d.[67] White Allom & Co. exhibited part of the Sutton Scarsdale suite of eighteenth-century chairs, including one of the double settees, dubbed a 'Love Seat'.[68] It would appear that such firms exhibited antique furniture and used the venue to offer copies to interested clients.

Continuing the tradition of previous decades, local firms supplied furniture and fittings for royal pavilions at exhibitions such as the reception rooms for the royal family at the 1901 Glasgow International Exhibition, fitted by Wylie & Lochhead and furnished with reproduction Georgian furniture. A versatile firm which thrived with 37,000ft² (3,437m²) of showrooms in Glasgow alone, Wylie & Lochhead was able to adapt and innovate, showing commercial variations of the Art Nouveau style. They were awarded a royal warrant as cabinet makers and upholsterers to Edward VII. Some of their production was in a watered-

Figs 9.58a & b The long-standing firm of George Trollope & Sons exhibited a mixture of antique and reproduction furniture at the St Louis fair, drawn from their own stock. The cabinet in the upper image was copied from one dated 1621, that belonged to the late Sir William Stirling, the chairs adapted from those at Knole. The lower image of the so-called 'Adams Room' shows furniture that owes more to the designs of Sheraton.
[Private collection]

cabinet maker François Linke was producing a limited range of furniture in distinctly English 'Chippendale' and 'Adam' styles and took a large stand at the exhibition, **Figs 9.53 & 9.54**.[64] Much of this furniture has yet to be identified, some today may well be mistakenly thought to have been made in England, although there will be a noticeable difference in the construction, the metal fittings and locks. Like other contemporaries, Bertram & Son put their own stamp on furniture they had bought from other makers, such as a Louis XV-style marquetry pedestal also by Linke.[65]

472

down Mackintosh style intended for a wider market at a reasonable price.[69] The press gave mixed reviews: one commentator noting that it was 'unquestionably the most important furnishing display [of the exhibition]'; another thought it was 'not suggestive of the greatest comfort'.[70]

In efforts to embody both tradition and political ambitions, there was a distinct contrast between the two styles of coronation chair ordered for Edward VII in 1902. In the light of Franco-British co-operation and the new king's well-publicised penchant for Paris, it is not surprising that two throne chairs were supplied by the Paris firm of Carlhian & Beaumetz who already had an established presence in London and had been recommended by Duveen, **Fig. 9.62**. At their Great Eastern Street shop 'every French style, from the François Premier to the Louis Seize and Empire' was fully represented.[71] It is not certain where the thrones were actually made, Paris or London, or if Carlhian themselves had the type of workshop capable of making such a sophisticated chair.[72] Now at Buckingham Palace, the thrones retain their original velvet cut with the royal cipher and the royal badges of Great Britain: the rose of England, the thistle of Scotland and the shamrock of Ireland.[73] In contrast, Edward VII also ordered a Gothic-style throne to an 1840s design by Pugin from Holland & Sons for Queen Alexandra's use at the coronation, **Fig. 9.63**.[74]

The trend for furniture-making firms, from the large London stores to small provincial companies, to offer comprehensively furnished interiors had increased greatly by the end of the nineteenth century.[75] For example, by the early 1900s Howard & Sons were advertising parquet flooring in Indian teak of a type made by Brownlee & Co. in Glasgow as well as oak wall panelling. Warings also provided panelled rooms. Howard & Sons offered a more comprehensive range but are best known today for their seat furniture, to the extent that, perpetuated by their takeover by Lenygon in 1935, every deep, comfortable upholstered chair is now attributed to them. Some have an enamel label with their name, others have the company name stamped on the brass castors. Firms such as the Army & Navy Stores, Maples, Hamptons, Waring & Gillow and Harrods expanded out to the provinces and overseas. Dropping the Gillow name, Warings opened a large new premises in Oxford Street in 1906, **Fig. 9.68**, and in the Champs Élysées in Paris the same year, as well as prestigious outlets in Brussels and Madrid. In a publication on the Franco-British Exhibition in 1908 Gillows listed an outlet in Montreal, advertising that 'Warings skill and resources are conspicuously exemplified in the work executed by them for the King and Queen', foremost amongst their royal clientele.[76] Hamptons, started by William Hampton in 1830, was expanded by his two sons to Pall Mall in 1869 and the firm bought up other cabinet-making firms, such as James Coulson & Co. of Lisburn in Northern Ireland in 1898 and subsequently the fifty-year-old

Fig. 9.59 **A 1910 advertisement showing a display at Wylie & Lochhead's Glasgow showrooms. The light-coloured furniture and panelling are in an eclectic Classical style.** [Frank Gorny]

Fig. 9.60 **Another Wylie & Lochhead showroom illustrates that traditional values of comfort and intimacy were still important in the first decade of the twentieth century. The overall style of the furniture is a revival of Louis XV Rococo.** [Private collection]

BRITISH FURNITURE

Goodall, Lamb & Highway in Manchester as well as 'the largest and most complete house furnishers in the North of England', Robson & Sons of Newcastle-upon-Tyne.[77] By the twentieth century Hamptons had huge premises, their extensive showrooms providing a complete home furnishing service. In 1903 they built a vast storage facility in Battersea, south of Chelsea Bridge. The frontage, with a gentle curve alongside a railway line, included workshops lit and ventilated by cast-iron windows of a style advocated by Loudon almost a century earlier. Photographs of the

Fig. 9.61 **In complete contrast to their Georgian reproductions, this rush-seated, walnut-inlaid oak armchair by William Birch of High Wycombe is an iconic example of 'Quaint' furniture designed by E.G. Punnett at the turn of the century.** [Bonhams]

Fig. 9.62 **One of a pair of throne chairs in the French Empire style, supplied by the Parisian firm of Carlhian & Beaumetz for the coronation of Edward VII at** Westminster Abbey in August 1902. [Royal Collection Trust © His Majesty King Charles III 2023, RCIN 2624]

Fig. 9.63 **A design of 1901 recording an original by A.W.N. Pugin in** *c.*1840. Edward VII ordered a copy of this throne specifying that it was to be made by Holland & Sons for the use of Queen Alexandra at the 1902 coronation. [Victoria and Albert Museum, E.6-1985]

474

workshops show no evidence of machinery although the veneering room had the latest pattern press and a chamber for heating the cauls, **Fig. 9.65**. In the upholstery shop, men are shown shaping the horsehair and webbing for chairs, the more genteel task of applying the gimp braid carried out by women, although many women carried out the unenviable task of French polishing in some establishments. Elder-Duncan in *The House Beautiful and Useful* referred to Warings as producers of 'Chairs and settees, upholstered in red velvet with fringed ends and studded with brass or copper nails'.[78]

Many firms both in London and the provinces combined making with retailing on a large scale. Harrods could boast of over one million square feet (102,000m^2) of retail space and had their own workshops, **Fig. 9.66**. Maples' premises on Tottenham Court Road was more of a three-sided palace than a department store, with possibly the largest concentration of retail furniture in the world, supported by at least four workshops. Having had a presence in Paris since *c.*1885, Maples opened their prestigious branch in the rue Boudreau in 1905. From 1900 they had been working with H.H. Martyn in Cheltenham, whose 12-acre (48,500m^2) site provided the space and efficient production for much of their contract work. Regional shops under the Maples banner subsequently opened in Bournemouth and Brighton. The firm won royal appointments from over twenty royal families, from the German empress to the sultan of Zanzibar, and the tsar of Russia to the king of Siam. George V furnished his favourite retreat, York House on the Sandringham Estate, with furniture supplied by Maples. The firm made furniture for the viceroy of India's palace at Simla in 1898 and was subsequently commissioned to furnish his palace in Delhi. The Dowager Queen of Portugal, an inveterate shopper in Paris, was invited to visit Maples' shop in rue Boudreau in 1901, where they held 'a very large stock of genuine English-made Furniture of the best finish & workmanship'.[79]

John Blundell Maple, the founder of the firm, wrote in the foreword to one of their large illustrated catalogues: 'chasteness of design – collections that constitute MAPLE'S an EXHIBITION WITHOUT PARALLEL IN THE WORLD'. Styling themselves 'the largest and most Convenient Furnishing Establishment in the World', Maples became one of the 'must see' sights of London. The firm encouraged visitors to pay a personal visit to their 30 acres (121,400m^2) of showrooms, all set out in different styles. Despite the growing power of mail order, even for bulky items of furniture, they offered to deliver up to a 50-mile (80-kilometre) radius with their own vans, suggesting that customers 'conveniently make use of these vans to send up goods requiring renovation'. It might be cynical to ask what they offered this 'service' for, their clients' convenience or to look for suitable models to copy! Notwithstanding the large stocks, the firm was cited repeatedly for the quality of its furniture.[80]

By the first decade of the century, James Shoolbred and other large furniture stores in London and the provinces offered everything that a household could require, from beds to pots and pans, decorations and carpeting. The Shoolbred furniture range included pieces in the ubiquitous commercial Art Nouveau style, similar to that of Liberty's, as well as simple oak furniture with carved Art Nouveau foliage. In April 1899, *The Cabinet Maker* reported that Shoolbred had extended their warehouse facilities. Set up as a limited company in 1913, the firm's success declined in the interwar period, closing in 1931. On a far smaller scale was S. & H. Jewell, founded in 1830 as mattress makers,

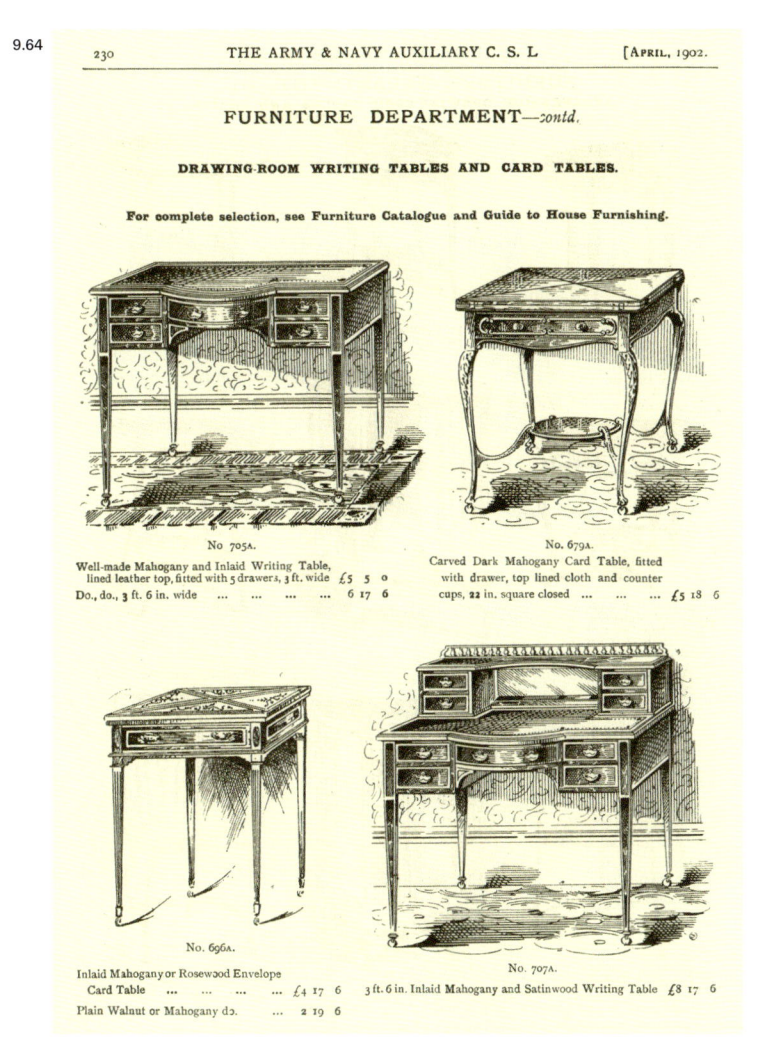

Fig. 9.64 **Not yet using photographic images, this page from the 1902 Army & Navy Stores catalogue shows engravings of 'Drawing-room Writing Tables and Card Tables', all almost certainly bought in from smaller, probably East End, firms.** [Look & Learn]

Fig. 9.65 **Everything is being finished by hand in this undated photograph of one of the cabinet shops at Hampton & Sons in Battersea. Twenty men are working at their benches, with an onlooker on the left and a supervisor in the background. The finished carcasses are then taken through to the veneering room.** [Butchoff archive]

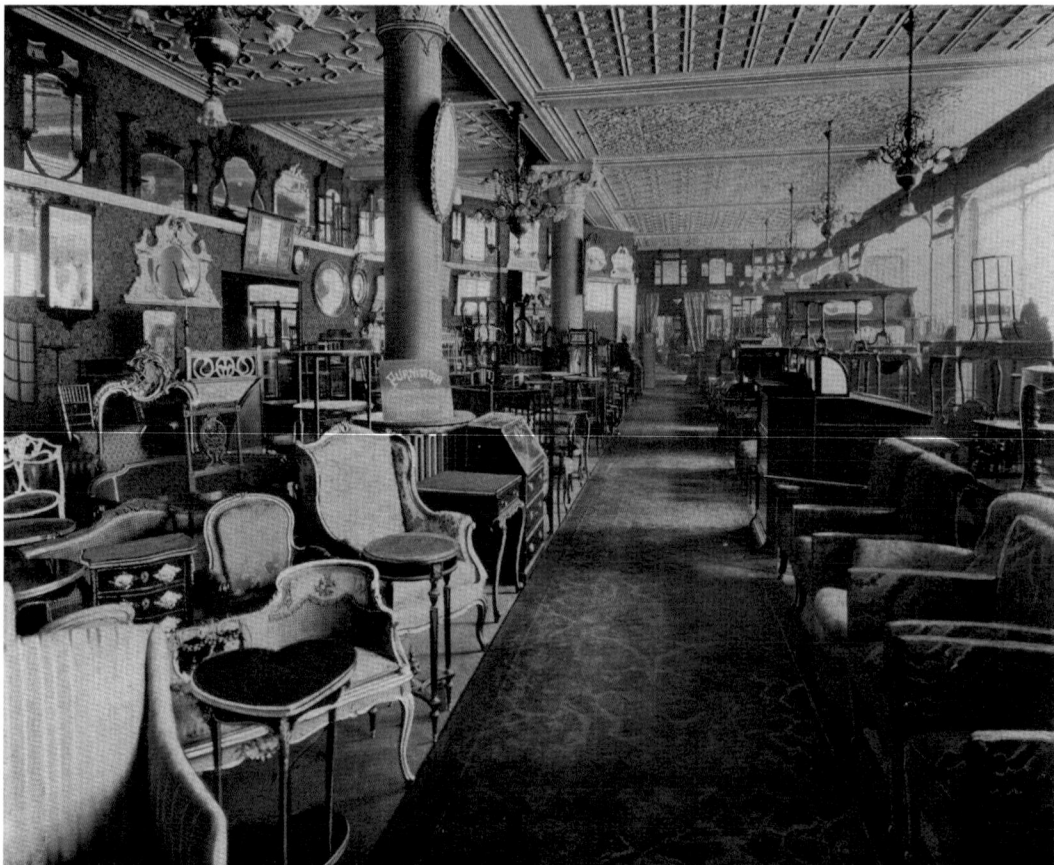

Fig. 9.66 **With over one million square feet (102,000m^2) of display space, this image of the Harrods Cabinet Department in *c.*1903 shows the extent of their modern French and English furniture display.**[81] [Look & Learn]

9.67

THE NEW ANNEXE OF MESSRS. OETZMANN AND CO.'S ESTABLISHMENT AT THE CORNER OF DRUMMOND STREET AND HAMPSTEAD ROAD.

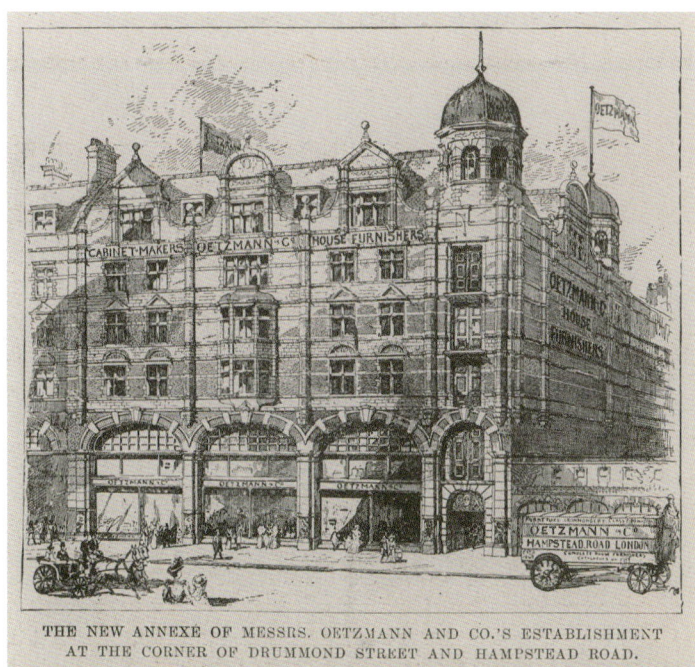

The new annexe, built from the plans of Mr. Fred Eales, of Welbeck Street, and extending down one side of Drummond Street, is very commodious. It includes seven spacious floors of showrooms and factory, surmounted by a fine cupola'd roof.

9.68

later cited as furniture makers. Jewell had the foresight to apply their name to much of, or possibly all, the furniture they handled, and it is unsure what they made, if indeed they were also makers, or what they bought in. Early pieces have a stamped brass plaque and by the 1870s they were using ivorine plaques or stencil stamps. The wide range of their furniture and the differing level of craftsmanship suggests that they were not actually makers but dealers, buying in new and old furniture which they renovated, adding their own label. The labels conveniently have an address, which allows some basic form of dating, not necessarily of the manufacture but of the time the piece was in stock, or sold.[82] In the provinces long-established firms such as Marsh, Jones & Cribb of Leeds battled against the larger stores until the 1930s, providing furniture at affordable prices and also antiques, becoming early members of the British Antique Dealers Association. The long-established firm Mawer & Collingham of Lincoln were typical of the larger provincial stores who supplied all household needs. The shop included a restaurant and the store was listed as a wholesale and retail

Fig. 9.67 **In this advertisement in** *The Illustrated London News*, **6 April 1901, the furniture manufacturers Oetzmann & Co. proudly show off their new 'commodious' establishment at the corner of Drummond Street and Hampstead Road in London.** [Look & Learn]

Fig. 9.68 **Making furniture since the eighteenth century, Gillows was merged with Warings in 1903. When the new 40,000ft² (approx. 3,700m²) building on Oxford Street opened in 1906, containing 150 specimen rooms, the red flag only sported the Warings name.**[83] [Alamy Stock Photo]

BRITISH FURNITURE

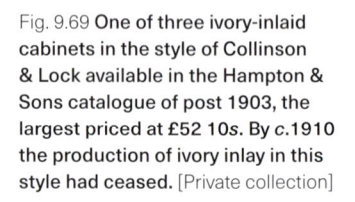

9.69

9.70

9.71

9.72

Fig. 9.69 One of three ivory-inlaid cabinets in the style of Collinson & Lock available in the Hampton & Sons catalogue of post 1903, the largest priced at £52 10s. By c.1910 the production of ivory inlay in this style had ceased. [Private collection]

Fig. 9.70 G.F. Bodley of Watt & Co. modernised the interior of Quenby Hall in Leicestershire in c.1905, the client content to mix seventeenth-century antique furniture from nearby C.B. Payne Ltd with reproduction furniture possibly made by Watts.[84] [Copyright *Country Life*/Future Publishing Ltd]

Fig. 9.71 A Maple & Co. catalogue, published before 1901, offering a wide range of furniture at different price levels. Such publications became increasingly important in maintaining and expanding business. [John Evans Bedford Library]

Fig. 9.72 A Shapland & Petter catalogue of 'China Cabinets of Artistic Design & High Class Manufacture', early 1900s. [Butchoff archive]

Fig. 9.73 Each of the three alternative styles of display cabinet from a Shapland & Petter catalogue of c.1901 has its own stock or pattern number. The company also offered cabinets in the Chinese Chippendale style.[85] [Museum of Barnstable and North Devon]

9.73

| CABINET Nº 1744. Height 6'9" Width 3'0" Depth 1'3" | CABINET Nº 1759. Height 6'4" Width 3'0" | CABINET Nº 1758. Height 6'3" Width 3'0" |

drapers, silk mercers, haberdashers, milliners, dressmakers, tailors, hatters, furriers, lacemen, clothiers, hosiers, glovers and general outfitters, carpet warehousemen, upholsterers and, last but not least, house furnishers and decorators.

Graham & Biddle were proud of their association with the past, advertising in *The Connoisseur* in July 1903 from their premises at Graham House, 463 Oxford Street, as the 'Only Surviving Partners of Jackson & Graham'. By then a department store working as complete house furnishers with what was by now an almost obligatory antiques department, they also retailed furniture from other makers. One example is a cabinet similar to a Gillows design of 1887, but with leather-embossed panelled doors, with decoration reminiscent of the ivory marquetry of Stephen Webb seen in the previous chapter, **Fig. 8.22**.[86] Graham & Banks, located nearby in 1905, at 445 Oxford Street, advertised as 'Antique Furniture, Modern Furniture, Chairs and Sofas'.[87] They also claimed descent 'from Jackson & Graham'. Clearly there was some competition between the two firms in the use of the distinguished name whose heyday had been between the 1850s and 1880s. An advertisement in *The Cabinet Maker* suggests that Graham & Banks may have been simply retailers. It showed a line drawing of a somewhat ponderous fall-front desk with Art Nouveau marquetry, beside a copy of a Georgian wing armchair. It read: 'here we have the rich tones of the mahogany relieved by inlay of the broad decorative character that has been cultivated of late by one or two of our leading manufacturers'.[88]

As worldwide trade developed, furniture catalogues played an increasingly important part in business-getting. In *c.*1905, the East End firm of Sewell & Sewell issued a comprehensive catalogue with 1,080 pages of designs.[89] Their premises in Worship Street was a cost-effective building with workshops, offices and a storeroom over ground-floor showrooms. The importance of catalogues, even for expensive luxury furniture, is illustrated by the catalogue issued by Hamptons of Pall Mall, elaborately bound with clasps imitating Renaissance hinges, and carrying stylised lettering influenced by the Arts and Crafts movement, **Fig. 9.75**. The firm had been registered with its new corporate name Hampton & Sons in 1897 holding a 'Great Inaugural Sale' the following year. The catalogue referred to the two blocks of its new 'vast Depository', which suggests that the catalogue dates to *c.*1903, the year the new stores

479

Fig. 9.74 In the early 1900s Hamptons estimated the complete cost of furnishing this 'Young Lady's Room' at £44 14s. [Butchoff archive]

Fig. 9.75 An elaborate undated catalogue published between c.1903 and c.1910, by Hampton & Sons of Pall Mall, bound with clasps imitating Renaissance hinges and carrying stylised lettering influenced by the Arts and Crafts movement.[90] [Butchoff archive]

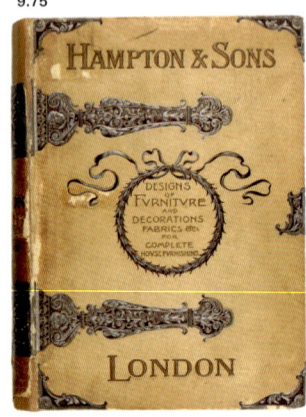

were opened.[91] It offered a full service as complete house furnishers.[92] The complete 'Young Lady's Room', could be purchased for £44 14s, almost half this being for the soft furnishings. The bedroom suite was described as being of 'Enamelled [sic] White...with Adams enrichments', **Fig. 9.74**. In 1903 Hamptons was taken over by Warings, but the brand name continued in use. A soft-bound catalogue 'Furnishing Schemes of Refinement and Character' was issued by Hamptons in 1907, the front cover, in colour, showed a young woman leaving a 'Colonial Adam Style' house. The introduction stated that: 'One of the chief charms of Colonial Adam is that, although the details are all in the same classical spirit, the style does not call for any attempt at academic accuracy...but affords ample scope for the play of individual thought and skill'. A contemporary design manual illustrated examples of a 'Colonial Georgian' and a 'Colonial Adam' style room, both being modern interpretations of the period.[93]

French furniture, mainly in the Louis XV taste with gentle curves and cabriole legs, continued in popularity well into the 1920s. London firms offered a wide range of luxury furniture from some of the best makers in Paris. Whereas Maples simply described their examples as 'French', Hindley & Wilkinson stated that their French furniture was specially commissioned, although their claim that their copy of the celebrated Oeben-Riesener *bureau du Roi* was made in their own workshops must be something of an exaggeration.[94] Certain manufacturers, such as Mellier, made French furniture in Paris and retailed it in London. Makers or retailers like Edmond Kahn pose more of a problem. Both Kahn and Hindley & Wilkinson passed off furniture by Linke and Sormani as their own and one has to assume that the original makers were complicit.[95] What Kahn actually made in-house is unclear.[96] He had established a business in London in 1892 with showrooms in London and Paris and was still in London in the 1930s with addresses at 6, 8 and 10 St Andrew Street, 18–21 Charlotte Street and 'a manufactory at 19–51 Gough Street'. The firm advertised in Paris as 'Kahn (E.) et Cie, meubles artistiques très soignés', and in London as 'E. Kahn & Co. Ltd., Manufacturers of Furniture and Upholstery, specialists in lacquered furniture, wholesale and export'.[97] A small catalogue of *c.*1900, 'Designs of English and French Artistic Furniture', with the initials 'E.K. & CO. Ltd.', illustrated familiar French reproduction furniture styles, much of it by François Linke. The firm also had access to a wide range of English furniture. Much of the Kahn stock has similarities to that often thought to be by Edwards & Roberts or Maple & Co., and it is unclear if it was bought in from smaller East End or provincial firms. A section of 'Decorated & Inlaid Satinwood' furniture includes a Carlton House desk as well as the model of satinwood dressing table offered by Hindley & Wilkinson, a copy of the Victoria and Albert Museum example shown in Chapter 5, see **Fig. 5.86**.[98] *The Cabinet Maker* supported the imports of French furniture by Kahn, writing a decade later: 'The traditions and training of the English craftsman preclude him from catching the spirit of the historic French styles. French furniture should be made by Frenchmen…'.[99] In 1907, prior to a stocktaking exercise, Kahn advertised a 'Great Reduction' of prices of between 15 and 33 per cent.[100]

The fall-front desk, **Fig. 9.78**, or *secrétaire à abbatant*, is an exceptional English copy of a celebrated piece of French furniture. The Chubb lock is stamped 128 Queen Victoria Street, which does not help the dating, since Chubb occupied that address from 1877 to 1941. However, the serial number '1650931' with the characteristic Chubb fish stamp, suggests a date between 1909 and 1914. A lock can always have been changed but close inspection confirms that the cabinet making is by an English hand, with constructional features not adopted in France, the most evident being the quarter mouldings in the drawers. The original desk was made by Jean-Henri Riesener for Marie Antoinette's private use at Marly in 1783. The desk was exhibited at the Bethnal Green Museum by Sir Richard Wallace between 1872 and 1875, where drawings were allowed which may have facilitated copies to have been produced. It is likely that the copy was made post 1900 when the original was on view again in the newly inaugurated Wallace Collection in Manchester Square.[101] The oval gilt-bronze panel on the fall front of

Fig. 9.76 **A four-poster bed with a Morant & Co. label, probably supplied to Buckhurst Park in *c.*1900. Based on a Hepplewhite design, it incorporates parts from a period George III bed.** [Christie's]

Riesener's desk and the burr veneer were not part of his original design but were added to replace marquetry by the French trade in the early nineteenth century.[102] The maker has copied the desk as he saw it, without knowing about the later embellishment, with painstaking accuracy and to the highest standards of British luxury craftsmanship. The fact that the inside of the copy is different to the original may have been to make it more practical or simply because when copied it was not possible to have the interior opened.

The long-established firm of Morant, styled Morant & Co. from 1890, was absorbed by Lenygon & Co. in 1909. Whereas much of Morant's later furniture was of a staid quasi mid-Georgian style, albeit of superb quality, Francis Lenygon looked back to the earlier periods of Carolean, Queen Anne and Palladian designs for inspiration. In 1909 he published *The Decoration and Furniture of English Mansions during the Seventeenth & Eighteenth Centuries*. A 1915 review of the book in *The Connoisseur* pointed out that the illustrations were based on the company's premises at 31 Old Burlington Street and highlighted the strong emphasis on the work of William Kent. Kentian reproductions are frequently attributed to the firm, often more in hope than reality (see Chapter 10 – 1910 to 1920). The George III style four-poster or tester bed, **Fig. 9.76**, with a Morant label was

Fig. 9.77 A beautifully made commode in well-figured mahogany. The locks are stamped 'Mellier & Co. London' but it is difficult to judge if the carcass was made in France or England. [Wick Antiques]

Fig. 9.78 Fitted with Chubb locks, this fall-front desk is an English copy of a writing desk or *secrétaire à abbatant* originally made by Jean-Henri Riesener in 1783, now at the Wallace Collection. Shown open here, the interior layout of the copy is a more practical arrangement than the Riesener original. [Private collection]

probably supplied to Robert H. Benson for Buckhurst Park in *c*.1900. Using parts of a George III original bed, it is based on Hepplewhite designs published posthumously in the third edition of The *Cabinet-Maker and Upholsterer's Guide*.[103] The innovative Morant bedroom suite, **Fig. 9.79**, has well-chosen satinwood veneers.

'The taste for antiques is largely on the increase', so proclaimed *The Connoisseur*.[104] Two features in the magazine in 1902 and 1905 discussed the antiques department of Warings, including retail prices, such as £25 for a 'Sheraton decorated settee' with four chair backs, in the manner of the Rossetti settee shown in Chapter 5, exhibited by Partridge, Lewis & Simmons at the Plaza Hotel, New York, in 1910 (see **Figs 5.89 & 5.90**). A new antiques showroom was opened by Warings in Oxford Street in 1904. Titles for their showrooms were misleading: 'Old English Furniture' was predominantly Dutch. 'Louis XV Furniture' was a room full of copies and pastiches. Robert Partridge, established as an antique dealer in London in the 1890s and in New York in 1912, was one of many dealers plying back and forth to New York to supply the growing demand for British antiques.[105] Arthur Avant, born in England in 1877, moved to the United States and set up his own shop in Manhattan in 1906, changing his name to Vernay; like many of his contemporaries, he plied between his shops in Piccadilly and New York, buying and selling antique furniture. Gill & Reigate, established in 1898, styled themselves 'Dealers in Antique & Modern Furniture, Artistic Decorators and Upholsterers'. Their extensive New Oxford Street and 'Soho Galleries' showrooms were furnished in the popular styles of the day. As well as restoration work, they exhibited a quantity of period furniture and a dining room of 'An Old Tudor House' at the 1908 Franco-British Exhibition. In 1924 they furnished the Royal Pavilion at Wembley for the British Empire Exhibition. By 1910, Gill & Reigate claimed to have 'the largest stock of genuine antiques in London', but also that 'particular attention has been given to "Reproductions"…Modern furniture exactly copied from the best designs of the sixteenth, seventeenth and eighteenth-century makers'. With showrooms in New York, Gill & Reigate were unequivocal that 'as Antique Dealers, we can select the finest models and accurately interpret them'.[106]

Some 'interpretations' may have gone further. In *Wycombe Memories*, the furniture maker Ralph Allan Janes wrote of the invention of the 'twisting machine' that it was very good for turning out large numbers of 'bastard chairs', **Fig. 9.82**. Such machinery facilitated the turning of the so-called 'barley-twist' type that had been used for chair back supports and legs in the late seventeenth century. Such an innovation greatly aided the copying of Charles II chairs, reducing manufacturing costs. Janes remarked that 'it was not long before I was asked to see if my men could not make

CHAPTER 9: 1900-1909

9.79

Fig. 9.79 **The superb choice of well-figured satinwood for this table, part of a bedroom suite, shows that the makers, Morant & Co., had access to the very best veneers available.** [Christie's]

Fig. 9.80 *The Drawing room at 3, The Close, Winchester, c.*1900, a watercolour by Beatrice Corfe. The Pembroke table in the centre is possibly a period example of the George III era, but the hexagonal example on the right in front of the French display cabinet is a modern interpretation of Georgian. On the left is a Moorish mother-of-pearl inlaid low table popularised by Liberty's and others. [Victoria and Albert Museum E.222-1955]

them look as old as the original pieces – rapidly ageing'. Janes had spotted a specialist in turning and spirals at a workhouse, and immediately employed him. He welcomed the new books available to help the amateur recognise fake furniture, but noted they were of more use to those wishing to deceive, as it helped them concentrate on making sure these easy-to-spot details were 'perfect'.[107]

Thomas Strange's *English Furniture, Decoration, Woodwork and Allied Arts: From the last half of the Seventeenth Century to the early Part of the Nineteenth Century* (1890), and Percy Macquoid's *A History of English Furniture* (1904–1908)[108] soon became known as the 'Faker's Bibles'. Janes, hungry for antique furniture to use as examples to copy, instigated a hunt around local antique shops and museums, the surreptitious use of photography acting as his 'sketch book'. He noted the provenance of suitable candidates for reproduction in a volume of Macquoid's, which led him to Gwydir Castle. At the castle, the Marquess of Lincolnshire willingly allowed Janes to take moulds and make drawings of furniture, and Janes made 'many interesting and beautiful Chairs, Court Cupboards, Tables and Stools', which he claimed were 'now gracing American, British and Russian homes'. In one instance 'an Antique Dealer in a very large way', his name delicately

9.80

483

withheld, asked Janes to extend a set of six Chippendale chairs to become a set of twenty-four. The match was perfect and easily obtained as the 'original' set of six had been made by Janes for a client only three weeks previously – they were not at all 'antique'! Janes confessed to 'going in for making and faking reproductions'. When the extensive Nicholls & Janes archive was sold at auction in 1969 it was purchased by the Victoria and Albert Museum.[109] The archive consists of over 20,000 photographs, drawings, blueprints and scale plans of a complete range of furniture. Other activities Janes described include a genuine Chippendale chair being given to a Bond Street firm with instructions to make a dozen to match – an unnamed connoisseur then found it difficult to say which was the original. Janes recalls making a fake William and Mary writing desk with the popular and expensive 'seaweed' or 'endive' arabesque marquetry in the style introduced into England in the 1680s. The desk was purchased by a well-known, but again unnamed, London antique dealer.

By no means all of Nicholls & Janes work was fraudulent. They exhibited a variety of furniture at the 1908 Arts and Crafts Exhibition in the Town Hall at High Wycombe, including not only chairs and a copy of a Gwydir Castle chair, but also a copy of a gate leg table, reproducing

9.81a

9.81b

Figs 9.81a & b **Two views of the Jockey Club in Buenos Aires, photographed in 1908. The furniture was supplied by Maples who referred to it as being in the Elizabethan style whereas more correctly the design is of William and Mary or early Queen Anne inspiration.** [Biblioteca Universidad de Oviedo]

Fig. 9.82 **A twisting lathe of *c*.1886** facilitated the basic shape, but as with most machine work, the 'barley-twists' needed finishing by hand. [Private collection]

Fig. 9.83 **Excavation and reconstitution of the fifteenth-century BCE Palace of Minos in Knossos by Sir Arthur Evans in 1900** was an opportunity to reproduce wooden copies of the unique stone throne chair. [Sotheby's]

Queen Anne and Chippendale-style tables, a settee and a 'Hepplewhite' toilet glass.[110] The firm made tables, chairs, larger items, such as sideboards, and giltwood seat furniture.

In 1899, the American-born sociologist and economist Thorstein Veblen discussed the rise of consumerism supported by the industrious middle and working classes.[111] The population was expanding rapidly with a surge in demand boosting the need for new furniture. A glance at an old map of London shows the exponential growth of the late Victorian and Edwardian terraced houses in fashionable areas such as Maida Vale and Brondesbury Park in the north or Battersea and Clapham in the south, to name but a few. Furniture for this market was made throughout Britain with exhibitions such as the Ideal Home Exhibition, established in 1908 by the *Daily Mail*, enabling buyers to see a wide choice of well-made furniture, most of the production in a watered-down, traditional style. The newspaper used the exhibition as an ingenious form of promotion, assuring themselves a useful stream of advertising revenue. The original exhibition slogan was a quote from the king. George V wrote: 'The foundations of the national glory are set in the homes of the people'.[112] In the furniture trade, numerous small workshops and factories in the provinces and especially in the East End of London were eager to fulfil the constant demand and were able to supply both middle class and luxury furniture in a wide range of styles and designs for every taste and pocket. This, and the amalgamation of many of the larger companies, makes it increasingly difficult to attribute unsigned pieces to a specific maker. The market for reproduction styles in particular was to continue well into the next decade and beyond, buoyed by new markets at home and abroad.

.1

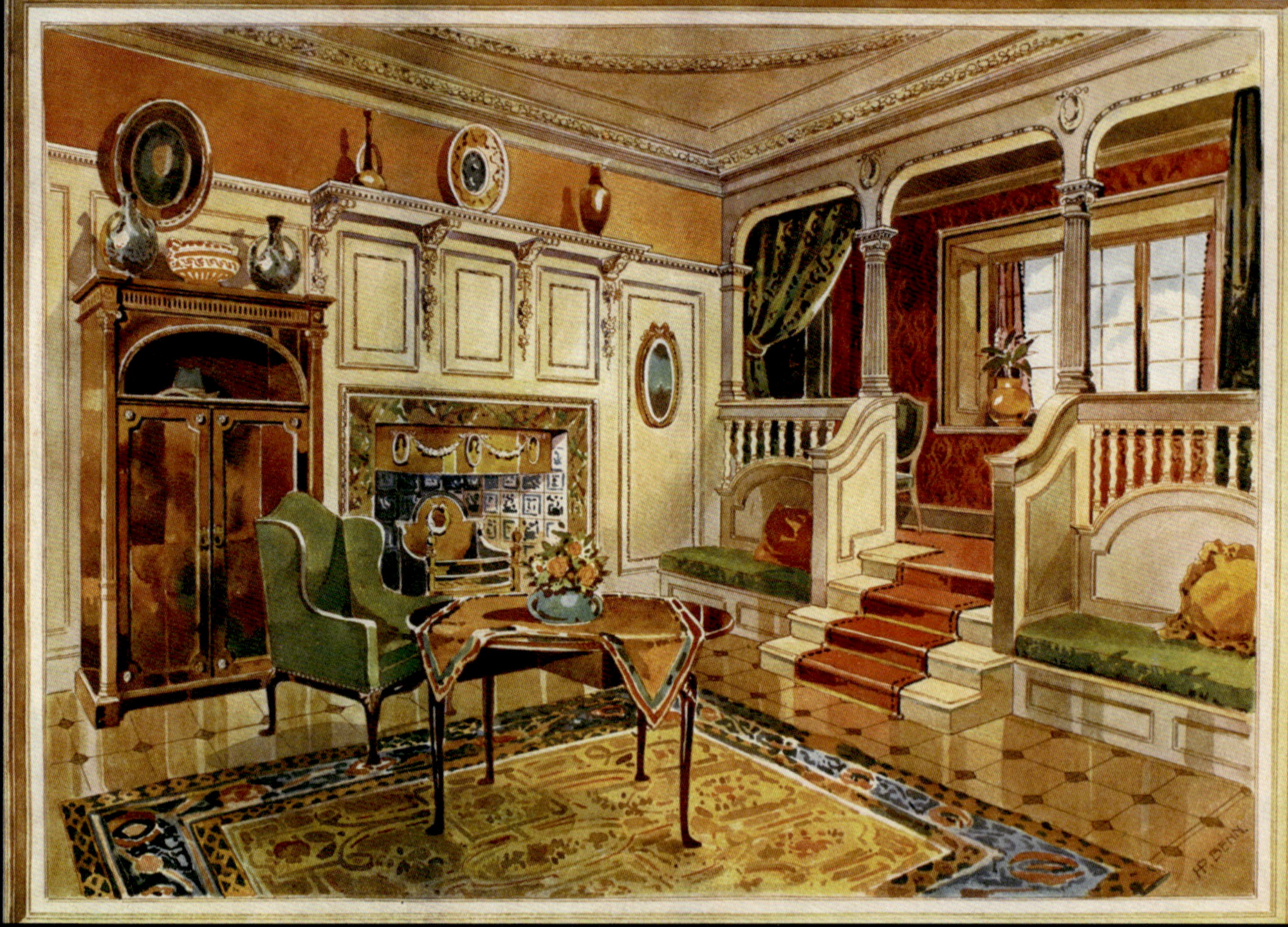

.2

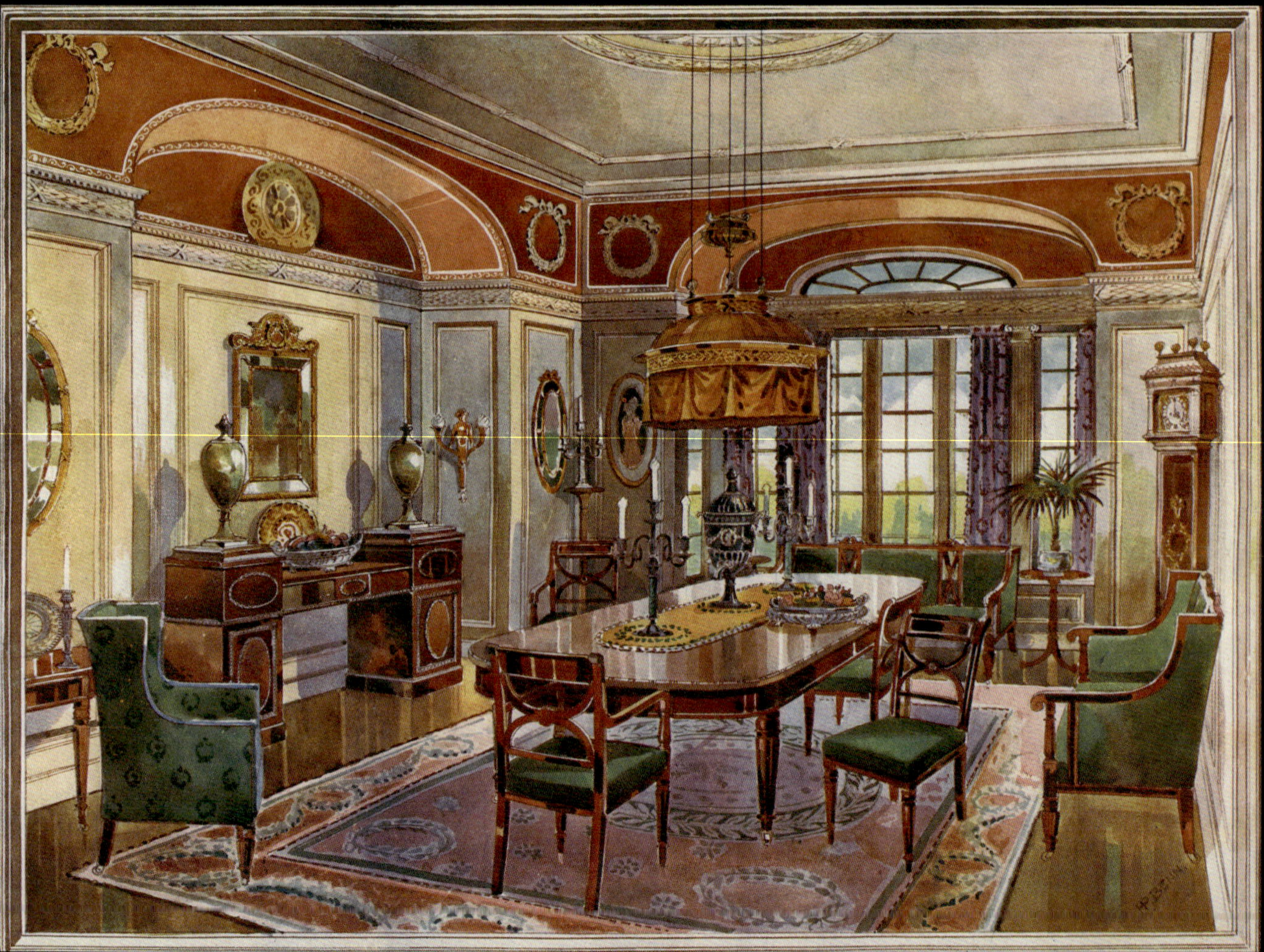

CHAPTER 10

1910–1920

'Designs are executed which Adam or Chippendale never conceived, but which they very well might have, and of which they would have no cause to be ashamed.'[1]

Reproduction furniture, pastiches and copies continued to be the mainstream of furniture production with a thriving home and export market. In 1910 Percy Wells highlighted a roll call of makers, designers and influencers of the pre-war period, working both in progressive and derivative styles.[2] One he mentioned was Frank Stuart Murray (1848–1915), who had worked for Waring & Gillow. When the firm's finances became uncertain, Murray left Warings with some of his colleagues and set up Durand, Murray & Seddon.[3] The new firm designed and made furniture for the ocean liner *Mauritania*, and worked as garden designers, for example at Polesden Lacey. Others noted by Wells were J.S. Henry, H.E. Marillier of Morris & Company, George Jack, Ernest Gimson, Charles Spooner and George Trollope & Sons. Spooner designed furniture that is often unashamedly derivative. Wells' preface pointed out the remarkable changes in methods of production over the previous twenty-five years: 'the term "Cabinetmaking" covers a much wider scope in craftsmanship than it did formerly.' Illustrations by Wells of a walnut sideboard by the Bath Cabinet Makers Company and one in oak by Skull of High Wycombe were in stark contrast to those by Ambrose Heal for example.[4]

The sideboard designed in 1912 by the architect Edwin Rickards (1872–1920), **Fig. 10.3**, is an imaginative reinterpretation of an eighteenth-century form. Rickards's concept is a full-blown Baroque extravaganza with Rococo additions in the Chippendale idiom, but unmistakably a reinvention. He has remodelled the Georgian sideboard or side table with accompanying pedestals in a pneumatic fashion and made them appear to interlock. The break with history is made complete by veneering the suite in quarter-veneered walnut instead of matched mahogany, which would have been the mid-eighteenth-century choice. Contemporary thinking wanted to encourage architects to be the arbiters of taste, 'the public must be encouraged to an understanding of what organic architecture means and weaned from the lures of the house decorator and the furniture dealer.'[5] Possibly Rickards was aware of the organic qualities of the 'Monocleid' cabinets by Sopwith of Newcastle, **Fig. 3.90a**. In contrast, the mahogany sideboard 'in Chippendale style' by Hampton & Sons is a more typical reproduction of the decade, **Fig. 10.4**, although could not be termed 'a copy'. Applied decoration such as that on the Hamptons sideboard could be outsourced, for example Lignine 'wood carvings' from the Ornamental Products Co. in Detroit, **Fig. 10.5**.

The two-volume publication by Edwin Foley, *The Book of Decorative Furniture* (1912), is an interesting insight into contemporary appreciation of antique furniture. A

Fig. 10.1 **'Scheme for a Georgian Hall'** by Henry Pringuer Benn. One of more than one hundred designs in *Style Schemes in Antique Furnishing* by Henry Shapland, first published 1909. [*Look and Learn*]

Fig. 10.2 **'Scheme for a late 18th Century Dining Room'** by Benn. [*Look and Learn*]

Fellow of the Institute of Decorative Designers, Foley and his son Conrad produced more than 1,000 drawings and watercolours. Foley's knowledge of furniture history was sketchy by modern standards and some of his illustrations were drawn in a manner that makes it difficult to be sure of the authenticity of the furniture (see **Fig. 10.8**). For example, the illustrations of a mahogany breakfront bookcase from an Irish collection with over-exaggerated applied Rococo carving and his impression of a pedestal sideboard of a type later reproduced by Hampton & Sons, with a variation by Waring & Gillow, do not have an authentic feel. Likewise, a Sheraton/Shearer breakfront wardrobe then owned by James Kirkley of Cleadon Park is unlikely to have been a period piece. Kirkley also owned an example of the 'Sheraton' painted satinwood dressing table of disputed date sold by John James to the South Kensington Museum (See Chapter 5), another of which later appeared in a Hindley & Wilkinson catalogue. Clearly Foley had some practical knowledge, writing that woodworm holes should not be straight like drill holes, but should 'wiggle'. He commented on the all too common practice of embellishing a plain eighteenth-century piece by carving foliage, as frequently seen

Fig. 10.3 **This inventive design for a sideboard, drawn in 1912 by Edwin Rickards, is an adaptation of the Baroque, Chippendale and Adam styles and unmistakably an early twentieth-century confection.** [RIBA]

Fig. 10.4 **Hampton's reinterpretation of the Chippendale style, stock number C9711, retailing at £98.** [Butchoff archive]

Fig. 10.5 **Almost unbreakable composite Lignine mouldings were available in all the popular styles from the Ornamental Products Co., Detroit, through British importers.** [Private collection]

Hamptons' No. C9711.
Carved Mahogany Sideboard in Chippendale style, fitted five drawers and two cupboards.   6 ft. 6 in. wide.

Fig. 10.6 **Hampton & Sons could supply a complete house in this style for £500. The price of the bureau on the left was £9 10s, the display cabinet £24 10s.** [Butchoff archive]

Fig. 10.7 **At the Anglo-American Exhibition in the summer of 1914, Green & Abbott exhibited variations of traditional English designs loosely based on furniture from the first half of the eighteenth century.** [*The Cabinet Maker*, 4 July 1914, p. 2]

on mahogany tripod tables. The after effect of this, known as 'carving up', leaves the remaining timber looking too thin and mean. Foley's early training appears to have been with Arthur Foley, founder in *c.*1867 of the Fisherton Machine Cabinet Works in Salisbury.[6]

The larger stores offered complete room settings modernising the period theme at competitive prices. Rooms of all styles at a range of quality and costs were available. A less expensive range by Hampton & Sons furnished a twelve-roomed house for £500, including servants' rooms, a kitchen and a bathroom, **Fig. 10.6**. Hamptons suggested furniture should be in rosewood for the drawing room with oak, walnut or mahogany in the dining room. Furniture of this type could have been supplied by any number of wholesalers, one possibility is Longstaff & Pitcher of Hampstead. The more expensive furnishings of the Hampton 'specimen

BRITISH FURNITURE

Fig. 10.8 Edwin Foley's watercolours of 1910 illustrated furniture purporting to have been made in the eighteenth century. An engraving of a very similar sideboard is illustrated in Litchfield, with a variation in a catalogue from E. Kahn.[7] Possibly it is only Foley's artistic interpretation which makes it appear that this is an early twentieth-century example. [Private collection]

Fig. 10.9 A well-made library bookcase with a Waring & Gillow brass label below the stamped number '8 7111'. The sides are inspired by elements from Chippendale's *Director*, plate LXVII. [Chuande Cao]

house' were shown at the main showrooms in Pall Mall, while the cheaper rooms were on view at their Whitcomb Street showrooms, **Fig. 9.74**. Comparing the illustrations in Hamptons' catalogues with those of Waring & Gillow suggests that by the 1910s the latter offered furniture of a better design and quality. A Waring & Gillow catalogue from *c*.1919 offered a small section of more extravagant furniture from the 'Gillow Galleries', with published prices for new English furniture ranging up to £395. For the more expensive furniture, heavily carved or lacquered, the price was on application only. Hamptons also offered a wide selection of well-made French furniture by Sormani and Linke, without disclosing the Paris makers' identity. So-called antique furniture illustrated by Hamptons (see Chapter 9, **Fig. 9.10**) appears dubious in the extreme, whereas on the evidence of their catalogue photographs, Waring's antique offerings appear more likely to have been genuine.

The six colour plates from *The Cabinet Maker* of 1907 shown in the previous chapter, **Figs 9.1 & 9.5a–e**, illustrate the possibilities and popularity of reproduction styles of the eighteenth century. Chippendale continued to be the most popular style, but the less complex forms of Adam and Hepplewhite designs became more sought-after and, with less carving and fretwork, were cheaper to produce. In 1920 *The Cabinet Maker* reported: 'genuine antique furniture is not…within the reach of everyone…Modern craftsmanship has, however reached such a pitch of excellence that reproductions…are now made which satisfy the most exacting demands'.[8]

Although there was an improvement in the standards of line drawings in magazines most illustrators, clearly not cabinet makers themselves, drew with a naivety that perpetuated the 'Quaint' style of previous decades. Many of the sketches of eighteenth-century furniture appear so weak that it is difficult to believe the illustrators were copying period pieces; they were adding too much of their own interpretation for the drawings to be considered accurate. The line drawings of the Cowtan & Sons display at the Anglo-American Exhibition at Shepherd's Bush in the summer of 1914, **Fig. 10.11**, were termed, regardless of the original designer, 'Chinese Chippendale', arguably one of the most popular styles in the first two decades of the

CHAPTER 10: 1910–1920

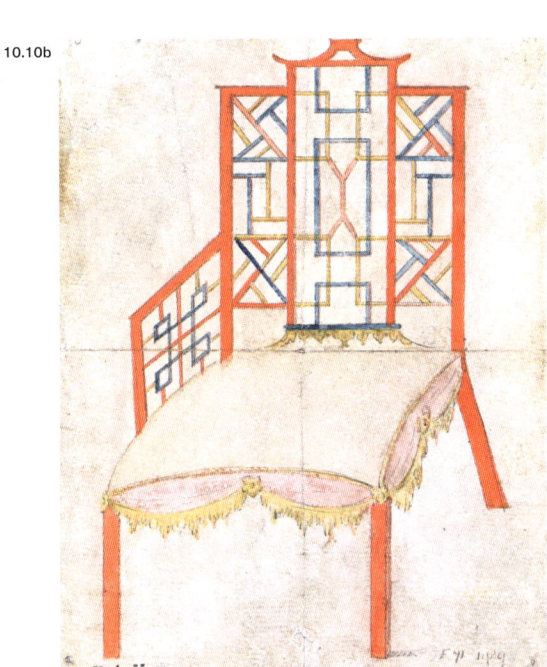

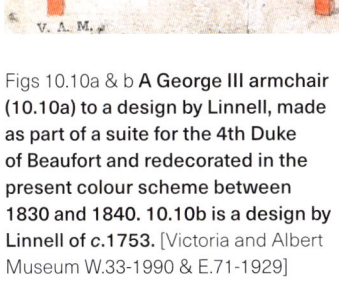

Figs 10.10a & b **A George III armchair (10.10a) to a design by Linnell, made as part of a suite for the 4th Duke of Beaufort and redecorated in the present colour scheme between 1830 and 1840. 10.10b is a design by Linnell of *c*.1753.** [Victoria and Albert Museum W.33-1990 & E.71-1929]

Fig. 10.11 **At the Anglo-American Exhibition at Shepherd's Bush in the summer of 1914 Cowtan & Sons exhibited reproduction furniture inspired by eighteenth-century designs by Chippendale and Linnell with varying degrees of authenticity and adaptation. The armchair is very close to the example in Fig. 10.10a.** [*The Cabinet Maker*, 4 July 1914, p. 3]

twentieth century. Most firms made furniture in this style, with varying degrees of success. In contrast, as an example of the eclecticism of the period, Green & Abbott's exhibits at the Anglo-American Exhibition featured a hybrid late seventeenth-century look which included a side table, with detailing sufficiently distinctive as to begin to identify a house style (**Fig. 10.7**).

There was little thought of war when the Geffrye Museum was opened in 1914 and the furniture trade was a hive of activity. Established by the London County Council, the museum was dedicated to the understanding of furniture and woodwork. It soon became a valuable resource for designers and makers working in the burgeoning East End furniture

Fig. 10.12 **A reimagining of the Chinese Chippendale style. The unknown maker has incorporated earlier Chinese lacquer panels.** [Sotheby's]

Fig. 10.13 **More reimaginings in the Chinese Chippendale style. Reverse glass paintings, in this case carefully designed to have a useful large area of silvered glass, were often made in Canton for export and had been popular since the eighteenth century.** [Sotheby's]

industry in and around Shoreditch. The new museum played a role in stoking interest in reproduction furniture. Loans of eighteenth-century Chippendale furniture by the Earl of Strathmore and Kinghorne and Sir Edward Feetham Coates served to heighten interest in the Chinese Chippendale style. Amongst other exhibitors, Restall, Brown & Clennell displayed a settee in the George II style at the opening of the museum. With a factory and studios in Bethnal Green and a well-positioned showroom in Great Russell Street near the British Museum, the firm's reputation grew rapidly. It had been established in 1905 with the backing of Greenwoods, antique dealers in Yorkshire and London. Advertising in *The Cabinet Maker* in 1907 the firm boasted 'High Class Productions in Decorated Satinwood and inlaid mahogany…', adding 'Our Goods are Money makers'.[9] As well as the perennially popular mid-eighteenth-century style, their showrooms were full of the type of reproduction Elizabethan and Jacobean furniture that had become popular in Britain and the United States. With a constant supply of genuine antique furniture passing through their hands, their designers and cabinet makers were able to study at first hand and produced a fine range of well-executed reproduction pieces. Their work ranged from imaginative copies of 'seaweed' or arabesque marquetry furniture to late Stuart-style chairs and satinwood pieces painted in the Neoclassical manner.

Prestigious London firms had a wide range of important patrons, including kings Edward VII, George V and later George VI, aristocrats such as the Duke of Devonshire and the Earl of Pembroke, and industrialists such as Lord Leverhulme.[10] The illustration of one of the throne chairs in the previous chapter, **Fig. 9.62**, supplied by Carlhian & Beaumetz on the recommendation of Duveen to the king in 1902 is an early example of this co-operation.

The Duveen Brothers played a prominent role in selling paintings, furniture and works of art, operating from high-profile addresses in London, Paris and New York.[11] In the early twentieth century, the guiding force was Joseph Duveen

Fig. 10.14 **A photograph from the Duveen archive of 'Amor's Cabinet', available for reproduction at a cost of £420.** [© J. Paul Getty Trust. Getty Research Institute, Los Angeles (2007. D.1)]

Fig. 10.15 **Duveen was able to supply this bookcase, inspired by plate LXI from *The Director*, with quatrefoil astragals. It was available with three or more doors in various sizes, for £264.** [© J. Paul Getty Trust. Getty Research Institute, Los Angeles (2007. D.1)]

Fig. 10.16 **A loose-leaf watercolour project in the Duveen archive for a display cabinet of mid-eighteenth-century inspiration.** [© J. Paul Getty Trust. Getty Research Institute, Los Angeles (2007. D.1)]

in London, his brother Henry running the business in New York.[12] The United States was their most significant market with clients such as Dodge, Frick, Huntington and J.P. Morgan, to name but a few.

The Getty Research Institute archive of Duveen material contains hundreds of carefully categorised photographs and watercolours of English and Continental antique and reproduction furniture of all ages.[13] The archive shows that the Duveens offered a considerable amount of reproduction furniture alongside period pieces and illustrates in part the co-operation between Duveen and various decorators. When the pair to an existing piece was not available, the desk not the right size or a set of chairs needed extending, Duveen had the contacts in England to supply exact copies as well as reproduction furniture in quasi-period styles. The archive also illustrates in part the co-operation between Duveen

Fig. 10.17 The form of this commode does not correspond to period examples; Duveen offered two at £120 each. The reverse is annotated 'Walnut & gilt commode Antique carcase'. [© J. Paul Getty Trust. Getty Research Institute, Los Angeles (2007. D.1)]

Fig. 10.18 Described as a wine table and made in walnut, the Duveen watercolour is marked on the reverse 'In stock' and available for £168 with seaweed marquetry. Although marked 'Reproduction' and 'Copy' it is not a model that existed in the eighteenth century. [© J. Paul Getty Trust. Getty Research Institute, Los Angeles (2007. D.1)]

Fig. 10.19 In a style attributed to Benjamin Goodison, Duveen offered one armchair and four gilt gesso chairs intriguingly described as 'very old copies'. Offered at £900 for the 'old' set, new copies would cost £95 each to make. [© J. Paul Getty Trust. Getty Research Institute, Los Angeles (2007. D.1)]

Fig. 10.20 The gilt gesso legs and feet of this extravagant English Baroque wing armchair, available new from Duveen, are somewhat in the manner of James Moore, c.1720. The scrolled 'wings' have more in common with a slightly earlier sofa at Penshurst Place. [© J. Paul Getty Trust. Getty Research Institute, Los Angeles (2007. D.1)]

and furniture makers and decorators such as Carlhian & Beaumetz, Lenygon, White Allom and dealers such as Moss Harris or Robert and Frank Partridge.[14] For example, one Duveen archive folder is headed 'Photographs English Furniture from Frank Partridge for E.J. Stotesbury' for Whitemarsh Hall in Pennsylvania, a project in which Duveen was heavily involved. A number of items in the Duveen and Partridge photographs are similar or most probably the same as the furniture illustrated by Macquoid in *A History of English Furniture* published between 1904 and 1908. Macquoid's illustrations were drawn from aristocratic houses, collectors and dealers alike.

These photographs helped clients decide on the models they wanted. One shows a mahogany bookcase, **Fig. 10.14**, which has the photographer's stamp on the reverse and the order number; the bookcase was photographed in situ in 1920 when part of the stock of Albert Amor,[15] an antique porcelain dealer who had previously been employed by Frederick Litchfield. The distinctive pattern of the glazing bars of the cabinet made it ideal for displaying ceramics, and the Duveens, who almost certainly bought porcelain from Amor, must have recognised an opportunity to offer a copy to his clients. The annotation on the back of the photograph asks what size reproduction is required, adding that it would take two months to make at a cost of £420. Watercolours and drawings were similarly used; a watercolour of a display cabinet shows a typical Edwardian adaptation of the late George II style, **Fig. 10.16**. It makes no attempt to be a period piece. The prospective client was offered a choice of size; it was 'proposed in guilt [sic] & Walnut', would take two months to make and retail at £390. A pencil drawing of another cabinet for the display of porcelain, with quatrefoil astragals, **Fig. 10.15**, is clearly inspired by, but not an exact copy of, plate LXI in Chippendale's *Director*.

A considerable number of the Duveen images are annotated 'reproduction' in pencil or ink on the reverse of the photograph and include the cost of production, others simply say 'genuine old'. The delivery time for copies was usually given, most pieces could be made in four to eight weeks. There appears to be a methodology in that some pieces are marked 'copy', others 'reproduction' but it is not always clear that this is the case. **Fig. 10.17** is a good example of a piece that would probably not have existed in the eighteenth century, although the reverse is marked somewhat alarmingly 'Walnut & gilt commode Antique carcase'. The walnut wine table, **Fig. 10.18**, is confusingly marked both 'Reproduction' and 'Copy' although as it is not a model that existed in the eighteenth century it strictly speaking is a pastiche. The popularity of late seventeenth- and early eighteenth-century styles is evident in the number of Duveen images available, some in stock, others made to order. This is particularly evident with seat furniture, with high back chairs that carry little favour today, settees and wing chairs in an extravagant style such as those once owned by the 1st Duke of Leeds.[16] A wing armchair with gilded and elaborately carved legs and apron, referred to as a 'bergere' [sic], is stylistically from the 1720s. At £69, it would take eight weeks to deliver from the date of order, **Fig. 10.20**. Red lacquer was a popular finish. A set of reproduction William and Mary high back chairs in red were held in stock. Single chairs were priced at £46 each, a matching chaise longue £90.[17] Another set is annotated: 'They are a fine model Lac & guilt & have a beautiful old tone on them & would look well anywhere they are placed'.[18] The Partridge folder in the Duveen archive contains numerous photographs of George II-style walnut and gilt parlour chairs, commonly used for dining, priced at £450 for a set of eight single chairs and a pair of armchairs, 'in process of finishing take 4 weeks to deliver'.[19]

Filed by category, the Duveen records include a photograph of the First State Room at the Lenygon showrooms at 31 Old Burlington Street opened in 1908. There were Lenygon workshops both in Old Burlington Street and in Newman Street.[20] By 1914 Lenygon employed twenty-two interior designers and decorators, painters, carpenters and upholsterers. The Lenygon showroom photograph in the Duveen archive was used as the frontispiece of Lenygon's 1909 publication, **Fig. 10.26**. A separate photograph of the bookcase to the right of the chimney is also in the Duveen archive – the annotation reads '2 in stock Reproductions of above £165 each'. This

Fig. 10.21 A photograph of this table is illustrated in the Cedar Room at the Lenygon showrooms and separately in Francis Lenygon's 1909 publication, p. 24. The same image, plus a bird's-eye view of the top, is in the Duveen archive, annotated on the reverse 'A reproduction W^m & Mary Walnut Centre Table £115. Take from 8 to 10 weeks to make'.
[© J. Paul Getty Trust. Getty Research Institute, Los Angeles (2007. D.1)]

10.22

10.23

10.24

10.25

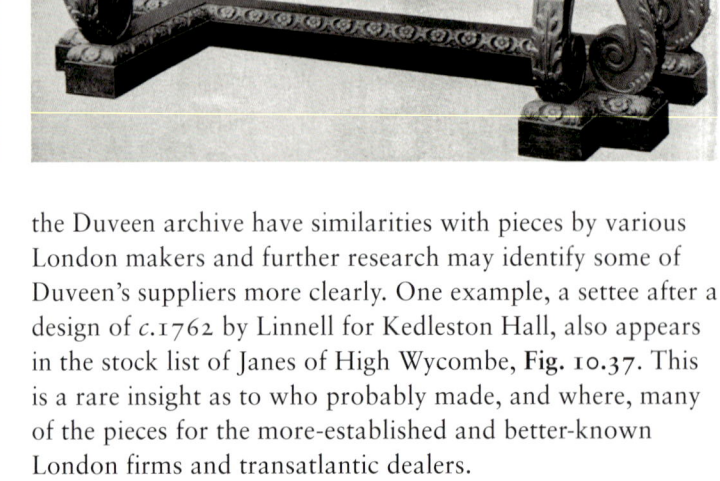

suggests that there was some association between Lenygon and Duveen, who appear to have been sourcing some of their furniture through the London decorating firm. In Lenygon's book, images marked copyright are pieces which have frequently been copied, and the Duveen stock photographs include several items illustrated by Lenygon, whether antique, copy or reproduction.[21] Alongside firms such as Partridge, Lenygon's success allowed them to establish a thriving business in New York in 1912, their client list a roll call of New York society.[22] Other items of furniture appearing in the Duveen archive have similarities with pieces by various London makers and further research may identify some of Duveen's suppliers more clearly. One example, a settee after a design of c.1762 by Linnell for Kedleston Hall, also appears in the stock list of Janes of High Wycombe, **Fig. 10.37**. This is a rare insight as to who probably made, and where, many of the pieces for the more-established and better-known London firms and transatlantic dealers.

Furniture supplied by Lenygon is distinctive and there is a consistency of style and sophistication in their pieces

Figs 10.22 & 10.23 Clearly labelled 'reproduction' in the Duveen stock book, the walnut display cabinet (10.23) was available for £114 or with seaweed marquetry for £152. The walnut card table (10.22), inspired by that illustrated on p. 158 in Macquoid's *The Age of Walnut*, was available at £53. [Both images: © J. Paul Getty Trust. Getty Research Institute, Los Angeles (2007. D.1)]

Fig. 10.24 A watercolour of a 'bureau-table' in the manner of Benjamin Goodison. The pencilled inscription on the reverse of the watercolour 'In Stock Genuine Old Kent mahogany writing desk with ormolu mounts' and significantly, 'Make to Pair £1,320'. [© J. Paul Getty Trust. Getty Research Institute, Los Angeles (2007. D.1)]

Fig. 10.25 A slab-top table illustrated in the Cedar Room at the Lenygon showrooms, the inspiration from a design of *c.*1740 by Matthias Lock. Charles Tozer supplied a similar variation without the lion mask, but with a more accurate rendition of the scrolled side supports.[23] [Private collection]

Fig. 10.26 The frontispiece of Lenygon's *The Decoration and Furniture of English Mansions during the Seventeenth and Eighteenth Centuries*, showing the First State Room, one of the firm's Mayfair showrooms at 31 Old Burlington Street. A reproduction of the cabinet was available for £165. Under the tabernacle mirror, one of the set of gesso Zodiac dining chairs (Fig. 10.28) is crammed next to an elaborate wing chair. [Private collection]

Figs 10.27a & b One of a pair of tables from the Royal Automobile Club, which was partly decorated by Lenygon between 1908 and 1911. The Vitruvian 'sea' scroll and fox supports centred by a mask typify the Palladian style indelibly associated with Kent designs. Illustrated in Lenygon's publication of 1909 (p. 38) this example[24] has the rare addition of a Lenygon stamp on one side: 'Made by Lenygon & Co Ltd'. [William MacKinnon, Three Centuries Antiques, Vancouver]

10.26

10.27b

10.27a

of the early twentieth century that may help to attribute unsigned furniture to them. The firm's extensive archives are held by Columbia University in New York, and this, along with Francis Lenygon's own publications, written for the firm by Margaret Jourdain, should help in attributing furniture made by, or made for, them.[25] Filled with black-and-white photographs, a copy of *The Decoration and Furniture of English Mansions* (1909) in the Victoria and Albert Museum has annotations on numerous illustrations of period pieces noting the owners' names, for example 'Lady Henry Grosvenor'. Many of the other illustrated items are marked 'Lenygon & Co. Ltd' and 'Copyright', for example **Fig. 10.25**, suggesting that Lenygon owned or had owned the pieces. These included period and reproduction models. Access to the eighteenth-century examples would have been the perfect opportunity for the firm to have copied them, or to incorporate details into their own designs. Margaret

Fig. 10.28 **A set of eighteen gilt and silvered dining chairs, a model by Lenygon that has similarities to a chair of 1730–36 at Temple Newsam House and to the richly carved cabriole legs of a set supplied to Stowe House from the same period. Each vase-shaped splat has a lacquered panel painted with a sign of the zodiac.** [Butchoff Antiques]

Jourdain's introduction to the second Lenygon book, *Furniture in England from 1660–1760* (1914) explained how the firm allowed any of the pieces in their collection to be photographed for the book, which meant that the images became widely available.

Francis Lenygon trained as a cabinet maker, then worked in the antiques business of Charles Duveen in London and from 1910 was, like many of his peers, working also in New York.[26] The gloriously extravagant set of eighteen dining chairs, **Fig. 10.28**, by Lenygon must have been part of an exceptional commission, with no expense spared. The shield-

Fig. 10.29 **A photograph from the Duveen archive with a note explaining: 'Pair of carved & gilt pedestals, reproductions of these [*sic*] in "Duke of Devonshire's" collection'. Copied from a model carved in 1735 by John Boson for Chiswick Villa at a cost of £5 each, Duveen was offering a pair for £78.** [© J. Paul Getty Trust. Getty Research Institute, Los Angeles (2007. D.1)]

Fig. 10.30 **A pair of armchairs in the so-called William and Mary style referencing the late 1690s, made by Charles Tozer, the tall backs with similarities to a model by Lenygon. The ebonised and parcel-gilt frames are supported on 'Braganza' or 'horsebone' legs. Such high back chairs had been made well into the reign of Queen Anne. There are fewer reproductions of high back chairs extant today, possibly because they were lighter framed than sturdier Georgian-style chairs and therefore more liable to damage. The elaborate caned backs and seats are more fragile, and today it is difficult to find the necessary skills to repair or replace them.**[28] [Bonhams]

Fig. 10.31 **An elegant giltwood sofa attributed to Lenygon & Morant in the firm's interpretation of the Queen Anne style.** [Mackinnon Fine Furniture]

or vase-shaped splats each have a sign of the zodiac painted on tole, a thin metal panel made of tin.[27] The back of each chair is ostentatiously carved and gilded in silvered gesso, the reverse of the painted zodiac splats with luxurious upholstery pads. An illustration of one of the side chairs can be seen in the frontispiece of Lenygon's 1909 publication (**Fig. 10.26**). The firm also held a range of the best-quality period furniture, and sold to museums and private collections. The pair of display cabinets very much in the style of Lenygon, **Fig. 10.38**, are an inventive 'Queen Anne' adaptation, the lower part inspired by a lacquer and gilt 'writing table' with a fine Japanese lacquer top and English japanned drawer fronts at Longford Castle.[29] The large slab table, with fox supports as a sign of welcome, **Fig. 10.27b**, is a rare example with a Lenygon stamp on the side but curiously not a copyright image in the Lenygon publication. Although very different in detail, it has similarities with an example in the style of William Kent, also at Longford Castle.[30] Underlining the importance and grandeur of furniture in the style of Kent, Lenygon's 1909 publication devoted a whole chapter to his work. In *c*.1912 Lenygon purchased the prestigious firm of Morant & Co., the two firms merging three years later as Lenygon & Morant.[31] Always of fine quality, furniture in a contemporary French style stamped only 'Morant & Co.' is not uncommon. Such examples are presumed to pre-date the Lenygon–Morant merger.[32]

The pedestal desk, **Fig. 10.33**, is a good example not only of Lenygon's house style, but of the enduring fashion for traditional English interiors. It was supplied by Lenygon for Lady Leconfield as part of the remodelling and furnishing commissioned for Petworth House in 1912, which included remodelling the proportions of some of the rooms. The furniture historian, Percy Macquoid, was a consultant to Lenygon & Morant, and the desk is a near copy of one then in the possession of J. Mallett & Son, illustrated in Macquoid's book *The Age of Mahogany*.[33] The nine locks all open with the same key – Lady Leconfield had the locks made to suit an existing Chubb key in her possession.[34]

499

10.32

10.33

CHAPTER 10: 1910–1920

10.34

Fig. 10.32 A fine pair of mahogany commodes in the Chippendale style, possibly retailed by Lenygon & Morant. Like most of the firm's work they are not signed or labelled. Adapted from plate XLIII in Chippendale's *Director* of 1754, they are likely to have been made by a middleman such as Frederick Parker, to be retailed by one of the larger London firms. [Sotheby's]

Fig. 10.33 A parcel-gilt pedestal desk in mahogany, supplied by Lenygon & Morant for Lady Leconfield's Sitting Room at Petworth House, Sussex. The same key is used for each drawer, the Chubb serial numbers on the locks show they were supplied in July 1912. [Private collection]

Fig. 10.34 Lady Leconfield's desk supplied by Lenygon to Petworth in 1912 shown in situ at Petworth in the 1920s, the room, including the plasterwork, redesigned by Lenygon. [*Country Life* / Future Publishing Ltd]

The large sofa in **Fig. 10.35**, made of finely carved mahogany with triton supports at either end after a 1762 design by John Linnell, was retailed by Maple & Co. Although a brass label stamped 'Maple & Company London Paris Buenos Aires' is attached underneath the seat rail, it was probably made in High Wycombe by Nicholls & Janes. A sketch of a similar settee by Linnell *c.*1762 was made for the 1st Baron Scarsdale for Kedleston Hall, **Fig. 10.36**.[35] At least two of the twentieth-century versions are known and probably more were made. It is design number 410 in the Nicholls & Janes archive and the firm also made a simplified version.[36] An almost identical sofa, is illustrated in Lenygon, marked with Lenygon's copyright.[37] The female arm supports on both models are the same although the back has been simplified, which may be due to a client's personal taste or for economy of time and material. Whereas the settee is a good copy of the 1760s original, Maples also retailed a pair of deeply upholstered *bergère* armchairs 'en suite', in a typical twentieth-century adaptation. Exuberant human arm supports had been a popular feature for carvers in the mid-eighteenth and nineteenth centuries, and can also be seen on a settee by Gerrard Robinson whose early work is discussed in Chapter 5.

In the 1910s the traditional English style was growing in fashion in Europe, and the British section of the 1913 *Exposition universelle et internationale* in Ghent had a considerable presence, with an allocation of approximately 13,000m² (142,000ft²) of floor space designed by Frank Brangwyn (1867–1956).[38] In England, continuing the

501

Fig. 10.35 This handsome mahogany settee, after an eighteenth-century design by John Linnell (see watercolour in Fig. 10.36), is similar to one made for the 1st Baron Scarsdale at Kedleston Hall. It bears a brass label stamped 'Maple & Company London Paris Buenos Aires'. The model compares to the design in Fig. 10.37 by Nicholls & Janes of High Wycombe. [Butchoff Antiques]

Fig. 10.36 One of a series of watercolour designs of *c*.1762 prepared for Baron Scarsdale at Kedleston Hall by John Linnell. [Victoria and Albert Museum E.140-1929]

Fig. 10.37 A settee adapted from Linnell's 1762 design by Nicholls & Janes. The firm further adapted the caryatid arm supports for a less elaborate variation. The settee was a model also illustrated in Lenygon in 1909. [*The Cabinet Maker*, 6 November 1915, p. 107]

Fig. 10.38 A pair of richly decorated gilt-gesso and red-japanned display cabinets in a style possibly made by, or for, Lenygon & Morant, probably just before World War I. The lower part is inspired by a japanned 'writing-table' of *c*.1725 at Longford Castle. [Butchoff Antiques]

tradition of using local firms to furnish royal pavilions, J. & B. Blower of Shrewsbury supplied furniture in the Jacobean and Georgian styles for George V's visit to the 75th Royal Agricultural Society fair in July 1914.

In the previous chapter, the exploits of Ralph Janes at Gwydir Castle underlined the increasing popularity of and demand for antique furniture, and clearly some firms were involved in fraudulent copies, namely – fakes. The extent of this skulduggery was highlighted in a notorious law case Shrager v. Dighton in 1924. The travesty of the proceedings and resultant judgement prompted Herbert Cescinsky to write *The Gentle Art of Faking Furniture* in 1931.[39] Copies and reproductions had been a large and honest part of the

10.38

furniture trade in Britain for decades but outright fakes can be difficult to spot, although it is hoped that the perpetrator will slip up in some way or another. More obvious to detect is furniture that has been transformed or made up from other pieces, such as the bureau cabinet in **Fig. 10.41**. The lower part is a genuine desk from *c*.1720, with later bracket feet. The upper part was made to order for the buyer in the workshops of this author's grandfather, C.B. Payne, in 1913. There was no intention to deceive. The mixture of styles shows the lack of awareness of period detail that was characteristic of the time, as the new top dates stylistically to the 1770s and the finished work is immediately recognisable today as a hybrid, known as a 'marriage'. The grain of the walnut sides of the upper and lower halves does not match, and the glazing bars are of a later Georgian style. The new upper part cost £5 out of a total invoice of £11 11*s*. The writing table in **Fig. 10.42** is an unsatisfactory marriage that has no historical precedent, but which typifies the desire for elaborate furniture for wealthy buyers. A pair of serpentine-fronted chests of drawers of the early George III period have been considerably altered, turned back-to-back and flaps added, possibly using old dining table leaves. The apron and elaborate giltwood stands appear to have been added to enhance the overall effect.[40] It was sold by Moss Harris to the 1st Baron Leverhulme for £2,500 in 1919, Macquoid describing it as English *c*.1750,

Fig. 10.39 The exuberant form and quality of finish of this set of twelve armchairs suggests an attribution to Lenygon. Two of the armchairs are oversize, each needing two people to lift them. The model is based on a set of mid-eighteenth-century giltwood and gesso seat furniture in the Royal Collection, with a matching settee in the Metropolitan Museum of Art.[41] The original set is thought to have been made for Stowe House and is now attributed to Benjamin Goodison (1700–1767).
[Adrian Alan Ltd]

and 'possibly by Thomas Chippendale'.[42] A group of *demilune* commodes of eighteenth-century origin but made up or altered probably c.1900 are now in the Lady Lever Art Gallery, one purchased from the dubious Orrock Collection.[43] Typically for the era, the design of the decoration was attributed to Michelangelo Pergolesi, the painting by Angelica Kauffman.

One of the most radical transformations must be a late eighteenth-century satinwood cabinet reputedly made by Seddon, Sons & Shackleton for Charles IV of Spain but never delivered. Seen in its original state in the photograph of c.1905, **Fig. 10.43**, a tradesman's mark of 1793 is the only clue to its date of origin.[44] Illustrated in Robinson's *English Furniture* in 1905, it was exhibited at the 1908 Franco-British Exhibition, loaned by the London antique dealer Robert W. Partridge.[45] In 1910, Partridge shipped the cabinet with more than sixty other pieces to New York on the *Lusitania*, staging a selling exhibition at the Plaza Hotel, the catalogue for which was entitled *The Furniture of Thomas Chippendale*.[46] The cabinet was subsequently broken up into separate pieces. One section, incorporating the allegorical painted figures of Day and Night, was remodelled as a secretaire, **Fig. 10.44**.[47] MGM Studios in Hollywood used the secretaire as a film prop. A commode made from parts of the centre of the eighteenth-century cabinet has also been recorded. In his exhibition in New York, Partridge also displayed what appears to be Rosetti's settee, see **Figs 5.89 & 5.90**. The 1910 catalogue described the satinwood suite of six chairs, two armchairs and a settee as having 'garden and river scenes and pastoral figure subjects by J. McNeill Whistler'.

In complete contrast to the traditional reproduction furniture that dominated the Edwardian era, in 1913 members of the Bloomsbury Group, notably Roger Fry

Fig. 10.40 **An advertisement of 1920 for Nicholls & Janes with reproduction furniture of a type widely made well into the century. Like competitors such as W. Mills & Sons, Fig. 10.58, Janes also made 'knock-down' furniture for export.** [Grace's Guide]

Fig. 10.41 **An early eighteenth-century bureau, the upper part made new at a cost of £5 in the workshops of C.B. Payne in 1913 to the client's design with no attempt to deceive. The glazing bars are of a later Georgian style, there is no attempt to match the walnut sides of the upper and lower parts.** [Author's collection]

Fig. 10.42 **A writing desk made up from two chests of drawers of the early George III period. Sold by the dealer Moss Harris to the 1st Baron Leverhulme for £2,500 in 1919, the carved and gilded wood of the new base is in a style popularised by firms such as White Allom or Lenygon & Morant.** [Butchoff archive]

with Vanessa Bell and Duncan Grant, established the avant-garde Omega Workshops in Fitzroy Square in 1913. The aim was to establish a more intellectual approach to design and to raise the decorative arts to the level of the fine arts. Although the firm received several private commissions, such as the 'Holland Park Lounge', **Fig. 10.46**, the concept was too advanced to gain traction and the company only lasted six years, being forced to close in 1919. As a result, examples of surviving furniture made by Omega are scarce and highly collectable. Most manufacturing for Omega was outsourced to professional craftsmen, such as the nearby workshops of J. Kallenborn & Sons for marquetry furniture and Harry Peach's firm, Dryad of Leicester, for tall cane-seat armchairs designed by Fry.[48] Fry also purchased second-hand furniture to be decorated at the Fitzroy Square workshop. Omega exhibited at the Ideal Home Exhibition in 1913, this commercial approach causing internal ructions.[49]

The 'Glorious Summer' was shattered by the outbreak

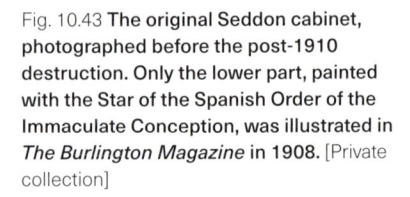

Fig. 10.43 **The original Seddon cabinet, photographed before the post-1910 destruction. Only the lower part, painted with the Star of the Spanish Order of the Immaculate Conception, was illustrated in** *The Burlington Magazine* **in 1908.** [Private collection]

Fig. 10.44 **A section of the upper part of the 1793 Seddon cabinet was transformed into a separate desk, post 1910.** [Bonhams]

and prolongation of war in August 1914. Far from being at peace by Christmas as had been hoped, furniture-making firms turned to war production. Waring's immediately put their fleet of motor lorries at the disposal of the War Office, **Fig. 10.48**. The hostilities created a nationwide demand for timber and other materials. Furniture firms like Bianco & Sons turned their hand not only to producing wooden parts for flying machines, such as the propeller workshop in one of Hampton & Sons' workshops, or the assembly shops of Waring & Gillow in Lancaster and Hammersmith, **Figs 10.49a–c**, but also to ammunition boxes and shell cases. Photographs of a Hampton workshop taken by Bedford Lemere in *c*.1916 show craftsmen and supervisors making aeroplane propellers of laminated wood as part of the war effort, with a woman helping in the finishing shop. Propeller making was one of the most exacting tasks, requiring the most experienced cabinet maker to create the perfect balance for the fixed-pitch laminated blades. Gillow's entire Lancaster factory was turned over to war production, making ammunition chests for the Royal Navy and propellers for de Havilland DH.9 aircraft. The war effort enabled Waring & Gillow to convert a £50,000 loss to a £50,000 profit by the end of 1914. By then the new Buenos Aires branch of Harrods was fully open but was suffering a loss of traditional business. Six years later Harrods' overall turnover in Argentina alone showed a substantial increase compared with the previous year, making a profit of almost £600,000.[50] Shapland & Petter, who made their own metalwork for furniture, made millions of artillery shells. Nicholls & Janes made ammunition boxes; Lebus made boxes and aircraft frames. Demand for the military effort increased and in 1918 Shapland & Petter announced that the entire workforce at

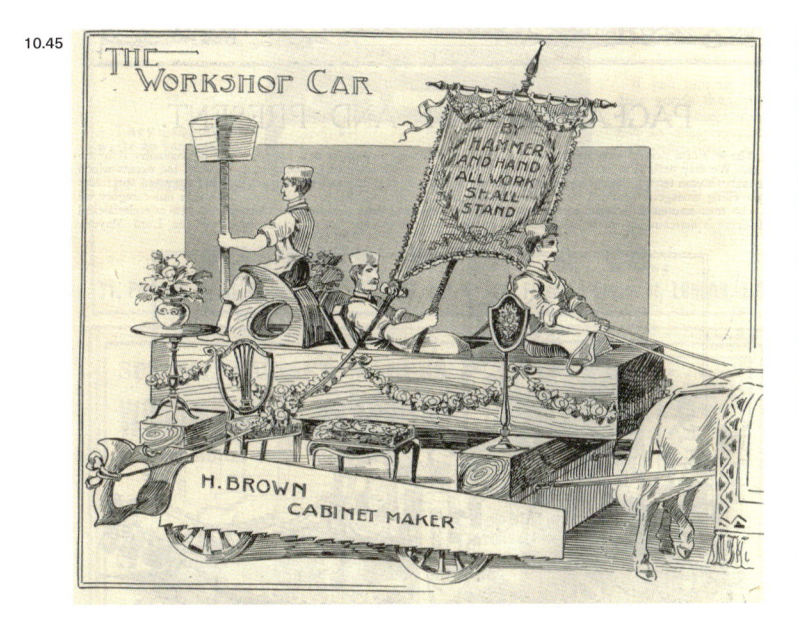

Fig. 10.45 **The calm before the storm.** One of a series of furniture makers' floats at the Lord Mayor's Show the week that Great Britain declared war. [*The Cabinet Maker*, 1 August 1914, p. 126]

Fig. 10.46 **A 'Lounge at Holland Park'**, furnished by The Omega Workshops of Bloomsbury. [Tate Images]

Fig. 10.47 **Maples' reinterpretation of the 'Adam' style** in this wartime advertisement has similarities to designs by Percival Hildesley. [*The Cabinet Maker*, 27 May 1916]

Fig. 10.48 **'A Waring's Van on Active Service! Somewhere in France'.** In August 1914, the fleet of Waring's motor lorries was immediately put at the disposal of the War Office. [*The Cabinet Maker*, 15 April 1916, p. 43]

their Raleigh Works was occupied with aircraft production. **Fig. 10.49c** shows a team of women working on the intricate assembly of a biplane wing in a Waring & Gillow factory in Lancaster.[51] The firm of B. Cohen & Sons of Curtain Road was an example of one of the smaller firms with such skills.[52] Hampton's workshop in Lambeth was turned over to war production, their fleet of lorries already used to transport munitions to the front line.

The full impact of war on the furniture trades was not immediate and, with a good supply of imported hardwoods still in stock, a limited furniture production continued. In 1914 there had been a noticeable increase in the stocks of mahogany and there were still 7,782 Honduras logs available in 1916. By 1916 furniture exports showed significant signs of improvement. Partly due to increased prices, furniture and cabinet ware in August amounted to a value of £57,719 against £36,643 the previous year. Records show that over one million tons of mahogany and other hardwoods and veneers were used in the cabinet-making industry between 1913 and 1915.[53]

In 1913 British furniture exports to all destinations had amounted to nearly £1.3 million and it was quickly understood that trade routes must be kept open to maintain export sales. An Act of Parliament banned the import of timber for furniture. Inevitably lack of imports, the enormous quantity of timber needed for the war effort, and the scarcity of soft and hard woods resulted in a dramatic increase in prices. The long-established wood brokers Churchill & Sim reported that in 1913 there had been 28,730 logs

Fig. 10.49a **Cabinet makers forming the laminated wood twin-blade propellors at Hampton's iconic warehouse just south of Chelsea Bridge, July 1916. The floor is deep in plane shavings.** [Bedford Lemere]

Fig. 10.49b **The final stages of polishing the laminated blades were entrusted to women and older craftsmen, seen here working on the finishing stages of four-blade propeller assembly at Hampton's Battersea premises in July 1916.** [Bedford Lemere]

Fig. 10.49c **Women in Lancaster assembling biplane wings at one of the Waring & Gillow factories.** [Bedford Lemere]

of mahogany available, the stocks down to 1,784 at the beginning of 1917. By 1915 the number of men called to the front and needed for the war effort meant that there was little new furniture being made. By 1916, 4,282 furniture makers had joined up but in many other cases their skills were needed for aeroplane construction at home. The lack of skilled hands further increased prices of new furniture as demand outstripped supply and there was more competition for antique furniture on the second-hand market in furniture stores and at auction, sending prices higher.[54] From 1914 there were restricted opening and working hours and the banning of all outside advertising lights or the lighting of shop windows. Early closing was introduced in October 1916. The lack of available energy supplies and falling demand in the furniture trades is evident in the publications of *The Cabinet Maker*. By 1917 the size of each issue had been reduced, with far less advertising. Editorial comment then concentrated on rattan production and soft furnishings, with little or no innovation in furniture design. By 1920 each weekly issue contained approximately thirty pages of advertisements for woodworking machinery, with timber suppliers buying most of the available space.

As a mark of respect, *The Cabinet Maker* began a roll call in 1915 of servicemen drawn from the furniture industry. Many gave their lives, won gallantry medals, or 'simply' volunteered for duty.[55] One survivor was Gordon Russell MC, who set up his own furniture-making business in the village of Broadway in 1922. Viscount Stansgate, Lieutenant William Wedgwood Benn, former chief of *The Cabinet Maker's* editorial department, a journal owned by Benn Brothers, was another highly decorated survivor. Four members of the Pratt family firm of Bradford served. Other servicemen cited had worked in High Wycombe, nine for William Birch and nine for William Bartlett & Sons. Bartlett had been makers of reproduction furniture, including in the Regency style, from c.1901 at their Sheraton Works.[56] The Denmark Street Works in London of William Birch had been almost completely taken over for war production by 1916.

Fig. 10.50 Skull's armchair appears to be inspired by one of c.1678 now at Ham House. Walter Skull of High Wycombe had contributed to the triumphal arch of chairs made when Queen Victoria visited the town in 1877. By the 1880s the firm had added a cabinet-making workshop. [*The Cabinet Maker*, 6 November 1915, p. 110]

Fig. 10.51 A small 'Adam-style' side cabinet made under the auspices of Lady Kinloch. The Classical medallions in cream and brown are painted on a light olive-green ground. [*The Cabinet Maker*, 29 July 1916, p. 82]

Fig. 10.52 A satinwood cabinet made by pupils at Queen Alexandra's Carving School at Sandringham. [Toovey's]

Walter Skull & Son, Lebus and many others also lost men to the front. Most of the men who fell are names who are otherwise probably unknown.[57]

The painted side cabinet in **Fig. 10.51** in the 'Adam style' was made by Tredagers, agents for the enterprising Lady Kinloch. Her project was set up in a Chelsea studio in 1916 under the supervision of Alexander Maclean to provide an occupation for artists whose work had been curtailed by the war. A complete range of well-made furniture was produced including desks, tables and chairs.[58] Other workshops were set up for disabled service personnel. For some years *The Cabinet Maker* staged a 'Christmas Cheer Fund' – an appeal to the trade for colleagues in need. The list of subscribers included familiar names such as Maples, Druce & Co., Skull and Hermann as well as the newly established Restall, Brown & Clennell. Princess Alexandra created a 'Technical School of Woodwork', originally established to train the children of Sandringham Estate workers and later turned into a carving school for ex-servicemen.[59] Some of the Sandringham work has a distinctive interlaced 'AA' cipher stamped below a crown and other pieces in satinwood, although not stamped, bear distinct similarities to the display cabinet in **Fig. 10.52**.[60]

Despite restrictions, furniture makers continued to advertise in an attempt to promote trade during the first two years of the war. William Whiteley had opened his new department store in Bayswater in 1911, claiming that the firm's 'beauty of design, skilfulness of workmanship & supremacy of value is unequalled'.[61] Like so many of the large stores, there is little evidence Whiteley's actually *made* their own furniture. As always, innovation was the key to attracting buyers. **Fig. 10.54** shows a shop window at the house furnishers John Anslow in Coventry. Anslow's hired actors dressed in Elizabethan clothing to add an air of authenticity. The Elizabethan theme was always popular and other Midlands firms such as the Boswell Studios and Brown & Smart in Nottingham also promoted the late Stuart style. The Carlyle Club, opened near Piccadilly Circus in 1914, was fitted out by Waring & Gillow in Elizabethan style with a suitably named and furnished 'Raleigh Room' and a 'Buccaneer Room'. G.H. & S. Keen and also Ebenezer Gomme, well known for their inventive chairs, were making modernised versions of George II settees by 1911, with a lower back adapted for the modern living room, as well as faithful copies of Charles II oak furniture, without any attempt to alter proportion or detail.[62]

Fig. 10.53 **A showroom of W. Bartlett & Sons, panelled and furnished in the seventeenth-century style. Similar room settings were adopted by firms such as E. Gomme and Walter Skull, but without a maker's mark it is difficult to distinguish the furniture of the various companies.** [*The Cabinet Maker*, 28 October 1916]

Fig. 10.54 **The shop window at Anslow Ltd in Coventry. The figures are local actors hired and dressed in Elizabethan clothing to enhance the look of authenticity.** [*The Cabinet Maker*, 3 July 2015, pp. 4, 11]

A limited number of exhibitions were mounted in the war years. The Economy Exhibition at the People's Palace in the Mile End Road in September 1916 showed a range of furniture made by the boys of the Shoreditch Technical Institute to designs by Percy Wells. Their work has a functional simplicity, a cross between designs of 1900 by Ambrose Heal and utility furniture of the 1940s. The 11th Annual Manchester Exhibition featured exhibitors such as Gomme, Gabe & Pass, Sadgrove and Briggs & Co. An exhibition of Arts and Crafts opened at Burlington House in October 1916 showing retrospective furniture by Reginald Blomfield, George Jack and Morris & Co. Gimson and the two Barnsleys were singled out for special mention. Despite admiration for furniture of the Arts and Crafts genre, there was criticism from high quarters. It was thought that by 1916 a cabinet maker served his generation better by using machinery to produce, for example, a sideboard at £25 than by hand making a version at 150 guineas (£157.50). The Bath Cabinet Makers Company had displayed their wares at Harrods and at Maples, but the factory was soon occupied making aeroplane parts. The company had flourished under the direction of Charles Richter whose philosophy was that machinery, far from being bad for the craftsman, freed him from repetitive tasks. There was still praise for the handmade: 'Mr. Gimson is so keen about good dovetails that he makes a pattern of them, and a very satisfactory pattern it is'.[63] Gimson and the Cotswold makers carried the Arts and Crafts movement through to the 1920s and 1930s, their style and methodology much revered today but the conflict between handmade and manufactured furniture continued. The principal architect of His Majesty's Office of Works, Sir Frank Baines,[64] declared at the 1920 Ideal Home Exhibition

10.55

10.56

10.57

10.58

Fig. 10.55 **A suggestion for a Smoking Room at a hotel or a club, the furniture selected from the stock of William Birch of High Wycombe who had softened their somewhat uncompromising Arts & Crafts style of the early 1900s.** [*The Cabinet Maker*, 28 October 1916, p. 65]

Fig. 10.56 **An illustration of an inlaid mahogany cabinet, available from Morris & Co. in 1912 for £40 10s. The upper tier is now less popular and may not have survived on extant examples.** [Private collection]

Fig. 10.57 **A china cabinet in satinwood, an exercise in eclecticism by R. & J. Waterer & Sons of Chertsey,** whose stamp is seen on furniture from the 1850s. Contemporaries would probably have termed the cabinet as 'Adam', whilst the feet are in the style of the early 1700s loosely known as 'William and Mary'. [Butchoff archive]

Fig. 10.58 **A bookcase made for export by W. Mills & Sons, in business since 1872. The design of the astragals has been adapted from Chippendale's *Director* and are made of brass, not in traditional moulded wood. This may be a useful indication in identifying other work by Mills. Morris & Co. offered a similar cabinet in 1912 for £35.** [*The Cabinet Maker*, 7 November 1914, p. 115]

that Arts and Crafts was 'useless' and in the same speech said that manufacturers' catalogues contained some of the most atrocious designs it was possible to produce![65] The term 'Arts & Crafts' was frequently misapplied; the Central School of Arts and Crafts, formed by the London County Council in 1896, was an invaluable training programme but much of the students' furniture was machine-made and often entirely derivative of Hepplewhite and Sheraton designs.[66] Another London County Council enterprise, the Hammersmith School of Arts and Crafts, also trained students to produce reproduction furniture in a manner more commonly associated with the 1920s and '30s.[67] No observer today would label the production of these and similar schools as 'Arts and Crafts', just as the twentieth-century output of Morris & Co. cannot be classified alongside the work of Gimson, the Barnsleys or Peter Waals.

In September 1914, The Furniture & Fine Art Depositories Ltd of Islington, by 'Royal Appointment to the King of Spain', advertised property formerly in the possession of the Duke of Sutherland and the Dowager Duchess of Newcastle. The firm sold a wide range of antique and contemporary furniture from 'Town and Country Mansions', paying customers' cab fares from any part of London. A review of the furniture trade reported that in 1916 there had been a ready market for high-class furniture. Prices were rising partly due to a shortage of labour and to an Act of

511

10.59

Fig. 10.59 **A boldly coloured watercolour in a Waring & Gillow catalogue of** *c.*1920, **illustrating the continuing popularity of furniture in the French Louis XIV style, eminently suitable to complement 'costly tapestries and expensive hangings'.** [Private collection]

Fig. 10.60 **The term 'oyster veneer' is beautifully illustrated on the walnut-veneered doors of this cocktail cabinet in a style made well into the 1930s and beyond. The top, with imitation Chinese clasps of** *c.*1680, **is stylistically 30 to 40 years earlier than the giltwood base.** [Nan Xu]

Fig. 10.61 **A gramophone case by The Aeolian Co., Ltd of New Bond Street. Veneered in expensive West Indian satinwood, the sides and top are painted in the Adam revival style. The volume is controlled by adjusting the right-hand door.** [Wick Antiques]

Fig. 10.62 **Displaying a novelty of design and function, Willingale's combined china and music cabinet was exhibited at the Central School of Arts and Crafts.** [*The Cabinet Maker*, 16 December 1916, p. 210, reproduced from *The Studio*]

Fig. 10.63 **A 'Music Cabinet in Walnut and Gold' that could easily be adapted as a cocktail cabinet. Appropiately surmounted by Oriental-style porcelain, Hildesley's wartime design is in the popular William and Mary style.** [Private collection]

Fig. 10.64 **Chapman's 'spirit, smoking and writer's cabinet', a forerunner of the ubiquitous cocktail cabinet.** [*The Cabinet Maker*, 24 June 1916, p. 257]

Parliament banning the import of furniture woods. There was a cautious optimism by the summer of 1918 that the war was soon to be at an end, but the following year there were still many craftspeople employed in the production of aeroplanes for the Air Ministry at a time when skilled labour was in short supply in the furniture industry and demand for new furniture was rising. Questions were asked in parliament to see if some of these men and women could be diverted back to furniture making.[68] The Central Aircraft Co. at the Palmerston Works in Kilburn kept the company name after the war but by the 1920s had a large stock of reproduction late Georgian furniture making good use of well-figured mahogany veneers.

Before the outbreak of war enterprising firms were designing furniture that could be easily crated for shipping and assembled at the destination. The East End maker, W. Mills & Sons, in business since 1872, advertised that they had 'considerable experience in the manufacture of high-class "K.D." [knock down] work for abroad'.[69] Their reproduction George III-style bookcase, **Fig. 10.58**, with well-figured flame mahogany doors has brass astragals cast in the Gothic style. An innovative feature, it is probable the glass would also have been supplied locally if exported abroad. It poses the question as to whether brass astragals were a unique feature of Mills' work or in more general use. As exports grew after the war there was a renewed interest in furniture that could be packed and shipped more efficiently. Much of the furniture exhibited at the 1920 Ideal Home Exhibition held at the Crystal Palace in Sydenham was of the 'knock down' type as part of the export drive but the exhibition also catered for 'people of considerable wealth looking for panelled interiors, costly tapestries and expensive hangings'.[70] Keeble of Carlisle House, established by Francis Keeble in London by 1866, were typical of the many firms supplying

513

Fig. 10.65 The Chippendale style generated admiration and critical observation. 'So unaffectedly do our manufacturers admire the styles created by the influence of Chippendale, Sheraton, Hepplewhite and the Brothers Adam, that they make and re-make, hash and re-hash, produce and reproduce the designs originated by the eighteenth-century.'[71] [Butchoff Antiques]

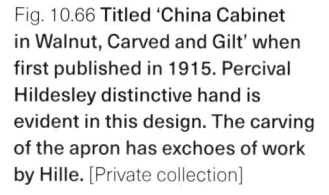

Fig. 10.66 Titled 'China Cabinet in Walnut, Carved and Gilt' when first published in 1915. Percival Hildesley distinctive hand is evident in this design. The carving of the apron has echoes of work by Hille. [Private collection]

Fig. 10.67 A showroom recreating an idealised Georgian interior mixing old and new. The display cabinet is the most easily identifiable as a modern reproduction. [Butchoff archive]

Fig. 10.68 A room at The Node, Hertfordshire, furnished in 1920 by Marsh, Jones & Cribb. [Historic England]

antique and modern furniture as well as panelling in popular styles.

Other innovations abounded. The Packflat Furniture Company produced furniture that could be assembled without the use of glue, screws or nails. William Bartlett & Sons exhibited dining tables, the legs of which unscrewed to be stored within the frame, echoing the practice of the eighteenth-century German cabinet makers Abraham and David Roentgen. Taking a step further than the fitted coromandel decanter boxes of the previous century, the East End firm, Chapman, Son & Co. of Charterhouse Buildings, made innovative forerunners of the ubiquitous cocktail cabinets that became so popular in the interwar period, **Fig. 10.64**. Like L.E. Jaccard of Clerkenwell who produced lacquer gramophone cabinets, Chapmans adapted the concept of decanter tables to make expensive and high-quality veneered and inlaid gramophone cases. A new task for the cabinet maker, gramophone cabinets were far more elaborate than most plain examples that survive today, such as those in a quasi-Adam style designed by Percival T. Hildesley. In 1915 Hildesley also designed an 'enclosed writing table', modelled on the concept of a late eighteenth-century square piano; such pianos are commonly seen transformed into writing desks. Many items of small, innovative furniture were made in the East End and sold anonymously by larger firms. When closed, the satinwood demi-lune side table in **Fig. 10.61** cleverly disguises a gramophone with record deck and a speaker.

BRITISH FURNITURE

10.69a 
10.69b

10.70

Figs 10.69a & b **Designs by Hildesley for a dressing table and a side table with an electric lamp first illustrated in** *The Cabinet Maker* **in 1915 and reproduced in** *English Furniture Designs* **in 1923.** [Private collection]

Fig. 10.70 **Hildesley's design for a sideboard in mahogany with pearwood. He has copied the fashion for a brass rail first seen in the mid-eighteenth century whilst the legs are of late seventeenth-century influence.** [Private collection]

The brass handle for the movement is seen on the left of the picture, the right-hand door opens and closes at will to adjust the volume. Called an Aeolian Vocalion, the company made cases available in all the popular styles. Newspaper advertisements for their range show that they produced a series of top of the line Vocalions in what they called 'period cases', designed to co-ordinate with the major periods of antique English furniture. Cases were available in all styles including 'Gothic, Jacobean, Queen Anne, William and Mary, Chippendale and Adams [*sic*]' and included Chinese-stye japanning.[72]

From 1915 *The Cabinet Maker* featured designs by Percival Hildesley, whose distinctive style did not become fashionable, due to the war, until they were re-published in

516

Figs 10.71a & b **One of a pair of George II-style, burr walnut, concertina-action, fold-over card tables. The detail of the rounded corner is typical of the style of Charles Tozer.** [Christian Davis Antiques]

Fig. 10.72 **A display cabinet by Hildesley, which although 'Chippendale' in influence, has an aura of Danish design. First illustrated in 1916, it was reproduced in** *English Furniture Designs* **in 1923.** [Private collection]

1920 and again in his *English Furniture Designs* of 1923. Details in Hildesley's wartime designs retained some of the Spanish influence evident in his 1907 watercolour *Hall in the Style of the Spanish Renaissance*.[73] Other details, such as the generous use of quarter-veneering, suggest that he was familiar with a cabinet designed by W.A.S. Benson exhibited by Morris & Co. at the 1908 Franco-British exhibition.[74] The Hildesley sideboard, **Fig. 10.70**, was re-published in 1920 with an editorial praising the lasting qualities of the design, wondering if in one hundred years' time it would be as sought after as one of the 'masterpieces of the eighteenth-century men'.[75]

Hildesley published eighty-seven designs in 1923, accompanied by scale drawings showing that he was familiar with the finer points of cabinet making and construction. The book included many designs that pre-date the war years, an interesting insight into the wartime delay of progressive furniture design.[76] A selection from the book in a distinctive, instantly recognisable hand, is shown in illustrations on these pages. The designs range from a sophisticated sideboard in mahogany with pearwood carving to a far more rustic look 'for a cottage living room'. Hildesley's foreword was written by Henry Shapland, a partner in Shapland & Petter. Shapland wrote in a heartfelt tone: 'So much has been written about fine antique furniture that we are in real danger of forgetting the existence of equally fine modern furniture…'. He continued: 'It is by no means sufficiently realised how great…English taste…[is] the standard throughout the civilised world.' Shapland added: '…French styles once held the field, but they have now been supplanted by English work, and France…readily buys English furniture.'[77] As well as a distinctly Spanish feel, entwined with an appreciation of

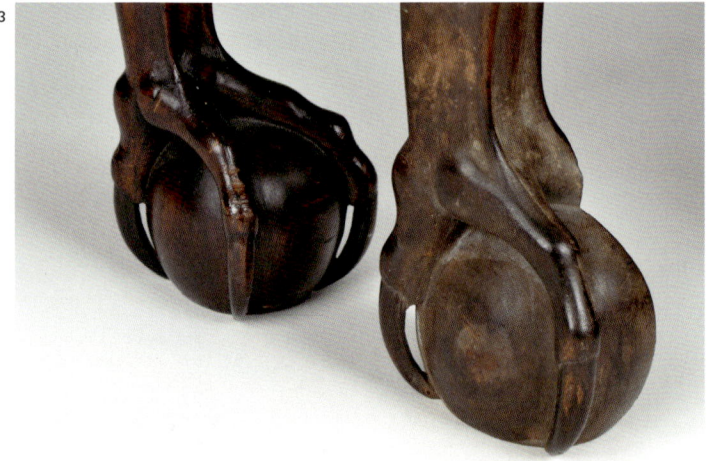

Fig. 10.73 **The claw foot of a dressing table by John Goddard of Newport, Rhode Island in 1763. The undercutting of the talons was an expensive, time-consuming practice and is rarely seen in reproductions.** [Winterthur Museum, Gift of Henry Francis du Pont]

Fig. 10.74 **A photograph in the Frederick Parker day books annotated '1904'. Sitting incongruously in a poorly manicured garden, this eighteen-piece suite in the manner of the Grendey suite at Stourhead is a mystery. Each has an old, well-worn seat suggesting that it is not a new set by Parker. Are some or all the pieces eighteenth-century originals?** [The Frederick Parker Collection]

Fig. 10.75 **A set of six carved walnut dining chairs in the style of the 1740s in the manner of Giles Grendey. The set includes a pair of armchairs in a typical interpretation by Charles Tozer in the early twentieth century. The model was also made by Frederick Parker who may well have been a supplier to Tozer.** [Sotheby's]

Fig. 10.76 **Like the original eighteenth-century model, formerly in the Percival Griffiths Collection, this pair of wide-seated armchairs are veneered in a fine choice of well-figured walnut. The construction and finish of the polish is in a style often attributed to Charles Tozer, but similar to later work by Hicks of Dublin.**[78] [Wick Antiques]

the William and Mary style, Hildesley's carefully executed drawings have an eye on the finer details of Chippendale and Adam furniture and the simplicity of Arts and Crafts. A more modern look for drawer handles and cabinet hardware was beginning to emerge by 1915, a style more in keeping with Hildesley's designs. Despite this distinctly new look to drawer handles, lines of fittings by hardware makers such as G.F. Thew of Liverpool, or the wares of the Birmingham firm of Timmings & Co., retained a strong Art Nouveau influence, even as late as 1920. Was this due to a surplus of stock after the war, or fashion?

Charles Tozer was first listed in 1891 as an 'Artistic Furniture Manufacturer'. Most recorded items of his furniture with his applied label are small tables, chairs and stools in walnut in what at the time was known as the Queen Anne style, which was also favoured by the designer Maurice Adams,[79] but he also supplied gilt gesso

CHAPTER 10: 1910–1920

10.77

10.78

Fig. 10.77 A fine pair of Cuban mahogany armchairs in the manner of Giles Grendey with distinctive 'shepherd's crook' arms, a model offered by Maples, branded as '"Chippendale"'. The vase splat is an extraordinary confection held at the rear by outstretched claws. In *Furniture of the Eighteenth Century*, Cescinsky illustrated a settee of similar form and referred to 'central splats...braced to the side balusters in a very peculiar manner'.[80] [Private collection]

Fig. 10.78 A generously proportioned walnut armchair with the label 'W. Charles Tozer 25 Brook Street London'. The elaborate back was possibly inspired by designs published in 1741 by William De La Cour in his *First Book of Ornament*. [Butchoff Antiques]

tables and lacquer furniture.[81] The term 'Queen Anne' was still a misnomer; it owes more to the early Georgian period, for example the pair of walnut card tables, one illustrated as **Fig. 10.71b**. Tozer furniture is usually well made and shows good attention to detail. It is likely that most of their labelled pieces, all typical of the reproduction era, date to the early twentieth century.[82] The card tables have a fully developed style of fold-over top, a sophisticated model copying the best elements of early George II original examples. Tozer has incorporated an elaborate concertina action which forms a veneered frieze when open, the top follows the shape of

519

Fig. 10.79 **Although at first glance modelled on an Adam-period *demi-lune* side cabinet, the twentieth-century date of this example is evident from the use of walnut veneers; satinwood or mahogany would have been the preferred choice in the George III period.** [Private collection]

Fig. 10.80 **A George III-style side cabinet with a Tozer paper label. Veneered in yew, it is probably a late example of their work, dating to well after World War I. Yew became** increasingly popular from the 1920s. Although used by Ince & Mayhew, it was not in common usage for veneers in the eighteenth century. [Woolley & Wallis]

Fig. 10.81 **The Dining Room at Tyntesfield with a set of thirty George II-style walnut dining chairs supplied by Baker of Bath *c*.1910. The firm also supplied chairs in the popular Chippendale manner.**[83] [*Country Life*/Future Publishing Ltd]

the rounded outset corners, another expensive feature. The tables are similar to an example of the 1730 to 1748 period by Benjamin Crook illustrated in Symonds.[84] Tozer and other makers and suppliers such as Gill & Reigate, Gillows, Harrods and Pratt, Thomas & Sons were subscribers to Symonds's 1929 publication. Did Tozer know of the extant card table before 1929, or does the model date to the post publication date of the 1930s? Although furniture by Tozer in the Queen Anne to George II style is the most commonly seen, a set of twelve green and cream-painted armchairs in the Regency style is known with applied ivorine labels stamped 'TOZER 25, Brook Street, London, W.1'. The maker, be it Tozer or one of his suppliers, has created an elegant model but probably not a direct copy.[85] Most applied labels by Tozer are stamped 'W. Charles Tozer' so this Regency set with a different label may be of a much later date.

In keeping with Georgian furniture of the 1730s to 1750s, most later copies of furniture with cabriole legs have either 'claw and ball' or lion's paw feet. The claw foot, either that of an eagle or *draco* (dragon) holding a sphere traditionally known as a pearl or ball, was one of the most common features of chair and table legs from the 1730s and was much favoured for reproductions in the twentieth century.[86] A traditional explanation but without substantiation is that the claw-and-ball foot was adapted, along with other Chinese influences on early eighteenth-century English furniture, from Chinese mythology. Likewise, the vase-shaped splats of George I and George II chairs, both period and copies, appear to follow Chinese porcelain forms. Well-made

CHAPTER 10: 1910–1920

10.82

Fig. 10.82 A walnut bookcase the lower part with laburnham oyster veneers, the proportions typical of early twentieth-century reproductions. The small glass panes of this and the cabinets illustrated by Hampton & Sons and Frederick Parker (Figs 10.83 & 10.84) are reminiscent of the Pepys bookcases at Magdalene College, Cambridge. [Wick Antiques]

Fig. 10.83 A William and Mary-style cabinet on stand available from Hampton & Sons, one of the more exclusive items marked 'Price on application'. [Hampton's catalogue]

Fig. 10.84 A display cabinet in the William and Mary style in the Frederick Parker day book, dated April 1914. [Frederick Parker Collection]

10.83

10.84

521

10.85

Fig. 10.85 **A pair of mahogany display cabinets of a novel shape complemented by carved decoration and Vitruvian scrolls in the George II style. Although the cabinet maker is not known, the locks are by Comyn Ching, a London hardware company founded in *c.*1750.** [Wick Antiques]

Fig. 10.86 **A japanned lacquer cabinet and an armchair of a type made by London firms such as Mandelbom or Herman & Phillips. The table is a modern urn stand imported in large quantities from China and many variations were shown at the British Empire Exhibition in 1924.** [*The Cabinet Maker*, 16 October 1920, p. 212]

Fig. 10.87 **Duveen had two of this model of cabinet on stand, of a similar style wholesaled by Kahn, to order at £300 each.** [© J. Paul Getty Trust. Getty Research Institute, Los Angeles (2007. D.1)]

Fig. 10.88 **Herman & Phillips specialised in mahogany furniture in the mid-eighteenth-century style whilst maintaining a good reputation for lacquer work.** [*The Cabinet Maker*, 25 September 1920, p. 767]

Fig. 10.89 **The enterprising firm of P. Mandelbom & Co. encouraged their craftsmen to study furniture at the Victoria and Albert Museum.** [*The Cabinet Maker*, 5 June 1920, p. 516]

BRITISH FURNITURE

10.90a

10734 Raised Lacquer Panel fitted to Chinese Chippendale Carved Frame, framework in dull old gilt.

10735 Raised Lacquer Panel fitted to Chinese Chippendale Frame, framework in dull old gilt.

DECORATIONS IN RAISED LACQUER, in BLACK, RED, GREEN, BLUE, or CREAM.

10736 Raised Lacquer Panel fitted to Chinese Chippendale Frame, framework in dull old gilt.

Fig. 10.90a The Kahn catalogue included such eccentricities as these extraordinary Chippendale-style mirror frames 'in dull old gilt' but instead of mirror glass they were fitted with lacquer panels, here priced in US dollars. [Arrowsmith Antiques]

Fig. 10.90b As well as copies, Kahn supplied a wide range of reproduction lacquer furniture in five different hues, also priced in US dollars for export. [Arrowsmith Antiques]

Figs 10.91a & b A chinoiserie lacquer dressing table in the Frederick Parker day book for 1914–1916. The cost price, in code, is annotated 'ready to Decorate as photo' [sic]. [Frederick Parker Collection]

10.90b

DECORATIONS IN RAISED LACQUER · in BLACK, RED, GREEN, BLUE, or CREAM.

10701 Queen Anne Bureau, in raised lacquer, with three drawers and interior fittings. 2 ft. 3 ins. wide.

10700 Queen Anne Bureau, in raised lacquer decorations, with four drawers and interior fittings. 2 ft. 6 ins. wide. 2 ft. 3 ins. wide. 2 ft. 0 ins. wide.

10702 Queen Anne Bureau, in raised lacquer, with two drawers and interior fittings. 2 ft. 0 ins. wide.

10.91a

10.91b

examples of an eighteenth-century claw show the long talons heavily undercut for realism (**Fig. 10.73**), but later, and in most reproduction pieces, the talons lie close to the ball, a making process involving less time, expense and skill.[87] In c.1920 in Britain a simple foot with the claw completely attached to the ball would cost some 25–30 (old) pence to carve. Another popular style of foot is that of a carved lion's paw; the lion being a sign of power and strength. The set of chairs in **Fig. 10.75** is in the style of Giles Grendey (1693–1780), an important cabinet and chair maker working in

10.92

10.94

10.93

Fig. 10.92 A lacquer display cabinet with suitably arranged chinoiserie-style glazing bars available from Frederick Parker. The identical form of cabinet was also available in plain mahogany. If the client wanted lacquer, it could be applied directly onto the mahogany substrate. [Frederick Parker Collection]

Fig. 10.93 Japanned furniture from the Queen Anne era is rare but was keenly copied in the early twentieth century. Although by the nineteenth century mirror glass could be produced in large sheets, here the maker has judiciously copied the old style of Vauxhall plate in two parts. Tozer are recorded as suppliers of japanned mirrors in the later George II style. [Sotheby's]

Fig. 10.94 Standing at just over 2m (6ft) high, this longcase clock, japanned in imitation of Chinese lacquer, has the iconic sounds of the 'Westminster chimes' from the Elizabeth Tower at the Palace of Westminster and the 'Whittington chimes' from St Mary-le-Bow. East End firms such as Kahn or Jaccard used specialists for this style of increasingly popular decoration. [Butchoff Antiques]

BRITISH FURNITURE

10.95

Fig. 10.95 **A chinoiserie cabinet designed in 1920 by Ray Hille, veneered in satinwood with japanned panels it mixes various elements from Chippendale's** *Director*. [Brother Decoration Group, Chongqing]

Fig. 10.96 **A 'Chinese Chippendale' Drawing Room illustrating chinoiserie furniture designed by Ray Hille. In the 1760s this type of furniture would have been made in mahogany but by** *c.*1910 Hille was using satinwood. The occasional table is topped by a bonsai tree. [*The Cabinet Maker*, 13 November 1920, p. 367]

Fig. 10.97 **A view of the Chinese Chippendale Drawing Room at Buckingham Palace photographed in 1914. The room was created in 1911 by Queen Mary, and Charles Allom of White Allom & Co. All the furniture, with the exception of the tabernacle mirror and the tripod table, date to the early 1900s. Battiscombe & Harris exhibited at the Building Exhibition at Olympia in 1920, making fibrous plaster mouldings and mirrors in popular eighteenth-century styles similar to the one shown here.** [© His Majesty King Charles III 2023, RCIN 2101874]

Fig. 10.98 **The Chinese Chippendale style was imaginatively adapted in the early twentieth century; this vivid red lacquer cabinet has all the quality and hallmarks of the Hille enterprise.** [Holly Johnson Antiques]

10.99

10.100

Figs 10.99 & 10.100 The ultimate British interpretation of chinoiserie. A chandelier in carved and giltwood burnished to a high degree, similar to the one in the Chinese Chippendale Drawing Room at Buckingham Palace, the room created in 1911 by Queen Mary, and Charles Allom of White Allom & Co. The Buckingham Palace chandelier is an eighteenth-century Thomas Chippendale design taken from Plate CLV of The Gentleman and Cabinet-maker's *Director*, 1756 titled 'Chandeliers for Halls etc.'. The watercolour by Arthur Reginald Smith (1871–1934) shows the room from another angle to Fig. 10.97 and looks towards the fireplace showing the room with green wallpaper and brightly coloured fabric on the comfortable, low armchairs. There is an abundance of Chinese figures including the lamp with the ubiquitous parasol shade.
[10.99: Butchoff Antiques; 10.100: His Majesty King Charles III, RCIN 926110]

Clerkenwell by *c*.1730. Grendey's work was frequently copied in the early twentieth century, often by Tozer. The set of six chairs, with their distinctive backs, is based on chairs believed to have been supplied by Grendey to the banker Henry Hoare at Stourhead.[88] Part of the house was gutted in 1902 and a much later image shows that reproductions replaced the originals.[89] Duveen had at least one example of this chair in stock with a settee *en suite* and Maples advertised the same model in walnut, also an armchair and a settee.[90] A side chair and a settee of this model are shown in Macquoid and like the desk discussed earlier, **Fig. 10.33**, were also the property of Messrs J. Mallett & Son.[91] A similar set with an unconventionally upholstered back to the settee, was photographed in 1904 in a garden setting, **Fig. 10.74**. The more conventional model settee was available from Duveen '2 Carved-3 back settees like [Fig.] 112 "Age of Mahogany"', at £80 each, the original again owned by Mallett.

By 1900, most fashionable firms were offering Chinese Chippendale-style furniture with English japanning. The return of interest in the Chinese taste was to become ever more popular with furniture of all types including clocks, **Fig. 10.94**. E. Kahn & Co. supplied 'raised lacquer' furniture in 'Black, Red, Green, Blue, or Cream Lacquer', influenced by Stalker & Parker's treatise in a style popular from *c*.1690 to 1760.[92] Kahn was praised 'for some of the best reproduction work to be seen in this country', **Figs 10.90a & b**.[93] The cabinet on stand with vibrant colouring in **Fig. 10.87**, was available from Duveen to order, priced at £300 each. Cream-coloured lacquer is inspired by a clothes press made in *c*.1775 by Thomas Chippendale for the actor David Garrick.[94] A resurgence in the early twentieth century saw many firms specialising in lacquer work, traditionally termed 'japanning'

529

in Britain to distinguish it from Chinese and Japanese wares. One of the specialist firms was P. Mandelbom & Co. of Playhouse Yard in the East End who kept '...staff in constant attendance at the Victoria and Albert Museum copying old designs'.[95] Herman & Phillips of Kingsland Road opened a new showroom in 1920 at 125 Curtain Road, exhibiting amongst other pieces the japanned furniture for which they had 'acquired an enviable reputation'.[96] All the lacquer furniture in a Hampton's catalogue is marked 'Price on application', suggesting that it was bought in from smaller East End specialists, the price liable to fluctuate.

The exotic satinwood chinoiserie display cabinet in **Fig. 10.95** is to a design by Ray Hille, a development of the firm's red, blue, black or ivory suites introduced in 1914. Her father, Salaman Hille, was a Ukrainian immigrant who started in the East End in 1906 by renovating and reproducing eighteenth-century furniture to a high standard, supplying larger firms such as Hamptons and Maples. Other variations of this cabinet were made by Hille, some with matching seat furniture and tables. The distinctive astragals are taken from a mixture of designs by Chippendale and a similar display cabinet formerly in the collection of Sir Basil Montgomery.[97] Hille also made complete suites of satinwood-veneered furniture including fashionable cocktail cabinets and *bergère* suites, all with the application of small distinctive japanned panels, and by the 1930s the company had established an international reputation. The cabinet in the contemporary engraving in **Fig. 10.96** has the same form and distinctive astragals, again with differing Chippendale

Fig. 10.101 **The modern furniture department at the Army & Navy Stores in 1915.** [Historic England]

Fig. 10.102 **A low cabinet by Frederick Parker who has produced a practical cabinet low enough to allow for a picture hang, the astragals adapted from the *Director*.** [Clive Edwards]

Fig. 10.103 **A chinoiserie cabinet by Frederick Parker drawing from elements of Chippendale's *Director*.** [Clive Edwards]

Fig. 10.104 Over 3m (10ft) wide this mahogany cabinet, possibly by Frederick Parker, has astragals adapted from Chippendale's *Director*. It breaks down easily for transportation; the three display sections are separate cabinets, locked together by the top and plinth which are each of one long piece. [Nan Xu]

Figs 10.105 & 10.106 The Frederick Parker archives contain images of designs number 0 to 265 dating from 1914–1916. Two of these models, illustrated here, appear to be richly inlaid with end-cut marquetry foliage. The commode is 1.4m (4ft 6in) wide, the display cabinet 1.8m (5ft 10in) wide. [The Frederick Parker Collection]

elements. The differences between the extant example and the engraving could be simply the artist's impression, or a variation by Hille or another East End maker.

One of the larger firms making reproduction furniture was Beresford & Hicks, established in 1891 with a factory in Hoxton and a showroom in Curtain Road, selling to large West End stores such as Heals and, in the 1930s and '40s, directly to the royal family. Two names well known in the furniture industry today are those of Frederick Parker (Parker Knoll) and Lucian Ercolani (Ercol), both known for their seat furniture and also cabinet making. Parker was the son of a cabinet maker who established his business in Shoreditch in 1869. By the 1900s the firm styled itself as 'Ship Furniture, Chair & Cabinet Manufacturers, Upholsterers, Antique Dealers'. In 1902 Parker supplied eighty chairs in the Chippendale style for the liner *Ophir* and 200 in the Hepplewhite style for the *Aquitania* in 1914.[98] Ercolani was the son of an Italian woodcarver whose family came to England in 1898. In 1910 he worked for Parker, then Gomme

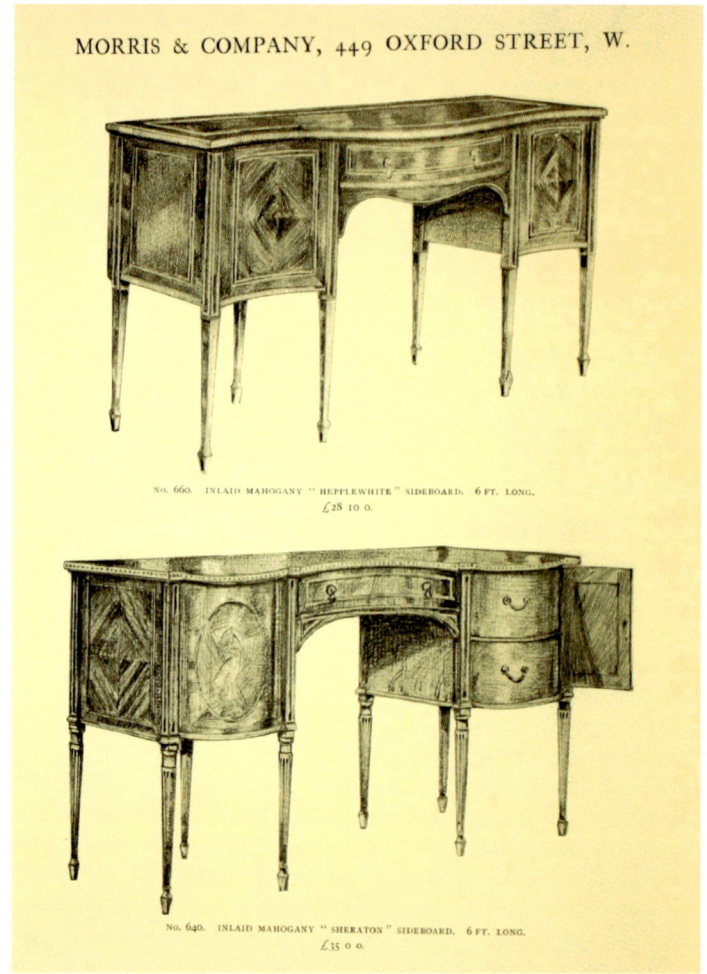

Fig. 10.107 The Leicester firm of Robert Johnson & Co. exhibited in a well-tried George II Revival format at the Buildings Exhibition at Olympia in 1920. The wall panelling, dining table and chairs were in Cuban mahogany. In contrast they also exhibited a bedroom simply painted in blue and grey. [*The Cabinet Maker*, 17 April 1920, p. 113]

Fig. 10.108 The Hepplewhite style was one of the most popular in the 1910–1920 decade. In principle the clean simpler lines were easier and cheaper to reproduce than more complex Chippendale designs. Numerous unsigned, unattributable sideboards in this style are to be found, for example retailed by Waring & Gillow, Hamptons and Morris & Co. Shaw Sparrow (1904) illustrated this mahogany sideboard by 'Robert Christie, Cabinet Maker', a rare example of a named maker working in the George III reproduction style. The brass rail acted as a splashback and, with the upper tier of small drawers, was often removed by later generations. [Private collection]

Fig. 10.109 A 'Hepplewhite' sideboard available from Morris & Co. in 1912 for £28 10s. The more complex 'Sheraton' example retailed at £35. [Private collection]

and ten years later established his own consortium with twenty men, trading as 'Furniture Industries'. Before 1914 Parker was doing considerable trade with mainland Europe and soon after the end of the war was in partnership with a firm in Malines, in Belgium: 'They were real old friends of ours and they were wonderful carvers'.[99]

The enlarging of the Boar Lane premises in Leeds of Marsh, Jones & Cribb in 1920 under the direction of a Mr Redman and a Mr Fenton is an indication of the robust health of the furniture trade. The company, which had been active building aeroplanes during and just after the war, were now fitting out ocean liners and providing complete panelled rooms. They bought the whole block either side of their existing seven-storey building, boasting five acres of showrooms.[100]

Imports of timber were increasing with over £410,000 worth of hewn and sawn mahogany alone shipped-in in April 1919. Japanese oak, plywood, knife- and saw-cut veneers of Cuban mahogany were now available to all trades involved in woodworking. Furniture production, although not back to pre-war years, had risen with exports in 1919 of £115,919 compared with £40,897 for the corresponding month in 1918. An increasing portion of the export trade was not luxury furniture. Grahame-White & Co. were applauded for the rapid increase in export of more utilitarian furniture to not only conventional markets such as New York but to the Middle East and Ghana (then termed the Gold Coast).[101]

Fig. 10.110 A watercolour by Percival Hildesley titled *A Reception Room in a London Town House*. The designer has incorporated old and new elements to create a modern interior in a traditional style at a time when old tapestries were again fashionable. [*The Cabinet Maker*, 27 March 1920]

Fig. 10.111 An armchair from a walnut and parcel gilt suite comprising ten chairs, a dining table, a side table, and a sideboard flanked by a pair of pedestals. The high quality and solid design suggest an attribution to a top London supplier such as Lenygon & Morant or Janes, the legs similar to a model by Frederick Parker. [Sotheby's]

Figs 10.112a & b The accoutrements contained in this finely figured mahogany dressing table by Waring & Gillow are stamped 'George Betjemann & Sons', with an ivorine plaque stamped 'Edward, Silversmiths to H. M. The King, 92 Buchanan Street, Glasgow'. It is an accomplished modernisation of Rudd's reflecting dressing table. Warings advertised this model at between £250 and £350 'according to the design of fittings'.[102] [Butchoff Antiques]

BRITISH FURNITURE

10.113

10.114

10.115

10.116

CHAPTER 10: 1910–1920

Fig. 10.113 **A later example of a ladies' dressing table with fittings supplied by the Goldsmiths' and Silversmiths' Company for the Nawab of Bahawalpur, Sadeq Mohammad Khan V. The silver fittings are hallmarked 1929 and 1930.** [Butchoff Antiques]

Fig. 10.114 **By 1920 interiors started to have a fresher, less cluttered look, often with vivid colours and always with an air of comfort. The tripod table in the foreground is one of a vast number seen today. The writing desk with elegant cabriole legs is a meeting of Louis XV and Hepplewhite.** [*The Cabinet Maker*, 9 October 1920, p. 65]

Fig. 10.115 **A mahogany display cabinet by James Henry Sellers, some of whose designs championed ziggurat stringing in ebony and satinwood, sometimes highlighted in red.** [*The Cabinet Maker*, 17 April 1920, p. 116]

Fig. 10.116 **A wardrobe designed by Sellers in beautiful quarter-veneered Cuban mahogany, the doors edged in ebony. The subtle serpentine front has the softness of line of case furniture made in the 1770s. Contemporary makers such as Fletcher, Lorimer and Simson used mahogany veneers in the same extravagant manner.** [Private collection]

Fig. 10.117 **Still popular amongst postwar makers and buyers in 1920, reproduction furniture in the sixteenth and seventeenth century styles was 'modernised', in this instance with dramatic upholstery colours. The blue is intended to tone in with the Chinese Kangxi-style vase and cover.** [*The Cabinet Maker*, 28 February 1920, p. 447]

10.117

The ancestry of the metamorphic dressing table can be traced back to the mid-eighteenth century. Originally a French conceit, known as a *poudreuse* or *table de toilette*, the concept was adapted by British makers but appears to have fallen out of favour in the early nineteenth century until revived and modernised a hundred years later. Examples from *c.*1900 have luxurious fittings of the highest quality either in hallmarked silver or silver plate, often incorporating turtle shell with silver filigree. **Fig. 10.112a** is based on the clean, simple lines of the late George III period, but others have a more elaborate casing, even in the provincial French Rococo style. Hepplewhite had been the first English designer to promote this form of table, with pull-out drawers and mirrors that tilted at various angles. The first known example

535

Fig. 10.118 There is a geometric simplicity to this chinoiserie settee, by Frederick Parker, available with armchairs *en suite*. The photograph is in the Parker day book for 1914–1916 and appears to anticipate the Art Deco settees designed by Oliver Hill for Mrs Albert Levy in 1927.[103] [Frederick Parker Collection]

Fig. 10.119 A 1920 design for a sideboard by the architect W.J. Palmer-Jones in an early anticipation of Art Deco, the style that takes its name from the *Exposition Internationale des Arts Décoratifs & Industriels Modernes*, held in Paris in 1925. [*The Cabinet Maker*, 10 April 1920, p. 65]

was illustrated in Hepplewhite's posthumously printed *The Cabinet-Maker and Upholsterer's Guide* of 1788.[104] Hepplewhite's widow, Alice, named this type of table 'Rudd's Table', a reference to Margaret Rudd, a courtesan and fraudster notorious in the 1770s.[105] The popularity of this style of table continued into the mid-twentieth century, later examples benefitting from electric lighting. An exceptionally luxurious later version, **Fig. 10.113**, was supplied to the Nawab of Bahawalpur, Sadeq Mohammad Khan V, by the Goldsmiths' and Silversmiths' Company in 1930. Each of the table's fittings bears his beautifully enamelled polychrome portrait.

In 1930, J.C. Rogers illustrated furniture by the best designers and furniture makers of the modern era.[106] The elegant display cabinet designed by George Jack in *c.*1890 (**Fig. 9.14**) and made in the William Morris workshops was illustrated alongside a Gimson cabinet.[107] Many of the designers are familiar names such as the Barnsleys, Ambrose Heal, John Stark and Sir Robert Lorimer, John Murray or W. Simpson, amongst a host of others; some had modernised the reproduction style that proudly showed its eighteenth-century origins. However by now Maurice Adams had discarded the reproduction 'King George V' style of his Grosvenor Range; he was no longer a 'Revivalist' but a 'Modernist'.[108] The furniture historian R.W. Symonds wanted to promote a Modern English Traditional School.[109] Working with Sir Edwin Lutyens' son Robert, the pair took contemporary design to the new movement of British 'Art Deco'.

Despite the implementation of a Luxury Tax in 1918, the furniture trade was buoyant in 1919. The value of exports of furniture and cabinet ware was just over £800,000, not surprisingly a huge increase over the war years, when exports fell to £297,000 in the last year of the war.[110] However the furniture trade by the end of 1920 did not meet the optimistic expectations of the beginning of the year. Business had fallen off and the air of post-war prosperity had dissipated. Manufacturers were caught in the spiral of falling sales and increasing demands for higher wages. The 1920s was a buyers' market, in stark contrast to the war years when dealers could sell all their stock at a time when there was little or no production due to the enormity of the war effort. Nevertheless, despite the market fluctuations and economic difficulties, British-made furniture at the luxury end of the scale was considered the market leader in terms of both taste and craftsmanship in the important markets of the world, from Australasia to North and South America.

More innovative furniture, however, and the seeds of the new aesthetic had been produced at the very end of the 1910s. The display cabinet in **Fig. 10.115**, designed by J.H. Sellers and first illustrated in *The Architect's Journal* in 1920, underlined Sellers' wish to borrow from the past by bringing it up to date, to make it 'a living Art in furniture' as quoted from his 1928 lecture to the Liverpool Architectural Society.[111] Using local firms such as William Henshall of Oldham for the cabinet work, by the 1920s some of Sellers' design work still seems to have had an eye on the eighteenth century, as seen in his elegant mahogany wardrobe (**Fig. 10.116**) but other pieces were more firmly in the Art Deco camp, the outline if not the decoration possibly influenced by the French designer Paul Follot.[112] It appears that Sellers and other contemporary designers had finally embraced a new approach to design and made 'a bold step towards rehabilitating that living tradition which was once our pride'.[113]

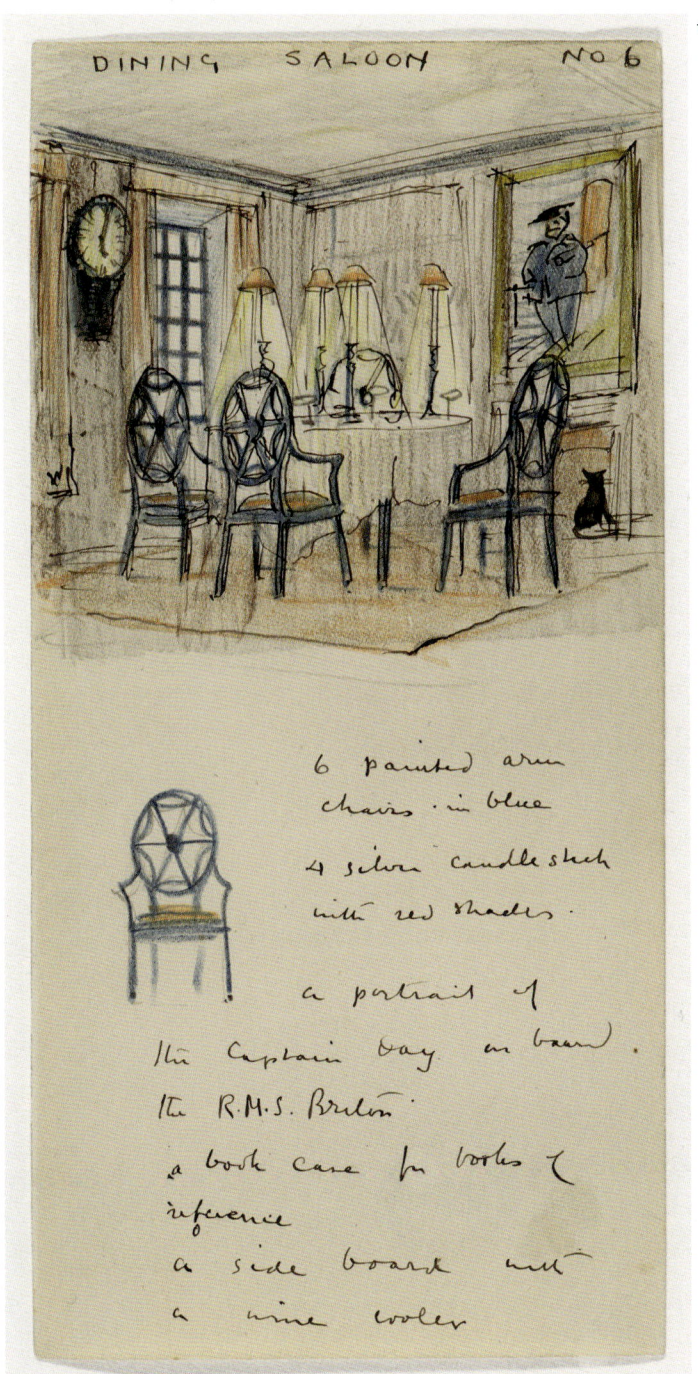

Fig. 10.120 The armchairs in this sketch by Lutyens for Captain Wetherspoon, dated 1919, are in a modernised Hepplewhite form also used by Oliver Hill at Essendon Place and Hampton Lodge. Lutyens' later furniture for the Viceroy's House, New Delhi, was also in a more traditional mid-Georgian to Regency style.[114] [RIBA 97515]

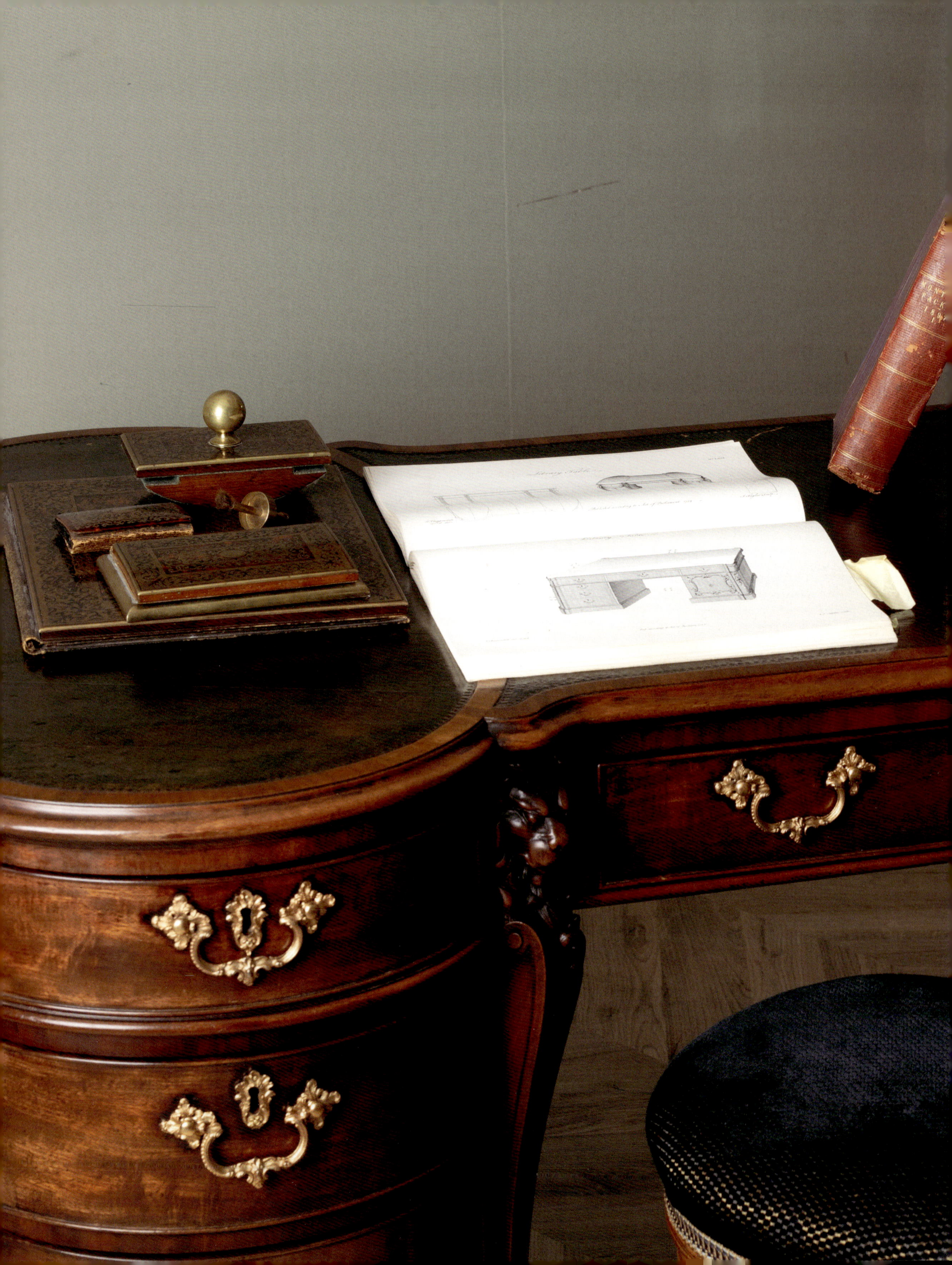

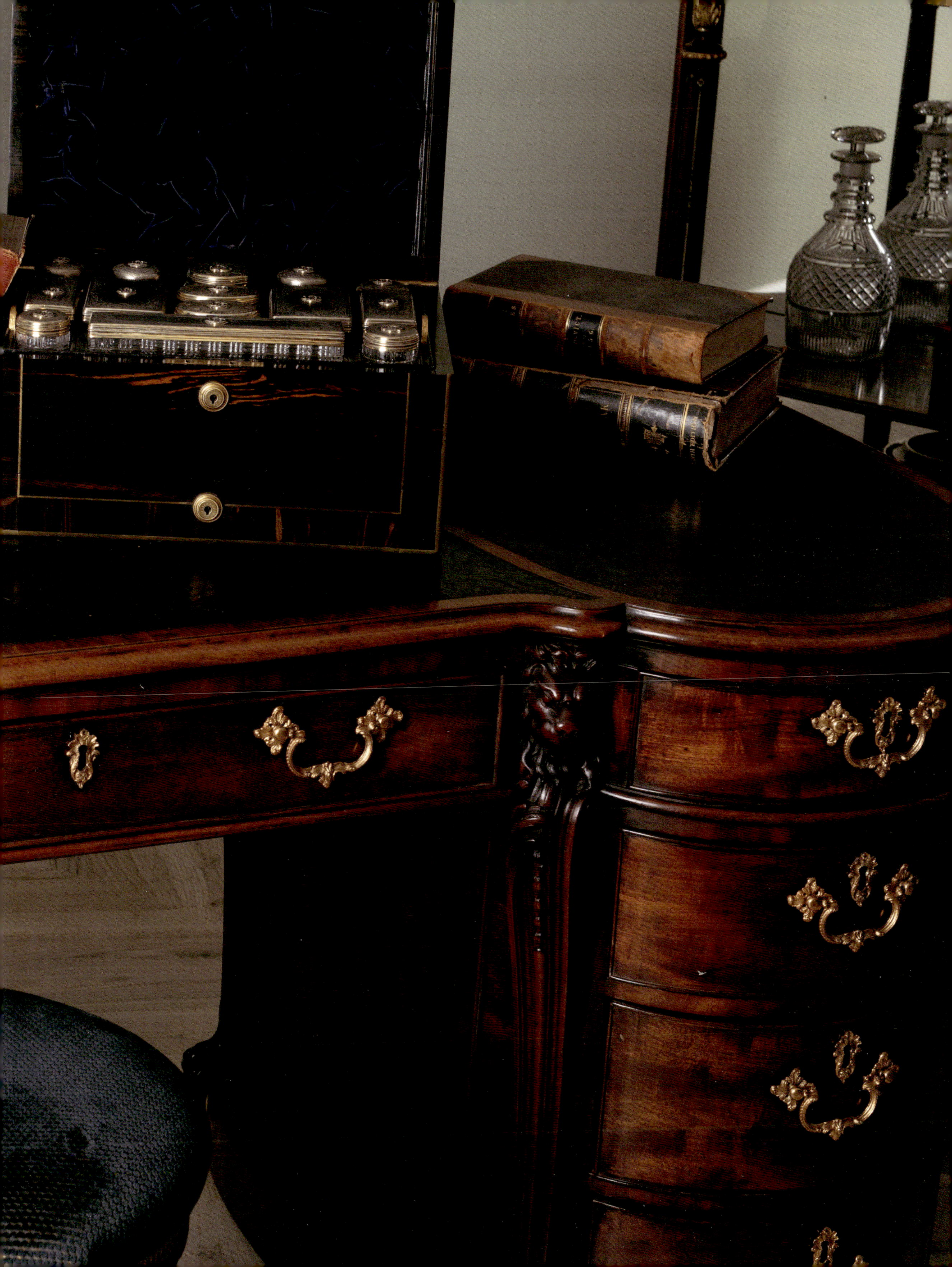

Endnotes

CHAPTER 1: 1820S

1. Smith 1808, p. vii.
2. See Stuart 2008, vol. 2, p. 349.
3. A later retailer's mark on the seat-rail is stamped simply 'Holden'.
4. See Heard and Jones 2019, p. 17. (The phrase is the title of the 1906 publication by L. Melville).
5. Wainwright et al. 1988 shows on p. 67 an identical foliate decoration, with the source, p. 137 of the Wilkinson Tracings (in the collection of Birmingham City Museum and Art Gallery) a record of Bullock's designs.
6. Inv. V/1836/37. I am grateful to the Trustees of Burghley House for the use of the image and to the curator, Jon Culverhouse, for providing the archive information.
7. Edwards 1969, p. 172.
8. Described by a Mr Bakewell as a 'beautiful Green Stone which is found in a part of the island of Angelsea [sic] the property of Mr George Bullock', *Liverpool Mercury*, 30 August 1811.
9. Family home of the portrait painter George Romney (1734–1802).
10. Brown 1835, p. 55.
11. See 'Tracings by Thomas Wilkinson, from Designs by the late Mr. George Bullock' 1820, Birmingham Museums Trust.
12. Christie's, London, 13–15 May 1819, lots 52–9.
13. Collard 1985, p. 111.
14. Wainwright 1988, 45.
15. Beard and Gilbert 1986, pp. 658–60. This book can now be viewed online at BIFMO.
16. See catalogue note for lots 800-803, Bonham's Chester, 9 July 2009. An 1893 inventory compiled by a Mr Salmon of Wilson & Co.
17. Stuart 2008, vol. 2, p. 276. George Romney's father purchased a quantity of mahogany from the firm in 1766.
18. Ackermann 1809–28, ser. 3, vol. 4, pl. 17, p. 185, March 1828.
19. The Metropolitan Museum of Art, 67.63.1.
20. 'Deus Nobis Haec Otia Fecit', meaning 'God has given us this ease'.
21. Dean 1989, p. 132.
22. Stuart records Lawson as having been apprenticed to Isaac Boulton, a chair maker of Lancaster. Stuart 2008, vol. 1, pp. 222–3.
23. See Macquoid and Edwards 1924, vol. 1, p. 237, Fig. 91.
24. See the Gillow archives, CWAC, E.S. 3603.
25. Sold at the Hamilton Palace sale, Christie's, London, 26 June 1882, lot 520.
26. Davis 2020, p. 261.
27. Christie's, London, 26 June 1882, lot 994. Sold for £1,081 10s to the dealers P. & D. Colnaghi & Co.
28. Davis 2020, p. 261 mistakenly refers to Alfred. Dakers 2011, p. 193.
29. Despite a lack of archival information about Hume's life and career, he is known to have been established at the following London addresses: 11 Crown Street, St Giles (1808); 34 Great Titchfield Street, Cavendish Square (1809–11); 4 Great Portland Street (1817); 4 Little Portland Street (1820); and 65 Berners Street (1837).
30. See: Christie's, London, 5 July 2012, lot 12.
31. I am grateful to Dr Diana Davis for this information.
32. Davis 2020, p. 247.
33. Beard and Gilbert 1986, p. 28.
34. RCIN 31308. See also a *pietre dure*-mounted *commode à vantaux* by Adam Weisweiler, RCIN 2593.
35. Bertie Greatheed, recorded in March 1803 (Royal Collection Trust note to RCIN 31308).
36. Gilbert 1978, pp. 134, 138, Fig. 212 and pl. 9. Another desk of this form, with wood marquetry, can be seen in a still-life painting by Nicolas Henry Jeaurat de Bertry, dated 1777 (Stair Sainty Gallery).
37. Thomas Parker was listed as a cabinet maker in Canterbury as early as 1796. See Gilbert 1996, p. 43.
38. See Christie's, London, 15 February 1990, lot 96, and De Bellaigue 1975, pp. 18–25.
39. National Trust, NT 1529727.
40. The two desks (RCIN 35289) are recorded as being delivered to the Royal Pavilion at Brighton in 1815 at £250 each. Eleven years later, they are illustrated in the North Drawing Room in John Nash's *Views of the Royal Pavilion*. Both desks are now at Windsor Castle.
41. The Wallace Collection, F479.
42. Robbins (auctioneers), 30 July 1827, lot 130.
43. Named mistakenly after Cardinal Mazarin, Chief Minister of France from 1642 to 1661. Most seventeenth-century examples would be approximately 100 cm wide.
44. In 1792, Stanislas-Aloys Straubharth of Paris invented and patented a 'boulle-style' stamping machine – the 'mosaïque polytipage'. See Payne 2018, p. 25.
45. Kirkham, P., 'Inlay, Marquetry and Buhl Workers in England c.1660–1850', *The Burlington Magazine*, Vol. 122, No. 927 (June, 1980), pp. 415-416, 419.
46. Hull 2006, p. 154.
47. Most sources cite the similar 1838 publication.
48. George IV was crowned on 19 July 1821. Scenes from the king's coronation banquet are illustrated in a watercolour by Denis Dighton in the Royal Collection (RCIN 913630), and a print in *The Gentleman's Magazine*, August 1821, pl. IV.
49. Edward Joy noted that Richard Price, a royal joiner, supplied the Court with walnut chairs decorated with 'twisted' turning between 1675–9. Joy 1969, p. 678, n. 8.
50. Smith 1826, p. iv.
51. Grüner 1846.
52. 'The style in which the Gothic predominates may be called, inaccurately enough, "Elizabethan", and the style in which the classical predominates over the Gothic, equally inaccurately, may be called "Jacobean". To save the time of those who do not wish to distinguish between these

periods of architectural uncertainty, I will henceforward use the term "Jacobethan"'. See Betjeman 1933, p. 41.
53. Comprising 158 plates, Smith's publication illustrates a large selection of furniture designed along Gothic principles, including beds, seating, tables, and bookcases.
54. RCIN 44196. Made to replace the original destroyed in the 1992 fire at Windsor Castle.
55. See Stuart 2008, vol. 1, p. 373, pl. 440. See also the Gillows 'Estimate Sketch Books', p. 1911. Stuart 2008 also illustrates in pl. 411 a similar bookcase, previously sold at Sotheby's, which she attributes to Gillows on this basis.
56. See 'Estimate Sketch Books', p. 1185; also illustrated in Boynton 1995, Fig. 170.
57. A fourth bookcase of similar design, made for Joseph Hanson, was illustrated in December 1799 as a rough sketch. See Stuart 2008, vol. 2, p. 133.
58. Robinson 1999, p. 71.
59. In Liverpool, Foster also completed the Gothic-style church of St Luke, at the top of Bold Street, and a Moorish-style arch at Edge Hill. His knowledge of Gothic architecture can no doubt be credited to his training under Wyatville. Lindfield 2016, p. 206.
60. Ibid.
61. See Stuart 2008, vol. 1, p. 251 and vol. 2; p. 373.
62. Roberts 2001, pp. 137, 357. The same legs can be seen on a circular table in Room 243, p. 360, Fig. 441. The historian and former Director of the Royal Collection, Sir Hugh Roberts inventoried the Morell & Seddon accounts in a wealth of detail.
63. Ibid., p. 357.
64. Seemingly identical to a table in the Victoria and Albert Museum, W.19-1962.
65. Victoria and Albert Museum, W.22:1 and 2-1959.
66. In late seventeenth-century Paris, such pewter or tin inlay was often silvered to give a richer hue.
67. Roberts 2001, p. 309, Figs. 368-9.
68. Morel's name disappears from the records in 1831, and the company of G. & T. Seddon, although awarded a Royal Warrant in 1832, had great difficulty in extracting the £200,000 from the Crown for the Windsor commission, leading to near bankruptcy in 1840. [BIFMO]
69. Victoria and Albert Museum, W.79-1975.
70. Beard and Gilbert 1986, p. 721.
71. Roberts, 2001, p. 37.
72. Joy 1977, p. 129.
73. Pugin's father was a French émigré draughtsman and drawing master who worked for John Nash.
74. Ackermann 1809-28, ser. 3, vol. 9, p. 183.
75. See Hope 1807, pls 9, 17, for a divan of virtually identical form, although in the Egyptian taste. Other design influences may have come from Sheraton 1791-3 and Percier and Fontaine 1801.
76. See Musgrave 1948, p. 38, no. 173; Ellwood 1995, pp. 129-205; Reade 1953, p. 46, pl. 42; and Beard and Gilbert 1986.
77. H. Fisher, Son & Co., 38 Newgate Street. Some plates dated 1827.
78. See Stuart 2008, vol. 2, p. 94.
79. Bamford 1983, p. 116.
80. Stuart suggests 'HH' could be Henry Howard, or Henry Holmes, both of whom were chair makers at Gillows. See Stuart 2008, vol. 1; pp. 227, 229, 291 and vol. 2, p. 243, for furniture with legs similar to the stools illustrated in this volume.

CHAPTER 2: 1830S

1. Queen Victoria to the Duchess of Sutherland. Gower 1883, vol. 1, p. 2, quoted in Yorke 2001, p. 11.
2. *Ayr Advertiser*, 29 August 1839.
3. Beard & Gilbert, 1986, p. 393. Trading as Hancock, Rixon & Dunt from 1838.
4. *The Times*, 11 and 13 August 1830. See also Webb 1921, vol. 2, p. 362.
5. King, Thomas, 1839 edition.
6. Joy 1977, p. 186.
7. RCIN 39564-5 and RCIN 57975.
8. Butchoff Antiques commissioned a report by Dr Adam Bowett, author of Bowett 2012.
9. Jaffer 2001, p. 373, fig. 142.
10. Stuart, 2008, Dust cover, vol. II.
11. Stuart 2008, vol. 1, pp. 302-3, plates 330, 332-3.
12. Loudon 1842, p. 1039.
13. Ibid.
14. Further research on Nixon can be seen in Davis, 2020.
15. Holley 1981, p. 66. From 1832, Pratt was also a royal trunk maker.
16. Loudon 1842, p. 1071, pl. 1970.
17. *Designs for window curtains & beds by William Smee and Son, Wholesale cabinet-makers & upholsterers* (Microfiche, GRI, 2627-350).
18. Loudon 1842, p. 1053, pl. 2092.
19. Could this be a Mr. Mallet of Dublin who carried out an 'Analysis of bricks'? See Loudon 1834-8, vol. 1, p. 317.
20. Renamed Lancaster House by Sir William Lever, 1st Baronet, after he purchased it in 1912.
21. Jaffer 2001, p. 372.
22. Gower 1883, vol. 1, p. 2, quoted in Yorke 2001, p. 11.
23. Sotheby's, Belgravia, 5 August 1981, lot 161.
24. Exhibition supplement, *The Illustrated London News*, 1 November 1851.
25. Stuart 2008, vol. 1, pp. 218, 224-6.
26. Bowett 2012, p. 4, pl. A2.
27. Joy 1969, pl. 53.
28. Staffordshire Record Office, D593/R/2/31/2.
29. The Duke and Duchess of Sutherland had visited Crozatier's foundry in Paris in 1837. See Payne 2018, p. 301.
30. Yorke 2001, p. 142.
31. Verlet 1987, p. 337. Foster's, 25-27 May 1843 and 21 July 1843 (Lugt 16621 and 17096).
32. Victoria and Albert Museum, LOAN: W.C.O.G.2.
33. De Bellaigue 1975a and De Bellaigue 1975b.
34. Nicolay 1956-9, vol. 2, p. 153.
35. Watson 1956, p. 214.
36. Verlet 1956, vol. 2, p. 78.
37. See De Bellaigue 1975a, p. 290.
38. Davis 2020, pp. 247-8.
39. Beard and Gilbert 1986, p. 34.
40. Payne, C., *Antique Collector*, January 1989, vol. 23, No.8, p. 17.
41. Gilbert 1978a, vol. 2, pp. 318-20, no. 395.
42. At Lotherton Hall. Gilbert 1978a, vol. 2, no. 395, pp. 318-20; Bellaigue 1975b.
43. Antique Collector, July 1937, p. 169.
44. Dr Clive Wainwright may have been the first to suggest that this style of table base was to designs by Richard Bridgens. See Davis 2020, p. 188, note 100.
45. Robinson 1979, p. 21. The table also has a paper label that refers to Lord & Baroness Beaumont of Glossop Hall, Derbyshire who were married in 1914.
46. Davis 2020, p. 176.
47. Ibid., p. 248.
48. Possibly Charles Hitchcock, a porcelain dealer.
49. Litchfield 1903, p. 221.
50. Christie's, London, 23 November 2006, lot 123.
51. De Bellaigue, 1975a, p. 292.
52. Ibid., p. 20, notes 563 pieces of white ware in the Baldock sale held on 21 July 1843.
53. Metropolitan Museum of Art, 1976.155.101.
54. Sotheby's, New York, 19 April 2007, vol. 2, lot 124.
55. Buccleuch Archives BS1.28, Baldock a/c no. 4.
56. RCIN 2369606.
57. Davis 2020. See also Sotheby's, London, 2 November 1990, lot 231, with extended footnote compiled by Christopher Payne. Also Payne 1989, pp. 17-20, Payne 2018, pp. 253-6, and Levy 2005.
58. See Davis 2020, p. 250.
59. Ibid., p. 250.
60. The *London & Provincial New Commercial Directory* (Pigot and Co.), 1826-7, lists the Webbs as cabinet makers. However,

60. their first listing, in the *Post Office London Directory* of 1825, is as upholsterers.
61. Sold Sotheby's, London, 16 March 1990, lot 54 and Bamfords March 2007, lot 1986.
62. BIFMO, auction catalogue of Pryor's bank, lots 585–6.
63. See Collard 1996. The 1851 Census gives an idea of the scale of the business, which recorded five cabinet makers, two Buhl cutters, two polishers and four brass finishers.
64. TNA, PROB 11/2092/350, 4 May 1849. Referred to in 'Raiding the Past: Furniture for the Anglo-Gallic Interior, 1800-1865', Dr Diana Davis, online lecture for The Furniture History Society, 28 June 2020.
65. Christie's, London, 19 April 1849.
66. Recording of their label varies slightly, with a truncated example in Payne 1981, p. 306.
67. See Payne 2018, p. 23.
68. BIFMO.
69. Loan: Gilbert .86:1, 2–2008. See Anna Maria Massinelli, *Hardstones*, London, 2000.
70. *Book of Prices* 1831, p. 20.
71. Account of June 16, 1836 lists: '12 Large carved Venetian Chairs & 2 stools to match...£160.0.0.'. (Burghley Archive, V/18836/37).
72. Payne 1981, p. 305.
73. Litchfield 1903, p. 233.
74. Davis 2020, p. 200, cites Baldock's insurance policy at Hanway Street. LMA: 553/122411, 18 May 1836.
75. Buccleuch Archives BS1.28 Baldock a/c no. 4.
76. RCIN 30006.
77. De Bellaigue, "Samuel Parker and the Vulliamys, purveyors of gilt-bronze*", *The Burlington*, Vol. 139, No. 1126, Jan., 1997, pp. 26-37.
78. Sold Sotheby's, 20 April 1937, lot 259, plate XLI.
79. Davis 2020, p. 237 (Fig. 8.10).
80. The Somerley desks are still at the house, in the Picture Gallery. The Powerscourt desk sold Christie's, London, 24-25 September 1984, lot 489.
81. Payne 1981, p. 108.
82. Payne 2013, pp. 88–89.
83. Christie's, London, 1849, 19 April, lot 582.
84. RCIN 861.
85. Christie's, London, 1849, 19 April, lots 72, 78.
86. Stuart 2008, vol.1, p. 229, pl. 222 and p. 387, pl. 466.
87. Joy 1977, p. 150.
88. Philip Hardwick material, Goldsmiths' Company Archive.
89. *The Furniture Gazette*, 8 November 1879, p. 319.
90. Joy 1977, pp. 104–5.
91. *Book of Prices* 1831, p. 21.
92. The base also has the date or serial stamp '1862', in what appears to be different tooling to the H. Winter stamp.
93. Sold Sotheby's, London, 10 December 2015, lot 201.
94. Victoria and Albert Museum, W.35:1 to 6-1980.
95. Morris 2018.
96. The author is grateful to Annabel Westman for her observations on this interior.

CHAPTER 3: 1840S

1. Quoted in Litchfield, 1903, p. 219.
2. *The Builder*, vol. 1, 1843, p. 423.
3. Litchfield, 1903, p. 220. A painting by Alfred Stevens of Collman's wife, Anne, is in the collection of the Tate Gallery (No1775).
4. Litchfield 1903, p. 217.
5. The chair was subsequently used for the State Opening of Parliament in 1901, the re-upholstery described in the Holland & Sons archives. The firm of J. and R. Webb had succeeded Charles Webb at 8 Old Bond Street in 1825 and is recorded as the maker of a Gothic-style extending dining table and matching sideboard.
6. See Holmes 2012, for a history of the house.
7. In 1845, Grüner was appointed 'advisor in art' to Queen Victoria. See Boekmann 1996, p. 1.
8. Joy 1969, pp. 677–85.
9. Christie's, London, 27-29 May 1987, lots 201–2.
10. RCIN 1562 and RCIN 44187.
11. Promoli (fl. 1840–1849) sold clocks, watches and coromandel-fitted boxes in Liverpool. The business was spoken of approvingly, and at length, in 1849 in the American publication *The Merchant's Magazine* and *Commercial Review*.
12. See Cooper 1987, p. 14, pl. 10.
13. Gow 1996, p. 15.
14. British History Online: Edward Walford, 'Tottenham Court Road', in Old and New London: Volume 4 (London, 1878), pp. 467–480.
15. Burghley Archives, FUR0299.
16. Patent No. 5418/1826. Science Museum Library.
17. Allwood 1996, pp. 90–7.
18. Burghley Archives, FUR0275a.
19. Quoted in Allwood 1996, p. 91.
20. The Survey of London records the Conservative Club in some detail, including the interior fixtures and furniture: 'All the woodwork is of oak and so was the furniture, a great deal of which was contemporary with the building and of considerable distinction. It was designed by Henry Whitaker, one of the small chairs and the long tables supported by pairs of griffins being illustrated [in] his book'.
21. Whitaker 1847, p. 11.
22. RCIN 41189 and RCIN 41203.
23. My thanks to Julie Biddlecombe-Brown at Raby for this information.
24. My thanks to Crispin Powell for showing these documents to me.
25. Morrison correspondence in the Buccleuch Archive.
26. Anderson, 'Robert Lorimer and Scott Morton & Company', in *Regional Furniture History*, 2005.
27. The books were shown to the author during a BBC *Antiques Roadshow* recording in Perth. First aired in Series 19, 16 March 1997.
28. Shrubland Hall archives.
29. A small Louis XV-style desk also has a Trollope label 'Duke of Buccleuch. Mr. Pye. April 26th '95'.
30. BIFMO.
31. Exhibition supplement, *The Illustrated London News*, 1 November 1851.
32. Kirkham 1989, p. 32 – extracted from *The Morning Chronicle*, 8 August 1850.
33. See Davis, 2020, p. 250.
34. In 1845, Geo. Blake & Co. were listed in the London Post Office Directory at 130 Mount Street, Berkeley Square. BIFMO.
35. Davis, 2020, p. 250.
36. 12 February 1880, Mr. Charles Blake, deceased.
37. Rothschild London Archive, XII/41/7A/90, XII/41/8/71 & others. I am very grateful to Diana Davis for generously sharing this information with me.
38. Metropolitan Museum of Art, 59.76, and Alnwick Castle, DNC 00223.
39. A silver plate inset on the lid is engraved 'Designed and Executed by/George Henry Blake/London'.
40. https://www.wikitree.com/wiki/Veitch-215
41. My thanks to Crispin Powell, archivist to the Duke of Buccleuch, for this and other related archival information. See also De Bellaigue 1975b, p. 24.
42. National Museums of Scotland, K.2012.26. See also Davis, p. 177.
43. For example, Metropolitan Museum of Art, 59.76.
44. Davis 2020, pp. 176 & 250.
45. Buccleuch Archive (Blake Bros. account, 29 February 1844).
46. Musée du Louvre, OA10453. A table of similar form is in the Metropolitan Museum of Art, 1975.1.2035. See Davis 2020, pp. 170–171.
47. Davis 2020, p. 129, pl. 31.
48. Davis 2020, noted this motif on the 17th-century tables by De Lucci sold by Baldock to the 5th Duke of Buccleuch, p. 177.
49. The Blake desk illustrated in T. Murdoch ed. (1992), *The English Versailles*, p. 125,

Fig. 121, mistakenly described as eighteenth century with alterations.
50. Baldock's connections in the ceramic trade meant that he was well positioned to exploit the fashion for porcelain-mounted furniture. He is known to have employed the Quaker artist Thomas Martin Randall at Madeley in Shropshire to embellish undecorated Sèvres and many of the porcelain panels and plaques used to decorate his furniture are closely allied to the work of Randall. Bonhams 20 November 2013, lot 259, & Bonhams, London, 11 March 2009, lot 114.
51. Two Baumhauer desks in the Huntington Library are approximately 160cm (63in) wide, some 25cm (approx. 10in) wider than the illustrated Baldock example. (Huntington Library, 27.132 and 27.137).
52. Huntington Library, 27.132.
53. De Bellaigue 1975a, p. 292. The Metropolitan Museum of Art, 58.75.48.
54. F71.
55. Generations later the Paris firm of Sormani exhibited the same model at the *Exposition Universelle* of 1900. See Payne, 2018, p. 172.
56. See Pradère 1989, pp. 125–7.
57. Charles Chubb, established in Portsmouth in 1818, expanded with workshops in London and Wolverhampton. The company kept meticulous records of the serial numbers of the locks they produced.
58. Sotheby's, New York, 30 October 2013, lot 38, and Sotheby's, London, 18 May 1977, lots 86–7 respectively. Lot 86 had an eighteenth-century carcass stamped J.L. Cosson.
59. I am grateful to Dr. Diana Davis for this information.
60. Bowett 2012, p. 128.
61. Stuart 2003, vol 1, p. 339.
62. 'Papier Maché Trays for Ibrahim Pacha', *Manchester Courier* and *Lancashire General Advertiser*, 6 October 1847, p. 635.
63. Edwards 2000, p. 6.
64. Mogg 1844.
65. *The Art Journal*, vol. 11, 1 January 1849, p. 306.
66. Kirkham 1989, p. 225.
67. Lomax 1997.
68. Allwood 1990, p. 4. The interior was first designed in 1836 or 1837 (Allwood 1990, refs. 7 & 9). Sopwith & Co. exhibited a modernised variation at the International Exhibition in 1873.

CHAPTER 4: 1850S

1. Founded in 1754, titled The Royal Society of Arts from 1908.
2. *The Art Journal*, 1849, vol. 11, p. 106.
3. Prince Albert was officially created Prince Consort in 1857.
4. *The London Gazette*, 26 February 1850, p. 534.
5. The records for the Royal Commission are at Imperial College, London. The Victoria and Albert Museum has an extensive collection of printed material relating to the exhibition.
6. Sir John Coghill (1766–1817).
7. Paxton, knighted in October 1851, had built the innovative but far smaller iron and glass conservatory at Chatsworth in 1837.
8. Published in 1854 by Joseph Nash, Louis Haghe and David Roberts as *Dickinson's Comprehensive Pictures of the Great Exhibition of 1851*.
9. Sadly, all three buildings were destroyed by fire – New York in 1856, Munich in 1931 and London in 1936.
10. *The Great Exhibition of 1851, A Commemorative Album*, 1850, HMSO, p. 117.
11. The Crystal Palace was removed from Hyde Park in the autumn of 1852 and re-erected in a modified form in Sydenham.
12. Victoria and Albert Museum, W.33-1976.
13. An early version made by Gillows for Broughton Hall in 1813 is illustrated in Stuart 2008, vol. 1, p. 249, pl. 247.
14. The 1857 exhibition was restricted to the fine and decorative arts. There had been an Exposition of British Industrial Art in Manchester in 1845.
15. Ferry 2003, pp. 175–188.
16. Jones had designed two Moorish houses in Hyde Park between 1845 and 1847.
17. In 1867, Jones published *The Grammar of Chinese Ornament*.
18. Victoria and Albert Museum, accession number 157&A-1864.
19. RCIN 41008.
20. Floud 1958, p. 36.
21. *The Art Journal*, 1875, vol. XIV, pp. 206–7.
22. Litchfield 1903, p. 223.
23. Ward, J., pp. 165–6.
24. Metropolitan Museum of Art, 1993.168, and the Newark Museum of Art, 92.72A-H.
25. Christie's, 26 June 1856, lot 172. 'A pair of magnificent slabs of malachite surmounting carved console tables, with cupids below.'
26. Buccleuch Collection Archives.
27. Wallis, T. W., *Autobiography of Thomas Wilkinson Wallis: Sculptor In Wood, And Extracts From His Sixty Years' Journal ...*, (1889), p. 82.
28. Ibid. pp. 84–5.
29. Ibid. p. 96.
30. The *New Zealand Journal*, no. 157, 3/1/1846, p. 96 & other advertisements.
31. Bowett 2012, p. 313. Work by Levien for Baron Lionel de Rothschild is noted in Chapter 5.
32. Michael Levien, 'The Furniture of J.M. Levien', Richard Gardner Antiques website, https://www.richardgardnerantiques.co.uk/shop/sold/ladys-work-table-by-j-m-levien/ (accessed September 2021), originally published in *The Connoisseur* magazine, January 1976.
33. Meyer, p. 30.
34. *The Illustrated London News*, 11 October 1851, p. 460.
35. BIFMO.
36. *The Art Journal Illustrated Catalogue of the Great Exhibition*, 1851, vol. 1, pp. 235, 326. The fountain was destroyed in the 1936 fire.
37. *Guide to the Great Exhibition*, Routledge, p. 214. An engraving is in *The Illustrated London News*, titled 'Large Log of Honduras Mahogany, Sold at Birkenhead', 6 April 1840, p. 228. In the early 1840s mahogany auctions in London were held at Garraway's Coffee House in Cornhill. *The Cabinet Maker*, 25 September 1920, p. 724.
38. See Victoria and Albert Museum, CIRC.20-1961.
39. See a watercolour by Maria Elisabeth Augusta (Lily) Cartwright of the Drawing Room at Aynhoe Park in November 1845, with a rocking chair apparently of strap steel (sold at Bukowski's, Stockholm, 3 December 2014, lot 931).
40. See Victoria and Albert Museum, CIRC.20-1961.
41. 22 April 1859, by a family friend, Louise Neergaard, née Olsen. The William Morris upholstery was given by Dorothea Melchior 13 years later. Both women were part of Anderson's dinner rotation system.
42. Andersen's Diary, 21/9/1870. Odense City Museums.
43. Presumably Porter & Co. of Welbeck Street.
44. Joy 1977, p. 279.
45. Aitken, W.C., *The Early History of Brass and the Brass Manufacturers of Birmingham*, 1866 (2019 reprint).
46. Still listed in 1886 in the *Furniture Gazette: Classified List of the Furniture, Upholstery, and Allied Trades*, 1 October, p.351.
47. *Illustrated Catalogue*, 1851, p. 70.
48. Ames 1968, p. 91, pl. 15.
49. Wyatt 1851, vol. 1, 'Marquetry Furniture by Messrs. Trollope of London', n.pag, pl. 75.
50. Weaver 1928, p. 247.
51. Gibbs-Smith 1950, p. 122.
52. *The Illustrated London News*, 1 November 1851, p. 557. A later version by Maples is shown in **Fig. 7.50**.
53. Victoria and Albert Museum, 25:1 to 3-1852.
54. Wornum 1851, p. 227.
55. Gere 1989, p. 249.
56. The journalist may have made an error, as he had in the caption for the adjacent 'Johnson' (Johnstone) table.
57. Joy 1977, p. 291.

58. Pinto and Pinto 1970, pp. 29–31.
59. Victoria and Albert Museum, nos. W.40-1952 & CIRC.35: 1-1958.
60. Design in the Patent Office, illus. Aslin 1962, pl. 7, the actual table pl. 8. Aslin notes the table is in the Victoria & Albert Museum but could not be found on the museum website.
61. *A Guide to the Great Exhibition*, 1851, p. 80.
62. See also Victoria and Albert Museum W.34:1, 2-1980.
63. The tables were sold, having been passed to the vendor by descent from Hicks. (Bonhams London, 26/11/2008, lot 194).
64. RCIN 169. Payment dated 10 July 1846, £25 4s, 'Mr Levien Fancy Table', RA, PA Ledgers, 1846/59.
65. One pair have a seemingly identical ebonised triform base as in the 1851 lithograph. Records of the Duke's purchases at the exhibition are in the Raby Archive, which is being catalogued at the time of writing.
66. *Great Industrial Exhibition*, 1853, p. 91.
67. Ibid., p. 92.
68. Loudon referred to the perennially popular davenport desk in his 1833 Encyclopedia as a 'devenport', a term used in the United States to describe an extending couch, or a narrow table. The true origins of the name are uncertain but traditionally a similar desk was made by Gillows for a Captain Davenport, their repeat orders classified under the name of the original owner.
69. Bevan 1877, p. 198. The natural material has erroneously been called tortoiseshell for many years, but actually comes from the shell of a turtle.
70. Now in the Coalbrookdale Museum, the table, catalogued and sold by this author at Sotheby's in 1987, was owned and loved by an avid furniture collector, Mrs. Wallace of Batheaston.
71. Victoria and Albert Museum number: 7247:1 to 13-1860.
72. *The Exhibition of Art Industry in Paris 1855*, p. xi.
73. Marlborough House housed the Museum of Ornamental Art in 1852, renamed the South Kensington Museum in 1856 and remodelled as a home for the newly married Prince and Princess of Wales in 1863. The artist is probably George Grey who decorated the porcelain plaque for Holland & Sons on p. 205.
74. *Furniture Gazette*, 1/7/1886, p. 246.
75. Edwards 1998, pp. 242–3.
76. Accession number 1987-86-1 & 2.
77. Yapp 1879, pl.VII.
78. Wyatt 1856, pt. 1, pp. 306–7.
79. Smee also exhibited in 1862, again 1878 & 1888. See numerous drawings in Joy 1977. By 1890 known as Smee & Cobbay. (BIFMO).
80. The design relates to an 1840 entry in Gillows' 'Estimate Sketch book' for 'An Oak Pedestal and Kidney Table' supplied to Ferguson and Co. See Sotheby's, London, 15 November 1996, lot 113.
81. Symonds and Whineray 1962, p. 196, pl. 221.
82. Victoria and Albert Museum, W.26-1972.
83. Sotheby's, London, 3 March 1956, lot 169. Handley-Reed cat. no. B7.
84. Robinson 1856, pp. xi–xiii.
85. See a drawing in the Metropolitan Museum of Art, 46.38.62.
86. RCIN 919477.
87. RCIN 12017, RCIN 12121 and RCIN 13109.
88. These, and other Parisian copies, are discussed in Payne 2018, pp. 95–233.
89. Payne 1981, pp. 297–317.
90. Notably H.A. Fourdinois. See Payne 2018, p. 352.
91. Copies of important French eighteenth-century furniture made in London for Hertford are the most celebrated, but others pre-date the Hertford commission by a few years. Notable are the two copies of writing desks made by the Master of Pagodas in red turtleshell, dating to between 1847 and 1850 (**Fig. 3.76**). Also a pair of unusual console tables, or tables *en chiffonière* or *en secrétaire*, the original model once attributed to Jean-François Leleu, but most probably by Bernard II van Risenburgh or Jaques Dubois, shown in Chapter 2, **Fig. 2.43**.
92. Hertford loaned twenty-six pieces of furniture from his own collection to the Paris *Musée rétrospectif*. See Payne 2018, p. 108.
93. Ingamells 1981, p. 42.
94. Morris 1910, Morris 1911, and Hughes 1987.
95. See the Wallace Collection object file, F250.
96. The Wallace Collection, F460.
97. Possibly Charles-Guillaume Winckelsen.
98. C.D.E. Fortnum, a patron of Webb & Forrest. See: Nicholas Penny, *Catalogue of European Sculpture in the Ashmolean Museum, 1540 to the Present Day*, Oxford, 1992, pp. 22–23. The author is grateful to Giles Forster for this reference.
99. Paid 24 October 1858. (Wallace Collection Archive ('WCA'), HWF/M4/5/13).
100. This unique copy was sold at Sotheby's, New York, 26 April 2007, lot 105 ($3,176,000).
101. The Wallace Collection, F307.
102. This author is grateful to the late Clive Wainwright for pointing out the existence of these invaluable glass photographic slides.
103. A photograph in the Royal Collection (RCIN 2906105), 'A Quiet Moment by Thompson', was shown at the first exhibition of the Photographic Society in 1854, which was visited by Queen Victoria and Prince Albert.
104. WCA, HWF/M4/5/9.
105. Report 1854, p. iv. This was observed in Wade 2012.
106. Now at Petworth House after having been sold at the Hamilton Palace sale, Christie, Manson and Woods, 17 June 1882, lot 994. National Trust, NT 485401.
107. Christie, Manson and Woods, London, 24–26 June 1913, lots 292, 294.
108. Another pair of 'coffre-forts', identical to the pair by Blake, were signed by Winckelsen, sold Sotheby's London, 16 March 1990, lot 150.
109. Seligman 1961, p. 102.
110. The Frick Collection, 1916.5.02 and 1916.5.03.
111. *The Frick Collection, Vol IX, French Furniture*, pp. 19–21, 1955.
112. Sotheby's, London, 2 November 1990, lot 231. (Including an extensive catalogue footnote compiled by the author.)
113. A pair of English copies, believed to be those made for Hertford, were sold Sotheby's, London, 2 November 1990, lot 247.
114. C. Demetrescu, in *Dossier de l'Art*, No. 224, December 2014, pp. 30–59.
115. Private collection and Payne 2018, p. 117.
116. My thanks to Clare Baxter for these references. See p. 261 and **Fig. 5.92**.
117. The total cost was £6,340, including £35 for packing, other items and £10 carriage.
118. The balance of £3,100 was paid on 24 October 1858.
119. The Wallace Collection, F461.
120. The Lisbon version was exhibited at the Pennington Museum Treasures exhibition in Los Angeles in 1976, before being acquired by Graus Antiques who then sold it to António de Medeiros e Almeida.
121. 'Among other examples of Boulle marqueterie [sic], of which Sir John possesses every kind, is a noteworthy replica of the Grand Cabinet, surmounted by a clock, with the arms of Bavaria held aloft by lions, which Boulle executed in 1713 and which now belongs to the Duke of Buccleuch'. See Morris 1910, p. 238.
122. Jacobsen et al. 2020, p. 189.
123. RCIN 31207.
124. *Illustrated Catalogue*, 1851, p.747.
125. Kirkham 1980, p. 417.
126. 17 February 1857, WCA, AR2/15G.
127. National Trust, NT 592846.
128. Christie's, London, 24 June 1913, lot 56.
129. In some references, the desk has been wrongly attributed to Litchfield & Radclyff as theirs is the only legible stand placard in the engraving.

130. The Wallace Collection, F424 and F425.
131. Cf. a drawing attributed to Boulle or Gilles-Marie Oppenord, in the Musée des Arts Décoratifs, 723 B1, and *Nouveaux Deisseins de Meubles et Ouvrages de Bronze et de Marqueterie*, pl. 5, published by Jean Mariette, *c.*1710.
132. Exhibitor number: 5839.
133. The presumed original model for the copies was sold from the collection of Lionel de Rothschild, Sotheby's, 'Catalogue of the Magnificent Contents of 148 Piccadilly', 19–22 April 1937, lot 259, p. XLI.
134. Payne 1989, pp. 88-89, 93. Recorded, possibly erroneously, as French-made.

CHAPTER 5: 1860S

1. Sala 1868, p. 361.
2. The preface to *The Penny Guide to the International Exhibition*, 1862, stated '"What to see", "How to see" and "Where to see" the principal objects of interest are questions which puzzle all who visit the International Exhibition for the first time'.
3. Chevalier 1862, t. VI, p. 248.
4. Cited in Bevan, 1877, p. 176. The export figure is the approximate equivalent of £40 million today.
5. Charles Dickens, in *Our Mutual Friend*, 1862, chapter II, opening paragraph.
6. Lamb died in 1903. His obituary in *The Journal of Decorative Art and British Decorators* read: 'His name was a synonym for the best in everything that he did from 1850–1885, and he towered over everybody in Lancashire and Yorkshire as maker of high-class furniture...to middle aged and older men connected with the furniture and decorating business, his name for fifty years stood as a landmark for all that was best in both spheres of industrial art.'
7. Muthesius 2009, p. 141.
8. Workman's name: 'Rushworth'.
9. Gilbert 1998, p. 237, and Sheraton, 1791–3, pp. 444–5.
10. Sold Christie's, London, 22–23 October 1979, lot 129.
11. Illustrated in *Antique Trades Gazette*, 18 February 2018, issue 2279, and sold by Andrew Smith and Son of Itchen Stoke.
12. See Payne 1981, p. 474.
13. In 1852, Henry Cole put on a course for women to learn chromolithography in order to illustrate museum objects.
14. Wyatt 1851–3.
15. *The Art Journal*, 1862, p. 57.
16. Two naturalistic oak sideboards with the coat-of-arms of the 3rd Earl of Eldon, one with a label, one attributed to T. Woodgate, were sold Christie's, 23 January 2007, lots 11 & 33.
17. *The Art Journal*, 1863, p. 272.
18. *The Furniture Gazette*, 7 October 1876, p. 211.
19. Yapp 1879, under pl. LXX.
20. Victoria and Albert Museum, CIRC.305:1-1965 and CIRC.66:1 to 5-1964.
21. Sotheby's, London, 13 June 2001, lot 131.
22. Now in the Shipley Art Gallery, TWCMS : N3575.
23. A bronze figure of Selkirk cast in 1885 could, out of context, be taken for an image of Crusoe.
24. Sold Sotheby's, London, 8 October 1982, lots 51–2. There were eleven chairs at the auction, presumably from an original set of twelve.
25. Butchoff Antiques, 2013, vol. 3, extracted from Waring 1862.
26. Symonds and Whineray 1962 p. 110, pl. 23. Symonds illustrates designs by Kendall in the Elizabethan style, pp.110–111.
27. Pollen 1912, pp. 308–309.
28. Sotheby's, London, 17 February 1984, lot 71.
29. 12 September 1863.
30. Burton 1999, pp. 108–9.
31. Hardman was joined by his nephew, John Hardman Powell, the stained-glass designer who married Pugin's daughter Anne in 1850.
32. For example, Gillow numbers 5206, 5210 and L17498.
33. Sala, G., *Notes and Sketches of the Paris Exhibition*, 1868, p. 352.
34. *The Gentleman's Magazine*, vol. CCXII, 1862, p. 664.
35. Meyer 2006, p. 114, pl. D13.
36. The locks were made by A. Mills in March 1862.
37. Such as the credenza exhibited in 1851 by Smee of Finsbury Pavement of exaggerated, almost pneumatic form. Smee also exhibited in 1862, 1878 and 1888. See numerous drawings in Joy 1977. By 1890, the firm was known as Smee & Cobbay (BIFMO).
38. Yapp p. 205.
39. *Building News*, 29 May 1868, p. VIII, at the Museum of Building Appliances, and 25 December 1868, p. 877.
40. The Higgins Art Gallery and Museum, HAGM:F.78.
41. Cescinsky 1931, pl. facing p. 124.
42. In traditional dealer parlance, such a set was traditionally known as a 'triad'.
43. From 1871, *Kelly's* records Cowtan and Mannoch as cabinetmakers at 314 Oxford Street.
44. Inv. no. F47-8.
45. Waring 1862, vol. I, pl. 40.
46. Symonds and Whineray 1962 p. 169, pls. 166–9.
47. TNA, AAD/1983/13 and AAD/1998/1.
48. Victoria and Albert Museum, W.29-1972.
49. Invoice to H.H. Vaughan Esq., December 1866. Private collection.
50. *Illustrated Catalogue*, 1862, p. 280.
51. See Symonds & Whineray 1965, pp. 71, 74, pls. 222–3.
52. The Holland & Son records show that the cost of the desk alone was £64 10s.
53. Victoria and Albert Museum, W.47:1, 2-1911 and W.47A&B-1911.
54. A letter written by Thomas Ross, Donald Ross's son, to the Victoria and Albert Museum in 1928, states that a suite of similar furniture exhibited by Ross at the Great Exhibition was believed to have been sold to Queen Victoria through an agent called Freyberg.
55. See Kjellberg 1989, p. 516.
56. John Lane is recorded working at 47 Sloane Street around 1820, and 174 Sloane Street after 1866.
57. Sala 1868, pp. 350-1.
58. The Marjoribanks family were on the list of guarantors for the purchase of the Soulages Collection for the South Kensington Museum in 1856. The 4th Marquess of Hertford also featured on the list.
59. Brinsden 2004, pp. 38–48.
60. A pair of larchwood cabinets, made for the duke by the Liverpool cabinetmaker George Bullock in 1817, is at Blair Castle.
61. Victoria and Albert Museum, W.47:1, 2-1911, W.47A&B-1911.
62. He exhibited horological objects in 1851.
63. Hamilton-Gordon, 1925, vol. 1, pp. 102, 125-6.
64. Victoria and Albert Museum, 240:1, 2-1887.
65. Litchfield 1907, p. 312.
66. Phillips, Son and Neale, London, 23–25 June 1886.
67. *The Times*, 22 June 1886.
68. *The Cabinet Maker and Art Furnisher*, 1 July 1886, p. 28.
69. Victoria and Albert Museum, 635:1 to 27-1870.
70. Special Loan Exhibition of English Furniture and Figured Silks Manufactured in the 17th and 18th Centuries.
71. Published on the Victoria and Albert Museum's online catalogue entry for 635-1870 (accessed October 2019).
72. The object's entry in Tomlin's *Catalogue of Adam Period Furniture* suggests that the superstructure is a later addition, an error in this author's opinion. See Tomlin, 1972, p. 179.
73. The white line painting is similar to that on the Ardgowan bed made by Gillows *c.*1801. See Stuart, 2008, vol. 1, p. 351, pl. 410.
74. Foley 1910, vol. 2, pp. 147-8, pl. opposite p. 148.
75. Litchfield 1907, opposite p.208.
76. *Official Illustrated Catalogue of the International Exhibition London 1862.* vol. II, The British Division, 1862, p. 47, no. 5862. Waring 1862, pl. 132.

77. Sheraton 1792, *The Cabinet-Maker and Upholsterer's Drawing-Book*, pl. 56.
78. Working from Bouverie Street in London, then George Street.
79. Acc. No. 352A-1870, Victoria & Albert Museum object summary.
80. Williamson 1919, p. 13.
81. Gere 1989, p. 282.
82. Collard 1985, p. 243, extracted from *The Architect*, vol. XVI, 8 July 1876, p. 19.
83. Williamson, 1919, p. 58.
84. Dunn 1904, p. 36. The author is grateful to Clive Wainwright and Francis Collard for pointing out Dunn's work during various conversations in the 1980s.
85. Ibid., p. 29.
86. The receipt in the Alnwick archives reads: 'Received of his Grace the Duke of Northumberland by payment of Wm Twopeny Eq [sic] Eighty-pounds being part-[?] of one hundred pounds for a design by me of a Table to be executed in Marqueterie representing the Five Senses. £80…now paid 20…paid before'.
87. 'causes of delay…through the decease of Henry Blake…being impossible to proceed…without good light, foggy weather increased the delay.' My grateful thanks to Clare Baxter at Alnwick for confirming this information, which was first brought to my attention by Clive Wainwright in the 1990s.
88. Victoria and Albert Museum, E.779-1968.
89. Alnwick Coll. no. DNC 00223.
90. My thanks to Clare Baxter and Lisa Little at Alnwick for this information.
91. Yapp 1878/9, pl. CXXXIII.
92. Beavan 1896, p. 55.
93. Ibid., p. 28.
94. The Holland records for the work between 1864 and 1872 fill eighty-eight double pages, Victoria and Albert Museum, AAD/1983/13, AAD/1998/1.
95. Beavan 1896, p. 55.
96. Victoria and Albert Museum, W.11:1 to 8-1972.
97. 'Cabinet by Holland & Sons, Probably Supplied to the Prince of Wales for Marlborough House, London'. In *Apollo* (Archive: 1925-2005) 151, no. 460 (1 June, 2000).
98. Christie's, London, 25 February 1971, lot 172.
99. Hope 1809, vol. 2, pp. 103, 113 (reversed).
100. Beavan 1896, p. 63.
101. Ibid., p. 56.
102. Ibid., pp. 44, 56.
103. Ibid., p. 76.
104. Beavan did not name the 'purple wood' inlay by its correct name of purpleheart; it might be assumed that his description of 'light Hungarian oak' was in fact Hungarian ash. See Ibid., p. 83.
105. More commonly termed 'purpleheart' today (*Peltogyne* spp.).
106. John Evan Bedford Library, University of Leeds, FEO/86.
107. Beavan 1896, p. 36.
108. Diary entry: 13 December 1864. Meyer, 2001, p. 87.
109. British patent no. 1,661 issued 29 June 1861. Edwards 2012, p. 411.
110. Dated 1866, now at The Metropolitan Museum, Accession Number: 2015.281a, b.
111. Illustrated in *The Art Journal*, 1867, p. 215. Meyer 2006, p. 198, E75, suggests that the wardrobe is inlaid but it is certainly stencilled decoration. See Bevan 1876–77, p. 201.
112. Bumpus, *Gazette des Beaux-Arts*, 1893, vol. 9, p. 427.
113. The 6th edition published in the United States in 1881, the 4th in London in 1887.
114. Koyama-Richard 2002. 'Such a wave unfurled over Europe and the United States, the Japanese effect offered to the world of art a long-awaited renewal'.
115. Victoria and Albert Museum, 8042:1 to 3-1862.
116. Victoria and Albert Museum, CIRC.38:1 to 5-1953.
117. Ames 1974.
118. The presence of a piano in the drawing room designed by Jones at the Priory is confirmed by an entry by George Lewes in his journal of 13 November 1863. Caroline Dakers supports a possible connection between Eliot and her partner with Owen Jones and Alfred Morrison. Dakers 2011, p. 235.
119. Quoted in Flores 1996, p. 320, n. 1249.
120. Exhibit number 826.
121. Third Day's Sale, 20 June 1882, lot 303, illustrated in the catalogue.
122. Art Institute of Chicago (1997.334); another example in the Carnegie Museum of Art (1997.21.1).
123. The Paris Universal Exhibition, 1867, p. 7. Review published by *The Art Journal*.
124. *The Art Journal*, 1871, p. 81.
125. *The Furniture Gazette*, 14 June 1873, p. 151.
126. Christie, Manson and Woods, London, 14 December 1885, lot 586.
127. *The Furniture Gazette*, 14 October 1876, p. 237.
128. In April 1873, *The Furniture Gazette* calculated that there were 48,333 cabinetmakers in Britain, of whom 8,667 were female.
129. Pollen quoted in Edwards 1998, p. 243.
130. Sala 1868, pp. 343-4. See also Edwards 1998, p. 253.
131. Ibid., pp. 363-369.
132. This serial number suggests that the locks were made in Chubb's Horseley Fields factory in Wolverhampton.
133. Pollen 1877, p. 177.
134. Victoria and Albert Museum, 548-1868.
135. Obituary in *The Journal of Decorative Art and British Decorator*, September 1903.
136. BIFMO (British and Irish Furniture Makers Online) https://bifmo.history.ac.uk

CHAPTER 6: 1870S

1. *The Spectator*, 23 November 1872, pp. 1486–7, quoted in Mordaunt Crook, 1999, p. 5.
2. It ran until 1896, then merged into *Furniture and Decoration*. Since commencing research for this publication, the resources of BIFMO have been put to good effect listing furniture makers mentioned in *The Furniture Gazette*.
3. Google & HathiTrust.
4. The walls are inspired by the frescos in the Villa Negroni, excavated in Rome in 1777.
5. Allwood 1988, p. 4.
6. *The Furniture Gazette*, 20 December 1879, p. 413.
7. Ibid., 22 September 1877, p. 225.
8. Ibid., 24 July 1880, p. 470.
9. Ibid., 22 November 1879, p. 356.
10. Ibid., 26 August 1880, p. 182.
11. Ibid., 19 August 1876, p. 117.
12. Ibid., 19 April 1872.
13. Ball 1978, p. 64.
14. Oliver 1966, p. 36.
15. *The Furniture Gazette*, 15 October, 1890, p. 291.
16. BIFMO records a Punch & Sons in Sedbergh, fl. 1870–1889, and Punch Brothers from 1886.
17. *The Furniture Gazette*, 16 June 1877, p. 398.
18. Ibid., 7 July 1877, p. 4.
19. For example, in 1877 Laverton & Co. of Bristol, still active in 1886, made an Italianate cabinet of 'excellent design and workmanship'. See *The Furniture Gazette*, 3 November 1877, p. 348.
20. *The Furniture Gazette*, 12 February 1876, p. 97.
21. Ibid., 13 September 1879, p. 219.
22. By 1882 it was titled: *The Cabinet-makers' Pattern-book: Being Examples of Modern Furniture of the Character Mostly in Demand from Original Designs by First-rate Artists: Issued as Supplements with the "Furniture Gazette"*.
23. Child, P.J., *How to make three fortunes and lose the lot. 100 years of family furniture.* (Private publication, 2001).
24. E. and F.N. Spon. The following year, Spon published Richards's *The Arrangement, Care, and Operation of Wood-working Factories and Machinery*.
25. *The Furniture Gazette*, 12 April 1873, p. 3.
26. Bevan 1876–77, p. 179.
27. Tabasco was selling for as low as one penny

ENDNOTES

per foot by December 1877. See *The Furniture Gazette*, 29 December 1877, p. 478.
28. Ibid., 12 April 1873, p. 3.
29. Ibid., 13 October 1877, p. 276.
30. Ibid., 29 December 1877, p. 478.
31. Ibid., 14 July 1877, p. 21.
32. Conway, 1882, p. 158.
33. In October 1877, 105 vessels sailed into Liverpool with almost 85,000 tons of timber, including large shipments of yellow and red pine from British North America. See *The Furniture Gazette*, 17 November 1877, p. 382.
34. Bevan 1876–77, p. 201.
35. *The Furniture Gazette*, 2 August 1879, p. 65. See also Ibid.,13 October 1877, p. 276, reporting mahogany imports were 54,463 tons in 1875 (value £317,920) and 27,486 tons in 1877 (value £253,228).
36. *The Journal of The Society of Arts*, 24 November 1871, p. 37.
37. Official Exhibition Catalogue, p. 153, Class II, No. 3053. Victoria and Albert Museum, MISC.127:1-9-1921.
38. For a comprehensive monograph on Collinson & Lock, see Edwards 2022.
39. Purchased by the Prince of Liechtenstein, who gave it to the Österreichisches Museum für angewandte Kunst, Vienna, in 1881.
40. Edwards, 2022, p. 64.
41. *The Furniture Gazette*, 19 August 1876, p. 112.
42. *English Guide*, 1878, p. 65.
43. Christie's, London, 4 April 1879, lot 204.
44. Yapp 1879, plate CXL.
45. Fitzwilliam Museum, M.15-1980.
46. Chubb set up in New York in 1882.
47. The house was demolished in 1891.
48. Jones 1856, Greek 3, pl. XVII.
49. See note to Bonhams, London, 19 March 2008, lot 175.
50. The locks are stamped 'IMPd Patent Lever'.
51. Bevan 1876–77, pp. 161–216.
52. Ibid., pp. 161–216.
53. Conway 1882, p. 160.
54. *The Furniture Gazette*, 5 July 1884, p. 6.
55. RCIN 36964.
56. *The Furniture Gazette*, 19 July 1873, p. 229.
57. See Metropolitan Museum, Accession Number: 1983.121.
58. *The Furniture Gazette*, 14 October 1876, p. 237.
59. In 1996, the club purchased its current premises at 4 St James's Square.
60. No pre-1840 directory entries have been traced for S. & H. Jewell of 29–31 Little Queen St, Holborn, although a billhead for furniture supplied by them to Standen, East Grinstead, Sussex, on 1 May 1894 states that they were founded in 1830. (British History Online).
61. City of Westminster Archives Centre.
62. Payne, 1989, p. 135.
63. Aslet, 1979, pp. 2084–87.
64. Christie's, London, 22 October 1979.
65. Jones 1997.
66. An engineering triumph, it took just three months to complete this, the largest roofed building in existence at the time, with a diameter of 426 ½ft (130m). See *The Furniture Gazette*, 19 April 1873, p. 24.
67. Baird 2016, p. 46. A fire at Alexandra Palace in June 1873 meant that some of the collection was lost, although the royal Sèvres porcelain was salvaged.
68. *The Furniture Gazette*, 31 May 1873, p. 119.
69. Ibid., 10 May 1873, p. 75.
70. Ibid., 3 March 1877, p. 131.
71. Ibid., 3 May 1873, p. 54.
72. Ibid., 3 May 1873, p. 58.
73. 'The Work of Christopher Dresser', published anonymously in 1899 by *The Studio*, vol. 15, p. 105.
74. A glass table designed by T.-J. de Thomon in 1808 made in Russia (Corning Museum).
75. *The Society of Arts*, 1879, pp. 126–7.
76. Victoria and Albert Museum, W. 18-1981.
77. Victoria and Albert Museum, 8277. A to M.
78. *The Cabinetmaker and Art Furnisher*, vol. 2, no. 13, 1 July 1881, p. 5.
79. *The Furniture Gazette*, 16 November 1878, p. 238.
80. *Illustrated Catalogue* 1878, p. 118.
81. Sotheby's, London, 4 May 1990, lot 123.
82. Sotheby's, London, 24–25 May 1995, lots 48–9, 54, 124, 129.
83. *The Illustrated Paris Universal Exhibition*, 16 November 1879, p. 329.
84. Gonse 1879, p. 396.
85. *The Society of Arts*, Artisan Reports on the *Paris Universal Exhibition* of 1878: Cabinet Work, 1897, p. 418.
86. Demolished in 1953.
87. The details of the suite are taken from the Holland ledgers in the Archive of Art and Design at the Victoria and Albert Museum, under the heading 'Furniture Exhibited at Paris'. The archives of Holland & Sons are one of the few fully preserved archives of an important British furniture maker.
88. Sir Richard Wallace died in 1890.
89. Edwards 2005, p. 127.
90. Possibly A.R. Hinton who worked with Wright & Mansfield.
91. Bevan 1876–77, p. 189.
92. *The Furniture Gazette*, 17 May 1873, p. 87.
93. *The Penny Magazine*, March 23, 1844, p. 107.
94. The cabinet with a brass label documenting the woods used was with Wick Antiques at the time of writing.
95. Hamilton-Gordon 1925, vol. 1, p. 192.
96. Meyer 2006, p. 214. No further reference given.
97. The pair of an even higher quality than the illustrated example were in the British trade 20–25 years go and were sold to the United States.
98. Victoria and Albert Museum, W.12:1-1982.
99. *The Cabinetmaker and Art Furnisher*, 1 July 1886, p. 23, illus p. 14.
100. The colour illustration example, sold at auction in Dallas in 2012, is stamped 'WRIGHT & MANSFIELD, 104 BOND ST. LONDON', and has an ivorine plaque 'JAMES PHILLIPS & SONS, LTD., FURNISHERS & REMOVERS, UNION ST., BRISTOL'. The Philips archives are in Bristol, ref. 8884 & 44439.
101. Although possibly circumstantial, the illustrated example was sold by Heritage Auctions, Texas in June 2012.
102. *The Cabinetmaker and Art Furnisher*, vol. 7, 1 July 1886, p. 23.
103. See Victoria and Albert Museum, W.12:1-1982.
104. Including large firms like Holland and Maples, and smaller companies like Jenks & Wood.
105. The armchairs, V&A accession number 240:1, 2-1887. The Pembroke table on loan at the time of writing to the Cannon Hall Museum, Barnsley. The panels accession numbers 232-1887, 234-1887, 235-1887.
106. See also Tomlin 1972, p. 129, see plates P/7, 8.
107. Victoria and Albert Museum, W.12:1-1982.
108. Victoria and Albert Museum, 240:1, 2-1887. A closely related suite made by Wright & Mansfield, consisting of a settee, armchair and three chairs, was offered for sale by Cheffins, Cambridge, 13 September 2018, lot 414.
109. Perceptively, Litchfield also noted that the light colour of satinwood, and wear and tear on a painted surface, could make such furniture difficult to date accurately.
110. Number 4588, followed by 'Ct' (cost), coded as 'VO/-'.
111. Written by hand as 'Apl 19/79'.
112. The 1881 census records him as employing 150 men. My thanks to Clarissa Ward for this information. She also notes that Mellier later moved next door to George Mansfield's family.
113. Humphreys 1908.
114. Sotheby's, 2 November 1989, lot 418.
115. Holman 1905, vol. 2, p. 203.
116. By 1866, there were approximately 10,000 Egyptian artefacts in the British Museum.
117. Anglo-Japanese Designs, c.1860 (pen & black ink & w/c on paper), Godwin, Edward William (1833-86) / Private Collection / The Stapleton Collection / Bridgeman Images. IMAGE number 0639.
118. The first *International Health Exhibition*, was held in South Kensington in 1884.
119. Haweis 1881, p. 42.
120. See Aslin, E., *The Aesthetic Movement*, 1969; Cooper, J., 1987, pp. 117-152.

121. For further information on Cottier see Petra Ten Doesschate, Chu et al. *Daniel Cottier-Designer, Decorator, Dealer*, 2021.
122. *Art of Furnishing*, 1880, p. 83.
123. *The Furniture Gazette*, 2 June 1877, p. 361.
124. Ibid., 19 September 1876, p. 186.
125. Ibid., 21 July 1877, p. 43.
126. Freer Gallery of Art and Arthur M. Sackler Gallery, F1904.61.
127. Williamson 1919, p. 89.
128. *The Furniture Gazette*, 28 June 1873, p. 188. The manager was a Mr D. Murray.
129. Victoria and Albert Museum, E.245-1963 (sketchbook).
130. Bedford Park is considered the first 'garden suburb'.
131. *The Furniture Gazette*, 17 May 1873, p. 91.
132. Aslin 1962, p. 84, pls 77, 80, 86–8.
133. London, 1876; United States, 1877.
134. Metropolitan Museum of Art, 1985.116.
135. Talbert 1971, p. 29.
136. See Payne 2018, p. 302.
137. See Payne 2018, pp. 94, 119, 314.
138. House of Lords Select Committee, *First Report from the Sweating* System, 11 August 1888, p. 430.
139. Ibid., pp. 281–282.
140. The exhibition as a whole covered over 50 acres (202,343m²).
141. *Gems of the Centennial Exhibition*, 1877, p. 91.
142. Bevan 1876–77, p. 182.
143. Onegin 2021, pp. 209–218.
144. Smith 1875, p. 164-6.
145. *The Furniture Gazette*, 26 August 1876, p. 122.
146. *Gems of the Centennial Exhibition*, 1877, p. 96.

CHAPTER 7: 1880S

1. Bevan 1876–77, p. 166.
2. Conway 1882.
3. Goodin & Morris 2017, p. 26. The piano designed by Alma-Tadema for Henry Marquand sold for 400 guineas in 1920, *The Cabinet Maker*, 31 July 1920, p. 221.
4. Guests included Mrs Gladstone, Lady Rosebery, the evangelist professor Henry Drummond, the 9th Earl of Elgin, the Countess of Elgin, Robert Farquharson MP, and the American Civil War correspondent, George Washburn Smalley.
5. *The Furniture Gazette*, 1 April 1885, p. 373. BIFMO records three firms making bamboo furniture of the same name.
6. Edis 1881, p. 100, pl. VI.
7. *The Furniture Gazette*, 2 June 1883, p. 392.
8. Ibid., 25 October 1884, p. 329, and 13 December 1884, p. 473.
9. Ibid., 1 April 1885, p. 200.
10. Kinchin 1985.
11. *The Furniture Gazette*, 3 November 1883, p. 266.
12. *Illustrated London News*, 16 August 1884.
13. Ibid., 1 May 1885, p. 266.
14. See Edwards 2005, p. 130.
15. *The Furniture Gazette*, 28 August 1880, p. 132.
16. For a table designed by Christie in 1891, see Chapter 8 – 1890s, **Fig. 8.78**.
17. Edis 1881, pl. 11.
18. In 1860, a carpet sweeper was invented by Daniel Hess of Iowa. It gathered dust with a rotating brush and a bellows. In 1869, the 'Whirlwind' was invented by Ives McGaffey of Chicago.
19. Edwards 2022, p. 39.
20. Edis 1881, p. 103.
21. Hamilton 1882, p. 39.
22. The Metropolitan Museum of Art, 2016.49.
23. Illustrated in *The Furniture Gazette*, 1 April 1885, p. 223.
24. Ibid., 7 July 1883, p. 8, and *The Cabinet Maker*, July 1883, p. 8.
25. *The Furniture Gazette*, 1 April 1885, p. 223.
26. Ibid., 3 January 1885, p. 18.
27. All quotes from *The Furniture Gazette*, 1 January 1886, p. 247.
28. Ibid., 11 February 1882, p. 90.
29. For example, Cheek et al. 1982.
30. This type of panel was published by C. & R. Light *Cabinet Furniture: Designs and Catalogue of Cabinet and Upholstery Furniture*, 1881.
31. *The Furniture Gazette*, 4 November 1882, p. 306.
32. Ibid., 17 July 1875, p. 33.
33. *The Artist*, vol. 23, 1898. A watercolour from Foley's two-volume publication *The Book of Decorative Furniture*, Vols 1 & 2, c.1910, is shown in **Fig. 10.8**.
34. Illustrated in *The Furniture Gazette*, 2 April 1881, p. 219.
35. Ibid., 29 January 1881, pp. 77, 93.
36. Ibid., 6 September 1879, p. 160.
37. Ibid., 18 August 1883, p. 111.
38. Ibid., 10 November 1883, p. 325.
39. Illustrated in ibid., 6 January 1883, p. 7.
40. A wide variety shown in Hasluck 1901.
41. *The Furniture Gazette*, 5 May 1883, p. 309.
42. Ibid., 5 January 1884, p. 2.
43. Ibid., 23 December 1882, p. 442.
44. *The Architect*, 41, 7 July 1889.
45. Original patent no. 6788.
46. Meyer 2006, p. 243.
47. Similar tables are now in use at St James's Palace. The partnership was dissolved in 1882, the business transferred to Morant & Co. in 1894.
48. Edwards 2022, pp. 172–3. Patrick Sandberg Antiques stock nos 4618 (Collinson) & 5951 (Filmer).
49. The British Museum, EA2481.
50. Hope 1807, pl. 7, and similar chairs in pl. 8 in situ in the Flaxman Room, Duchess Street.
51. See Ibid., pl. 20, nos 3, 4, as well as with different decoration to the back and arms and shown in situ in the Aurora and Cephalus room in pl. 7.
52. Sold Phillips, Fonthill Abbey, September 1823, lots 1171–3.
53. Stamped with a workman's name 'F.A. Hinkworth' and '066'. Christie's, London, 24 April 2008, lot 52.
54. Edis 1881, pl. 8, illustrates a version with the back fully upholstered.
55. Extracted from Balfour, Eustace, *Sheraton's Furniture*, pp. 190–6.
56. Cescinsky 1931, p. 133.
57. Litchfield 1921, p. 130.
58. *The Furniture Gazette*, 14 January 1882, p. 19., 11 February 1882, p. 92, and 17 February 1883, p. 112.
59. House of Lords Select Committee, First Report from the Sweating System, 11 August 1888, p. 11.
60. Ibid., p. 212.
61. *The Building News*, 27 April 1883, p. 543
62. Ibid., 20 November 1880, p. 311.
63. Ibid., 15 January 1881, p. 42.
64. Phillips, Son and Neale, June 1886 and July 1887.
65. 'It is difficult…to give and adequate idea of the magnificent collection of art cabinet work which was thus brought to the hammer'. There were reports 'Of Chippendale and Sheraton…there were… charming genuine examples, as well as modern reproductions. The workmanship of every article was perfect, even down to the minutest detail'. *The Furniture Gazette*, 1 July 1886, pp. 245–6.
66. *The Furniture Gazette*, 17 June 1882, pp. 382–3.
67. In reference to a Gothic suite by Jackson & Graham, *The Furniture Gazette*, 19 July 1873, p. 151, and Edis 1881, p. 115, respectively.
68. *The Furniture Gazette*, 3 May 1884, p. 353, July 1886, p. 246.
69. Litchfield 1903, p. 220.
70. *The Furniture Gazette*, 1 February 1888, p. 37. Geoff & Gully and Brook & Co. in Exeter suffered severe damage by fire and water in August 1882. Howard & Sons suffered a warehouse fire in January 1884. White & Co. was badly damaged by a gas explosion in Percy Street. Ibid., 10 July 1880, p. 30.
71. George Manton and Co. of Birmingham folded with £14,577 of liabilities.
72. *The Furniture Gazette*, 1 October 1886, p. 351.
73. Printed in London by Remington and Co. and in Paris by Librarie de l'Art.
74. Fourdinois had exhibited this model in Paris

75. Lot 1805. Reported in *The Scotsman*, 11 July 1882. I am grateful to Clarissa Ward for this reference.
76. *The Furniture Gazette*, 1 October 1886, p. xii.
77. Brown, *The Furniture Gazette*, 26 July 1884, p. 66. Maple & Co., Bowett 2012, p. 309.
78. *The Furniture Gazette*, 28 July 1884, p. 68, 7 July 1883, p. 2, 18 August 1883, p. 116, 5 March 1881, p. 154.
79. Leeds Museums and Art Galleries. See FHS Newsletter no. 165, February 2007.
80. *The Furniture Gazette*, 5 March 1881, p.154.
81. Pascoe, Charles Eyre, Boston, 1891, p. 400.
82. Edwards 1995.
83. Published by *The Cabinet Maker & Art Furnisher*, 1 June 1881.
84. *The Furniture Gazette*, 15 April 1882, p. 234.
85. Ibid., 28 July 1884, p. 66.
86. 'Beith is becoming a large and noted centre for high-class furniture', *The Furniture Gazette*, 9 April 1881, p. 231.
87. In 1888, the average rate of pay for a cabinet maker at Maple & Co. was 9 pence per hour, Lebus paid between 6½ pence and 1s 3 pence per hour. Extracted from House of Lords Select Committee, First Report from the Sweating System, 11 August 1888, pp. 751–2.
88. Payne 2018, p. 243.
89. Hindley & Wilkinson undated catalogue, post 1887.
90. See ibid., pp. 160–4.
91. *The Graphic*, 10 January 1880, p. 55.
92. House of Lords Select Committee, First Report from the Sweating System, 11 August 1888, p. 230. (Witness Henry Miller).
93. House of Lords Select Committee, First Report from the Sweating System, 11 August 1888, p. 749.
94. House of Lords Select Committee, First Report from the Sweating System, 11 August 1888, pp. 444, 733.
95. Thompson & Co. subsequently had a business association with Harrods.
96. Barty-King 1992. Records of Maples are held by the Victoria and Albert Museum.
97. *The Furniture Gazette*, 1 September 1883, p. 154.
98. Ibid., 29 March 1884, p. 253. The compiler also noted that there was an increasing amount of Austrian bentwood furniture being imported into India.
99. For example, a table attributed to Collinson & Lock without substantiation, sold at Bonhams, London, 21 April 2015, lot 141. Graham & Biddle advertised in *The Connoisseur* in July 1903 to show that they also sold antique furniture.
100. *The Furniture Gazette*, 12 June 1881, p. 385.
101. *Magazine of Art* in 1883, vol. VI, pp. 190–6.
102. *The Furniture Gazette*, 10 March 1883, p. 170.
103. Pascoe 1891, pp. 404–5.
104. Messrs Howard and Sons' Furniture. *The Illustrated London News*, vol. 73. London: The Illustrated London News & Sketch Ltd, 1878, p. 40.
105. *The Furniture Gazette*, 24 November 1883, p. 361.
106. Booth 1891, vol. 1, p. 315.
107. Ibid., p. 320. The finer knife-cutting machines were made by John Pickles & Sons, Royd Iron works, Hebden Bridge.
108. House of Lords Select Committee, First Report from the Sweating System, 11 August 1888, pp. 26, 209, 212 & 218.
109. Aslin 1962, p. 51.
110. This pastime carried on well into the twentieth century. This author's forebears learnt to carve at night school in the 1930s.
111. There were four ducal seats in the area: Worksop Manor, owned by the dukes of Norfolk; Welbeck Abbey, owned by the dukes of Portland; Thoresby Hall, owned by the dukes of Kingston; and Clumber House, owned by the dukes of Newcastle.
112. Bowett 2021.
113. House of Lords Select Committee, First Report from the Sweating System, 11 August 1888, p. 382.
114. They had previously exhibited at the *International Inventions Exhibition* in London in 1885, and at the *International Exhibition of Navigation, Commerce and Industry* in Liverpool in 1886.
115. In 1899 Goodall amalgamated with the furniture maker James Lamb and the wallpaper manufacturer Heighway, renamed Goodall, Lamb and Heighway.
116. Victoria and Albert Museum, CIRC.35:3-1962, and National Trust, 1214009. Pointedly, Edwards does not include this cabinet in his publication *Collinson & Lock*, 2022.
117. Aslin 1962, pl. 98.
118. *The Furniture Gazette*, 22 September 1887, p. 231.
119. *The Furniture Gazette*, 17 March 1881, p. 167.
120. Hampton serial numbers are presently not identifiable.
121. The 1882 *Post Office Directory* recorded Jetley, Victor and Gustave, upholsterers at that address. G. Jetley occupied 55 South Audley Street from 1925 and their label is frequently seen on George II reproduction furniture.
122. This cabinet was deaccessioned from the Centennial Museum at the University of Texas, El Paso, to benefit the Museum Collections Fund (accession no. #CF-172).
123. Victoria and Albert Museum W.20:1, 2-1971. Family tradition records that the cabinet cost £500 to produce.
124. *The Pall Mall Gazette*, June 1886, 'Occasional Notes', p. 3. Cited in Edwards 2012, p. 426.
125. By 1902, Webb had adapted his Renaissance-style marquetry designs to the modern trend for Art Nouveau. See Edwards 2022, p. 99, fig. 4.6.
126. Sotheby's, London, 19 July 1985, lot 115. Another version, recorded as being in the Victoria and Albert Museum, is stamped 'Collinson & Lock, London 822', but these numbers are not identified, unless it is a later annotation for Gillows, dating it to between 1871 and 1872, which would seem improbable.
127. Edwards 2020, p. 78, fig. 4.154.
128. See Hayward et al. 1965, p. 217, pl. 819.
129. *Examples of Furniture & Decoration by Gillows*, p. 136.
130. One of many examples is Rawlinson's application for a patent 'for the improvements of treating bone to give it the appearance of ivory'. *The Furniture Gazette*, 8 December 1877, p. 431. Also, 7 July 1887, p. 18.
131. Sotheby's, London, 19 July 1985, lot 116, & 8 June 1990, lot 111, the latter stamped 'London 1747'; a seemingly identical table is in the Victoria and Albert Museum, W.32-1954.
132. Payne 2018, pp. 34–5.
133. Some of the furniture designed by Aitchison for Leighton House, in ivory-inlaid ebonised wood, was sold at Christie's, 8 July 1896, lots 137–140.
134. Beavan 1896, p. 30.
135. *The Furniture Gazette*, 28 April 1883, p. 289, 12 May 1883, p. 325.
136. Ibid., p. 326.
137. Beavan 1896, p. 26.
138. Victoria and Albert Museum, W.23:1 to 4-1927.
139. Naylor 1971.
140. De Bellaigue 1974, vol. 1, p. 330.
141. See Payne, 2018, p. 226.

CHAPTER 8: 1890S

1. Interview with Edward Linley Sambourne, 1893. Hilly Sloan, The History Guide, https://thehistoryguide.co.uk/journal/
2. Formerly the Geffrye Museum in Shoreditch, the heart of the East End furniture trade, opened in 1914.
3. *The Lady* (1892) extracted from Beavers, p. 12.
4. No. 13, vol. II, p.1, November 1890.
5. 198–212 Westminster Bridge Road, styling themselves as 'Cabinet Makers, Upholsterers, Carpet Warehousemen &c'.
6. The table is likely to be RCIN 34022.

7. *The Furniture Gazette*, 15 January 1892, p. 13.
8. Ibid., 15 October 1892, p. 198.
9. First published posthumously in 1896. Robert Louis Stevenson had revisited the comfortable concept of Darby and Joan in *Songs of Travel and Other Verses*.
10. *The Cabinet Maker and Art Furnisher*, 23 January 1919, p. 159.
11. Shakespeare, N., *Six Minutes in May*, Vintage, 2018, p. 213.
12. Aslet 1982, pp. 185, 321, and Aslet 1984a, pp. 80–4, and Aslet 1984b, pp. 446–49.
13. Victoria and Albert Museum, V&A Circ 40:1 to 10-1953. (Historical context note.)
14. Rubens 1986, p. 70.
15. December 1900, p. 161.
16. The Edward Barnsley Workshop is still thriving in Petersfield, Hampshire.
17. Charles Rennie Mackintosh, James Herbert MacNair (1868–1955), Margaret Macdonald (1864–1933) and her sister, Frances (1873–1921). See the website of the Charles Rennie Mackintosh Society for a detailed bibliography.
18. Livingstone 2016.
19. Ellwood 1911.
20. *The Art Journal*, 1900, pp. 133–34, 281.
21. See *Art Journal*, 1900, p. 127.
22. John Harris Heal had established the firm in 1810, moving to 203 Tottenham Court Road in 1818.
23. Cardwell et al. 1898. Preface by Sir Walter Besant.
24. Ibid., pp. 185–7.
25. The house taken over in 1899 by another firm of furniture dealers, Messrs Keeble Ltd, until 1936. The late seventeenth-century house was destroyed by bombing in May 1941.
26. Cardwell et al. 1898, p. 190.
27. Agius 1978, p. 146. (Agius does not cite the source.)
28. Litchfield 1921, p. 186.
29. Victoria and Albert Museum, W.53-1984. British Galleries, Room 125, Edwin and Susan Davies Gallery, case 1.
30. Coke 28 May 1891, p. 42.
31. Now the Rhinefield House Hotel, Hampshire. The Moorish Smoking Room photographed by Bedford Lemere, September 1891 (BL11220).
32. Victoria and Albert Museum, craftsman file, Hamptons, undated photocopy of an advertisement with no date or publication reference.
33. The chairs have similarities with an early eighteenth-century precedent formerly in the collection of Sir George Donaldson. See Macquoid & Edwards 1924, p. 224, fig. 61.
34. *The Furniture Gazette*, 2 July 1894, p. 103.
35. Grade II Preston Manor was restored and enlarged by Charles Stanley Peach in 1905 and contains an important collection of furniture open to the public.
36. Victoria and Albert Museum, W.20:1, 2-1971.
37. The catalogue is undated, the sale later advertised in *The Times*, 5 November 1898. I am grateful to Clive Edwards for this information.
38. *Leamington Courier*, 21 June 1892.
39. Hall 1996a.
40. Sold to the Metropolitan Museum of Art by the founder's grandson, Charles Albert Hindley, for £50. Microulis 2001.
41. Sir John Soane's Museum, XF196.
42. *The Furniture Gazette*, 15 March 1892, pp. 52–3.
43. Ibid., 15 February 1892, p. 28.
44. *The Cabinet Maker and Art Furnisher*, June 1898.
45. *The Furniture Gazette*, 15 October 1892, p. 199.
46. Kirkham et al. 1987, pp. 21, 45.
47. Kirkham 1982, p. 228.
48. Booth 1891, p. 190
49. *The Furniture Gazette*, 15 October 1892, p. 198.
50. See Payne 2018, p. 405.
51. After the merger the Johnstone name appears to have been occasionally used until c.1911 just before Lenygon purchased Morant & Co.
52. Stamped on the top drawer 'George Prince of Wales', the reverse has a Prince of Wales's feathers brand above a 'G'. RCIN 28727.
53. *The Furniture Gazette*, 15 June 1893, p. 108.
54. Ibid., 15 April 1893, p. 306. It is not clear if the Levasseur working in London at this time was a scion of Étienne Levasseur, whose family production of mainly Boulle-inspired furniture was popular in England and France in the late eighteenth and early nineteenth centuries. *The Gazette* of 1893 listed his first initial as 'L.'; BIFMO records an 'L.' Levasseur of 336a Oxford Street in 1886.
55. *The Cabinet Maker and Art Furnisher*, June 1892. Listed as Antiques Dealers of 13 Newman Street, c.1910 (Leeds University the British Antique Trade).
56. BIFMO and *The Furniture Gazette*, 15 April 1893, p. 306.
57. BIFMO, see also Vaughan 1984.
58. The premises had been the home of Beresford & Hicks, manufacturers of reproduction furniture, who exhibited furniture at the British Industries Fair from c.1922 until 1947.
59. *The Furniture Gazette*, 15 April 1893, p. 306.
60. BIFMO. His son, also William, patented a folding table 'The Pulgrave Combination Luncheon & Card Table' extracted from Christopher Clarke Antiques, makers archive.
61. The Royal Commission Official Catalogue of the British Section Chicago Exhibition, 1893, Presentation Copy, p. xix.
62. In December 1891 the firm sold a set of 'patent circular Dining tables' for use at Windsor Castle. They are described as 'A set of Wainscot oak patent circular Dining tables 5' 6" diameter, expanding to form two tables of 6' 4" diameter [...] and 7' 6" diameter — also extending to 25 ft in length when in the 7' 6" width [...] As per estimate £116 —' in a firm's invoice in the Lord Chamberlain's Bill Book, TNA, LC 11/286. Several other extending tables by the firm are also in the Royal Collection, e.g., inventory numbers 29898 and 29943. See Morris 2018, p. 5, n 19.
63. *Grace's Guide to British Industrial History* (online).
64. Edwards 1995 cited a visit in 1895 to London by the American Furniture Manufacturers Exposition Association, who tried to evaluate the commercial advantages of shipping furniture to Britain in knocked down (unassembled) form, p. 210.
65. *The Furniture Gazette*, 16 January 1893, p. 258.
66. This practice was innocently explained to this author in the 1970s.
67. Booth 1891, pp. 175–76, 179. More than 4,000 men were under the age of nineteen, more than 20,000 between twenty and fifty-five, and almost 3,000 over the age of fifty-five. The wood-carving industry accounts for another 6,000, and carvers and gilders 4,000. More than two thirds were born in London. There were 45,200 cabinet makers employed in 1861, rising to 51,400 a decade later with a drop to 46,200 in 1881, rising to 56,200 in 1891.
68. *The Furniture Gazette*, 15 November 1890, p. 297.
69. Pevsner, Nikolaus (1964). *Pioneers of Modern Design*, p. 152.
70. *The Furniture Gazette*, 15 January 1892, p. 3.
71. BIFMO.
72. Sotheby's, Belgravia, 12 November 1975, lot 123.
73. Sotheby's, London, 9 July 2019, lots 7, 16, 19, 178.
74. 1 February 1913, p. 168.
75. John Nicholsons, Auctioneers, Haslemere, 14 May 2008.
76. Christie's, London, 6 June 2006, lot 607.
77. Macquoid and Edwards 1953, p. 275, fig. 152. One of the chairs was described 'In the thick set armchair there is an interesting mixture of style. The splat and top rail are marked by strong rococo influence but the finely carved lions' heads holding writhing

78. Christie's, South Kensington, 21 November 2006, lot 457, and 24 November 2015, lot 34.
79. See Gilbert 1996, p. 395, pl. 780. Sold Christie's, London, 13 January 1997, lot 105.
80. Information and photographs kindly shown to the author by D. Wells, February 2016.
81. See Hayward and Kirkham 1980, p. 79, fig. 229, and Vardy 1744, pl. 43. For a Kentian copy, see Christie's, London, 27 November 2007, lot 54.
82. BIFMO. The present-day values of such sums are difficult to equate, but £1 million in the early 1890s would be approximately £122 million today.
83. A comprehensive study is in Barty-King 1992.
84. See Wood 1994, pp. 244–46, figs. 231, 234, 236.
85. Roberts 1995, p. 124, extracted from Ackerman, 1814.
86. The inner panels would have veneer on the outside and a counter veneer on the inside to keep the door from warping or shrinking. Well-made examples would have the secondary planks running with the grain in alternating directions for added stability.
87. Clive Wainwright and Francis Collard in discussions with this author. Both objects are discussed and illustrated in Collard 1985, pp. 246, 248, 258.
88. Victoria and Albert Museum, W.29-1976. Given by Sir Colin Anderson.
89. The 'Empire' table was perhaps from Sargent's studio as it appears in his 1902 portrait of Evelyn, Duchess of Devonshire.
90. Two Temple Place, London WC2.
91. Collard 1985, p. 249.
92. Ibid., p. 245 & *The Cabinet Maker*, January 1895. Another, at Balls Park, Hertfordshire, is illustrated in M. Jourdain *Regency Furniture* (1948 ed.), pl. 163 and repeated in R. Edwards & P. Macquoid, *The Dictionary of English Furniture*, rev. ed., 1954, vol. III, p. 133, fig. 24.
93. Litchfield 1892, p. 206.
94. A cutting in the National Portrait Gallery's British Picture Framemakers 1600–1950 project files, dated c.1914, refers to Peake as 'the modern Grinling Gibbons'. The Archbishop of Canterbury said to Peake, 'You are the living Grinling Gibbons' (Brixton Free Press, 30 May 1924).
95. Haweis 1882, p. 106.
96. Aguis 1978, pp. 37–38.
97. Brook 1889, p. 29.
98. Hampton & Sons undated catalogue, pp. 73, 81, stock numbers C4215 & 4249 at £18/10s & £32/10s.
99. South London Press, 13 August 1904.

'Mr Peake is a professor in wood carving and has many pupils eager to learn the intricacies of the work, and who soon get the artist's fire in their blood as they see the flowers and fruit grow and come to life under their hands.' *Kentish Mercury*, 24 March 1899, 'Mr Peake's wood carving, and especially his groups of fruit and flowers, formed an especially attractive feature. Botanists who inspected the work expressed warm admiration of the truthfulness to nature, exquisite delicacy of execution and artistic taste displayed in grouping.'

CHAPTER 9: 1900–1909

1. Elder-Duncan 1907, p. 101.
2. The Frederick Parker Chair Collection is held by the London Metropolitan University.
3. Callmann 1999, p. 348. Ellen Callmann pointed out that Bardini was openly reusing old parts to make up furniture and it was many years later that his pieces were wrongly sold on as 'antiques'.
4. Wood 1994, pp. 207–208, plates 196–200.
5. Jennings 1902, pl. 27.
6. The illustrated example is 109×167.5×71cm/43×66×28in (h×w×d). The other example is 94×152.5×67cm/37×60×26½in. Sold Bonhams, 20 November 2013, lot 150.
7. A collection of Hicks furniture, together with the original receipts, was sold by Herm & Wilkinson of Dublin in May 1996.
8. Reported in *The Irish Times*, 8 August 1998.
9. Eastwood, p. 12. Extracted from *Arts and Crafts Society of Ireland: Journal of Proceedings*, 1896, Dublin 1896, p. 24.
10. Eastwood notes that several Hicks pieces were offered at Christie's, *Cabinteely House*, 5 & 6 November 1984 and *Glenaulin Chapelizoid*, 29 & 30 April 1985.
11. Metal fittings, however, would usually be made by a specialist colleague.
12. Victoria and Albert Museum, CIRC.593A-1966.
13. Still trading today as Christopher Pratts, Regent Street, Leeds.
14. *Country Life*, 30 October 1900, The Paris Exhibition.
15. Among the many pieces Janes made for Lutyens were miniature furnishings for Queen Mary's Dolls' House between 1921 and 1924.
16. Published by John Hogg, 1903.
17. Bennett 2005.
18. Bennett 2005, p. 112, fig. 6.26 & p. 114, fig. 6.28. Shapland design number R1371. Hamptons catalogue, c.1900-1910, number C 4066.
19. In 1924, Shapland and Petter merged with the Barnstaple Cabinet Company. Continuing in business until 1999, the firm was the largest privately owned employer in Devon, with a staff of approximately 900 during the 1990s.
20. See an album of 'Antique English, French & Spanish furniture', dated 1902 held in the Metropolitan Museum library, Accession number 62.619.51.
21. Hindley & Wilkinson Ltd., architectural decorators, designers, upholsterers & manufacturers of high-class furniture, p. 38, pl. IX.
22. *The Furniture Record and Furnisher*, November 1902, p. 547.
23. *The Cabinet Maker and Complete House Furnisher, Wycombe Memories*, R.A. Janes, 4 August 1951, p. 422.
24. Collated from the Christian Davis Antiques website.
25. *A Collection of Ornamental Designs applicable to Furniture, Frames & the Decoration of Rooms in the style of Louis 14th on 24 Plates chiefly after Thos. Chippendale*.
26. 'Sheraton's Furniture', *The Magazine of Art*, vol. 6, p. 190.
27. Cescinsky 1931, pl. 203.
28. Chippendale, T. 1966 reprint, pl. XV.
29. A single side chair is in the Victoria and Albert Museum. It is described as dating to c.1755–60 and having come from Westwood House, Worcestershire, but assuming it is period, it more likely dates to the 1740s. See Victoria and Albert Museum, W.24-1951.
30. Christie's, London, 18 October 2017, lot 583.
31. Gloag and Hackenbroch 1958, p. 27.
32. *The Cabinet Dictionary*, 1803, p. 146.
33. Christie's, 12 November 1999, lot 41.
34. Christie's, London, 4–5 March 1909.
35. Claxton Stevens & Whittington 1983, p. 72. Tomlin 1972, p. 134, shows a similar chair with minor variations; and a painted version is in Macquoid 1908, vol. 4, fig. 102.
36. Williamson 1919, p. 28.
37. See Harris 2001. (Victoria and Albert Museum, set W.35-1919).
38. Eilish Munday noted there were between eighty-three and eighty-five employees approximately a decade later. *Irish Furniture*, pp. 10-12.
39. Macquoid 1938, p. 228, fig. 209.
40. Hicks made a cabinet of similar form, see Christie's, 13 March 2012, lot 386.
41. Victoria and Albert Museum, W.12:1-1930
42. GRI Special Collections, 2007.D.1 (bx.496-497). The extensive collection of photographs and watercolours in the Duveen archive are not dated and for the

43. Moore 2005, p. 23.
44. See Weber 2014, p. 495, for an almost identical console table.
45. Kirkham 1987, p. 15.
46. Smith and Rogers 2006, p. 32. A report in *The Cabinet Maker* is an aide to comparing the size of the Lebus workforce and can be measured against a 1901 census. 52,660 men and women were employed in England and Wales as cabinet makers, with a slight drop to 50,974 by 1911. (18 July 1914, p. 73.)
47. Hazel was not commonly used for case furniture. The term may have been used as a marketing ploy by Maples, who imported American red gum, which was known as satin walnut. See Bowett 2012, p. 95.
48. 'The influence of Commerce', *The Illustrated London News*, 17 June 1893. Cribs of a similar height can be seen, held by Cobbett & Co.; see *The Cabinet Maker*, November 1892, p. 130.
49. House of Lords Select Committee, *First Report from the Sweating System*, 11 August 1888, p. 572.
50. *The Cabinet Maker*, 3 June 1916, p. 185.
51. Bullock n.d., p. 41.
52. Penick and Long, 2019, extracted from *The Architectural Review*, p. 83.
53. Heal's *Plain Oak Furniture*, catalogue, 1898. In conversation, Oliver Heal kindly pointed out that Heal's also outsourced from other makers such as Frederick Parker.
54. *The Furniture Gazette*, 13 April 1893, p. XV.
55. The four Bath Cabinet Makers' Company pieces and Howard study illustrated in *The Art Journal*, 1900, pp. 133, 134, 280, 281 and 135, respectively.
56. National Trust NT 202013. See Bowett 2009, p. 229, pl. 5.7. The eagle with wings outstretched in a distinctive manner has been attributed to Benjamin Goodison and Francis Brodie.
57. GRI 2007 D.1. (bx 531-533). Cf.: Victoria and Albert Museum W.21-1945.
58. White Allom were eighteen blocks away at 19 East 52nd Street by c.1914.
59. Spielmann 1906, p. 31.
60. Ibid., p. 35.
61. Ibid., p. 309.
62. Ibid., p. 312.
63. William Birch Ltd were awarded a Gold Medal at the New Zealand International Exhibition in 1906 and 1907.
64. See Payne 2018, p. 450.
65. Sold Christie's, London, 25 September 1986, lot 288. (Linke index number 134.)
66. Dumas 1908, no page number. Presumably this was an adaptation of the French *duchesse brisé*.
67. Agius 1978, pp. 146-7.
68. It is not known if White Allom reproduced this model, the original attributed to Thomas How (active 1710-33). Original examples are at The Metropolitan Museum, Temple Newsam, the Frick Collection and the Cooper-Hewitt Museum.
69. Kinchin 1985.
70. *The Cabinet Maker and Art Furnisher*, August 1901, p. 35; *The Art Journal*, 1901, p. 241.
71. *The Cabinet Maker and Art Furnisher*, April 1893, p. 275.
72. The comprehensive Carlhian and Beaumetz archive is in Special Collections, Getty Research Institute.
73. RCIN 2624.
74. Jervis notes a 'State Throne Chair' made by Hollands made at a cost of £238 10s for the opening of parliament in 1901. Jervis 1970, p. 46. In 1911 George V commissioned Morris & Co. to make a pair of X-frame throne chairs covered in red velvet in mid-seventeenth-century style for the newly renovated Throne Room at Holyroodhouse (RCIN 2650), and a pair with carved fame for the Investiture of the Prince of Wales. (See Morris & Co. catalogue pp. 39, 40.)
75. For further information see Edwards 2013, pp. 1-17.
76. *Franco-British Exhibition: Illustrated Review*, Chatto & Windus.
77. Agius 1978, p. 162.
78. Elder-Duncan 1907, pp. viii, 33; p. 111 for Waring.
79. Handwritten letter dated 8 June 1901. Casa Real archive (Lisbon), CX 7004/6979.
80. The company made good use of satinwood, supplying a long set of Hepplewhite-style dining chairs in solid satinwood for Woburn Abbey. The set is a *tour de force* of the craftsman's skills, satinwood is a notoriously difficult timber to work, the grain running in all directions; easy enough in a veneer but very difficult to work in the solid. My thanks to Anthony Beech Furniture Conservation at Burghley House for this insight.
81. The heart-shaped table on the left is a model by Zwiener of Paris.
82. June 2020, in conversation with Christian Davies and Geoffrey Boyes-Korkis, the latter a nephew of Stephen Jewell, still active in the family business.
83. This image c.1914.
84. Hall 1996b, p. 197. See also Edwards 1994, p. 174
85. No. 2281.
86. Bonhams, London, 22 November 2005, lot 197.
87. *The Connoisseur*, vol. 11, 1905.
88. January 1899, illus. Agius 1978, p. 90.
89. See Agius 1978, p. 161.
90. Like many catalogues at this time, it is not dated. However, Hamptons write that the 1903 depository in Battersea is nearly complete and they write of delivery 'vans' suggesting that it was prior to them establishing a motorised fleet of lorries.
91. Grace's Guide dates the catalogue as 1894.
92. 'All goods are marked in plain Figures, for cash, without discount'.
93. Wells & Hooper 1910, pls 39, 42.
94. The original was started in 1760 by J.-F. Oeben and delivered to Versailles by his successor J.-H. Riesener in 1769 (Inv. V3750).
95. Linke did allow selected contemporaries to reproduce his bronze mounts under licence, see Payne, 2003, pp. 438-9.
96. The Paris *Bottin* records a Léon Kahn working as a bronze chaser in Paris in 1900.
97. Payne 2018, p. 405.
98. Kahn catalogue R 1066.
99. *The Cabinet Maker*, 5 September 1914, p. 280.
100. *The Cabinet Maker*, 13 July 1907 (supplement), p. xi.
101. F303.
102. Jacobsen et al. 2020, p. 173.
103. Plates 58 and 61.
104. *The Connoisseur*, 1902.
105. In 1910 Robert W. Partridge opened a gallery with large display windows at 180 New Bond Street.
106. Agius, p. 146.
107. *The Cabinet Maker*, 26 October 1918, p. 76; *Wycombe Memories*, R.A. Janes, 4/8/1951, pp. 422-23.
108. The four volumes were titled: *The Age of Oak*, *The Age of Walnut*, *The Age of Mahogany* and *The Age of Satinwood*.
109. Sold Sotheby's, London, 3 February 1969. The farsighted Charles Handley-Read contributing towards the purchase price.
110. *Bucks Free Press*, 2 June 2017, p. 40.
111. *The Theory of the Leisure Class: An Economic Study of Institutions* (1899); *The Theory of Business Enterprise* (1904).
112. Edwards 1994, p. 174.

CHAPTER 10: 1910–1920

1. *The Cabinet Maker*, 27 March 1920, p. 747.
2. Wells & Hooper 1910, p. 258.
3. J.R. Davidson, *A European Contribution to California Modernism*, Berlin, Boston: Birkhäuser, 2019, pp. 13-35.
4. Wells & Hooper 1910, pls XXXL & XL.
5. *The Building News*, 26 February 1915, p. 234.
6. An early design of a lumpy Gothic-style cabinet by Foley was illustrated in 1880, criticised for being veneered rather than made in solid wood. *The Furniture Gazette*, 27 November 1880, p. 334. Earlier designs by Foley in the Queen Anne style appeared

in the *Gazette* on 21 August 1880.
7. Litchfield 1907, p.259. Kahn number R 845.
8. *The Cabinet Maker*, 5 June 1920, p. 516.
9. *The Cabinet Maker*, 27 July 1907, Supplement v.
10. After the death of the collector James Orrock in 1913, Lord Leverhulme purchased much of his furniture. Several pieces from Orrock's collection are illustrated in *Old English Furniture*, Fenn & Wylie, 1920 (Batsford reprint), for example plates LXIII & LXIV.
11. The firm was established by Joel Duveen in 1868, closing in 1964.
12. Charles Duveen traded as 'C. Charles' and later in New York as 'Charles of London'.
13. Both the Duveen and the Carlhian archives are held in the Special Collections department of the Getty Research Institute at the J. Paul Getty Museum. Duveen Brothers' stock documentation from the dealer's library, 1829–1965. Series VII. Photographs, 1898–circa 1960. Series VII.D.
14. Allom had been involved in building flying boats during the war and after hostilities ended he opened a gallery in New York, like Partridge and Duveen, plying back and forth from London. Tragically, some London dealers were drowned when the *Lusitania* was torpedoed in 1915 off the Irish coast. Partridge, a strong swimmer, survived.
15. A.C. Cooper number 9194 'Attendance at 31 St. James St'. 'Adam Book Case', October 1920.
16. A pair of elaborate high back chairs were sold by the Duke of Leeds, Christie's 10 June 1920, lot 114, bought by the dealer Moss Harris.
17. GRI 2007 D.1. (bx 531-533), nu. 40-41.
18. GRI 2007 D.1. (bx 531-533), nu. 46-47.
19. GRI 2007 D.1. (bx 531-533), nu. 12-13.
20. Dew 2015.
21. GRI 2007 D.I. (bx 17), nu. 022.
22. In 1935 Lenygon & Morant took over the long-established business of Howard & Sons, concentrating on seat furniture.
23. Lenygon 1909, p. 37; Christie's, 5 July 2011, lot 306. Cf. a side table at Oving, Cornforth. J., *Inspirations of the Past*, 1985, pl. 95.
24. Sotheby's 26–28 June 2001, lot 305.
25. *The Decoration of English Mansions during the Seventeenth and Eighteenth Centuries* (1909) and *Furniture in England from 1660 to 1760*.
26. Dew 2015, p. 2. J.M. Duveen & Co., 'antique furniture dealers', re-opened their premises at 4 Water Street, Liverpool. *The Cabinet Maker*, 27 May 1916, p. 174.
27. Referred to in French as *tôle peinte*.
28. Cf. Bowett 2002, p. 154, pl. 8:46. Bowett describes this leg as 'horsebone', a term of uncertain origin. Bowett 2002, pp. 100–101, pls 3:55–3:57.
29. For the original table see *Country Life*, 26 December 1931, p. 716, pl. 3.
30. *Country Life*, 12 December 1931, p. 681, pl. 7.
31. The British Antique Trade Directory cites the purchase as 1913, Dew 2015 as c.1912.
32. See Christie's, London, 27 April 2006, lot 152.
33. Macquoid 1906, p. 180, fig. 155. The unusual gilt drawer panels and distinctive feet are also similar to a commode, p. 182, fig. 156. For similar panels and feet see Macquoid & Edwards, 1924, Vol. I, p. 134, fig. 32.
34. The locks are numbered from 1675675-83. The Chubb order book for order no. B6377 reads: '9 21/2 Mortise Till, 1" to Pin/ to key sent, no new keys'. The curious entry, dated 23 July 1912.
35. See Hayward and Kirkham 1980; an unsigned drawing of the sofa may be found in Harris 1973, pls 98–100.
36. Victoria and Albert Museum, Furniture, Textiles & Fashion Department, craftsman file, H1254.
37. Lenygon 1909, p. 69. A George III example was acquired by the Philadelphia Museum of Art in 1929, 1929-161-1.
38. Brangwyn had trained under Mackmurdo and William Morris, and in 1895 Siegfried Bing had commissioned him to decorate the exterior of his Galerie L'Art Nouveau.
39. See Harrison Moore 2011.
40. Macquoid 1906, p. 151, fig. 133.
41. RCIN 33392, and the Metropolitan Museum of Art, 24.136.1, respectively.
42. For a detailed analysis of the transformations see: Wood 1994, pp. 310–14.
43. Ibid., pp. 283–309. For an extensive selection of photographs of furniture from the Orrock Collection, see Shaw Sparrow, *The British Home of Today*, New York, 1904.
44. Gilbert 1997, pp. 3–4.
45. Written up in glowing terms in *The Burlington Magazine* in July 1908. The article only included the lower part of the nine-foot-high cabinet, an unfortunate prelude to its eventual fate.
46. Published by the Cranford Press, George Pulman and Sons, Limited. (Undated, c.1910.)
47. Christie's, 19 November 1987, lot 125. Bonhams, 7 March 2012, lot 133.
48. Shone 1999, p. 139. A pair sold Sotheby's, Belgravia, 12 November 1975, lot 136. V&A MISC.2:3-1934.
49. For further reading see: Anscombe, 1981 *Omega and After* and Collins, 1984 *The Omega Workshops*. Also, Gerstein, A. 2009 *Beyond Bloomsbury: Designs of the Omega Workshops 1913–1919*.
50. *The Cabinet Maker*, 4 December 1920, p. 570. In the same year Harrods took over The South American Stores (Gath & Chaves) Ltd.
51. *The Cabinet Maker*, 21 September 1918, p. 261.
52. Massil 1997, p. 24.
53. *The Cabinet Maker*, 23 September 1916, p. 273, 29 January 1916, p. 87.
54. *The Cabinet Maker*, 22 August 1914, p. 205, 6 January 1917, p. 8, 23 December 1916, p. 232.
55. Second Lieutenant Cecil Ambrose Heal, eldest son of Ambrose Heal was fatally wounded in Belgium, 3 July 1915. Ambrose Heal & Edith Heal, with Charles A. Bernau, *The Records of the Heal Family*, privately printed and published, 1932. There were many others, such as Lieutenant Charles Allom, d. 20 October 1917.
56. *The Cabinet Maker*, 20 November 1915, p. 151, 29 January 1916, p. 89.
57. John Arthur Bates (1897–1978), who started working as a cabinet maker for Warings in 1911 fought in Belgium. *FHS Newsletter*, no. 191, August 2013, p.4. This authors' grandfather, C.B. Payne, tried in vain to keep one of his key workers, Beeston, in his Melton Mowbray furniture workshop. (*The Cabinet Maker*, 11 November 1916, p. 121.) This chapter can only touch on the huge effort by service men and women who sacrificed so much.
58. *The Studio*, vols 69–72, pp. 69–70. A bedroom suite from the Kinloch family, one piece signed 'Silas', was sold Bonhams, 27 April 2017, lot 332.
59. A selling exhibition of 170 items of 'Hand-Made Furniture' from the school was held at Walker's Galleries, New Bond Street, 3–29 April 1933.
60. Christie's, 25 September 2007, lot 371 and Sotheby's, Crossrigg Hall, 13 September 1994, lots 39–44.
61. *The Cabinet Maker*, 3 July 1915, p. 2.
62. In 1926 Keen made a set of six gilt chairs for George V, RCIN 33499, to match a set of armchairs bought by George IV.
63. *The Cabinet Maker*, 4 November 1916, p. 89.
64. Baines, born in Stepney was apprenticed to C.R. Ashbee. He created several estates in the London area in the Arts & Crafts idiom.
65. *The Cabinet Maker*, 28 February 1920, p. 443
66. See illustration *The Cabinet Maker*, 12 June 1920, p. 569.
67. Other schools such as in High Wycombe and in Tanner Street in Shoreditch and Birmingham, trained disabled men who also produced furniture in a similar vein. *The Cabinet Maker*, 31 July 1920, pp. 218–19.

68. Hansard vol. 116, 5/6/1919.
69. *The Cabinet Maker*, 7 November 1914, p. 115.
70. Ibid., 6 March 1920, p. 548.
71. Ibid., 27 May 1916, p. 169.
72. See: *The Sketch*, 29 October 1919; *Daily News*, 5 November 1919; *Country Life*, 12 March 1921, p. xciv.
73. *English Furniture Designs* was reissued in Spanish in 1929.
74. See: *Franco-British Exhibition Illustrated*, p.205.
75. *The Cabinet Maker*, 28 February 1920, p. 443. The design is of the same genre as a display cabinet by Hildesley in *The Cabinet Maker*, 20 January 1917, p. 42.
76. Hildesley 1923. Marquetry designs by William Chase and A.J. Rowley at The Rowley Gallery in 1915 were, like the Hildesley drawings, early signs of what would later be deemed 'Art Deco'.
77. Shapland, ex-chair of the Design and Industries Association was also a former editor of *The Cabinet Maker*. In 1926 he wrote *The Practical Decoration of Furniture*, and in 1938, *A Key to English Furniture*.
78. See Macquoid & Edwards 1924, vol. I, p. 225, fig. 63.
79. Adams furniture was made in Gloucester and shown in Portman Square, London. His works *My Book of Furniture* was published in 1926 and *Modern Decorative Art* in 1930.
80. Vol. 2, p. 66. & *English Furniture from Gothic to Sheraton*, 1937, p. 167.
81. A green lacquer bureau bookcase is at Shaw's Corner, National Trust. (NT 1274804).
82. Tozer also retailed French furniture, for example a Louis XVI-style mahogany cylinder desk. Christie's, 5 April 2000, lot 71.
83. BIFMO. The entry extracted from *The Cotton Archive at the Museum of the Home*. The stamp 'Made by Charles Baker, Chippendale House, Wells Road, Bath' has been recorded.
84. Symonds, *English Furniture from Charles II to George II*, 1929, p. 47, fig. 25.
85. Christie's, 24 April 2008, lot 460.
86. The earliest I have found, dating to between 1725 and 1740, is illustrated in Bowett, 2009, p. 172, pl. 4:56.
87. On the nandj.org.uk website (accessed May 2021), one of the firm's carvers, John Hudson, recalls that in the 1930s the wage for carving a claw and ball foot was between 25d and 30d each.
88. Lennox-Boyd 1998, pp.37–38, pl. 24.
89. RIBA images, RIBA18170.
90. GRI Special Collections 2007, D.1 (bx. 496-497). Another image is annotated 'These chairs were made by Thomas Chippendale for Baron de Gestas who was the French Ambassador to London' (box 531-533, nu. 149).
91. Macquoid 1906, pp. 129–30, pls 111–12.
92. John Stalker and George Parker published *Treatise of Japanning and Varnishing* in 1688.
93. *The Cabinet Maker*, 28 August 1915, p. 181.
94. Part of a suite, Victoria and Albert Museum Accession number W.22:1to 8-1917.
95. *The Cabinet Maker*, 5 June 1920, p. 516 (illustration).
96. *The Cabinet Maker*, 25 September 1920, p. 767 (illustration).
97. Macquoid & Edwards 1924, vol. I, p. 164, fig. 27.
98. *See* BIFMO.
99. Parker Archive, London Metropolitan University, *The History of the Company*, typewritten interview with T.C.P. Parker (undated), p. 7.
100. *The Cabinet Maker*, 21 February 1920, p. 380.
101. Ibid., 15 May 1921, p. 348, 20 March 1920, p. 659.
102. This is almost certainly the same table in an undated Waring & Gillow catalogue of c.1920. Catalogue no. 233, p. 200.
103. This style of settee was modernised by Oliver Hill in 1927 (RIBA 29319).
104. Also shown in a simplified form in the *Cabinet Maker's London Book of Prices*. Published again in 1797, Sheraton claimed that by 1803 it was 'not much in present use'.
105. My thanks to Clive Edwards for pointing this out.
106. Rogers 1930.
107. Ibid., p. 37.
108. For the contrasts in Maurice Adams' work, see Victoria and Albert Museum W.49-1934 and W.96-1978.
109. When Symonds published *English Furniture from Charles II to George II*, in 1929, the five-page list of subscribers included Lutyens' father and son, Geoffrey and John Duveen, Arthur Brett, Tozer, Gillows and Waring & Gillow.
110. *The Cabinet Maker*, 13 November 1920, p. 364.
111. Quoted in Evans, S., *Furniture History*, vol. 6, 1970, p. 85. See also Morley, C., *FHS Newsletter* 207, August 2017, pp. 2–8.
112. In 1928 Follot became a director of Waring & Gillow at their branch in Paris.
113. Rogers 1930, p. 1.
114. For example, RIBA 97617 and 97623 amongst others.

Although not signed, this finely executed marquetry panel has all the hallmarks of the work of Jackson & Graham. The panel of shells is framed by marbled veneer, termed today 'Macassar ebony', the stylised floral inlays with delicate ivory highlights. The foliate decoration is inspired by Owen Jones (1809–74), whose extensive travels in Europe culminated in a detailed study of form and decoration at the Alhambra in Spain. Traces of Jones' work in *The Grammar of Ornament* (1856) remain in the framing of the cabinet, such as the three-leaf vertical foliage along the top; the marquetry is formalised, in keeping with several of Jones' plates for Greek ornament. Jackson & Graham have produced a commercial interpretation of the late Owen Jones' designs. No precise date can be given for the cabinet, although the door has a brass lock by Chubb numbered 800354, a sequence that dates to between 1875 and 1880. The single door of the cabinet encloses a range of ash-veneered drawers for storing shell specimens. Conchology, the collecting of shells, can be traced back to Antiquity. The Dutch East India Company had been importing shells into Europe since the seventeenth century and the craze for conchology in the form of grottoes, cabinets of curiosity and still-life paintings was widespread: Margaret of Valois commissioned a shell grotto at Issy-les-Moulineaux; the "Grotto of Tethys" was built at Versailles in 1665; and, a century later, Louis XVI had a shell cottage built at Rambouillet for Marie Antoinette. Jackson & Graham's composition of the marquetry panel has similarities with the work of, amongst others, the Dutch artist Balthasar van der Ast (1593/4–1657) and the French painter Jaques Linard (1597–1645). Marquetry cutters at Jackson & Graham were highly skilled and this panel appears to be either a copy of a presently unrecorded image or a composite from various sources. The early shell artists working in oils produced highly coloured panels. The monotone colouring of the panel suggests that the unnamed marquetry cutter was working from an engraving. Amongst the wide variety of shell specimens depicted are Junonia, Troschel's Murex, Common Spider Conch, Abalone, Pod razor shell and sea urchin.

Bibliography

Ackermann 1809–28
R. Ackermann, *Repository of Arts, Literature, Commerce, Manufactures, Fashions and Politics*, 3 ser., 40 vols, London.

Adams 1926
M. Adams, *My Book of Furniture*, London.

Agius 1978
P. Agius, *British Furniture, 1880–1915*, Woodbridge.

Aitken 1866
W.C. Aitken, *The Early History of Brass and the Brass Manufactures of Birmingham*, London.

Aldrich 1990
M. Aldrich (ed.) *The Traces: Royal Decorators 1768-1899*, London.

Allwood 1988
R. Allwood, 'Luxury Furniture Makers of the Victorian Period', *Antique Collecting*, vol. 23, no. 2, pp. 4–8.

Allwood 1990
R. Allwood, 'Thomas Sopwith of Newcastle 1803–1879', *Furniture History* 26, pp. 1–9.

Allwood 1996
R. Allwood, 'Machine Carving of the 1840s, and the Catalogue of the Patent Wood Carving Company', *Furniture History*, vol. 32, pp. 90–126.

Ames 1968
W. Ames, *Prince Albert and Victorian Taste*, New York.

Ames 1974
K. Ames, 'The Battle of the Sideboards', *Winterthur Portfolio*, vol. 9, pp. 1–27.

Art of Furnishing 1880
Anon., 'The Art of Furnishing. III. The Drawing Room', *The Art Amateur*, vol. 3, no. 4, pp. 81–83.

Aslet 1979
C. Aslet, '"A Mini Mentmore"', *Country Life*, vol. 166, no. 4299, pp. 2084, 2087.

Aslet 1982
C. Aslet, *The Last Country Houses*, London and New Haven CT.

Aslet 1984a
C. Aslet, 'Kinloch Castle, Isle of Rhum I', *Country Life*, vol. 176, no. 4538, pp. 380–84.

Aslet 1984b
C. Aslet, 'Kinloch Castle, Isle of Rhum II', *Country Life*, vol. 176, no. 4539, pp. 446–49.

Aslin 1962
E. Aslin, *19th Century English Furniture*, London.

Baarsen 1993
R. Baarsen, 'French Furniture in Amsterdam in 1771', *Furniture History*, vol. 29, pp. 114–28.

Baird 2016
C. Baird, *Showcase Britain: Britain at the Vienna World Exhibition 1873*, Bern.

Ball 1978
J. Ball, 'John Manuel & Son of Sheffield', *Furniture History*, vol. 14, pp. 62–65.

Bamford 1983
F. Bamford, 'A Dictionary of Edinburgh Wrights and Furniture Makers 1660–1840', *Furniture History*, vol. 19, pp. 1–137.

Barty-King 1992
H. Barty-King, *Maples Fine Furnishers: A Household Word for 150 Years*, London.

Beard & Gilbert 1986
G. Beard and C. Gilbert, *Dictionary of English Furniture Makers, 1660–1840*, Leeds.

Beavers 1999
D. Beavers, *Preston Manor*, Royal Pavilion Libraries & Museums.

Bennett 2005
D. Bennett, *Shapland & Petter Ltd of Barnstaple*, Barnstaple.

Bevan 1876–77
G.P. Bevan (ed.), *British Manufacturing Industries*, 15 vols, London.

Beavan 1896
A.H. Beavan, *Marlborough House and its Occupants Past and Present*, London.

Betjeman 1933
J. Betjeman, *Ghastly Good Taste*, London.

Boekmann 1996
D. Boekmann, 'Ludwig Grüner, Art Advisor to Prince Albert', unpublished thesis, University of East Anglia.

Book of Prices 1831
Anon., *The London Cabinet Makers' Book of Prices*, London.

Booth 1891
C. Booth (ed.), *Labour and the Life of the People*, 2 vols, London.

Bowett 1999
A. Bowett, *English Furniture, 1660–1714: From Charles II to Queen Anne*, Woodbridge.

Bowett 2009
A. Bowett, *Early Georgian Furniture, 1715–1740*, Woodbridge.

Bowett 2012
A. Bowett, *Woods in British Furniture Making, 1400-1900: An Illustrated Dictionary*, London.

Boynton 1995
L. Boynton, *Gillow Furniture Designs, 1760–1800*, London.

Brinsden 2004
J. Brinsden, 'Furniture Makers in Eighteenth Century Aberdeen: An Introduction', *Regional Furniture*, vol. 18, pp. 30–48.

Brook 1889
R. Brook, *Elements of Style in Furniture and Woodwork*, London.

Brown 1835
R. Brown, *The Rudiments of Drawing Cabinet and Upholstery Furniture*, London.

Bullock n.d.
W. Bullock, *Timbers for Woodwork*, London.

Burton 1999
A. Burton, *Vision and Accident: The Story of the Victoria and Albert Museum*, London.

Callmann 1999
E. Callmann, 'William Blundell Spence and the Transformation of Renaissance Cassoni', *The Burlington Magazine*, vol. 141, no. 1155, pp. 338–48.

Cardwell et al. 1898
J.H. Cardwell et al., *Two Centuries of Soho: Its Institutions, Firms, and Amusements*, London.

Casey 2005
C. Casey, *Dublin: The Buildings of Ireland*, London and New Haven CT.

Centennial Exhibition 1876
Anon., 'The Centennial Exhibition. I', *The Art Journal*, new series, vol. 2, pp. 161–68.

Cescinsky 1931
H. Cescinsky, *The Gentle Art of Faking Furniture*, London.

Chevalier 1862
M. Chevalier, quoting Prosper Mérimée, *Considérations sur les applications à l'Exposition universelle, Exposition universelle de 1862 : rapports des membres de la section française du jury international sur l'ensemble de l'Exposition*, Paris, 1862, t. VI, p. 248.

Cheek et al. 1982
R. Cheek et al., *Newport Mansions: The Gilded Age*, Dublin NH.

Chippendale 1754 & 1762
T. Chippendale, *The Gentleman and Cabinet-Maker's Director*.

Claxton Stevens & Whittington 1983
C. Claxton Stevens and S. Whittington, *18th Century English Furniture: The Norman Adams Collection*, Woodbridge.

Coke 1891
T. Coke, *Hearth and Home: An Illustrated Weekly Journal for Gentlewomen*, published weekly, London.

Collard 1985
F. Collard, *Regency Furniture*, Woodbridge.

Collard 1996
F. Collard, 'Town & Emanuel', *Furniture History*, vol. 32, pp. 81–89.

Conway 1882
M.D. Conway, *Travels in South Kensington with Notes on Decorative Art and Architecture in England*, London.

Cooper 1987
J. Cooper, *Victorian and Edwardian Furniture and Interiors: From the Gothic Revival to Art Nouveau*, London.

Dakers 2011
C. Dakers, *A Genius for Money Business, Art and the Morrisons*, Yale.

Davis 2020
D. Davis, *The Tastemakers – British Dealers and the Anglo-Gallic Interiors, 1785–1865*, Los Angeles.

Dean 1989
J. Dean, 'The Regency Furniture in the Liverpool Town Hall', *Furniture History* 25, pp. 127–44.

De Bellaigue 1974
G. de Bellaigue, *The James A. de Rothschild Collection at Waddesdon Manor: Furniture, Clocks and Gilt Bronzes*, 2 vols, Fribourg.

De Bellaigue 1975a
G. de Bellaigue, 'Edward Holmes Baldock, Part 1', *The Connoisseur*, vol. 189, pp. 290–99.

De Bellaigue 1975b
G. de Bellaigue, 'Edward Holmes Baldock, Part 2', *The Connoisseur*, vol. 190, pp. 18–25.

Dumas 1908
F.G. Dumas, *The Franco-British Exhibition: Illustrated Review*, London.

Dunn 1904
H.T. Dunn, *Recollections of Dante Gabriel Rossetti and His Circle*, London.

Edis 1881
R.W. Edis, *Decoration & Furniture of Town Houses*, New York.

Eastlake 1895
E. Eastlake, *Journals and Correspondence of Lady Eastlake*, vol. 2.

Edwards 1969
R. Edwards, 'George Bullock as a Sculptor and Modeller', *The Connoisseur*, vol. 171, pp. 172–73.

Edwards 1994
C. Edwards, *Twentieth-Century Furniture: Materials, Manufacture and Markets*, Manchester.

Edwards 1995
C. Edwards, 'British Imports of American Furniture in the Later Nineteenth Century', *Furniture History*, vol. 31, pp. 210–16.

Edwards 1998
C. Edwards, 'The Firm of Jackson and Graham', *Furniture History*, vol. 34, pp. 238–65.

Edwards 2000
C. Edwards, *Encyclopedia of Furniture Material, Trades and Techniques*, Aldershot and Brookfield.

Edwards 2005
C. Edwards, *Turning Houses into Homes: A History of the Retailing and Consumption of Domestic Furnishings*, London.

Edwards 2011
C. Edwards, 'Tottenham Court Road: The Changing Fortunes of London's Furniture Street', *The London Journal*, vol. 36, pp. 140–60.

Edwards 2012
C. Edwards, 'Improving the Decoration of Furniture: Imitation and Mechanization in the Marquetry Process in Britain and America, 1850–1900', *Technology and Culture*, vol. 53, no. 2, pp. 401–34.

Edwards 2013
C. Edwards, 'Complete House Furnishers: The Retailer as Interior Designer in Nineteenth-Century London', *Journal of Interior Design*, vol. 38.

Edwards 2022
C. Edwards, *Collinson & Lock, Art Furnishers, Interior Decorators and Designers, 1870-1900*.

Edwards & Ramsay 1958
Ralph Edwards and L.G.G. Ramsay (eds), *Early Victorian, 1830–1860*, London.

Elder-Duncan 1907
J.H. Elder-Duncan, *The House Beautiful and Useful*, London.

Ellwood 1911
G.M. Ellwood, *English Furniture and Decoration, 1680–1800*

Ellwood 1995
Giles Ellwood, 'James Newton', *Furniture History*, vol. 31, pp. 129–205.

English Guide 1878
Anon., *The English Guide to the Paris Exhibition, 1878*, London.

Ferry 2003
K. Ferry, 'Printing the Alhambra: Owen Jones and Chromolithography', *Architectural History* 46, pp. 175–88.

Field & Bunney 1905
Horace Field and Michael Bunney. *English Domestic Architecture of the 17th and 18th Centuries*, 1905.

Fleming & Honour 1977
J. Fleming and H. Honour, *The Penguin Dictionary of Decorative Arts*, London.

Flores 1996
C.A.H. Flores, 'Owen Jones, Architect', unpublished thesis, Georgia Institute of Technology.

Floud 1958
P. Floud, 'Furniture', in Edwards and Ramsay 1958.

Gems of the Centennial Exhibition 1877
Anon., *Gems of the Centennial Exhibition*, New York.

Gere 1989
C. Gere, *Nineteenth-Century Decoration: The Art of the Interior*, New York.

Gibbs-Smith 1950
C.H. Gibbs-Smith (ed.), *The Great Exhibition of 1851: A Commemorative Album*, London.

Gilbert 1978a
C. Gilbert, *Furniture at Temple Newsam House and Lotherton Hall*, 2 vols, Leeds.

Gilbert 1978b
C. Gilbert, *The Life and Work of Thomas Chippendale*, Bristol.

Gilbert 1996
C. Gilbert, *Pictorial Dictionary of Marked London Furniture 1700–1840*, Leeds.

Gilbert 1997
C. Gilbert, 'Seddon, Sons and Shackleton', *Furniture History*, vol. 33, pp. 1–29.

Gilbert 1998
C. Gilbert, 'A Few Seddon Gleanings', *Furniture History*, vol. 34, pp. 226–37.

Gillows 1904
Gillow & Waring Ltd, *Examples of Furniture & Decoration by Gillows*, London.

Gloag & Hackenbroch 1958
J. Gloag and Y. Hackenbroch, *English Furniture with Some Furniture of Other Countries in the Irwin Untermyer Collection*, Cambridge MA.

Gonse 1879
L. Gonse (ed.), *L'Art Moderne à l'Exposition de 1878*, Paris.

Goodin & Morris 2017
A. Goodin and K.M. Morris (eds), *Orchestrating Elegance: Alma-Tadema and the Marquand Music Room*, Yale.

Gow 1996
I. Gow, 'Mary Queen of Scots meets Charles Rennie Rennie Mackintosh: Some Problems in the Historiography of the Scotch Baronial Revival Interior', *Furniture History*, vol. 32, pp. 1–32.

Gower 1883
R. Gower, *My Reminiscences*, 2 vols, London.

Great Industrial Exhibition 1853
Anon., *Official Catalogue of the Great Industrial Exhibition*, Dublin.

Grüner 1846
L. Grüner, *The Decorations of the Garden-Pavilion in the Grounds of Buckingham Palace*, London.

Guide 1851
A Guide to the Great Exhibition: containing a description of every principal object of interest: with a plan, pointing out the easiest and most systematic way of examining the contents of the Crystal Palace, London.

Hall 1996
Melanie Hall, 'James Plucknett of Warwick and Leamington Spa', *Furniture History*, vol. 32, pp. 159–78.

Hall 1996
Michael Hall, '"Furniture of Artistic Character": Watts and Company as House Furnishers, 1874–1907', *Furniture History*, vol. 32, pp. 179–204.

Hamilton 1882
W. Hamilton, *The Aesthetic Movement in England*, London.

Hamilton-Gordon 1925
J. Hamilton-Gordon and I. Hamilton-Gordon, *We Twa*, 2 vols, London.

Harris 1973
E. Harris, *The Furniture of Robert Adam*, London.

Harris 2001
E. Harris, *The Genius of Robert Adam: His Interiors*, London and New Haven CT.

Harrison Moore 2011
A. Harrison Moore, *Fraud, Fakery and False Business: Rethinking the Shrager versus Dighton 'Old Furniture Case'*, London and New York.

Haweis 1881
H.R. Haweis, *The Art of Decoration*, London.

Hayward et al. 1965
H. Hayward et al., *World Furniture*, H. Hayward (ed.), London.

Hayward & Kirkham 1980
H. Hayward and P. Kirkham, *William and John Linnell*, London.

Hasluck 1901
Paul N. Hasluck, *Bamboo work: comprising the construction of furniture, household fitments, and other articles in bamboo*, London.

Heard & Jones 2019
K. Heard and K. Jones (eds), *George IV: Art and Spectacle*, London.

Hildesley 1923
P.T. Hildesley, *English Furniture Designs*, London.

Holman 1905
W.H. Holman, *Pre-Raphaelitism and the Pre-Raphaelite Brotherhood*, 2 vols, London and New York.

Holley 1981
D. Holley, 'Upholstery Springs', *Furniture History* 17, pp. 64–67.

Holmes 2012
S.E. Holmes, *The Paradise of Furness: The Story of Conishead Priory and its People*, Ulverston.

Hope 1807
T. Hope, *Household Furniture and Interior Decoration*, London.

Hope 1809
T. Hope, *Costume of the Ancients*, 2 vols, London.

Hughes 1987
P. Hughes, 'Replicas of French Furniture made for the 4th Marquess of Hertford', *Antologia di Belle Arti* 31–32, pp. 50–61.

Hull 2006
L. Hull, *Britain's Medieval Castles*, Westport.

Humphreys 1908
A.L. Humphreys, *Catalogue of the Collection of Works of Art at Minley Manor*, privately published.

Illustrated Catalogue 1851
Anon., *The Art Journal Illustrated Catalogue: The Industry of All Nations*, London.

Illustrated Catalogue 1862
Anon., *The Art Journal Illustrated Catalogue of the International Exhibition*, London.

Illustrated Catalogue 1878
Anon., *The Art Journal illustrated catalogue of the Paris International Exhibition*, London.

Ingamells 1981
J. Ingamells (ed.), *The Hertford Mawson Letters: The 4th Marquess of Hertford to his Agent Samuel Mawson*, London.

International Exhibition Report 1906
Anon., *Report of His Majesty's Commission for the International Exhibition, Saint Louis 1904*, London.

Jaffer 2001
A. Jaffer, *Furniture from British India and Ceylon*, London.

Jacobsen et al. 2020
H. Jacobsen et al., *Jean-Henri Riesener: Cabinetmaker to Louis XVI & Marie-Antoinette*, London.

Jennings 1902
H.J. Jennings, *Our Homes, and How to Beautify Them*.

Jervis 1968
S. Jervis, *Victorian Furniture*, London.

Jones 1856
O. Jones, *The Grammar of Ornament*, London.

Jones 1997
R. Jones, 'Arthur Foley: A Nineteenth-Century Cabinet Manufacturer in Salisbury', *Regional Furniture*, vol. 11, pp. 42–49.

Joy 1969
E. Joy, 'The Royal Victorian Furniture-Makers, 1837–87', *The Burlington Magazine*, vol. 111, no. 800, pp. 677–84, 687.

Joy 1977
E. Joy, *English Furniture 1800–1851*, London.

Kinchin 1985
J. Kinchin, 'The Wylie & Lochhead Style', *The Journal of the Decorative Arts Society, 1850 to the Present*, vol. 9, pp. 4–16.

Kirkham 1980
P. Kirkham, 'Inlay, Marquetry and Buhl Workers in England, *c.* 1660–1850', *The Burlington Magazine*, vol. 22, no. 927, pp. 415–16, 419.

Kirkham 1982
P. Kirkham, 'Furniture-Making in London *c.* 1700–1870: Craft, Design, Business and Labour', unpublished thesis, Westfield College.

Kirkham 1989
P. Kirkham, *The London Furniture Trade, 1700–1870*, London.

Kirkham et al. 1987
P. Kirkham et al., *Furnishing the World: The East London Furniture Trade, 1830–1980*, London.

Kjellberg 1989
P. Kjellberg, *Le Mobilier Français du XVIIIth Siècle*, Paris.

Koyama-Richard 2002
B. Koyama-Richard, *Japon Rêvé. Edmond de Goncourt et Hayashi Tadamasa*, Paris.

Lee 1980
A. Lee, *British Regional Employment Statistics, 1841-1971*, Cambridge.

Gilbert 1998
C. Gilbert, 'A Critical Survey: The Curator's View', in *Masterpieces of English Furniture: The Gerstenfeld Collection*, Edward Lennox-Boyd (ed.), London.

Lenygon 1909
F. Lenygon, *The Decoration & Furniture of English Mansions during the Seventeenth & Eighteenth Centuries*, London.

Levy 2005
M. Levy, 'E.H. Baldock and the Blake Family: Further Evidence', *Furniture History Society Newsletter*, no. 158, pp. 1–3.

Lindfield 2016
P. Lindeld, *Georgian Gothic: Medievalist Architecture, Furniture and Interiors, 1730–1840*, Woodbridge.

Litchfield 1903
F. Litchfield, *The Illustrated History of Furniture*, London and New York.

Litchfield 1921
F. Litchfield, *Antiques, Genuine and Spurious. An Art Expert's Recollections and Cautions*, London.

Livingstone 2016
K. Livingstone (ed.), *C.F.A. Voysey Arts & Crafts Designer*, London.

Lomax 1997
J. Lomax, 'Buying Antiques in Early Victorian Leeds: The 1843 Exhibition', *Furniture History*, vol. 33, pp. 275–85.

Loudon 1834–38
J.C. Loudon, *The Architectural Magazine*, 5 vols, London.

Loudon 1842
J.C. Loudon, *An Encyclopaedia of Cottage, Farm, and Villa Architecture and Furniture*, London.

Macquoid 1904–1908
P. Macquoid, *History of English Furniture*, 4 vols, London and New York.

Macquoid & Edwards 1924
P. Macquoid, and R. Edwards, *The Dictionary of English Furniture*, 3 vols, London and New York.

Massil 1997
W. Massil, *Immigrant Furniture Makers in London 1881–1939*, The Jewish Museum.

Meyer 2001
J. Meyer, 'Trollope and Sons – Makers and Exhibitors of Fine Furniture', *The Journal of the Decorative Arts Society 1850 to the Present*, no. 25, pp. 87–96.

Meyer 2006
J. Meyer, *Great Exhibitions: London, Paris, New York, Philadelphia 1851–1900*, Woodbridge.

Microulis 2001
L. Microulis, 'The Furniture Drawings of Charles Hindley and Sons, 134 Oxford Street, London', *Furniture History*, vol. 37, pp. 67–90.

Mogg 1844
E. Mogg, *Mogg's New Picture of London, and Visitors' Guide to its Sights*, London.

Moore 2005
A. Moore, *Francis de Groot: Irish fascist, Australian Legend*, Alexandria NSW.

Mordaunt Crook 1999
J. Mordaunt Crook, *The Rise of the Nouveaux Riches: Style and Status in Victorian and Edwardian Architecture*, London.

Morris 1910
A.F. Morris, 'Sir John Murray Scott's Collection in the Rue Lafitte, Paris', *The Connoisseur*, vol. 27, pp. 231–40.

Morris 1911
A.F. Morris, 'Sir John Murray Scott's Collection in the Rue Lafitte, Paris, Part II', *The Connoisseur*, vol. 29, pp. 215–22.

Morris 2018
K. Morris, 'A Patent Worth Protecting: Jupe's Improved Expanding Dining Table, *Furniture History Society Newsletter*, no. 209, pp. 2–7.

Morris & Company 1912
Specimens of Furniture and Interior Decoration: Morris and Company Decorators, Ltd, 'By Royal Warrant Furnishers to H.M. The King'.

Muirhead 1918
F. Muirhead, *London and its Environs*, London.

Munday 1999
E. Munday, *Irish Furniture*, symposium papers presented at the Victoria & Albert Museum, Furniture History Society, 6 February 1999, London.

Musgrave 1948
C. Musgrave (ed.), *The Regency Festival: Regency Exhibition Catalogue*, Brighton.

Muthesius 2009
S. Muthesius, *The Poetic Home*, London.

Naylor 1971
G. Naylor, *The Arts and Crafts Movement*, London.

Neto 2017
Maria João Neto, Monserrate Revisited – The Cook Collection in Portugal

Nicolay 1956
J. Nicolay, *L'art et la manière des maîtres ebénistes français au XVIIIe siècle*, Paris.

Nicholson 1826
P. Nicholson, *The Cabinet Maker, Upholsterer and Complete Decorator*, London.

Oliver 1966
J.D. Oliver, *The Development and Structure of the Furniture Industry*, London.

Pascoe 1891
C.E. Pascoe, *London of To-day*, Boston.

Patent Wood Carvings 1845
Anon., *Patent Wood Carvings*, London.

Payne 1981
C. Payne, *19th Century European Furniture*, Woodbridge.

Payne 1989
C. Payne, 'Baldock, Beckford, Bridgens and Bullock', *Antique Collecting*, January 1989.

Payne 1989
C. Payne (ed.), *Sotheby's Concise Encyclopedia of Furniture*, London.

Payne 2003
C. Payne, *François Linke 1855–1946: The Belle Epoque of French Furniture*, Woodbridge.

Payne 2018
C. Payne, *Paris Furniture: The Luxury Market of the 19th Century*, Saint-Rémy-en-l'Eau.

Penick & Long 2019
M. Penick and C. Long (eds), *The Rise of Everyday Design: The Arts and Crafts Movement in Britain and America*, London and New Haven CT.

Percier & Fontaine 1801
C. Percier and P.-F.-L. Fontaine, *Recueil de décorations intérieures*, Paris.

Pinto & Pinto 1970
E. Pinto and E. Pinto, *Tunbridge and Scottish Souvenir Woodware*, London.

Pollen 1912
A. Pollen, *John Hungerford Pollen*, London.

Pradère 1989
A. Pradère, *French Furniture Makers: The Art of the Ébéniste from Louis XIV to the Revolution*, Los Angeles.

Reade 1953
B.E. Reade, *Regency Antiques*, London.

Recollections 1851
Anon., *Recollections of the Great Exhibition of All Nations*, London.

Report 1854
Anon., *First Report of the Department of Science and Art*, London.

Reports 1856
Anon., *Reports on the Paris Universal Exhibition*, London.

Reynolds 1905
J. Reynolds, *Discourses Delivered to the Students of the Royal Academy*, London.

Roberts 1995
H. Roberts, 'The First Carlton House Table?', *Furniture History*, vol. 31, pp. 124–28.

Roberts 2001
H. Roberts, *For The King's Pleasure: The Furnishing and Decoration of George IV's Apartments at Windsor Castle*, London.

Robinson 1979
J.M. Robinson, 'Carlton and the Stapletons: The History of a Recusant Family', *The Connoisseur*, vol. 202, p.21.

Robinson 1856
J.C. Robinson, *Catalogue of the Soulages Collection*, London.

Robinson 1999
J.M. Robinson, 'Knowsley Hall, Lancashire, A Seat of the Earl of Derby', *Country Life*, vol. 193, no. 15, pp. 70–75.

Rogers 1930
J.C. Rogers, *Modern English Furniture*, Country Life, c.1930.

Rubens 1986
G. Rubens, *William Richard Lethaby: His Life and Work 1857–1931*, London.

Sala 1868
G.A. Sala, *Notes and Sketches of the Paris Exhibition*, London.

Seligman 1961
G. Seligman, *Merchants of Art, 1880–1960: Eighty Years of Professional Collecting*, New York.

Sheppard 1960
F.H.W. Sheppard, *Survey of London: St James's Westminster, Part 1*, 2 vols, London.

Sheraton 1791 & 1793
T. Sheraton, *The Cabinet-Maker and Upholsterer's Drawing Book*, London.

Shone 1999
R. Shone, *The Art of Bloomsbury: Roger Fry, Vanessa Bell and Duncan Grant*, Princeton.

Smith 1808
G. Smith, *Collection of Designs for Household Furniture and Interior Decoration*, London.

Smith 1826
G. Smith, *The Cabinet-Maker and Upholsterer's Guide*, London.

Smith 1875
W. Smith, *Examples of Household Taste*, New York.

Smith & Rogers 2006
J. Smith and R. Rogers, *Behind the Veneer: The South Shoreditch Furniture Trade and its Buildings*, Swindon.

The Society of Arts 1879
Artisan Reports on the Paris Universal Exhibition of 1878, London.

Spielmann 1906
I. Spielmann, *Royal Commission: St. Louis International Exhibition, 1904: The British Section*, London.

Stuart 2008
S. Stuart, *Gillows of Lancaster and London, 1730–1840*, 2 vols, London.

Symonds & Whineray 1965
R.W. Symonds and B.B. Whineray, *Victorian Furniture*, London.

Talbert 1971
B.J. Talbert, *Gothic Forms. Examples of Ancient and Modern Furniture*, London.

Tomlin 1972
M. Tomlin, *Catalogue of Adam Period Furniture*, London.

Vardy 1744
J. Vardy, *Some Designs of Mr. Inigo Jones and Mr. Wm. Kent*, London.

Vaughan 1984
A. Vaughan, *The Vaughans. East End Furniture Makers. Three Hundred Years of a London Family*, London.

Verlet 1956
P. Verlet, *Les meubles français du XVIIIe siècle*, 2 vols, Paris.

Verlet 1987
P. Verlet, *Les bronzes dorés français du XVIIIe siècle*, Paris.

Wade 2012
R.J. Wade, 'Pedagogic Objects: The Formation, Circulation and Exhibition of Teaching Collections for Art and Design Education in Leeds, 1837–1857', unpublished thesis, University of Leeds.

Wainwright et al. 1988
C. Wainwright et al., *George Bullock: Cabinet Maker*, London.

Waring 1862
J.B. Waring, *Masterpieces of Industrial Art & Sculpture at the International Exhibition*, 3 vols, London.

Watson 1956
F.J.B. Watson, *Wallace Collection Catalogues: Furniture*, London.

Weale 1858
J. Weale, *Old English and French Ornaments*, London.

Weaver 1928
L. Weaver, 'Tradition & Modernity in Craftsmanship, Part II,' *The Architectural Review*.

Webb 1921
E.A. Webb, *The Records of St. Bartholomew's Priory and of The Church and Parish of St. Bartholomew the Great, West Smithfield*, 2 vols, Oxford.

Weber 2014
S. Weber (ed.), *William Kent: Designing Georgian Britain*, London and New Haven CT.

Wells & Hooper 1910
P. Wells and J. Hooper, *Modern Cabinetwork, Furniture, And Fitments*, London and New York.

Westgarth 2009
M. Westgarth, 'A Biographical Dictionary of Nineteenth Century Antique and Curiosity Dealers', *Regional Furniture*, vol. 23, pp. 57–191.

Whitaker 1847
H. Whitaker, *The Practical Cabinet Maker & Upholsterer's Treasury of Designs*, London.

Williamson 1919
G.C. Williamson, *Murray Marks and His Friends*, London and New York.

Winternitz 1966
E. Winternitz, *Musical Instruments of the Western World*, London.

Wood 1994
L. Wood, *Catalogue of Commodes*, London.

Wornum 1851
R.N. Wornum, 'The Exhibition as a Lesson in Taste', in Illustrated Catalogue 1851.

Wyatt 1851–53
M.D. Wyatt, *The Industrial Arts of the Nineteenth Century*, 2 vols, London.

Wyatt 1856
M.D. Wyatt, 'On Furniture and Decoration', in Reports 1856.

Yapp 1879
G.W. Yapp, *Art Industry: Furniture, House Fittings and Decorations*, London.

Yorke 2001
J. Yorke, *Lancaster House: London's Greatest Townhouse*, London.

Two distinct and contrasting styles of marquetry showing the skills of the nineteenth-century marqueteur. Above is the top of the centre table formerly in the collection of Hannah de Rothschild, the base with three boldly modelled gilt-bronze dolphin supports (see Frontispiece p.5), on the right, a recently identified marquetry table veneered in satinwood probably designed for Alfred Morrison. The 'Old French' floral inlay of the Rothschild table dates to the 1840s and is inlaid with polychrome marquetry on a quarter-veneered ebony ground with flowers, birds and butterflies divided by six grotesque masks in the style associated with André-Charles Boulle. The other table is highly stylised and is a radical new form of design by Owen Jones reminiscent of his influential *Grammar of Ornament* of 1856.

By the mid-nineteenth century, refinements to earlier techniques and more sophisticated tools allowed up to twelve examples of the same marquetry element to be made by assembling up to twelve sheets of veneer in a single packet for cutting. The shading in hot sand was still carried out separately on each piece and, once completed, the numerous pieces of the design were assembled and inserted into the background veneer. This process encouraged the development of specialised marquetry workshops that produced ready-made marquetry and was a labour-intensive process, requiring extremely precise design resulting in a more perfect execution than most previous techniques. The marquetry of the Rothschild table is of a type closely associated with the London firm of Blake and was possibly supplied to the Rothschild family by Edward Holmes Baldock. The more formal, stylised marquetry table with outset lobes was almost certainly made by Jackson & Graham for 16 Carlton House Terrace between 1867 and 1870. It shows the radical aesthetic of Owen Jones comparable to the armchair **Fig. 5.119**. The table is thought to be part of a group of furniture made for Morrison and later exhibited at the London International Exhibition of 1874 as a tribute to the late Owen Jones, who as a young man had been a friend of Morrison's father, James.

Index

Arab Room **348**; 348, 381
Abbot Hall Art Gallery and Museum 252
Abbot of Colchester 191
Abbotsford 66; 24, 39, 67
Abelard, Peter 295
Abercrombie, Sir Robert 140
Aberdeen, 1st Marquess of 341
Aberdeen, Lady 256, 315, 318–19, 341
Abraham 515
Ackermann, Rudolph 29, 31, 43, 54, 56, 423
Acts of Parliament 507, 511–12
Adam 232, 256, 290, 314, 434, 443, 448, 463, 514, 518
Adam, James 256, 514
Adam, Robert 243, 256, 281, 346, 428, 430, 438, 444, 447–48, 461, 514
Adam, William 256, 514
Adams, Henry 364
Adams, Maurice B. 366, 414, 518, 537
Adelaide, Queen, wife of William IV 91
Adelphi Hotel, Liverpool 393
Aeolian Co. Ltd 512
Air Ministry 512
Aitchison, George 296, 297, 381, 382
Aitken 188
Albert, Prince 122, 124, 132–33, 163, 167, 171–72, 174, 191, 196, 198, 213–14, 216, 225, 248, 256, 265
Alcock, Sir Rutherford 272–73
Aldersgate Street 52
Alexander II, Tsar of Russia 347
Alexander Palace, St Petersburg 406
Alexandra Palace, London 225, 349
Alexandra Park Company 305
Alexandra, Princess of Denmark 264, 268, 509
Alexandra, Queen 267–68, 473–74
Alhambra Court 175
Alhambra Palace, Spain 381, 555
Alice Maria, Lady 279

Allan, Sir William 67
Allcroft, John Derby 233, 242–43, 374
Allen & Manooch 407
Alliance Cabinet Makers' Association 391
Allom, Charles 468, 527, 529
Alma-Tadema, Anna 341
Alma-Tadema, Lawrence 323, 328, 341, 343, 355, 384–85
Alnwick Castle **265**; 152, 219–20, 231, 261, 265
Alsop, Uriah 352
Ames, Kenneth 275
Amor, Albert 495
Andersen 279
Andersen, Hans Christian 186, 190
Angus, James Barr 406, 412
Angus, William 363
Angus & Co. 414
Anne, Queen 499
Annear, James 161, 163
Anslow, John of Coventry 510
Anslow Ltd, Coventry **510**; 510
Antique & Foreign Furniture Co. 353
Apsley House, Hyde Park Corner, London **345**; 74, 345
Aquitania 531
Architectural Carving Works 130
Argenteuil, Héloïse d' 295
Armdale Castle 24
Armitage, George Faulkner 383, 456
Armstrong, Sir William 289, 305
Army & Navy Stores **530**; 473, 475, 530
Arrowsmith, Arthur 366
Arrowsmith, Henry 366
Arrowsmith, William 366
Art Furnishers' Alliance 355–56
Art Furniture Company 239, 325
Art Workers' Guild 379, 385–86, 399, 454

Arthur, Prince (Duke of Connaught and Strathearn) 287–88, 307
Arts and Crafts Exhibition Society 379, 385–86, 399, 407, 416
Arts and Crafts Society, London 457
Arts and Crafts Society of Ireland 449
Arundel Castle 132
Ashbee, C.R. 397–400
Ashburton, Lord 364
Aslin 372
Aston Hall 39, 42
Astor, 1st Viscount 235, 438
Astor House 438
Atholl, 4th Duke of 253
Atkinson & Co. **393**; 368, 391, 393–94
Attingham Park 52
auctions:
 Baldock (1843) 74, 87, 196, 198
 Christie's 83; (1849) 90; (1880) 151; (1851) 169
 Erlestoke Park, 1832 32
 Hamilton Palace Collection 275; (1882) 360–2
 Heritage Auctions, Texas (2012) 546
 Hertford (1913) 218
 Mellier & Co. 361
 Nicholls & Janes (1969) 484
 Plucknett, James (1908) 467
 Robbins auctioneers (1827) 538
 Rothschild (1937) 223
 Taylor, George Watson (1825) 220
 timber auction, Liverpool (April 1873) 290–91
 Town & Emanuel 91, 100, 101; (1849) 91,
 Wilkinson (1892) 412
 Wright & Mansfield 322; (1886) 257, 259, 359; (1887) 320, 323, 359
Audas & Leggott of Hull 327
Aulmont, Femme 220
Avant, Arthur 482

Baccarat 307
Bailey, Edward 66
Bailey & Co. 408
Baines, Sir Frank 510
Baird 305
Baker of Bath 520
Baldock, E.H. 24, 36–37, 74, 76–8, 83, 85–7, 89, 95, 99, 100, 119, 126, 133, 138, 144, 152–61, 163, 169, 198, 220, 223, 400, 563
Baldock, W. 456
Balfour, Eustace 368
Balmoral Castle **213**; 212–14, 428
Bamburgh Castle 305
Bamford, G. 21
Banting, France & Co. 174–75, 184
Bantings 358
Barbedienne, Ferdinand of Paris 198, 202, 359
Barbedienne foundry, Paris 313,
Barchard, Francis 195
Bardini, Stefano 444
Barfield, Samuel 456
Barker & Co. 443
Barlow, Francis 455
Barnard, Bradley 339
Barnett Moss, London 353
Barnsley, Ernest and Sidney 397–98, 451, 510–11, 537
Barnsleys' workshop, Pinbury **397**; 397
Barrie, J. 191
Barrow, John 208
Barry, Sir Charles 43, 55, 72, 124
Bartholomew & Fletcher 443
Bartlett & Sons **510**; 412, 508, 510, 515
Barton, J.S. 291
Bastendorff & Co. 343
Bates, T.H. 191
Bath, 4th Marquess of 235
Bath Cabinet Makers Company 398–99, 455, 468, 487, 510

INDEX

Bath House, Piccadilly 315
Batley, Henry W. 285, 287, 296, 313, 327
Battiscombe & Harris 527
Battle Abbey 24, 39
Baumhauer, Joseph 149, 154, 156–57, 159
Beakey, Patrick 197, 283
Beakey & McDowell 283
Beaufort, 4th Duke of 491
Beaumanor Hall **126**; 122, 126
Beaumont, 8th Baron 79
Beavan 261, 264, 267
Beavis, R. 188, 193
Beckford, William 36, 77, 106, 356
Bective, Earl of 279
Bedford, Francis 237
Bedford, John 575
Beeching, Mr 370
Beer, Rachel 393
Befort of Paris 91, 222
Bell, John 201, 203
Bell, Vanessa 505
Bellaigue, Geoffrey de 77, 386
Belle Vue House, Chelsea **343**; 341, 343
Belton House 58
Belvoir Castle **34–5**; 33, 36–7, 43, 72–3, 132
Benjamin, H.L. 410, 412
Benn, Henry Pringuer 407, 487
Benn, Lieutenant William Wedgwood 508
Benn Brothers 508
Bennett, George 441, 455
Benson, Robert H. 482
Benson, W.A.S. 385–86, 408, 471–72, 517
Bérain, Jean 38–9, 151, 153
Beresford & Hicks 531
Berkeley Hotel, London **400**; 381, 400
Berkeley Square, No. 15 297
Berlin Woolwork 206
Bertram, William of Dean Street 352, 460
Bertram & Son 255, 423, 430, 460–61, 468, 472
Berwick, Lord 52
Bessant, Charles 460–61
Bethnal Green Museum 220, 258, 291, 293, 481
Betjemann & Sons 374, 378, 533
Bettridge, James 167
Bevan, Charles 201, 226, 235, 240, 269, 304, 306, 347, 351
Bevis, Richard 270
Bianco & Sons 506
Biedermeier 268
Bihan, P. Le 172
Biltmore, North Carolina 575
Binns, Joseph 39
Birch, William 330, 356, 398, 399, 470, 474, 508, 511
Birch & Co. 408
Birley, Samuel 175, 227–28
Birmingham City Museum and Art Gallery 22
Blackie & Sons 206
Blain & Son 127
Blair Castle 24
Blake, Charles 151–52, 245, 261
Blake, George Henry 149, 151
Blake, Henry 152, 261
Blake, James 151
Blake, Robert 25, 87, 144, 151

Blake family/workshop 77–80, 83, 85, 87–8, 91, 94, 100, 144–45, 149, 151, 153–54, 156, 159, 169, 214–15, 218–20, 3241, 243–44, 265, 563
Blanchard, Francis and Arentina 212
Blenheim 257
Blois, Château de 322
Blomfield, Reginald 454, 510
Bloomsbury Group 504
Blow, Detmar 397
Blower, J. & B. 502
Blyth, James 1st Baron 440
Blyth & Sons 369, 384
Bodley, G.F. 478
Boer War 456
Bolton, Matthew 24
Bolton Hall 24
Bonaparte, Napoleon I, Emperor of France 23, 113, 117, 220
Bonaparte, Napoleon III, Emperor of France 55, 215, 281, 298
Bonaparte, Prince Napoleon 298
Booker family 283
Booth, Charles 369, 370
Booth, Lorenzo 43
Boson, John 499
Boswell Studios 510
Bott, Thomas 264
Boughton House 160, 219, 241
Boulle, André-Charles 19, 32–3, 36–7, 99, 145, 214–16, 218–20, 222–23, 245, 257, 298, 333, 562
Boulton family 132
Boulton, Matthew 233
Bourbon kings 85
Bourgogne, Duchesse de 222
Bowen 396
Bowhill House **144**; 79, 87, 93–4, 140–41, 144, 196, 223
Boyton Manor 31
Braddyll, Colonel 124
Bradley, I. 322
Bramah, Joseph 110–11, 315, 344
Brangwyn, Frank 398, 501
Brassey, Henry 298–99, 302, 308, 312
Braybrooke, 3rd Baron 91
Brew 351
Brew & Claris 349–51, 361
Brewer, Cecil 399
Bridge Wharf on the River Taw, Barnstaple **466**; 466
Bridgens, Richard 24–5, 39, 42, 44, 72, 78–9, 83–7, 89, 106, 115, 119, 132, 161, 163–64, 175, 206, 374
Briggs & Co. 510
Brighton Pavilion 21, 32, 52, 176, 286
Bristol, 1st Marquess of 75
British Antique Dealers Association 477
British Commissioner House, Vienna 307
British Consul, Tokyo 272
British Horological Institute 256
British Museum 323, 325, 328, 355–56, 492
British Patent Office 285
Britnell, J. 415
Broadwood & Sons 453
Brook House, Park Lane, London 252, 315–18
Brook, Rupert 353
Brookshaw, George 256, 417, 424
Brotherton Library 575
Broughton Hall 61

Brown, Richard 23–4, 26
Brown, W.S. 361, 363
Brown & Smart of Nottingham 510
Brown Brothers, Edinburgh 312
Brownlee, James 466
Brownlee & Co. 466, 473
— City Saw Mills 466
Bruce, Lady Augusta 213
Bruce, Tyndall 125
Brun, Charles Le 36
Brunelleschi, Filippo 322
Brustolon, Andrea 92, 130
Buccleuch, 5th Duchess of 78, 141–42, 166, 181, 196
Buccleuch, 5th Duke of 77–9, 84, 87, 95, 99, 100, 130, 132–33, 140–41, 143, 152–54, 159, 161, 163, 214, 216, 219–20, 223
Buchanan Street Tea Rooms, Glasgow 399
Buchschmid & Gretaux 455
Buck, Adam 431
Buckingham, Duke of 77
Buckingham House
Buckingham Palace (form. Buckingham House) **286, 527**; 67, 116, 124, 129, 143, 168, 174, 286, 416–17, 468, 473, 527, 529
— Garden Pavilion **129**; 129
— Octagon Library, **421**; 416, 421
Buckingham Street, No. 15 **237–38**; 237
Buckler, J. & J.C. 52
Bullock, George 22–6, 37, 39, 43, 63, 65, 110, 132, 135, 235
Bullock, William 19, 23, 63, 467
Bullock & Wilkinson 71
Bullough, Sir George 346, 394
Bulwer-Lytton, Edward 124
Burges, William 233–39, 273, 302, 325, 381, 400
Burghley House **131, 137, 138**; 22, 37, 43, 92, 95, 126–27, 130–32, 136–38, 169, 183
Burgundy, Duke of 233
Burlington, 3rd Earl of 463–64
Burn, William 125, 132, 141
Burne-Jones, Edward 234, 279, 296, 298, 352, 385, 404
Burns, Robert 230
Burrowes & Son 363
Burton Constable Hall 183
Burty, Philippe 272
Buscot Park 436, 439
Bushloe House, near Leicester 356
Bute, 3rd Marquess of 381
Butler, Michael 447, 461–63
Butterfield, Henry 341–42
Byng, George 19

Caldecott, William 45, 184
Calder, John 175
California Redwood Company 361
Callot, Jacques 87, 91, 154
Calvert, Dr 186
Cambridge, Duke of 176
Cambridge House, No. 94, Piccadilly 303
Cambridge Street Works 188
Cambridge University 175
Camelford House 219
Campbell, John 2nd Marquess of Breadalbane 77
Cannon Hall Museum 259
Cantor Lectures 344

Capel, Henry 331
Capel, James 331
Capel Art Furniture showrooms, Great Titchfield Street **331**; 331
Cardiff Castle 233, 381
Carlhian & Beaumetz of Paris 411, 473–74, 492, 495, 575
Carlin, Martin 84, 158–59, 206, 236, 254
Carlisle House 399
Carlton Hotel, London 439
Carlton House 32, 52, 55, 115, 176, 481
Carlton House Terrace 438
— No. 16 275, 278, 298, 302, 563
— No. 21 267
Carlton Towers 79, 80, 106, 461
Carlyle Club, Piccadilly Circus 510
Carr, John 47
Carroll, Lewis 286
Casa-Museu Medeiros e Almeida, Lisbon 218–20
Castell Coch 381
Catherine Cranston's Luncheon Room, Glasgow 400
Cavamelli, Alfonso of Rome 162, 165
Cave, Walter 398, 467
Cavendish, Lady Frederick 267
Cawley & Co. 353
Cellini 270
Census (1881) 369
Central Aircraft Co. 512
Central School of Arts and Crafts 511–12
Century Guild of Artists 369, 372–73
Cerceau, du 324
Cescinsky, Herbert 357, 458, 502, 519
Chambers, Sir William 290
Champs Élysées, Paris 473
Chant, G. 408
Chapman, Son & Co. 512, 515
Charbonne, Paris 359
Charlecote Park, Warwickshire **84**; 77, 85, 91, 106, 130, 181
Charles, B. 306
Charles, Richard 272, 303
Charles II, King 45
Charles IV, King of Spain 504
Charles X, King of France 50, 52
Charles the Bold 232–33
Chateau-sur-Mer, Newport, Rhode Island 305
Chatsworth 183, 190, 195, 235
Chaucer, Geoffrey 264, 267, 300
Chequers Court, Great Chamber **441**; 441
Chesterfield Gardens, No. 7 **393**; 393
Child & Hinde 290
Ching, Comyn 315, 333, 347, 352, 359, 523
Chippendale, Thomas **359**; 37, 44, 47, 61, 69, 141, 166, 168, 232, 257–58, 260, 290, 315, 353, 363, 386, 394, 406, 411–12, 422, 436, 443–44, 448, 454, 456–58, 463, 472, 484, 490–92, 495, 501, 504, 511, 514, 518, 527, 529–32
Chiswick House 463–64
Chiswick Villa 499
Cholmondley Castle 24
Christie, Robert 347, 349, 436, 439, 532
Christie's 83, 90
Christofle of Paris 252
Chubb 94, 111, 160, 165, 167, 281, 298–99, 301, 315, 335, 555

567

Chubb & Son 355-56
Churchill & Sim 361, 507
Cipriani 314, 317
Clandon Park 95, 223
Claremont 83
Clarence House 248
Clarke 181
Clarke, Thomas 333
Clay, Henry of London 168, 187
Clementine 290
Cleveland, Duchess of 197
Cleveland, Duke of 181, 197
Cliffe Castle, Yorkshire **342**; 341-42
Cliveden 235, 438
Cluny Museum 281
Clyde Canal, Glasgow 466
Coalbrookdale 202, 359
Coalbrookdale Iron Company **203**; 168, 203
Coalbrookdale Museum of Iron, Shropshire 201
Coalport 85, 89
Coates, Sir Edward Feetham 492
Cobden-Sanderson, T.J. 386
Coghill, Sir John 173
Cohen & Sons 409, 507
Cohn 290
Cole, Henry 171, 202, 275, 279, 287, 292
Collard & Collard 285
Collard, Francis 91, 260
Collcutt, Thomas 290-91, 293, 296, 327, 329, 372
collections:
  Alcock, Sir Rutherford 272
  Armstrong, Sir William 305
  Bowhill 87
  Buccleuch 79, 86, 94, 144, 196, 214, 219, 220, 541
  Clarke, Purdon 383
  Coghill, Sir John 173
  Connaught, Duke of 380
  Devonshire, Duke of 499
  Frick 219, 542, 543
  Gilbert 36, 91
  Griffiths, Percival 518
  Hamilton Palace 360, 547
  Hamilton, Duke of 214
  Handley-Read 240
  Handley-Read, Charles 264, 309
  Hertford 218, 220
  Ionides 263, 382
  Jones 400, 544, 575
  Joules Soulages 213
  Lever 434
  Londesborough 22
  Mill, Sir Charles 214
  Minley Manor (formed by Bertram Wodehouse) 322, 324
  Newstead Abbey 48
  Normanton, Earls of 223
  Northumberland, Duke of 214
  Orrock 504, 552
  Parker, Frederick 12, 550
  Philadelphia Special Collections 575
  Rothschild 95, 163, 543
  Royal 52, 66, 100, 125, 196, 198, 206-7, 214, 504, 538, 539, 542, 549
  St Maurice 383
  Wallace 12, 37, 160, 215, 218-20, 222, 245, 481, 482, 538, 542, 543
  Westminster, Duke of 287
  Wimbourne, Lady 162

Collier & Plunknett 399
Colling, James Kellaway 202, 205
Collinson, Frank of Doncaster 177, 293, 360
Collinson & Lock **336, 402**; 239, 267, 290-91, 293, 296, 305, 313, 325-29, 334, 336, 339, 344, 348-49, 352, 355, 360, 362-63, 366, 368-70, 372-74, 378-80, 401-2, 404, 407, 413, 439, 455, 468
Collman, Leonard 339
Collman, Leonard William 119, 468
Colombo, Claudio 205
Columbia University, New York 498
Compton, Lord Alwyne 404, 406
Congreve, General Sir Walter Norris 374
Conishead Priory **125**; 105, 124-25
Connaught, Duke of 267, 380
Conrath & Sons 366, 438
Conservative and Unionist Club 110
Conservative Club 130
Constable, Lady 183
Conway, Moncure D. 341
Conyngham, 2nd Marquess of 230
Cook, James 364
Cook, Sir Francis 176
Cookes, William 86, 156, 159, 171, 185
Cookes & Sons **181**; 177, 181
Coombe Abbey 222
Cooper & Holt 304, 336, 339, 357
Cooper Hewitt Museum, New York 205
Cooper, Henry 346
Cooper, J. & H. 407
Cooper, John 346
Cope 359
Cope & Collinson 204, 315, 380
Cope & Timmins 253
Copeland 268
Copeland & Garrett 163, 165, 173
Corfe, Beatrice 483
Corfield, John 37
Cornwallis, Lord 250
Cottier, Daniel 326
Coulson & Co. 403, 473
Cowden Castle, Falkirk 317
Cowie, William 456
Cowtan 241, 243
Cowtan & Sons 243, 490-91
Cox 306
Cox & Son 133, 338
Cox & Yemen 440
Coxon, Robert 394
Crace 21, 56, 213, 225, 233, 283, 287, 302, 358, 366
Crace, Frederick 21
Crace, J.D. 285
Crace, John 286
Crace, John Dibblee 236, 438
Crace, John Gregory 55, 124, 189, 190, 193, 195, 213
Crace & Son 128, 235, 267
Crace family 124
Cragside 305
Crane, Walter 352, 379, 382
Cranston & Elliot 363
Craven, 2nd Earl of 220, 222
Cribb & Son 399
Crom Castle 78
Crook, Benjamin 520
Crosse 281, 256
Crouch, Joseph 407-9, 415
Croxteth Lodge, Liverpool **368**; 368
Croydon Cabinet 309

Crozatier, Charles 74, 215
Crystal Palace, Sydenham (see also: Exhibitions) 175, 359, 366, 407, 513;
— exhibition building **170**; 171
— Egyptian Court 175
— Greek Court 175
Cucci, Domenico 36, 77
Cuddesdon College 212
Currie, Raikes 322
Curries & Co. bank 322
Curtain Road, No. 117 411

D'Arcy, William Knox 404
D'Oyly Carte, Richard 349
Daguerre, Dominique 55
Dalkeith Palace **99**; 94, 99, 133, 141, 143
Daly, John 363
Dalziel, William 69
Daneway House workshop 454
Dante 338
Darby, John and Joan 394
Darmanin, Joseph 72
Dasson, Henry 215, 219, 264, 333, 335, 361, 364, 575
Davey, R. 290
Davidson, George 399
Davis 79, 87, 90
Davis, C.E. 264
Davis, John Scarlett 106
Davis, O.W. 327
Dawkins-Pennant, George H. 115
Day & Son 175, 228-29, 236
De La Cour, William 519
De Lucci, Antonio and Lucio 77, 100, 154
Dean, George 575
De Vere Gardens, No. 14 **343**; 343
Debenham & Hewitt 353
Decorative Arts Building 471
Decorative Arts Committee 468
Deepdene, The 94
Defoe, Daniel 230
Delhi Durbar 309
Demontreuil, Jean 183
Denning, David 398
Department of Science 218
Derby Day, Epsom 230
Derby House, Grosvenor Square 444
Derby-Allcroft, John 236
Derby, Countess of 444, 447
Design and Industries Association 399
Devonshire, 6th Duke of 124, 128, 190, 195
Devonshire, Duke of 176, 235, 492, 499
Devonshire House 190
Dexheimer, Philippe and Adam (also Dexheimer Frères) 222-23
Dibdin, Thomas 61
Dickens, Charles 186, 225-26
Diehl, Guillaume 242
Dixwell, Charles 30-1, 59
Dodge 493
Dolmabahçe Palace, Istanbul 65
Dovestone, Bird & Hull 226, 330
Dovestone, Davey, Hull & Co. 350, 352
Dowbiggin & Son 187, 335
Dowbiggin, Thomas 66-7, 183, 246, 285
Dreschler, Carl 215
Dresser & Holme 355
Dresser, Christopher 228, 272, 285, 288, 296, 302, 305, 307, 325, 355-56, 383-84
Dromore Castle 327
Druce & Co. 389, 509

Drumlanrig Castle 87, 92-3, 132, 141
Dryad of Leicester 505
Dublin Museum 408
Dubois, Jacques 85
Dubois, René 385-86
Dubut, Jean-François 158, 160
Duckinfield Astley, Francis 47
Duke of Buccleuch 91
Duleep Singh, Maharaja 383
Dumfries House 37
Duncan 443
Dungannon, 2nd Viscount 36
Dunn, Henry Treffry 260, 263
Dunn, Nathan 169
Dunrobin Castle 25
Durand, Murray & Seddon 487
Dutch East India Company 555
Duveen 158-60, 462, 468-69, 473, 493-96, 523, 529
Duveen, Charles 498
Duveen, Henry 493
Duveen, Joseph 219, 492
Duveen Brothers 492
Dyer, John 267
Dyer & Watts 268, 271

Eagan, J. 283
Essex, Earl of 177
East India Company 175
Eastlake, Charles Locke 272, 325, 330, 336, 338
Eastman Photographic Materials **399**; 399
Eastnor Castle **118**; 119
Eastwood, Fiona 449
Eaton Hall **52**; 52, 53, 56
Ebbutt, Alfred Charles 309, 312
Écuries de l'Hôtel Bourbon 76
Edis, Colonel Sir Robert 344, 347, 349, 352, 356, 360
Edward VII, King 267, 449-50, 472-74, 492
Edward (Silversmiths to H.M. The King) 533
Edwards, John 154
Edwards & Roberts 90, 97, 250, 255, 314, 330, 357, 371, 389, 399, 436, 438, 443, 481, 575
Egan, James 200
Eglinton Castle 43
Eglinton Tournament 43, 65
Eglinton, Earl of 200
Egremont, Lord 270
Egyptian Hall, The 23, 63
Elcock, George 371
Elder & Co. 347
Elder-Duncan 475
Eliot, George 275
Elizabeth Tower, Palace of Westminster 525
Elkington, Mason & Co. 125, 204
Ellel Grange, Lancashire 304
Ellesmere, 2nd Earl of 143
Elliott, James 413
Ellmore, W.T. 343
Ellwood, George Montague 398, 407-8, 468
Elveden Hall 383
Ely, Bishop of 404, 406
Emanuel, Edward 90-91
Emslie, Alfred 258, 341-42
Érard 85, 152
Ercolani, Lucian (Ercol) 531

568

INDEX

Erlestoke Park 32–3
Estall, W.J. 225–26, 371
Etzensberger & Co. 350
Eugénie, Empress 268
Evans, Brooke 231
Evans, Edward Bickerton 241
Evans, Sir Arthur 485
Ewart & Son 291
Exeter, 2nd Marquess of 126, 130, 132, 136
exhibitions:
  Antwerp
  Exposition Internationale d'Anvers (1885) 383; (1894) 403
  Birmingham
  Exhibition of the Industrial Arts and Manufacturers (1849) 167, 168
  Brighton
  Regency Festival Exhibition, Brighton Pavilion (1948) 58
  Bristol
  Industrial and Fine Art Exhibition (1884) 352
  Chicago
  World's Columbian Exposition (1893) 360, 379, 403, 413, 575
  Cork
  Industrial Exhibition (1883) 363
  Dublin
  Dublin exhibition (1882) 363
  Great Industrial Exhibition (1853) 202; 185, 197, 201–2, 283
  International Exhibition of Arts and Manufactures (1865) 270, 282, 283, 299
  Royal Dublin Society Exhibition (1850) 185; (1864) 201
  Edinburgh
  International Forestry Exhibition (1884) 361, 363
  Ghent
  Exposition Universelle et Internationale (1913) 501
  Glasgow
  International Exhibition (1901) 399, 472
  High Wycombe
  Arts and Crafts Exhibition (1908) 484
  Leeds
  International Exhibition (1839) 19
  exhibition of antique and modern furniture (1881) 361
  Liverpool
  International Exhibition of Navigation, Travelling, Commerce and Manufactures (1886) 372–3
  London
  Ancient and Modern Carving, Albert Hall 1880) 370
  Anglo-American Exhibition (1914) 489, 490, 491
  Art Workmanship Exhibition (*also* Exhibition of Works of Art Applied to Furniture), Albert Hall (1881) 366
  Arts & Crafts Exhibition (1888) 352, 386; (1889) 385–86, 395; (1890) 397, 412, 415; (1899) 399; (1916) 510
  Bethnal Green exhibition (1875) 407
  British Empire Exhibition (1924) 482, 523
  Colonial and Indian Exhibition, Albert Hall (1886) 346, 351, 384

Crystal Palace Electrical Exhibition (1892) 407
Dunn's 'Chinese Museum' (1842) 168; 168
Economy Exhibition, the People's Palace, Mile End Road (1916) 510
Franco-British Exhibition (1908) 471; 468, 470–73, 482
Furniture Exhibition, Agricultural Hall (1883) 353–54, 365, 383
Furniture Trades Exhibition, Agricultural Hall, Islington (1893) 412
George IV: Art & Spectacle, Queen's Gallery, Buckingham Palace (2020) 21
Great Building Exhibition at Olympia (1920) 532; 527, 532
Great Exhibition (*also* Crystal Palace Exhibition) (1851) 172, 188, 196, 198, 201; 45, 71, 74, 125, 132, 146, 163, 164, 166–69, 171–75, 177, 180, 181, 183–89, 191, 193, 195–98, 200, 201, 203, 206, 222, 225, 229, 230, 250, 291, 293, 308, 373
Home Arts and Industries Association, Royal Albert Hall (1884–1913) 386
Ideal Home Exhibition (1913) 505; (1920) 510, 513
International Exhibition (1828) 19; (1862) 221, 56, 100, 143, 174, 175, 184, 186, 201, 202, 220, 222, 223, 225–31, 233–36, 242–44, 247, 248, 250–53, 257–261, 270, 272, 273, 285, 308, 342, 344, 373; (1871) 290; 278, 281, 287, 290, 292–93, 296; (1872) 292, 303, 330; (1874) 301–2, 307
International Exhibition, Crystal Palace (1884) 359
International Fisheries Exhibition (1883) 348; 345–48, 351
International Health Exhibition (1884) 347–48; 346–48, 373
International Inventions Exhibition (1885) 383
Kenton & Co. exhibition (1891) 396
Paris in London, Earl's Court (1902) 468
Royal Society of Arts' Exhibition of Manufacturers (1845) 167
Shoreditch Art Furniture Exhibition (1898) 407
South Kensington Loan Exhibition (1862) 275
Wool Exhibition, Crystal Palace (1881) 366
Manchester
Art Treasures Exhibition (*also* 11th Annual Manchester Exhibition) (1857) 175, 177, 216, 510
Fine Art and Industrial Exhibition (1882) 352
International Exhibition (1837) 19
Manchester exhibition (1867) 339
Royal Jubilee Exhibition (1887) 372, 397
Melbourne
Melbourne exhibition (1881) 366
Munich
General German Industrial Exhibition (1854) 174

New York
World's Fair (1853) 174
Newcastle
Royal Jubilee Exhibition (1887) 415
Norwich
Norwich Festival (1884) 346
Paris
11th (Quinquennial) exposition (1849) 171
Expositions des produits de l'industrie française (1798–1849) 19
Exposition Internationale des Arts Décoratifs & Industriels Modernes (1925) 536
Exposition Universelle (1855) **203–4, 269**; 185, 187, 201, 203–5, 225, 235, 237, 256, 261, 267–70, 278, 279, 281, 283, 292, 298–99, 381, 413; (1878) 288, 300, 309–10; 215, 285, 287–88, 296, 298, 300, 301, 303, 306–10, 312–14, 328, 329, 331, 346, 355, 364, 413, 546, 547; (1900) 399, 407, 413, 452, 468
Musée rétrospectif (1865) 214, 215
Philadelphia
Centennial Exposition (1876) **336–38**; 258, 291, 296, 307, 318, 321, 329, 334, 336–39, 352
Plymouth
Library furniture exhibition (1885) 361
Shrewsbury
Royal Agricultural Show (1914) 502
St Louis
Louisiana Purchase Exposition (*also* St Louis World's Fair) (1904) **470, 472**; 469, 470, 472
Vienna
World's Fair (1873) 278, 279, 281, 289, 291, 296, 304–6, 329–30
Warwick
Royal Agricultural Show (1892) 402, 404
Eyles, Henry of Bath 191, 195
Eyot Works 386

Fairbank, G.W. 303
Fairs, Thomas 142–44, 148
Falkland, 10th Lord 74
Farmer, Robert 104
Faulkner, Kate 385
Feetham of Clifford Street 258, 336, 359
Fell, Lawrence 61
Fell & Newton 132, 136
Fenton 532
Ferox Hall, Tonbridge 370
Fetherstonhaugh, Sir Harry 37
Fetteresso Castle, Stonehaven 318–19
Filmer, T.H. 355
Fine Art Society 383
Fingall, Lady 449
Fisherton Machine Cabinet Works, Salisbury 304, 489
Fitz Cook, H. 187
Fitzwilliam, 5th Earl of 74
Flatpack Furniture Company 515
Flaxman, John 184, 256
Fletcher, J. 188, 535
Floud, Peter 176
Flower, Wickham 263, 352
Foley, 4th Baron 152
Foley, Arthur 304, 489

Foley, Conrad 488
Foley, Edwin 259, 353, 487–88, 490
Foley, Thomas Henry 151
Follot, Paul 537
Fontaine, François-Léonard 19
Fontainebleau, Château de 322
Fontainebleau, Palace of 215
Fonthill House 106, 274–75, 298
Forest, Lockwood de 349
Forrest 83
Forster Graham 291
Fortnum 215, 218
Foster & Cooper 289, 414
Foster, John 51, 347
Foster Jr, John 48
Fourdinois, Henri-Auguste 177, 203, 225, 361
Fox, George 341
Fox, T. 176
François I, King of France 322
Freeman, W. & C. 83–4, 86, 175
Freud, Sigmund 371
Frick, Henry Clay 219, 493
Frogmore House 226; 226
Fry, Roger 504–5
Fry of Dublin 230, 283
Furniture & Fine Art Depositories Ltd 511

Gabe & Pass 510
Gaigneur, Louis Constantin Le 37–9
Galleons Hotel, Royal Albert Docks 369
Galleries for Antiques, Pall Mall 400
Garden Pavilion, Buckingham Palace 43, 125, 129, 559
Garnier, Pierre 249
Garrick, David 529
Geffrye Museum 491
George III, King 21, 235
George IV, King 21, 32, 37, 43, 45, 48, 50, 52, 55, 65, 71, 77, 95, 99, 133, 174, 220, 233
George V, King 450, 475, 485, 492, 502
George VI, King 492
George & Son 229–30, 233
Getty Research Institute 493
Gibbons, Grinling 183, 232, 439, 441
Gibbs, William 236
Giles & Co. 361, 472
Gill & Reigate 456, 482, 520
Gillespie, J.P. 69
Gillows (*see also*: Waring & Gillow) **288, 380, 402, 477**; 20, 22, 24, 28–32, 37, 46–7, 49, 52, 59, 61, 63, 68–9, 72, 74–5, 77, 104–5, 122, 124, 130, 146, 165, 167, 183, 185, 208, 213, 226, 228, 233–36, 242, 246–47, 250, 252, 272, 283, 285, 287–88, 290, 296, 300, 302, 304–5, 307, 309, 313, 318–19, 321–22, 325, 330, 332–35, 344–49, 352, 355, 357–58, 366, 368, 371, 379–381, 383, 391, 393, 402–4, 468, 477, 479, 520
Gimson, Ernest 396–98, 415, 451, 454, 487, 510–11, 537
Gladstone, William 341
Glasgow, Earl of 140
Glaspalast, Munich 174
Glena Cottage 200
Glynlliffon 31
Gobelins workshop 32, 36
Goddard, John 518
Godfrey, R.W. 256

Godwin, Edward William 239, 260, 272, 275, 296, 325–31, 334, 343, 347, 349, 394
Goertz, Heinrich Ludwig 66, 233
Goldschmidt-Rothschild family 163
Goldsmiths' and Silversmiths' Company 535–36
Goldsmiths' Hall **101**; 73, 75, 101–3, 132
Gomme, Ebenezer 510, 531
Goodall & Co. 368–69, 372
Goodall, Lamb & Highway 474
Goode, William 355
Goodison, Benjamin 494, 497, 504
Goodwood House 156
Goodyer of Regent Street 455
Gore House, Kensington 33, 172, 214–16, 218–20
Gosford Castle 106, 115
Gould, Frank Jay 339
Gouthière 215
Government School of Design 202, 228
Goyer, Jean 386
Graham & Banks 444, 447, 479
Graham & Biddle 366, 399, 401, 403, 479
Graham, Mrs E. 359
Graham, Peter and Forster 274
Graham-White & Co. 532
Grand Hotel, London 369
Grand Rapids factories, Michigan 464
Grand Union Canal, Kentish Town 464, 466
Grange, Ellel 226
Grange, The 189, 212
Grant, Duncan 505
Grants 363
Gray, George 205
Great Marlborough Street, No. 13 52
Great Shalimar, The 173
Great Tew Park 24, 125, 132
Grecian Gallery 23
Green & Abbott 489, 491
Greenwood & Sons of Tudor House, York 461, 492
Gregory & Co. **468**; 305–6, 356, 360, 366, 368, 468, 413, 468–69
Grendey, Giles 463, 518–19, 524, 529
Grey, George 202, 204
Grimani family 115
Grohé Frères 225, 264
Grosvenor, Lady Henry 498
Grosvenor family 56
Grosvenor Hotel, Shaftsbury 231
Grosvenor House 287
Grosvenor Square, No. 1 296
Grüner, Ludwig 43, 124–25, 129, 174–76, 186–87
Guéret Frères, Paris 359
Guild of Art Craftsmen 398
Guinness family 283
Guisachan 252, 256
Guishan 317
Gutta Percha Company 193
Gwydir Castle 483, 502

Hackney Furnishing Company 410
Haddo House, Aberdeenshire **342**; 256, 315, 318, 341, 342
Hall (retailer, Manchester) 253
Hall, Keith 133
Hall, Thomas 312
Hall, William 397

Halse, Thomas 393
Ham House 509
Hamilton 317
Hamilton Palace 33, 257, 275
Hamilton, 10th Duke of 32–3, 36, 140, 275
Hamilton, 11th Duke of 214, 216, 218
Hamilton, 12th Duke of 275
Hammersmith School of Arts and Crafts 511
Hampton, William 473, 488, 507–8
Hampton & Sons **476, 508**; 368, 374, 476, 261, 283, 400–1, 403–4, 413, 439, 443, 446, 448–49, 453, 455, 472–74, 476, 478–80, 487–90, 506, 508, 521, 530, 532
Hancock & Rixon 65
Handicrafts workshop 457
Handley-Read, Charles 264
Hanson, Samuel 69, 257
Hardman Trading Co. Ltd 195, 233
Hardwick, Philip 73, 75, 101–2, 105
Harewood, Earl of 361
Harewood House 436
Hargreaves, John 201, 203
Harland & Fisher 236
Harlaxton Manor 43
Harper & Sons 409, 439
Harris, Moss 495, 503, 505
Harrods 417, 424, 473, 475, 506, 510, 520
— Cabinet Department **476**; 476
Hasenauer, Karl Freiherr von 305
Hatfields (bronzists) 215, 218, 386
Hatfield House 403, 413, 472
— Great Hall 472
Hausburg, Friedrich Ludwig 121, 125
Hauteville House, Guernsey 320, 322
Haweis, H.R. 325
Hawker, Alice Ernestine 247, 249
Hawkins, Samuel 185, 189
Hay, J. 307
Hayball, Arthur 175
Hayes, President 318
Haymount, Holcombe Brook, Greater Manchester **404**; 404
Heal, Ambrose 399, 467, 487, 510, 537
Heal, John Harris 188
Heals 233, 347, 394, 399, 444, 531
Helena, Princess 160, 163
Helms, Harry 370
Henderson, Alexander 436
Henry, C.J. 305
Henry, J.S. **460**; 312, 398, 407, 460, 467–68, 487, 497
Henry Clay Frick House, Fifth Avenue, New York 468
Henry of Battenberg, Princess 352
Henshall, William of Oldham 537
Hepplewhite, George 258, 320, 322, 411, 420, 422–23, 430–33, 443, 454, 481–82, 514, 535–36
Hepplewhite, Alice 536
Herford, Marquess of 169
Herman & Phillips 523, 530
Herns, Harry 318
Herring & Sons (also & Co.) 184, 296
Herrmann, Henry **414**; 414, 509
Hertford, 3rd Marquess of 37
Hertford, 4th Marquess of 33, 90, 145, 149, 162, 171, 184, 214–16, 218–20, 222
Hertford House **215**; 215, 219, 315

Hever Castle 235
Hewetson & Milner 365
Hewett 359
Hewson & Hornby 365
Hicks, Harry 449
Hicks, James 447–49, 518
Hicks, John Isaac 195–96, 198
Highclere Castle 43
Hildesley, Percival 507, 512, 515–18, 533
Hill, Oliver 536–37
Hille, Ray 515, 527, 530–31
Hille, Salaman 530
Hillsborough Castle 411
Hindley, Charles 72, 406, 411
Hindley, Charles Jr 411
Hindley, Edward 411
Hindley & Sons of London 122, 148, 190, 213, 215, 404, 406
Hindley & Wilkinson **395**; 258, 262, 364–66, 386, 394–95, 411–12, 415, 456, 458, 480–81, 488
Hinton Ampner 37, 91, 315
His Majesty's Office of Works 510
Historic England Archive 363
Hitchcock 83
Hittorff, Jacques Ignace 175, 229
Hoare, Henry of Stourhead 529
Hobbs & Co. 261, 315, 420
Hobson, Edward 47
Holborn Restaurant 366
Holdsworth, Samuel 361
Holiday, Henry 238
Holland, Henry 25, 101, 105, 272, 391
Holland & Sons **310**; 67, 74, 130, 163, 185, 187, 189, 191, 202, 205, 207–8, 213–14, 226, 233–35, 241, 243, 246–50, 252, 256, 261, 264–65, 267–68, 271, 283, 292, 305, 310, 313, 315, 333, 344, 347, 349, 350, 358, 366, 397, 450, 473–74
Holland Park **507**; 507
Holme, Charles 355
Holme & Co. 383
Home Arts and Industries Association, The 386
Hood, Robin 232
Hope, Thomas 24–5, 56, 61–3, 78, 94, 264, 356, 360, 436, 439
Hope-Edwards family 244–45
Hopper, Thomas 43, 106, 115
Hornby Castle 347
Horne, Herbert 369
Horstead Place, Sussex **212**; 212
Horstman, Mr and Mrs 452
Hortense, Queen of Holland (aka Eugénie Hortense Bonaparte) 76
Hotel Carol I, Romania 369
Hotspur, Sir Harry 230
House of Commons 213
House of Lords **123**; 122, 176, 213, 466
— Prince's Chamber **123**; 122
Houses of Parliament 124
Howard, John 67
Howard & Sons **337**; 138, 213, 229, 242, 283, 285, 335–37, 354, 366, 368, 404, 415–16, 468, 473
Hoyle, Henry of Sheffield 175, 184
Hugo, Victor 381
Hume, Robert (father) 32, 33, 36–7, 73, 87
Hume, Robert (son) 32
Hummerston Brothers 361

Humphrey 359
Hunt, Holman 323
Hunt, Robert 174
Hunt, T.F. 110
Hunt, William Holman 326
Hunter, R. 327, 353, 365
Hunter, W. & J.R. 303
Hutchins & Sons of Weymouth 412

Ickworth House (also Ickworth Park) **284**; 74–5, 284–85, 395
Ida, Lady **436**; 436
Ince 406
Ince & Mayhew 448, 520
Ingledew, Charles 247
Institute of Decorative Designers 488
Ionic Temple, Yorkshire 468
Ionides, Mrs Luke **383**; 380, 383
Ionides families 385
Irving, William 127
Ishbel, Lady Aberdeen 317
Issy-les-Moulineaux 555

Jaccard, L.E. 515, 525
Jack, George 368, 372, 386, 395–97, 415, 454–55, 471, 487, 510, 536
Jackson & Graham **204, 269, 347**; 198, 269, 195, 198, 201, 203–5, 213, 225–26, 229, 233, 247–48, 257, 268–69, 272, 274–76, 278–79, 281, 283, 285, 287, 291–93, 295–96, 298–99, 301–2, 307–9, 312, 322, 335, 347, 349–52, 356–57, 359–60, 366, 370, 479, 555, 563
Jackson & Sons 72, 168
Jacob, George 55
Jacob, Thomas 298
Jacoby, Julius 312
James, John 258–59, 488
Janes, Ralph Allan 456, 469, 482–84, 496, 502, 533
Jeckyll, Thomas 272, 327
Jenks & Holt 365
Jenks & Wood 358
Jennens & Bettridge 133, 167–68, 187, 247
Jensen, Gerrit 241
Jetley 378
Jewell, S. & H. 304, 475, 477
Jockey Club, Buenos Aires **484**; 484
John the Fearless 232–33
Johnson, Thomas 455
Johnson & Co. **532**; 532
Johnstone, John 116
Johnstone, Jupe & Co. 116–17
Johnstone, Norman & Co. 355, 361, 368, 384–85, 411, 413–14
Johnstone & Jeanes 113, 116, 143, 175, 189, 213, 235, 240, 303, 312–13, 320, 339, 355, 357–58, 366
Jones, Arthur James of Dublin 174, 177
Jones, George 45
Jones, Inigo 141
Jones, John Lambert 174
Jones, Marsh 361
Jones, Owen 175–76, 184, 240, 246, 271–72, 274–75, 278, 291–92, 296, 298–99, 301, 304, 309, 319, 555, 562
Jones & Co., J.A. 361
Jones & Cribb of Leeds 288
Jordan's Carving Works 133
Jourdain, Margaret 498
Joy, Edward 53, 190

INDEX

Judges' Lodgings Museum, Lancaster 104
Jupe, Robert 113, 116–17, 167, 355, 358, 413

Kahn, Edmond 364, 410–11, 481, 490, 523–25, 529
Kahn & Co. 481, 529
Kallenborn & Sons 505
Kane, Gregory 202
Kauffman, Angelica (Angelika Kauffmann) 314, 317, 388, 430–31, 447, 449, 504
Keats, John 264, 267
Kedleston Hall 496, 501–2
Keeble, Francis 513
Keen, G.H. & S. 510
Kelmscott Manor 260
Kendal, Milne & Co. 339, 371
Kendall, Thomas 177, 181, 231
Kendell, John 226–27
Kendell & Co. 227–28, 356
Kenilworth Castle **181**; 177, 181
Kensington Palace 329
Kent, Duchess of 213, 226
Kent, William 185, 421, 463–64, 468–69, 481, 499
Kenton & Co. 395–97
Kerr, John 423
Khedive of Egypt 309
Kimbel & Cabus 296
Kinfauns Castle 61
King, Thomas 29, 31, 66–7, 69, 72, 105, 247
King, William 177
Kingsley, Charles 404
Kinloch, Lady 509
Kinloch Castle, Isle of Rùm 346, 394
Kintore, 8th Earl and Countess of 133
Kirkham 409
Kirkley, James 488
Kirkley, Thomas 259
Klaftenberger, C.J. 256
Knebworth House **128**; 124, 128
Knight, Thomas 226, 228, 264, 268, 356
Knollys, Miss 264
Knowle Cottage 247
Knowsley Hall 48
Kodak building, Glasgow 399
Kohn, Jean-Baptiste 400

La Fontaine, Jean de 80
Lackenby, A. 327
Ladies' Work Society 415–16
Lady Lever Art Gallery 504
Laing Art Gallery, Newcastle 230
Lamb, Edward 116
Lamb, Elizabeth 1st Viscountess of Melbourne 39
Lamb, James 225–26, 230, 256, 283, 286, 309, 371–74, 378
Lancaster School of Art 372
Lane, John 250, 254
Lane, Thomas 187
Lannark Park 47
Lansdowne, 3rd Marquess of (Henry Petty-Fitzmaurice) 74, 77, 86, 90
Lasenby, Arthur 272
Lauderdale, Earl of 140
Lavati 186
Laverton & Co. 352
Law Brothers 408
Lawson, James 30–1

Lawson, Robert 31
Lawson, Sir Wilfred MP 296
Laycock Abbey 415
Leake 195
Lebus, Louis and Harris 364, 443, 464, 506, 509
Leconfield, Lady 499, 501
Lee, Arthur and Ruth 441
Leeds, 1st Duke of 495
Leeds Public Library 361
Leggott, Charles 327
Lehmann, Frederick 297
Leicester, Earl of 177
Leigh, Lord and Lady 181
Leighton, Lord 400
Leighton House 195, 300
— Arab Hall **382**; 381–82
Leinster, Duke of 174
Leleu, Jean-François 158, 160, 250
Lemere, Bedford 286, 506
Lemere, Henry (Harry) Bedford 343, 347, 349, 363, 368, 382
Lennon, Thomas 449
Lenygon, Francis 473, 481, 495, 498
Lenygon & Co. 481, 495–99, 501, 504
Lenygon & Morant 499, 501–2, 505, 533
Leo, Daniel 47
Lethaby, William 395, 397, 454
Levasseur, E. Jr 412
Levasseur, Étienne 37, 87, 298, 333, 361, 458
Levasseur, L. & E. 412
Leverhulme, 1st Baron 492, 503, 505
Levien, Johann Martin 125, 160–61, 163, 183, 186, 196–98, 237–39, 244, 392
Levins, James 449
Levy, Mrs Albert 536
Lewes, G.H. 275
Leyland, Frederick 327
Liberty's 273, 325, 355–56, 380–81, 383–84, 394, 398, 452, 455, 475, 483
Liberty's Furnishing and Decoration Studio 356
Light, C. & R. 212, 364
Ligneureux, Martin-Eloi 37
Liley & Wood 346
Linard, Jaques 555
Lincolnshire, Marquess of 483
Linke, François 364, 404, 411, 412, 469, 470, 472, 481, 490, 575
Linnell, John 421, 433, 461, 491, 496, 501–2
Linton Park 250
Liobi, E. 399
Lironi, Peter 289
Lismore Castle 124, 128
Litchfield, Frederick 83, 119, 176, 257, 259, 322, 357, 400, 438, 470, 490, 495
Litchfield, Samuel 83, 101, 257, 313, 400
Litchfield & Radclyff 257
Livadia, Imperial Yacht **349**; 347, 349, 439
Liverpool Architectural Society 537
Liverpool Town Hall 29, 31
Lochhead, William 346
Lock, George 293, 360, 378, 380, 407
Lock, Matthias 141, 378, 458, 497
Londesborough family 22
London County Council 491, 511
London Society of Cabinet Makers 422
Longford Castle 463–64, 499, 502
Longleat House 235

Longstaff & Pitcher 353, 489
Lonsdale, 2nd Earl of 77
Lonsdale, Richard 105
Lord Mayor of London 327
Lord Mayor's Show 507
Lorimer, Sir Robert 339, 363, 535, 537
Lormier, Alfred 279, 281, 292, 298, 322, 366
Loudon, John Claudius 68–9, 71, 116, 169, 247, 474
Louis XIV, King of France 33, 36, 77
Louis XV, King of France 364
Louis-Philippe, King of France 83, 203
Louise, Princess 176, 180, 329
Lucraft & Son 313
Lucy, George Hammond 77, 91, 181
Lumbus, William 196
Luscombe, William 100
Luton Hoo 315
Lutyens, Robert 451, 453, 537, 553
Lutyens, Sir Edwin 451–53, 537, 550, 553
Lygon Arms, The, Broadway, Worcestershire 452

Macartney, Mervyn E. 471–72
Macintosh of Macintosh 140
Mack, Williams & Gibton of Dublin 104–5
Mackay's of Durham 138
Mackintosh, Charles Rennie 383, 398–99, 452–53, 455
Mackmurdo, Arthur Heygate 369, 372–73, 388, 399
Maclean, Alexander 509
Macquoid, Percy 459, 462, 483, 499, 495, 497, 503, 529
Macquoid, Thomas Robert 189
Madame Tussaud's 439
Madryll Cheere, Charles 28
Magdalen College, Oxford 323
Magdalene College, Cambridge 521
Maison pompéienne, Paris 298
Maisons-Laffitte villa 339
Mallett, John 472, 529
Mallett & Son 499, 529
Manchester City Art Gallery 378
Manchester Town Hall 330, 372–73
Mandelbom & Co. 523, 530
Mansfield, George Needham 257
Manuel, John (Jr) 288
Manvers, 3rd Earl of 232
Manwaring, Robert 458
Maple, Harry 364
Maple, John Blundell 364, 422, 466, 475
Maple & Co. 116, 258, 293–94, 439, 348, 351, 355, 358, 361, 364, 366, 368–69, 379, 404, 420, 422, 427–28, 431–32, 444, 452, 454, 457, 463–64, 466–67, 473, 478, 480–81, 484, 501–2, 507, 510, 519, 529–30
Maplesden, Ernest H. 354
Margaret of Valois 555
Marie Antoinette, Queen of France 254, 257, 275–76, 481, 555
Mariette 245
Marillier, H.E. 487
Marjoribanks, Sir Dudley Coutts 252–53, 256, 259, 315–16, 318–19, 344
Marks, Murray 259–60, 461
Marlborough House **267**, **390**; 261, 264, 267–68, 383, 391, 411
Marly, Chateau de 481

Marochetti, Baron 186
Marochetti, Carlo 184
Marot, Daniel 127
Marquand, Henry Gurdon 384–85
Marris & Norton 360
Marsh, Jones & Cribb 226–27, 235, 269, 356, 361, 477, 515, 532
Marsh Court, Hampshire 451–52
Martyn, H.H. 475
Mary, Queen 527, 529
Mason, Augustus 397
Master of the Pagodas 160, 162, 167
Mathilde, Princess 313
Matifat, Charles 202
Mauritania, ocean liner 487
Mavers **413**; 413
Mawe & Co. 383
Mawer & Collingham 477
Mawson, Samuel 214, 216
Maximilian II Emanuel, Elector of Bavaria 220
Mayhew 406
Mayhew & Ince 444, 447
McCallum & Hodson 188
McDowell, Hugh 197
McDuff 38–9
McGowan Brothers 363
Medici family 228
Meissen 229
Mellier, Charles 322, 480
Mellier & Co. 324, 361, 470, 482
Ménagerie, Château de la 222
Mentmore Towers 43, 163
Mérimée, Prosper 225
Merley House 162
Messenger & Sons 168
Metcalfe, Lady Alexandra 'Baba' 394
Metropolitan Museum of Art 30–1, 459, 504
Mewès & Davis 315
MGM Studios, Hollywood 504
Michelangelo 270
Middleton, Sir William 142, 144, 148
Mikado Company 412
Miles, Henry 154
Miles & Edwards 79, 154
Millet of Paris 243, 246, 575
Mills, Sir Charles 161, 214–15, 219, 363
Mills & Sons 505, 511–12
Mills of Bradford 175, 513
Milne, James 372
Milne & Co. 372
Milton, John 264, 267, 300
Milton Hall 385
Minley Manor **324**; 322, 324
Minos, Palace of 485
Mintons of Stoke-on-Trent 204
Mitchell & Rammelsberg Furniture Co., Cincinnati 336
Model & Co. 354
Mol, Van 368
Monbro, Georges-Alphonse-Bonifacio 160–61, 322
Monserrate Palace **236**; 176, 236
Monson, 3rd Baron 417
Montacute House 394
Montgomery, Sir Basil 530
Montigny, Philippe-Claude 250, 336
Moore, James 494
Moore, William 447
Moore & Hunton 354
Morant, Boyd & Blandford (*also* Blanford) 333, 335, 366, 374

Morant, George of London 24–5, 32, 36–7, 76, 78–80, 83, 85, 89, 92, 94, 106, 129–30, 135–36, 138, 141, 143–44, 156, 160, 162, 169, 176, 198, 213, 285, 305, 411, 462, 482
Morant & Boyd 208, 212
Morant & Co. 333, 335, 409, 430, 481, 483, 499
Morant & Sons 72, 74, 125, 129, 132
Mordan, Sampson 110, 315
Mordaunt, Sir Charles 231
Morel, Nicholas 52, 72
Morel & Hughes 26, 59
Morel & Seddon 31, 48–55, 71, 163, 165
Morgan, J.P. 493
Morison, James 133, 140–44
Morison family 185
Morris, Marshall, Faulkner & Co. 234, 237, 263–64
Morris, William 190, 213, 234–35, 260, 272, 279, 298, 312, 315, 325, 327, 353, 373, 382, 385–86, 388, 404–5, 415–16, 451, 457, 467, 536
Morris & Co. **471**; 260, 326, 330, 349, 352, 368, 385–86, 395–97, 404, 455, 471–72, 487, 510–11, 517, 532
Morrison, Alfred 33, 274–75, 278, 298, 302, 562
Morrison, James 563
Morton, William Scott 339
Morton & Co. **338**; 338–39
Muckross Abbey 200, 202
Muckross House 200
Mulready, William 202
Munster, Countess of 89
Murch, Arthur 264
Murch, Sir Jerom 264
Murray, Captain H.B. 250
Murray, Charles Fairfax 296
Murray, Frank Stuart 487
Murray, John 537
Murray, Michael 449
Museum of Decorative Art 246
Museum of the Home 391
Myers, George 189

Napoleon's Egyptian Campaign 63
Nash, John 21
Nash, Joseph 171, 173
National Archives 246
National Art Training School, London 288
National Museum of Ireland 448
National School of Woodcarving 344
Natural History Museum, London 174, 225, 373
Naval and Military Club, St James's 303
Nawab of Bahawalpur, Sadeq Mohammad Khan V 535–36
Naylor, John 195
Neatby, W.J. 407
Needs, J.T. 315
Nesfield, William 222, 323
New Longwood 26
New Town Hall, Westminster 361
New York Crystal Palace 177
New Zealand House 183
Newborough, 2nd Baron 31
Newborough, 3rd Baron 122
Newcastle, Dowager Duchess of 511
Newsam, Temple 361
Newstead Abbey 48
Newton, James 58, 61

Nicholl, S.J. 305–6
Nicholls, Thomas 438
Nicholls & Janes 453, 484, 501–2, 505–6
Nicholson, Peter & Michael Angelo 58–59, 61, 167
Nicolay, Jean 76
Nicoll, T. 188
Nienhaus, Bernard 420
Nixon, James 69
Nixon, T. 201
Node, The, Hertfordshire **515**; 515
Norfolk, 13th Duke of 132, 461
Norfolk House **10**; 11, 72, 132
Norman & Stacey 455
Norman Shaw 352
Normanton, Earls of 95, 223
North & Sons 356
Northumberland, 2nd Duke of 26
Northumberland, 3rd Duke of 26, 36, 59, 77
Northumberland, 4th Duke of 214, 230, 261, 265
Northumberland, 6th Duke of 366
Northumberland, Duchess of 219
Northumberland House 26
Norton Priory 106
Nosotti, Charles Andrea 242–43, 313, 361
Nosotti & Co. 360–62
Noyon Cathedral 237
Nutter, Joseph 361
Nye, Edmund 164, 191

O'Connor, Jeremiah of Killarney 200
Oakeshott, G.J. 379
Oakley, George 25, 28–9
Oeben, Jean-François 116, 151, 153, 244–45, 412, 423, 480
Oetzmann, J.R. 361
Oetzmann & Co. **477**; 348, 361–62, 368, 477
Ogden, Henry 313, 364
Old Bond Street, No. 8 **411**; 411
Old Swan House, Chelsea **352**; 263, 352
Oliver & Sons 290, 359
Omega Workshops of Bloomsbury 505, 507
Ophir 531
Ordnance Wharf, Lambeth 189
Ornamental Products Co., Detroit 487–88
Osborne House **392**; 74, 105, 130, 133, 174, 188, 304, 335, 392
Osler, F. & C. 306–8
Osler, Thomas 185, 188, 306–9
Osmond 409
Ottoman Empire 393
Owston, Hiram 356

Pacha, Ibrahim 167
Paine, James 142
Palais de Justice, Rouen 56
Palais du Trocadéro, Paris **300**; 300
Pallas 175
Palmer-Jones, W.J. 536
Palmer, Harold 392
Palmer, Henry 191
Panama Canal 361
Pantin 308
Papworth Hall 28
Paris Commune of 1871 214
Park & Cunningham 363

Parker, Frederick 443, 501, 518, 521, 524–25, 530–33, 536
Parker, Samuel 95
Parker, Thomas 37–9
Parnell, William 334
Partington, Edward, 1st Baron Doverdale 459
Partridge, Frank 495–96
Partridge, Lewis & Simmons 263, 482
Partridge, Robert W. 495, 504
Parvis, Giuseppe 384
Pascoe, Charles 368
Passe, Crispijn de 236
Pateman 409
Patent, Jordan 133
Patent Wood Carving Company 127, 130, 193
Pawsey & Payne 218
Paxton, Sir Joseph 43, 173
Payne, C.B. 503, 505
Payne & Co. 288, 478
Peach, Harry 505
Peake, James 439, 441
Pellegrini, Francesco 115
Pembroke, Earl of 492
Pennethorne, Sir James 261
Penrhyn Castle **108–9**; 106, 115
Penrose, F.C. 285
Percier, Charles 19
Percy, Sir Henry 230
Pergolesi, Michelangelo 447, 504
Pericles, Prince of Tyre 268
Perrin 409
Perry, Matthew C. 272
Petersen, Ole 279, 281, 295, 301
Petter, Henry 455
Pettitt & Co. 575
Petty-Fitzmaurice, Henry see: Lansdowne, 3rd Marquis of
Petworth House **501**; 33, 499, 501
Pevsner 415
Phipps, C.J. 361–3, 393
Phipson, Emma 339
Photographic Society 216
Pincon & Prolisch 256
Plas Glynllifon 122
Plaza Hotel, New York 263, 482, 504
Plucknett, James of Warwick 398, 402–4, 467
Plucknett showroom, Warwickshire **467**; 467
Polesden Lacey 487
Pollen, John Hungerford 231–32, 279, 281, 298–99
Porden, William 53, 56
Porter, John 187
Portugal, Dowager Queen of 475
Powerscourt, 7th Viscount 223
Pownall Hall, Cheshire 369, 372
Poynter, Edward 236, 288, 344
Pratt, Christopher 452, 455, 508
Pratt, Henry 127
Pratt, Samuel 69, 116, 126–27, 131
Pratt, Thomas & Sons 520
Preston, William 226, 228
Preston Manor, Brighton 403
Prignot, Alexandre Eugène 195, 198, 201, 203–5, 226, 236, 247, 296, 298, 366
Priory, The, Regent's Park 275
Prisse d'Avennes 381
Promoli, August 125
Protât, Hugues 177, 225–26, 373
Provence, comtesse de 216, 220

Prussia, King of 183
Pugin, Augustus Charles 52
Pugin, A.W.N. 47, 51–6, 106, 115, 119, 122, 124, 130, 189–90, 193, 195, 212–13, 233–34, 473–74
Pugin, Edward Welby 56, 212–13, 235
Punch 286, 329
Punch Brothers 288
Punnett, E.G. 398, 407, 471, 474
Pyghtle Works of Bedford 398

Quaritch, Bernard 287
Queen Alexandra's Carving School, Sandringham 509
Quenby Hall, Leicestershire **478**; 478

Raby Castle **32**, **47**, **139–40**; 32, 46–7, 132–33, 139, 141, 144, 160, 196–97, 337
Radnor, Earls of 463
Radnor House 346
Railton, William 122
Rambouillet 555
Rampendahl of Hamburg 172
Randall, John 89, 227–28
Randall, Thomas Martin 86, 156
Rayner, Samuel 192
Read, Charles Handley 309
Redfearn 83
Redman 532
Regent, Prince 37, 38
Regent's Park 21
Regnart, Horace 364
Reid & Sons 361
Rembrandt 338
Renishaw Hall **436**; 436
Resolute, HMS 318
Restall, Brown & Clennell 492, 509
Rhinefield House, Hampshire 400
Richards, John 290, 365
Richardson, C.J. 184–85, 187
Richmond, William Blake 380, 383
Richter, Charles 468, 510
Rickards, Edwin 487–88
Riesener, Jean Henri 90, 215–16, 220, 254, 275–76, 305, 411–12, 480–82
Ripon, Lord 299
Risenburgh, Bernard I van 153, 220
Risenburgh, Bernard II van 85
Robbins & Randall 89
Roberts, James 212–13
Robertson & Son, Thomas 366
Robins, John 406
Robinson, Frederick S. 504
Robinson, Gerrard 171, 230–33, 438, 441, 501
Robinson, R. 274
Robinson & Son 289
Robson & Sons 415, 474
Roentgen, David 515
Roentgen family 416
Rogers, George A. 126, 370
Rogers, Harry 176
Rogers, J.C. 536
Rogers, Mark 270
Rogers, William 163, 176, 180–81, 370
Roman Court 175
Romney, George 29
Rooke 296
Rosebery, 5th Earl of 341
Rosenberg 246, 248
Ross, Donald 249–50, 254–55
Ross, Thomas Henry Gallic 250

Ross Castle 200
Rossetti, Dante Gabriel 234, 236–37, 260, 263–64, 279, 298, 323, 325, 353, 382, 388
Rothschild, Baron Ferdinand de 163, 275, 386
Rothschild, Baron Meyer de 43
Rothschild, Hannah de 562
Rothschild, Lionel de 95, 152
Rothschild family 100, 183, 296
Rottman & Stone 380, 394
Rottmann, Strome & Co. 327
Rouher, Eugène 225
Roux, Alexander 177, 225
Royal Agricultural Hall, Islington 410
Royal Automobile Club 497
Royal College of Art 454
Royal Commonwealth Society 68
Royal Institute of British Architects 175, 397
Royal London Yacht Club, Cowes 369
Royal Navy 506
Royal Pavilion, Brighton 66, 95, 99, 183
Royal Society 344
Rubens 338
Rudd, Margaret 533, 536
Ruddle 201
Ruskin, John 32, 34, 99, 373, 385, 457
Russell, Gordon 451–52, 508
Russell, John Scott 305
Russia, Empress of 406
Rutland, Duchess of 36
Rutland, Duke of 132
Rutland, dukes of 33, 43
Rutter, Edward 215–16

Sackville, Lady 219
Sadgrove 510
Sageot, Nicolas 153
Sala, George 234, 252, 279
Salisbury, Marquess of 413
Salisbury Cathedral 318
Salt, Titus 235, 269
Salvin, Anthony 43, 74, 110
Sambourne, Edward Linley 293, 329, 332, 403, 405, 415–16
Sambourne, Marion 332
Samuel, Henry 415–17, 421–24,
Sandringham Estate 509
Sanspeur, Jean 232
Saphin, Peter 220
Sargent, John Singer 436
Sassoon, Siegfried 393
Saunier, Claude Charles 169, 206, 236
Savoy Hotel 430
Savoy Theatre 349
Sayer, Roger 260
Scarisbrick Hall 124, 130, 236
Scarsdale, 1st Baron 501–2
Schinkel, Karl 174–75, 186
School of Art, South Kensington 379
School of Woodcarving 370
Science Museum 174
Scone Palace 24
Scott, Baillie 398
Scott, George Gilbert (Jr) 329, 332
Scott, James 236, 247
Scott, Sir Giles Gilbert 231
Scott, Sir John Murray 218–20, 222
Scott, Sir Walter 24, 43, 177
Scott, Thomas 236, 247
Scottish Equitable Life Assurance Society 140

SCP Ltd 412
Second Schleswig War (1863–1864) 279
Seddon, George 30, 52, 63, 165, 226, 320, 325
Seddon, J.P. 398
Seddon, Thomas 165, 234, 325
Seddon & Co. 205, 257
Seddon & Shackleton (*also* Seddon, Sons & Shackleton) 259, 320, 322, 504
Seddon & Sons 65, 164, 205, 233–36, 357
Selbourne, 1st Earl of 331
Seligmann, Germain 219
Seligmann, Jacques 219
Selkirk, Alexander of Fife 230
Sellers, James Henry 535, 537
Semper, Gottfried 202, 205
Sèvres 89, 315
Sewell & Sewell 353, 384, 479
Shacklock, G. 177
Shakespeare, William 230, 233, 264, 267–68, 300, 338–39
Shapland, Henry 455–56, 487, 517
Shapland & Petter **451**; 401, 451, 453, 455, 478, 506, 517
Shaw Sparrow, Walter 532
Shaw, George 371
Shaw, Norman 234–35, 260, 305, 327, 330
Shearer, Thomas 422–23, 488
Sheffield School of Design 175, 184
Sheraton, Thomas 25, 30, 39, 47, 164, 167, 207–8, 226, 257–60, 317, 322, 345, 346, 351, 357, 389, 404, 406, 411, 417, 422, 430–31, 443–44, 446, 448, 454, 458, 460, 463, 472, 488, 514
Shoesmith 415
Shoolbred & Co. **338, 393**; 327–39, 346–47, 349, 365–66, 369, 393
Shoolbred, James 272–73, 285, 287, 292, 313, 327–29, 338, 391, 394, 397, 415, 475
Shoreditch Technical Institute 510
Shottesbrooke Park 416
Shrager v. Dighton (1924) 502
Shrubland Hall, Suffolk 24, 74, 142, 144
Shuckburgh Hall **127**; 127
Shuttleworth, Joseph 290
Siam, King of 475
Sims, George 283
Sinclair Galleries 400
Sitwell, Sir George **436**; 436
Skull, Walter of High Wycombe 487, 509–10
Skull & Son 453, 509
Skutterskelfe Hall 74
Slane Castle 230
Slocombe, Charles Philip 261, 265
Smee, William 69, 206, 247, 312, 365
Smee & Son **196**; 167, 176, 196
Smith, Arthur Reginald 529
Smith, George 19, 43–4, 46, 51, 67, 101–2
Smith, Guy and Rose 416
Smith, John Moyr 296, 325, 327
Smith, Walter 338
Smiths 352
Snell & Co. 184, 186
Soane, Sir John 406
Society for the Protection of Ancient Buildings 397

Society of Arts 171, 308, 315
Society of Arts and Crafts 416
Society of Upholsterers, Cabinetmakers etc. 260
Sollier brothers 270
Solon, Marc-Louis 308
Somerley House, Hampshire 95, 223
Sommerard, Alexandre du 281
Sopwith, Jacob 169
Sopwith, Thomas 168–69
Sopwith & Co. 166, 487
Sormani 364, 411–12, 481, 490
Soulages, Jules 213
South African parliament 347
South Kensington design school 233
Spain, King of 511
Sparrow, John 306
Spiers and Son 184, 213
Spooner, Charles 487
St. Cloud, Palace of 411
St George's House 339
St James's Palace 65–6, 346, 444
St James's club 130
St Margaret's Mansions **371**; 371
Stafford, Marquess of (later the 2nd Duke of Sutherland) 53
Stafford House **76, 101**; 71–2, 74, 76, 91, 101, 132, 176
Stafford Terrace, No. 18, Kensington **332, 405**; 329–30, 332, 405
Stalker & Parker 529
Standen House, West Sussex 368, 372, 401, 455
Stanmore Hall **405**; 395, 404–5
Stansgate, Viscount 508
Stark, John 537
Statistical Society 370
Steevens, John 188, 230
Stephanoff, James 421
Stephenson, Robert Louis 168
Stirling, Sir William 472
Stokes, J. 60
Stokesay Court, Shropshire **374**; 242, 374
Stoneleigh Abbey 181
Story & Co. **467**; 443, 467
Story Bros. & Trigg 443
Stotesbury, Edward 468, 495
Stowe House 498, 504
Strahan, Robert 72, 201
Strahan & Co. 200, 282–83, 462
Strange, Thomas 483
Strathmore and Kinghorne, Earl of 492
Strawberry Hill House, Twickenham 44
Street, George Edmund 212–13, 327
Stuart & Smith 202
Stubbs, George 72, 75
Styan, Francis 201
Sudbourne Hall 315
Suez Canal 381
Sullivan, Louis 456
Summer Palace, Beijing 353
Sumner, Heywood 385–86
Sussex, Duke of 174
Sutherland, 2nd Duke of (*see also:* Staffordshire, Marquess of) 71, 74, 77, 91, 132, 176
Sutherland, Duchess of 72, 143, 176
Sutherland, 4th Duke of 511
Swan House, Chelsea 382
Sweden, Crown Princess of 449
Swing Riots 65
Symon 288

Symonds, R.W. 537
Symonds and Whineray 246
Syon House 461

Tabard Inn, Bedford Park 330
Talbert, Bruce 226, 268, 272, 287, 296, 298, 308–9, 312, 325, 330, 334, 368–373
Talbot, Mr 267
Taprell, Stephen 76, 162
Taprell, Holland & Son 162, 164–65
Tatham & Bailey 66
Tatton Park **75**; 74–5
Taylor, Alphonso Warrington 237
Taylor, E.A. 455
Taylor, Fisher & Blunt 365
Taylor, George Watson 36, 220
Taymouth Castle 77
Technical School of Woodwork 509
Teck, Prince & Princess of 254
Tempest, Stephen 61
Temple Newsam House 78, 498
Tenniel, John 286
Tennyson, Alfred 268
Tessier, Louis 73
Tew Park **134**; 134–35
Thackeray, William Makepeace 171, 325
The Close, No. 3, Winchester **483**; 483
Thew, G.F. 518
Thirsk Hall 49
Thomas & Sons 520
Thompson & Co. 365–66
Thompson, Charles Thurston 87, 216
Thonet, Michael 187
Thoresby Hall 230
Thornton, Alfred James 247, 249
Thornton, Richard Napoleon 208, 246–49
Timms & Webb 439
Toft, Charles 300
Tomline, G. 183
Toms, Josiah 100
Toms & Luscombe 95, 99–100, 220, 222–23
Tottenham House **106**; 106
Tower House **237**; 237, 239
Town & Emanuel 22–3, 37–9, 83, 90–2, 95, 97, 100–1, 130
Town Hall, Belfast 349
Townsend House, Chelsea **340, 343**; 341, 343
Tozer, Charles 449, 497, 499, 517–20, 525, 529
Trapnell & Gane 352, 398
Treasurer's House, York 222
Tredagers 509
Tredescant, John 193
Trevor, Page & Co. 346
Trianon 33
Trier & Co. 412
Trimmings & Co. 518
Trojan War 432
Trollope & Sons **472**; 213, 233, 267, 269, 292, 313, 472, 144, 188, 193, 240, 246, 267–71, 283, 470, 472, 487
Trotter, William 60–1
Tudor House, Hampstead **355**; 355
Tupper, D. 320, 322
Turnbull, Ralph 161, 163
Turner, J.M.W. 67, 106
Turton, William 61
Tweedmouth, 1st Baron 253

Tweedy, Thomas 171, 230, 232–33
Tyntesfield House **286**, **520**; 236, 286, 520

Udal & Sons 289
Urquhart family 402, 404

van der Ast, Balthasar 555
Vandale 229
Vanderbilt II, George 575
Vandercruse, Roger 151, 153
Vassal Webster, Sir Godfrey 39
Vaughanx, Alfred 412
Vaughanx, Henry 412
Veblen, Thorstein 485
Veitch, John 141, 153
Veneering, Mr and Mrs 225
Verlet, Pierre 76
Vernay 482
Versailles 215, 555
Vert 261
Viardot of Paris 393
Viceregal Lodge, Dublin 462
Viceroy of India's palace, Delhi 475
Viceroy of India's palace, Simla 475
Viceroy's House, New Delhi 537
Vickers & Rutledge 461
Victoria, Princess 449
Victoria, Queen (1837–1901) 21, 53, 65, 72, 77, 83, 90, 92, 100, 105, 124, 132–33, 141, 161, 163, 171–72, 174, 176, 180, 183–84, 188, 191, 196, 198, 200, 214–16, 219, 225, 233, 235, 248, 256, 264–65, 286, 309, 335, 346, 372, 411, 441, 450, 509
Victoria and Albert Museum 30–1, 52–3, 110, 115, 175–76, 226, 230, 246, 250, 254, 258–59, 261–62, 264, 318, 320–21, 372, 379, 400, 461, 463, 481, 484, 498, 523, 530
Victoria Cabinet and Chair factory, Beith 363
Victoria Mary, Princess of Teck 411
Vigers, Allan F. 396
Villa Borghese 468
Villa Grüneburg, Frankfurt 163
Vinland, Newport Rhode Island 352, 404
Viollet-le-Duc, M. 234
Vivares, François 458
Voysey, C.F.A. 383, 385, 397–98, 407, 451, 454, 457, 467
Vulliamy, Benjamin 95, 99

Waals, Peter 511
Waddesdon Manor 275, 385–86
Wadmore & Baker 370
Waines, William 289
Wainwright, Clive 250, 261

Waldorf Hotel, New York 439
Wales, Prince of 200, 233, 261, 264, 268, 305, 315, 346, 383–84
Wales, Princess of 261, 288, 305, 309, 313, 346, 411, 444
Walford, Edward 126
Walford & Donkin 239
Walker, Anthony 458
Walker, W. 364, 366
Walker, William (also Walker & Sons) 290, 303, 364, 366
Walker-Munro, Mabel 400
Wallace, Lady 218, 315
Wallace, Sir Richard 218, 220, 310, 314–15, 361, 407, 481
Wallace & Co. 288, 409
Wallis, George 278
Wallis, Thomas Wilkinson 176, 183
Walpole, Horace 44
Walpole, Horatio, 3rd Earl of Orford 181
Walton, George 399, 400, 408
Walton & Co. 400
Walton Hall, Warwickshire 231
War Office 506–7
Ward, John 353, 386
Waring, John Burley 175, 228, 235
Waring, S.J. 400
Waring & Gillow **470**, **477**, **508**; 401, 455–56, 470–71, 473, 477, 487–88, 490, 506–8, 510, 512, 532–33
Waring & Sons **444**; 229, 246, 364, 368, 381, 439, 444, 473, 475, 480, 482, 506–7
Warwick, 3rd Earl of 115
Warwick Castle 115, 181
Washington, George 113, 117
Waterer & Sons 511
Waterhouse, Alfred 329–31, 372–73
Watson 191
Watson, Francis 76
Watson, John 250
Watt, James 39
Watt, William 234, 313, 328–29, 331
Watts & Co. 275, 306, 326–27, 332, 352, 478
Watts-Dunton, Theodore 260
Weale, John 141, 458
Webb, John **196**; 83, 87, 90–91, 119, 122, 169, 171, 184, 187, 196–97, 212–13, 215–16, 218–20, 261
Webb, Philip 212, 234, 263, 325, 381–82, 396–97, 405, 454
Webb, Richard 87
Webb, Stephen 296, 378, 380, 401, 403, 413, 455, 479
Webb & Cragg 87, 126
Webb & Forrest 215, 218
Webster, Thomas 186

Wedgwood 226, 251–53, 256, 258, 268, 279, 283, 300, 303, 313, 315, 317–19, 378
Weisweiler, Adam 215, 248, 361
Welby 53
Wellington, 1st Duke of **345**; 74, 113, 117, 345
Wells, Percy 487, 510
Wentworth Woodhouse **75**; 72, 75
Wern Fawr, Harlech 399
Wernher, Lady 315
Wernher, Sir Julius 315
Wertheimer, A. 219
Wertheimer, Samson 100, 201, 275
West End Cabinet-makers' Society 371
Westmacott, H.S. 183
Westminster Abbey 474
Westminster, 1st Duke of 287
Westminster, Palace of 55, 130, 189, 195
Westwood Park **459**; 458–59
Wetherspoon, Captain 537
Wharton, Edith 441
Whishaw, Francis 171
Whistler, James McNeill 263, 327, 504
Whitaker, Henry 74, 105, 110, 130, 133
Whitbourne Hall **241**; 241
White, Arnold 370
White & Parlby 183
White Allom & Co. 468–69, 472, 495, 505, 527, 529
White House, Shiplake 399
Whiteley, William 510
Whitemarsh Hall, Wyndmoor, Pennsylvania 468, 495
Whitestock Hall 24, 28
Whittington Hall **105**; 105
Whytock, Edinburgh. 313
Whytock & Co. 237
Wickham Hall **392**; 392
Wigg, W.C. 287
Wilde, Oscar 322–23, 353, 363
Wilkinson, Charles 75
Wilkinson, M. 281
Wilkinson, Thomas 22
Wilkinson, W. & C. 65, 101
Wilkinson, William 75
Wilkinson & Son(s) 69, 73, 102, 411–12, 415–16
Willcox, James Morris of Warwick 181, 183, 231
William IV, King 53, 65, 77, 233
Williams & Gibton 105
Williamson, Henry 103, 105
Willingale 512
Willow Tearooms, Glasgow 453
Willson, Mathew 111
Willson, Thomas 111
Wilson & Co. 185

Wimbourne, Lady (née Lady Cornelia Spencer-Churchill) 162
Winckelsen, Charles-Guillaume 219, 361
Windle, W. 355, 370
Windsor Castle **55**; 32, 47–8, 50–5, 65, 67, 71, 73, 116, 119, 124–25, 165, 174, 206–7, 220, 355
Windsor Great Park 233
Windus family 106
Winfield & Sons (also R.W. Winfield & Co.) 186, 188, 191
Winter, H. 115
Winter, James 208
Winter & Son 20
Witley Court 151
Wodehouse, Bertram 324
Wolfe, Catherine 352, 404
Wolterton Hall, Norfolk 181
Wood, Henry 206
Wood & Hemmons 368
Woodfall, Henry 394
Woodgate 229
Woodruff, Thomas 174–76
Woodworth, Edith 371
World War I 219, 452, 467, 502, 505, 507, 510, 512, 520
World War II 8, 101
Wrest Park **116–17**; 116–17
Wright, Alfred Thomas 257
Wright, P. 148
Wright & Mansfield **337**; 223, 225–27, 251–53, 256–60, 278–79, 281, 283, 303, 313, 315, 317–22, 329–30, 332, 334, 336–37, 342, 344, 357–59, 361, 366, 400, 416, 443, 575
Wrotham Park **157**; 19, 152, 156, 159
Wyatt, Benjamin 72, 74
Wyatt, Lewis 74
Wyatt, Sir Matthew Digby 175, 205, 229, 259–60
Wyatville, Sir Jeffry 50, 55
Wyburd, Leonard 355–56, 384, 416
Wylie, Robert 346
Wylie & Lochhead **473**; 346–47, 455, 472–73
Wyman 247, 290

Yapp, George 176, 229, 230, 233, 237, 247, 261, 296
Yarmouth, Earl of 37, 39
York Cottage, Sandringham Estate 475
York House (later Stafford House) **444**; 119, 444
York, Duke of 411

Zisa Palace, Palermo 382
Zwiener of Berlin 469

A Very Handsome Mahog[an]y & inlaid Carlton Shaped Writing Table
4 ft 6 wide x 2 ft 3 deep 2 ft 6 high table part
back part 3 ft 3 from ground.
with Brass gallery. int of
£40

Satinwood & mahog[an]y inlaid writing Table
4 ft 0 wide x 2 ft 0 deep 30 gnis

Almost 1,400 drawings are contained in three bound letterpress volumes compiled for Edwards & Roberts by George Dean who had previously been with Wright & Mansfield. The images are a form of counterproof, transferred onto translucent paper by using water soluble iron gall ink used before the invention of carbon paper in *c*.1900. Most are instantly recognisable as being by Edwards & Roberts in their familiar house styles adapted from eighteenth-century precedents. Many have the profuse foliate painted decoration or 'marquetrie' inlaid into a mahogany, rosewood, or satinwood ground, for example the 'Carlton Shaped Writing Table' and the 'Satinwood and mahogany inlaid Writing Table' shown above. The Chippendale-inspired sideboard, wine cooler and armchair on the right are also typical of carved mahogany furniture associated with Edwards & Roberts. It is clear that the drawings were not for manufacturing purposes but represent models that the firm was able to procure for prospective clients; they are precise and to a high standard of accuracy and a large number have overall measurements. The volumes include proposals for aspects of room settings, including 'cozy corners', chimney pieces, and clocks, Dutch furniture, and a small number of antique pieces, others openly noted as made up from old parts.

Several pages have a small cachet with the Edwards & Roberts name and address such as the one shown on the right on what would appear to be a table of mid-nineteenth-century origin. One drawing shows a reading stand with a carved date of 1893 but, apart from this, the books are not signed or dated. The dated stand occurs towards the end of one volume, suggesting the bulk of drawings are from the 1880s and possibly not much later that 1893. Another aide to dating is a 'Proposed Stand for Chicago Exhibition' and another shows the Riesener commode from the Jones Collection at the Victoria & Albert Museum, which would indicate a date of post 1882, when the collection was first put on public display. Its inclusion in the books suggests that Edwards & Roberts were able to source a copy for prospective clients and, in addition to the George III-style reproductions, a number of the illustrated pieces are models of French furniture. Although not labelled as such, these can be identified as being by Millet, Dasson, Linke and other Parisian makers of *meubles de luxe*; some drawings are marked 'C&B', a reference to the prestigious firm of decorators, Carlhian & Beaumetz, based in Paris, London, and New York, suggesting a commercial link between them and Edwards & Roberts. These drawings underline the role of Edwards & Roberts as furniture retailers, but the images of English-style furniture offer no clues as to the maker. Some drawings may correspond with furniture sent to George Vanderbilt II for Biltmore, North Carolina, receipted in 1896 and 1898. Edwards & Roberts furniture is frequently stamped, usually on a drawer, but many pieces have the firm's pre-printed paper label and a few have the firm's small ivorine plaque. It is not clear if the style of stamp or label used by Edwards & Roberts is an aide to dating or if it indicates a piece was made in their own workshops, or sourced by them from suppliers making to the firm's specific requirements.

Two of the books are part of the extensive collection compiled by the late John Bedford and now housed in the Brotherton Library. A further book by the same London stationer, T. Pettitt & Co., is held in the Athenaeum of Philadelphia Special Collections. [Brotherton Library, Bedford Collection MS 2241/7/4/9]

Frontispiece: **Detail of an elaborate centre table formerly in the collection of Hannah de Rothschild, Countess of Rosebery and Archibald Philip Primrose, 5th Earl of Rosebery.** A similar configuration of gilt-bronze dolphin supports can be seen in a circular table in the State Drawing Room at Stafford House, supplied by Edward Holmes Baldock in 1837, Fig. 2.25. The marquetry cutter is unrecorded although work by the Blake family is frequently associated with furniture supplied by Baldock. The dolphin, a symbol of French monarchy, became a frequent adornment of both furniture and added mounts on porcelain from the 1820s. The top is shown on p.564. [Sotheby's]

pp.16/17: **Green baize was used traditionally for gaming tables and writing surfaces and here the original faded baize is still in place.** Gillows frequently used engraved brass alphabetic tablets. See also, Figs 1.2a–c. [Butchoff Antiques]

pp.538/539: **Detail of the Chippendale-style mahogany desk Fig. 8.63a, showing the reverse side with a bank of four graduated drawers in each pedestal.** On the desk, to the left is a 'buhl' desk set with an ink blotter; on the right, a brass-bound coromandel-veneered dressing case by Asprey. Established in 1781 as a silk printing business, Asprey soon moved into supplying luxury items and opened its flagship store on New Bond Street in 1841, advertising their 'articles of exclusive design and high quality, whether for personal adornment or personal accompaniment and to endow with richness and beauty the table and homes of people of refinement and discernment'.

Endpapers: **The detailed ink and watercolour designs of 'An improved expanding table...' submitted by Robert Jupe, who applied for the patent in March 1835.** See Fig. 2.82a.

© 2023 Christopher Payne
World copyright reserved
ISBN 978 1 78884 174 0

The right of Christopher Payne to be identified as author of this work has been asserted by him in accordance with the Copyright, Designs and Patents Act 1988.

All rights reserved. No part of this publication may be reproduced, stored in a retrieval system, or transmitted in any form or by any means electronic, mechanical, photocopying, recording or otherwise, without the prior permission of the publisher.

The author and publisher gratefully acknowledge the permission granted to reproduce the copyright material in this book. Every effort has been made to trace copyright holders and to obtain their permission for the use of copyright material. The publisher apologises for any errors or omissions in the text and would be grateful if notified of any corrections that should be incorporated in future reprints or editions of this book.

British Library Cataloguing-in-Publication Data
A catalogue record for this book is available from the British Library

Printed in Belgium
for ACC Art Books Ltd, Woodbridge, Suffolk, UK
www.accartbooks.com

ACC ART BOOKS

FIG. 12.

FIG. 13.

FIG. 19.

FIG. 15.

FIG. 22.

FIG. 20.